THE
CAMBRIDGE EDITION OF
THE LETTERS AND WORKS OF
D. H. LAWRENCE

THE LETTERS OF D. H. LAWRENCE

Vol. I: September 1901 – May 1913
James T. Boulton

Vol. II: June 1913 – October 1916
George J. Zytaruk and James T. Boulton

Vol. III: October 1916 – June 1921
James T. Boulton and Andrew Robertson

Vol. IV: June 1921 – March 1924
Warren Roberts, James T. Boulton and Elizabeth Mansfield

Vol. V: March 1924 – March 1927
James T. Boulton and Lindeth Vasey

Vol. VI: March 1927 – November 1928
James T. Boulton and Margaret H. Boulton, with Gerald M. Lacy

Vol. VII: November 1928 – February 1930
Keith Sagar and James T. Boulton

All published

THE LETTERS OF D. H. LAWRENCE

THE LETTERS OF
D. H. LAWRENCE

VOLUME VIII
Previously Uncollected Letters
General Index

EDITED AND COMPILED BY
JAMES T. BOULTON

CAMBRIDGE
UNIVERSITY PRESS

PUBLISHED BY THE PRESS SYNDICATE OF THE UNIVERSITY OF CAMBRIDGE
The Pitt Building, Trumpington Street, Cambridge CB2 1RP, United Kingdom

CAMBRIDGE UNIVERSITY PRESS
The Edinburgh Building, Cambridge CB2 2RU, UK http://www.cup.cam.ac.uk
40 West 20th Street, New York, NY 10011–4211, USA http://www.cup.org
10 Stamford Road, Oakleigh, Melbourne 3166, Australia
Ruiz de Alarcón 13, 28014 Madrid, Spain

First published 2000

Printed in the United Kingdom at the University Press, Cambridge

Typeface Ehrhardt MT 10/12 pt   *System* QuarkXPress™   [SE]

A catalogue record for this book is available from the British Library

ISBN 0 521 23117 5

This volume is dedicated to the memory of
two men
who, in their distinctive ways, enriched
scholarship associated with
D. H. Lawrence

GEORGE LAZARUS (1904–1997)
WARREN ROBERTS (1916–1998)

CONTENTS

Preface   *page* xi

Acknowledgements   xiii

Note on the text   xv

   Cue-titles   xv

Previously uncollected letters   1

Additional letters   113

Corrigenda and addenda, Volumes I–VII   117

Index, Volumes I–VIII   133

PREFACE

This final volume of *Letters* has a threefold purpose: to publish letters both to and from Lawrence (and two from Frieda Lawrence) which came to light too late to be entered in their correct chronological positions, as well as a few already printed elsewhere but uncollected; to acknowledge and correct textual errors in the first seven volumes, and offer some additional information in annotation; and to provide a comprehensive critical index for the entire edition. It is hoped that this last – especially through the inclusion of general topics – will greatly enhance the value of the edition among a wide readership.

ACKNOWLEDGEMENTS

I am grateful to all who have shared the determination of those directly involved in the undertaking to produce an edition of Lawrence's *Letters* as complete as circumstances permit. A few owners have preferred to exercise their right not to make their possessions available for the edition; they may perhaps publish their manuscripts after this final volume appears; but to those who have magnanimously given my fellow-editors and me the privilege of printing the letters in their care or ownership, I am particularly indebted.

Inevitably in an undertaking as complex as seven volumes of letters, errors were committed or left uncorrected, and editorial ignorance was revealed. During the lifetime of the project, moreover, much new information came to light, particularly arising from the admirable scholarship of Lawrence's three 'Cambridge biographers', John Worthen, Mark Kinkead-Weekes and David Ellis. The interplay between editors and biographers has proved of immense mutual advantage. Known errors in the text are corrected and such new information as is thought relevant provided, in the 'Corrigenda and Addenda' below. Regrettably it was considered impracticable fully to record the transfer of manuscripts from one owner to another so none has been attempted.

I wish to thank most warmly those careful readers who took the trouble to respond to my plea for help in assembling the 'Corrigenda and Addenda'; they wrote from many countries. Together with readers who directed me to the whereabouts of additional letters or information, they deserve my gratitude and are listed here (if I have omitted any, I apologise profoundly): J. B. Allen, Helen and the late Carl Baron, Nicola Beauman, Harold F. Brooks, the late Margaret H. Carpenter, Edward Chaney, Sarah Chapman, Krzysztof Z. Cieszkowski, Richard Grenville Clark, Louis Cottam, David Cram, Gordon Crandles, Keith Cushman, Tony Davies, Emile Delavenay, Paul Eggert, David Farmer, Allen Freer, Jay A. Gertzman, Anne Gildea, Vincent Giroud, Kevin L. Glick, Bonnie L. Grad, Elizabeth W. Harries, Andrew Harrison, Cathy Henderson, Michael Herbert, Paul Hogarth, George J. Houle, Rosemary Howard, Ellen V. Howe, Virginia Hyde, Takeo Iida, Christa Jansohn, Frederick R. Jeffrey, Dorothy B. Johnston, Mara Kalnins, M. Uding-van Laarhoven, Jane Lillystone, Jonathan L. E. Long, Hannah M. Loewy-Kahler, Islay de Courcy Lyons, Brenda Maddox, John Martin, Dieter Mehl, Jeffrey Meyers, Francis Miller, the late Kenneth Muir, the trustees of John Middleton Murry, J. T. Needham, Margaret

Needham, David Norton, Edmund D. Pollinger, Gerald Pollinger, Christopher Pollnitz, Anthony Powell, Lawrence Clark Powell, Peter Preston, K. Ramseur III, Mrs J. Rintoul, H. E. Robbins, Janice Robinson, Anthony Rota, Dominic Rowland, Keith Sagar, Hans-Wilhelm Schwarze, Stuart O Seanoir, Michael Silverman, Roy Spencer, Michael Squires, Bruce Steele, Jack Stewart, Richard Storey, Ronald Tullius, Leslie Cauvel Watson, Christopher Wickham, Helen E. Wilcox, David Wishart, Louise Wright and Ornella de Zordo.

Some deserve particular mention: Michael Black who conceived and boldly initiated the project at the Press, Andrew Brown and his colleagues who sustained it; my co-editors – Gerald Lacy, Elizabeth Mansfield, the late Warren Roberts, Andrew Robertson, Keith Sagar, Lindeth Vasey and George Zytaruk – who committed years of expertise, energy and enthusiasm to the enterprise; and the University of Birmingham which has housed the editorial centre for more than two decades. Gratitude is also specially due to David Milson, Peter Robinson, Kevin Taylor and Chris Hamilton-Emery for their invaluable computer skills; John Worthen for translations from German and, with Michael Black and Lin Vasey, for constant advice, encouragement and scholarly assistance; and, most of all, my wife for her active participation in the project as typist, co-editor and proof-reader, and for her unfailing support over many years of endeavour.

JTB

NOTE ON THE TEXT

A full statement of the 'Rules of Transcription' and an explanation of the 'Editorial Apparatus' are provided in Volume I, pp. xviii–xx. The reader may, however, like to be reminded that the following symbols are used in the presentation of letters:

[ ]   indicates a defect in the MS making it impossible even to conjecture what Lawrence had written. Where a reconstruction can be hazarded or a fault corrected, the conjecture or correction is shown within the square brackets.

[. . .]   indicates a deletion which cannot be deciphered or a postmark which is wholly or partly illegible

MSC = autograph manuscript copy
TMS = typed manuscript
TMSC = typed manuscript copy
TSCC = typescript carbon copy

CUE-TITLES

Cue-titles are employed both for the manuscript locations and for printed works. The following appear in this volume.

A. Manuscript locations:

Anon	Anonymous
Broxtowe	Broxtowe Borough Council, Nottinghamshire
Copley	James S. Copley Library, California
CUL	Cambridge University Library
Davies	Dr David Davies
Dean	Dr Winton B. Dean
Fath	Mr Creekmore Fath
Forrester	Mr Norman J. Forrester
Forster	the late Mr W. Forster
GU	Georgetown University, Washington D. C.
Holt	Mrs Frances Holt
Houle	Mr George J. Houle
Hughes	Mr Robert D. Hughes
Jermy	Mr P. J. Jermy
Lauer	Dr Gerhard Lauer

Meerwein	Professor Dr. Med. Meerwein
NLA	National Library of Australia
NLMD	Nederlands Letterkundig Museum en Documentatiecentrum
NWU	Northwestern University
NYPL	New York Public Library
Price-Williams	Dr Douglass Price-Williams
Roberts	the late Dr F. Warren Roberts
Schulson	Mrs Claudia Strauss Schulson
Segal	Mr Ronald Segal
TCD	Trinity College Library, Dublin
UN	University of Nottingham
UR	University of Reading
UT	University of Texas at Austin
Wanning	Professor Emeritus Andrews Wanning
Wells	Mrs Rosalind Wells
Whitworth	the late Mr Robin Whitworth
YU	Yale University

B. *Printed Works*

(The place of publication, here and throughout, is London unless otherwise stated.)

DHLReview	*The D. H. Lawrence Review.* Fayetteville: University of Arkansas, 1968–83; Newark: University of Delaware, 1984–93; University of Texas at Austin, 1994–2000; State University of New York at Geneseo, 2000–
Gertzman and Squires	Jay A. Gertzman and Michael Squires, 'New Letters from Thomas Seltzer and Robert Mountsier to D. H. Lawrence', *DHLReview*, xxviii (1999), 53–77
Huxley	Aldous Huxley, ed. *The Letters of D. H. Lawrence.* Heinemann, 1932
Letters, i.	James T. Boulton, ed. *The Letters of D. H. Lawrence.* Volume I, September 1901–May 1913. Cambridge: Cambridge University Press, 1979
Letters, ii.	George J. Zytaruk and James T. Boulton, eds. *The Letters of D. H. Lawrence.* Volume II, June 1913–October 1916. Cambridge: Cambridge University Press, 1981

Letters, iii.	James T. Boulton and Andrew Robertson, eds. *The Letters of D. H. Lawrence*. Volume III, October 1916–June 1921. Cambridge: Cambridge University Press, 1984
Letters, iv.	Warren Roberts, James T. Boulton and Elizabeth Mansfield, eds. *The Letters of D. H. Lawrence*. Volume IV, June 1921–March 1924. Cambridge: Cambridge University Press, 1987
Letters, v.	James T. Boulton and Lindeth Vasey, eds. *The Letters of D. H. Lawrence*. Volume V, March 1924–March 1927. Cambridge: Cambridge University Press, 1989
Letters, vi.	James T. Boulton and Margaret H. Boulton, with Gerald M. Lacy, eds. *The Letters of D. H. Lawrence*. Volume VI, March 1927–November 1928. Cambridge: Cambridge University Press, 1991
Letters, vii.	Keith Sagar and James T. Boulton, eds. *The Letters of D. H. Lawrence*. Volume VII, November 1928–February 1930. Cambridge: Cambridge University Press, 1993
Nehls	Edward Nehls, ed. *D. H. Lawrence: A Composite Biography*. 3 volumes. Madison: University of Wisconsin Press, 1957–9
Roberts	Warren Roberts. *A Bibliography of D. H. Lawrence*. 2nd edition. Cambridge: Cambridge University Press, 1982
Tedlock, *Lawrence MSS*	E. W. Tedlock, *The Frieda Lawrence Collection of D. H. Lawrence Manuscripts: A Descriptive Bibliography*. Albuquerque: University of New Mexico, 1948

PREVIOUSLY UNCOLLECTED LETTERS

NB The distinctive number allocated to each letter indicates its chronological position in relation to others published in Volumes I–VII. A number followed by 'n' associates the letter with the annotation to a particular text.

7a. To Alvina Lawrence, [31 October 1903]

Text: MS UN; PC v. Thorney Abbey - North East; Postmark, [Peter]borough OC 31 03; Unpublished.

[31 October 1903]

[1]Off to Skeg[ness]. Broken our journey in Peterboro here.

xx   DHL

10a. To Alvina Lawrence, [5 March 1904]

Text: MS UN; PC v. Worksop Priory Church; Postmark, Eastwood MR 5 04; Unpublished.

[97 Lynn Croft, Eastwood]
[5 March 1904]

Dear Tim,

Thanks so much for the Joey,[2] it was a very nice card. Could you send me his home next. I guess you were very pleased to hear of Nell's success.[3] I didn't know what Nottm views you had, but thought perhaps you'd like this. Are you coming at Easter?

Your loving coz   DHL

10b. To Alvina Lawrence, [9 March 1904]

Text: MS UN; PC v. St. Mary's Church, Nottingham; Postmark, Eastwood MR 9 04; Unpublished.

[97 Lynn Croft, Eastwood]
[9 March 1904]

Thanks very much for Highbury,[4] it was a v. good view. You have not this card, I think. We've had a lovely day today. Don't send me views of Brum town, please. Send me Warwick or Kenilworth or Coventry, if you can. You don't mind me asking you, do you Tim? All send love.

Yours   DHL

---

[1] DHL's correspondent was his cousin, Alvina ('Tim') Lawrence (1880–1968). See *Letters*, i. 68 n. 3.

[2] Most likely a picture of Joseph Chamberlain (1836–1914), thrice Mayor of Birmingham, MP from 1885, Chancellor of the University of Birmingham from 1901, etc. (see letter following).

[3] Mary Ellen Allam (b.1886), daughter of James and Mary Ellen Allam and step-sister to Alvina Lawrence, Alvina was living with the Allams in Kings Heath, Birmingham. See i. 199 n. 4; 231 n. 3.

[4] Joseph Chamberlain's opulent house in Italianate Gothic style, with 100 acres of elaborately laid-out gardens; it is located in Moseley, Birmingham ('Brum'), close to Kings Heath (see previous letter n. 3).

12a. To Thomas A. Smith, [30 December 1904]

Text: MS Jermy; PC v. Eastwood Hall; Postmark, Eastwood DE 30 04; Unpublished.

[97 Lynn Croft, Eastwood]
[30 December 1904]

What are you[1] doing at Leicester – enjoying yourself, I hope.

Two stupid young girls are grinning over each (that's one) word I write –
Centre girls, too.[2] Isn't our Eastwood charming, you must form quite an
exalted opinion of it – and the inhabitants including

Yrs.   DHL

Happy New Year.

138n. To D. H. Lawrence from Ford Madox Hueffer, 15 December 1909

Text: MS (copy) UN; John Worthen, *D. H. Lawrence: The Early Years 1885–1912* (Cambridge, 1991), pp. 221–2.

84 Holland Park Avenue, W.
Dec 15 09.

Dear Mr Lawrence,

[3]I have now read your novel, and have read it with a great deal of interest,
which, in the case of a person who has to read so many MSS as I do, is in
itself a remarkable testimonial. I don't think I could use it in the 'English
Review' for several reasons, the chief of them being its inordinate length. As
you know, I like to publish a serial in four numbers, and a quarter of your
book would take up almost half the Review. But I don't think that this great
length would militate against its popularity with the public, for both the
public and the libraries like long books. Properly handled, I think it might
have a very considerable success, and I don't think that in these matters I am
at all a bad judge; but a great deal depends on its being properly handled,
and if you are sending the MSS to a publisher, I should advise you to try one
of the most active – that is to say one who already has the ear of the public.
As you must probably be aware, the book, with its enormous prolixity of

---

[1] Thomas Alfred Smith (1886–1966), DHL's close friend and later his fellow-student at
University College, Nottingham. See *Letters,* i. 6–7,142–3 n. 7.

[2] I.e. girls from the Pupil-Teacher Centre at Ilkeston, Derbyshire, which DHL attended part-
time, March 1904–July 1905.

[3] Ford Madox Hueffer (later Ford) (1873–1939), novelist and, at this time, editor of the *English
Review* which he founded in December 1908. He had published five of DHL's poems in the
November 1909 issue of the *Review,* and offered to read 'any of the work I like to send him'
(i. 138). DHL sent him the *White Peacock* MS and immediately on receiving this response,
forwarded it to William Heinemann as stated in his letter to the publisher, 15 December 1909
(i. 148–9).

detail, sins against almost every canon of art as I conceive it. It is, that is to say, of the school of Mr William de Morgan – or perhaps still more of the school of Lorna Doone.[1] But I am not so limited as to fail to appreciate other schools than my own, and I can very fully admire your very remarkable and poetic gifts. I certainly think you have in you the makings of a very considerable novelist, and I should not have the least hesitation in prophesying for you a great future, did I not know how much a matter of sheer luck one's career always is. With this in view I should advise you in approaching a publisher to promise him at least the refusal of several of your future works. This means that he will be encouraged to make efforts with your first book with some confidence that if it succeeds you will not immediately abandon him for another firm,

Yours Sincerely   Ford Madox Hueffer

143a. To Sydney Pawling, 19 January 1910
Text: MS Segal; Unpublished.

12 Colworth Rd, Addiscombe, Croydon
19 Jan 10.

Sydney S. Pawling Esq.
– Wm. Heinemann
21 Bedford St W.C.
Dear Sir,[2]

I shall be glad to call on you on Friday next if you will allow me to come at 12.30 instead of 12.0.

Yours faithfully   D. H. Lawrence

155. To Sydney Pawling, 27 April 1910
Text: MS Segal; Huxley 1–2.[3]

12 Colworth Rd, Addiscombe, Croydon
27 April 1910

Dear Mr. Pawling,

With reference to your letter of the 25th.: – I think the novel[4] is complete and final in its form as I have sent it you; also I think you will not find it actually so lengthy as the weight of the M.S. might lead one to suppose. The

---

[1] William Frend de Morgan (1839–1917), collaborator with William Morris and author of long, digressive and elaborately plotted novels; *Lorna Doone* (1869), the celebrated novel of romantic adventure by R. D. Blackmore (1825–1900).

[2] Sydney S. Pawling (1862?–1923), publisher; partner to William Heinemann. See *Letters*, i. 158 n. 4.

[3] Previously published text corrected from MS: cf. i. 159.

[4] *The White Peacock.*

book is, I believe, much shorter than *Tono-Bungay* – about the length of *Jane Eyre*, or rather less, I estimated it. I will delete as much as I can in phrases and perhaps here and there a paragraph from the proofs, but there are now no passages of any length that I could take out.

I have written about a half of another novel:[1] I wonder what you would think of it.

                                     Yours Sincerely   D. H. Lawrence

Sydney S. Pawling Esq
31 Bedford St. – W.C.

186. To Sydney Pawling, 18 October 1910

Text: MS Segal; Huxley 4–5.[2]

                                     12 Colworth Rd, Addiscombe, Croydon
                                                              18 October 1910

Sydney S Pawling Esq
21 Bedford St W.C.

Dear Mr Pawling,

I am glad, and much relieved, to hear that you have the MSS of the S[aga] of S[iegmund][3] in your hands – (By the way, don't you think the title idiotic? I am a failure there. How would 'The Livanters' do?) I shall wait with some curiosity to hear your opinion of the work. It contains, I know, some rattling good stuff. But if the whole is not to your taste, I shall not mind, for I am not in the least anxious to publish that book. I am content to let it lie by for a few years. Of course, you have only got the rapid work of three months. I should want, I do want, to overhaul the book considerably as soon as you care to return it to me. I am not anxious to publish it, and if you are of like mind, we can let the thing stay, and I will give you – with no intermediary this time – my third novel, 'Paul Morel',[4] which is plotted out very interestingly (to me), and about one eighth of which is written. 'Paul Morel' will be a novel – not a florid prose poem, or a decorated idyll running to seed in realism: but a restrained, *somewhat* impersonal novel. It interests me very much. I wish I were not so agitated just now, and could do more.

When you say 'the plates of the *White Peacock* were sent from New York' – do you mean the plates of the cover design, or what? I am a trifle curious. I *do* want that book to make haste. Not that I care much myself. But I want my

---

[1] *The Trespasser.*
[2] Previously published text corrected from MS: cf. *Letters*, i. 184–5.
[3] I.e. *The Trespasser.*
[4] Later *Sons and Lovers.*

mother to see it while still she keeps her live consciousness. She is really horribly ill. I am going up to the Midlands again this week-end.

But you will think I have a sort of 'Mr Bunbury.'[1]

I don't want to bother you to write, but let me know about the second
novel when you're ready, please.

Yours truly   D. H. Lawrence

212. To Arthur McLeod, 23 December 1910

Text: MS Broxtowe; *Letters*, i. 213.

[12, Colworth Road, Addiscombe, Croydon.][2]
23 Dec 1910

Dear Mac,[3]

Nice of you to remember that I wanted those Latin poems: I'd forgotten
myself: which makes it all the pleasanter now.

If you've already got this Everyman vol – I wont write in it, and then you
can give it someone else.[4] But if you've not read 'Our Lady's Tumbler'
– it is rich, it is a nonsuch. I read it to my mother in bed two months ago. –
And the boys gloat over the 'Three Thieves.' Give it them for composition.

Be jolly!

Yrs   DHL

---

[1] In Wilde's *Importance of Being Earnest* (1899), the imaginary character Bunbury serves as a
pretext for visiting a variety of places.

[2] DHL used headed 'mourning' notepaper edged in black(his mother died on 9 December
1910).

[3] The opening sentence of this letter was given in *Letters*, i. 213; the MS has since become available giving the full text. DHL's correspondent was Arthur William McLeod (1885–1956), his
colleague and closest friend at Davidson Road School, Croydon.

[4] The volume was *Aucassin and Nicolette and other Mediaeval Romances and Legends*, trans.
Eugene Mason (Everyman, September 1910). Its contents include 'Our Lady's Tumbler', a
story of the faithful minstrel-tumbler whose devotion to the Blessed Virgin was such that she
appeared to him in his lifetime and, at his death, 'gathered [his soul] to her bosom' and transported it to heaven. In ways that would amuse DHL's pupils, 'The Three Thieves' illustrates
the proverb (quoted at the end of the story) that 'Bad is the company of thieves'.

437a. To Irene Brinton, [9 May 1912]
Text: Sotheby's Catalogue, 22 July 1983, Item 458; PC v. Trier - Dom u. Liebfrauenkirche;
Postmark, Trier 9 5 12; Unpublished.

Hôtel Rheinischer Hof, Trier
[9 May 1912]

. . . [1]have been here about a week. I was staying in Metz, but had to quit,
because they said I was a spy, an English officer, and they were going to
arrest me. I, who don't know a fortress from a factory. It's too bad . . . Tell
Peg to send one or two grinning photos to my sister at Eastwood, there's a
dear . . .

Love   D. H. Lawrence

613a. To Katherine Mansfield, [21 July 1913]
Text: Maggs Bros Catalogue 1071 (1986), Item 106.

28 Percy Avenue, Broadstairs
Monday

Dear Mrs Murry,[2]

I hope you found my book at your new address. You must come down here
this coming week-end – How are you fixed up now? – . . . Frieda is bothering
you about her children. You will help, wont you? The best way is to get one
of the boys to bring Monty to you – Monty Weekley[3] . . . He is 13 years old –
so you'll ask one of the bigger boys of the Preparatory School for
him[4]. . .Try and get Monty to see you, will you? Then Frieda might meet
him at your house. – We will get a little flat for you in Bavaria, for a month,
in return – not in return, but it seems rotten to drag you into our troubles,
one straightway thinks of reparation . . .

D. H. Lawrence

[In a pencilled postscript Lawrence apologises for not enclosing a sovereign for Monty Weekley, as promised in the letter, and adds] I am thick
headed with the thunder.

DHL

---

[1] DHL had met his correspondent, Irene Brinton, from Hampstead, when she, with her sister
Margaret ('Peg' or 'Meg') was staying – as he was – at the boarding-house, Compton House
in Bournemouth, January 1912 (*Letters*, i. 350 n. 1).
[2] Though addressed here as 'Mrs Murry', Katherine Mansfield (1888–1923) and John
Middleton Murry (1889–1957) did not marry until 1918; they had lived together for 16
months when DHL and Frieda met her on 9 July 1913 (ii. 31–2, 31 nn. 5 and 6).
[3] Frieda's eldest child, Montague (1900–82). He later recalled that Frieda took him to a teashop
in West Kensington and introduced him to 'a fascinating young woman who had a charming
and rather enigmatical smile. This was Katherine Mansfield' (Nehls, i. 198). Subsequently
she delivered messages from Frieda to her children.
[4] Colet Court, West Kensington, preparatory school for St. Paul's (Nehls, i. 197).

641a. To John Middleton Murry, 30 August 1913

Text: MS NYPL: Unpublished.

Irschenhausen, (Post) *Ebenhaüsen*, Oberbayern.

30 August 1913.

Dear Murry,

Your last letter was really the low-water mark. I hope you're better by now. I count the weeks for you quite apprehensively – Sept, Oct and Nov. – it's a long time. But you'll perhaps be able to hang on till then. It is definitely settled we stay here till Sept 23rd: then Viva l'Italia. – I liked your review of those poets.[1] You can do it jolly well. I wish I could.[2]

Frieda and I are struggling on. We have just reached the point where we cease to murder each other. I've taken my hands from her throat, and she's taken her hands from mine, and we are staring at each other, round eyed and full of wonder at finding ourselves still here and alive. I think she treats me very badly, but I have assumed the forbearance of a Christian martyr, and manage to hug it round me for an odd ten minutes, like a cloak of protection. I am sorry to say it is flimsy, and soon rips. I should like a box of tacks to tack down my wits, which seem to have turned up at the edges like ruinous oil-cloth, and I am always falling over 'em. – a box of tin-tacks to tack my wits down and hold 'em steady – danke schön.

I've written one or two things about which I know nothing – like a somnambulist. F. says they aren't bad. I've begun a novel on the same principle:[3] it's like working in a dream, rather uncomfortable – as if you can't get solid hold of yourself. 'Hello my lad, are you there!' I say to myself, when I see the sentences stalking by.

That's *my* Klagen.[4] I look to Italy to wake me up. Think of me as the Sleeping Beauty. But fancy if the Sleeping Beauty had walked in her sleep. God knows what princes she mightn't have run up against in the passages. Oh Lord!

It has been wonderful weather here: such a vally full of the delicatest sunshine, and in the woods all spangles and glitters among the shadows. The chicory is still blue as blue. If I send Katarina any, it will die, because it crumples up in fifty minutes, and is no more. Then in the green cut grass by the wood-edge and in the broad green places by the roadside, there are

---

[1] Murry had probably sent a copy of the review which would appear on 12 November 1913 in the *Daily News* entitled 'Three Poets' (John Helston, W. H. Davies and Arthur Symons). See George Lilley, *A Bibliography of . . . Murry* , 1974, C43.

[2] could.] could do it.

[3] 'The Sisters'.

[4] 'complaint'.

autumn crocuses standing such a lot, each one slim and separate and mauve-pink among the vivid green. I like their name: Herbst Zeitlosen.[1] Sometimes I gather a bowlful of them. They open out so wide and spikey. I think they are a bit uncanny: rather like a Miriam:[2] or like a virgin of thirty years.

We had one letter from Campbell, saying you had abused him.[3] But he wrote very nicely and fatherly to us.

I *do* wish you two could come to tea to-day – I should be so thankful. The Mädchen has made such good Kringels[4] and cakes, and it's a bit rainy, and so still. I should[5] fearfully like a talk with you, John Middleton Murry, and your K[atherine] M[ansfield]. Three months is a long time before you come to Italy. I've got an awful wish that you were here today.

In about a month's time, I am going to have a play published.[6] It's a good one. You must look out for it, and say nice things about it to people. How is your novel, Katarina, and your head, J.M.? I feel frightfully like the parish priest and the doctor mixed, where you two are concerned. Doesn't it amuse you?

I suppose you are fixed quite fast out there in London. If it gets very bad, Murry, chuck up before you go to pieces, and we'll manage somehow, when you come out – don't put the last straw on, during those three infernal months. Are you making arrangements for breaking loose? Have you mentioned your flight at the *W[estminster] G[azette]*?[7] Couldn't you do, say, a third of your work for them, in Italy? It wouldn't be so much, would it? Three weeks on Tuesday we depart. Rather land yourself in a financial hole, than in a physical or mental breakdown. Chuck that stuff in London as soon as you can.

'For we're all nice folk, yes we are —
And all hot stuff – tra-la-la —[8]

By jove, Kringeln just hot out of the pan, they *are* good.

Frieda will write the rest to you.

Auf wiedersehen, Ihr zwei[9]   D. H. Lawrence

[1] 'Meadow Saffron'.
[2] Perhaps the Israelite Miriam of Numbers xii rather than the character in *Sons and Lovers* based on the friend of DHL's youth, Jessie Chambers (1887–1944).
[3] Charles Henry Gordon Campbell (1885–1963), Irish barrister, introduced to the Lawrences on 26 July 1913 by Murry and Katherine Mansfield (*Letters*, ii. 51 and n. 1).
[4] 'girl . . . fancy biscuits'.
[5] should] feel
[6] *The Widowing of Mrs Holroyd*, published on 1 April 1914.
[7] Murry was a full-time reviewer for the *Westminster Gazette*.
[8] Unidentified
[9] DHL presumably intended to say: 'Goodbye to both of you'.

655a. To John Middleton Murry, 30 September 1913
Text: MS UN; Unpublished.

Albergo della Palme, *Lerici*, Golfo della Spezia
30 Sept 1913.

My dear Murry,

Now we've found a place – a four roomed cottage in a big vineyardy
garden, tucked in a tiny bay, almost alone, under great hills of olive woods.
One runs out onto a bit of sand and into the water. There is only one other
house, a pink fisherman's cottage. The bay is shut in, nearly, by black rocks
and rocklets. The Mediterranean is very blue. There is a boat. The cost is 60
francs a month, furnished, and 25 francs for a woman who sleeps in the
fishing village 20 minutes off, and who does all work and washing. It is
simply perfect. I think of sitting in my kitchen, a little fire of olive-wood
burning in the wide open chimney, a bottle of wine in its rush singlet, and
hearing the waves wash at night, softly: – then of getting up in the morning
and going out to bathe and run back through the garden.

One goes by train – via Genoa, to Spezia, thence by steamer over the gulf
to here, Lerici – then in a rowing boat round the headlands.

How much longer before you come? You can stay with us while we find
you another such a house. We've looked at a lot of apartments – not bad –
here. But our house is the best. You come as quick as you can, and we find
you something as good. There are plenty of decent apartments – but I *love* a
little house.

I had a note from Campbell – he said your visit had been psychological. –
Frieda and I are going to be frightfully happy in the villino at Fiascherine. I
have been acutely unhappy – I seem to have a bent that way – I am a fool. – I
walked from Schaffhausen - Zürich - Lucerne - over the Gotthard - Airolo,
Bellinzona, Lugano, Como. It was beautiful, but Switzerland is too milk
chocolaty and too tourist trodden.[1]

We must stay here another 8 days. The proprietor is getting in his crops
at our villino. And I want so much to go.

Why doesn't Katharina write to us? – Are you stopping still 3 months in
London –

Love from us to you – D. H. Lawrence

Write to us here

---

[1] Cf. *Twilight in Italy*, ed. Paul Eggert (Cambridge: Cambridge University Press, 1994),
209:36–7: 'Lucerne and its lake were as irritating as ever: like the wrapper round milk chocolate.' (The quotation is from 'The Return Journey' which was completed and sent for typing
on 19 October 1915.)

**659a. To John Middleton Murry and Katherine Mansfield,
[10 October 1913]**
Text: MS Anon; PC; Postmark, Lerici 10. 10. 13; Unpublished.

[Lawrence begins]

Lerici per Fiascherino, Golfo della Spezia, Italy
[10 October 1913]
Dear Murry,

I feel as if I had written you at least five times and you haven't answered.
Perhaps I exaggerate, but – . – We *have* got an adorable place here – you
couldn't beat it on the face of the earth. Here is your place to bask and laze.
And it is nearly November, and warm as July – pure sunshine all day, and a
soft, delicious sea, and figs still ripe – If you write to us, then I'll tell you all
about it. – I know one place in Lerici you could have – good, cheap. I'll
enquire about more if you will say whether you come or not.

Yrs   DHL

[Frieda Weekley begins]
Dear K[atherine] –

Has any letter of yours gone astray I wonder? Or what are you doing? Are
you desperately bursting with plans of Halls or anything? Write to me and of
the brats, if you can[1] – It's the most difficult thing to imagine that there are
places where it is'nt summer like here, real summer – I wonder if you'll
come – We are looking for places for you. –

Yrs   F.

Orange blossom in the garden!!

674a. To Mitchell Kennerley, 19 November 1913
Text: MS Anon; Unpublished.

Lerici per Fiascherino, Golfo della Spezia, Italia
19th Nov. 1913
Dear Mr Kennerley,[2]

I received this morning your letter and the agreement, which latter I
return now. I also send by the same post the typewritten-copy of the play,
which I received a little while back, and let lie, not knowing you wanted me
to go over it. However it is done now. I dont think there are many alterations.

---

[1] Katherine Mansfield acted as a go-between for Frieda and her children. In *'Not I, But the
Wind . . . '*, Frieda recalled: 'She . . . tried her best to help me with the children. She went to
see them, talked to them and took them letters from me. I loved her like a younger sister' (p.
86).
[2] Mitchell Kennerley (1878–1950) became DHL's American publisher with the publication of
The Trespasser in May 1912; he published *The Widowing of Mrs Holroyd* on 1 April 1914.

The play seems to me pretty complete now, as it stands. I am sorry that it is a play of unbelief – a bit cynical in conception. One has no right to be cynical.

I am quite content with the agreement. It pleases me very much to think the play will be published one day. I wish I were there to see it.

I do hope also that one day you may find my writing a good speculation. But I think you will. My thanks for advertising *Sons and Lovers* so widely. I do like the reviews. But – bisogna dar tempo al tempo.[1]

If the proofs of the play have gone in before this corrected MS arrives, then no matter. What alterations there are, are not important. But they go to improving the surface. One can feel so much better when one can go straight forward over a plain typed copy – as over proofs.

Yours Sincerely   D. H. Lawrence

745n. To D. H. Lawrence from Douglas Clayton, 3 July 1914
Text: MS UN; Unpublished.

54 Birdhurst Rd, Croydon.
July 3. 1914.

Dear Lawrence.[2]
1) I enclose M.S. of *New Eve & Old Adam* This has not yet been typed so I have no record of its words
2) Also, – *The White Stocking*: 7,904 words (I like the *4*!) (Pinker had the typed copy of this.)
3) *Love among the Haystacks* has never been here.
4) *The Sick Collier* } sent to you at the Cearne July 9. 1913.
   2,500 words   } (In a later letter you refer to certain M.S.S.
5) *Once*   } having been sent on from Cearne (July 14, to
   3,427 words   } Margate.)
I have made a fair copy of the following list to put with the M.S. for ready reference in the future & we will keep it up to date.

*

List of works sent & what befell them.
1) *New Eve & Old Adam* MS. Sent Selwood Terrace July 3. 1914
2) *Sick Collier* (2,500) M.S. also typescript Sent Cearne July 9. 1913
3) *Fly in the Ointment* (2,029) Sent MS & typescript Cearne July 9. 1913

---

[1] 'one mustn't rush things'.
[2] DHL's correspondent, Douglas Clayton (1894–1960), was a jobbing printer who typed many of DHL's MSS; his uncle-by-marriage, Edward Garnett, had introduced DHL to him (*Letters*, ii. 30 nn. 1 and 3). In this letter (of which the MS is incomplete) Clayton was replying to DHL's of 2 July 1914, written from 9 Selwood Terrace, South Kensington, the home of Gordon Campbell (ii. 187, 190). (The Cearne, which Clayton mentions, was Edward Garnett's home at Edenbridge in Kent.)

4) *Once!* (3,427) Sent MS & Typescript Cearne July 9. 1913.
5) *Honour & Arms.* (9,601) Sent to Italy November 11. 1913
          Typescript sent to Margate July 1913.
6) *Blind Gods that do not spare*[1] (9,500) Sent M.S. & typescript Cearne
     Vin d'Ordinaire July 9. 1913.
7) *The Rose Garden* (5,200) Original M.S. at 54 Birdhurst Rd.
          Typescript sent Margate July 18. 1913.
8) *The Christening* (3,317) Original MS at 54 Birdhurst Rd
          Typescript sent Margate July 18. 1913
9) *Strike Pay* (3.427) Original M.S. at 54 Birdhurst Rd
          Typescript went to Lawrence at Margate, 14 July 1913.
10) *Her Turn* (2.075) Original M.S at Birdhurst Rd
          Typescript to Lawrence 14 July 1913
11) *The White Woman*[2] (7,400) Original M.S. at Birdhurst Rd
          Typescript sent July 18 1913 to Lawrence at Margate.
12) *The Daughters of the Vicar.* (18,980) M.S. at Birdhurst Rd
          Typescript sent Aug 1/13 to Margate.
13) *Two Marriages.*[3] (?) Untyped. M.S. at Birdhurst Rd Croydon
14) *The Primrose Path* (5,480) M.S at Birdhurst Rd
          Typescript Aug. 5th to L. acknowledged from Hampstead.
15) *The White Stocking* (7,904) M.S to Lawrence at Kensington July 4 1914
          Typescript to Pinker[4] (July? 1913)
     Poems M.S. of set of Poems are at Birdhurst Rd

785a. To Alfred Sutro, 10 September 1914

Text: MS Dean; cited in Jeffrey Meyers, *D. H. Lawrence: A Biography* (1990), p.158.

The Triangle, Bellingdon Lane, Chesham, Bucks
10 Sept 1914

Dear Mr Sutro,[5]

Your cheque for ten pounds *was* like a sudden fall of manna this morning. I was picturing myself fleeing towards a barracks to enlist, pursued by the wolf from the door, who should sit outside the barracks gate waiting for my return with the honorable little paper 'It is certified that D. H. Lawrence

[1] Early title for 'Vin Ordinaire'.
[2] Early title for 'The Witch à la Mode'.
[3] Early version of 'Daughters of the Vicar' (Roberts C214).
[4] James Brand Pinker (1863–1922), DHL's literary agent 1914–19.
[5] Alfred Sutro (1863 – 1933), dramatist and translator, had heard that the Lawrences 'were very badly off' (*Letters*, ii. 213 and n. 2). He at once sent them a cheque for a loan of £10. See two letters following.

presented himself for enlistment at the Aylesbury barracks, but could not be sworn in owing to weakness of chest.' – That's what one is given, to save one's honor. Somebody called the farm labourer in the next cottage 'milky,' because he didn't go to serve his king and country. So, in a great state, he drove off on the baker's cart, to show 'em what milk he was made of. But late at night he came home again, and when I said, 'But didn't you enlist, then?' he came at me and pulling a paper from his pocket, threw it without a word on the table. It was – 'on account of bad teeth.'

We were almost at our last gasp, now, my wife and I, but confidently expecting something to turn up. So I wrote to Pinker, the agent. I am already in his debt, but the publisher is in my debt, so that Pinker promised me something, if I would be patient. There is due to me about £50. True, it is all I have in the world, and various debts to pay – not very big ones. It is all I have to live on and to hope for. And it hasn't come yet. But even as a prospect, it is something, and you may have somebody more hard up than we are. Please let me keep the ten pounds, because I need them. But as for the more substantial help – the quails after this manna[1] – I would be glad of it, if I were not depriving another poorer man still.

If you are a Knight or a baronet, please forgive me, because I am not sure.

Yours Sincerely   D. H. Lawrence

786a. To Alfred Sutro, 13 September 1914

Text: MS Dean; Unpublished.

The Triangle, Bellingdon Lane, Chesham, Bucks
13 Sept 1914

Dear Mr Sutro,

It has just dawned on me that you must have lent me the £10 of yourself. I did not realise it at first. Your letter came as such a shock – I had no idea that Mary Cannan had written of our reduced state[2] – so that I thought that somehow you were acting on the behalf of some society – and I felt a bit awkward.

Please let me thank you very sincerely for lending me the money. It came at a tight moment, out of the skies, so that it scarcely occurred to me to thank you yourself, at the time.

I am   Yours Very Sincerely   D. H. Lawrence

---

[1] Cf. Exodus xvi. 12–13; Numbers xi. 31–2.

[2] Mary Cannan, née Ansell (1867–1950), m. (1) 1894, (Sir) James Barrie (1860–1937), dramatist; divorced 1909 (2) 1910, Gilbert Cannan (1884–1955), novelist and dramatist (see *Letters*, ii. 208 n.1, 213). The Cannans were close friends of DHL at this time.

798a. To Alfred Sutro, 16 October 1914
Text: MS Dean; Unpublished.

Bellingdon Lane, *Chesham*, Bucks
16 Oct 1914

Dear Mr Sutro,

I suppose you are aware that the Royal Literary Fund have joyfully given me £50.[1] Did they begrudge it me, the good old creatures? Never mind, I will live on their charity gently for a month or two.

Will you let me send you back your cheque, which came in so helpfully a while back. I am just as grateful for it as if I kept it. It is registered in my mind a gift.

Yours Sincerely   D. H. Lawrence

898a. To Lady Ottoline Morrell, [c. 10 April 1915]
Text: MS UT; Unpublished.

[Greatham, Pulborough, Sussex]
[c. 10 April 1915][2]

[Frieda Lawrence begins]
Dear Lady Ottoline,

Yes, do come any day, stay the night if you can, it makes it much less of a rush for you – I am sorry you are not very well, it makes me so cross to be seedy! Will you feel it very much leaving London?[3] We think that every week there will be an excursion train to Garsington! I must'nt write any more because the postman is here for the letters – We will have a lovely talk when you come and dont do too much –

In haste Frieda

God be merciful to us and dont send us any Meynell when you come!

[Lawrence begins]

We shall be so glad to see you. I am writing my 'philosophy' now. It is coming! Thank God. It will be real – thank heaven. I feel the thing is getting under weigh – the new England.

---

[1] Sutro actively promoted DHL's application for support from the Royal Literary Fund: see *Letters*, ii. 224 – 5 n. 4; iii. 227, 251.

[2] The letter is dated with reference to DHL's invitation to Lady Ottoline Morrell (1873–1938), on Good Friday, 2 April 1915, to 'come down–but not till after the middle of next week', an invitation repeated on 8 April (ii. 312, 314). He reported to her, also on 8 April, that he had 'begun again' writing his 'philosophy' (then entitled 'Morgenrot', later 'Le Gai Savaire'), while on 10 April, recovering from an indisposition, he was well enough to send 'the first chapter of my philosophy' to Kot for typing (ii. 315, 317).

[3] Philip Morrell M. P. (1870–1943) and Lady Ottoline moved to Garsington on 17 May 1915.

You will stay the night, for sure.

Love   DHL

916a. To Marjorie Wilkinson, 5 May 1915
Text: Michael Silverman Catalogue Six (1992), Item 33; Postmark, Pulborough 5 May 1915;
Unpublished.

[Greatham. Pulborough. Sussex.]
5 May 1915

Dear Sir[1]

Yes you may have my permission to print the 'Corot' poem in your anthology.[2]

Yours truly   D. H. Lawrence

950a. To Unidentified Recipient, 11 July 1915
Text: MS Meerwein; cited in J.Worthen, *D. H. Lawrence: The Early Years 1885–1912*,
pp. 63–4.

Greatham. Pulborough. Sussex.
11 July 1915

Dear Sir,

Thank you for your letter regarding the spelling in the *Prussian Officer*. The difficulty is, that one reads with the eye, as well as with the ear. Consequently 'dosta' is read as one word, and the mind mechanically halts, saying 'What strange word is this?' And to pull up the mind like that is fatal. Have you ever tried reading dialect – those Yorkshire stories one used to see, or even William Barnes' poetry?[3] It is difficult, even painful, because of the mental effort of interpreting into sound new connections perceived by the eye. Unless the effect of sound is conveyed simultaneously with eye-picture, there is discrepancy and awkwardness. Think how many people can read Molière with pleasure, who wouldn't understand a word of it, on the stage, through hearing. This will tell you how secondary the ear is, even in reading[4] speech.

---

[1] DHL had mistakenly assumed that his correspondent was masculine. Marjorie Wilkinson, who had written to him, was a graduate of the University of London who had been commissioned to produce an anthology, chiefly of verse but with some prose, for the use of children. She wrote also to Rupert Brooke, Masefield, Bridges, de la Mare, Binyon, Housman and many others. Her plans were defeated by wartime stringencies; the anthology was never published.

[2] The poem first appeared in *Love Poems and Others* (1913).

[3] William Barnes (1801–86) was renowned for his poems in the Dorset dialect; see his *Collected Poems*, 1879.

[4] reading] hearing

I never liked the *ter* I use. Often, I used 'ta'. But that even creates a false impression. It reads too sharp, tà. One must compromise, since the convention of word-form is fixed to the eye. The ear will understand all kinds of variation – but the eye wont. Print is so arbitrary. Have you ever read Milton in the old 1680 form?[1] It is the only way to read Milton. The eye is happy then.

Thank you for your letter. I would gladly use 'dosta' if I thought it would be instinctively understood, would not cost an effort.

Yours Sincerely   D. H. Lawrence

1009a. To John Wilson, 6 October 1915

Text: MS Anon; Unpublished.

[1, Byron Villas, Vale-of-Health, Hampstead, London.]
6 Oct 1915

Dear Sir,[2]

Thank you for your card intimating your wish to subscribe for three copies of the *Signature*. I don't quite know what you mean by 'scope etc.' But if you will send subscription of 7/6 to the *Signature*, 12 Fisher St, Southampton Row, they will send you at once three copies of the number already issued, and three copies each of the remaining five numbers, as they appear, fortnightly, hence until Christmas.

If there is anything else you would like to know, will you please ask me in detail.

Yours faithfully   D. H. Lawrence

1156. To Lady Ottoline Morrell, 1 February 1916

Text: MS GU; *Letters*, ii. 521–2.

Porthcothan – St Merryn – N. Cornwall
1 Feb. 1916

My dear Ottoline,[3]

---

[1] DHL's reference is unclear since the only edn of Milton in 1680 was a re-issue of *Paradise Regain'd [and] Samson Agonistes* (1671). In view of his concerns in this letter it is possible that he had seen David Masson's facsimile edn (1877) of *Paradise Lost* which stimulated interest in Milton's idiosyncratic spelling. (DHL had visited Lady Ottoline Morrell at Garsington in mid-June 1915; perhaps in her library he had seen this or another 'old spelling' edn.)

[2] The recipient was most likely John Gideon Wilson (1876–1963), bookseller, formerly with Constable & Co., then with Jones & Evans, and finally chairman and managing director of John & Edward Bumpus, 1941–50. DHL reported the enquiry from Jones & Evans, for three copies of *Signature*, on 7 October 1915 (*Letters*, ii. 407).

[3] The text of this letter printed in Volume II relied on Huxley; the MS has since become available; the present text is complete and accurate. Annotation to the text in ii. 521–2 is not repeated here.

Here I send you the MS. of the poems. It is complete except for that poem 'Snapdragon' which was published in the first *Georgian Anthology*. I will send you that on, and you will insert it in the right place, according to the index, will you? Tell me if you like the poems. You see they make a sort of inner history of my life, from 20 to 26. Tell me if the inscription will do.

This MS. is for America really. Will you send it on to my agent, *J. B. Pinker, Talbot House, Arundel St, Strand W. C.*, in a few days? I have sent him the duplicate MS. for the English publisher. But keep this as long as you want it.

You will find enclosed also three little MS. books, from which these poems were chiefly collected. The black book is a new scribble – but the red college note books – they *are* my past, indeed. Will you let them lie with my other MS. at Garsington. But read the poems first in the type-written MS; they will make a better impression.

I send you also, Petronius. He startled me at first, but I liked him. He is a gentleman, when all is said. I have taken a great dislike to Dostoievsky in the *Possessed*. It seems so sensational, and such a degrading of the pure mind, somehow. It seems as though the pure mind, the true reason, which surely is noble, were made trampled and filthy under the hoofs of secret, perverse, undirect sensuality. Petronius is straight and above board. Whatever he does, he doesn't try to degrade and dirty[1] the pure Mind in him. But Dostoievsky, mixing God and Sadism, he is foul. I will send your books back by degrees. A thousand thanks for them. And that Egyptian book of Mlle. Baillots is a real pleasure. Please give her my thanks for it.

I am getting better – at last I've got a solid core inside me. I've felt so long as if I hadn't got a solid being at all. Now I can put my feet on the ground again. But it is still shaky. I believe that milk casein stuff is *very* good; also the Brands.

Heseltine and his Puma are not very happy I think. But let the affair work itself out: that is the only way.[2]

When do you think you may be coming down. We had a perfect day on Sunday, when we could see the ships far out at sea, and we were all so happy. But it has gone sad again.

Would you rather have had your title in the inscription? After all, it is to you the inscription is written, not to your social self.

Heseltine is gloomy about conscription. When one thinks out, away from

---

[1] dirty]bla[cken?]
[2] For Philip Heseltine and Minnie Lucy ('Puma') Channing, see *Letters*, ii. 442 n. 3 and 481 n. 2 respectively.

this remoteness, how horrible it is! But there, it is no good: why should one
waste oneself.

Frieda sends her love, and I mine. I hope you are feeling better.

Yours   D. H. Lawrence

1299a. To Augusta de Wit, 22 October 1916

Text: MS NLMD; M. Uding-van Laarhoven, '"Oh, I wish it was spring in the world of
man . . . ": Twee brieven van D. H. Lawrence (1885-1930) aan Augusta de Wit (1864-1939)',
Opstellen over de Koninklijke Bibliotheek en andere studies (Hilversum, 1986), pp. 466–7.

Higher Tregerthen, Zennor, St.-Ives. Cornwall.
22 Oct. 1916

Dear Madam,[1]

I have asked Duckworths to send you a copy of my *Widowing of Mrs
Holroyd*, also of my first volume of poems. My first novel *The White Peacock*
might be of some use to you: it is about farm-life and middle-class life
mixed: the second, *The Trespasser*, is about a violinist in the Covent Garden
orchestra: *Sons and Lovers* is the third. My last novel, *The Rainbow* was sup-
pressed by the authorities here for *immorality*, and so cannot be obtained.
There remains only a book of short stories, *The Prussian Officer*, which has
only one or two tales dealing with the common people, and a book of Italian
Studies. These are all my works – excepting a book of poems this year, called
Amores. Duckworth is the publisher of them all. I would send you the lot,
but have no money. Living by these writings, I am always hopelessly poor.

I should like to read your 'Orpheus in a Malay Village' in German. I am
sorry I cannot read Dutch. But in English or German or French I should
enjoy reading anything you have written.

There is need enough, as you say, for poets, men and women, in days like
these. But the world is like a child that is ill, which screams and kicks when a
doctor approaches to touch its pain. The last thing the world will bear nowadays – at least in England – is the touch of a genuine poet.

I am glad you are speaking of Hardy.[2] He is our last great writer. Bennett
is only a journalist, in comparison, and Masefield is, a good deal of him, spurious. Wells, in his *Tono Bungay*, *Love and Mr Lewisham*, *The History of Mr*

---

[1] Anna Augusta Henriette de Wit (1864–1939), Dutch novelist and short-story writer; for over
  30 years she had reviewed publications in German and English for the Dutch press; her most
  famous work was *Orpheus in de dessa* (Amsterdam, 1903) ('Orpheus in a Malay Village'). For
  further details see James T. Boulton, 'Editing D. H. Lawrence's Letters: The Editor's
  Creative Role', *Prose Studies*, xix (August 1996), 217–19.
2 She had been in correspondence with Hardy (as well as with Hans Carossa and Richard
  Hughes) (see M. Uding-van Laarhoven, *art. cit.*, p. 466).

Polly, is really very good, dealing with lower class life, don't you think? to me, he is better than Bennett, who leaves out the *toughness* which the common people never really lack. Bennett's is coward's writing: he is really a journalist, a time-server.

There are a few odd books of the English working classes that are very revealing: like Niel Lyons *Sixpenny Pieces*, and *Arthur's*. Then there is one good Scotch novel *The House with the Green Shutters* – as well as Barrie's sentimental *Window in Thrums* and *Sentimental Tommy*.[1] But perhaps you know these things quite as well as I do. If so, please forgive the intrusion.

Yours Very Sincerely   D. H. Lawrence

You can get Wells' books, and the *House with the Green Shutters*, and many other modern ones, for sevenpence each, 'Nelsons Sevenpenny Series.' They are quite decent, if you don't know them.[2]

1332a. To Esther Andrews, [17? December 1916]

Text: MS Wanning; Louise E. Wright, 'Dear Montague: Letters from Esther Andrews to Robert Mountsier', *DHLReview*, xxvi (1995–96), 177.

[Zennor, St. Ives, Cornwall]
[17? December 1916][3]

[Esther Andrews, writing to Robert Mountsier on 19 December 1916, reported a letter from Lawrence asking 'what day we were coming', and continuing:][4] Please ask Mountsier to ask his sister to lend John Edler the copy of the *Rainbow*[5] - I have written him (John) [. . .] sent him back his $3 & told him I [. . .] would lend him the book for *one week only*. I wish Mountsier would write to his sister at once.

---

[1] Alfred Neil Lyons (1880–1940), *Arthur's* (1908) and *Sixpenny Pieces* (1909); George Douglas Brown (1869–1902) (pseud. George Douglas), *The House with the Green Shutters* (1901); (Sir) James Barrie, *A Window in Thrums* (1889) and *Sentimental Tommy* (1896).

2 On 28 January 1917, in *Nieuwe Rotterdamsche Courant*, appeared Augusta de Wit's highly appreciative review of *The Widowing of Mrs Holroyd*, in which she also treated *The White Peacock*, *Sons and Lovers*, *Love Poems* and *Amores*.

3 Mail appears to have been delayed between London and Zennor; when he wrote this letter DHL had not received Esther Andrews' written on Friday, 15 December; his letter, arriving in London on Tuesday, 19 December, may therefore have been written on Sunday 17th.

4 Esther Andrews (1880–1962), was an American, a student of art at Yale and now a journalist; she partnered DHL's friend who was later to become his agent, the American Robert ('Montague') Mountsier (1888–1972). They were to spend Christmas together at Higher Tregerthen; she alone later visited the Lawrences there in May 1917. She did relief work in France toward the end of the war and probably there met Canby Chambers (d.1958), whose wife she became in 1919. (For a fuller account see Louise E. Wright, *DHL Review*, xxvi.167–75.)

5 Mountsier had two sisters (obituary, *New York Times*, 25 November 1972); the one referred to here was Mabel who lived at his address in New York. Edler is unidentified.

1372n. From Frieda Lawrence to Esther Andrews, [9? February 1917]

Text: TMSC Anon; Unpublished.

[Zennor, St. Ives, Cornwall]

[9? February 1917][1]

Dear Esther,

For once I feel quite as desperate as you – *If* America comes in, well then there *is* no America in our sense; Is it at all a game? I dont understand it. It all rings false this sudden anger – as if it were factitious. We get letters and forms about passports, but the home office does not know itself what to do at present, it's bloody – I will let you know about coming to London – We want to go if it is at all possible to America unless war is declared, but I think it wont be – Is'nt all this done to pacify the Allies? – I feel there is a great swindle going on *somewhere* – Monty mustnt go – Tell him how *cold* the water is, and I *don't* like heroes – *Three ships* have been torpedoed *just here*, gone, the men seen struggling in the water (Stanley saw them) for a few minutes, I tell you it's *very* bad I won't go unless in a safe American boat – *unwar* – But I am so miserable really, as if absolutely nothing mattered – You must'nt go to America either yet, till things settle a little bit – But I daresay you are frightfully restless – Of course you can come here as you know – We will be as happy as we can – After all *damn* them – We are not them! 'Thank God I am not like my neighbour!' Gilbert Cannan has had a breakdown – He is in a Hampstead nursing home – I respect him for it – hes is so poor too – Mrs. Carswell got on your nerves[2] – There is a certain scotch impudence about her at times, *very* trying – I suppose London is vile and the blitheness on top is so *sickening*! But make yourself *sick* with it all, quite sick, then it will go and we shall come out like daisies, fresh and smiling new hope – I want to go to London on the *22nd* just for 3 or four days – I shall stay with Campbell – I wish you could be here with Lawrence – Where will you go, if you must give up your rooms? The gin has cheered us – I was so *happy* before the American blow –

Frieda

---

[1] Frieda's letter – providing background material to DHL's two letters of 9 February 1917 – was probably written on that day. It was clearly later than 2 February when USA broke off relations with Germany and after the ships were sunk off Zennor on 6th (see *Letters*, iii. 88); Frieda comments on Gilbert Cannan's breakdown reported in Kot's letter received and replied to on 9th (iii. 89–90); she remarks that she will stay in London with Gordon Campbell from whom a 'friendly' letter had arrived on 9th (iii. 90); and her letter obviously pre-dates the news – which DHL had received by 12 February – that the Lawrences' application for passports had been rejected (iii.90).

[2] Catherine Carswell (1879–1946), novelist, close friend since 1914 of the Lawrences and, later, DHL's biographer. m. 1915, Donald Carswell (1882–1940), barrister.

1377a. To Augusta de Wit, 22 February 1917

Text: MS NLMD; M. Uding-van Laarhoven, *Opstellen over de Koninklijke Biblioteek en andere studies* (1986), pp. 467–8.

Zennor, St. Ives, Cornwall
22 Feb. 1917

Dear Augusta de Witt,

I have received today your letter dated 13/2, but no other letter has reached me. The *Yale Review* came just after Christmas, with a little notification that it was part of a mail captured by the Germans, and consequently delayed. The letter, I suppose, was lost in the capture. I am sorry. You have then received the books which I asked the publishers to send you?

I shall be very happy for you to translate some of my work for Holland. I shall have to let my agent arrange any business that is necessary, but I shall ask him to fix any copy right charge at a minumum. You will hear from him in a day or two.[1]

'The Hunter' in the *Yale Review* interested me very much.[2] This same subject, the primal cruelty which undoubtedly belongs to all life, the duality of the tiger and the deer, the surge and glitter of intermingled play and blood-destruction, all through life, seems to me the core of the mystery. And you had created the whole atmosphere of the jungle most vividly and beautifully. How do you know it so well? I wish to God man would only hear that note in the chirping of the crickets 'a merry sweetness, most gentle.'[3] Then the change of heart would have come over the mankind of today, for which one craves most passionately. Oh, I wish it was spring in the world of man, as it is, nearly, in the world of nature. The birds are already singing. But when will the change come over mankind? One wants it, oh, so much, to move with a delicate, happy gentleness, such delight of sensitive bliss. But there is only the greatest ugliness and hatred, even a morbid evil destructiveness in the soul and will of people, that one wonders, here, in England, that the very grass doesn't die. – But the change will come – we shall still be happy and know the merry gentleness of humanity.

D. H. Lawrence

---

[1] DHL sent Augusta de Wit's letter immediately to Pinker, with the suggestion that he should not 'charge much, if anything' (*Letters*, iii. 95). However, no translations of DHL's works were ever published by de Wit.

[2] Her story (a translation of 'De jager', 1912) appeared in the *Yale Review*, v (January 1916), 397–408. Its action is set in the Malayan jungle; its theme may be roughly expressed in the translator's words: 'the one lust for life and for death which hurls every strong one upon every other strong one' (p. 406).

[3] DHL quotes from a sentence towards the end of de Wit's story (p. 408).

1386a. To Harriet Monroe, 9 March 1917
Text: TMSC Anon; Unpublished.

Higher Tregerthen, Zennor, St. Ives. – Cornwall.

9 March 1917

Dear Harriet Monroe,[1]

Thank you for your letter with the copy of the 'Resurrection' poem, and the cheque for five pounds. I return the original version of the poem. I like it much better than the one you had, but you use which you like.[2] I enclose two or three other poems. They are all out of the new book. You will use them if you care for them.[3] None has been published before, either in England or in America. But my new book will come out, I suppose, in June or July. I will let you know. If you want any more poems from me, which I don't suppose you do, will you tell me.

It is spring, with new sunshine and such a delicate wind off the sea. The road to America on a day like this looks so exquisite and ethereal, a blue Semplegades[4] of sky and ocean, it seems surely there is bliss beyond. I am confident we can find the Blessed Isles, if we go about it the right way. We must find the Blessed Isles, at least catch sight of them rising up in the distance, before we die. It is our business.

D. H. Lawrence[5]

---

[1] Harriet Monroe (1860–1936), American poet and editor; founder of *Poetry: A Magazine of Verse* (Chicago) in 1912.

[2] The versions of the poem to which DHL refers cannot be identified with complete certainty. 'Resurrection' had a complicated history. DHL had sent one MS of the poem (Roberts E346b) to Harriet Monroe on 26 October 1915 (*Letters*, ii. 417); a second, extensively revised MS (Roberts E346a), was submitted via Hilda Aldington in October 1916 (ii. 664–5), for publication in *Some Imagist Poets* (1917), edited by Amy Lowell. When Lowell decided not to include the poem in her anthology it is more than likely that she passed the MS, or typed copy, to Monroe for *Poetry*. Monroe then returned to DHL the two versions of the poem which were now in her possession; he in turn, sent one back to her with this letter; but which was deemed 'the original version' is unclear. The poem which Monroe published in *Poetry*, June 1917, is faithful to neither of the MSS mentioned here.

[3] No poem from the 'new book'– *Look! We Have Come Through!* (November 1917) – was published in *Poetry*. At least four were offered by DHL: 'The Doe at Evening' (published as 'A Doe at Evening' in *Look! We Have Come Through!*); 'Frost Flowers'; 'Rabbit Snared in the Night'; and 'People'.

[4] The word is puzzling. DHL, who was not an expert typist, may have intended 'Symplegades', thus making reference to the Cyanean Rocks, the two movable rocks where the Bosporus and Black Sea meet and between which Jason passed in his search for the Golden Fleece. ('Cyanean' means 'blue-coloured'.)

[5] According to a typed note on the original, Harriet Monroe replied to this letter on 12 June 1917.

1389a. To Hilda Aldington, [23? March 1917]

Text: H. D., *Bid Me To Live* (1960), p. 51.

[Higher Tregerthen, Zennor, St. Ives, Cornwall]
[23? March 1917]

Dear [Hilda],[1]

There is no use trying to believe that all this war really exists. It really doesn't matter. We must go on. I know that [Richard] will come back. Your frozen altars mean something, but I don't like the second half of the Orpheus sequence as well as the first.[2] Stick to the woman speaking. How can you know what Orpheus feels? It's your part to be woman, the woman vibration. Eurydice should be enough. You can't deal with both. If you go on –

1404a. To Robert Nichols, 21 April 1917

Text: Takeo Iida, 'Lawrence's 21 April 1917 Letter to Robert Nichols', *DHLReview*, xx (Spring 1988), 69–70; Kazuo Nakahashi, *D. H. Lawrence* (Tokyo, 1955).

[5, Acacia Road, St John's Wood, N.W.]
21 April 1917

Dear Nichols[3]

Heseltine says you are ill in hospital. I am here until Monday, or Tuesday. Will somebody ring me up here and tell me at what time I can see you on Monday?

Yrs   D. H. Lawrence

1410a. To Hilda Aldington, [?April–May 1917]

Text: H. D., *Bid Me To Live*, pp. 57, 80, 139.

[Higher Tregerthen, Zennor, St. Ives, Cornwall]
[?April–May 1917]

We will go away together where the angels come down to earth . . . Kick over

---

[1] In her autobiography in the form of a novel, *Bid Me To Live*, Hilda Aldington (1886–1961) cast herself as Julia Ashton, her husband, Richard Aldington (1892–1962) as Rafe, and DHL as Frederico (or 'Rico'). Because the characters and events in the novel so closely relate to actuality, and because we know that DHL had just heard from her (*Letters*, iii. 105), it is legitimate to assume (as Professor John Worthen argues in a forthcoming article in *DHLReview*, Vol. 30) that the text quoted here is, if not a verbatim transcript, at least close to DHL's original.

[2] DHL was in correspondence with Hilda Aldington about the anthology, *Some Imagist Poets* (Boston and New York, 1917), to which both had contributed. DHL's reference is probably to one of her poems in the anthology, 'Eurydice' (*Collected Poems 1912–1944*, ed. Louis l. Martz, Manchester: Carcanet Press, 1984, pp. 51–5).

[3] Robert Malise Bowyer Nichols (1893–1944), poet and dramatist. DHL would remember visiting him in hospital, suffering from shell-shock, in 1915. Philip Heseltine (pseud. Peter Warlock) (1894–1930), friend to both men, had taken DHL there (ii. 442 nn. 2 and 3).

your tiresome house of life, our languid lily of virtue nods perilously near the pit . . . love-adept, you are a living spirit in a living spirit city.[1]

1441a. To Esther Andrews, 23 August 1917

Text: TMSC Anon; Mark Kinkead-Weekes, 'Humour in the Letters of D. H. Lawrence',
Lawrence and Comedy, ed. P. Eggert and J. Worthen (Cambridge, 1996), pp. 180–2.

Zennor, St. Ives, Cornwall
23 Aug. 1917

Your letter came two days ago: glad you are in a room of your own, and feel better. – Montague sleeps sounder than the Seven Sleepers,[2] though his dreams are inconsequent beyond measure. – Everything in the world at large is nauseating: labour gone back on Stockholm, miners having made a volte face[3] – but the miners like the war, they are rich and safe. – Somehow I don't care. Labour is a bad egg to start with. One looks to it just to help to stop the war, that is all. But it won't even do that. – Yet the end is not far off. The unseen ministers of grace[4] are working out the close of this business, ministers of disgrace notwithstanding. – I feel a bit triumphant somewhere, as after a hard struggle with the impervious fiend. – We shall come to America when the war is over. The cup of Europe is drunk empty, we can't go on sucking at the dregs.[5] – How I shall get any money is a problem. But problems work out.

Here in Zennor – first, Frieda has been in bed for three weeks with bad neuritis in her leg, much pain and everything wretched. But it is getting better. – The weather has been beautiful, I have worked in the hay, and bathed on Sundays. One can't swim here, the sea is never calm enough, among the rocks. The gardens are rolling and teeming with vegetables, and a row of sweet-peas of all colors. There are at present 25 fat marrows plumping under the roaming leaves, the tomatoes by the tower are just turning red, beans and peas hang in festoons, the whole place is like a harvest festival, I

---

[1] These extracts, scattered in Hilda Aldington's novel, may well have come from the same letter (as Professor Worthen has suggested).

[2] It is possible that, in her letter received on 21 August, Esther Andrews had mentioned the *Seven Arts* magazine for which she was seeking short stories (see *Letters*, iii. 142), and that prompted DHL's reference to the seven youths of Ephesus who, according to legend, died following the Decian persecution in 250 A.D. and awoke after 230 years, dying soon after.

[3] An international Peace Conference was to be held in Stockholm; German Socialists would be present; and this provoked acrimonious debate as to whether British trades unionists should attend. On 10 August the Miners Federation supported their going, but on 20 August by a small majority the miners reversed their earlier decision, thus ensuring the defeat of the proposal at the Labour Party Conference on 21st.

[4] *Hamlet* I. iv. 39.

[5] Cf. Isaiah li. 17, 22 (A.V.).

never saw such prolific fat of the land. – Puma and Heseltine came down:[1]
wan and unhappy she, crazy he: stayed a fortnight in the bungalow, she
hating it; now have disappeared utterly. Starr[2] says mysteriously 'Mum's the
word.' It is all the sheerest nonsense. Gray is at Bosigran, painting his cup-
boards.[3] The Starrs are at Treveal.

Last night they gave a concert in St. Ives: the Starrs: in St. Ives' Pavilion.
It was called a Concert Play 'East and West' – composed by Starr. I went
down with the Hockings: W[illia]m H[enr]y, Mary, Mabel, Stanley.[4] It was
too dreadful. There was a violin solo: then Meredith intoned[5] a dreadful
poem of his own concoction: 'Oh East is East and West is West and *ever* the
twain shall meet,' fearful.[6] He wore a long night-gown of dark green cotton
with a white mark in it: and the violin moaned faintly from behind a curtain,
pained. Starr has no ear, and was [ ]. Then he was to have had an 'original'
character, Old Rowe, the old man who looks after the mines at Treveal – who
scared Gray and Heseltine, and gave Starr a bottle of rum, you remember.
At the eleventh hour, old Rowe said he was buggered if he was going, one
fool was enough, no need to make it two. The resourceful Meredith,
however, in the afternoon came upon an elderly weed singing in the streets
of St. Ives, gave him sixpence and his tea, and wherever, on the programme,
it said 'Daddy White, an Original Song, composed by Himself' – appeared
this piece of street refuse, in Lady Mary's cotton kimono, and yowled a
street song, putting up his hand occasionally, automatically, as if someone
had given him a penny. The audience, many of whom had paid 3/3 for a
seat: seats 1/2, 2/2, 3/3, were merely pained: Lady Hain,[7] patroness of this
affair, and Lady Hain's musical daughter exceedingly so. Then Lady Mary
sang 'The Rosary' rather faintly and blankly.[8] Then Starr recited 'the Bells'
– giving a brief fore speech 'This magnificent poem by Edgar Allan Poe is
one of the most wonderful in the English language. Edgar Allan Poe was a
master of transcendental music, *far* greater than Shakspeare – etc.' – Then

---

[1] See *Letters*, iii. 36 and n. 1.

[2] Meredith Starr and Lady Mary, née Grey (1881–1945), daughter of 8th Earl of Stamford, m.
1 March 1917 (divorced 1930).

[3] Cecil Gray (1895–1951), composer and music critic; he lived at Bosigran Castle, Morvah,
near Pendeen (see iii. 128 and n. 1).

[4] The Hocking family were farmers and neighbours of the Lawrences (see iii. 64 n. 1).

[5] intoned] sang

[6] Cf. Rudyard Kipling, 'The Ballad of East and West' (1892) [' . . . is West, and never the twain
. . .'].

[7] Née Catherine Hughes, m. Sir Edward Hain (1851–1917), shipowner of St Ives. Their daughter was Kate (b. 1885).

[8] Several songs have this title; this may have been the sentimental song by Ethelbert Nevin (cf.
iv. 102n).

he recited the poem. It went awfully flat. People giggled a little at the winkle-winkle tinkle-tinkle business, then Meredith started to hop, he stamped at the 'Bells bells bells – – ' and jumped 'Bells!' and leaped into the air 'Bells!!!'[1] It was most astounding. Unfortunately the Cornish *couldn't* laugh: they were too pained.

Then came 'Scene I. Leila and Majnoun – the Persian Romeo and Juliet (a) Dawn (b) Dusk.' – Leila lay on a couch, hair brushed out, orange butter-muslin frock, while Starr recited – intoned – read from a little book, another poem of his 'The red of dawn approacheth, The night doeth sound retreat – – ' ending each verse 'the love of your lily-white feet.' After a long poem, Lady Mary awkwardly awoke and gauchely got up and he kissed her – exit left. – re-enter Right: Starr lies down to sleep, she invokes him; he awakes (he wears a crimson satin coatee and a pale blue turban) – kisses her – exit left – Song by Daddy White 'Peek-a-bo' – Violin Solo. – 'Scene II, James O'Reilly Adventurer, and bride, Spanish Gipsy – Lady Mary and Meredith Starr.' – She in one of Frieda's frocks and the black silk shawl, sat very uncomfortably on the camp-bed (on which was our Ott[oline] bed-cover)[2] and very gawkily tried to fan herself with a big paper fan. Meredith, shirt and trousers and sash, read-intoned recited from a little book a long long poem about himself, every verse ending 'The Admiral's daughter Lulu.' Pained wonder on the part of everybody. So ended Scene II. – Song Daddy White. 'Scene III. Queen Sheba The Angel of Destiny.' Lady Mary, with her hands drooping and shoulder shrugging recites a short poem by Meredith, of how she loves and does not love: Meredith's occult form looms behind the curtain 'Thou shalt etc – ' Lady Mary sinks on the couch, Meredith bursts forth from the curtain, in his blue bed-gown with spots 'I am The Angel of Destiny, I govern you by fear.' – recites his own grandeur – exeunt omnes. – Violin Solo by Trevor White. – (a) African Dance: Starr, in a table cloth, stamps and stares (b) Indian Serpent dance – Starr in a towel, prances and undulates his arms. (c) Greek Flute dance – Starr, with his

---

[1] Poe's poem (1849) would give Starr abundant opportunity for physical display:
　　How they tinkle, tinkle, tinkle,
　　In the icy air of night!
　　While the stars that oversprinkle
　　All the Heavens, seem to twinkle
　　With a crystalline delight . . .
　　To the tintinnabulation that so musically wells
　　From the bells, bells, bells, bells,
　　Bells, bells, bells –
　　From the jingling and the tinkling of the bells.
'Bells' recurs on innumerable occasions thereafter.
[2] A gift from Lady Ottoline Morrell in February 1916 (see ii. 538).

hands to his mouth, in trousers and sash, capers like figures on a Greek Vase. (d) Short Violin Solo.

After that, I, and,[1] most of the audience, left. – William Henry was almost in tears. We ate chip-potatoes in a side street, and drove home, black darkness, and howling storm of rain, rain like waves of the sea: William Henry shouting at the horse 'Rose – co-o-ome up' then continuing in a heartbroken voice 'How! And have we come out of a night like this, and all – –'

– I had to give you this in full, as it is the greatest event in Zennor for some time. – Starr must have made quite a bit of money out of it. The takings must have been about £15 or more – one third for Red Cross – £10 for Meredith, from which he was going to give 6d to the weed – and the violinist was a good deal of a musician and a gentleman. – £9-19-6 for Meredith. – I want my money back – my 1/2.

Chatto & Windus are doing the poems.[2] – Cecil Palmer wrote about the novel:[3] thinks it would be impossible to publish publicly – only wishes he were rich enough to bring it out for pleasure – but isn't – and there's the end. Qu'importe![4] There's no other publishing news.

Let us know your movements.

D. H. Lawrence

Why didn't you answer Frieda's letter?[5]

1512a. To The Librarian, Cambridge University Library, [24 January 1918]

Text: MS CUL; PC; Postmark, Newbury 24 JA 18; Unpublished.

[Chapel Farm Cottage, Hermitage, nr Newbury, Berks]
[24 January 1918]

I send my full name as requested

David Herbert Lawrence[6]

---

[1] TMSC reads 'and, and'

[2] Chatto & Windus published *Look! We Have Come Through!* on 26 November 1917 (Roberts A10).

[3] DHL heard from Palmer on or about 21 August 1917 (cf. *Letters*, iii. 151) and received the MS of *Women in Love* from him on 25 August.

[4] 'What does it matter!'

[5] Her letter is unlocated.

[6] *Look! We Have Come Through!* was the first of DHL's works to be catalogued in Cambridge University Library; cataloguing involved recording an author's full name; hence the request to DHL and his reply. The University Librarian to whom the postcard was returned was Francis John Henry Jenkinson (1853–1923).

1662a. To Cyril Beaumont, 28 November 1918
Text: MS Anon; Michael Silverman Catalogue, 1998.

Mountain Cottage, Middleton-by-Wirksworth, Derby
28 November 1918

Dear Beaumont,[1]

Have you any idea when you are going to publish that little volume of verse of mine, called *Bay*? It seems a long time since you took the MS. [Did you return to Pinker] that other MS. of verse, 'All of Us'? [If you still have it, please send it to me at Mountain Cottage.]

D. H. Lawrence

1663a. To Selina Yorke, 2 December 1918
Text: MS Schulson; Unpublished.

Mountain Cottage, Middleton-by-Wirksworth. Derby.
2 Dec. 1918

Dear Mrs Yorke,[2]

I understand well enough that sometimes one *can't* go out when one has promised. Such a lot of complex things go to one's make-up now, and it isn't easy to live. Heavens, don't apologise to me. Though we haven't known each other very long, yet, in a way, I believe we know one another pretty well, Arabella and you and me. And the things of the moment don't matter. The moment is a tiresome affair, very tangled. At the back one is free and friendly all along. That's how I feel. – With Hilda, I feel one could never speak to her any more as to a human being who would simply understand: she really has lost her own self. That's why one is hopeless about knowing *her*. It is somehow too late. – As for ourselves, I think we run a bit loose at times, but we come back. Hilda doesn't.

I am alone here. Frieda is still in Hermitage. She is coming to London this week, I think: staying in Catherine Carswell's house – Holly Bush House, Holly Mount, Hampstead N. W. 3. You will hear from her. – I am trying to get stories and things done to save *our* situation. Oh poverty! – But really, it doesn't bother me. One day we shall win through. – I hope A's

---

[1] Cyril William Beaumont (1891–1976), bookseller and publisher; published *Bay*, 20 November 1919 (Roberts A12).

[2] Selina Yorke, expatriate American, of whom little is known, was the mother of the Lawrences' friend, Dorothy ('Arabella') Yorke (b. 1892). Arabella had spent two weeks with them in Derbyshire in June 1918 (see *Letters*, iii. 173 n. 3, 256). She had just begun what was to prove a long relationship with Richard Aldington, which contributed to his separation in 1919 from his wife, Hilda Doolittle ('H.D'.) (see iii. 31 n. 1).

Selfridge cartoon[1] goes well – it was nice. We'll have a nice and festive meeting soon, shall we? I should love to be gay and jolly a bit.

I expect I shall be in London again soon. I invoke the gods for you: – you invoke them for me. We'll have a little gay triumph yet. Never mind – this is low water mark.

affectionately   D. H. Lawrence

No, no Mr.[2]

1768a. To Cyril Beaumont, 16 July 1919
Text: Michael Silverman Catalogue Seven, 1992, Item 32, Plate IV; Unpublished.

Chapel Farm Cottage, Hermitage nr. Newbury. Berks
16 July 1919

Dear Beaumont

I return the proofs. I thought when you sent the MS. you did so *before* setting up at all: hence the big change in 'Guards'.[3]

It is a pity to put 'Town' before 'Last Hours.'[4] The movement is supposed to be from the old pre-war days, and from the old country pre-war sleep, gradually into war. But if it is really important you can break the order.

Do please continue to send me proofs. I promise not to alter more than a word or so – and this cannot mean much delay: especially at the rate you get on at. I believe you intend this to be one of my posthumous works . . .

1934a. To Baroness Anna von Richthofen, [3 March 1920]
Text: MS Houle; PC v. Vista dell'Etna da Taormina; Postmark, Taormina 4 3 20; Unpublished.

Fontana Vecchia, Taormina, Sicily
3 March.

[5]I have found such a beautiful house here, with a big garden on the hillside. Frieda is still in Capri – I hope she will arrive by steamer at Messina on Saturday – She will love this place. She wanted to come to Sicily. I will write soon.

Love   DHL

---

[1] Unidentified, but cf. Corrigenda and Addenda, ii. 418 n. 2.

[2] Perhaps Mrs Yorke had addressed DHL as 'Mr'.

[3] DHL sent Beaumont the MS of '18 poems – à propos the war', on 21 April 1918 (*Letters*, iii. 233, 237); over a year later, on 18 June 1919 (iii. 365), DHL returned 'MS.' (perhaps meaning the typescript), pointing out that he had 'altered the Hyde Park', which – as 'Guards! A Review in Hyde Park, 1913' – is the opening poem in *Bay*.

[4] In *Bay*, 'Last Hours' precedes 'Town'.

[5] DHL's correspondent was Frieda's mother (1851–1930).

1959a. To Stanley Unwin, 2 April 1920
Text: TMSC UR; Unpublished.

Fontana Vecchia, Taormina, Sicily.
2 April 1920

Dear Mr Unwin,[1]

I had your letter of March 24th.[2] Sorry those Education Essays which I would have finished and given to you are in my big luggage, which has been on the way from London since November 14th and hasn't arrived *yet*. Such are railways here. Be warned. When it comes, I will do the essays as I promised and let you see them. The novel[3] is only $\frac{1}{2}$ finished and the end must be prayed for.

What I want to ask you, however, is whether you would like to consider an MS. on the Foreign Legion – in Algiers and Lyons – by a man who hated it and deserted from it. It isn't *war* experiences – just peace, or rather at home life in the Foreign Legion, rather awful, and very improper. The man who did the book is in a monastery here in Italy – I think in its unliterary way, it's jolly good; straight and simple. I believe the bare record of the life that happens would be too strong for an English public. But I know M[agnus] wouldn't mind how much you cut, if you found it necessary, as he isn't literary. What he would like is to sell the book right out for a sum down – English rights presumably.

Will you tell me what you think of this.

Yours   D. H. Lawrence[4]

---

[1] Stanley Unwin (1884–1968) founded the publishing firm of George Allen & Unwin Ltd in 1914.

[2] Unwin had been in touch with Barbara Low – who was then acting as DHL's London agent – about the publication of essays originally invited by George Freeman, editor of the *Times Educational Supplement*. DHL submitted four essays; they were rejected by Freeman on 1 January 1919; on 24 March 1920, in a letter to DHL, Unwin expressed an interest in seeing 'sufficient matter to form a volume' (TMSC UR). He also enquired about a novel which he understood DHL had not yet placed with a publisher.

[3] *The Lost Girl*.

[4] Unwin replied on 8 April (TMSC UR), encouraging DHL to let him see Maurice Magnus's MS: 'The fact that it *isn't* war experiences is to the good, for war books are very much at a discount just now.' For the later, extremely complex negotiations relating to the publication of Magnus's MS, see Louise Wright, 'Disputed *Dregs*: D. H. Lawrence and the Publication of Maurice Magnus' *Memoirs of the Foreign Legion*', *The Journal of the D. H. Lawrence Society* (Eastwood, 1996), pp. 57–73.

1964a. To Baroness Anna von Richthofen, [9 April 1920]
Text: MS Houle; PC v. Catania: Panorama dal porto; Postmark, Taormina 12 4 20;
Unpublished.

Catania
– 9 April

That screwed-in tooth of F[rieda's] came out, so we have had to run to
Catania. What a wild town it is! about 1 hour from Taormina, quick train.
The coast is lovely. We are becoming so brown, both of us, with the sun. I
heard from my sister she has sent parcels to you and Else.[1] I shall try to send
you a pair of shoes – if it is allowed – Shall they be same size as Frieda's? –
Remember me to Marriannchen[2] – she is a young lady now, I hear.

Love from both   DHL

1976a. To Stanley Unwin, 4 May 1920
Text: MS UR; Unpublished.

Villa Fontana Vecchia, Taormina, (Messina)
4 May 1920

Dear Mr Unwin

I am posting to you today, by registered post, the first half or more of
Magnus' book on *The Foreign Legion*, of which I wrote to you. The second
half is finished, and Magnus will no doubt forward it to you himself. It[3] contains an account of the Legion at Lyons, and the desertion and escape from
France.

I think the book is a good, simple record, genuine every bit – a really good
document. No doubt it is too simple and explicit. But M. won't mind how
much you cut it, if you have to cut it. In fact what he wants is to sell you the
MS. outright for a sum down, leaving you every right over it, for you to do as
you like with it. Myself, I cant help respecting the work for its simple bareness. I like even its amateurishness. – The whole amounts to about 90 thousand words.

My luggage is still 'somewhere' on the railway between Turin and here.
It annoys me terribly. The weather is sweltering hot, and I am stuck in
winter clothes. – I suppose, however, it *must* come eventually, when I have
kicked up a large enough row. And *then* I shall send you an MS. of mine.

---

[1] The Baroness's eldest daughter, Else Jaffe (1874–1973).
[2] Marianne Jaffe (b. 1905), Else's eldest child.
[3] MS reads 'I'.

Meanwhile this of Magnus'. Let me know what you think of it as soon as possible.

Yours Sincerely   D. H. Lawrence[1]

1990a. To Stanley Unwin, 15 May 1920
Text: MS UR; Unpublished.

Fontana Vecchia, *Taormina*, (Messina).
15 May 1920

Dear Mr Unwin

At last my luggage has come, and I have those essays on Education. You would like, I believe, about 30,000 words. I will do them at once.

I find also the complete MS. of those *Studies in Classic American Literature*, some of which appeared in the *English Review* – from November 1918 to June 1919. I never sent out this MS. If you would care for it, I will send it you. But first, if you haven't seen those essays, glance through the ones in the *English Review* – that is, if you are interested at all. I should think the whole thing will contain 80,000 words.

I hope you received Magnus' MS. on *The Foreign Legion*. The other part is being sent. Please write to me about it.

Yours   D. H. Lawrence

Post is extremely bad here – a letter to England takes anything from 8 to 25 days.[2]

---

[1] DHL's letter was acknowledged on 10 May; Unwin promised to study Magnus's MS 'carefully' when it arrived (TMSC UR).

[2] Unwin replied on 31 May (TMSC UR):

> Dear Mr. Lawrence,
>
> My hearty congratulations upon the receipt of your luggage! I look forward to receiving the essays on Education at an early date and am quite sure they will be interesting.
>
> Yes, I remember the Studies in Classic American Literature which appeared in "The English Review", but the subject frightened me for I don't think it is one in which we could interest any large number of readers. On the other hand, if you have the MS. available I should be delighted if you would send it to me for I have no doubt whatever that I could make satisfactory arrangements for you for it's publication in the States, and probably at the same time provide for the importation of an edition with our imprint for sale in this market. This method would have the advantage of ensuring that the work was copyrighted in the U. S. A.
>
> We have studied the MS. on The Foreign Legion which you kindly sent us, but we do not feel that we should be able to obtain a sufficient sale for it to cover the present exorbitant costs of production. We have, however, taken the liberty of showing it to an American Publisher and when we have his reply will write to you further.
>
> Yours sincerely

2019a To Stanley Unwin, [17 June 1920]
Text: MS UR; PC; Postmark, Taormina 17 6 20; Unpublished.

Taormina.

17 June.

Have your letter – am sorry nothing doing about Magnus' *Legion* manuscript. Let me know if anything is happening to it, because I will have it sent to another publisher if not. If you should by chance have made any arrangement with an American for it, and want the 2nd half, write direct to Maurice Magnus, c/o Thomas Cook & Son, Strada Reale, *Valetta*, Malta. But let me know as soon as possible. And you remember Magnus wants to be anonymous, and to sell outright for a sum down.

I am doing the Education book – about 30,000 words, I think you said. At any rate, that is about the length I intended.

I shall wait till I hear from America, about the *Classic American Literature* MS. – And I will arrange the American publication of the Education book – have agreements over there which I must keep. – Expect the MS. will take me about another week.

Yrs   D. H. Lawrence[1]

2020a. To Hubert Foss, [23 June 1920]
Text: MS Anon; Unpublished.

Fontana Vecchia, *Taormina*, Sicily.

24 May 1920[2]

Dear Mr Foss[3]

Thank you for your letter. I should really like to be serialised in *The Queen*: such a relief after *English Review*s, highbrow and *Nash*. But is it just a random suggestion?

Anyhow I send the MS. of *The Lost Girl*. I am under contract with Secker – he will publish in book form.[4] If within the next ten days or so I cable you 'Send MS. Secker,' will you be so good as to post it across to [him][5]? It will be at least 8 days coming to you, I [sup]pose. If you have no word from me, do [let?] *The Queen* see the book. Secker has already written to me for this carbon copy MS. But he has the original, so don't know why

---

[1] In his reply (TMSC UR) on 25? June, Unwin declared that, because he did not believe Magnus's book would 'make a success', he had written to him and offered to return the MS wherever Magnus directed.

[2] DHL implicitly acknowledges his dating error in the next letter to Foss (below), 23 July 1920.

[3] Hubert James Foss (1899–1953), assistant editor of *Land and Water*. He did not succeed in arranging for the serialisation of *The Lost Girl*.

[4] Martin Secker (1882–1978) published the novel in November 1920 (Roberts A16).

[5] MS damaged.

he wants this. Anyhow I should like the *Queen* to see it: would be fun if she printed it. So I send it to you. You will be so good as to send it across to Secker, 5 John St., Adelphi, if I cable you – won't you. – And if ever you should want to cable me, *Lawrence, Taormina, Sicily* is enough.

Yours Sincerely   D. H. Lawrence

2032a. To Stanley Unwin, [6 July 1920]
Text: MS UR; Unpublished.

Fontana Vecchia, Taormina, Sicily
July 6th[1]

Dear Unwin

I am sending complete MS. of 'Education of the People' to Jack Squire today: he said he *might* make some extracts for *The London Mercury*. I asked him, if he was going to use any parts, to have them typed from the original, and then to let you have my MS. complete as it stands. Probably he won't use any of the stuff for his *Mercury*[2] – too much quicksilver for him. He likes his mercury not too mercurial.

It makes an amusing and serious little book, I think. One day it will probably sell fast: ought to. Don't feel under the slightest obligation about it. If you have the least hesitation, let me have the MS. back.

But this is the *only* MS., so please take care of it. I will arrange America myself. You can invent a new title as you please. I don't want any advance, but you must give me a decent royalty.

Hope you'll like the book. But if you don't, let me know, and I'll arrange its' disposal elsewhere. No bones broken anyhow.

Yrs   D. H. Lawrence

J. C. Squire, *The London Mercury*, Windsor House, Breams Buildings, E. C. 4.

Heaven knows how the post is at your end just now - spasmodic at my end.[3]

---

[1] '1920' was added in an unknown hand.

[2] (Sir) John Collings Squire (1884–1958) was editor of *London Mercury*, 1913–34; DHL's forecast proved to be accurate.

[3] Unwin acknowledged DHL's letter on 14 July (TMSC UR) and then wrote again on 15 October (TMSC UR):

> We have read ['Education of the People'] with interest and should like to be identified with its publication. Our difficulty is to see how under existing conditions it can be published at a price that people would pay for such a small book and at the same time yield a margin after paying the cost of printing, paper and binding, let alone the "decent royalty" to which we quite agree you are entitled.
> We have taken great pains to go into the matter and enclose a specimen page which the printers have set up and also our office estimate of the costs of production.
> . . . To leave a reasonable margin to all concerned the book ought to be published at, at

2048a. To Hubert Foss, 23 July 1920

Text: MS Anon; PC; Postmark, Taormina 24 7 20; Unpublished.

Fontana Vecchia, *Taormina*. Sicily

23 July 1920

Dear Mr Foss

Have you received the MS. of my novel *The Lost Girl*, which I posted to you exactly a month ago, on the 23rd. June, by registered manuscript post. I should be glad to know.

If you have this MS., and Secker wants it to make corrections in his uncorrected copy, please let him have it. But if *The Queen* would like to see the book, and if 'She' could read it in a week or so, perhaps let her have it *first*, because if once Secker gets it there is no knowing when he will part from it again: he would only *need* to keep it a few days.

Hope it has arrived.

Yrs   D. H. Lawrence

2053a. To Thomas Seltzer, 1 August 1920

Text: MS Fath; Postmark, Taormina 2. 8. 20; Unpublished.

Fontana Vecchia, *Taormina*, Sicily

1 August 1920

Dear Seltzer[1]

I have the first set of galleys[2]– yesterday – find few mistakes so far – one or two words. – Also your letter of 16 July.

I hope *The Century* has the MS. by now, and that they will be quick.[3] I told them, if they reject the book, to give the MS. to Robert Mountsier, or to you. Mountsier is a friend. He is leaving Paris on Aug 11th for New York: perhaps you know him. He is a journalist, a New York man. He has agreed to look after my affairs in America, and I have given him full powers. He is a nice man, I hope you'll get on with him. – I want him to give *The Lost Girl* to the *Metropolitan*, if the *Century* rejects it – and if the *Met.* turns it down, then you

least, 7/6d, but at that figure its sale would be very much restricted, and furthermore, it would look horribly expensive . . . .

We have much enjoyed reading the MS and are retaining it in our safe, pending instructions as to what you would like done with it . . .

You might return the enclosed estimate at your convenience as we like to keep them on our file for future reference.   Yours very truly

[1] Thomas Seltzer (1875–1943), DHL's principal American publisher. m. 1906, Adele Szold (1876–1940).

[2] The arrival of *Women in Love* galleys from Seltzer is confirmed in DHL's diary; see Tedlock, *Lawrence MSS* 91. See also Letter 2115a below.

[3] DHL is here reiterating his strategy to serialise *The Lost Girl* in either *The Metropolitan* or *The Century*, in USA, and *The Queen* in England; he had already told Seltzer of it on 18 July (*Letters*, iii. 571). His efforts failed.

go ahead with it as fast as you like. – I sent a MS copy to London to *The Queen*, but damn the post, it hasn't arrived. Luckily I sent Secker's copy by hand.[1]

I am sending to Mountsier my complete MS. of *Studies in Classic American Literature*, which he is to give to you when he lands – he sails on the *Rotterdam* from Boulogne – Aug 11th. Cecil Palmer, of Palmer & Hayward, 14 Bloomsbury St., W. C., asked me to let him publish in London.[2] But when you have read the MS. you will see I don't care about its being done by a small English publisher – at least, I'd rather it came in America first.

Huebsch wrote that he is handing you the MS. of *Studies* – and he more or less says goodbye to me.[3] I agree with you, about sticking to one publisher as far as possible, and shall not try to place anything in America before coming to you: except magazine stuff. The *Dial* has a couple of trifles.[4]

I am doing another novel: errant and amusing but not improper.[5] – But we are going away – my wife to Germany to her people, I knocking about. We'll be back here, God willing in October – early Oct.

[PS][6] on galley 11. line 5. *step*, not stop.

        galley 12. Chap. III. line 5 come *over* dark, not *after* dark
        galley 20. line *16* offence
        "   24. *hand* not head – as queried
        "   33. line 45. mocking *and* objective
        "   34. *pale* blue (correction)
        "   for *Vergine della Rocche* put *Virgins of the Rocks*
        "   40. line 18 *inequality* not equality
        "   last line but one. *volume*
        "   41. line 3. *flask*
        "   44. lines 43 – *bloody* not bloody –
        "   and 47 misgiving

---

[1] Compton Mackenzie transported Secker's copy of *The Lost Girl*: see DHL's diary for 15 June 1920 (Tedlock, *Lawrence MSS* 90).

[2] DHL had sent 'the complete MS' of *SCAL* to Palmer on 23 July 1920 (*Letters*, iii. 577–8).

3 Benjamin W. Huebsch (1876–1964), a New York publisher; he told DHL on 8 July (iii. 544 n.1) that he was handing *SCAL* over to Seltzer. DHL said 'goodbye' to him on 21 April 1923: see Letter 2798a below.

[4] The 'trifles' were 'Adolf' and 'Rex' published in *Dial*, September 1920 and February 1921 respectively.

5 The reference is to *Mr Noon*; DHL recorded it as begun on 7 May 1920 (Tedlock, *Lawrence MSS* 90) and again on 31 May (iii. 537), and variously described it as 'a comedy' and 'rather amusing, but rather scandalous' (iii. 626, 639).

6 The MS lacks complimentary close and signature. The corrections to the galleys of *Women in Love* were clearly a postscript but written at a right angle to the address at the head of the letter. To locate DHL's corrections see *Women in Love*, ed. David Farmer, Lindeth Vasey and John Worthen (Cambridge, 1987), pp. 30:35, 35:6, 55:23, 67:2(?), 87:39, 90:12, 91:17, 103:35/6, 105:37, 106:1, 115:1, 115:4.

2107a. To Baroness Anna von Richthofen, [12 October 1920]
Text: MS Houle; PC v. Venezia–Canal Grande e Palazzo dell'Accademia; Postmark, Venezia
12. X. 1920; Unpublished.

Venice.
12 Oct.

Frieda arrived after quite a good journey on Sunday evening – she loves
Venice. We are having a tea-party today, and I shall have my tea from my
lovely cup and saucer. Such nice things F. brought. – We leave for Rome on
Sunday.

Love from us both.   DHL

2112a. To John Lane, 22 October 1920
Text: MS UT; Unpublished.

Villa Fontana Vecchia, *Taormina*, Sicily.
22 October 1920

Dear Mr Lane[1]
Your letter has reached me here today. I left Venice a week ago. If I had
known sooner, I would have stayed and done the book, because Venice is
intriguing and irritating. But I can't go back now I am home: at least, not
yet. In the New Year. I must write on the spot – most of the stuff, at least.
But if you care to send me proofs of the Brangwen drawings, I will see if I
can make a start: and if I make a start, I will certainly go to Venice in January
or February, and finish, because of something that interests me there.

Edward Hutton is in Florence,[2] at the Washington Hotel, if you like to
ask him to do the book.

I tell you, I'll say definitely about my tackling it when I've seen the pictures: if you think fit to send them.

Yrs   D. H. Lawrence

2112b. To Stanley Unwin, 22 October 1920
Text: MS UR; Unpublished.

Villa Fontana Vecchia, *Taormina*, Sicily
22 Oct 1920

Dear Mr Unwin
I have your letter today – understand your position: though 2/9 seems a

---

[1] The publisher, John Lane (1854–1925), offered DHL £150 'to write a little book on Venice'
(*Letters*, iii. 615); it was to be illustrated by Frank Brangwyn (1867–1956), a painter whom
DHL greatly admired (iii. 620 and n. 1).
[2] Edward Hutton (1875–1969) had published *Venice and Venetia* with Methuen (illustrated by
Maxwell Armfield) in 1911; 2nd edn 1923.

small price for a cloth-bound book. Must you have a cloth binding, for example?

However, let it lie awhile in your safe, till we see how things go. Secker is publishing my novel on November 1st.

I return your estimate sheet.

Yrs   D. H. Lawrence

2115a. To Thomas Seltzer, [late October 1920]

Text: *New York Times*, 1 May 1986.

[Fontana Vecchia, *Taormina*, (Messina), Sicily]
[late October 1920][1]

Tell Manson there's no substitute for the right word.

2115b. To Stanley Unwin, 3 November 1920

Text: MS Davies; Unpublished.

Villa Fontana Vecchia, *Taormina*, Sicily.
3 Nov. 1920

Dear Mr Unwin,

Would you be so good as to send me the MS. of the little 'Education of the People' book, after all – by registered manuscript post.

Yours   D. H. Lawrence[2]

2122a. To Norman Douglas, 16 November 1920

Text: MS YU; Unpublished.

Fontana Vecchia, *Taormina*, Sicily
16 Nov 1920

Dear Douglas,[3]

I heard from Don Mauro the other day that Magnus had committed suicide.[4] Today I receive the Malta newspaper with a paragraph – he was

---

[1] On 18 October 1920 DHL received 'full proofs of *Women in Love*' from Seltzer (*Letters*, iii. 613); it is assumed that, after reading proof, he wrote to Seltzer towards the end of the month. Harold Matson (1898–) (later a New York literary agent), was employed by Seltzer to see the novel through the press; he had corrected something written by DHL, thus prompting this retort.

[2] Unwin replied on 18 November 1920 (TMSC UR) that the MS was being returned as requested.

[3] DHL had known his correspondent, the novelist and essayist, George Norman Douglas (1868–1962), since 1913 when Douglas was assistant editor of the *English Review*. He was Maurice Magnus's literary executor and heir to his literary property.

[4] Magnus died on 4 November 1920; DHL's informant was Don Mauro Inguanez, a monk from Monte Cassino, the friend whom Magnus trusted to carry out his final wishes concerning his literary effects. Cf Letter 1959a and n.4 above.

found in a white suit dead on his bed in his room at Notabile, having taken poison. En voilà fini.[1]

Here it rains heavens hard and I get rather sick of it. But at any rate there is the open sea in front, and quiet.

How do you like Mentone?

I had a letter, when I got back here, from John Lane, asking me to do the book on Venice. I said too late this year, might have a shot in spring – but no further answer.

Sicily dead-alive – and the journey here hell on earth – nothing rosy in any direction at the moment.

Hope you're well.

Greetings from both   D. H. Lawrence

2150a. To Baroness Anna von Richthofen, [7 January 1921]

Text: MS Houle; PC v. Sala dei Matrimoni – Filippo Figari (dettaglio) Il Suonatore; Postmark, Cagliari -8.1. 21; Unpublished.

Cagliari
7 January

We have come to Sardinia for a few days – wonderful place, the good old world here

love   DHL

2160a. To Sara Teasdale, 28 January 1921

Text: MS Anon; Unpublished.

Villa Fontana Vecchia, *Taormina*, Sicily
28 Jan. 1921

Dear Sara Teasdale,[2]

It was a pleasure to get *Flame and Shadow*. There are such sensitive delicate songs: almost too sensitive: nerve-bare. One almost winces. One must harden ones heart at last, or die of it. As for me, it resolves into a long fight. And so one sees the sword in everything, and the fighting-fury: even in squills and Arcturus and phlox and asters of Connecticut.[3] For me an aster

---

[1] 'What an ending.'

[2] Sara Teasdale (1884–1933), American poet; awarded the Pulitzer Prize, 1917. She had sent a copy of her sixth book of poems, *Flame and Shadow* (1920), to DHL; he mentioned it to Mountsier on 25 January 1921 and, on 28th, asked him to forward this letter to her; DHL did not know her address (*Letters*, iii. 654, 657). Sara Teasdale was a close acquaintance of Louis Untermeyer who had written to DHL and received a reply from him in September 1920 (iii. 595); perhaps Untermeyer had encouraged her to send her poems. m. 1914, Ernst B. Filsinger (divorced 1929).

[3] The poems to which DHL was alluding are: 'Blue Squills' (*Flame and Shadow*, p. 71); 'Arcturus' (p. 25); 'White Fog' (p. 24); 'August Moonrise' (pp. 45–6).

shakes her hair like a savage woman soldier, and a phlox lurks through the
night like an Indian spy. It's a question of mode. And the mode becomes all a
fight.

I lend your poems, and people like them so much.

Yours Sincerely   D. H. Lawrence

2217a. To J. B. Pinker, 28 April 1921
Text: MS NWU; Unpublished.

Ludwig-Wilhelmstift, *Baden-Baden*, Germany.
28 April 1921.

Dear Pinker

Thank you for your communication received yesterday – enclosing
Harrison's answer to you. I strongly object to Harrison's mischievous note.[1]
Of course when we dissolved our agreement I informed him. But since the
story in question was placed by you, he knows quite well he is legally bound
to complete the transaction with you. I am writing to him now, asking him to
pay up to you at once.

Yours[2]

2270a. To Thomas Seltzer, 1 July 1921
Text: MS Fath; Unpublished.

[Hotel Krone, Ebersteinburg, bei Baden-Baden][3]
1 July 1921

Dear Seltzer

Your letter of July 15 today.[4] – I had the ten copies of *Psychoanalysis and
the Unconscious* – and thanked you.

I daren't write much, because Mountsier pounces on me if I go between
him and his publisher – I expect him here on Tuesday, by the way – and we
shall walk across the Black Forest to Constance, then cross the lake and go to
Innsbruck, and so to my sister-in-law's place not far from Salzburg. Don't
know how long we shall stay. I shall send address next week.

---

[1] The note from Austin Harrison (1873–1928) is missing. It presumably concerned his alleged
failure to pay for the publication of DHL's story, 'The Blind Man' in the *English Review* (July
1920), of which he was editor, and his involvement in placing the story in the American periodical, *The Living Age* (August 1920) (Roberts C72). DHL had questioned Pinker about the
matter as early as 9 December 1920 (*Letters*, iii. 635) and twice since (iii. 645, 690). For
Pinker's initial explanation see iii. 650 n. 1.

[2] DHL's signature has been cut from the MS.

[3] DHL used the hotel's headed notepaper.

[4] 'June 15' must have been intended; DHL received the ten copies of *Psychoanalysis* and
acknowledged them on 3 June 1921 (iii. 732).

Aaron's Rod is finished. I await Mountsier and will then get it typed. It is moderate size – like *Lost Girl* – but I don't know if you'll like it.

The American publication of the *History* is at *my* disposal – or Mountsiers.[1]

I'll come to America when the gods let me – mein innerliches Schicksal – mein inneres Schicksal.[2] I have to wait upon it. – But I doubt if ever I could lecture. I should hate the people's faces, and want to say 'Go home, swine!'

Bennett is a cad – praises me in private, lets me down in public. May Sinclair is a funny little marm. I *do not like* W. L. George, and do not wish him to take my name into his mouth – or on to his pen.[3]

I have done the book to follow *Psychoanalysis and the Unconscious*: I should think 30,000 words: to be called *Child Consciousness* (or Human Consciousness).[4] I wrote it all away in the woods here, in pencil: thank goodness undecipherable to anybody but myself. To me it is extraordinarily important – But what I think and what other folks think are different affairs. I shan't have it typed yet.

I get annoyed over that Medici Press book.[5] They've got to agree to something different – a different sort of book – or I shant do it. I will do 'Italian Pictures for Children' – but not a vague and fuzzy 'Child's Book on Art' circumscribed by the Medici Press illustrations – 20 damned 3-color reproductions, no drawings, no wood-cuts, no missal, no architectural photographs – Can't be done. *A childs book on Art* such as they want means a thousand things they won't and cant furnish. I'm not going to pile up words about unrepresented objects. A child's book on art must have the letterpress most accurately relative to the illustrations.

But this is the point of my letter. For the Sardinia book my friend Jan Juta has painted eight illustrations;[6] – very good, very original, very novel, and brilliant. I sent them to Stuttgart to a color-printer. He says they will come

---

[1] No American edn of *Movements in European History* ever appeared.

[2] 'my inward fate – my inner destiny'.

[3] Bennett was capable of private generosity (see *Letters*, iii. 472 and n.) but DHL did not trust him; later he regarded Bennett as a 'pig in clover' (vi. 342). In 'The Bad Side of Books' DHL coupled him with the novelist May Sinclair (1863–1942) as raising 'a kindly protest' against the suppression of *The Rainbow*. In 1913 DHL had expressed a liking for the novelist and journalist, Walter Lionel George (1882–1926), considering him 'one of the funniest men in London' (ii. 108).

[4] A version of this title persisted until 8 October 1921 (iv. 96); it became *Fantasia of the Unconscious* soon after (iv. 103).

[5] DHL had been invited in June 1921 'to do a "Child's Book on Art" for the Medici Society' (iv. 24–5). The proposal came to nothing (iv. 66).

[6] Seltzer published *Sea and Sardinia* in December 1921; Secker's edn followed in April 1923 (Roberts A20).

out beautifully, 4-color process: and that the cost of engraving each plate, size 13 x 10 cm., is *600 Mark*. The Medici Press estimate was £5. See the difference. I await now to know the cost of 2000 printed copies. – The engraving of 8 blocks would cost 4800 Mark.

Secker, who is so farthingless to hear him talk, faints at the word color illustration. I absolutely want the pictures included. It would make a startling christmas book. I want you to authorise us to go ahead, and then Secker will have to pay his share, or go to hell. Book would have to be about 22 x 14 cm. size. More about this the moment Mountsier arrives.

Yrs   D. H. Lawrence

Ludwig-Wilhemstift, *Baden-Baden* always finds me.

2280a. To Baroness Anna von Richthofen, [16 July 1921]

Text: MS Houle; PC v. Meersburg Eingang x. Alt. Schloss; Postmark, Meers[burg] 17. 7. 21; Unpublished.

Meersburg.

Samstag.

Wie war es dann gestern? – und wie bist du heute? Wir gehen immer herum – waren jetzt im alten Schloss hier: nun trinken Meersburg Rot-wien im Garten am See. – Emil hat telegrafiert dass die Pässe *können* morgen kommen: nicht sicher. – Der Tag ist nicht klar, doch sehen wir die Alpen. Konstanz ist viel billiger wie BadenBaden.

Viele Grüsse   DHL

[Meersburg.

Saturday.

How was it then yesterday? – and how old are you today?[1] We go round a good deal – just now were in the old castle here: are now drinking Meersburg red wine in the garden by the lake. – Emil[2] has cabled that the passports *could* come tomorrow: not sure. – The day is not clear, but we can see the Alps. Constance is much cheaper than BadenBaden.

Many greetings   DHL]

---

[1] The Baroness was 70 on 14 July.
[2] Emil von Krug (1870–1944), whom Frieda's younger sister, Johanna (1882–1971) married in 1923 after divorcing her first husband.

2288a. To Baroness Anna von Richthofen, [27 July 1921]

Text: MS Houle; PC v. Möserboden g. d. Karlinggletscher 1968 m.; Postmark, [. . .] 27 VII 21;
Unpublished.

[Villa Alpensee, Thumersbach, Zell-am-See, bei Salzburg]
Mittwoch

Wir vergnügen uns sehr hier – waren gestern auf dem Hunstein – 2110[1]M –
und einen so wunderschönen Blick auf alle Schneeberge. Wir waren elf
Stunden weg, und gar nicht zu müde. Das Wetter ist wundervoll schön. Ich
hoffe es ist nicht zu heiss für dich in Baden – möchte wissen wie es dir geht.
Der Amerikaner ist in Wien. Hoffentlich geht er bald wieder nach Paris: wir
sind viel besser ohne ihn. Ich schicke dir gleich deine Photografien – nicht
klar genug ausgekommen.

Belli Saluti   DHL

[*Wednesday*

We are enjoying ourselves very much here – were up the Hundstein yesterday – 2110 metres – and such a wonderful view over all the snowy mountains. We were away eleven hours, and not at all too tired. The weather is
wonderfully fine. I hope it is not too hot for you in Baden – would like to
know how you are. The American is in Vienna.[2] I hope he'll soon go back to
Paris: we're much better without him. I'll be sending you your photographs
– haven't come out clearly enough.

Warm regards   DHL]

2306a. To Baroness Anna von Richthofen, [10 August 1921]

Text: MS Houle; PC v. A. Feuerbach, *Francesca da Rimini e Paolo*; Postmark, [. . .];
Unpublished.

[Villa Alpensee, Thumersbach, Zell-am-See, bei Salzburg]
10 August

Immer noch das wunderschönste Wetter: aber wir sind etwas faul geworden,
und machen keine grosse Anstrengungen. Heute gehen Frieda und ich an
die Jagdhütte und schlafen da: kommen morgen mittag wieder zum Essen
und Geburtstag. Die grosse Hitze ist vorbei: hoffentlich ist es besser bei dir
in Baden. Kannst du wieder im Garten sitzen? Ich bin jetzt fleissig: habe

---

[1] The figure '6' has been inserted in an unknown hand over 'o' in 2110.
[2] DHL's American agent, Robert Mountsier, had been with the Lawrences since 5 July 1921
(*Letters*, iv. 50).

meinen Roman von England ausgeschrieben, und mache es fertig.[1] Montag reisst Mountsier weg, nach Paris. Er war 14 Tage in Budapest: ein unruhiger Kerl. Alles geht uns gut hier.

Viele herzliche grüsse   DHL

[Still the most beautiful weather: but we've grown rather lazy, and don't make any great efforts. Today Frieda and I are going to the hunting-lodge and sleeping there: coming back tomorrow mid-day for lunch and birthday.[2] The great heat is over: I hope it's better with you in Baden. Can you sit in the garden again? I'm busy just now: have my novel sent out from England, and am finishing it. Mountsier leaves on Monday, for Paris. He was a fortnight in Budapest: a restless fellow. All is well with us here.

Many affectionate greetings   DHL]

2324a. To Baroness Anna von Richthofen, [22 August 1921]

Text: MS Houle; PC v. Innsbruck , Hofkirche, König - Arthur - Gruppe; Postmark, Innsbruck [. . .]2 VIII [. . .]; Unpublished.

[Innsbruck]
Montag.

– Wir reisen morgen früh von Osterreich – adieu Nordland, adieu Alpen. Es war schön und man fühlt sich traurig – Schreibe du ein Wort nach Florenz –

DHL

Der Arthur immer Frieda's Idéal.

[Monday
– We set out tomorrow from Austria – adieu Land of the North, adieu the Alps. It was nice and one feels sad – Write a word to Florence –

DHL

Arthur always Frieda's ideal.[3]]

---

[1] DHL's German in this sentence is strange and unclear. Literally he says that he has written out his novel about England – but he did not write it out at this stage and *Aaron's Rod* is not a novel *about* England. He received the typescript of the novel on 7 August *from* England (*Letters*, iv. 65); the translation has been adjusted to accord with this fact, in the belief that where DHL wrote 'ausgeschrieben' ('written out') he intended 'ausgeschickt' ('sent out').

[2] Frieda's 42nd birthday.

[3] The English King Arthur is shown in full armour on the verso of the card.

2325a. To Baroness Anna von Richthofen, [25 August 1921]
Text: MS Houle; PC v. Firenze–Ponte Vecchio (Taddeo Gaddi); Postmark, Firenze 25 VIII 21;
Unpublished.

32 Via dei Bardi. Firenze
25 Aug.

Wir sind gestern Abend angekommen – waren ein Tag in Verona. Wir
haben eine schöne Wohnung in einem ganz alten Palazzo über dem Fluss –
das Haus das man sieht, abgeschnitten. – Ein wunderschöne Terrasse mit
Blumen[1] und zitronen, über dem Wasser, und gerade gegenüber vom Uffizi
und Palazzo Vecchio und Dom. Schade das du es nicht sehen kannst. Die
Frieda ist selig.

Mila Saluti.   DHL

[We got here last night[2] – spent a day in Verona. We have a beautiful flat in a
really old Palazzo overlooking the river – the house one can see, cut off.[3] – A
wonderful terrace with flowers and lemons, above the water, and straight
across from the Uffizi and Palazzo Vecchio and Cathedral. Pity that you
can't see it. Frieda is blissfully happy.

Warmest greetings   DHL]

2331a. To Baroness Anna von Richthofen, [5 September 1921]
Text: MS Houle; PC v. Firenze–Vergine che adora il Figlio–Lippi; Postmark, Firenze - 5. 9.
21.; Unpublished.

[32 Via dei Bardi, Florence]
Montag

Schade dass du wieder krank wärst – bist du wirklich wieder ganz kräftig?
Uns geht es gut. Ja, es ist ganz gesund hier über den Fluss – und nicht zu
heiss. Wir sitzen und gucken das ganzes Leben von Florenz an – Männer im
Wasser, Boote, die Leute die uber die Brücke endlos fahren. Aber es ist doch
eine lärmige Stadt – fürchtbar. Die Florentiner haben Lärm wirklich gern.
– Jetzt wäscht ein Bub einen Teppisch im Arno, und die Farbe strömt wie
Blut aus – ; und es geht Cavalerie vorbei, und zwei Madchen, die Furchtbar
angst haben in der engen Strasse, verstecken sich hinter einem Wägerle: so
macht *jeder* Soldat dass sein Pferd springt und hupft in der Nähe von den
Mädchen, die sterben vor Angst. – So geht's.

Saluti cari.   DHL

---

[1] Blumen]blumen
[2] Letters 2325 and 2326 both confirm their arrival on 25 August; DHL must have intended to
write 'tonight' ('heute Abend') and not 'last night' ('gestern Abend').
[3] DHL put a cross over the building - cut in two by the edge of the card - on the extreme left of
the picture on the verso.

[Monday

Shame that you were ill again – are you really quite strong now? We're fine. Yes, it's really healthy here above the river, and not too hot. We sit and watch the whole life of Florence – men in the water, boats, the people who drive endlessly over the bridges. But it certainly is a noisy town – frightful. The Florentines are really fond of noise. Just now a boy is washing a carpet in the Arno, and the colour streams out like blood – ; and cavalry are going past, and two girls, who are terribly frightened in the narrow streets, hide behind a little wagon: so every soldier makes his horse leap and prance near the girls, who are dying of fright. – That's how it is.

Love.   DHL]

2343a. To Baroness Anna von Richthofen, [21 September 1921]

Text: MS Houle; PC v. Siena–Stazione Ferroviario–Scala; Postmark, Siena 21. 9. 21; Unpublished.

[Siena]
21 Sept

Wieder unterwegs – Siena wunderbar schön, aber das Wetter *heiss*. Wir gehen Rom, Montecassino, und Capri – kommen in ungefähr zehn Tagen an[1] Taormina. – Ist die Anni schon dabei?

tanti belli saluti   DHL

[Underway again – Siena wonderfully beautiful, but the weather *hot*. We go to Rome, Montecassino, and Capri – arrive in Taormina in about ten days. – Is Anni[2] already there with you?

many warm regards   DHL]

2345a. To Baroness Anna von Richthofen, [29 September 1921]

Text: MS Houle; PC v. Firenze - Cattedrale; Postmark, Taormina 30 SET 21; Unpublished.

Taormina
29 Sept.

Wir sind gestern Abend angekommen – furchtbar müde, nach so vielen Reisen – aber Gottfroh dass wir wieder zuhaus sind. Unsere Fontana Vecchia ist wirklich schöner wie man es errinnert – so wunderbar, das Meer ganz offen zum Ost, wie ein Fenster auf einer anderer Welt. Wie geht's dir?

---

[1] an] nach
[2] Unidentified

Unsere Grazia und Carmelo, alle, fragen nach dir. Carmelo hat noch einen Baby, Ciccia kriegt auch einen.

DHL

[We got back last night – fearfully tired, after so much travelling – but thank God glad that we are home again. Our Fontana Vecchia is really lovelier than one remembers – so wonderful, the sea wide open to the east, like a window on to another world. How are you? Our Grazia and Carmelo, everyone, asks after you. Carmelo has another baby, Ciccia is expecting one too.[1]

DHL]

2376n. To D. H. Lawrence from Martin Secker, 1 December 1921
Text: MS Copley; Unpublished.

NUMBER FIVE JOHN STREET ADELPHI
December 1. 1921

Dear Lawrence.[2]

Many thanks for your letter. *Aaron's Rod* has just reached me, and I will read it during the coming week. Meanwhile, I want you to send me the collection of short stories.[3] The new edition of *Women in Love* will be ready in a few days now, and I hope to see it selling steadily into the new year. My advice is to follow up this very controversial book with the volume of short stories, which will secure a library circulation again. *Aaron's Rod* could follow in the late spring or so, and all you will sacrifice is the simultaneous publication with America which is of no great importance – in fact it will please Seltzer.[4] Please let me know if you agree to this.

In round figures *The Lost Girl* sold 3000. *Women in Love*, so far, 1500 (no library sale.) I want ultimately to see your sales double that of the former, and if as I imagine may be the case, *Aaron's Rod* is difficult in places, I think this is the judicious sequence of publication to adopt.

Yours sincerely   Martin Secker

---

[1] Grazia Cacópardo and her son, Carmelo and daughter Francesca ('Ciccia'); her son Francesco ('Ciccio') was DHL's landlord at Fontana Vecchia.

[2] Secker was responding to DHL's letter of 23 November 1921 which told him that the MS of *Aaron's Rod* had gone to Curtis Brown; for Secker's information DHL cited Mountsier's and Curtis Brown's forecast that he would 'refuse to publish it' (*Letters*, iv. 129).

[3] It would be entitled *England, My England*, published by Seltzer, October 1922, and by Secker in January 1924 (Roberts A23).

[4] Seltzer published *Aaron's Rod* in April 1922, Secker in June 1922 (Roberts A21).

2395a. To Baroness Anna von Richthofen, [19 December 1921]
Text: MS Houle; PC v. Venise.–Leonardo De Vinci. Etude pour la Sainte Famille du Louvre;
Postmark, Taormina 19 DEC 21; Unpublished.

[Fontana Vecchia, *Taormina*, (Messina), Sicily]
19 Dez.

Heute sind Schlips Halstuch, Kalender, Schürze, Schnupftuch, Bild und alles schön angekommen. Ich trage schon den Schlips – steht mir gut. – Else's Brief haben wir auch. Sie macht was sie will – aber du solls die zwölf Tausend für dich behalten. Alles geht gut hier – wir bekommen einen Truthahn mit Castanien hier zuhaus Weihnachts abend – essen im Palazzo Atenasio Weihnacht. Lassen alle sich freuen.

DHL

[Today arrived safely tie, scarf, calendar, apron, picture and everything. I'm already wearing the tie – suits me nicely. – We have Else's letter too. She does what she likes – but you should keep the twelve thousand for yourself.[1] Everything is fine here – we're having a turkey with chestnuts at home on Christmas Eve – eat in the Palazzo Atenasio on Christmas Day.[2] Let everybody enjoy themselves.

DHL]

2397a. To Norman Douglas, 20 December 1921
Text: MS YU; Unpublished.

Fontana Vecchia, *Taormina*, Sicilia
20 Decem. 1921

Dear Douglas

Apparently the shades of Magnus are going to give us no peace. Michael Borg[3] and Don Mauro both wrote and asked me if I would help to get the *Legion* MS. published. I said I would try in America, – thought I could do nothing in Europe. – I don't know who really is responsible for the MS. But I set to to write an introduction giving all I knew about M[agnus] – not unkindly,[4] I hope. I wanted also portraits of him and of his mother –

---

[1] DHL had accepted an offer from Dr Anton Kippenberg (1874–1950), of Insel Verlag (Leipzig), of 18,000 marks for a German edition of *The Rainbow* and had instructed him to send the money to the Baroness; Frieda thought her mother should keep only 12,000 and give the remainder to her family. See *Letters*, iv. 132,136.

[2] The 'Ciccio Atenasios' were members of a group in Taormina whom the Lawrences met on social occasions (cf. iv. 101).

[3] Michael Borg was Magnus's close friend and principal creditor in Malta.

[4] The two words, 'not unkindly', were underlined in green and an exclamation mark added in the margin, most probably by Douglas after he had read DHL's 'Introduction' to which he took strong exception.

photographs. Do you agree to my doing this? I wish *you* would do it, really, and let me stand clear. If you will do it, I will write to an American publisher for you. – If you don't want, then I'll go ahead, rather unwillingly. Can you tell me about the Hohenzollern myth? – who was the mother, and who the grandfather.[1]

If I went ahead, I should propose to an American publisher to buy the thing outright – for whatever he'd give: 400 dollars, or more if possible. Then if you could agree with Michael Borg to let the Malta debts be paid first – about £60, I believe – then out of what remained I could have a bit for my introduction and the money he owes me – some £23 you know – or even if I had just £20 to clear the debt – and you the rest. I've got an agent in New York[2]– he might manage something. I should like Michael Borg to be paid: he is poor enough, and Magnus should never have let him in. And even if you only got about £20. it is better than a slap in the eye.

But to tell the truth I'd like best to be out of it altogether. If you'll do an introduction to catch the public eye – American – why, you might effect a sale.

I am so very sick of Taormina, that I hope to sail away to New Mexico in January or February,with Frieda. Oh I am so sick and surfeited of Europe, so tired, so tired.

I hope you are well, and cheerful, and working. I won't mention Christmas.

D. H. Lawrence

In my introduction I give a sketch of Magnus as I knew him in Florence, Montecassino, here, and Malta. In the first of course you figure, under a disguised name: along with me. The only vice I give you is that of drinking the best part of the bottle of whiskey, instead of the worst part, like me. Do you mind at all?[3]

---

[1] See *Letters*, iv. 186 n. 1.

[2] Robert Mountsier.

[3] Douglas replied on 26 December 1921. The full text of his letter (MS UT) is given because it was from this that DHL quoted in his own letter to the *New Statesman* on 20 February 1926 (v. 395–7) and it has been claimed that he misrepresented Douglas by the extracts selected: see Louise Wright, in *The Journal of the D. H. Lawrence Society*, 1996, pp. 62ff.

Florence
26 Dec 1921

Dear Lawrence,

I am writing from Volterra -- wonderful old place -- but will be back in Florence ere long. So many thanks for yours of the 20th.

Damn the Foreign Legion. As literary executor of M[agnus] (appointed 4 years before his death, and once again later on) and as *co-writer* of that MS, I applied for it to Borg on the 27 April, and also earlier, immediately after M's death, and again, *via* the U.S. Consul in Valletta. Couldn't get an answer out of him. I then had an editor, or rather publisher, who

2406a. To Norman Douglas, 5 January 1922
Text: MS YU; Unpublished.

Fontana Vecchia, *Taormina*, Sicilia
5 Jan 1922

Dear Douglas

I feel rather like you about that 'Dregs' business.[1] I haven't heard from Michael Borg – But I have written the little prefacing Memoir. Will you please tell me who the imperial grandfather was supposed to be? – Frederick or Wilhelm I: and what then was the *mother's* name – and [. . .] who was the grandmother? – And who was Mr Magnus the father? And was our M. born in America.[2]

Tell me these things if it doesn't bore you. Then if Michael Borg *does* send the MS., I'll try to get the whole thing published like this: sell the 'Dregs' outright for what I can get, agreement to be signed by you, Borg, and publisher: and you can settle the money between you. I will try to make something for myself out of my preface only. And shall I sell American rights only, and leave *you* to dispose of English rights, and *you* write *your* memoir for that? Or shall I sell English rights with American? – Always of course supposing I sell anything at all, and haven't just wasted my time once more.

Hellishly cold here, and me with a touch of flu. Frieda greets you and sympathises.

D. H. Lawrence

would have taken it on, and all the profit would have gone to Borg, as Magnus wrote me about his great kindness to him. I was going to do a memoir of him. Latterly, Grant Richards [publisher] has applied to me for it. I referred him to Borg, who has answered him back that the MS has gone to the U.S.

I bet you the Foreign Legion is going to "give me peace." Whoever wants it, may ram it up his exhaust-pipe. I have done my best, and if Borg had sent it on to me then, the book would be published by this time, and Borg about £30 or £50 the richer. Some folks are 'ard to please. By all means do what you like with the MS. As to M. himself, I may do some kind of memoir of him later on -- independent, I mean, of Foreign Legions. Put me into your introduction -- drunk and stark naked, if you like. I am long past caring about such things, and if you surround M-- with disreputable characters, why, it may end in persuading those American fools that he was a saint. What does it matter, any how, what one writes for those people?

Pocket all the cash yourself: Borg seems to be such a fool that he don't deserve any.

Or put yourself into connection with Grant Richards, if you like to have further complications.

I'm out of it, and, for *once in my life*, with a clean conscience.

New Mexico? What next! You'll come back neurasthenic. Everybody does, who sets foot on that absurd continent. Why not Burma, or Indo-China?

Much love to Frieda! I am amazed at your enduring Taormina all these months.

Yours always Norman Douglas

[1] What later appeared as *Memoirs of the Foreign Legion* was entitled 'Dregs' by Magnus.
[2] He was born in New York City.

2422n.3. To D. H. Lawrence from Benjamin Huebsch, 31 December 1921

Text: TMS Copley; Unpublished.

116 West 13th Street, New York City
December 31, 1921.

Mr. D. H. Lawrence,
Villa Fontana Vecchia,
Taormina, Sicily.

Dear Lawrence,

I enclose a copy of a letter to Mountsier, with which I enclosed statements of sales.[1]

These were rather insignificant in volume, except for "The Rainbow," of which 1116 copies were sold in the last semi-annual period. The royalty on this item amounts to about $836.00. This sale, by the way, represents practically the entire edition printed. It was limited to advance subscriptions.[2]

I am glad that you liked the appearance of the book.

Yours truly   B W Huebsch

2443a. To Earl Brewster, [10? February 1922]

Text: MS Holt; Unpublished.

[Fontana Vecchia, *Taormina*, (Messina), Sicily]
[10? February 1922]

[3]I really think that we shall come. We shall sail either on the *Osterley*, on Feby 26th or on the *Omar*, same line, March 5th. – both from Naples – Or else we shall sail from Malta, if there is an available ship and if it is any cheaper . . . I shall cable you the boat, whatever it is.

---

[1] For his enclosure – the copy of Huebsch's letter to Mountsier also of 31 December 1921 – see *Letters*, iv. 169 n.5. DHL thanked Huebsch for his letter on 28 January 1922 (iv. 182).
[2] For Huebsch's justification for limiting the edn to subscribers, see iv. 106 n.2.
[3] DHL's correspondent, Earl Brewster (1878–1957), was an expatriate American painter whom he first met in April 1921 on Capri and who was now living in Kandy, Ceylon. Writing to his wife, Achsah Barlow Brewster (1878–1945), on 14 February 1922, Brewster quoted (seemingly verbatim) the text of this 'letter from Lawrence' which had arrived the previous evening.

2444a. To Albert Stopford, [c. 12 February 1922]
Text: MS Houle; Unpublished.

Fontana Vecchia
[c. 12 February 1922][1]

Dear Stopford,[2]

Thank you very much; we will come on Wednesday. About tonight I am not sure, one feels so cold and unexpansive. Bitter the sky, with almond blossom.

Benedicite   D. H. Lawrence

2452a. To Albert Stopford, [17 February 1922]
Text: MS Houle; Unpublished.

Fontana Vecchia, *Taormina*
Friday[3]

Dear Stopford,

So tiresome of us – but I find we must leave for Palermo on Monday morning, so have got a wild time packing and making an inventario of the house with Carmelo.[4] Do please forgive me if I ask you to let me off the Sunday luncheon I planned. I am sorry – but all is now just a whirl at Fontana Vecchia.

I hope *The Rainbow* will please you. This is the only copy of this edition which I have signed.

Thank you so much for the jolly meetings.

Yours   D. H. Lawrence

---

[1] DHL told Mary Cannan, 12? February 1922: 'Albert Stopford is here' (*Letters*, iv. 191). It is assumed that he had recently arrived. In the same letter DHL remarks: 'It is so cold. The almond blossom is out, and looks and *feels* like snow.' It seems likely, therefore, that this letter is of approximately the same date.

[2] Stopford (b. 1860), an art dealer, was a member of a collateral branch of the earls of Courtown whose family name was Stopford. See iv. 191 n. 3.

[3] The Lawrences left Taormina for Palermo on Monday, 20 February 1922; hence the conjectural date for this letter.

[4] Carmelo Cacópardo.

2456a. To Albert Stopford, [c. 19 February 1922]
Text: MS Houle; Unpublished.

[Fontana Vecchia]
[c. 19 February 1922][1]

Dear Stopford –
   Benedicite – addio – I shall see you again one day
   This is Carmela whose photograph we promised her should be taken.[2]
Dear Stopford, if it is a nuisance, say the camera is broken.

addio DHL

2456b. To Baroness Anna von Richthofen, [23 February 1922]
Text: MS Houle; PC v. [mosaic from Monreale Cathedral]; Postmark, Palermo 23 . II 1922;
Unpublished.

Palermo
Donnerstag

So, wir sind weg – waren gestern in Monreale hier – heut' Abend mit Schiff
nach Neapel. Es ist schlechter Wetter gewesen, aber heute wieder Blau. Ich
schau nur vorwärts, rückwärts darf nicht gucken. Die Ruth Wheelock, die
Amerikanerin, kommt mit nach Neapel – und da finden wir auch andere
Freunden. Else wird Monreale gut errinnern – so schön.

Wiedersehen. DHL

[*Palermo*
Thursday

So, we're off – were here in Monreale yesterday – tonight by boat to Naples.
The weather has been bad, but today blue again. I look forwards, mustn't
look back. Ruth Wheelock, the American, comes to Naples with us[3] – and
there we'll find other friends too. Else will remember Monreale well – so
lovely.

Wiedersehen   DHL]

---

[1] DHL's message was evidently written shortly before the Lawrences left for Palermo on
20 February.

[2] DHL wrote his message for 'The Hon. Albert Stopford', on a calling card bearing the printed
name, 'Mr D. H. Lawrence'. With the card (delivered by Carmela Cacópardo) he enclosed a
photograph of Frieda, himself and a third person, presumably Stopford; perhaps Carmela
had acted as photographer using Stopford's camera, with the promise that she would be
repaid by a photograph of herself.

[3] Ruth Wheelock (1891–1958), a secretary in the American Consulate in Palermo; she had
typed *Sea and Sardinia, Mr Noon* etc.

2494a. To Baroness Anna von Richthofen, 12 April 1922
Text: MS Houle; PC v. Kandy from Lady Horton Walk; Postmark , Kandy 12 [. . .]22;
Unpublished.

[Kandy]
12 April 1922
Liebe Schwiegermutter,
    Ich schicke dir Heute ein Paket mit Thee, Kakao, Chocolat, und Gewurz
– echt Ceylonese Gewurz. Hoffentlich erhaltest du es bald, und ohne Zoll.
Wir gehen herum – fahren um 24^{n} nach Australien. Du sollst ein bisschen
Gewurz herum schenken! F[rieda] grüsst.

DHL

[Dear Schwiegermutter,
    I send you today a parcel with tea, cocoa, chocolate, and spice – genuine
Ceylonese spice. I hope you get it soon, and without paying duty. We're
wandering on – travelling to Australia on 24th. You ought to pass on some of
the spice! F sends greetings.

DHL][1]

2565a. To Baroness Anna von Richthofen, [15 August 1922]
Text: MS Houle; PC v. Maori Whare. N. Z. F. G. R. 6122; Postmark, [. . .]; Unpublished.
[Frieda Lawrence begins]
Wellington, New Zealand
15. August
Der weiteste Punkt von Dir, liebe mère! Wir sitzen und frühstücken!

F

[Lawrence continues]
Nächster Schritt: Heimwärts   DHL

[The furthest point from you, dear mother! We are sitting having breakfast!
F
Next step: homewards[2]   DHL]

---

[1] The Baroness responded on an undated postcard (MS Houle) after receiving DHL's parcel:
    Mein lieber Schwiegersohn!
        Just was my lettre gone! – then came your kind rich gift. How nice will it be to drink
    with my old ladies of your Wohl! [health!] – Many thank – I am now in good spirit – after all
    sweet and good things. –
                                            Love for ever   your Schwiegermutter
[2] The Lawrences were on their way, on *R. M. S. Tahiti*, to San Francisco where they arrived on
    4 September. (The verso of the card shows a Maori meeting-house, a wooden building with
    maori carving on the gable.)

2576a. To Baroness Anna von Richthofen, [22 August 1922]

Text: MS Houle; PC v. Tahiti - Feï ne s'en fait pas - *We should worry*; Postmark, Pap[eete] 23–8 22; Unpublished.

Papeete – Tahiti.

22 Aug.

Wir liegen hier über Nacht – sehr schöner Fahrt – Insel und Meer zauber-haft – aber die kleine Stadt verdorben – Morgen gehen wir im Auto in den Bergen – Es ist warm, aber nicht zu heiss. Französisch hier – auch viele Chinesen.

DHL

[We're moored here overnight – very lovely voyage – island and sea magical – but the little town spoilt. Tomorrow we're going by car into the mountains – It's warm but not too hot. French here – a lot of Chinese people too.

DHL]

2582a. To Laura Forrester, [5 September 1922]

Text: MS Forrester; PC ; Postmark, [San Fran]cisco [. . .] 1922; Robert Darroch, 'More on Lawrence in Australia', *DHLReview*, xx (Spring 1988), 41, 45.

[Palace Hotel, San Francisco]

5 Sept.

[1]Had a good voyage, but thankful to be on land again. San Francisco a fine town, but bewildering and deafening – we've been motoring round this afternoon. Best wishes from both.

D. H. Lawrence

2589a. To Baroness Anna von Richthofen, [10 September 1922]

Text: MS Houle; PC v. The California Limited; Postmark, Albuquerque SEP 10 1922; Unpublished.

Sontag 10 Sept

Unser Zug – wir essen hier – erste Stazion in New Mexico

DHL

[*Sunday* 10 Sept

Our train[2] – we eat here – first station in New Mexico

DHL]

---

[1] On board *S.S. Malwa* from Fremantle to Sydney, May 1922, the Lawrences had met the English migrants, Laura Forrester and her husband Arthur Denis Forrester (1898–), a hosiery worker from Nottingham. The Forresters visited them at 'Wyewurk', Thirroul, and photographs suggest that a cordial relationship had developed (see *DHLReview*, xx. 48–59; see also Nehls, ii. 140–1, 157–8).

[2] Referring to the colour picture of 'The California Limited' on the verso.

2606a. To Laura Forrester, [20 September 1922]
Text: MS Forrester; PC v. Mesa Encantada; Postmark, [. . .] SEP 20 1922; Darroch,
DHLReview, xx (Spring 1988), 41, 46.

Taos. *New Mexico.*
[20 September 1922]

Well here we are *at home* again – in a long little house of sun-baked brick
called 'Adobe' – but furnished very fine and 'arty.' Pity you can't see us. We
are just making peach jam, and this morning took our first ride on horse-
back. It is a horse country – everybody rides – sort of wild west. It is still
quite hot, especially in the sun, but the rains are beginning. F[rieda] loves it,
but I feel a stranger still. Greet everybody and send news.

DHL

2613a. To William Siebenhaar, [24 September 1922]
Text: Nehls, iii. 108; Telegram.

[Taos, New Mexico]
[24 September 1922]

Greatly impressed. Go on without delay.[1]

2629a. To Thomas Seltzer, 18 October 1922
Text: Joseph M. Maddalena Catalog 8, Item 123; Postmark, Taos OCT 20 1922; Unpublished.

[Taos, New Mexico]
18 October 1922

I had your letter last evening. What a curse about *Sons and Lovers.* I wish so
much we could have recaptured it.[2] *Ulysses* hasn't come yet[3] – it will arrive. I
only heard three days ago that it was a wildly expensive $25 book. Hope you
were able to borrow it, and didn't have to buy it. Let me know. Anyhow
please charge everything to me, when you make up the accounts. I'm expecting *Fantasia* now: and *England my England* you say in about another week.
Would you be so good as to post me one or two copies of *England my England*

---

[1] On 21 June 1922 DHL had encouraged William Siebenhaar (1863–1937) to translate the first
50 pages of a novel, *Max Havelaar* (1860), by Multatuli (pseud. for Eduard Douwes Dekker,
1820–87); DHL offered to use them to arouse the interest of a New York publisher (Knopf)
(see *Letters*, iv. 240 n. 2, 270). He received the translated pages on 24 September (iv. 309) and
replied at once with this telegram.

[2] DHL was keen to transfer American publication of *Sons and Lovers* from Mitchell Kennerley
(publisher of the first US edn) to Seltzer.

[3] DHL had requested a copy on 22 September 1922 (iv. 306).

direct from your office, and send on to me the remaining six or so. I'll put in a list of addresses. Mountsie[r] told me you had MS. of *Birds Beasts*. I must tell him what you say, and he must produce it. I want to make it complete. I have got *Studies in C[lassic] A[merican]- Lit.* and am going over them. I want you to do them in the spring. Is that your intention? I think we'd better have a shorter title: 'The American Demon' – or 'The American Daimon' – and keep *Studies in C.A. Lit.* as a sub-title. What do you think?

I have done *Kangaroo*. I must keep in the war-experience episode.[1] I have done a good bit of re-writing: now it is a final form. I think it is good: the *deepest* of my novels. I'll send this MS. to Mountsie[r] and get him to have the overwritten pages – or good many – typed out, then he must give you the MS., and you must write me *fully* what you think. I don't hear from Secker and Curtis Brown. I trust neither of them – and in spite of my flat forbidding them to go ahead with the three novelettes – Secker calls them *Ladybird*[2] – I've a misgiving that they'll go their own ways and pretend to have had my letter too late. [ ] Secker is such a slow-coach, I doubt if he'd be ready before January. But I don't feel easy on his score. Tell me how you plan the spring publications. I want you to do the *Studies* for one: and Secker may rush us into the *Ladybird* book. Then there is *Kangaroo* and *Birds Beasts*. What do you propose? I send you a (to me) rather squilchy letter from a Californian mystic[3] who sends monthly Epistles to his devotees. You'll see what he says about *Psychoanalysis and the Unconscious*, and judge if it is worthwhile?

Thank you so much for the invitation East. I like this *country* so much, I think we shall stay right on till spring, at least. Don't fix your coming for last week in December, as we may be away seeing Indian dances at San Domingo. But you might come and see them with us. Lots of fun, as they say here. I think probably Mountsier will come to Taos – not sure – He talks of seeing Kennerley for *Sons and Lovers* royalties. Write me always when there is any news, and I'll be sure and keep [you] posted.

---

[1] Chapter XII, 'The Nightmare'.
[2] Secker published the 'novelettes' as *The Ladybird, The Fox, The Captain's Doll*, in March 1923; on 11 April 1923 Seltzer published *The Captain's Doll: Three Novelettes* (Roberts A24).
[3] Unidentified. The enclosure is missing.

2692a. To Thomas Seltzer, 16 January 1923
Text: MS Fath; Unpublished.

Del Monte Ranch. *Questa*. New Mexico
16 Jan. 1923

Dear Seltzer

I was glad to hear from Adele Szold that she liked *Mastro-don*.[1] I feel so
deeply for it myself. I have just revised the *Novelle Rusticane*, whose title I
changed from 'Black Bread' to *Little Novels of Sicily*.[2] John Macy of the
Nation wrote asking for short stories from me, and for foreign short stories.[3]
So I sent him – or Mountsier did – the whole *Novelle Rusticane* MS., asking
him to select a story and then hand on at once the complete MS. to you. If it
doesn't come, in about a week's time, ask him. Mountsier thinks these *Little
Novels* would be more popular than *Mastro-don*, and therefore best published first. I don't know myself. It is your affair.

I am going over the MS. of *Studies in C[lassic]. A[merican]. Literature*
which MS you will receive in a day or two. Mountsier also showed me the
contracts for these *Studies*, and *Kangaroo*, and *Captain's Doll*. You must do
all you can in the way of agreeing with him about these contracts, and what
you find you truly can't do, you must plainly write to him, and also to me,
and I will settle. As far as England goes, the scale of royalties is not abnormal. And you know, on *Women in Love*, I do think you should have made a
scale, not a dead level 10%.[4]

But listen. So long as you really believe in me and are 'innerlich' loyal, I
will not go back on you nor let Mountsier go back on you.[5] And as I said
before, I only want us to be just with one another. We are men first, and contractors of business second.

After all I like the Merrild black-and-white *Kangaroo* jacket best: the one
Mrs Seltzer liked. The three are done – and I like them very much: trust you
will too.[6] I shall be glad if you can put a bit of work in the Danes' way.
Götzsche is beginning to paint me today. He has done a very amusing black-
and-white of me and Merrild and him on ponies here. We might get that

---

[1] Seltzer published DHL's translation of Verga's *Mastro-don Gesualdo* on 13 October 1923
   (Roberts A28).
[2] This decision cancelled a proposal originally made in April 1922 (*Letters*, iv. 232).
[3] Macy (1877–1932) was literary editor of the *Nation*, 1922–3.
[4] In his letter to Seltzer, 4 January, DHL remarked that Mountsier spoke of 'some contracts he
   had drawn up, starting with a 15% royalty'; DHL added: 'I don't know how that affects you'
   (iv. 367).
[5] Seltzer had been at 'daggers drawn' with Mountsier since at least September 1922 (iv. 298).
[6] Merrild designed jackets for *Kangaroo*, *Studies in Classic American Literature* and *The
   Captain's Doll*; Seltzer bought all three (see Letter 2707n below) but used only the last.

into some journal. I sent one or two of Merrild's black-and-white drawings to *The Dial* along with my review on Sherman's *Americans.*

It is lovely weather here – all sun, and the snow *almost* gone. We continue to be busy with things round about the place. I am sure I should never do any creative work here: only critical. Mountsier wants me to do with him a collection of best short stories, with notes, for University use: go halves on royalties – he to do all the correspondence and business. I don't know if I shall do it. Feel[1] I am being made use of a bit.

I don't think I shall stay here longer than March: then to Old Mexico. If you can find out anything about the country, tell me. Mountsier suggests coming along, but I think we'll go alone.

I had your letter from San Francisco – realise you felt a bit dreary in California. Ach! The Warner *money* would have been nice, but the film would have been sickening, so all for the best.[2]

You haven't told me what you think of *Kangaroo.*[3]

Greet Adele Szold. – We've got a new (old) pony, piebald, *pinto.* He creaks as he goes. – Mountsier spends nearly all his day up in his bedroom composing an article on The Economic Situation in Europe, from sheaves of newspaper clippings. By the time he has read the last clipping the situation has bust up and started on a new career. Poor M.!

Be greeted.

D. H. Lawrence[4]

2692a n. To D. H. Lawrence from Thomas Seltzer, 26 January 1923
Text: TMS Copley; Gertzman and Squires, 56–60.

5 West Fiftieth Street, New York
January 26, 1923

Mr. D. H. Lawrence
Taos, N,M.

Dear Lawrence:

Congratulations on KANGAROO! It is superb. Entirely different from any of your other novels. I knew that if you ever wrote about the War you would say something that nobody else said, in a way that nobody else could; but I never thought that you would put it in a novel. I need not tell you how glad I am that it is in a novel, because in that form it will get the widest

---

[1] Feel] Fell
[2] It is not known to what film this refers.
[3] DHL had sent 'the last words of *Kangaroo*' to Seltzer on 4 January (*Letters,* iv. 367).
[4] See letter following for Seltzer's reply.

hearing. For myself, your book means a great deal. Every new book of yours carries one forward. One does not remain on the same spot as with most of our other writers. The two chapters that affected me deeply are "Struthers" and "Kangaroo", and the next one, about your War experiences. I mention the War element in your novel particularly because it is so close to us but of course it is by no means the whole novel. You have the whole country Australia in it, its depression as well as its fascination. It was a stroke of genius to put the War against such a background. The contrast between the vast silence of that large uninhabited country and the noise of the War intensifies both. And then there is the whole world besides. The Odyssey of the human soul as seen through the individual soul of Richard Lovatt and the revelation of the dark God. I think I am intimate with your dark God, I seem to know him, and let others laugh, it won't affect me and I hope it won't affect you. They will not laugh for long, I am sure.

The manuscript is bad in parts, some errors must have crept in in transcription. I will let you have galley proof and you can fix it up. What I can guess at myself I will have corrected here in the office.

I got home at nine o'clock Tuesday, the 16th. Of course a pile of work awaited me, and I had no time to write until now. Yours is the first letter I am dictating. My trip was quite worth while. Everywhere I went the bookdealers greeted me with "D. H. Lawrence." You have many enthusiastic admirers in Los Angeles and in San Francisco, and through out the West and Middle West. In Chicago, one of the literary lights told me that he had just spent an evening in which the chief topic of conversation for several hours was D. H. Lawrence. I wonder if you remember, some three years ago I wrote you that you would come into your own. Well, you have, apparently, already. WOMEN IN LOVE continues to sell well and there is a steady demand for your other books. What I am glad to see especially is that there is a constant small sale for SEA AND SARDINIA. I shall probably have to print a second edition soon of PSYCHOANALYSIS AND THE UNCONSCIOUS. ENGLAND, MY ENGLAND has received praise from practically all reviewers so far. If you are interested I will send you some of the clippings. FANTASIA OF THE UNCONSCIOUS they do not understand, or do not want to understand. In San Francisco I met an insistent little lady reviewer who had written a rather snippy review of FANTASIA, and she would discuss this book with me endlessly, though I had very little time; I had important other things to do. Nevertheless, it will do some good, as she lectures on your book. It has affected her strongly in spite of herself, and she feels she must fight back. This will no doubt create some readers, and when FANTASIA OF THE UNCONSCIOUS gets enough readers it will begin to be appreciated. It too, is having a steady moderate sale.

Nobody whom I met in Los Angeles and San Francisco knew much about Mexico. I went to the Chamber of Commerce in Los Angeles and spoke to the man who is supposed to know a good deal, but he proved very disappointing. He said that the two chief points of interest in Mexico are Mexico City and Gaudalajara, about fourteen hours from Mexico City. I think you can make the trip comfortably on about three hundred and fifty to four hundred dollars for each person, but I will find out the exact cost of the fare from the Mexican Consul here, and will write you about it soon.

I suppose Mexico is calling you, and you must go. If you change your mind and want to come East, you will have a nice house in Stamford, Connecticut, the country house of our friend I told you about. They are going to Europe and the house is at your disposal for the whole summer, so that even if you come East in June you will have the house. It is a nice place, not pretentious at all, just pleasant. It is possible also that there will be another house of theirs vacant on the same grounds, and if that is the case we may be able to stay there also, for a couple of months. Adele and I would like it very much.

In Chicago I received word from the office, asking where the third novelette "Ladybird" is. You know that Mountsier, when he gave me "The Fox", took away "Ladybird" to submit to the *Cosmopolitan*. The two other novelettes are in page proof, and we cannot go on. It puts me in a predicament. We have pretty nearly our entire Spring list complete, and not a single work of yours is in such shape that we can announce a definite publication date. It is absurd. Did Mountsier get my telegram about "Ladybird"?

I had a letter from John Macy of the *Nation* about little novels, returning all the stories. He wrote Mountsier, so you know the situation. No, by all means, if "Mastro-Don" is all that you and Adele think about it we must begin with this novel. Short stories even at best hardly ever sell as well as a novel that is successful, and if you have a big novel "Mastro-Don", why naturally, that should come first. I will try to read it soon.

I had never meant to pay you only ten percent on WOMEN IN LOVE, contract or no contract. I had given orders before that you are to be paid fifteen percent on all copies above five thousand, counting also the copies of the limited edition that we sold, so that after less than four thousand of the new edition, you will be getting fifteen percent, but as regards all of your books, I find that our ten percent up to five thousand is perfectly fair. I have gone into this thing carefully and I find that the best results for you and for me can be obtained on this basis only. I could explain to you in detail but it will only weary you. You will believe me if I say that it is so. I should feel miserable if we were "contractors of business" only, just as you would. Wit[h] you I absolutely refuse to be that, and that alone. As to my being "innerlich" loyal to you, you know that I am, don't you? You don't want me to make protestations. But I want to say this, the relation between us with regard to your books is perfectly natural, in the natural course of things, but any interference by a third person is unnatural, unnecessary, and create[s] needless fuss and inconvenience both to you and me. It must be stopped even if the feelings of somebody are hurt, and the only way to do it is to put an end to it once for all. No half measures will do. I will be miserable. It is unwise. And I am afraid I will have to make you uncomfortable occasionally against my will if the thing is not put a stop to. It is the right thing, it is the just thing. You know that it is, and if something unpleasant has got to be done it is neither your fault nor mine; it is the fault of the person who occasions all this.

We have had about four different changes of weather since my return; very cold, warm, very cold, snow and rain on the same day – a sort of indeterminate weather now. This is New York, you are lucky not to be here at this season.

Editing a volume of best stories is not for you, rather cheap. Furthermore, for use in a college one must be connected with some educational institution, because in textbooks it is usually an exchange of favors between educators. You buy my textbook, and I will buy yours; no outsider shall infringe. So I have my doubts about the advisability of it, even if it were the kind of work you ought to do. You will not let yourself be used, of course not.

Remember me to Frieda Lawrence. I should like to see you soon again.

Yours   Thomas Seltzer

2698n. To D. H. Lawrence from Thomas Seltzer, 1 February 1923
Text: TMS Copley; Gertzman and Squires, 60–6.

5 West Fiftieth Street, New York
February 1st, 1923

Dear Lawrence:

Soon after writing to you I received your letter of January 19th and your special delivery of January 23rd.[1] I communicated with Hearsts International at once and found that THE CAPTAIN'S DOLL had not yet been scheduled. As they arrange their schedule three months ahead this

[1] This letter should therefore be read in conjunction with *Letters*, iv. 369–72.

means that it cannot appear before June. I then sent off your cable to Curtis Brown setting the date as August. The editor of Hearst's promised me to do his best. The reason for its taking so long is that the size of the story is rather unusual and they are finding difficulty in getting the space for it. But I'll do my best to get them to print it in June, and we can release the book as soon as the story appears in the magazine. Before I left for New Mexico the editor promised to publish it in time for March publication of the book. So I did not bother any more. But evidently they need looking after. They have a new managing editor[1] who is friendly to me and a great admirer of your work, so I think he'll do all in his power to accomodate us.

Did you get the page proof of THE CAPTAIN'S DOLL and THE FOX? I sent you uncorrected proof. The printer has the corrected copy. Do you like the fountain pen? If it is too hard or unsatisfactory in any way, return it to me and I'll change it for the kind you like.

The package came with the manuscripts of STUDIES, LADYBIRD, LITTLE NOVELS OF SICILY, Merrild's three jackets, Götsche's amusing sketch, the thousand contracts AND the letter of Mountsier, a copy of which I am enclosing.[2]

The impudent good for nothing! The cheek and vulgarity of him. The penny soul. After this there was only one thing for me to do. I enclose my reply also.[3] I could not do otherwise and retain my self-respect. He has ruled himself out. He does not belong with people like you and me. We are not going to haggle eternally over dollars and cents. We'll be just to each other and act with dignity. It is impossible to act with dignity with Mountsier meddling.

Evidently he has been playing up the contract of WOMEN IN LOVE as his big trump card. My last letter disposed of that. You know under what circumstances the contract was drawn up. It was the first of your books I accepted. Neither you nor I expected a sale above 5000. It was to be a limited edition. It cost several thousand dollars to produce. It would be some time before I could even get back the investment. Surely it wasn't a profiteering proposition. Now that it turned out that the book is selling I am not so petty as to take advantage of a contract. I don't conceive of our relation as merely one of dollars and cents. I leave that to Mountsier.

He says something about TOUCH AND GO and THE WIDOWING OF MRS. HOLROYD. What about them? The royalty due on TOUCH

[1] Carl Hovey (see Letter 2707n. below).
[2] Missing.
[3] Missing.

AND GO up to date is $3.43. I don't think the sale of MRS. HOLROYD has yet covered the amount I paid for the stock and the plates. I bought the play because I wanted to get all your books I could and subsequently bring them under one imprint. What's the great "financial expert" talking about?

Why, if another agent had represented you, would I not have gotten THE LOST GIRL? You gave me the option on it in the contract of WOMEN IN LOVE. You wrote me promising it to me absolutely. Does he think that you would go back on your word? Did he not ask me to show him the contract of WOMEN IN LOVE and was it not only after he saw the option clause that he finally gave me the manuscript of THE LOST GIRL? Did he not dilly-dally as he always does, so that Secker got ahead of us and we lost considerable sales on account of it? A nice mess he would have made if he had the free disposal of THE LOST GIRL.

He talks about other agents. I have dealt and am dealing with almost every literary agent of any account. They have all been very nice to me. They cooperate with me and are often helpful. They don't haggle. None of them has shown himself as petty as Mountsier, none has dared to be bossy with me. We agree on the main points, then a contract is drawn up, a short, sensible contract, not the crazy Authors' League and hair splitting lawyer's contract, and all is done. Everything else they leave to me. They don't meddle, they don't attempt to print the book for me, to publish it, to advertise it and to sell it. If they can help me they do it, unobtrusively. I have not yet lost a single author I wanted to keep through the treachery of an agent. They have all been satisfied with the way I handled their books and whether I was protected by an option clause or not they have so far always given me the author's new books. Mountsier alone is dissatisfied. This proves his utter incompetence. For if I have given satisfaction in other cases surely I must have done so in yours. You know that there is not another author on my list for whom I have worked so hard and with so much devotion, to whom I have given so much of the best that there is in me. And everybody, except those who are greedy to snatch for themselves the results accomplished by the hard work of another, recognizes that we have done well, unusually well, in fact. But Mountsier doesn't see it. A nice literary agent he is.

He complains of my advertising. What we have done before the censorship case you know.[1] Since then WOMEN IN LOVE has featured for months as news in papers all over the country, and in editorials and special articles. Perhaps another publisher would have bought up all the newspapers

---

[1] An unsuccessful attempt was made in September 1922 to prosecute Seltzer as the publisher of *Women in Love* and the anonymous *Young Girl's Diary*. See *Letters*, iv. 292 n.1, and 296.

and excluded all other news. Or perhaps Mountsier thinks that the best form of advertising is to tell the reviewers that AARON'S ROD is so poor a novel that he and other friends of yours had tried to keep you from publishing it. When I was in San Francisco the hotel where I stopped was invaded by reporters who came to interview me when they learned I was in the city. They came early in the morning and interviewed me when I was still in bed, they interviewed me at breakfast, at all hours of the day, and my last goodbye before I left for the East was to a reporter.

Mountsier hates me because I am not a mere merchandiser but appreciate your books in and for themselves and *he* did not until a lot of people said so; he hates me because I not only advertise that you are a genius, and the greatest writer in the English language, but because he knows that I believe it, and that my response is direct, from within, which is what gives me the courage to publish it abroad; while he – well, I need not tell you that he is utterly incapable of seeing the greatness and the beauty of your writings. I shall continue to declare in my advertisements that you are a genius whenever I think it appropriate. You *are* the greatest writer in English and I personally don't know any foreign author either whose works give me the same sense of bigness as yours do, from whom I get such a feeling of personality, of life and worthwhileness. Mountsier says, "Lawrence's works speak for themselves." When did they begin to speak for themselves to *him*? AARON'S ROD spoke so loudly to him that he couldn't bear the noise and wanted to stop it. Like so many who do not see the real essence of your art SONS AND LOVERS has remained your "best novel" to him and THE LOST GIRL your next best. Has he changed his mind now, has he suddenly seen a light?

Well, Mountsier need not fear that I have done you harm with the way I advertised you. If you had been with me on my trip you'd have heard the bookdealers all over, and private people too: "You have made Lawrence." "You have made Lawrence." Of course I did not make you. You made yourself. I could not have made you as I have made you if your works were not what they are. But their meaning is clear enough. Your works "speak for themselves!" How clever in Mountsier! And we stupid publishers go and spend thousands of dollars every month in advertising to tell the people what the works tell about themselves.

It is too absurd. I don't at all like to say all this. You don't need it, I am sure. You know it all without my saying it, don't you? But since I am wound up let me finish. The truth is, the people have learned to respect my opinion about books. More and more people know that my opinion of a book deserves a hearing. Some critics too have a great regard for what I say. Even most of the hostile critics have a sneaking regard for my opinion and it enrages them. Inferiority complex.

Shall I then keep quiet? Shall I, whenever a new novel by Lawrence or René Maran appears, whisper in six point type: – "Kangaroo: it speaks for itself."[1]

To think of Mountsier telling me what is appropriate, teaching me good manners – a bully who can write a bullying, vulgar letter like this to a decent man.

All the arrangements I have made with Mountsier in the past I will allow to stand. But on your future books I wrote you in my last letters what I consider a fair graded royalty – 10% on the first 5000 and 15% above. I based this statement on the actual figures of last year's business. We had a good year. And if I find this year that I can increase your royalty to 15% from the start I will do so, and let you have the additional royalty of 5% on the first 5000 of each book at the end of the year. If we have great prosperity there will be a bonus also, which is a reasonable business arrangement based on what the state of the business permits. In a word, I am not greedy. I'll do what is right.

I can't bear to look at these long, foolish contracts I received. I'll have a contract drawn up which will protect you in every respect. This is thoroughly satisfactory, most frequently used, and we'll get along with it all right.

Of course I'll let you have a say whenever the question of moving picture rights arises. But if quick action is necessary and you cannot be reached in time you don't want me to miss a chance.

The royalties due you from June to January 1st amount to $4286.46. Not bad. Added to your royalties of the first half of the year, the total of royalties for 1922 is more than $6000. Mountsier's haggling made a difference of about $300. Isn't it stupid? From a business point of view I must count every dollar and every penny, because it would make a difference of thousands of dollars a year which the firm could not afford to lose. But for your representative to haggle over this is pure pettiness – and worse, a lack of desire to cooperate, to help me do the best for you.

Curtis Brown writes me that Secker has at last decided to publish SEA AND SARDINIA. I am glad of that. He will print it himself.[2]

---

[1] René Maran (1887–1960), African novelist, perhaps the most influential among earlier writers of the modern African novel. His masterpiece, *Batouala* (1921), awarded the Prix Goncourt, had been translated from the French by Adele Seltzer and published by Seltzer in 1922.

[2] Secker's edn appeared in April 1923; Seltzer had published the book in December 1921 (Roberts A20).

I tried to get the two books of Melville in every bookshop I visited on my trip and in New York. They cannot be obtained. I am advertising for them now. I will also try to get the Spanish book on Mexico.[1]

Have not yet seen Mexican consul.[2] Will do my best to find time in a few days.

I like THE CAPTAIN'S DOLL and STUDIES jackets. Don't care for the KANGAROO one.

I will write soon again about the order in which the new books are to be published.

Best regards to Mrs. Lawrence.

Yours   Thomas Seltzer

2707n. To D. H. Lawrence from Thomas Seltzer, 17 February 1923
Text: TMS Copley; Gertzman and Squires, 66–8.

5 West Fiftieth Street, New York
February 17, 1923

Mr. D. H. Lawrence
Del Monte Ranch
Questa, N. M.

Dear Lawrence:

So the Mountsier chapter is ended.[3] I realize how awful it was for you. It was awful for me too, but perhaps not quite so bad. But it had to be gone through with. Now I am sure it will be all right between you and me.

My last letter may explain part of Mountsier's bad conscience.[4] I wonder if he hasn't done anything dirtier behind our backs. Time will show.

If your arrangement with him did not specify that he is to receive a commission permanently, then by all means discontinue the commission. It is all wrong that he should be getting it, besides he should not get any commission at all on WOMEN IN LOVE, as he did not place this book. I had a talk with lawyer Stern and am fairly convinced that his advice at the start was bad.[5] I think I might have managed to get SONS AND LOVERS from Mitchell Kennerley if I had been able to treat with him some two years ago.

---

[1] See *Letters*, iv. 345 and n.3; 383 and n.1.
[2] DHL wanted to know 'what the travelling is like' in Mexico (iv. 369).
[3] This letter should be read in conjunction with Letters 2704, 2705 and 2707 in which DHL both breaks his connection with Mountsier and tells Seltzer that he has done so (iv. 375–9).
[4] See Letter 2698n above.
[5] DHL told Seltzer on 3 February 1923 (iv. 376) that Mountsier was 'starting a lawsuit against Kennerley' to recover royalties on *Sons and Lovers*, using Benjamin H. Stern of the legal firm Stern and Ruben.

Now the book is out in the cheap edition and what arrangement he made and whether it is possible to take away the cheap edition rights even when we get back the book from Mitchell Kennerley, I do not know. Stern says that Kennerley's lawyer promised to give him a definite answer in two weeks and hopes that Kennerley will turn over the book to us without going to court. Would it be so! Even with the cheap edition on the market it would still be nice to have the book for the collected edition of your novels.

THE RAINBOW becomes ours automatically six months after serving the notice. If you let me have the dates of the expiration of the contracts of the other books, I shall see that notice is served in time.

I will be glad to attend to the business with Stern myself and keep you informed of every step and of course not do anything of importance without your consent, except in such cases where a quick decision is to be made. This will save you a lot of time and unnecessary trouble. When you are in New York, if the matter is still pending, it will be easy for you to get in touch with Stern personally.

Carl Hovey, managing editor of Hearst's magazines, has consented to let us print THE CAPTAIN'S DOLL book whenever we want, irrespective of the date of publication in the magazine, so now it can be released. I want, however, to have another talk with him before releasing the stories for book publication.

I sent Merrild a check for $120. for the three jackets, $40. a piece. This is a very good price. I do not think the KANGAROO jacket will show up well among other books, but I will keep the jacket anyway.

The best thing for Götsche, is to do a decorative, not a picture jacket, for BIRDS, BEASTS and FLOWERS. The size is $6\frac{5}{8} \times 8\frac{1}{2}$. The first thing I read of your BIRDS, was of course 'Bubbles'.[1] It is a joy! When Adele came in I showed it to her, and she was enchanted.

For the present, the following is the order of publication: THE CAPTAIN'S DOLL about March 15; STUDIES the first or second week in April; BIRDS will have to be postponed to the Fall. It is too important a book not to get the best sale for it, and it will get the best sale only if published early in the Fall, say the middle of September or perhaps a little later. KANGAROO too, ought to be published about that time. However, I will have all your books set up as soon as possible so that if we decide to publish them before, we can do so. I shall see that Curtis Brown gets all information with regard to dates of any book of yours. I will try to work together so as not to conflict with each other. I would also like to publish THE WHITE

---

[1] I.e. 'Bibbles'. (Seltzer published *Birds, Beasts and Flowers* on 9 October 1923).

PEACOCK some time this year, and THE RAINBOW when we get it.

I will send you the contracts soon containing the seven-year term clause and will let you have transfer of copyright with the contracts, so that you will be completely protected. I do not want to influence you about your English publisher, but I have my suspicions about twenty and twenty-five percent. If Secker expects to do any advertising, how in the world can he afford these royalties? We will talk about this when you are in New York. I shall probably go to England some time this year and if you want me to, I will do anything I can to get you the right terms and the right publisher.

If you want me to help you in the matter of income tax, I can arrange it for you if you let me know the exact amount.

Terry's "Guide to Mexico" has gone off to you and so has the "Oxford Book of Ballads".[1] It seems as there is no such thing as the "Oxford Book of Songs"; there are two books, the Ballads and another one, which I had ordered for you.[2]

I saw Walter Pach the artist the other day to find out something about Mexico.[3] He was in Mexico for a few months last year, lecturing on art. He spoke very interesting on Mexico. I will write you about it in my next letter, soon.[4]

2722n. To D. H. Lawrence from Thomas Seltzer, 24 February 1923
Text: TMS Copley; Gertzman and Squires, 69–71.

5 West Fiftieth Street, New York
February 24, 1923

Mr. D. H. Lawrence,
Del Monte Ranch,
Questa, N. M.

Dear Lawrence:

Your letter of February 17 just came. Also the corrected proofs of LADYBIRD. My last letter answers most of your questions, I think.

Yes, you had better withdraw your account from the Charleroi bank. I will open an account for you in the Chase National Bank, Metropolitan Branch, New York.[5]

---

[1] *Oxford Book of Ballads* (1910), ed. Sir A. T. Quiller Couch. For Terry, see iv. 374 n. 4.
[2] There was an *Oxford Song Book*, ed. Percy C. Buck, (OUP, 1916 and often reprinted); DHL had requested a copy in January 1923 (iv. 373). On 13 February (in a letter not available for publication) he thanked Adele Seltzer for 'the music books'.
[3] Walter Pach (1883–1958), American artist and author.
[4] For DHL's reply, see iv. 393–5.
[5] See iv. 384.

After April 1st, if you want to keep the money due you as royalties from July 1 to December 31 in the Seltzer corporation, I will pay you the usual interest of 6% yearly. If not, do you want me to invest it in safe securities? It would be a waste to let so much money lie idle in your bank or at the low interest which a bank pays. I shall see that you always have a balance of about $2,000.00 in your bank for your open account. This is enough, don't you think so?

Please let me know if the English publisher has set a definite date for the publication of the Verga novel. I'll read it as soon as possible. This book also should be an early fall publication and be brought out simultaneously here and in England.

My plan now is to have the same format for BIRDS, BEASTS AND FLOWERS as the English edition of LOOK WE HAVE COME THROUGH, which I like very much. Be sure I'll do my best to make a good-looking book. I have not yet read all the poems, but from what I have read, you are justified in laying so much store by it. So I want to give it the proper dress. It will be all right. Early next week I'll probably have the complete typescript to send to you.

Your telegram appeared in the newspapers complete exactly as you sent it.[1] An omission of one word only – "guileless," before "Daughter." – Not my doing but the newspaper editors'. Evidently they feared libel suit.

I saw Jonathan Cape yesterday. He is eager to get your books. Will pay 15% on the first ten thousand and 20% above, and 300 lbs advance on every book. From what he told me, although he was careful not to say anything against Secker, there is no chance of your books getting the reading public they ought to have in England as long as they are in Secker's hands. I don't like to urge you to change you[r] publisher, but I am anxious that your books should get the right treatment in England. It is of course highly important. Anyway my advice is not to hurry in this matter. Cape may not be quite the right man; but he certainly would push your books. I'd like to talk this thing over with you carefully.

Next Tuesday I'll see the lawyer again about SONS AND LOVERS, and will write you immediately.

Since you are going to spend a couple of months in Mexico, you will obtain all the information you want in Mexico City, and there is no need for me to give you the bit I was able to gather. Walter Pach says one must be careful about one's food in Mexico, but he was there in the summer.

Is THE WHITE PEACOCK now free for publication at any time?

---

[1] See *Letters*, iv. 379.

All the best things for you and Frieda Lawrence.

Yours,   Thomas Seltzer

[1]Acting Assistant District Attorney Pecora made a statement in the papers the day after Ford's attack that he is not likely to take any further action against Women in Love because he knows he cannot secure its suppression.[2] Sumner doesn't know what he is talking about. The only one that can bring an indictment in New York is the District Attorney and Pecora is the real district attorney, Banton being only a figure head.[3] Sumner tried to get the District Atty to bring an indictment before the Grand Jury after he lost the case in the Magistrate's Court. Banton turned him down flat.

TS

Judge Ford, by the way, is known as a gas bag and a poor judge whom the other judges try to relegate to his proper place by giving him petty cases only.

2730n. To D. H. Lawrence from Thomas Seltzer, 3 March 1923

Text: TMS Copley; Gertzman and Squires, 71–4.

5 West Fiftieth Street, New York
March 3, 1923.

Mr. D. H. Lawrence,
Del Monte Ranch,
Questa, New Mexico.

Dear Lawrence:

Your letter of February 22nd received.

Mitchell Kennerley's lawyer is ill with pneumonia and so the decision about SONS AND LOVERS is delayed. Stern assures me that he will see him as soon as he is back in the office. I will let you know immediately when there is any news of importance.

The enclosed card of Lincoln Steffens will introduce you to Robert Haberman, an Hungarian-American and a newspaper man in Mexico City who Steffens says is much liked and knows people whom you will want to

---

[1] From hereon the letter is in Seltzer's own hand.
[2] Ferdinand Pecora (1882–1971), Chief Assistant District Attorney, New York County, 1922–30; later Justice of the Supreme Court of New York. In February 1923 Justice John Ford of the New York Supreme Court had resurrected the case brought by John S. Sumner, of the Society for the Suppression of Vice, against Seltzer as the publisher of *Women in Love* and *A Young Girl's Diary* which Magistrate George W. Simpson had dismissed on 12 September 1922. Sumner got his indictment in July 1923 but only against two books, not *Women in Love*.
[3] Joab H. Banton (1869–1949), District Attorney for New York County, 1922–9.

meet.[1] You will have no difficulty, Steffens says, in locating him among the newspapers in Mexico City. Lincoln Steffens is a very well known journalist and writer here. He has been in Mexico a number of times and he has written out on the card an itinerary for you. This is for a quick trip. I suppose you will not follow it as you mean to spend some time in Mexico. You will, of course, make Mexico City your headquarters. The last three cities marked on the card I suppose you will visit on your way to New York after returning to Mexico City.

I have not yet been able to make out Stern. I will rent a strong box for you in a bank where you can keep all your important papers. The less lawyer the better. I only use them as a last resort in an extreme emergency.

I will read MASTRO-DON GESUALDO soon and will try to bring the book out simultaneously with its publication in England. I think the middle of September is a better date than August.

Almost all of BIRDS, BEASTS AND FLOWERS is now typewritten and a copy will go off to you early next week. I will have it forwarded special delivery so that you will be sure to get it before you leave.

I thought my letter of February 17th explained that there was to be no interior decoration for BIRDS, BEASTS AND FLOWERS but only a decorative jacket.

Your contracts with Huebsch have a seven year term clause, have they not, and notice must be served at the expiration of the seven years. Six months after serving notice the books are free. That is my understanding of it and I think I am right.

The contracts and the assignments of copyright will be ready early next week and I will try to let you have them before you leave. After signing them please return them, and your copies I will put in your box. If the contracts are not ready in time, I will see that you get them in Mexico City but I shall try to have them before.

Please send me the Huebsch contracts, if possible. I will get in touch with Huebsch and will let you know.

I think now that all questions are answered. In addition to the fact that I am overwhelmed with work, some questions cannot be answered immediately because there is a good deal of information to be obtained which takes time; so please be patient and be sure that all the information you desire will be given you at the earliest possible moment.

I want to say again that I think it very wrong and absurd that Mountsier should receive a commission for the rest of his life. He has done nothing

---

[1] See *Letters*, iv. 406 and n. 2, 410.

whatever to further your affairs as regards your books. You had your publisher, and it was a simple matter to let me have the manuscripts and publish them at the most favorable time. Nothing Mountsier ever did was helpful, but many things he did were an obstruction. He did do something perhaps worthwhile in placing things with the magazines but for this he has been paid. My suggestion is that you pay him a lump sum of $200. or $300. just as an employe[e] who is dismissed is given two or four weeks' notice with pay until he finds another position. That's as fair as can be. There is no reason on earth why Mountsier should expect different treatment. As far as I am concerned it, of course, does not affect me directly, but I do not want him to take advantage of you. Don't let him do it.

Judge Ford has been making a tremendous fuss. Last Sunday all the New York papers had prominent front page news of a meeting he called together at the Astor Hotel at which he announced that he would introduce a law making any book obscene which contains even a single passage that is regarded as obscene. This would practically outlaw the entire book business. He got the backing of powerful names and organizations: the Catholic Church, the Boy Scouts Movement, the Prohibition Forces. Being a practiced politician the law might be railroaded in spite of its absurdity, unless it is counteracted by an opposition movement. So we got together and are forming an Anti-Censorship League. The majority of the public it seems clear are strongly opposed to censorship, but nevertheless this law might be passed just as prohibition was passed if it is not fought. The conservative "Times" last Tuesday came ought with a strong editorial against the proposed law, so did other papers. We will have practically the whole press with us I think and, no doubt, the law will either be killed or will never even get to the stage of being introduced, but it means a lot of hard work and is taking my time.

WOMEN IN LOVE is a big seller. It already sold over 12,500 exclusive of the limited edition and I have ordered a fourth printing. It will soon outstrip Batouala.

I hope you have recovered from your cold.

Remember me to Frieda Lawrence.

Yours   Thomas Seltzer

2736a. To Albert Curtis Brown, 26 February 1923
Text: MS Lazarus; Cablegram; Tedlock, *Lawrence MSS* 97.

[Taos, New Mexico]
26 Feb. 1923[1]

LCD Browncurt, London
Proceed *Ladybird* released March publication.

Lawrence[2]

2740n. To D. H. Lawrence from Robert Mountsier, 6 March 1923
Text: TMS Copley; Gertzman and Squires, 74–5.

Taos, New Mex.
March 6, 1923.

Dear Lawrence,

I have your letter of the 3rd, asking me to put into writing that I am satisfied to accept ten per cent of all your receipts from Seltzer for this current year and to promise to send back to you your manuscripts and papers as soon as I go east.

You asked me to write you what I wanted in way of settlement, but neither by word of mouth nor by letter have I asked you for any particular settlement – and by no means did I ask you, as one of your letters seemed to indicate that you thought I did, for a permanent commission on your royalties. In this connection you mentioned that "Women in Love" was outside of my contracts; yes, you made the original contract with Seltzer, but consider that there were also such matters as "Sons and Lovers" and "The Trespasser" that I worked with on your behalf although I was not responsible for the original contracts – or lack of one in the case of the former – and drew nothing from them.

You have decided what you wish to pay me, and when it is paid there is an end to it so far as I am concerned. I express no dissatisfaction with the settlement; I express dissatisfaction in connection with certain things in your writings and with your allowing yourself to fall a prey to Seltzer by signing his contracts in place of the ones drawn up by Mr. Stern and me – certainly the "Women in Love" contract and various words and doings on Seltzer's part should have been sufficient warning. And you appear to be throwing away your chance to get "Women in Love" back under your control.

---

[1] The previous day DHL had written to Curtis Brown telling him that Seltzer 'had got "The Captains Doll" [*The Ladybird*] released, and that he proposed to publish it March 15th' (*Letters*, iv. 399; see also Letter 2629a above and p.57 n. 2). DHL added that he would 'get in to Taos' and send Curtis Brown a cable. This he did.
[2] A note on the MS reads: 'Received 2. 27. 23 C.B.'

Since you wish it in writing here is my promise to accept your settlement, to give your own words to me, of "ten per cent of all receipts from Seltzer for this current year" and the return of "all manuscripts and papers belonging to me as soon as you go east."

Robert Mountsier

2754a. To Baroness Anna von Richthofen, [16 March 1923]

Text: MS Houle; PC v. C. Spitzweg. Flurschütz; Postmark, Taos MAR 18 [. . .]; Unpublished.

[Taos, New Mexico]
16 März

Heute kam dein Brief vom 25 Februar: es dauert lang. Ach, so traurig ist Europa. Wir gehen Morgen früh zu Taos – Montag kommen an Santa Fe: Mitwoch an El Paso, der Grenz: und Freitag abend Mexico City. Hier ist tiefe Schnee – da wird es heiss sein. Ich gehe gern, vom Winter weg. Wenn wir in Mexico kommen, schreibe ich dir sofort. Man ist weit von Europa, doch duftet Elend in der Luft.

Bleib wohl. DHL

[Today came your letter of 25 February: it took a long time. Oh, how sad Europe is. We're going to Taos tomorrow morning – Monday arrive at Santa Fe: Wednesday at El Paso, the border: and Friday night Mexcio City. Here it's deep snow – there it will be hot. I'm glad to go, away from winter. When we get to Mexico, I'll write to you at once. One is a long way from Europe, but the smell of its misery is in the air.

Keep well. DHL]

2755a. To Adele Seltzer, 18 March 1923

Text: MS Fath; Postmark, Taos MAR 20 1923; Unpublished.

Ufers' house. *Taos.*
Sunday 18 March 1923

Dear Adele Szold

We have got so far:[1] left Del Monte in deep snow and the tail end of a cyclone. It was rough. Frieda cured for ever of her desire to live in a cave: myself cured for the time being of wild west, desert, freedom, simple life, the soil, and all that sort of thing. At the moment I want to be a *signore*. I

---

[1] DHL and Frieda made a brief stopover at the home of the artist Walter Ufer (1876–1936) and his wife Mary Monrad Frederiksen Ufer, mutual friends of the Danish painters, Knud Merrild and Kai Götzsche.

want to be a Don: Don Lorenzo: with ten peones.[1] I want to have a silk shirt and silver buttons on a short coat. I almost want to have a gold ring. Crude America is very crude. The spirit of place, uncurled and uncombed, is a disagreeable thing, here. Curled and combed it is no better. It is a devastating country: lays waste to the soul and gradually hardens the heart. I want to go away. We'll see what Mexico is like.

We leave in the morning for Santa Fe: leave Santa Fe on Tuesday night: leave El Paso on Wednesday afternoon: arrive Mexico City, *Deo Volente*!, on Friday night. I had a telegram from Witter Bynner that he can't leave Santa Fe until tomorrow week.[2] So we shall just go ahead. I refuse to hang round. Am rather glad to go alone. I've ordered the Drawing Room[3] as a slight set-off to Del Monte Ranch.

I wonder if the American continent altogether is a vast negative field, active in the downthrow of life as long as life will let itself be thrown down, and as soon as life starts again to live, and spring-time comes, doomed, America, to disappear again into silence, a sort of inertia.

Or can America become ever positive?

Vediamo![4]

I sent you yesterday a brass tray I got from Ceylon. This is a gift from us to you.

I will send you a tiny trunk to *5 West*,[5] with the sheepskins and arctics.[6] Merrild just gave me some [moth balls], and I put them in the trunk.[7] Would it trouble you too much to put one or two in? [Frieda adds] Merrild has some. (We put some in !)

[Lawrence continues]

It grieves me very much to leave Bibbles.[8] But Merrild and Götzsche are staying on here in Taos till May, and she knows them, and is lively with them. And if we remain in Mexico I will have Götzsche or Mrs Freeman[9] bring her to us. I can't trail her round hotels. If we had a house to go to I would take her at once.

---

[1] Servants, originally slaves (usually Mexican).

[2] The Lawrences were joined in Mexico City, on 26 March, by the American poet, Harold ('Hal') Witter Bynner (1881–1968) and his close friend Willard ('Spud'/'Spoodle') Johnson (1897–1968), journalist and editor..

[3] A private compartment in a Pullman railway carriage.

[4] 'Let's see!'

[5] I.e. 5 West Fiftieth Street, New York, Seltzer's business address.

[6] Fur-lined waterproof overshoes.

[7] Merrild . . . trunk] I forgot yesterday to get moth balls

[8] DHL's 'little black dog' (*Letters*, iv. 408).

[9] Elizabeth ('Bessie') Wilkeson Freeman (1876–1951), girlhood friend of Mabel Luhan; DHL often expressed the hope that she would visit Mexico (e.g. iv. 392, 413, 443).

Would you hate having these two books sent to Götzsche's father for me.[1]
Thomas said Farewell. I go no further than

auf wiedersehen   D. H. Lawrence

[Frieda continues]

I am sorry you are so busy, is'nt it too much? Thomas is *not* to worry
about Lawrence – he *does* trust him and Thomas knows it, but you see it
seems a little rough on Hübsch,[2] just as he is making a little money, we *know*
that Thomas would make a lot *more* for us – Think of us and wish us luck –

F

Hope you will like the tray, Mountsier wanted it badly!

2757a. To Baroness Anna von Richthofen, 20 March 1923

Text: MS Houle; PC v. Snug as a Bug in a Rug. Pueblo Indian Papoose; Postmark, Santa Fe,
MAR 20 1923; Unpublished.

Santa Fe.
20 March 1923

Wir sind so weit gekommen – schon wärmer – sind mit Freunden hier –
F[rieda] hat Indianische Perlen-Mocassins gekauft, und eine sehr feine
Serape – ein blanket, alle Farben. Wir gehen heut ' abend – und kommen
Morgen an El Paso – der Grenz. Ich reise immer gern, mochte wieder
Blumen und Blätter sehen: hier in dieser Höhen, kommt zu viele Schnee
und gibt zu viele Wüste.

Bleib gesund.   DHL

[We've got so far – warmer already – are here with friends[3] – F. has bought
Indian pearl-mocassins, and a very fine serape – a blanket, all colours. We're
leaving tonight – and tomorrow get to El Paso – the border. I always love
travelling, want to see flowers and leaves again: here at this height too much
snow falls and there is too much desert.

Keep well.   DHL]

---

[1] The books are unidentified; the 'nice letter' DHL received from Götzsche's father was probably to thank him for them (*Letters*, iv. 463).

[2] Seltzer and Huebsch were in dispute over rights to publish *The Rainbow* and *Women in Love*;
DHL's action in sending Letter 2798a below to Huebsch, via Seltzer, was clearly intended to
confirm Frieda's assertion of DHL's loyalty.

[3] The Lawrences were staying with Witter Bynner.

2762a. To Baroness Anna von Richthofen, [21 March 1923]
Text: MS Houle; PC v. International Bridge between El Paso, Texas, and Juarez, Mexico;
Postmark, El Paso MA[. . .] 2[. . .] 192[. . .]; Unpublished.

– El Paso
Mittwoch

Wir gehen heut Morgen über den Grenz – letztes Wort vom U. S. A. – Alles
geht gut.

DHL

[Wednesday

This morning we cross the border – last word from the U. S. A. – Everything
is going well.

DHL]

2772a. To Laura Forrester, [4 April 1923]
Text: MS Forrester; PC v. Volcan Popocatepetl. Mexico. Popocatepetl Volkan. Mexico.;
Postmark, Mexico D. F. 4 – ABR 1923; Darroch, *DHLReview*, xx (Spring 1988), 41-4.

Mexico City
4 April

– Your letter came on to us here – do you really think to establish yourself in
Australia? We are moving around in this queer country, before we make up
our minds to sail for England. Mexico City is just inside the tropics, but
7300 ft up, on a plateau, so not too hot. Sydney seems far away. – You don't
tell us what sort of business you are in. But I'm sure you are wise to occupy
yourself – you ought to be busy.

Many greetings   DHL

2772b. To Baroness Anna von Richthofen, [4 April 1923]
Text: MS Houle; PC v. Pyramid of the Sun at San Juan Teotihuacán, Mexico; Postmark,
Mexico D. F. 4 ABR 1923; Unpublished.

[Hotel Monte Carlo, Avenue Uruguay 69, Mexico City]
4. April

Wir waren gestern hier in San Juan Teotihuacán – in auto gegangen, mit den
zwei Amer. Freunden. Es ist merkwurdig, viel mehr so wie Pompei – so
gross und still. Wir waren auf dem Pyramid, und sahen das ganzes Thal
Mexicos herum liegen: cultiviert, aber leer, und viele viele zerbrochene
Häuse, in den Revolutionen ruiniert. – Mexico City habe ich nicht gern –
halb Americanisch, halb Span-Indian-Armenviertel, und sehr lärmig. Wir
gehen morgen an Cuernavacá, 120 Km. – Immer schlimme Nachrichten
von Europa, in den Zeitungen.

Bleib gesund.   DHL

Wir waren Sonntag am Stierkampf – liefen davon – es war grässlich

[We were here in San Juan Teotihuacán yesterday – went by car with the two American friends.[1] It is strange, much more so than Pompeii – so large and silent. We were on the Pyramid, and saw the whole valley of Mexico lying there, cultivated, but empty, and very many ruined houses, destroyed in the revolutions. – I don't like Mexico City – half American, half Spanish-Indian districts of the poor, and very noisy. We're going tomorrow to Cuernavaca, 120 km. away. Always bad news from Europe, in the papers.

Keep well.   DHL

We were at the Bullfight on Sunday – ran away – it was horrible]

2798a. To Benjamin Huebsch, 21 April 1923

Text: MS Fath; Unpublished.

Hotel Monte Carlo. Mexico City.
21 April 1923

Dear Huebsch

Your note with nothing in it has just come.

I understand you go round wiping your eyes, in New York, because of the injustice done you by me, complaining of my lack of integrity and gratitude, etc.

I don't forget, Huebsch, that you said to Robert Mountsier that I was a *liar*, and that you could prove it: and then you *didn't* prove it.[2] Nor could you. – Nor do I forget.

As for the precious $200, I am very glad to give them back. It was very kind of you to collect them, but it would have been kinder still if you had earned for me enough royalties not to leave me so absolutely poor, for several years. And it is by no means kind to turn the dirty $200 into an insult. Kindly accept them back. If they were more than two hundred, just let me know.[3]

---

[1] Bynner and Johnson.

[2] In a letter to Seltzer, 19 March 1923, DHL had made the same allegation against Huebsch and threatened: 'I will write and remind him of it' (*Letters*, iv. 412).

[3] With the MS of the letter is a cheque (dated 21 April 1923) for $200 payable to Huebsch on DHL's account with the Charleroi Savings and Trust Co. It is not clear, however, what unwelcome debt or obligation DHL was repaying. In January 1920 he received a cheque from Huebsch for the equivalent of $100 representing 'a gift' from Louis and Jean Untermeyer and Emile Tas (iii. 445); then in April 1920 Huebsch sent '150 dollars that Gilbert [Cannan] collected for me' (iii. 511). Perhaps DHL's memory led him to believe that the combined sums made up 'the dirty $200'.

After which I shall be glad to have nothing more to do with you. – But don't forget, in your turn, that I have a tongue in my head, and teeth too, that I can use upon occasion.

Yours faithfully   D. H. Lawrence[1]

2841a. To Baroness Anna von Richthofen, [10 June 1923]
Text: MS Houle; PC v. [photograph of Chapala foreshore]; Unpublished.

Chapala. Jal.
12 June 1923[2]

Meine liebe Schwiegermutter

Gleich kommt dein Geburtstag – ich schicke dir ein Bisschen Geld, und hoffe es geht dir fein und gut. Wir haben deinen Pfingsen Brief: du bist eine alte weisse Huhn mit deinem Brut herum. Gleich kommen die zwei Läufigen über Meer, und du kannst klucken und schimpfen wie unsere *Amarilla*, unsere gelbe die ist Prima donna im Huhnhaus hier, unter den Banana-bäumen. Mein Roman geht gut – mehr wie halb fertig, im ersten Schreiben. Heut ist Sonntag – in der Nacht viel Regen – jetzt heisse Sonne, – Markt-tag – Frieda hat viel Obst gekriegt – Mangos, guavas, tunas, pitayas, melonen, zupotes, chirimoyas. Aber besser sind Badenen Kirschen wie alle diese Tropische Fruchte. Im Bild ist es auch Sonntagmorgen – Holy – cambous uber den Zee gekommen – Peonen mit Sarapen uber den Schulter. – Am Ende des Monats fahren wir weg. Freue dich über deine Alter.

DHL

[My dear Schwiegermutter

Soon it will be your birthday – I send you a bit of money, and hope that things are going nicely and well with you. We have your Whitsun letter: you are an old white hen with your brood around you. Soon the two running

---

[1] DHL recorded in his diary for 21 April 1923: 'Wrote Huebsch and sent him back 200 dollars' (Tedlock, *Lawrence MSS* 98); this accords with his letter to Seltzer on 25 April 1923: 'I sent back that charity money, and told [Huebsch] what I thought of him' (*Letters*, iv. 432). However, a week later DHL wrote again to Seltzer: 'Hope you got my letter enclosing the one to Huebsch, with cheque to Huebsch, paying him back. Mind you send this' (iv. 437). The present MS is accompanied by an envelope addressed by DHL to Huebsch (and presumably sent to Seltzer), but it is unstamped. This, together with the absence of bank endorsement on the cheque or other visible evidence that the cheque was paid into a bank account, creates the suspicion that Seltzer forwarded neither the letter nor the cheque. No further communication is known between DHL and Huebsch.
[2] This date conflicts with DHL's reiterated remark that he was writing on a Sunday; Sunday was 10 June; it is assumed that '12' was an error.

overseas will come, and you can cluck and scold like our *Amarilla*, our yellow one who is Prima Donna in the henhouse here, under the banana-trees. My novel is going well[1] – more than half done, in the first draft. Today is Sunday – a lot of rain in the night – now hot sun – Market-day – Frieda has got masses of fruit – mangoes, guavas, prickly pears, pitahayas, melons, sapodilla plums, custard apples. But Baden cherries are better than all these tropical fruits. It is Sunday morning in the picture too – Holy – coming over the lake – peons with serapes over the shoulder. – At the end of the month we're leaving. Rejoice over your age.

DHL]

2847a. To Thomas Seltzer, [22 June 1923]

Text: MS Fath; PC v. photograph of Lawrence and Frieda; Unpublished.

Chapala.
22 June

Dear Thomas

Novel done, save for last three chapters – me got a cold so postponing finishing it. We leave this house on the 30th – may stay a few days in the hotel Arzopalo – like the Lake – still hanker after a little farm here – am going round looking at possibilities, with Winfield Scott.[2] If see anything promising, shall come back here in Sept. – early Sept. – probably not go to Europe at all – don't want to go. Feel like making a little life here on this lake. – Don't give Murry anything of mine for that snivelling *Adelphi*.[3] – Various people have *offered* me houses – so dont go to any expense. Anyhow only something tiny. Do you know anything of Elmer Harden[4] – offers to show us Greek plays in *Franconia* New Hampshire.

Hope you're well. Au revoir

DHL

Sent you 'Whitman' with piece added: hope you like it.[5]

---

[1] Then called 'Quetzalcoatl', later *The Plumed Serpent*.

[2] Manager of the 'shabby, but pleasant' Hotel Arzapalo.

[3] DHL received the first issue of *Adelphi c.* 15 June; it contained an extract from *Fantasia of the Unconscious*; but he thought the whole production 'knock-kneed' (*Letters*, iv. 458, 462).

[4] Perhaps Elmer Stetson Harden, author of *An American Poilu* (1919) etc.

[5] After early re-writing, the essay on Whitman first appeared in *Nation and Athenæum*, July 1921 (Roberts c83); 'three pages of a new ending' were substituted in February 1922 (iv. 197–8, 257); and a week before this letter, DHL agreed – apparently at Seltzer's request – to 'go over the "Whitman" essay again' (iv. 457).

2866a. To Baroness Anna von Richthofen, [15 July 1923]
Text: MS Houle; PC v. Picking Cotton; Postmark, New Orleans JUL 16 1923; Unpublished.

New Orleans.
Sunday

Wir bleiben ein Paar Tage hier – sehr schwül – eine alte, gebrochene Stadt –
trübselig – mit den grossen, wüsten, braunen Mississippi schwer wie den
Styx. Hab' es nicht gern - ugh! Fahren Mitwoch nach New York – mit
Seltzer – Immer näherer.

DHL

[We're staying here a few days – very sultry – an old, broken-down town –
melancholy - with the great, desolate brown Mississippi oppressive as the
Styx. Don't like it – ugh! Wednesday we go to New York – with Seltzer –
Closer and closer.

DHL]

2904a. To Baroness Anna von Richthofen, [25 August 1923]
Text: MS Houle; PC v. American Falls; Postmark, Niagara Fa[lls] AUG 25 19[. . .];
Unpublished.

Niagara.
25 Aug.

Heute bin ich hier – schön, aber verdorben – modern. – Mittagsessen mit
der Mutter von Mabel Sterne – reiche, alte, traurige Frau – du bist tausend-
mal schöner – und mehr lustig. Hast du F[rieda] gesehen?

DHL

[Today I'm here – beautiful, but corrupt – modern. – Lunch with Mabel
Sterne's mother – rich, old, sad woman[1] – you are a thousand times lovelier
and more cheerful. Have you seen F.?

DHL]

2912a. To Baroness Anna von Richthofen, [12 September 1923]
Text: MS Houle; PC v. A Prize Flock, Cawston Ostrich Farm, South Pasadena, Calif.;
Postmark, Los Angeles SEP 13 1923; Unpublished.

Los Angeles
12 Sept.

– Ist die Frieda noch da in Baden-Baden? Ich habe noch nichts von ihr: ich
darf kaum an Deutschland denken. Hier ist alles ganz kummerlos und ein

[1] Sara Cook Ganson (d. 1933).

Bisschen dumm. – Man *braucht* ja seiner Kummer, sonst wird er leer. – Ich sah den Eclipse der Sonne, Montag: es ist wunderbar, wie eine andere Welt: seltsam ist es. Ich bin noch nicht wieder *da*. – Hier in California geht man immer in Auto und so weit. Ich bin müde. Was thut Ihr alle? Ich denke immer an Euch.

DHL

[– Is Frieda still there in Baden-Baden? I still have nothing from her: I scarcely dare think of Germany. Here everything is utterly worry-free and a bit stupid. – One *needs* one's worries, otherwise one grows empty. – On Monday I saw the eclipse of the sun: it's wonderful, like another world: peculiar, it is. I'm still not *back* yet. – Here in California one always goes by car and such a distance. I am tired. What are you all doing? I'm always thinking of you.

DHL]

2912b. To Charlotte Becker, [12 September 1923]
Text: MS Martin; PC v. All Ages, Cawston Ostrich Farm, South Pasadena, Calif.; Postmark, Los Angeles SEP 13 1923; Unpublished.

Los A.
12 Sept.

[1] – Just got back from Sta Barbara from seeing eclipse – very impressive – like another life-glimpse – this world still a bit unreal. Saw also those 7 destroyers on rocks – gruesome:[2] Hovering on one foot wondering where next – but have been so busy motoring here.

My zoo interest still holds – there's a circus in the street.

D. H. Lawrence

Greet the LIBRARIAN –

2918a. To Baroness Anna von Richthofen, [22 September 1923]
Text: MS Houle; PC v. [Ostrich with eggs]; Unpublished.

Los Angeles
Samstag 22 Sept.

Meine lieber Schwiegermutter
– Ich denke viel an dir und Deutschland. Ist die Frieda noch da? Ich hätte von ihr einen Brief von London: nicht mehr. Und England, sagt sie, gefällt

---

[1] DHL's correspondent was an old friend of Mabel Luhan; she lived in Buffalo which he had visited 22–7 August 1923.
[2] See *Letters*, iv. 497 and n. 1.

ihr wenig. – Es muss furchtbar in Deutschland sein: ein Schauer! Wie kann es so sein, das ein grosses ganzes Volk so nieder-gewurfen ist? So ein miserables Schicksal versteh ich gar nicht. Ich hasse ja die Europäische Menschenwelt, dass es so gemein und Muthlos ist. Ich *kann* nicht wieder kommen, während es so eine Schamhöhle ist. Man könnte wie ein Hund aus Ohnmacht und Ferne heulen. Muth verloren ist alles verloren, und Europa hat seinen Lebensmuth verloren. – Frieda muss es so machen dass dein Gelt aus England kommt monatlich an der Bank. – Ich gehe mit dem Däne Götzsche nächste Woche nach Mexico, um eine Wintersheimat zu finden. Wir gehen die Western-Küste entlang, von Guayamas auf dem Gulf of Mexico, bis Culiacan und Mazatlan und Tepic. Hoffentlich finden wir etwas schön und weit von der Welt, wo noch der HerrGott herrscht, und nicht der Mensch. – Wir waren bei den Ostrich-farm hier in der Nähe. – Heute Abend hören wir *Aida*, und essen mit Freunden ein Abschieds-mahl, Immer noch Abschied.

Bleib wohl.   DHL

[*Saturday 22 Sept.*

My dear Schiegermutter
– I think a good deal about you and Germany. Is Frieda still there? I had a letter from London from her: nothing else. And she says she doesn't like England much. – It must be dreadful in Germany: makes one shudder! How can it happen that an entire great people is so cast down? I really don't understand such a miserable fate. I do hate the European world of men for being so vulgar and despondent. I *can't* come back, while it's such a pit of shamefulness. One could howl like a dog from helplessness and distance. Courage gone means everything gone, and Europe has lost its courage to live. – Frieda must arrange it so that your money from England comes to the bank monthly. – I'm going next week to Mexico with the Dane Götzsche, to find a home for the winter. We're going along the west coast, from Guayamas on the Gulf of Mexico, to Culiacan and Mazatlan and Tepic. I hope we'll find something nice and a long way from the world, where the Lord God still rules, and not man. – We were at the Ostrich-farm not far from here. Tonight we will hear *Aida*, and have a farewell dinner with friends. Yet another goodbye.

Keep well   DHL]

2918b. To Frieda Lawrence, [22 September 1923]
Text: MS Houle; PC v. [Peacock in full display]; Unpublished.

Los Angeles.
Sat. 22 Sept.

I think we leave on Monday – Götzsche and I: go down to Guaymas, on the Gulf of California – and on to Navajoa, where an old Swiss has a ranch.[1] If don't like it there, proceed to San Blas – if not there, then to Tepic, which is not very far from Guadalajara, though the railway does not connect all the way. It's time now we found a place for the winter – and better not California: this all so on the outside, and *so* empty inside. – Tonight I am taking Danes, Johnsons and Böterns[2] to *Aida*. Remember that last awful performance? – America has 'recognised' Mexico, and they say it's very safe. – Bessie Freeman isn't yet here. – When you come, I think Merrild would like to come with you to Mexico, though he doesn't want to stay long: like Del Monte. – I had your letter from London. *Don't trust 'em –* that's my perpetual warning. Keep your heart safe hidden somewhere, and smile and be nice without giving anything away. One can live a very pleasant easy life here: but nothing to it. Wonder where you are?

L.

2922a. To Frieda Lawrence, [24 September 1923]
Text: MS Houle; PC v. [Three ostrich chicks]; Unpublished.

Los Angeles.
24 Sept.

These are baby ostriches on the ostrich farm near here – aren't they nice!

Götzsche and I set off tomorrow – I've got the tickets. We call at Palm Springs for a night – then on to Nogales, the frontier – then down to Guaymas, on the Gulf. I'm really going to look round carefully. – You, if you get bored in Europe, come out to Los Angeles and stay in Palm Springs till I've found a place – which I hope won't take long. I don't think I shall come back to Europe whatever happens. I've turned in my return ticket to New York, to get the money back. – The world is so wearisome. So come as soon as ever you wish – Los Angeles is only two days from Mazatlan. You can stay near Mrs Freeman – Palm Springs. California; – If you come here, write to Merrild – at 628 W. 27th St. Also write to

---

[1] In a letter to Knud Merrild, 15 October 1923, Kai Götzsche reported that he and DHL 'went to see the Swiss who has a silver mine in the mountains in a rather tiresome landscape of forest-covered mountains' (Merrild, *A Poet and Two Painters*, 1938, p. 336).

[2] Götzsche and Merrild; Harry Roland Johnson (1880–1972), a geologist, and his wife Olivia (see *Letters*, iv. 481n); J. Winchell Böttern, a Danish painter, and his wife Anna (iv. 507 n. 1).

Mrs James Forsyth, 1540 South Wilton Place, Los Angeles.
– She is very nice and will do anything for you she can.[1] He is a Scotchman –
banker. – When you come down to Mexico Merrild would like to bring you
– to come with you. People have been very nice here – and its very sunny all
the time, never too hot. It's a selfish place – live for the moment – but not
false. It's not so altogether bad. – But the world wearies me till my bones
ache inside my limbs – worldliness wearies me so. – I wish I heard from you
again before I left. – Don't stay any longer in Europe if you don't want to. –

L.

2923a. S. S. Koteliansky, [25 September 1923]

Text: MS Houle; PC v. [Cactus]; Postmark, Palm Springs SEP 27 1923; Unpublished.

Palm Springs.
25 Sept.

On the way to Mexico – tell F[rieda] we stopped off here to see Mrs
Freeman, and missed her – but saw the house, and Mrs Birge's.[2] This is
queer pale desert country. I prefer New Mexico really and Old. – I do hope
you dont get tired of forwarding the mail to F. She will soon be coming this
way again. I don't know what I should write to your *Adelphi*.[3]

Many greetings   DHL

2926a. Frieda Lawrence, [28 September 1923]

Text: MS Houle; PC v. [Old Mexican woman]; Postmark, Correos 29 SEP 23; Unpublished.

Guaymas.
28 Sept

Got here this morning – a pretty harbour, rather like Lerici – but the old
delapidated stubborn Mexican feeling. I think we go on in two more days to
Navajoa, then up to the ranch of the Swiss, among the mountains. We might
stay there the winter – we will see. – It is hot here – sun *very* hot – breeze
cool from the sea. – I hope your cold is better – wonder if you got to
Germany. Come west when you feel like it.

L.[4]

---

[1] DHL had enjoyed the Forsyths' kindness and was 'full of gratitude' to them (*Letters*, iv. 505).
[2] A friend of Bessie Freeman; they were both originally from Buffalo.
[3] DHL later described Kot as 'the busy bee of the *Adelphi*, Murry the sort of queen bee' (iv. 556). DHL frequently contributed to the periodical both before this letter and as late as February 1927 (Roberts c151).
[4] DHL addressed the card c/o Koteliansky at 5, Acacia Road, St Johns Wood.

3002a. To Thomas Seltzer [12 January 1924]
Text: MS YU; Cablegram; Unpublished.

[110 Heath St. Hampstead, NW3]
[12 January 1924]

ALL RIGHT ACCEPT LAWRENCE[1]

3049a. To Adele Seltzer, [11 February 1924]
Text: MS YU; PC v. Baden-Baden–Altes Schloss; Postmark, Baden-Baden
11 2 24; Unpublished.

BadenBaden
11 Feb.

Sunny frosty weather here – everybody frightfully poor, yet the country feels stronger, people more alive. I never get a word from Thomas – *must* hear about the income tax.[2]

DHL

3055a. To Adele Seltzer, 14 February 1924
Text: MS YU; Unpublished.

Ludwig Wilhelmstift, *Baden-Baden*
14 Feb. 1924

Dear Adele

Failing to get any answer from Thomas, the only thing is to come to New York and do things for myself.

We expect to be back in London by the 26th of this month, and to be in New York by the 10th March. I suppose that is time enough to pay the income tax. Probably Miss Brett will come with us, but Murry can't come till early April.[3] So we may wait for him in the east, and go on to New Mexico when he arrives.

---

[1] DHL was replying to a cablegram from Seltzer, 11 January 1924 (TMSC YU):
'All is well Disregard Secker Brown tattle Make no entangling alliance Try keep Adelphi for ourselves Will do my best for it Had five thousand dollar offer cinema Women Love Shall I accept Cable THOMAS SELTZER'
DHL referred to the cable in a letter 22 January (see *Letters*, iv. 558 and n. 4).

[2] DHL had not heard from Seltzer for 6 weeks and did not know 'whether he has put me any of the money he owes me into the bank, and whether he will pay my income tax' (iv. 583).

[3] Hon. Dorothy Eugenie Brett (1883–1977), artist and DHL's disciple; she did accompany the Lawrences to USA in March 1924 whereas Murry failed them.

Send me a line care Curtis Brown – and perhaps you might suggest an inexpensive hotel in New York.

Yrs   DHL[1]

---

[1] Partly in response to this and partly to DHL's letter, 22 January 1924 (*Letters*, iv. 558-9), Seltzer wrote on 23 February (TMSC YU):

Dear Lawrence:

I have been waiting until I can write you at length and tell you all the things you might want to know, but I do not want to wait any longer, as I am anxious for you to have word from me before you leave for New York.

For weeks a great deal of my time was taken up with that terrible case [a threatened prosecution for publishing 'unclean' books], which reached a crisis some time ago. It is not settled yet, but there is a possibility that a settlement will be reached soon. At any rate, I am no longer as troubled about it as I have been. A good deal of politics has entered into this matter. Very strong influences were at work on the side of suppression. Fortunately, I have very powerful friends who may be able to counteract these influences. We shall see.

I'll tell you all about Secker, SEA AND SARDINIA, and MASTRO-DON GESUALDO when I see you. The reason I cannot bring the matter to a head with Blackwell is because he wants me to guarantee the British copyright, which I am unable to do. I have tried to see the agent who claims to represent the Verga family, but so far have been unable to see him. I shall make a special effort to do so at once and if I can get this matter arranged, I will take up the offer of Blackwell by which you can get your full royalty.

THE BOY IN THE BUSH has come. I'll read it and send it to the printer immediately. When does Secker expect to publish it?

MEMOIR OF MAURICE MAGNUS typescript was sent to you on January 25th to Hampstead.

Adele and I are reading QUETZACOATL. It is a miracle. I hear that Witter Bynner is furious. No wonder. But you could not do otherwise -- you told the truth, and it is a marvel. If he didn't want it, he should not have put himself in your way.

The article, "The Proper Study", was published in the January issue of Vanity Fair and check for $100., which I received for it was placed to your credit in the Chase National Bank, also check for $100, from Gotzsche was placed to your credit there. You now have a balance of about $600. in the bank. I cannot tell you the exact figure because it is a holiday and my book-keeper is away. I will put some more in soon, so that you will have enough for your expenses.

Your income tax statement will be made out in the office and will be paid when due.

Business last year was not very good, but January and February of this year have shown a great improvement.

The little book on you by Seligmann will be published next week. I expect the pamphlet edition to come in Monday. I will immediately send you a copy and hope it reaches you before you leave. If it doesn't, tell your mother-in-law to keep it for herself, not to return it. The cloth edition will be out a few days later. We sell the paper cover book for 25c and the cloth bound for 75c. In each case I shall probably lose on the sale of this book, but I want to have as large a distribution for it as possible, so I don't want to make the price any higher. The only thing Seligmann lacks is a sense of humor. If he had that he would be a perfect interpreter. Even so, he has done a splendid piece of work.

I am so glad that I'll see you and Frieda soon again. So of course is Adele.

I am sending a copy of this letter also to England, in case you go there before leaving for New York.

Greetings. Yours,

3118n To D. H. Lawrence from Thomas Seltzer, 7 May 1924
Text: TMSC YU; Unpublished.

May 7, 1924.

Mr D. H. Lawrence,
Taos, New Mexico.

Dear Lawrence:

I just received your letter and jacket and Secker's proof of THE BOY IN THE BUSH. The jacket is fine. Now we can use it, except that the lettering will have to be made more prominent. As it was before, it was impossible. It would have cost a fortune to reproduce. Also the boy's legs were too impudently to the fore. It would have made a disagreeable impression, and we must not antagonize people with a jacket. They are more retiring now, and altogether the jacket is far better. I am pleased with it.

I have been wrestling with the proof of THE BOY to accommodate Miss Skinner and will now compare it with your revised Secker proof....

You would, I think, have enjoyed being at Miss Kameny's wedding, at least for a few minutes.[1] It was rather old-fashioned, though it did not have the flavor and the character of a Jewish wedding in Russia. And there was no nonsense, no weeping or that sort of thing. Miss Kameny and her man were quite happy and were not afraid to show it. Youth is still youth, Lawrence, even in this damned rotten age.

I am still at a loss about THE RAINBOW. The lawyers don't know their minds. But I shall bring it to a head soon. It may be necessary to do some expurgating. I will write you as soon as I know definitely.

Barmby has, I suppose, kept you informed of the payments he has received. Business does not show any improvement yet. I doubt whether a decided change for the better can be expected before the Fall. My advice to you is to be as economical as you can, for although you will probably make enough out of royalties to keep you comfortable, still in times like these it is best to keep as large a reserve as possible.

That was a handsome thing of Mabel to do, give Frieda the ranch. I hope you'll both like it a lot.

Goetzsche is through with his painting job. We gave him a bit of work to do which will keep him for a week.

Yours,

---

1 She was probably Seltzer's personal secretary; cf. *Letters*, v. 39.

3228a. To Katharine Throssell, 12 September 1924

Text: MS NLA; PC v. Threshing Wheat with Goats, Santa Fe, New Mexico; Postmark, Taos
SEP 15 1924; Tetsuhiko Kamimura, 'A Lawrence Postcard to Katherine Throssell',
DHLReview, xxvii (1998), 65-7.

Del Monte Ranch. *Questa*. New Mexico

12 Sept 1924[1]

Your letter of July 29 came yesterday, and the song for my wife: nothing
more. We couldn't try the song yet. I hope the books will turn up, and I'll do
anything I can. As for songs, we are both *very* fond of them. We used to sing
in the evenings a good deal. Do you know the Hebridean Songs?[2] – My wife
now owns this little ranch at the foot of the Rockies – very lovely, and not
your 'America' at all. – But for the winter we are going down to Old Mexico.
This is 8000 ft up, and cold later on. – No, I thought you were too feminine
about *Kangaroo*. You'll probably like *Boy in the Bush* better. I haven't heard
from Miss Skin[ner] these last few weeks: don't know why. *Boy* has very
good *Times* review, but all *me*.[3]

DHL

A bonny baby![4]

3264a. To Baroness Anna von Richthofen, [14 October 1924]

Text: David Schulson Autographs Catalog; PC v. Native American woman; Postmark, Taos
OCT 14 1924; Unpublished.

[Taos, New Mexico]

[14 October 1924]

We stay here until Wednesday. On the 20th, we will already be in Mexico
City. Again it is warm and beautiful here and F[rieda] weeps for her
ranch . . . Mabel [Dodge Luhan] travels to New York on the 20th . . .

DHL[5]

---

[1] An extract from this letter (as published by the recipient, the Australian author, Katharine
Susannah (Prichard) Throssell) was included in Volume V of the *Letters*; in the absence of the
MS and other reliable evidence, it was misdated. See Letter 3126.

[2] Marjorie Kennedy-Fraser's *Songs of the Hebrides* (1909) (see *Letters*, iii. 164 and n. 6; v. 570
and n. 2).

[3] His embarrassment at being almost the sole focus of attention from the reviewer – the author
and journalist, Harold Hannyngton Child (1869–1945) – in the *Times Literary Supplement*, 28
August 1924, was conveyed to Mollie Skinner on the day following this letter (v. 123).

[4] It is presumed that Katharine Throssell had sent a photograph of her two-year-old son (see iv.
272 – 3). By 'bonny' DHL may have meant either 'handsome' or (in northern usage) 'well
fed', or even both.

[5] The original text is said to be in German.

3356n. To D. H. Lawrence from Thomas Seltzer, 7 February 1925
Text: TMSC YU; Telegram; Unpublished.

February 7, 1925

Mr D. H. Lawrence
c/o British Consulate,
1 Avenue Madero,
Mexico D F Mexico

Is it true you are giving books to Knopf   I cannot believe it   I will pay your royalties don't fear but your hurt my chances   You endanger all if you leave me

Thomas Seltzer[1]

3367n. From Frieda Lawrence to Friedrich Jaffe, [5? March 1925]
Text: MS Roberts; Unpublished.

Hotel Imperial, Mexico City
[5? March 1925]

Lieber Friedel,

Hier sind wir Gott sei Dank,nachdem Lawr in Oaxaca totkrank war mit Malaria, Influenza; es war *schlimm* und in diesem Land, das ich verfluche *keine* Hilfe – die mexik. Doktor kamen *einfach* nicht, ob aus Indolenz oder Angst der Verantwortung aber auf mir allein lag alles, ich tat eben was ich konnte und hab ihn durchgebracht und dann muß ich sagen half mir die amerikan. Kolonie *sehr*, mit Autos und allem, aber Gott steh allen Weißen bei in diesem Land – Ich selbst bekam auch Malaria, Fieber jede Nacht; nur die See sagen sie heilt Malaria, also nehmen wir das nächste Schiff – Wir hatten vor im *Mai* zur ranch aber *Höhe* ist schlecht für L jetzt – aber gieb die Hoffnung nicht auf und vielleicht können wir mit deiner Mutter Ferien in Europa aufbringen – daß dir Amerika *nicht* gefällt freut uns – der Seltzer ist nicht so schlimm, aber nachdem er *klein* mit Lawr anfing schwoll ihm der Kamm er wollte zuviel, wollte ein *großer* Verleger sein, es reichte nicht dazu bei ihm, er hatte nicht die Kraft und nun ist er immer in Geldschwierigkeiten und bezahlt uns nicht, so hatten wir letztes Jahr wening Gelf aber ich hoffe dies Jahr mehr mit *Knopf* – Mabel Luhan ist eine interessante Frau aber im Grunde ein *Zerstörerin*, das ist ihre Grundnatur und am Ende hat man genug – Ich freue mich ganz närrisch auf Europa, ich hab es satt endlich die *Wilden* wie die Großmutter sagt – ich bin augenblicklich für die höchste Kultur!! Lawrs Roman war fertig ehe er zusammenbrach – es ist ein großer Roman – Bleib Du nur gesund – das Amerika saugt die Kraft, die lebendige,

---

[1] DHL responded on 15 February 1925: see *Letters*, v. 213.

wenn man nicht zur Maschine wird wie der Rest – also in ein paar Tagen
geht's nach Europa

                                        Alles Gute   Deine Tante Frieda
    Law grüßt

[Dear Friedel,[1]
    Here we are, thank God, after Lawrence was deathly ill in Oaxaca with
malaria, influenza; it was *bad*, and in this country that I curse, *no* help – The
Mexican doctor *simply* didn't come, either out of indolence or fear of
responsibility; but everything was on my shoulders alone; I did what I could
and have brought him through – and I do have to say the American colony
helped me *very much*, with cars and everything, but may God help all the
White People in this country. I myself got malaria, too, fever every night;
they say only the sea heals malaria, so we're taking the next ship – we had
planned to go to the ranch in *May* but the *altitude* is bad for L. now – but
don't give up hope and maybe we can have a vacation in Europe with your
mother – we're glad that you *don't* like America – Seltzer is not so bad, but
after starting *small* with Lawr he got a swelled head. He wanted too much,
wanted to be a *big* publisher, he didn't have it in him, he didn't have the
strength, and now he always has money problems and doesn't pay us, so we
had little money last year, but I hope for more this year with *Knopf* – Mabel
Luhan is an interesting woman but basically destructive, that's her true
nature and in the end you've had enough – I'm madly looking forward to
Europe, I'm finally fed up with the *savages*, as Grandma says – at the
moment I'm in favour of the finest culture!! Lawr's novel was finished before
he broke down – it is a great novel. Stay healthy – America saps your
strength, your life; if you don't turn into a machine like all the rest – it's off
to Europe in a few days

                                        Best wishes   Your Aunt Frieda
    Lawr sends greetings]

---

[1] Friedrich ('Friedel') Jaffe (b. 1903), Else Jaffe's eldest child and Frieda's nephew; he was in
   USA as an exchange student; he joined the Lawrences at the ranch in June 1925 (see *Letters*, v.
   269). Subsequently he changed his surname to 'Jeffrey' and became an American citizen.

3404a. To Joseph Foster, [c. 24 April 1925]

Text: Joseph Foster, *D. H. Lawrence in Taos* (Albuquerque, 1972), p. 233.

[Kiowa]

[c. 24 April 1925][1]

Do come and see us. Next week perhaps . . . Could you bring us some meat from Cummings?[2]

3416n To D. H. Lawrence from Thomas Seltzer, 8 May 1925

Text: TMSC YU; Unpublished.

May 8, 1925.

Mr. D. H. Lawrence,

Del Monte Ranch,

Taos, New Mexico.

Dear Lawrence:

I have only just learned that you are back on the Ranch. So you evidently did not go to England, as you expected to. We forwarded some mail to you c/o Curtis Brown, London, and also sent you a copy of LITTLE NOVELS OF SICILY there.

THE LITTLE NOVELS have been greeted with enthusiasm and good reviews still continue to come. It will probably have a steady sale in any case, and a good sale if business improves soon. But now nothing is selling much except "The Constant Nymph" and "Arrowsmith", and I doubt if they are going as big as best sellers usually do.[3]

Until I can pay you all I owe you, I have no right to try to persuade you to let me publish all your books. So that your suggestion that I share you with another publisher, may not be a bad scheme temporarily. However, if you should consent to have me publish your books exclusively, with the exception of the novelette [*St. Mawr*] you have already sold to Knopf, my friends may be willing to finance me for the purpose, so that I could let you have a substantial sum in advance for each book and thus secure your royalties beforehand to a large extent.

Please let me know what you think of this plan. If you consent, I will begin trying to raise a fund for this purpose immediately. This will of course

---

[1] The writer and Taos resident, Joseph O'Kane Foster dated his visit to the Lawrences on 'a nice day in May or June' (*D. H. Lawrence in Taos*, p. 233); he also quoted DHL (p. 236) as saying that they had 'bought a buggy'. The buggy was bought between 15 and 21 April 1925 (*Letters*, v. 239, 244) and was clearly a recent acquisition when Foster visited Kiowa. If, then, the visit took place in May and the letter was written up to a week before that, it can reasonably be dated c. 24 April.

[2] Albert Cummings, the Taos butcher (cf. v. 64 and n. 5).

[3] *The Constant Nymph* (1924) by Margaret Moore Kennedy (1896–1967); *Arrowsmith* (New York, 1925) by Sinclair Lewis (1885–1951).

not interfere with my gradual payment of the old debt to you. As soon as
business conditions improve, it will be possible for me to clear the debt
entirely. We have good books that sell steadily, and in normal times I should
be doing very well.

Sentiment apart – and I am not ashamed to confessing to a feeling in the
case of your books which has nothing to do with business – I am very
anxious to keep you on my list. You seem to belong there naturally. If you
have this feeling the least little bit as I have it in a large measure, you will do
your utmost to help to find a way for us to keep together.

Yours,[1]

3416n To D. H. Lawrence from Thomas Seltzer, 23 May 1925
Text: TMSC YU; Unpublished.

May 23, 1925.

Mr. D. H. Lawrence,
Del Monte Ranch,
Questa, New Mexico.
Dear Lawrence:

I have your letter of May 13th. I was very sorry to hear of your illness and
hope you are quite well now.

What do you mean by I did not show you confidence for confidence?
Please do tell me. This is not a rhetorical question. I want to know what is in
your mind. Tell me specifically. I have no idea what you are referring to.
Having made the charge, you must substantiate it if you can.

Yours,[2]

3439n. To D. H. Lawrence from Thomas Seltzer, 2 July 1925
Text: TMSC YU; Unpublished.

July 2, 1925.

Mr. D. H. Lawrence,
Del Monte Ranch,
Questa, New Mexico.
Dear Lawrence:

Your letter was a great relief to me. I had your word and I believed it of
course. But the announcement was so strange, I naturally was puzzled.[3]

---

[1] DHL's reply, 13 May 1925 (*Letters*, v. 253), prompted Seltzer's letter which follows.

[2] DHL's reply is missing.

[3] Presumably DHL replied to (what he described to Curtis Brown as) Seltzer's 'expostulation'
(v. 271) and denied Knopf's claim to be 'exclusively' his publisher (v. 271 n. 1); this then was
Seltzer's relieved response.

I had been meaning to publish this fall THE WHITE PEACOCK and MOVEMENTS IN EUROPEAN HISTORY. If you have no objection, I might still add THE WHITE PEACOCK to our fall list and publish the History next year. I want to go slowly with the publishing of more books by you until the account is paid up or at least considerably reduced.

When I get on my feet completely, I will go down to your ranch to see you and try to reestablish our old relations. I have an idea that you will feel more comfortable when that happens. I certainly will.

Write me and tell me about yourself, and remember me to Frieda.

Yours,

3453a. To Joseph Foster, [c. 26 July 1925]
Text: Foster, *D. H. Lawrence in Taos*, p. 239.

[Kiowa]
[c. 26 July 1925][1]

Do come up sometime. I've been in bed again with a chill. Nothing much . . . Bring some books. Whatever you have. Gibbon. *The Decline and Fall*. I feel like reading something heavy.

3579 n.2. To D. H. Lawrence from Adele Seltzer, 7 December 1925
Text: TMSC YU; Unpublished.

December 7th, 1925.

Dear Lawrence:

The letter copy of which is enclosed, was received by us today, and we have informed the writer that the matter of the translation is in your and the agent's hands.[2]

Where are you? In England? Or have you gone into the Continent and down to Italy?

Greetings to you and Frieda.

Cordially yours,

---

[1] Foster associated this letter with summer 1925. He referred also to the very heavy rainfall at that time, two bridges being washed away in the Taos region. Writing to Ida Rauh, 26 July 1925 (*Letters*, v. 282), DHL similarly mentioned a cloud-burst and a bridge having 'gone down' between Taos and Raton. Hence the conjectural date for his letter.

[2] The unsuccessful enquiry from Dr Nanette ('Nettie') G. Katzenstein (1889–) read as follows (TMSC YU):

Zurich, 14th of November, 19[25].

RE.THOMAS SELTZER. NEW YORK

Sir,

Having read THE LOST GIRL by D.H.Lawrence with the greatest interest, I trust just this book would have a sure success in Germany.

I beg you to let me kindly know, if the rights of translation are still obtainable and also the conditions in connection with them.

3806a. To Phyllis Whitworth, 2 September 1926
Text: MS Whitworth; Unpublished.

'Duneville', Trusthorpe Rd. *Sutton on Sea*. Lincs
2 Sept. 1926

Dear Mrs Whitworth[1]

Will you please write to me to this address, to let me know when you would care to talk over with me the production of *David*. I expect I shall be coming to town one day next week.

Yours Sincerely   D. H. Lawrence

3824a. To Phyllis Whitworth, 11 September 1926
Text: MS Whitworth; Unpublished.

Sutton-on-Sea.
11 Sept 1926

Dear Mrs Whitworth

Many thanks for your letter. We leave here on Monday, and I expect to be in London by Thursday next. So if you would send me word to:

30. Willoughby Rd, *Hampstead*. N. W. 3.

I could meet you and Mr Atkin whenever you wish.[2]

Yours Sincerely   D. H. Lawrence

3841a. To Phyllis Whitworth, 24 September 1926
Text: MS Whitworth; Unpublished.

30 Willoughby Rd, Hampstead, N. W. 3.
24 Sept. 1926

Dear Mrs Whitworth

I have received your letter, forwarded from Sutton, only today. I did send you this address when I left there – but perhaps you did not get it.

I shall see Secker today, and shall ask him if he can send you a copy of *David*.[3]

---

footnote from page 95 (*cont.*)

Having your kind answer, I shall ask my German publisher to negotiate with you on that subject.

Truly yours,
Schifflande 10, Zurich, Switzerland   (signed) DR. NETTIE KATZENSTEIN

[1] Phyllis Whitworth, née Bell (1884–1964), theatrical producer; founded the 'Three Hundred Club' in 1924; in 1926 she agreed to its amalgamation with the Stage Society (which was responsible for the production of *David*, 22–3 May 1927). m. 1910, Geoffrey Whitworth (1883–1951), critic, dramatist and founder of the British Drama League.

[2] Robert Atkins (1886–1972), actor and stage-director. He was expected to – but in the end did not – produce *David*.

[3] Secker published the play in March 1926.

I am leaving for Italy next Tuesday, so the time is now rather short. Tomorrow we are going to dinner with W. J. Turner, who, I believe, is a friend of yours.[1] And I might see you on Monday morning, at your convenience. Will you let me know? There is unfortunately no telephone here.

I am sorry there has been this delay, owing to the change of address. But perhaps we can still manage a meeting.

Yours Sincerely   D. H. Lawrence

3841b. To Phyllis Whitworth, [24 September 1926]
Text: MS Whitworth; Unpublished.

30 Willoughby Rd, Hampstead, N. W. 3.
Friday

Dear Mrs Whitworth

You will have had my letter saying we are leaving for Paris on Tuesday. Mr Atkin has suggested Monday evening for a meeting – and I have kept that open. I should like to see you too, if you could manage it. Perhaps we could meet after dinner in some café for an hour or so, seeing this is the last opportunity.

Martin Secker will have posted you a copy of *David* today – if he didn't forget, and I hope he didn't. If he did, would you remind him? at

5 John St. Adelphi. W C 2

I hope then that I may see you.

Yours Sincerely   D. H. Lawrence

3842a. To Phyllis Whitworth, 25 September 1926
Text: MS Whitworth; Unpublished.

30 Willoughby Rd, Hampstead, N. W. 3.
25 Sept. 1926

Dear Mrs Whitworth

Many thanks for your invitation. We will be at the Chandos restaurant at 1.0 on Monday, in the new room.

This will reach your house this evening. Mr Atkins had suggested Monday evening, but lunch-time is just as well for me.

Yours Sincerely   D. H. Lawrence

---

[1] Walter James Turner (1889–1946), Australian poet and music critic, resident in London; drama critic of *London Mercury*, 1919–23. Author of *The Hunter and Other Poems* (1916), *The Dark Fire* (1918), etc. His play, *Smaragda's Lover* was performed by the 300 Club on 22 February 1925, in the Court Theatre; the cast included Ernest Milton, Esmé Percy and Peter Creswell, with all of whom DHL would become concerned.

3846a. To Grace Farrand, 29 September 1926
Text: MS Hughes; Postmark, Paris 29 -9 26; Unpublished.

[49, Bd. Montparnasse. Paris.]
29 Sept 1926

Dear Mrs Farrand[1]

So sorry I walked off with the key – hope it didn't put you out. We had a very pleasant journey – a smooth sea, and not a great crowd.

Many thanks for all your kindness

Yours Sincerely   D. H. Lawrence[2]

3890b. To Phyllis Whitworth, 15 November 1926
Text: MS Whitworth; Unpublished.

Villa Mirenda, *Scandicci* (Florence)
15 Novem 1926

Dear Mrs Whitworth

I wonder why Robert Atkins funked *David* – found it a bit too heavy for him, I suppose. I sent him the music for it, about a month ago, but he never answered.[3] You might get the music sheet from him, it will do for February, if you don't mind. – As a matter of fact, though he is a nice man and I liked him I doubt very much if he's subtle enough for *David*. He's perhaps wise to leave it alone.

I'm glad you're doing *Mrs Holroyd* first.[4] It is a simpler proposition. If only the English winter didn't make me chesty, I'd hop over like a bird for the production. But I must certainly come for *David* – tell me in plenty of time when I can be of any use. So perhaps I'll stay here, where it's warmer

---

[1] DHL addressed his letter to 'Mrs P. Farrand' but the occupants of Carlingford House, 30 Willoughby Road, Hampstead, London NW3, were Grace Farrand and her husband Frederick George Farrand. Presumably Grace Farrand was the landlady at that address where the Lawrences had been staying, 16–28 September 1926 (cf. *Letters*, v. 536–45). Catherine Carswell reported their being 'in rooms in Hampstead' (Carswell 242); the Lawrences were conveniently placed for seeing certain friends and had indeed thrown a party for a small number including the Carswells and Kot on 27th, the night before they left for Paris (Carswell 245).

[2] On the front of the envelope DHL wrote: 'Contains a key - contient un clef', together with his name and his address in Paris; on the verso, there is a wax seal (for a description of the seal see iv. 190). Attached to the MS is a scrap of paper on which he wrote: 'D.H.Lawrence, Villa Mirenda, *Scandicci*, Florence, Italy', the address to which he went on leaving Paris on 1 October.

[3] See v. 557. The music is printed in *The Plays*, ed. Hans-Wilhelm Schwarze and John Worthen (Cambridge, 1999), pp. 587–601.

[4] The 300 Club production (under the direction of Phyllis Whitworth) of *The Widowing of Mrs Holroyd* took place in the Kingsway Theatre on 12, 13 and 19 December 1926. The producer was Esmé Percy.

and sunnier, till after Christmas. – If I can help in *any* way, from a distance, with *Mrs Holroyd*, do let me know.

How are you? still full of all kinds of perplexities, or sailing on a pleasant quiet sea? The latter, I hope: though it's not so easy.

Remember me to your husband – I can always see his alert look. And you shouldn't have been so distant with Bonamy Dobrée, he's very nice really.[1]

Best wishes from my wife and me.

Yours Sincerely   D. H. Lawrence

3900a. To Edgell Rickword, 30 November 1926
Text: MS Anon; Michael Silverman Catalogue, 1998.

Villa Mirenda, *Scandicci* (Florence)
30 Nov. 1926

Dear Mr Rickword,

Thanks for the Cunninghame Grahame book – I'm sure it will interest me, and shall be glad to have a shot at reviewing it.[2] It's nice to say what one thinks.

Do send me a list of titles of books I might do, if it is not troubling you too much.

Yours Sincerely   D. H. Lawrence

3921a. To Phyllis Whitworth, 20 December 1926
Text: MS Whitworth; Unpublished.

Villa Mirenda, *Scandicci* (Florence)
20 Dec 1926

Dear Mrs Whitworth

I was frightfully interested in the photographs and press-cuttings of *Mrs Holroyd*. The people seem not to have had a good time looking at it, poor darlings! As a matter of fact, it's years since I even read the play, so I can't remember it very well. But probably they're right about the last act: too much death, and life not given a look in. If it were to be done again, I'd have a shot at re-modelling the end. You see the play was written fifteen years ago when I was pretty green. – Anyhow I'm glad it was so well done, and very grateful to you for giving it a show. – I will write to Esmé Percy and thank him.

---

[1] Bonamy Dobrée (1891–1974) was then Lecturer in English, University of London; later he was Professor in Cairo and in the University of Leeds (see *Letters*, v. 558 n. 1). DHL told him about Atkins' decision not to produce *David*, on 15 November, and in the same letter jocularly recalled 'that fiaschetto [mini-disaster] of a lunch in that pub. with you and Mrs Whitworth and the others' (v. 577).

[2] DHL reviewed Graham's *Pedro de Valdivia, Conqueror of Chile* (1926) in *Calendar*, iii (January 1927), 322-6, edited by Edgell Rickword (1898–1982). For DHL's opinion of Graham see v. 590.

David will take more work to put on the stage. Unless the skies fall on me, I shall certainly come and help as much as I can. So let me know in time, won't you?

How did Dobrée respond to your olive twig? He hasn't written me? Did he fly away from it, with a ruffling of feathers? I can just see him.

I do hope you weren't disappointed in the reception *Mrs Holroyd* got. It seems hard lines, after such noble hard work. But you have my gratitude, really.

All good wishes from me and my wife.

Yrs   D. H. Lawrence

I sent you a 1/- *Glad Ghosts* for a Christmas Card the other day.[1] If it doesn't come, it'll be because the Italian post has absorbed it.

3941a. To Phyllis Whitworth, 12 January 1927
Text: MS Whitworth; Unpublished.

Villa Mirenda, Scandicci (Florence)
12 Jan. 1927

Dear Mrs Whitworth

Thanks for your letter – Hope your show went off gaily, and brought you a good purse. What an energetic woman you are!

About *David*, it'll suit me very nicely if it's put back to April. The more the spring is advanced, when I come to England, the better for me. But you'll let me know, won't you?

Best wishes for all your enterprises.

Sincerely   D. H. Lawrence

3981a. To Millicent and Mary Beveridge, and Mabel Harrison, [22 March 1927]
Text: MS Anon; Postmark, Ravello 23. 3. 27; Unpublished.

'Cimbrone', Ravello, Salerno
Tuesday

Dear Milly and M[ary] and M[abel][2]

I got here[3] last night – bus from Vietri, winding round all the little bays in

---

[1] The story was published by Ernest Benn, 1926 (Roberts A36): limited edn 6/-, ordinary 1/-.

[2] Anne Millicent ('Milly') Beveridge (1871–1955), Scottish painter whom DHL met in Sicily in 1921 and who painted his portrait (see *Letters*, iii. 671). Mabel Harrison, a fellow-artist, lived in Paris. In February 1927 the two painters and Milly's sister Mary had rented the Villa La Massa, near Villa Mirenda.

[3] DHL had joined Earl and Achsah Brewster who were living in the Palazzo Cimbrone, a palatial house with extensive gardens containing numerous statues, owned by Ralph William Ernest Beckett, 3rd Baron Grimthorpe (1891–1963).

the sunset – crawling up in a carriage here in the dusk. It's brilliant sunny weather – The mauve irises are out in the garden – We have tea in the little moorish court, where the rose-garden is and the two little bronze deer. – All the statues are still here – and more and more indoors – I'm getting quite frightened of them. – I sleep in a big brass bed that looks intended for the harem rather than for the isolated pasha – and the chambermaid valets me, carries off my clothes and my self-ironed flannel trousers – and irons 'em – or gets 'em ironed – again. Cheek! Luxurious breakfast in bed – but too many tiles and statues by far.

The Brewsters are leaving on the 28th – so he and I will probably do a bit of a tour for a week or so – then back to the Mirenda.[1] It's very dramatic landscape here, but I prefer San Paolo Mosciano. I wouldn't want to live here.

Rome I found *very* irritable and irritating – don't go there – we motored to Ostia on the sea – vile place – *never* go there.

I hope you are all happy, painting successfully. The sun is a good thing.

au revoir, then   DHL

4008a. To Phyllis Whitworth, 30 April 1927
Text: MS Whitworth; Unpublished.

Villa Mirenda, Scandicci (Firenze)
30 Aprile 1927

Dear Mrs Whitworth

Many thanks for your letter. I will try to be in London by next Saturday or Sunday – May 7th. or 8th. – And then we must do what we can about that play.

Is £300 much or little in these cases? Seems a fair sum to me.

I will write again precisely.

Au revoir   D. H. Lawrence

4010a. To Phyllis Whitworth, 4 May 1927
Text: MS Whitworth; Unpublished.

Villa Mirenda, Scandicci. Florence
4 May 1927

Dear Mrs Whitworth

Alas, I've got a cold, and shant be able to travel if it sticks. I've had a

---

[1] DHL set off, with Earl Brewster, on 28 March on a walking tour, looking at Etruscan remains; he returned to the Mirenda on 11 April.

perfect hell of a time this last year with bronchials, so have to be careful. It's sickening.

If I don't turn up, you'll know why. But I'll write again.

Sincerely   D. H. Lawrence

4019a. To Phyllis Whitworth, 13 May 1927
Text: MS Whitworth; Unpublished.

Villa Mirenda, *Scandicci*, Florence
13 May 1927

Dear Mrs Whitworth

Your letter came today. I am more sorry than I can say about my not coming to *David*. This infernal cold got mixed up with a return of malaria, owing to the hot damp weather, and it's just kept me a rag – though it's the malaria chiefly. If only the journey weren't so long, I'd risk it. But I would hate to arrive and have to go to bed and be a nuisance to somebody. As it is, I'm deaf as a lump of wood, with quinine. Really no luck!

Tell Mr Milton to cut as he thinks best:[1] perhaps the whole of Scene III – a good deal of Saul's long speech – and then anything that makes the movement drag. I wish I had been there, to see if the long speeches, especially Samuel's, I mean not only his prayer, those towards the end too – if they dragged. If they really go over, I'd be glad if they weren't cut – because I didn't want the effect of the play to be snappy, rather slow and archaic-religious. But if that doesn't really succeed, then cut the longish mouthfuls and spit it out quick and sharp. Anything rather than let it be long-drawn-out and a nuisance. They say the long-drawn-out last act of *Mrs Holroyd* spoilt that production. – As for clothes, there is very little in it: for the men, a short sleeveless shirt, to the knee: over that, on occasion, a longish loose-sleeved coat [in?] cotton or wool, may be coloured, tied in at the [waist?] – then, on occasion, a burnous mantle. For the women, a long sleeveless shirt, loose or tied, and sometimes a shorter, wide-sleeved coloured coat.

My wife and I should so much have liked to come to your party. If only I'm a bit more solid, I shall still dash over. No luck, really!

Yours Sincerely   D. H. Lawrence

---

[1] The producer, Ernest Milton (1890–1974), inserted a note in the programme: 'In order to bring the Play within the time limit of a single performance, the Producer has, to his regret, been obliged to omit the whole of Scenes iii and x.'

4021a. To Millicent Beveridge, [16 May 1927]
Text: John Wilson Catalogue Seventy; Unpublished.

Villa Mirenda, Scandicci, Firenze
Monday, 16 May

I very nearly started off on Saturday – then at the last minute my courage failed me – I thought, what if I get stuck in bed in London, what a frightful bore and bother for other people. . . . I had a letter from Mrs Whitworth urging me to come, and saying they wanted my help. I felt rather bad about it. . . . Yesterday your padrona asked me to go over, and when I went, began showing me old chair-legs that were rickety or broken, telling me the electric light was broken, saying a glass was missing etc.[1] I heard her, and then told her what I thought of her – short and sharp – and left her gasping 'ma!' in the doorway. . . . Yesterday Orioli came with Reggie Turner – they were very pleasant. Osbert Sitwell and Edith are here, at Monte Guffone.[2] . . . The hot weather is rather lovely. I was out in the woods by eight oclock this morning – so fresh and fine. . . . The place is all a white flutter with cistus, and the broom is lovely, a soft, warm queer perfume it has. Pity you left so soon. You should stay till the wheat is cut.

4032a. To Phyllis Whitworth, [c. 27 May 1927]
Text: MS Whitworth; Unpublished.

[Villa Mirenda, Scandicci, Florence]
[c. 27 May 1927]

time?[3] I should like very much to see what the actors looked like – even if there are no snaps of scenes.

I'm sending you my last book, in commemoration of *David*'s production.[4] You needn't read it, though.

I hope when we come to England you'll still give your party, and assemble if possible David and Saul and Michal[5] and all, for us. That would be great fun.

---

[1] At the Villa La Massa (see Letter 3981a n. 2 above) vacated by Millicent Beveridge c. 12 May 1927 (*Letters*, vi. 62).

[2] Guiseppe ('Pino') Orioli (1884–1942), bookseller and publisher (published *Lady Chatterley's Lover*, 1928), and Reginald Turner (d. 1938), expatriate writer, were close friends of DHL. For the Sitwell family and their Castello di Montegufoni, near Florence, see v. 468 and n. 3, 472, 474.

[3] MS incomplete; p.1 of the letter is missing. The date given to the fragment takes account of letters written on 27 May to Koteliansky and Nancy Pearn in response to their reports on the performance of *David*.

[4] The book was probably *The Plumed Serpent* (1926): it was unlikely to have been a copy of *Sun* (limited to 100 copies); *Glad Ghosts* had been sent to Phyllis Whitworth for Christmas 1926; and *Mornings in Mexico*, though finished, was not published till June 1927.

[5] Parts played by Robert Harris, Peter Creswell and Angela Baddeley, respectively.

And you spent £400! To me it seems a lot. If I were rich I'd fob out: but catch me being rich.

I expect we shall stay here till end of July – then perhaps to England.

All good wishes   D. H. Lawrence[1]

4065a. To Caroline Ashby, 15 July 1927

Text: MS Price-Williams; Unpublished.

Villa Mirenda, *Scandicci*, (Firenze)

15 July 1927

Dear Mrs Ashby[2]

Miss Brett is still at the ranch – or with Mabel Lujan in Taos – alternating between the two places. c/o Mrs Mabel Lujan: *Taos:* New Mex. always gets her. She seems to be having a good time – and writes frequently.

Would you do me a favour – and ask any of your archaelogical friends if they know where I could get photographs of Volci – Vulci – the etruscan site: north of Tarquinia? I particularly wanted photographs of the Ponte della Badia, and the Castello, and the Coccumella – but Alinari, Brogi, Anderson and Moscioni haven't got them. I hope I am not presuming on your kindness.

We are going to the mountains in Austria as soon as I can take my damned thrice damnèd bronchials on a journey – they have broken down again.

I'll ask Brett why she never answered you.[3]

Yours Sincerely   D. H. Lawrence

---

[1] In an undated letter (MS Whitworth) to Phyllis Whitworth, Frieda expressed herself about the reception accorded to *David*: 'I am so cross on your account, you must feel very sore after all your work – Is almost every body so "canaille"? We had such enthusiastic letters about the production of "David" and then the press! It seems a real cabal. Naturally people like St John Ervine and such small fry are afraid of "flame", it would frizzle them up hard enough. I was so *very* sorry not to see it! And treating you like that!! But *do* go on fighting, *dont* give in, we have got to win! . . . How *slow* England is and static and never a move on! When I first came to England they acted Barry 30 years ago and they act him still – . . .'

[2] Caroline May Ashby, née Price-Williams (1869–1950), m. 1921, Thomas Ashby (1874–1931), distinguished archaeologist and Director of the British School at Rome, 1906–25. After ceasing to be Director he continued to reside in Rome. Ashby wrote the text to *Forty Drawings of Roman Scenes by British Artists* (published by the British Museum, 1911) which included *Ponte della Bardia, Vulci* by Samuel James Ainsley, the picture which – on subsequent advice from Ashby – DHL proposed to Secker should illustrate the section on Vulci in *Sketches of Etruscan Places.* See *Letters,* vi. 105 and n. 2.

[3] DHL conveyed the enquiry to Brett immediately, via Mabel Luhan: see vi. 101.

4066a. To Phyllis Whitworth, [15 July 1927]
Text: MS Whitworth; Unpublished.

Villa Mirenda, *Scandicci*, Florence
15 July

Dear Mrs Whitworth

We want to leave in about ten days for Austria – but near Villach. I'm not sure of the address. We think to be in the Isartal – at Irschenhausen, about 20 miles from München, for the month of *September*: and near Villach for *August*.

But send a line to us to[1] my mother-in-law

Frau Baronin von Richthofen, Ludwig-Wilhelmstift, *BadenBaden*

That will quickly get us, and we'll fix up a meeting either in Austria or in the Isartal. I shall be glad to see you and Mr Whitworth again.

Sincerely   D. H. Lawrence

4071a. To Caroline Ashby, [22 July 1927]
Text: MS Price-Williams; Unpublished.

Villa Mirenda, *Scandicci*, Firenze
Friday

Dear Mrs Ashby

Very many thanks to you and Dr Ashby for the help about Vulci. I am doing a book of *Sketches of Etruscan Places* – just light sketches – I shall get the Ainsley print from the Brit Museum.

Am still in bed, as my bronchial hemorrhage keeps coming back. I wish we could leave – It is very hot – though cooler out here than in Florence.

I hope I may meet Dr Ashby and you one day.

Again thanks

Sincerely   D. H. Lawrence

Pity the snaps are so cloudy.

4107a. To Phyllis Whitworth, 12 August 1927
Text: MS Whitworth; Unpublished.

Hotel Fischer, *Villach*, Kärnten
12 Aug. 1927

Dear Mrs Whitworth

We had your letter forwarded from Baden this morning: so sorry you are going so soon: I thought you were here till September. I was ill in Italy – crawled here a week ago – am better, but not up to a long journey, or we'd

---

[1] us to] us from Salzburg to

come to Salzburg now. We mean to come at the end of the month. I suppose
Villach is too far out of your way? – certainly there's nothing thrilling to see
here. But it's a pity if we miss you.

I sent a wire this morning – do hope you had it.

Many greetings from us both.

D. H. Lawrence

How is the Salzburg festival?

Do you get much out of it?

4157a. To Erich von Kahler, [1 October 1927]

Text: MS Lauer; PC v. Kirche in Icking; Postmark, Munchen 1.10.27; James T. Boulton,
'Editing D. H. Lawrence's Letters', *Prose Studies*, xix (August 1996), 215.

[Irschenhausen, *Post Ebenhausen*, bei München]

Saturday

– [1]We have been expecting you every day – I hope Frau von Kahler isnt
really ill. Surely you had my wife's letter! We leave on Tuesday morning for
Baden – and I have a book for you. Tomorrow I will ask Anna to telephone –
she's in München now.[2]

D. H. Lawrence

4220a. To Thomas MacGreevy, 5 December 1927

Text: MS TCD; Postmark, Scandicci -9. 12. 27; Unpublished.

Villa Mirenda, *Scandicci*, Florence

5 Decem 1927

Dear Mr McGreevy[3]

My agents Curtis Brown made a proper contract with the Wishart people

---

[1] DHL's correspondent, Erich von Kahler (1885–1970) was well acquainted with the
Richthofens (see *Letters*, vi. 149-50,167), a close friend of Alfred Weber (his former teacher)
and of Frieda's sister, Else Jaffe. m., 1912, Josephine Sobotka. Born in Prague he took
German citizenship in 1929 but emigrated in 1938 to USA where he later held professorial
appointments at Cornell and Princeton. His circle of friends included Thomas Mann,
Hermann Broch and Albert Einstein; his many publications focussed particularly on cultural
history, literary criticism and the historical development of the human consciousness. Author
of *The Germans* (1937), *Man the Measure* (1943), *The Meaning of History* (1964), etc. Kahler's
correspondence with Mann was published (in translation) as *An Exceptional Friendship*
(Cornell, 1975).

2 Anna had been Edgar Jaffe's servant; she had looked after the Lawrences since they arrived in
Irschenhausen on 31 August (vi. 139, 141).

3 Thomas MacGreevy (1893–1967), poet, critic, translator and eventually Director of the
National Gallery of Ireland (1950–63). (DHL addressed him at the Ecole Normale Supérieure
in Paris.)

— I believe so, at least — and I've heard no more.[1] I think the Rickwords are quite nice young fellows[2] – no money of course – not very business-like. It's no good being severe or businesslike with them. I suppose they'll get the book out some day; and if they make any money, they'll no doubt pay. I got a very few belated pounds from them the other day for some *Calendar* stuff.[3]

But if they said they'd give you £5 in cash, and *you have their letter* – then tell them you're hard up, and will they please pay the £5 because you need it – and say you've asked me about it, and I say, surely they can keep their word to the extent of £5: it's hardly worth breaking it, at the price.

But you'll never bully anything out of these young people, as far as I know them. Though surely in God's name they'll divide the royalties fairly – if they get any. That they can be made to do, by my agent or anybody else's. If they're dividing the 15% 'equally,' then every scrutineer gets the same. That is the usual, and right, way. But they must tell you. Only don't write huffily, it's no good. Get your £5 if you can, and then let us all whistle for a while.

Yours Sincerely   D. H. Lawrence

4409. To Arthur Wilkinson, [25 April 1928]
Text: MS Anon; PC; Postmark, Scandicci 28. 4. 28; cited in *Letters*, vi. 385.

Villa Mirenda.
25 April.

[4]Can't understand why you haven't sent a line to say how you are, all of you. And your peasants have only had a p.c. from Paris. – All well here – very quiet – today a lovely day, perhaps the real spring-summer will set in. We leave here about May 15th, for Switzerland. Frieda is determined to keep on this flat – a staggerer! – so if ever you want to pop over and inhabit it, here it will be, all ready.

The Miss Beveridges have been in Florence about a fortnight – leaving next Wednesday. The Salvestrinis[5] have a new baby – very tiny but all right. We've had rather a lot of visitors.

DHL

I suppose you had my letter?[6]

---

[1] The contract related to the collection of critical essays, *Scrutinies*, edited by Edgell Rickword and published by Wishart & Co. in March 1928 (Roberts B24); DHL contributed the chapter on Galsworthy (*Letters*, vi. 67, 136), MacGreevy that on George Moore.

[2] By 'the Rickwords' DHL presumably meant Rickword himself and his co-editor of *Calendar*, Douglas Mavin Garman (1903–).

[3] DHL's review of Walter Wilkinson's *Peep Show* and V. V. Rozanov's *Solitaria* had appeared in *Calendar* in July 1927 (Roberts C156).

[4] The MS was not available when an extract from this letter was printed in vi. 385.

[5] A peasant family on the Mirenda estate.

[6] See vi. 361–2.

4553a. To Alan Steele, 29 July 1928

Text: MS Anon; Sotherby's catalogue of sale, 17 July 1997, lot 287; Unpublished.

Kesslematte, *Gsteig b. Gstaad*, (Bern), Switzerland
29 July 1928

Dear Sir,

[Orioli sent to DHL Steele's letter cancelling the order for 80 copies of *Lady Chatterley's Lover*. Since the order was not] provisional [and since 72 copies have already been posted] I don't see how you can so confidently withdraw. [Steele should hold the copies; DHL has asked a friend to call with a taxi to collect them] and to repeat the call every day until all the seventy-two copies are collected.[1]

Thanking you for your courtesy.   D. H. Lawrence

4613n. To D. H. Lawrence from Maria Cristina Chambers, 9 August 1928

Text: MS Wells; Michael Squires, 'Two Newly Discovered Letters to D. H. Lawrence', *DHLReview,* xxiii (Spring 1991), 32–4.

43 Hillside Road, *Elm Point*, Great Neck. N.Y.
9 August 1928

Senor Lawrence!!

[2]I've played a monstrous joke on myself! Just think! Several of my friends have your new novel already – some of them over a week and *mine* are not here yet. Haven't been able to get even a peep at Lady Jane. My friends are having a colossal revenge; trying to chafe my tender self in all sorts of ways.

You see, I wrote them all a very emphatic letter and made it very clear and on my oath, that Lady Chatterley's Lover was not going to be on the lending branch of my book case, not to anyone! And now? Do you think a single wretch of them lets me even touch your book?– And you should hear them relate the story. Todos me dícen que ando camino á la *carcel* y que me prepare á ir derecha al infierno–y etc etc. –[3]

All of which makes my anxiety to read your last novel, grow beyond any other anxiety I can think of at this moment. –

---

[1] See *Letters,* vi. 476–7.

[2] Maria Cristina Chambers (d.1965), Mexican, wife of American Henry Kellett Chambers, senior editor of *Literary Digest* (see vi. 210 n. 3). She became one of DHL's regular correspondents from November 1927, a devoted admirer and, later, anxious to replace the New York office of Curtis Brown as DHL's American agent. To a limited extent she succeeded in this endeavour (see vii. 524–5, 551, 624 n. 1). She met DHL once only, in early July 1929 (see vii. 351 and n. 1, 357 and nn. 1 and 2).

[3] 'Everyone tells me that I'm heading for prison and that I should prepare myself to go straight to hell–and so on'.

And also, and this is the real purpose of this letter. It occurs to me, you should know about a certain bookseller here who is already anxious to get a number of copies, speculate with them, corner the market, as it were, and make money el Señor Lawrence should have, if anyone. –

If such a thing is going to be, why can't I 'corner the market' here for you and perhaps help to make your first million – or would it be the second? – At any rate, something seems to tell me the gods will use me in some way to help in the realization of that most noble and deserving dream of yours. "to have a place where we could live, & a few people could stay, to make a *life* together." Oh! Señor Lawrence! And how this poor soul of mine *hopes*, *hopes, hopes*, she might be one of them!!

But back to the practical. I'll tell you just all I know about the book-seller. This morning, a friend telephoned to say, she had gone into a second-hand book-shop on Lexington Avenue, near 26th Street. That while there, a man noticing the book she had under her arm (your new novel, she had just gone to get at the P.O.), said to her:

"Would you mind telling me where you got that book?" To which she felt a bit embarrassed – being a timid soul although thirsting for life – and replying without giving the man any information, saying it wasn't hers or some other stupidity. Well then, the man who told her he was a book-seller, explained he was most anxious to get as many copies as he could of it, asked her if she would sell it and ended by telling her she had a *book under her arm worth* $50.00!

Now Señor Lawrence! Why don't you do something about it. You just tell me what to do or how to go about it and I am at your service. I feel you're going to make a lot of money with Lady Jane and why should the booksellers get it away from you!

Am not afraid of *la carcel*.[1] And am free to do as I like. Let *me* sell the books & let them all come to me and pay for them, if they want them.

Can't get to town to-day but mañana, sin falta,[2] very early I'll take a train straight to the book-shop on Lexington Ave, find out who the man is, get to him, take his order (I understand he is offering to pay more than 10.00 a piece for them) take the order and his check for it, send the order in myself at the usual 10.00 price, send *you* the surplus of the amount direct, when I have an address, and then if anything happens in the mean time, meaning if I really know people who will pay 50.00 a piece for the books, then when they get here, I will return the merchant his money, tell him I can't get any books

[1] 'prison'.
[2] 'tomorrow, without fail'.

for him etc etc. Is this practical? Any way I'm going to do it on my own responsibility. And please don't scold.

About my own copies of your precious novel. I have thought possible, you, in your great kindness to me, kept my two books, knowing I intended going over to London for August. I can't think what else could happen to them.

Am sending some orders to Orioli to-day & I'll tell him about it.

Not a word from el Señor Lawrence for ages! Está usted mejor?[1] And I hope I have not been to[o] implicit[2] and lost the gift – the greatest the gods have given me – la luz de plenilunio en la ventana de mi alcoba de enferma![3]

I've written you a letter to Villa Mirenda, saying I had decided to wait and see if Life would have me at your rancho in the winter. I know the rancho now. Yes. Black-eyed Susan and Timsy are great friends of mine already.[4] And they tell me of their trials and I can't understand how they can wait much longer for Mrs Lawrence to pet them once more. –

Am I becoming [morbid?]? I am actually thinking for the first time, what your wife might think of my inviting myself to her place? In my great simplicity of purpose and desire it hadn't occurred to me your wife might not want me. But if such is the case, know, that by hook or by crook I'm going to catch you both somehow, somewhere and bring my *little stove*.

If this letter gets to you it will be only because God is great. – Haven't the least idea where to address it. –

Be sure to find out about weather conditions in this wretched New York, if you intend coming next month. We are having a very late summer, weather is impossible, the heat 90 & over with burning humidity. Torrential rains & then horrible heat. This weather burns me up & I long for the mountains and high altitude. Is there a little ranch near Taos I might buy? And how much? How you must laugh at me!! And still! I might be more lorn than I am.

Always grateful   Maria Cristina Chambers[5]

---

[1] 'Are you better?'

[2] Cf. DHL to Maria Chambers, 24 April 1928: 'I think you and I instinctively turn to the same thing, the life implicit instead of the life explicit. And the life implicit is embodied and has touch: and the life explicit is only ideas, and is bodiless' (*Letters*, vi. 378).

[3] 'the light of the full moon in the window of my sickroom!'

[4] DHL's cow and cat at Del Monte Ranch, Questa, New Mexico.

[5] DHL replied on 25 August 1928 (vi. 521–2).

**4828. To Arthur, Lilian, William and Frances Wilkinson,
20 December 1928**
Text: MS Anon; *Letters*, vii. 80–1.

Hotel Beau Rivage. *Bandol.* Var. France
20 Dec 1928[1]

Dear Wilkses

Well we must write you for Christmas, remembering last year, and San
Paolo and all. It is rather sad to be in a hotel, and homeless – yet perhaps also
it is rather a relief. You know we've given up the Mirenda – finished. – I
heard Miss Kent wants to sell her house and go and take our apartment:[2] but
selling her house won't be easy.

We are here in this quite pleasant little hotel by the sea – it's been sunny
nearly all the time, and good for my health. Of course I still cough like a
brute, but am much stronger. I think Frieda's two daughters will come for
Christmas – and after, we *may* go to Spain. But we are very undecided.
Frieda says she wants a house – but she doesn't know where, – and you can't
have a house nowhere. – Where does one want to live? tell me if you can! –
How do you like London? I hear of you giving shows at Heals, and showing
A[rthur]'s pictures, and selling them – beato lui! So, that's all to the good.
And I suppose Bim and Pino get more melodious every day! – We shall have
to see you before long, to see all the strides taken. What a game life is!

This is Happy Christmas to you all – and ricordi cari of last year and year
before – and I hope we shall meet fairly soon, to hear everything.

tante belle cose!   D. H. Lawrence

5033a. To Barbara Weekley, [ante 6 April 1929]
Text: Nehls, iii. 189.

[Hotel de Versailles, 60 Bvd. Montparnasse, Paris XV]
[ante 6 April 1929][3]

Don't let her [Elsa Weekley] marry a man unless she feels his physical presence warm to her ... Passion has dignity; affection can be a very valuable
thing, and one can make a life relationship with it.

---

[1] The full text of the letter became available after *Letters* vii was published; annotation provided
in vii. 80–1 is not repeated here.
[2] Cf. vii. 19 and n. 5.
[3] Barbara Weekley, Frieda's elder daughter, associated this letter with the time when her sister,
Elsa's wedding was in prospect; DHL knew in December 1928 (vii. 69) that Elsa would be
married 'in March or April'; this letter was probably written in the early months of 1929,
before the wedding on 6 April.

5095a. To Hilda Aldington, 20 May 1929
Text: MS YU; Unpublished.

Hotel Principe Alfonso, *Palma de Mallorca*, Spain
20 May 1929

Dear Hilda[1]

Yours today – I don't mind coming into an Imagist anthology in my Sunday clothes, if you want me to – otherwise I'd rather be out in the wide wide world. Was Hughes the man I met?[2] *What* a dull and portentous and take-it-all-seriously man! Aldous Huxley and I ragged him, and his wife – pretty à la poupée[3]–was amused–nice little image she was. I might send you one or two poems which are being excluded out of my *Pansies* – which I've just given to Secker – because they are 'improper'– which they aren't. *Pansies* is a new book of poems. Can I put a cod's-piece among the images, or not? Anyhow I've got nothing else just now to offer – and can't send you these till I get copies from London – *Demon Justice*[4] etc. – quite representative in my opinion. – Glad R[ichard] is well–is he with Bridget? – I hear from Arabella, she too is in Paris.[5]

I expect we'll be here another fortnight – Yes, how well I remember our charade – with you for the apple tree – and that wine-coloured dress – and R. with a chrysanthemum for a fig-leaf – chic!

Belle cose! – from both   D. H. Lawrence[6]

---

[1] Hilda Aldington was seeking contributions for her 1930 *Imagist Anthology* and had approached her old friend DHL (they had known each other since 1914). He responded positively as the further letter from him on 10 August 1929, reveals (see *Letters*, vii. 414–15 and Roberts E319.1). Hilda Aldington originally possessed 'a bundle of letters' from DHL but Richard, her husband, confessed that he had burned them (her unpublished 'Compassionate Friendship', MS YU, p. 61). In a letter to him, 4 May 1949, she remarked: 'I have only one letter that I can find . . . I think the only one I have left from Lawrence. It is from Palma de Mallorca and dates 20 May, 1929' (Richard Aldington Papers, Special Collections, Morris Library, Southern Illinois University at Carbondale).

[2] In March 1929, when researching for his book *Imagism and the Imagists* (1931), the American academic Glenn Arthur Hughes (1894–1964) interviewed DHL who was staying with Aldous and Maria Huxley at Suresnes, Seine (see vii. 223 and n.5).

[3] 'in a doll-like way'.

[4] 'Demon Justice' was one of the poems sent to Hilda Aldington with DHL's letter of 10 August. It seems that a copy (draft?) of the poem may have been included with the present letter.

[5] Richard Aldington separated from Hilda in 1919 to live with Dorothy ('Arabella") Yorke; Brigit Patmore (1882–1965) was subsequently his mistress.

[6] The existence of this letter was drawn to my attention by an unpublished paper delivered at the 'H. D. Centennial Conference' in 1986 by Professor Janice Robinson.

ADDITIONAL LETTERS

Three further letters became available at a very late stage in the production of this volume. Professor John Worthen drew my attention to the first, Emeritus Professor Jay A. Gertzman to the second and third; I am greatly indebted to them both. I am grateful, too, to Nottingham County Library and Columbia University for agreeing that the letters should be published.

207a. To Nurse Broadbent, 21 December 1910

Text: MS Nottinghamshire County Library; Unpublished.

12, Colworth Road, Addiscombe, Croydon.

21st Dec 1910

Dear Nurse,[1]

The book is not to be published yet – held over till Spring on account of elections etc[2] – so I venture to send you the little picture. Don't scold me. I've had my eye on it for a week. As soon as I caught sight of it in the shop-window I said to myself 'That's pretty' – and the next thought was 'Nurse would like it.'

I often think of you – and dream: but, mein Gott, I wish I could be delivered of dreams.

You were very good to my mother, kind and loving: and she was fond of you. I shall never forget it. I think I loved my mother more that I ever shall love anyone else. You do not know how much we were to each other. And these days crawl over me like horrid tortoises. Oh dear!

Sister and I are going to Brighton on Saturday for the week. I want things to be as moderate for her as possible.

I hope you'll have a jolly time this Christmas. I wish life could be warmer and richer for you. Don't think me impertinent.

Au revoir, then. I shall see you again, I am sure.

Yours   D. H. Lawrence

---

[1] Nurse Broadbent was the district nurse at the time of Lydia Lawrence's fatal illness; to some extent she was the model for 'Nurse Broadbanks' in DHL's play *The Merry-go Round* which was started in late November–early December 1910. In the opening stage-direction the character is described as: 'the parish nurse . . . a well-built woman of some thirty years, smooth haired, pale, soothing in manner; (*The Plays*, ed. Hans-Wilhelm Schwarze and John Worthen, Cambridge, 1999, p. 113 and 622 n.).

The letter (on mourning notepaper) was delivered by hand perhaps by Ada Lawrence after her Brighton holiday with DHL; the (unstamped) envelope is addressed: 'Nurse Broadbent, Hilltop, Eastwood, Notts'.

[2] *The White Peacock* was published in New York on 19 January 1911 and in London on 20th.

4446a. To George Macy, 2 June 1928
Text: MS (Photocopy) Columbia University, Vanguard Press Archive; Unpublished.

Villa Mirenda – *Scandicci* (Florence)
2 June 1928

Dear Mr Macy[1]

Yes, I had your cable, and sent it at once to Curtis Brown, who replied he had written instructions to Rich in New York: that is weeks ago. But Alfred Knopfs' were hanging fire about an expurgated edition of *Lady Chetterley's Lover* – so perhaps that tied up Rich. I don't know quite how they're going to expurgate it. I hear Mrs Knopf wanted to publish the book, her fellow directors very much *didn't*. – If you can get the MS. from Edwin Rich of Curtis Brown Ltd. – see what you can make of it. I also wrote him direct, some weeks ago, to treat with you about it. I don't mind how *much* I expurgate, if it can be done without taking the sense away from the book. Probably it can't. – Most men seem horrified of the book – you'd think none of 'em had got or ever had had a John Thomas as big as a wax match. Blue funk! I don't understand men. The women come up to the scratch much better.

As to future work, heaven knows. I get fed up with the wee willy winkie public and publishers. Maybe I have to offer Alfred Knopf another book – nothing more – and I'm not sure even of that. I think the Knopf firm are a bit frightened of me. They'll be fairly shuddering after *Lady Chatterley*. Bah! Don't you feel scared at all? A publisher who wasn't scared, and who dared, and who could hold out like the devil, might get past very well with my books. But I'm no great catch to any hasty all-in-a-moment Johnny who wants his money quick, and nothing else.

Probably you've already talked to Edwin Rich. If you haven't, it's his fault. But do talk with him, and let me know. I'd love to have a good fighting publisher. Poor little Seltzer, I was sorry about him. But I shall never *drift* into popularity and sales. It's a fight. But my God, why not! And though Mrs Knopf likes my work, I don't believe the others of her firm do. They funk it too. So you see more or less where you are: or I am.

I've just done the last proofs of *Lady C.* – so should be sending it out in ten days' time. I *hope* it'll make 'em howl – and let 'em do their paltry damnedest, after.

Yours Sincerely   D. H. Lawrence
Address me   c/o Curtis Brown, 6 Henrietta St, Covent Garden,
London, W. C. 2

---

[1] George Macy (1900–56), New York Publisher, had shown interest in publishing a limited edition of *Lady Chatterley's Lover* (in 1929 he founded the Limited Edition Club).

4631a. To Jacob Baker, 1 September 1928

Text: MS (Photocopy) Columbia University, Vanguard Press Archive; Unpublished.

(Kesselmatte. Gsteig b. Gstaad) c/o Curtis Brown Ltd, 6 Henrietta St.
London W. C. 2.
1 Sept 1928

Dear Mr Baker[1]

I had your letter on Monday, and immediately cabled "Withold Knopf Two Sent."[2] I sent the three books actually only yesterday, as I had to get them from Italy. They were put in a paper cover with a title I invented for them – *Joy Go With You* – and I wrote an inscription on each one to save customs – so I hope they will arrive safely. But I hear that *Lady C.* is being held up. I shall send no more to America.

[3]Rich varies what he considers my obligation to Knopf. One letter he says *two full-length books* and the next *two novels*. I thought *The Woman Who Rode Away* was a full-length book, and knocked off one of the obligations, but he says no. So the point remains to settle, whether it is *two full-length books* or *two novels*.

Anyhow you will have to make the contract for *Lady C.* with Rich.

Perhaps you have been able to get copies of *Lady C.* in New York. The Holliday Bookshop received five copies, and the Phoenix two. They all want more, but I shall not send. When I hear you are going ahead with your edition I will let have list of orders for America. I have only a few left of my edition, and can easily dispose of them over here.

Yours Sincerely   D. H. Lawrence

---

[1] Managing editor of Vanguard Press; he had shown interest in publishing a New York reprint of *Lady Chatterley's Lover* at $10 to thwart possible piracies. This letter should be read in association with *Letters*, vi. 525–7, 538–9.

[2] The cable with this text, dated 27 August 1928, is in the Vanguard Archive.

[3] '→Mr' has been inserted in the MS in an unknown hand.

CORRIGENDA AND ADDENDA

VOLUME I

Genealogy (*et passim*) *For* John Arthur Lawrence *read* Arthur John Lawrence

xxvii *For* c.15 November 1910 *read* 1 August 1910

20 l.29 *For* 1912 *read* 1913

22 n. 1 The boarding-house was on South Parade, Skegness

22 n2 *For* 1908 *read* 1909

23 n.2 The reference is possibly to a postcard reproduction of the drawings of cats as human characters by Louis Wain (1860–1939)

23 n.3 The exam was the Pupil Teachers' Exam, July 1903

26 ll.21 and 24 *For* c.25 *read* 17

26 n.1 *Delete The English Language* (1886 . . . *or*

29 n.3 *For* financée *read* fiancée
     For c.1900 *read* c. 1903–4

30 ll. 27 and 30 *date to read* [**c. 13 September 1906**]

36 n.1 *For* Samual *read* Samuel

46 n.2 *For* Ada Rose . . . 1944) *read* Ellen ('Nellie') Staynes (d. 22 April 1908)

69 n.2 *For* (from 1911) *read* (from 1910)

70 ll.28 and 31 *date to read* [17 August 1908]

71 l.25 *For* remainds *read* reminds

81 l.34 Cf. D.G. Rossetti's poem 'Mary Rose', in *Ballads and Sonnets* (1881)

82 l.24 *For* times *read* time

129 n.2 *et passim* *For* MacCartney *read* Macartney

133 n.3 *For* in December *read* on 28 December

137 ll. 1 and 3 date to *read* [1911?]

139 n.3 *For* destroyed all *read* destroyed almost all

148 l.26 *Insert* MS Segal;

159 Letter 155 *See* viii. 3–4 above

161 n.3 *For* Holt *read* Mason

167 l.33 *For* your *read* you

172 n.4 The story is the fragment now entitled 'Matilda Wootton' (MS in the Bancroft Library, Berkeley, California)

175 n.4 *Delete*

176 n.5 *For* Sallie A....Pattie *read* Sarah ('Sallie') Annie Hopkin, née Potter (1867–1922), ardent feminist. Presented as Patty

184–5 Letter 186 *See* viii. 4–5 above

196 n.1 Information from David Cram makes it possible to identify the originals of DHL's two poems. 'Self-Contempt' is based on 'Selbstverspottung' and 'Near the Mark' on 'Nahe am Ziel', to be found in _Die Lieder eines ägyptischen Bauern_, ed. Heinrich Schäfer (Leipzig, 1903), nos. 57 and 101. (An English translation of Schäfer's book by Frances Hart Breasted was published in Leipzig, 1904, as _The Songs of an Egyptian Peasant_.)

224 n.2 _For_ Lettice Berry _read_ Ada Krenkow

244 n.1 _For_ 1918 _read_ 1919

263 Letter 260 dated by DHL 29 April, actually written 29 May

278 n.4 _For_ (b.1886) _read_ (1886–1913)

279 n.2 _to read_ See _Love Among the Haystacks_, ed. John Worthen (Cambridge, 1987), p.247, 161:1 n.

286 n.1 _For_ Unidentified _read_ Gussie Cooper, a neighbour of Laura Macartney

306 n.5 _Add_ Dolcie Rutter was one of DHL's fellow-students at Nottingham University College

312 l.17 _For_ 12 Colworth _read_ 16 Colworth

315 n.1 _For_ (1892–) _read_ (1892–1981)

324 n.5 _For_ genuis _read_ genius

331 n.2 _To read_ MS UN LaB 203.

339 n.4 _For_ Parrender _read_ Parrinder

342 l.3 Cf. Charles Wolfe, 'The Burial of Sir John Moore at Corunna' (1817), ll.11–12 ['But he lay . . . With his martial cloak around him']

345 n.1 _Delete_ 'A Prelude'

346 n.1 _For_ Scheinen _read_ Scheinin

350 n.1 _See_ viii. 6 and n. 1 above

354 n.2 _to read_ Mrs and Miss Haley, from Harrogate

374 n.3 _For_ Underwood _read_ Brinsley

391 n.3 _For_ Luke 46 _read_ Luke xxiii.46

392 ll.1and 4 _For_ [7 May 1912] _read_ [8? May 1912]

400 l.4 Professor John Worthen believes that Letter 442, though correctly dated, was sent to Garnett by DHL with Letter 452, while Frieda's note on p. 410 dates from some uncertain time in June or July 1912

404 l.24 _For_ known _read_ know

415 ll.8,14 _For_ Freidas/Freida _read_ Friedas/Frieda

420 n.1 _To read:_ Probably 'The Christening', 'Delihah and Mr Bircumshaw' and 'A Blot' (first version of 'The Fly in the Ointment')

421 n.1 _For_ (b.1900) . . . (b.1902) . . . (b.1904) _read_ (1900–82) . . . (1902–85) . . . (1904–98).

430 n.3 The two 'lost' MSS were 'Fortified Germany' I and II; they had been retained by De la Mare; see *Twilight in Italy*, ed. Paul Eggert (Cambridge, 1994), pp. 7–15

432 ll. 5, 7, 15 and 18 *date to read* [7 August 1912]

434 n.2 *For* soldier *read* Soldier

440 n.3 *For* 1926 *read* 1927

443 l.4 *For* send *read* sends

443 ll. 11 and 14 *date to read* [28 August 1912]

447 l.15 The three articles were 'Christs in the Tirol', 'Chapel Among the Mountains' and 'A Hay Hut Among the Mountains'

451 l.19 *Add note:* MS torn

454 l.25 *Add note* Nellie   cf. p. 231 n.3

466 n.2 *For* unfinished *read* unwritten; *for* Country *read* Countryside

487 Letter 526 The addressee was DHL's father, Arthur John Lawrence; the letter may have been written *c.* 2 December

491 n.3 *For* 1864–1920 *read* 1860–1920

494 n.1 *For* bitter *read* better

505 n.1 *For* Persevalli *read* Marconi

507 l.25 The 'short tale' was probably 'The Overtone'

520 nn. 2 and 4 *For* Almgrem *read* Almgren

544 n.4 *See* Abercrombie, *Thomas Hardy*, p.19: '. . . putting the art of his fiction under the control of a metaphysic'

550 n.3 *Delete* Templeman

VOLUME II

xv l.31 *For* 1955 *read* 1956

xvi l.23 *For* Gaythorne *read* Gathorne

xix l.27 The address was 4 Downshire Hill

xxi l.32 Bellingdon (now Hawridge) Lane

4 l.5 *For* Lady *read* Mary, Lady

4 l.28 *et passim* *For* Spezia *read* La Spezia

21 n.3 and 26 n.8 *For* 'Once' *read* 'New Eve and Old Adam'

24 l.18 *For* Nabel *read* Nebel

30 n.2 *For* Unidentified *read* Perhaps 'Lessford's Rabbits' and 'A Lesson on a Tortoise'

44 n.3 The stories were: 'The Fly in the Ointment' and perhaps 'The Shadow in the Rose Garden' and 'The Old Adam'

94 n.4 *For* Woman *read* Women

131 n.6 To *read* Edward Hayter Preston, journalist, editor of *The Cerebralist* (1913) and friend of Pound

142 n.2 *To read*: The surviving fragment of *Sisters II* (printed in *The Rainbow*, ed. Mark Kinkead-Weekes, Cambridge, 1989, p. 479), concludes with a glimpse of Ben Templeman. In the next version, 'The Wedding Ring' – not under way until February 1914 – 'the Templeman episode' was replaced by an affair with 'Charles' Skrebensky. This name appears in the surviving pages of 'The Wedding Ring' which were incorporated into the MS of *The Rainbow* where it is changed to 'Anton' (cf. ibid, p.xxvi)

147 l.26 and n.4 *For* Lady Mary *read* Mary, Lady

150 l. 20 Letter 708 should perhaps be dated **[21–2 February 1914]**

157 n.1 *For* Aleister . . . 1947) *read* Hans Henning von Voigt (pseud. Alastair) (1887–), artist and illustrator; published *Forty-three Drawings by Alastair* (1913), etc.

160 l. 8 Letter 715 should perhaps be dated **[c. October 1913]** (see John Worthen, *Cold Hearts and Coronets: Lawrence, the Weekleys and the von Richthofens*, University of Nottingham, 1995, pp. 17–18)

180 l.14 *For* . *read* a

180 n.4 *For* 301–4 *read* 291–305; *for libro read libero*

181 n.2 *For* p. 12 *read* p. 8

190 n.1 *Add after* found: (though a section was incorporated into the MS of *The Rainbow*)

206 Letter 774 For Amy Lowell's letters to DHL, see *The Letters of D.H.Lawrence & Amy Lowell, 1914–1925*, ed. E. Claire Healey and Keith Cushman (Black Sparrow Press, Santa Barbara), 1985

209 l.14 *For* as *read* an

214 Letter 787 Marsh bought Gertler's *Agapanthus* before the end of August 1914 (C. Hassall, *Edward Marsh*, 1959, p. 370); therefore this letter may have been written earlier than shown

217 n. 4 *For* 'Where deep . . . grows' *read* 'In the dark foliage the gold oranges glow'

224 l.14 *For* ehrrte *read* ehrte

225 l.10 *For* them *read* then

244 l.24 *For* conservation *read* conversation

247 n.4 *For* Constant *read* Constance

253 n.3 Murry's suggestion (Nehls, i.240) that DHL met Lady Ottoline *c.*13 August 1914 was possibly inaccurate; the meeting may have occurred as much as 3–4 months later

255 n.1 *Add* For impressions of DHL's stay at Greatham, *see* Francis Meynell, *My Lives* (1972), pp. 86–8

280 l.28 *For* but *read* by

291 l.27 *For* Furbank, ii.11 *read* C.L. Ross, *Review of English Studies*, N.S. xxvii (1976), 290

307, 309 Doubt has been cast on the ordering of Letters 887 and 890, with the suggestion that their positions should be reversed

331 n.1 *For* Brooke *read* Brooke's death

350 n.4 *For* Unidentified *read* Gertrude Speedwell Massingham, née Black (b. 1888?), daughter of Arthur Black and niece of Constance Garnett; m. 1914, Harold John Massingham (1888–1952), author and journalist

353 l.31 Their visitor was Lady Cynthia Asquith

357 n.1 *For* Lord Alfred Harmsworth *read* Alfred Harmsworth, Lord

364 n.4 *For* (1892) *read* (2nd edn, 1908)

396 l.2 *For* Unpublished *read* cited in Ross, *RES*, N.S. xxvii.291

407 n.2 *Add* See also *Reflections on the Death of a Porcupine and Other Essays*, ed. Michael Herbert (Cambridge, 1988), 261:32 and n.

418 n.2 *to read* 'I walked to Selfridge . . . and had a crayon sketch for 1/6d done of myself. The draughtsman is extraordinarily clever – he does them in 3 minutes' (Lady Cynthia Asquith's (unpublished) diary entry, 26 October 1915)

435 n.5 *For* Howard *read* Heward

463 n.4 His letter to Pinker, 8 December 1915 (MS NYPL) establishes that Biart-Bellens was from Antwerp, a 'Belgian Refugee' wanting to 'complete his library' while in England

475 l.24 The editor was Carl Hovey (cf. p.216 n.4)

481 n.2 *For* Lucie *read* Lucy

488 l. 29 *For* spendid *read* splendid

493 n.3 *For* 'Samson and Delilah' *read* 'The Horse-Dealer's Daughter'

503 ll.3–6 Cf. T.S. Eliot: 'This speaks to me of that at which I have long aimed, . . . to write poetry which should be essentially poetry, with nothing poetic about it, poetry standing naked in its bare bones, or poetry so transparent that we should not see the poetry, but that which we are meant to see through the poetry, poetry so transparent that in reading it we are intent on what the poem *points at*, and not on the poetry...To get *beyond poetry*, as Beethoven, in his later works, strove to get *beyond music*. We never succeed, perhaps, but Lawrence's words mean this to me, that they express to me what I think that the forty or fifty original lines that I have written strive towards' (F.O. Matthiessen, *The Achievement of T.S. Eliot*, 1947, p. 90)

531 n.2 *Delete* See

540 l.11 *For* its *read* it

547 l. 5 *For* meat *read* meal

570 n.3 *For* Sophie *read* Sonia ('Sophie')

576 n.2 *Delete Twilight in Italy* and/or

608 n.4 *For* 367 *read* 184

611 l.18 *For* Delany 226–7 *read* K. Sagar, *DHLReview*, vi (1973), 306

637 Letter 1265 Professor Mark Kinkead-Weekes believes – despite DHL's
    clear dating – that this letter was written on 21 October 1916. That date
    would fit with DHL's having abandoned typing by 13 October (Letter
    1296) and deciding to have the typing done in Pinker's office (cf. Letter
    1299)

638 Letter 1267 If, as now seems likely, DHL visited Mylor on 22–3 July,
    this letter would be dated **[25 July 1916]**

VOLUME III

xvii l.19 *For* 11 April *read* late April

xx l.23 *Insert* March 1919 'Fenimore Cooper's Leatherstocking Novels' in
    English Review

xxi l.4 *For* Foye *read* Forge

xxi l.17–19 *For* 15 August...Mapledurham *read* 22 August 1919
    Mapledurham Joined by Rosalind Baynes, and by Godwin Baynes
    c. 25–26 August 1919

xxii l.18 *Delete* meets...Young

xxii l.25 *For* 29 January 1920 *read* ante 17 January 1920

xxii l.34 Add 19–21 February   Montecassino

xxiii l.32 *For* 2–5? August 1930 *read* 2–4? August 1920

29 n.2 *For* Horse Dealer's *read* Horse-Dealer's

31 l.2 *For* stands *read* stand

32 n.3 *For* Cynthis *read* Cynthia

56 n.1 *Add* Cf. Psalms cxxiv. 4–5

58 l.25 *For* is *read* in

65 n.1 *Add* For an analysis of the evidence that Mountsier might have been
    a spy, see Louise E. Wright, 'D. H. Lawrence, Robert Mountsier and the
    Journalist Spy Controversy', *Journal of the D. H. Lawrence Society*,
    1992–93 (1994), pp. 7–21

87 n.1 *For* Unidentified *read* The song is sung by David Pew, the blind
    beggar in R.L. Stevenson's play, *Admiral Guinea* (1884). See Stevenson's
    Works ed. E.Gosse (1907), xiv.171, 176, 178 etc.

101 n.1 *Add* and had written an intelligent review, recently re-discovered,
    of *The Rainbow* for the *Daily Telegraph*, which was set up in galley but
    never printed

110 l.25 *For* g *read* give

115 n.2 *Add* DHL had seen Sallie in Nottingham

122 n.1 *For* 1894 *read* 1849

130 n.4 Lady Mary was the daughter of Rev. Harry Grey, an unemployed remittance-man, who lived with and, in 1880, married (his third marriage) a South African 'coloured' lady, Martha Solomons, in Wynberg, Cape; he succeeded to the earldom of Stafford in 1883. Grey died in 1890; Lady Mary was sent, probably by the Cape Board of Executors, to complete her education in Europe

139 n.2 *For* H ' *read* Hand'

187 n.1 *Add* DHL had met Whibley through Lady Cynthia Asquith on 28 October 1915 (Asquith, *Diaries* 94)

197 n.1 *For* Unidentified *read* Almost certainly Gray's housekeeper

222 n.3 *For* the Marsdens, *see* John Worthen, *D. H. Lawrence: The Early Years 1885–1912* (Cambridge, 1991), pp. 83, 85–6

244 n.2 *For* Unidentified *read* the novelist, Dorothy Richardson (1882–1957), and her husband, Alan Odle; according to her *Selected Letters*, ed. Gloria G. Fromm (University of Georgia Press, 1995, p. 583) DHL later wrote 'a letter & postcard' to her but their whereabouts are unknown

249 n.1 *For* 244 *read* 224

256 l.12 *For* 1818 *read* **1918**

259 n.2 *For* Ripley *read* Nottingham Road, Eastwood

291 l.5 The 'friend' was Herbert Watson cf. iii.101 and n.1

293 n.1 *To read* The reference is to the archangel Michael, the dragon-slayer

296 l.10 *For* n'importe *read* m'importe

298 l.4 *For* [11 November 1918] *read* **[18 November 1918]**

302 l.31 *For* Butterfly *read* Butterley

305 n.3 *Add* Lady Cynthia Asquith recorded in her (unpublished) diary for 26 November 1918 that, after she and DHL had lunched together, 'he insisted on forcing his way into [Augustus] John's studio and remained there all through my sitting. Between those two beards I nearly got Fou Rire ['an attack of uncontrollable laughter']. He said John made him talk Latin so 'dead' was he. He kept muttering 'mortuus est' – 'mortuus est' and condoling John on the fact that the baby he had just painted was so obviously a corpse – He said my portrait was an impertinence – he couldn't bear its pipe-clay look and summed up by saying 'Let the dead paint their dead'

306 l.1 The recipient was probably Nancy Henry

326 n.1 *For* Humphry *read* Humphrey

352 l.32 *For* SIU *read* UN

357 l.14 *For* skv *read* sky

359 l.2 *For* Your *read* You

377 l.1 The recipient may have been Robert Nichols whom DHL wished to consult about lecturing in America.

382 l.6 *For* [11 **August 1919**] *read* [18 **August 1919**]

389 l.14 *For* mind *read* mine

400 n.1 *For* Unidentified *read* Hermann Schaff, a friend of Huebsch and perhaps involved in publishing

400 n.2 *Add* Jane Burr pseud. for Rosalind Mae GuggenheimWinslow (1881-)

407 n.4 *For* Mason *read* Masson

409 l.15 The letter may have been written on 10 or 11 November when DHL had abandoned the idea of a ship; cf. Letter 1838.

418 l.13 Despite DHL's clear spelling on other letters, the name of the Pension should be 'Balestri'.

421 l.13 The letter should probably be dated [4?–6? **December 1919**]

444 l.11 The 'arch-scandalmonger' was Gwen Galata (wife of the Pretore of Capri, Giovanni Galata); DHL arranged for a copy of *The Rainbow* to be sent to her (iii. 484 and n. 3). She appears as Mrs Ambrosio in Mackenzie's *Vestal Fire* (1927)

446 l.2 ''e don't know where 'e are' is the title and recurring line of a song (c. 1890) by Frederick Eplett and Harry Wright, part of the repertoire of the renowned music-hall artist and Cockney impersonator, Ernest Augustus ('Gus') Elen (1862–1940)

453 l.2 *For* TMSC *read* MS

454 l.21 *For* Salaro *read* Solaro

467 l.24 *For* Unpublished *read* cited in K. Sagar, *The Life of D. H. Lawrence* (1980), p. 113

470 ll.7, 12 The letter may have been written on 30 January 1920, given the likelihood that Katherine Mansfield's letter to Murry was written on 7 February, not 9th

471 n.1 *For* (1892–) *read* (1892–1984)

474 l.15 In view of the reference in Letter 1925 to Duckworth, Secker and *The Rainbow*, this letter should probably be dated 4 February 1920

479 l.17 Mackenzie published Letters 1936 and 1937, both written on the same day and conveying similar information, claiming that both were addressed to himself. However, DHL's diary with its reference to his having sent 'Brett Young his Lire 50' on 9 March 1920 (Tedlock. *Lawrence MSS* 89), confirms that Letter 1936 was not written to

Mackenzie but to Brett Young. (It should be remembered that, though Piccola was owned by Mackenzie, it was being rented by Brett Young.)

491 n. 4 *For* (1897–) *read* (1897–1991)

494 ll.27–8 Cf. 'The lilies and languors of virtue/ . . . the raptures and roses of vice', Swinburne, 'Dolores' (in *Poems and Ballads*, 1866), ll. 67–8

500 l.31 *For* collaps. *read* collaps –

510 n. 1 *Delete* has not survived

529 n.2 *For* be *read* he

550 l.24 *For* Unpublished *read* cited in K. Sagar, *Life of D. H. Lawrence*, colour plates p. 3

551 n.2 *Add* (d. 1938)

557 l.7 *For* Ciccio's *read* Ciccio is

561 n.1 *For* Melony *read* Meloney

594 n.3 *To read* The teenage schoolboy, Réné Mari, with whom Douglas was touring

621 l.24 *Add n. 3:* Don Mauro Inguanez was the 'Don Bernardo' in DHL's memoir of Magnus; he had just written to tell DHL of Magnus's suicide

630 n.2 *For* former *read* latter

638 l.5 *For* American *read* America

665 l.16 'the Burr' was the nickname for Elizabeth Humes, Juta's American fiancée; cf. iv. 25 n.6

672 n.2 Cyril Kay Scott, pseudonym for Frederick Creighton Wellman, painter, and husband of Evelyn Scott; cf. p. 692 n.3

675 n.2 *For* 'may have...1921' *read* included 'Medlars and Sorb Apples', *New Republic*, 5 January 1921 (Roberts C75)

676 l.5 *Add note* Ivy Litvinov had been in Copenhagen, summer 1920; in early 1921 she was in Estonia where Litvinov was Soviet Ambassador (J. P. Carswell, *The Exile*, 1983, p. 98)

683 n.3 *Add* For a photograph of the portrait, see Nehls, ii. frontispiece

699 l.18 *For* days *read* says

703 l.30 Achsah Brewster recorded in her private memoir called 'The Child' (i.e. Harwood Brewster) that when she and Earl Brewster met DHL, they asked where he was staying; he answered: 'With Anna di Chiara and Ferdinando in Anacapri. She is a perfect hostess, and one-eyed Nannina the best cook on the island. I fear Nan has given her own room to me, done in robin-egg blue, satin and lace bedspread, a wide terrace in front! I take my bath in a long, white porcelain tub like a coffin for a young girl.' Achsah Brewster's own description of the di Chiaras, in the same memoir, confirms DHL's impressions. She writes of Anna as

having 'an active mind' and 'ideas of her own . . . a fascinating and
cultured woman . . . picturesque and charming,' with a 'discerning
taste', and of Ferdinando as 'young and handsome . . . of dreamy, artistic
yearnings', a sensitive 'idealist'

712 n.2 *For* (1913–) *read* (1912–90)

716 n.3 *To read Die Traumdeutung* (Leipzig, 1900) was translated by
Abraham Brill; David Eder translated *Uber der Traum* (1901) under the
title *On Dreams* (1914)

728 l.3 Cf. Psalms ciii. 5: 'youth is renewed like the eagle's'

VOLUME IV

xxiii l.24 *For* 7 October *read* 6 October

xxiii l.33 and xxiv l.1 *For* 17 November *read* 16 November

8 l.38 *et passim For* Anna *read* Annie

9 l.38 Alexander was head of Ormond College, University of Melbourne

18 ll.23–4 *For* and Seltzer published *read* and in April Seltzer had published

79 l.9 *Insert* n.1: Murry had published a hostile review of *Women in Love* in
the *Nation and Athenaeum*, 13 August 1921 (see R. P. Draper, *D. H.
Lawrence: The Critical Heritage*, 1970, pp. 168–72)

81 l.1 *For* Nelly *read* Nellie

81 n.4 *For* Unidentified *read* Gino Sansani

107 n.7 *For* 21 *read* 11

110 n.4 *For* had gone . . . Mexico , and *read* had moved to Taos, New
Mexico, where there was an art colony, and

124 n.3 *For* (1918–) *read* (1918–97)

146 l.19 *For* [**10 December 1921**] *read* [**11 December 1921**]

164 l.19 *For* **Jack** *read* **John**

182 n. 1 *For* Jung *read* Jung and particularly of Freud

217 n.2 *For* Anna Louise *read* Annie Louisa

218 n.3 *For* Unidentified *read* Victor Cunard (d. 1960), *Times*
correspondent living in Rome

231 l.14 *date to read* [**21 April 1922**]

233 ll.30–1 The pianist was Fr Stefano (later Stephen) Moreno, a very
talented musician and composer (Joseph Davis, *D. H. Lawence at
Thirroul*, Sydney, 1989, pp. 85–6)

236 l.29 *et passim For* W[est] *read* W[estern]

236 n.1 *For* 1878 *read* 1876

240 l.22 *Add n.3* Cf. Nehls, iii.105–6

251 n.2 *For* Australian Prime Minister *read* Premier of Western Australia

257 n.2 *For* 'Adolf' never . . . it *read* 'Adolf' appeared in *Insel Almanach für das Jahr* 1924, pp. 118–32, translated by Franz Franzius

283 l.9 *date to read* [**15 August 1922**]

286 l.35 In 'Travel seems to me a splendid lesson in disillusion' there may be an echo of R.L. Stevenson's 'Sightseeing is the Art of Disappointment' in *The Silverado Squatters* (*Works*, 1906, ii.199) to which DHL probably alluded a week later (in Letter 2583)

291 l.16 *date to read* [**8 September 1922**]

316 ll. 8–9 Mountsier's sister was Mabel Mountsier (1871–1976); a graduate of California State College, California, Pennsylvania, M.A. from Columbia University, New York, some postgraduate work in Oxford, and for many years head of the English Department of Jacoby School, N.Y. She was occasionally consulted by her brother about the correctness of linguistic usage for USA in DHL's MSS. Ed. *Singing Youth: An Anthology of Poems by Children* (New York, 1927)

317 n.1 *Delete* in heart

317 n.4 *For* second *read* third

327 l.25 *For* I makes *read* It makes

331 l.20 *For* D.H. *read* DHL

339 n.3 *For* Unidentified *read* Eshref Shevky (1893–1969) and his wife Marion née Christenson. Shevky had recently graduated with a Ph.D. in Physiology at Stanford University; he became a leading anthropologist, interested in the Indians of New Mexico

387 l.20 *date to read* [**15 February 1923**]

419 n.2 *For* led *read* participated in

446 n.1 *For* Unidentified *read* An American family staying at the hotel with Bynner

447 l.19 *For* Lupe *read* Lupa

475 n.1 *To read* DHL probably referred to George Robert Stow Mead (1863–1933), writer on theosophy and gnosticism; many of his writings were published by the Theosophical Publishing Society

499 l.29 *For* to able *read* to be able

499 n.2 *et passim* *For* O'Keefe *read* O'Keeffe

510 l.12 *For* Arnos *read* Amos

524 n.2 *For* John . . . 1925) *read* John Russell ('Jack') Skinner (1881–1925)

554 l.17 *For* **Frederick** . . . **Mrs Carter** *read* **Frederick and Mary Carter**

555 n.1 *For* December *read* No. 8, Summer

567 l.21 *For* that *read* than

587 Letter 3064: *See* Letter 4692 (vi.583–4)

VOLUME V

6 l.8 *For* on Capri *read* in Ravello

11 l.21 *For* sent *read* send

39 l.26 Most likely Miss Kameny was Seltzer's personal secretary; he went to her wedding in May 1924; see viii. 89 above

39 n.1 *For* parent's *read* parents'

57 n.2 *For* Elizabeth *read* Elisabeth

67 n. 1 *For* (1894–) *read* (1894–1982)

90 n.1 *For* throught *read* through

98 l.11 *For* **1914** *read* **1924**

111 l.28 *For* this *read* their

116 l.12 *For* don't But *read* don't. But

119 l.16 *For* I'll come *read* I'll not come

125 n.1 *Insert* and Freud *after* Jung

133 l.8 *For* autombile *read* automobile

142 l.27 *For* be . no *read* be no

153 l.6 *For* to to *read* to go to

184 n.1 *For* Xatanzaro *read* Catanzaro

211 n.1 *For* must *read* may

237 l.15 *For* Do know *read* Do you know

254 l.23 *For* sent *read* send

255 l.9 *For* it it *read* it in

256 n.2 *For* Danish *read* Norwegian

288 n.4 *For* (1884–) *read* (1884–1966)

299 l.14 Though DHL wrote 'Consulich', he was referring to the Cosulich Line

321 n.2 *For* D'Auréuilly *read* d'Aurevilly

355 n.6 *For* Unidentified *read* The vegetarian restaurant in Tottenham Court Road much frequented by writers and artists

362 n.4 *For* educated in Birmingham *read* studied medicine in the University of Birmingham

364 l.8 *For* vaguer *read* voguer

370 n.1 *For* 3551 and n.1 *read* 3552 and p. 342 n.2

396 l.6 *For* the full text of Douglas's reply, see viii.49 n.3 above

403 n.1 *For* Paris *read* London; Mabel Harrison lived in Paris

419 n.2 *For* (1874–c. 1950) *read* (1875–1950)

486 n.2 *For* antiquity *read* antiques

491 n.1 *Add* See Mark Amory, *Lord Berners* (1998)

518 l.22 and 519 l.12 DHL's repeated use of the phrase 'so very bracing' to

describe the Lincolnshire coast, may derive from his memory of the famous and widely displayed poster produced in 1908 by John Hassall (1868–1948), depicting a 'Jolly Fisherman' and carrying the slogan: 'Skegness is so bracing'

525 n.1 *For* Unidentified *read* Harold Stanley ('Jim') Ede (1895–1990), assistant to the Director of the Tate Gallery, 1920–36; lived at 1 Elm Row, Hampstead (see Letter 3809); a collector of modern art, especially Gaudier-Brzeska; created Kettle's Yard in Cambridge (see his *Way of Life: Kettle's Yard*, Cambridge, 1984), (obituary, *Independent*, 23 March 1990)

550 n.2 *For* Rockfort *read* Rockford

558 l.23 *For* Women *read* Woman

559 n.2 *For* though *read* thought

578 l.34 *For* lighting *read* lightning

622 n.1 *For* Murry *read* Murray

634 n.6 *For* 642 *read* 624

651 l.18 *For* go the *read* go to the

656 l.5 *For* **Hopkin** *read* **Hilton**

VOLUME VI

xxix l.39 *For* rea *read* tea

xxx l.34 *For* Kirchenleider . . . Eines *read* Kirchenlieder...eines

xxxii ll.22–3 *For* German . . . *Stories read Die Frau die davon ritt*

1 l.30 *For* the the *read* the

50 l.29 *For* pornographico *read* pornografico

54 n.3 *For* Rickwood *read* Rickword

95 l.13 *Insert paragraph*: And, as for you, how are you? Of course you are not bathing in the lake? The doctor says my haemorrhage was brought on by sea-bathing, which I've been doing at Forte.

95 ll.21–3 *Delete* The doctor . . . write.

101 l.25 *For* Ashly *read* Ashby

101 n. 3 *For* Unidentified *read* Mrs Caroline May Ashby, née Price-Williams (1869–1950), wife of the former Director of the British School at Rome, Thomas Ashby (1874–1931)

105 n.3 *For* bought *read* leased

125 n.1 to *read* ['Bowle'] cold punch

129 n.1 *For* novels *read* short stories

130 n.2 *For* rubbish *read* nonsense

132 n.2 *For* 1942 *read* 1924

199 n.2 Else Jaffe did translate the novel; Kippenberg rejected her translation

214 n.5 *For* (b. 1904) *read* (1904–94)

218 n.2 *For* murding *read* murdering

231 n.2 *For* DHL's letter to MacGreevy see viii.106–7 above

238 n.2 *Delete* bleak

239 l.14 *For* belive *read* believe

246 n.1 *Add* Eckart Peterich (1900–68), writer and poet; he published a very successful German guide to Italy in three volumes and, in the first, mentioned DHL and Huxley among famous visitors to Forte dei Marmi

246 n.2 *For* (1920–) *read* (1920–92)

254 n.2 *For* 1876 *read* 1871

270 n.3 *For* 'In Love' *read* 'In Love?'

275 n.3 *to read* Else Jaffe's translation of the volume excluded 'None of That' but included 'The Princess'

300 n.4 *For* (1927) *read* (1928)

315 n.2 *to read* . . . in Dickens' *David Copperfield* (1850)

342 l. 7 *For* eassay *read* essay

343 n.6 *For* 1886 *read* 1868

350 l.18 *For* go the *read* go to the

369 n.3 *Add* It seems increasingly likely that DHL's correspondent – despite his signature – was the Bristol bookseller and friend of Charles Lahr, William Dibben (cf. K. Hopkins, *The Corruption of a Poet*, 1954, p. 97)

371 n.3 *Add* In her *Tuscan Childhood* (Penguin, 1995), p. 210, Kinta Beevor remarks that, following the Fascist occupation of Poggio Gherardo during WWII, 'almost everything of value had disappeared, including letters to my parents [the Waterfields] from D. H. Lawrence.'

385 l.21 *For* women *read* woman

388 n.3 *For* Potency of Man *read* Potency of Men
        For waves over my *read* waves o'er my

401 n.1 *For* Bogey between *read* Bogey Between

421 n.4 *For* 1928 *read* 1929

444 n.1 *For* mutul *read* mutual

462 l.26 DHL reproduced Achsah Brewster's response almost verbatim in the opening paragraph of 'Nobody Loves Me' which appeared posthumously in *Life and Letters*, v (July 1930), 39–49 (see *Phoenix* 204) (Roberts C203)

480 l.9 *For* £1.345.00 *read* L1,345.00

485 l.32 *For* ever *read* every

492 l.28 *For* .hem *read* them

503 n.1 It is possible that, instead of 'William Congreve . . .', DHL was referrring to Dobrée's forthcoming review of *The Woman Who Rode Away* volume, which would be published in the *Criterion*, September 1928

524 n.2 *For* Kirchenleider . . . Eines *read* Kirchenlieder . . . eines

562 l.31 Salem – a famous boarding-school for *boys* – is in the Black Forest, not Bavaria

584 l.4 *For* indeed arrive *read* arrive safely

595 n.2 *For* than *read* then

600 l.29 *For* ² *read* ⁴

609 n.2 *To* 'Spurrier' *add* Stephen Spurrier R.A. (1878–1961), painter and illustrator

616 n.1 *Add* For the contents of the volume and the background to it, see C. Jansohn and D. Mehl, 'D.H. Lawrence and the Insel-Verlag', *Archiv*, cxlii (1990), 38–60

VOLUME VII

xxvi l.21 *For* Hotel Nouvel *read* Nouvel Hôtel

32 n.4 'Voigt' was Frederick Augustus (Fritz August) Voigt (1892–1957), author of *Combed Out* (1920), *Hindenberg* (1930), etc.; later influential London correspondent of the *Manchester Guardian*, and editor of *Nineteenth Century and After*, 1938–46

70 l.27 *For* (Photocopy) HU *read* University of Arizona, Tucson

70–1 n.3 *For* Jarell *read* Jared. Jared B. French (1905–88), American painter (see an essay on him by Nancy Grimes, *Art in America*, November 1992)

79 n.2 *For* (1896–) *read* (1896–1994)

179 l.22 *machine à plaisir* (quoted also in *Studies in Classic American Literature*, 1923, p. 100), a phrase from *Mademoiselle de Maupin* (1835) by Théophile Gautier, chap. ix.

201 n.2 *to read* Gerald Basil Edwards (1899–1976) was an admirer of DHL, protégé of Murry, friend of Stephen Potter and latterly a novelist himself; his *Book of Ebenezer Le Page* was published in 1981

223 n.1 *For* Gasset *read* Grasset

346 n.1 *For* Petterich *read* Peterich

426 n.2 *For* 5314 *read* 5214

444 n.1 *to read*: Carter married Mary Hamilton MacQueen (b.1895), 20 July 1922. His reluctance to mention her to DHL is understandable: he had begun divorce proceedings; indeed in August 1929 (about the time of DHL's letter) she was alleged to be engaged in an adulterous relationship. They were divorced in October 1931. (See Richard Grenville Clark, *Frederick Carter: Life and Works*, Guildford, Phoenix Books,1993)

468 n.4 *For Adelphi read New Adelphi*

521 l.11 *For* bedroon *read* bedroom

596 n.3 Dr Kurt Fiedler was Curtis Brown's representative in Berlin, 1929–33. He translated *St Mawr* into German, offered it to Kippenberg but had it rejected (see C. Jansohn and D. Mehl, *Archiv*, cxlii, 51–2)

641 l.10 *For* Baons *read* Baous

653 n.1 *Add* For a first-hand account of the situation at the Villa Robermond and of DHL's funeral, see the letter from Robert Nichols printed in Sybille Bedford, *Aldous Huxley* (1973), i. 225–8

INDEX

All titles of paintings and writings by Lawrence are gathered under his name.

Names of Lawrence's correspondents appear in BLOCK CAPITALS.

No distinction is made between a reference in the text or in a footnote.

See under Croydon, Eastwood, London or Nottingham for localities, public buildings or institutions etc. associated with each.

Information given in 'Corrigenda and Addenda' above is included, without distinction, under relevant entries in the index.

In the analysed entries normal conjunctions, prepositions, verbs etc. showing the relation of each item to the main entry are omitted.

The following general topics are indexed; they appear in italicised *BLOCK CAPITALS*:

Animal(s)
Architecture
Aristocracy
Art/Artists
Autobiography/Biography
Bible, The
Birds
Blood
Capitalism
Censorship
Childhood
Christianity
Civilisation
Communism
Conflict
Conservative(s)
Criticism/Critics
Cruelty
Death
Democracy
Dialect
Drink
Education
Evil
Fascism
Film (including Cinema)
Flowers
Food
Friendship
Health
Hinduism/Hindus
Homosexuality
Industry

Insects
Jew/Jewry
Journalism
Labour
Lawrence's Reading
Letters (Writing of)
Literary Agents
Love
Marriage
Money
Music
Newspapers
Novel/Novelist
Painting
Photographs
Poetry
Politics
Prayer
Public, The
Publishers
Rananim
Religion
Reviewers/Reviews
Sexuality
Socialism
Solitude
Spiritual, The
Symbols/Symbolism
Theatre (actors, drama etc)
Travel
War
Youth and Age

The following abbreviations are used throughout the Index:

A Propos   *A Propos of Lady
                     Chatterley's Lover*
All Things   *All Things Are Possible*
B in B   *The Boy in the Bush*
BBF   *Birds, Beasts and Flowers*
EME   *England, My England and
                     Other Stories*
Etruscan Places   *Sketches of Etruscan Places*
Fantasia   *Fantasia of the Unconscious*
Foreign Legion   *Memoirs of the Foreign
                     Legion*
Gesualdo   *Mastro-don Gesualdo*
Hardy   *Study of Thomas Hardy*
LCL   *Lady Chatterley's Lover*
Little Novels   *Little Novels of Sicily*
LWHCT   *Look! We Have Come
                     Through!*
M in M   *Mornings in Mexico*
Movements   *Movements in European
                     History*
MS   manuscript

My Skirmish   *My Skirmish with Jolly
                     Roger*
P and O   *Pornography and Obscenity*
Paintings   *The Paintings of D. H.
                     Lawrence*
Porcupine   *Reflections on the Death of a
                     Porcupine and Other Essays*
Psychoanalysis   *Psychoanalysis and the
                     Unconscious*
S and L   *Sons and Lovers*
S and S   *Sea and Sardinia*
SCAL   *Studies in Classic American
                     Literature*
T and G   *Touch and Go*
TS   typescript
Twilight   *Twilight in Italy*
W in L   *Women in Love*
Widowing   *The Widowing of Mrs.
                     Holroyd*
WWRA   *The Woman Who Rode Away
                     and Other Stories*

Abarbanel, Nathalia Clara Ruth (Nathalia
    Crane), Seltzer's 'infant prodigy', {v}48
    Janitor's Boy and Other Poems, {v}48,
    343
Abbey, Edwin Austin, {i}116
Abbotsbury (Dorset), *see* Old Coast Guard
    Station
Abbott, Miss, {ii}577–8, 585, 664
Abercrombie, Catherine, {ii}85, 92, 113, 120
Abercrombie, Lascelles, {i}362, {ii}2, 85, 92,
    113, 136, 175
    at Italian peasant wedding, {ii}116, 118;
    sharp mind, {ii}118, 119–20; 'The End
    of the World' paltry and vulgar,
    {ii}176–7; reviews *S and L*, {ii}177; on
    Hardy {ii}198
    Emblems of Love, {i}362;
    'The End of the World', {ii}176–7;
    Mary and the Bramble, {ii}177;
    New Numbers, {ii}136, 155, 176;
    The Sale of St Thomas, {ii}177;
    Thomas Hardy, {i}544, {ii}198
Aberdeen (Scotland), {v}228, 287

Aberdeen (Washington), {vi}212, 431, 433
Abraham, {iv}90, 198
Abraham, Dr Felix, {vii}287, 335
Abruzzi (Italy), {iii}8, 214, 585–7, 602,
    {v}184, 471
Académie Française, {v}550, 578–9
Academy, *see* London 11, Royal Academy
Academy, The, {i}107, 241, {ii}29
*Account of the Natives of the Tonga Islands,
    An*, *see* Martin, J.
Account of the Pelew Islands, An, *see* Keate, G.
Achsah, *see* Brewster, A. B.
Acrobats, The, *see* Gertler, M.
Acton, Arthur Mario, {v}625
Acton, (Sir) Harold Mario Mitchell, {vi}2,
    11, 214, 223
    The Last of the Medici, {vi}470, 591
Ad Astra (Vence), {vii}2, 12–15, 626
    DHL resistant to, {vii}630–2; 'will go
    for a month or so', {vii}635–6; comfort-
    able in, {vii}638–47; gradual disenchant-
    ment before leaving, {vii}649–52
Ada, *see* Clarke, L. A.

'Adam and Eve', Juliette Huxley embroiders, DHL contributes to, {vi}313, 316, 344, 375, 403, 460
Adam Bede, see Eliot, G.
Adam Cast Forth, see Doughty, C. M.
Adams, Ethel, {i}319
Adams, Eldridge, untrustworthy publisher, {vii}233, 236, 239, 272, 390–1, 445
Adams, Franklin P., {iv}16
Adams, Mrs, {i}319, 348, 351
Adderley, Hon. Rev. James Granville, *Epiphany*, {i}364
Addey, Dr William Fielding, treats DHL for pneumonia, {i}330–4, 337, 340–2; advised DHL against marriage, {i}361
Addington (Surrey), {i}250
Addiscombe (Croydon), {i}241, 298, 330
Adelaide (Australia), {iv}10, 237–8, 241, 243, 249; DHL visits art gallery in, {iv}273
Adele, *see* Seltzer, A.
Adelphi (The Adelphi Press) {iv}15, 20, 432, 485, 499, 519, 529, 565, 575, 585, 595, 593, {v}17, 43, 74, 87, 205, 240, 322 356, 383, 464, 575, 582
  Murry creates as vehicle for DHL's views, {ii}31; 'Indians and an Englishman' in, {iv}298, 432; 'Spirits Summoned West' in, {iv}327; published no Verga translations, {iv}447; Kot business manager for, {iv}454, 556, {v}16, {viii}86; DHL considers 'feeble', 'knock-kneed', disappointing, {iv}458, 462, 480–1, 483, {v}18, 231, {viii}81; Murry should be satirical in, {iv}500; DHL might work with Murry on, {iv}522; story by Mabel Luhan offered to, {iv}545; DHL writing articles for, {iv}549–50; DHL might be partner in Adelphi Press, {iv}556–9; DHL annoyed by Murry's articles in, {iv}572; stories not to be offered to, {v}26; 'Indians and Entertainment' in, {v}36; 'does one no good', {v}49;'The Dance of the Sprouting Corn' in, {v}57; Murry rejects 'On Coming Home', {v}94; 'The Hopi Snake Dance' in, {v}103, 110, 116,170, 173; in financial crisis, {v}170; DHL expects demise of, {v}226; not keen to publish Mexican essays in, {v}242; writes review for, {v}301; Murry's 'A Simple Creed' in, {v}328; DHL refuses back numbers of, {v}348; Molly Skinner's story revised for publication in, {v}351, 419; Murry told to 'throw the *Adelphi* to the devil', {v}368, 370, 372, 374; DHL refuses to publish again in, {v}380, 385–6, 432; Murry announces closure of, {vi}47, 55; source of financial backing for, {vi}83; 'fell through the holes in its own socks', {vi}181; 'beshitten', {vi}247; DHL's contempt for, {vi}382
  see also New Adelphi, The,
Aden, {iv}204, 206, 208, 211
Adler, Cyrus, *The Jewish Encyclopaedia*, {ii}385
'Adonis', *see* Aldington, H.
Adonis, DHL allegedly regarded by female disciples as, {iii}179; 'life-bringer', {vii}519
Adrian, *see* Secker, A.
Adriatic Sea, {v}311
Adriatic, R.M.S., {ii}437
Adventures of Hajji Baba, see Morier, J. J.
Adventures of Maya the Bee, The, see Bonsels, W.
Aegean Sea, {vii}545
Aeschylus, {ii}298, 301
  Prometheus Bound, {ii}248, 283–4; *Prometheus Unbound*, {ii}248
Aesop, {ii}552
Afric, *see* Wilkinson, Mrs
Africa, {ii}107, 631, {iii}233 312, 338, 412, 416, 438, 448, 488, 491–2, 525, 655–6, {iv}239, {vii}23, {viii}120, 220
  DHL might visit, {iii}449, 460, 462–3, 526, 626, {vii}28, 166, 494; scirocco from, {iv}122; the negation of what England represents, {iv}219; too costly to visit, {vi}317; isolated if living in, {vii}465
  see also South Africa
After Lenin, see Farbman, M.
'After the Fireworks', *see* Huxley, A.
Aga Khan III, {vii}15, 652–3
Agag, {vii}189

Agapeto, {v}530
Agnes, *see* Holt, A.
Aïda, {viii}84–5
Aigle (Switzerland), {vi}279, 285, 314, 374,
    380, 473–4, 493, 502
Aiken, Conrad, *The Pilgrimage of Festus,*
    {iv}494
Aiken, Robert, *see* Atkins, R.
Aimard, Gustave, *see* Gloux, O.
Ainley, Henry, {iii}411
Ainslee's, {vi}270
Ainsley, Samuel James, {vi}105,
    {viii}104–5
Ainslie, Robert, {vi}287
Ainsworth, William Harrison, {i}5
Airships, {ii}10, 651, 657
    'like a bright golden finger..among a
    fragile incandescence of clouds',
    {ii}389–90; 'gleaming like a new great
    sign in the heavens', {ii}394; 'gleaming
    golden like a long-ovate moon', {ii}396
AITKEN, WILLIAM MAXWELL, LORD
    BEAVERBROOK, {iii}39, {v}383,
    {vi}11, 271, 616
    orders three copies of *LCL,* {vi}479;
    needs *Rainbow* to complete his collec-
    tion, {vi}479, 491, 497; Gerhardie and,
    {vi}616
    Letters to {vi}479
    Letters from {vi}479
Aix-en-Provence (France), {vii}623
Ajaccio (Corsica), {vii}183, 190–1
Ajanta Caves (India), {v}519, 561, {vi}72,
    208
Ajanta Frescoes, The, {ii}483, 505
    DHL and Russell give copy to Ottoline
    Morrell, {ii}488–90; 'the most perfect
    things I have *ever* seen', {ii}489
Aked, Rev. Charles Frederic, {i}44
Akin, Colonel Albert D., {v}202, 213, 263
Akin, Jean Harmon, {v}202, 215
AKINS, ZOË, {ii}10
    Papa: An Amorality', 'full of life and go',
    {ii}145
    Letters to {ii}396–7
Alain, *see* Insole, A.
Alamos (Mexico), {iv}506, 510
Alamosa (New Mexico), {iv}338, 354

Alan, *see* Chambers, A.
Alaska (USA), {v}394, 429, 440
Alassio (Italy), {vi}361, 366–8, {vii}611
    'chronic hole, awful', {v}347; Barbara
    Weekley stays in, {v}349–50, 352, 356–7,
    369, 371, {vi}329–30, 340, 367, 371, 377;
    Frieda goes to, {vi}361, 367 {vi}366–8,
    371, 377; DHL in, {vi}375
Albany (Western Australia), {iv}496
Albenga (Italy), {v}397
    Huxleys' car breaks down in, {vii}164,
    167, 169, 171
Albert, *see* Boni, A.
Albidia, *see* Marcus, A.
Albuquerque (New Mexico), {v}343, 497,
    510, {vi}36
    income tax office in, {iv}559, {v}39, 46
Aldington, Frances Perdita, {iii}349
ALDINGTON, HILDA ('H. D.'), {ii}2,
    203, 206, 210, 514, 541, 645, {iii}37, 56,
    72, 178, 253, {v}104, 426, {vi}42,
    {vii}349
    DHL contributes to Imagist anthologies
    edited by, {ii}664–5, {vii}414–15,
    {viii}112; 'physical apprehension' in
    poems by, {iii}30–1; poems 'The God'
    and 'Adonis' 'good', {iii}84; MS of
    LWHCT sent to, {iii}94, 102; very sad,
    {iii}105; DHL offered use of flat by,
    {iii}170–1, 189–90, {vi}467; possible
    member of Andes group, {iii}173;
    representative of new world of 'knowl-
    edge and being', {iii}180; appears happy
    in Cornwall, {iii}254; left Cornwall,
    {iii}280; not trusted, {iii}308; has child,
    {iii}314, 347, 349; model for Miranda in
    Cournos novel, {v}433; refuses to
    divorce Aldington, {v}443, 475; DHL's
    letters in autobiographical novel by,
    {viii}23–4; 'lost her own self',
    {viii}28
    Bid Me To Live, {viii}23–4;
    'Eurydice', {viii}23
    Letters to {vii}414–15, {viii}23–4,
    112
ALDINGTON, RICHARD, {i}256, {ii}2,
    203, 206, 210, 467, {iii}31, 190, 349,
    454, 457, {v}104, 180, 476, 482, 550,

{vi}1, 158, 467, 532, {vii}17, 15, 349, 652, {viii}23, 28, 112
irreverence of war poem by, {ii}232; glamour of war getting hold of, {ii}644; portentous letter from, {iii}197; sent to France, {iii}233; Amy Lowell lectures on, {iii}253; poems in *New Paths* with DHL, {iii}261; on leave from France, {iii}313; not easy to get on with, {iii}449; facilitates publication of 'Rex' for DHL, {iii}536; *Lost Girl* for, {iii}617; DHL fails to write foreword for play by, {iv}242; Amy Lowell entertains DHL and, {v}197; invited to tour Etruscan sites, {v}427; model for 'Arnold' in Cournos novel, {v}433; living with Dorothy Yorke, {v}443, 469, 475, {viii}112; writes leaders for *TLS*, {v}469; DHL visits, {v}505, 507; invited to stay in Villa Mirenda, {v}518, 534, 542–3, 548–9, 552; advises on publication of Mabel Luhan's memoirs, {v}550, 578–9, 602, 615; helps to distribute *LCL*, {vi}12–15, 488–9, 491–2, 494–7, 499–500, 503, 510–15, 517–20, 529–30, 544–5, 603, {vii}600; Port-Cros with DHL, {vi}18–19, 519, 542, 544, 569, 573, 578, 585–96, 600–4; writes pamphlet, *Indiscretion*, on DHL, {vi}44, 64–5, 221; offers DHL financial help, {vi}220–1; considers *LCL* 'feather in the cap of the 20th Century', {vi}480, 484–6, 497; and Brigit Patmore, {vi}590, {viii}112; invited to contribute volume to Orioli's series, {vii}416, 504, 540, 564–5, 573, 578; possible contributor to 'The Squib', {vii}498, 516; *Story of Doctor Manente* sent to, {vii}558
D. H. Lawrence: An Indiscretion, {vi}44, 64–5, 221;
Death of a Hero, {vii}558;
Images, {ii}427
Letters to {iii}410, 536, {v}426–7, 542–3, 577, {vi}42–4, 64–5, 220–1, 474–5, 485–6, 488, 497, 514, 528–9, 578
Letters from {v}602–3
Aldous, *see* Huxley, A.
Aleister, *see* Crowley, E. A.

Aleppo (Turkey), {vi}342
Alessandro, Ellide, {ii}141
Alexander the Great, {ii}48
Alexander, Arthur, {iv}67
Alexander, Francesca, {iv}545
Alexandria (Egypt), {iii}669–70
Alexandria, see Forster, E. M.
Alfred, *see* Knopf, A. A.; Weber, A.
Alfreton (Derbyshire), {i}27, 34
Alfreton Park (Derbyshire), {i}34
Algiers (Algeria), {iii}673, 678, {iv}127, {v}343, {viii}30
Algonquin Hotel (New York), {iv}16, {v}301
Alicante (Spain), {vii}273, 276, 282–3, 286
Alice's Adventures in Wonderland, see Carroll, L.
Alice, *see* Flewins, A.; Henderson, A. C.
Aligarh (India), {i}8, 77, {vii}193
Alinari, Fratelli, {iii}603, 697, {vi}40, 48, 50, 77, 79, 85, {vii}368, 508, {viii}104
Alires, Frederico, {v}39, 264, 266, 269
All Things Are Possible, see Shestov, L.
Allam, James, {i}231, {viii}1
Allam, Mary Ellen, {i}231, 233, 442, 444, 444, 454, 461, 484, {viii}1
Allam, Nellie, *see* Allam, M. E.
Allan, Dolly, {iii}378, 581
Allanah, *see* Harper, A.
Allcock, Kitty, {iii}258–9
Allen, Clifford, {ii}551
Allen, J. A., & Co., {vi}512, 515, {vii}47–8
Allen, James Lane, {i}88
Allied Artists Association, {ii}46, 186
Almanach, see Borzoi, The, or *Insel Almanach*
Almgren, Antonia, {i}475, 537, 539, 547 estranged wife of Swedish artist, {i}18; pseudonyms 'Mrs Anthony', and 'Tony Cyriax', {i}520; stays with Lawrences, {i}522, 524–6, 530, 535–6; Frieda considers 'a sensationalist' and 'doesn't like', {i}533–4, {ii}139; model for English 'blonde signora' in *Twilight in Italy*, {ii}414
Tony Cyriax, *Among Italian Peasants*, {i}520
Almgren, Gisela, {i}520, 533, 538
Almgren, Per Johan Hugo, {i}18, 520, 533–4
Almora (India), {v}484, 519, 561

Along the Road, see Huxley, A.

Alongshore, see Reynolds, S.

Alpha, *see* Barlow, A.

Alps, {v}366, {vi}189
DHL walks over, {i}20, {ii}184;
honeymoon near, {i}413, 415, 426; Villa
Jaffe gives beautiful views of, {i}541,543,
547, 552, 553, {ii}57, 59; awful in rain,
{iv}65; less enervating on Swiss side of,
{vi}317; DHL heading for French,
{vi}407, 416, 419, 421–2; in Swiss,
{vi}468, 474, 509, 554, 562; DHL feels
better south of, {vii}332, 394, 453, 487;
in Austrian, {viii}42; leaves Austrian,
{viii}44

Alstyne, Frances Jane Van, {i}62

Altounyan, Ernest, {ii}403

Altrincham (Cheshire), {iii}430, 477, 483,
487

Altrincham Stage Society, produce
Widowing, {iii}428, 430, 477, 510

Amalfi (Italy), {v}343, 345, 649–50, 653,
{vi}27, 30
'marvellous', {iii}464; lovely coast,
{iii}469; Hotel Cappuccini in, {iii}633;
Mediterranean influence southwards
from, {iv}97

Amazon river, {iii}315
see also Bates, H. W.

Ambergate (Derbyshire), {i}35, {iii}259,
312, {vii}261

Ambergris, see Crowley, E. A.

Amblecoate (Amblecote) (Staffordshire),
{i}64, 373, 379

Ame d'Enfant, see Margueritte, P.

America, {i}220, {ii}2, 58, 98, 100, 117, 133,
135, 165, 193, 210, 230, 271, 354, 373,
393, 555, {iii}33–4, 142, 157, 227, 239,
280–1, 318, 356, 393, 425, 471, 483, 493,
501, 515, 548, 563, 565–6, 584 588, 606,
608, 620, 634, 640, 654, 658, 689, 701,
719, {iv}100, 186, 196, 213, 270, 355,
359, 368, 374, 399, 495, 543–6, 550, 567,
572–3, 574, 576, 582, 584, {v}32, 78,
174, 266, 270, 314, 347, 391, 397, 449,
457–9, 497, 545, 613, 642, 654–5, {vi}31,
52, 120, 179, 225, 266, 324, 404, 438,
485, 502, 542, {vii}62, 113, 226, 250–1,
268–9, 272, 302, 387, 445, 469, 471,
485–8, 557, 600, {viii}34, 48, 50, 90, 92
Pound returning to, {i}166; Press
Cuttings Co. of, {i}226; reception of
White Peacock in, {i}313, {iii}547, 653;
Trespasser published in, {i}430, {iii}653;
young Italian men going to, {i}536,
{ii}148–9, 153; publication of *Widowing*
in, {ii}77, 136, 143, 152; people not
'priggish conceited' in, {ii}146; Amy
Lowell returns to, {ii}216; 'Honour and
Arms' sold in, {ii}222–3, 256; when rich
DHL will go to, {ii}224; Lowell sends
typewriter from, {ii}227; DHL's hopes
will remain out of war, {ii}394; *Twilight*
published in, {ii}398, {iii}323, {vii}158,
265–6; *EME* published in, {ii}406;
DHL tries to go to, {ii}413–14, 417–20,
428, 432, 436–8, 440, 443; only hope
for world, {ii}415; publication of
Rainbow in, {ii}429, 480, 561, {iii}467;
DHL wants to start 'a new germ of a
new creation' in, {ii}438; 'bad, but..it
has a future', {ii}441; DHL postpones
visit to, {ii}446, 474, 565; has £60 to
go to, {ii}447; publication of poems
in, {ii}509–10, 560–1, {iii}15; DHL
afraid of, {ii}527; feels like Columbus
viewing shadowy, {ii}556; 'soulless',
{ii}612; 'splendid' in remoter parts,
{ii}645; *W in L* in, {iii}1, 11–13, 16, 391,
394–5, 400, 410, 456, 467, 482, 485, 455,
629; *SCAL*, {iii}4, 156, 160, 201, 209,
247, 270, 299, 324–5, 388,397, 405–7,
456, 556, 563, 565, 578, 582, 645,
{iv}197–8, 343, 355, 490; DHL wants to
transfer his life to, {iii}8, 25, 27, 144;
potent symbol, {iii}9; DHL's reputation
in, {iii}13; Mountsier acts for DHL in,
{iii}16, 476–7, 504, 577, {iv}29,
{viii}35; USA 'won't declare war',
{iii}88; breaks off relations with
Germany, {viii}20; declaration of war
makes USA 'a stink-pot', {iii}124;
'negative pole' of 'world's spiritual
energy', {iii}136; DHL wants to come
to, {iii}140, 143, 157, 305, 314, 322, 324,
326, 331, 333, 347, 364, 370, {viii}24;

'courage of ultimate truth in', {iii}141; 'the New World', {iii}143; DHL doesn't believe in 'Uncle Samdom', {iii}144; passports refused for, {iii}160; *LWHCT* in, {iii}238, 254–5, 323; *Bay* not published in, {iii}238, 585; DHL would love 'living lavishness' available in, {iii}348; prepared to lecture in, {iii}362, 364, 367; confident of being self-supporting in, {iii}369; expects imminent departure for, {iii}372, 374; deterred by thought of lecturing in, {iii}376, {viii}41; sickened by thought of, {iii}383; *New Poems* in, {iii}386, 399; DHL abandons visit to, {iii}388; expects to make money in, {iii}397; Huebsch the only 'white' publisher in, {iii}400; attempt to publish *All Things* in, {iii}393–4, 397–8, 400, 403, 433–4, 437–9, 441, 455–6, 470, 508; DHL needs agent in, {iii}473; film rights possible in, {iii}546; attempt to serialise *Lost Girl* in, {iii}560, 562, 564, 572, 627, 629, 638, 646, 667; *S and L* in, {iii}576, {iv}27, 47, 107, 121, 123, 129, 131, 137, 276; rights on 'The Fox' in, {iii}619, 651, {iv}10; 'The Blind Man' in, {iii}635, 650; tangle of affairs between publishers in, {iii}651–2; DHL feels must visit, {iii}659, 661, 664–6, 670, 672, 676; DHL proposes to 'write for', {iii}664, {iv}97; hopes to arrive in with '£300 clear', {iii}668; depends on, {iii}678; has to abandon 'for the present', {iii}683–5, 688, 695–6; advice not to publish *Movements* in, {iii}713; Scott's *Narrow House* is last word by white, {iii}733; DHL's visit 1922–3 to, {iv}1–17 *passim*; *Aaron's Rod* in, {iv}25, 95–6, 258–9, 276; 'Wintry Peacock' published in, {iv}31; DHL decides against going to, {iv}58; apprehensive about, {iv}73, 97; *Psychoanalysis* 'written for', {iv}85–6; DHL prefers to approach from Pacific {iv}95; publishing 'bad' in, {iv}104; DHL demands information on his publications in, {iv}107–8; *Fantasia* in, {iv}109, 255; DHL anxious about his

dollars in, {iv}110, 113, 121, 145, 268; Mabel Luhan invites DHL to, {iv}110–1, 120–1, 123, 125–6, 138; intends to go New Year 1922 to, {iv}111–12, 114, 127–66 *passim*; important to write American stories in, {iv}121; England hated in, {iv}132; journey expensive to, {iv}137; *EME* in, {iv} 145; Mountsier discouraging about Taos, {iv}150; sense of future in, {iv}157; DHL feels he '*can't*' come to, {iv}168, 171, 173, 177, 180–2, 190, 202, 207; 'utter unreality' of, {iv}171, 485; DHL to go east before going west, {iv}175; negation of what Englishmen represent, {iv}219; disenchantment with Ceylon reopens possibility of visit to, {iv}224–30, 235, 244, 246–7, 251, 253; DHL 'in diametric opposition' to, {iv}226; no one to know DHL arriving in, {iv}257, 259, 267; journey to, {iv}272, 274–81, 284, 286; goes 'with dread' to, {iv}273; DHL forecasts labour troubles in, {iv}277; arrives in 'the land of the free', {iv}287, 289–92; if DHL accepted in, then belongs to, {iv}299; predominance of will in relationships in, {iv}305, 311, 313–14; spontaneous life absent from, {iv}311; lacks 'understanding mildness' of Europe, {iv}325; DHL made to 'feel hard' in, {iv}349, 387; 'biggest *bully* world has yet seen..not a sympathetic country', {iv}352; 'blank nothing' replaced inside life in, {iv}362, 365; expensive, {iv}372; DHL not disappointed in, {iv}398; feels imprisoned in, {iv}415; *Kangaroo* published in, {iv}428, 489; money and possessions insignificant for Indians, predominant for whites in, {iv}452; *Plumed Serpent* ('Quetzalcoatl') DHL's 'real novel' of, {iv}457, {v}6, {vi}400; hopes not to stay long in, {iv}471; Frieda leaves, DHL stays in, {iv}479–90; '*genuine*' USA evident in Buffalo, {iv}492; 'voice of America' silent, {iv}499; 'foolish and empty', {iv}500; spiritually exhausting, {iv}503; DHL feels 'great disgust' for,

America (*cont.*)

{iv}518; *B in B* in, {iv}524, 549, 597;
rather than England, DHL would prefer
to be in, {iv}552, 560; DHL hated in
London more than in, {iv}556; Curtis
Brown to be DHL's agent in, {iv}559;
DHL glad to return to, {iv}595, 597;
returns mainly for business reasons,
{v}1–2; glad to be back in Taos, {v}28;
city and village-life 'empty and stupid'
in, {v}63; meditation important in Asia,
action in, {v}75; Navajo country is 'real
old savage', {v}113; 'iron backbone' of,
{v}184; DHL doesn't know all about,
{v}198; makes one feel 'leathery in one's
soul', {v}272; DHL hates 'the real USA,
Chicago and New York and all that',
{v}277; has had his 'whack' of, {v}278,
291, 304, 307; 'living feeling' absent
from ordinary people of, {v}294;
journalism preferred to creative writing
in, {v}307–8; Italy relaxing after tension
of, {v}343, 345, 357, 364, 382, 384, 425,
429; *Porcupine* in, {v}375, 378, 381, 387,
{vi}363, {vii}401; essential to be 'tough'
in, {v}387; DHL feels 'revulsion from',
{v}389, 453; only when tired of Europe
will DHL return to, {v}412, 416, 421–2,
438; *David* in, {v}454, 623, 638; not
good for DHL, {v}468; DHL not
attracted to, {v}485, 491–2; England
'not so scratchy as', {v}530; DHL's life
really in Europe, not in, {v}585, 651;
shrinks from, {v}600, 606; may soon
come to, {v}629; doubts if he will come
to, {vi}28; DHL's 'real inside doesn't
turn towards', {vi}58; 'good fighting
country', {vi}72; Osbert Sitwell's
loathing of USA makes DHL want to
return to, {vi}73; DHL would prefer 'a
hyaena house' to living in, {vi}79;
sometimes tempted to return to, {vi}82,
86; Europe 'a dud' makes DHL almost
long for, {vi}182; in Spring 1928 might
come to, {vi}208, 210, 212, 242, 296–7;
'tough..anarchic and soulless – but not as
mercenary as Italy', {vi}219; copies of
LCL allocated to, {vi}242, 265, 282, 314,
318, 320, 322, 328, 331, 401–2; DHL
postpones visit to, {vi}299; may visit,
{vi}338, 345, 349, 358, 362; commission
taken by booksellers in, {vi}343; danger
of censorship in, {vi}364, 408; orders for
LCL from, {vi}371, 377, 381, 385, 393,
408, 415–16, 418; reactions to *LCL* in,
{vi}375, 484, 504–5, 547–53, 555, 575,
607; Keyserling's *Marriage* read chiefly
in, {vi}419; copies of *LCL* mailed to,
{vi}428–98 *passim*, 508, 511, 518, 526,
532, 545, 566, 567–8, {vii}25, 35, 108,
137, 184; Vanguard Press offer to
distribute *LCL* in, {vi}525–7, 530, 532,
539, 545–6, 565, 568, {vii}35, 39, 42,
{viii}115; copies of *LCL* confiscated by
US Mail, {vi}530–2, 537, 550, 579, 608,
{vii}89, 132; *Escaped Cock* in, {vi}539,
598, {vii}426, 499, 504, 531, 551, 586;
DHL postpones exhibition of paintings
in, {vi}553, 559, 564, 574, 580; 'no real
spunk' left in, {vi}566; 'so absolutely
unbrave', {vi}576; DHL wants *Collected
Poems* to appear in, {vi}607, {vii}27, 38,
65–6, 182, 238, 243, 315, 320, 324;
pirated editions of *LCL* in, {vi}608,
{vii}30, 35, 38–40, 42, 45–8, 57, 77, 85,
105, 115, 210, 217, 219, 233–4, 307–8,
311–12, 321, 335, 375, 497–8; 'Cocksure
Women' bought by *Forum* in, {vi}609;
sales of Huxley's *Point Counter Point* in
{vii}21; 'so irritating', {vii}27; DHL
feels great hostility in, {vii}55; not
'paradise', {vii}94; DHL's reputation
might endanger *Paintings* in, {vii}138–9,
145, 168, 300, 337, 343–5, 353, 505, 551;
DHL would like to visit, health permit-
ting, {vii}197; not well enough to travel
to, {vii}203, 205, 213, 312; not 'quite
time' for visit to, {vii}277; *Paintings* will
sell easily in, {vii}279, 321–2; DHL
'belongs to Europe, not to USA',
{vii}287; 'authorities are so hateful' in,
{vii}290, 312; *Pansies* in, {vii}315, 320,
568; 'robot inhumanity' in, {vii}438;
'time ripe again' for DHL's work in,
{vii}503; DHL's literary affairs 'a mess'
in, {vii}520–2; seems more distant than

Babylon or Nineveh, {vii}547; enraged
by Europe DHL will try to return to,
{vii}574, 594–5, 617, 633, 637; Wall
Street crash, {vii}578, 582, 586; DHL
feels unwelcome in, {vii}636–7; 'devas-
tating', {viii}76; recognises Mexico,
{viii}85
American Caravan, The, see Brooks, V. W.
American Express, {iii}140, 159, 721, {iv}39,
44, 75–6, 79, {v}298, {vi}531, 547
American Merchant, S. S., {vi}13, 450
American Review, see North American Review
Americana, see, Mencken, H.L.
Amfiteatrov, Aleksander Valentinovich,
{ii}155, 168
Amorality, see Akins, Z.
Amour, Terre Inconnue, see Maurice, M.
Amsterdam (Netherlands), {iii}349, 620
Amy, *see* Lowell, A.
Anacapri, {iii}438,443, 496, 513, 558, 579,
{iv}138, {v}627, 629, 630, {vi}22, 89,
92, 111, 317, {vii}22, 28, 48, 68, 155,
170, 250, 362
Anacoreti nelle Tebaidi (LaTebaide), see
Lorenzetti, P.
Anatomy of Melancholy, The, see Burton, R.
Anchor (Shipping) Line, {vii}586
Ancient Art and Ritual, see Harrison, J.
Ancient History of the Near East, The, see Hall,
H. R.
Ancient Spanish Ballads, {i}205
Anderson, James, {vi}48, 85, 89–90,
{viii}104
Anderson, Sherwood, {vi}180
Winesburg, {iii}426
Andes Mountains, {iii}8, 173, 174–5, 265,
316, {vii}377
Andrew, *see* Dasburg, A. M.
ANDREWS, ESTHER ('HADAFFAH'),
{iii}56, 72, 75, 77, 79, 85, 102, 124–5,
132, 144, 162, 199
'doing some journalism', {iii}25; 'not
really a journalist', {iii}27; 'an artist..we
liked her very much', {iii}28; 'nice',
{iii}34, 37; *Women in Love* TS on loan
to, {iii}44, 51; stays with Lawrences,
{iii}64; depressed, {iii}65, 159;
'Hadaffah', {iii}66–8; possible recruit

for Rananim, {iii}87; unhappy about
Mountsier, {iii}93; visits Catherine
Carswell, {iii}130–1; seeking stories for
Seven Arts, {iii}140, 142, {viii}24; one of
women representing 'threshold of a new
world', {iii}180
Letters to {viii}19–20, 24–7
Andreyev, Leonidas, *Silence and Other
Stories,* {i}349, 353;
To the Stars, {iii}532
Angeles y Velarde, {iv}526–7
Angelico (Fra), Guido di Pietro, {ii}266, 275,
298, {iii}248, 341, 420
The Last Judgment, {ii}263, 301
Angell, Mrs, {vi}157, 199
Angell, (Sir) Norman, *Why Freedom Matters,*
{iii}113
Angulo, Jaime de, {iv}585–6, {v}23, 28, 37,
41–2, 94, 102, 136
Angulo, Lucy ('Nancy') de, {v}23, 102
ANIMAL(S), 'a great purpose which keeps
the menagerie moving onward..while the
animals snap and rattle by the way',
{i}57; Sarah Bernhardt 'a gazelle with a
beautiful panther's fascination and fury',
{i}59; DHL pulls his ears 'as long as a
donkeys, with mad metaphors', {i}86;
school-children 'malicious young
human', {i}93; 'pale deer flee' in
Richmond Park, {i}120; 'intruding like a
muddy shaggy animal', {i}188; DHL's
aunt 'like a bison with a skirt on', {i}224;
'Man's the animal baby "who won't be
happy till he gets it"', {i}252; 'people
dodging out of the way like hares',
{i}356; old man 'blorts like a bullock',
{i}377; Frieda 'a lazy animal', {i}495;
deer 'fly with great bounds' when
disturbed, hare 'dances round in wild
bewilderment', {i}543; 'hare lobs among
the grass', {i}553; deer jump 'up and
down to get the wet out of their jackets',
'squirrels simply hang out by their tails
like washing', {ii}63; 'deer go trotting
through the sun-dapplings', {ii}65; 'I
feel as if my heart would jump out of my
chest like a hare at night', {ii}156; Van
Gogh should have 'set the angel of

ANIMAL(S) (*cont.*)

himself clear in relation to the animal of himself', {ii}298; 'a rat..slithers along in the dark, pointing its sharp nose..contains a principle of evil', {ii}311; DHL 'run to earth, like a fox they have chased till it can't go any further', {ii}500; 'a mole, a creature that feels its way and doesn't think', {ii}547; Allies 'feed like enormous rats' on Germany's dismemberment, {ii}603; Englishmen will be 'whipped up like dogs to fasten on the body of Germany', {ii}609; people are 'rats..sewer-rats, with all the foul courage of death and corruption', {iii}21; Lloyd George 'clever little Welsh *rat*', {iii}48; 'little pigs infinitely gayer and more delicate in soul' than lambs, {iii}124; republics 'imaginary chickens of an addled egg', {iii}139; Paradise 'just a hare listening to the inaudible', {iii}160; DHL as politically innocent 'as the rabbits of the field', {iii}168; various animal (rabbit, hare, fox, weasel, field-mice etc) 'footmarks in the snow' vividly described, {iii}328; Europe 'a dead dog' which stinks, England 'a dead dog' which died of 'love disease like syphilis', {iv}114; DHL considered 'a possible animal sketch-book later', {iv}169; bedouins 'like animals, Arabs - wonderful', {iv}211; in Australia, 'you clatter round like so many mechanical', {iv}264; numerous Mexican servants in house seem to have holes 'like rabbits', {iv}453; Huichole Indians 'like animals from another world', {iv}529; in London DHL 'like a wild animal in a trap..like a caged coyote', {iv}542; 'a machine [New York] is perhaps less distressing than a dying animal: London', {v}17; only 'unison' among wild animals is 'of avoiding one another', {v}67; Squire a 'suburban rat', a 'dirty dog', {v}91, {vii}376; snake dances, {v}100; on DHL's ranch, {v}258-9, 266; Bynner applies feline imagery to DHL, {v}384, {vii}575 ; embroidery of

'peacock, kid, and deer among the vines!', {v}478; DHL posits Edenic painting with God 'disappearing in a dudgeon, and the animals skipping', {v}639; *Porcupine* 'not a paying', {vi}28; DHL not 'tough and snorting like a war-horse', {vi}56; Austrians 'like sea-lions, so inert and prostrate', {vi}126; 'red stag..leaving his inquisitive rump in sight, for a hunter to shoot at', {vi}146; deer darting past tree-trunks 'like a little Persian painting', {vi}154, 158; cow-bells 'like village shop-bells', {vi}158; characteristics of 'man-animal', {vi}161-2; Arlen like 'dog that people throw stones at by instinct', {vi}221; DHL 'a lamb at last', {vi}321; 'perhaps..public is not such a dumb', {vi}403; peasants 'sunk into the earth, like moles or voles', {vi}527; 'I feel like a badger..on Wimbledon Common..trying not to be caught', {vi}601; book about 'censor-animal' affects DHL as if 'watching a great unchained ape fumbling through his hairs for something', {vi}613; old mare and bull terrier at Haggs Farm, {vi}618; Secker 'more like a mouse than a rabbit', {vii}163; if DHL has sixth sense, Murry 'animal with only four', {vii}166; England unlike Australia 'where none of the animals bite', {vii}180; doctor claims 'animal man' in 'state of change', {vii}466, 470; 'duality of tiger and deer' illustrates 'primal cruelty' in all life, {viii}21; 'howl like a dog from helplessness', {viii}84

Anita, *see* Schreibershofen, A. von

Anita, Annie, *see* Hinke, A. von

Ann Veronica, see Wells, H. G.

Anna Karénina, see Tolstoy, L.

Anna of the Five Towns, see Bennett, E. A.

Anna, Edgar Jaffe's servant, {vi}139, 141-3, 147-50, 154, 156, 158, 166, {viii} 106

Annecy (France), {vi}396-7, 402, 406-7

Annenheim (Austria), {vi}108, 125, 129, 141

Annesley (Nottinghamshire), {i}35, {v}243, 592

Anni, {vi}149, {viii}46

Annunzio, Gabriele d', {ii}26, 180, 247, 595, {iii}40, 733
'cruder' than my *Trespasser*, {iii}41; 'a sensationalist, nearly always in bad taste', {v}276
La Fiaccolo sotto il Moggio (*The Light under the Bushel*), {i}505;
Il Fuoco (*Flame of Life*), {iii}43, {v}175;
L'Innocente, {iii}40, 43;
Trionfo della Morte (*The Triumph of Death*), {iii}43, {v}276;
Vergine della Roche (*Virgins of the Rocks*), {iii}43, {iv}492, {viii}36

Ansell, Walter, {i}314

Antarctic, {i}517, {iv}242

Anthologia Hebraica, {iii}679

Anthologia Helvetica, {iii}679

Anthony, Mrs, *see* Almgren, A.

Anticoli-Corrado (Italy), {iii}536, 551–2, 574, 578, 579–81, 583–8, 687, 695, {iv}52, 80, 111, 127, 138

Antigone, see Sophocles

Antipodes, {iv}282–3

Antoinette, Marie, {iv}589–90

Anton Francesco, *see* Grazzini, A.

Antonio, 'hotel boy', {vii}296

Aosta (Italy), {ii}184–5

Apache country, {iv}298, 300–3, 312

Apache Indian Reservation, {iv}298, 303, {vi}299

Apaches, {iv}296–7, 303, 309, 313, 432

Apennine Mountains (Italy), {ii}116, 120, 122, 124, 126–7, 156, {iii}450, {iv}84, {v}485, 548, 563–5, 630, 633

Aphrodite, {i}94, {iii}38–9, 395, 496, 562

Apocalypse de Jean, L', see Loisy, A. F.

Apocalypse Unsealed, The, see Pryse, J. M.

'Apocalypse Unveiled, The', *see* Pryse, J. M., ;
see also Lawrence, D. H., *All Things Are Possible*

Apple Orchard, see La Condamine, R. C. de

Apuleius, *The Golden Ass*, {vi}262

'Aquarium', *see* Lowell, A.

Aquitania, R. M. S., {iv}20–1, 593–4, 596–600, {v}15

Arabella, *see* Yorke, D.

Arabia, {i}73, {ii}528, {iv}212

Arabian Nights, {i}310, {iii}414, {iv}7, 208–11, 213, 527, {vi}37

Arabian Sea, {iv}208, 213

Aran Isles, {iv}38

Archer, E., *see* Lahr, C.

Archer, Esther, *see* Lahr, E.

Archer, William, {i}112, {vi}49

Archipenko, Alexander, {iv}548

Architectural Review, The, {vii}4, 269, 295

ARCHITECTURE, 'curves in Greek', {ii}162–3; 'Painting is *not* architecture' and 'puerile' to pretend otherwise, {ii}263; nation is 'great architecture of living people', {ii}379; sculpture 'a part of', {iii}46

Archuleta, Rufina ('Lufina', 'Ruffian', 'Ruffina'), {v}8, 38, 233, 242, 244–6, 251, 254, 258–9, 507, 530, {vi}436
painting by Brett of, {v}42; DHL's names for, {v}49, 231, 510; 'short and fat and twenty, waddles like a duck', {v}239; ordered to leave by Frieda, {v}266, 268–9; 'a risky bit of goods', {v}510; cackles like a chicken, {vi}86; 'nasty', {vi}211, 255, 550

Archuleta, Trinidad, {v}8, 230–4, 242, 245 251, 254, 258, 264, 266, 491, {vi}436, 550
painting by Brett of, {v}42, {vi}233; 'chaste as a girl, with his two plaits', {v}239; drives the buggy, {v}244, 246, 249, 259, 268; sent away, {v}266, 269; cackles like a chicken, {vi}86; elopes with Agapeto Concha, {vi}211; singer and dancer, {vii}277

Ardnaree (Kandy, Ceylon), {iv}179–221 *passim*, 243, 266, 279

Ardours and Endurances, see Nichols, R. M. B.

Aretino, Pietro, {vii}141
I Ragionamenti, {vi}343

Arezzo (Italy), {vi}48, 75, 79, 88–9, 93, 182, 302, 317, 344, 508, 538, 566

Argegno (Italy), {iii}591, {iv}190, 195

Ariel Poems, see Faber & Faber

ARISTOCRACY, {ii}4, 12, {iv}10, 357
  miners' wives aristocrats 'to the backbone', {i}379; Frieda delighted by
  contact with English, {ii}51; 'life itself
  is an affair of', {ii}254; the'new-born'
  will be 'aristocrats, and as wise as the
  serpent in dealing with the mob',
  {ii}273; 'aristocracy of people who have
  wisdom' essential, {ii}364; political
  system must include 'elected', {ii}371;
  aristocrats and plebeians exist, 'born,
  not made', {ii}379; as 'pernicious' as
  democracy but 'much more dead',
  {ii}593; 'what good are the aristocrats'
  having 'sold the vital principle of life to
  the mere current of foul affairs',
  {iii}118; Sicily always ruled by 'foreign
  incoming', {iii}517; DHL believes in
  'divine right of natural', {iv}226;
  owners of 'big shops' are Australian,
  {iv}249; Socialists more than aristocrats
  dislike *Pansies*, {vii}451
Aristophanes, {i}525
Arizona (USA), {iv}142, 294, 362, {vi}282
  Hopi Snake Dance in, {v}5, 82, 98–101,
  109, 132, 150
Arkansas (USA), {vii}395
Arlen, Michael, *see* Kouyoumdjian, D.
Arles (France), {iv}565, 568
Armitage (Staffordshire), {i}64
Army, the, {i}168, 194, 215, 356, 384, 391,
  416, {ii}21, 153, 184, 206, 218, 240–1,
  377, 384, 388, 403, 527, 599, 602, 628,
  {iii}28, 60, 61, 91, 129, 291, 294, {iv}76,
  133, 229 {v}459, {vi}131, 226, {vii}383,
  460
  DHL might be 'hooked into, {ii}614; his
  hatred of medical examinations by,
  {iii}1, 136, 286–9; medical examination
  for, {iii}130–2, 135, 250, 279 279, 281,
  283–4; DHL wouldn't 'do anything for',
  {iii}135; ordered out of Cornwall by
  police and Army Command, {iii}168–9,
  175, 189, 281
  see also Military Service Act
Arne, *see* Garborg, A.
Arno river (Italy), {iii}419–24, 602,
  {iv}83–4, (v)443, 448, 453, 564, 582,

585, 643–5, {vi}75, 111, {vii}181, 465,
  478, {viii}46
Arno Vale Farm (Nottingham), {i}500
Arnold, Matthew, {ii}12
Arnold, Sir Edwin, *The Light of Asia*, {i}5,
  46, 256
Arrowsmith, see Lewis, S
Arroyo Hondo (New Mexico), {v}82, 248,
  283
Arroyo Seco (New Mexico), {v}82
Art, see Bell, A. C. H.
Art and Progress, {vii}503
Art and Ritual, see Harrison, J.
Art Chronicle, The, {ii}46
Art et Décoration, {vii}503
Art News, {iii}129
Art Nonsense, see Gill E.
ART/ARTISTS, 'artistic principles and
  such-like jargon', {i}44; 'Art and the
  Individual', {i}53, 55, 63, 66, 72; *'feeling'*
  essence of, {i}99; Gissing on, {i}107;
  Hueffer's story has 'more art than life',
  {i}141; DHL envies Rachel Annand
  Taylor's art, {i}179; verses 'fingered by
  art into a grace the experience does not
  warrant', {i}187; *Trespasser* 'execrable
  bad art', {i}229; 'most folk are artists
  where their own ends are concerned',
  {i}242; Meredith's *Tragic Comedians*
  clever but 'not a work of art, too turgid',
  {i}250; Garnett on DHL's 'creative art',
  {i}324; 'erotic literature must be in the
  form of high art' (Hueffer), {i}330, 339;
  Trespasser must be 'work of art' though
  false to fact, {i}359; 'literature..the
  glorious Art..preys upon the marrow in
  our bones', {i}417; 'art..seems like
  grammar' (Frieda), {i}479; DHL's
  'motto..Art for my sake', {i}491; for
  Collings to fear 'female element..not
  good for [his] art, {i}503; Middleton
  unfair about 'women and art', {ii}97; art
  of some poets is 'of self hate and self-
  murder', {ii}101; Tolstoy's *Kreutzer
  Sonata* true to experience 'but not art',
  {ii}114; necessary 'to fuse ones physical
  and mental self right down, to produce
  good art', {ii}115; Whitman 'neither art

nor religion nor truth', {ii}130; men and women drawing closer to one another the only way to re-vivify art, {ii}181; Van Gogh on, {ii}298; 'each work of art..must give expression to the great collective experience, not to the individual', {ii}301; 'art..is indirect and ultimate', {ii}391; Masters' poetry 'always stated, not really art', {ii}503; 'conveyors of art' (like Heseltine) next in importance to artists, {ii}540, 549; Dostoevsky's novels 'great parables..but false art', {ii}544; work of art is 'act of faith', {ii}593, 602; opposition of 'life stubborn against death' creates 'the pure resultant, absolved, art', {ii}638; 'the great articulate extremity of art' in Gertler's *Merry-Go-Round*, {ii}660–1; people want 'senses gratified in art', {iii}20; USA more developed in 'decadence and non-emotional aestheticism', {iii}30; futuristic art expresses 'pure sensation *without concepts*', {iii}31; direct experience must be re-created into art otherwise life itself vulgarised, {iii}35; best English art 'the subtlest and loveliest and most perfect in the world', {iii}41; 'Yankee "art"..contains the spirit of puerile self-magnification', {iii}141; artist must be 'free soul', {iii}281; society 'coldly indifferent' to artist, {iii}325–6; DHL asks if 'colony of rather dreadful sub-arty people' in Taos, {iv}111, 324; obscure style 'befits the magic art', {iv}556; 'artists - writers - ..only people..capable of imaginative international understanding', {v}88; DHL doesn't 'care a button for neat works of art', {v}200; 'I can't bear art that you can walk round and admire..I hate the actor and audience business', {v}201; artists 'most lively hating one another', {v}273; 'pretty sound attitude to art' in Barnes Foundation, {v}296; 'art always gilds the pill', {v}423; DHL sickened by artists 'who make art out of antipathy to life', {v}627; world needs 'a few courageous artists', {vi}327; 'art has

to reveal the palpitating moment or the state of man as it is', {vi}600; 'all art is *au fond* symbolic, conscious or unconscious', {vii}476; *White Peacock* 'sins against almost every canon of art' (Hueffer), {viii}3; essential qualities for child's book on art, {viii}41

Arthur, King, {ii}492, 495–6, 498, 505, 507, {viii}44

Artsybashev, Mikhail Petrovich, {ii}247
    Sanine, {ii}33, 70

Arzapalo Hotel (Chapala), {iv}436, 467, 473, 511

As You Like It, see Shakespeare, W.

Ascona (Switzerland), {iv}39, {vi}207, 213

ASHBY, CAROLINE MAY, {vi}101
    illustration for *Etruscan Places* sought from, {viii}104
    Letters to {viii}104–5

Ashby, Thomas, {vi}101
    Forty Drawings of Roman Scenes by British Artists, {vi}105, {viii}104–5

Ashdown Forest (Sussex), {i}526, 538

Ashenden, or the British Agent, see Maugham, W. S.

Ashwell, Lena, {ii}17, 201

Asia, {iii}488, {iv}586, {v}75

Asolo (Italy), {iv}189

Aspects of the Novel, see Forster, E. M.

Asquith, Elizabeth, *see* Bibesco, E.

Asquith, Herbert ('Beb'), {ii}54, 63–4, 89, 93, 129, 336, 386, 419–20, 438, 453, 527, 587, {iii}91, 518, {iv}32, 34, 235, {v}190, {vi}71
    DHL meets, {ii}36, 48, 49; paucity of work as barrister, {ii}109; enlists, {ii}267, 287; slightly wounded but 'spell-bound' by war, {ii}359–60, 376; on sick-leave, {ii}400, 405; visits DHL, {ii}435; concussed, {ii}443, 466; DHL seeks advice and friendship from, {ii}600–1; DHL asks for poems by, {iii}27, 33; a poet but deadened by tradition, {iii}38; recovered in physical health, {iii}157, 201, 265; *Lost Girl* sent to, {iii}617; works with publishers, Hutchinson, {iv}32, 36, 354; lunch with, {v}324; might care for *LCL*, {vi}358–9

Asquith, Herbert ('Beb') *(cont.)*
  Poems 1912–1933, {ii}41;
  The Volunteer and Other Poems, {ii}487,
  {iii}27, 33, 38
Asquith, John, {ii}339, 386, 527, {iii}91,
  {iv}34
  'fat and smiling', {ii}63; 'Manly', {ii}64;
  'the jonquil', {ii}89; "don John',
  {ii}129; DHL theorises about autistic
  condition of, {ii}335–7, 438, {iii}118,
  201
Asquith, Katherine, {ii}363, 368, 398,
  {iii}177
ASQUITH, LADY CYNTHIA, {ii}2–4, 12,
  16–17, 61 178, 195, 205, 353–4, 363, 372,
  435, 443, 450, 453, 535, {iii}1, 3, 12, 14,
  51, 226, 318, {iv}2, 7, 36, {vi}10
  DHL meets, {ii}36, 41, 48, 51–2, 54, 62;
  epistolary style to, {ii}106; her second
  child, {ii}198; 'wearies' DHL 'a bit',
  {ii}289: DHL offers theoretical advice
  about son John, {ii}335–8, {iii}118, 201;
  'a nature hard and sad as rock', {ii}339;
  unhappy at husband's absorption by war,
  {ii}359–60; 'hard, stoic, elemental sense
  of logic and truth' is 'real beauty' of,
  {ii}368; DHL's soul 'fizzing savagely'
  despite rebuke from, {ii}385; subscribes
  to *Signature*, {ii}398, 405, 411–12;
  brothers killed in action, {ii}414–15,
  649; helps DHL over passports,
  {ii}418–20, 431; model for character in
  'The Thimble', {ii}420, {iii}50; lectured
  on love and war, {ii}424–5; an 'over-
  loose letter' to, {ii}432; urged to join
  DHL in USA, {ii}437–8; perhaps does
  care about 'the difference between life
  and death', {ii}455; DHL wants help
  with Foreign Office from, {ii}466;
  'queer, absolved relationship' between
  Lawrences and, {ii}527; DHL seeks
  advice about military service, {ii}600,
  606–7; DHL differs on subject of war
  with, {iii}32–3; challenged on issue of
  peace and war, {iii}38–40; DHL offers
  to dedicate collection of poems to,
  {iii}49–50, 221, 227, 234; DHL seeks
  dedicatee for *W in L*, {iii}55, 220; DHL

seeks help from over passports to USA,
  {iii}69–70, 77, 90; DHL fears letters
  found 'something ridiculous' by, {iii}91;
  urged to stick by 'own soul, and nothing
  else', {iii}118; offers to help over
  expulsion from Cornwall, {iii}170, 172,
  177, 186, 188, 207; DHL dreams about,
  {iii}195, 247–8, 333; sends £5, {iii}217;
  Bay dedicated to, {iii}234, 237, 242, 248,
  287, 366, 395, 462, 465, 494; helps with
  application to Royal Literary Fund,
  {iii}265; becomes secretary to Barrie,
  {iii}272, 287, {iv}34, 312 353; *T and G*
  shown to, {iii}301, 305, 311, 315, 333;
  pregnant, {iii}333, 336, 358–9, 366; son
  born, {iii}389, 394–5; ill and depressed,
  {iii}370, 429; *S and S* for, {iv}193, 207,
  235; authorship, {iv}353, {v}324; sense
  of failure in, {v}324, 332; encouraged to
  buy *LCL*, {vi}358, 360
  The Black Cap, {v}590, 613, 631, 636,
  647, 654, {vi}21, 29, 71, 347, {vii}507;
  The Flying Carpet, {v}324;
  The Ghost Book, {v}339, 341, 360, 385,
  388, 400, 415, 424–5, 449, 590, 599, 631,
  {vi}140, {vii}445, 507;
  'The Woman's View', {iv}353
  Letters to {ii}62–4, 88–9, 106–9, 128–9,
  267–9, 286–7, 334–8, 367–9, 375–6,
  378–81, 385–6, 397–400, 405, 411–12,
  414–15, 418–19, 420–5, 431–2, 436–8,
  454–5, 465–7, 475, 486–7, 491, 526–7,
  573–4, 587, 600–1, 606–7, 648–9,
  {iii}26–7, 32–3, 38–40, 49–50, 55,
  69–70, 90–1, 117–19, 132–3, 157–8, 168,
  176–7, 182–3, 186–8, 195, 201–2, 206–7,
  211, 217, 219–21, 227–8, 234, 237–8,
  241–2, 247–8, 252–3, 264–5, 272, 282–3,
  287–8, 293–4, 305, 311, 333, 358–9, 368,
  389, 394–6, 417–18, 429, 447, 461–3,
  494, 517–18, {iv}32–4, 207, 233–5, 284,
  353–4, 424, 570, {v}189–90, 339, 424–5,
  {vi}71, 358–9
Asquith, Margaret ('Margot'), {ii}487,
  {iii}33
Asquith, Michael, {ii}198, 338, 339, 372,
  438, 527, {iii}91, 293, 359, 370, {iv}34
Asquith, Raymond, {ii}363, {iii}177

Asquith, Rt. Hon. Herbert Henry {ii}41, 48–9, 363, 453, 487, {iii}26, {iv}32 Prime Minister in Coalition Government, {ii}342, 379; introduces conscription, {ii}495; issues terms for peace, {ii}557; 'derelict', {ii}612; 'his real *decency*', {iii}39, 46–8

Asquith, Simon Anthony Roland, {iii}359, 389, 394, {iv}34

Asquith, Violet, *see* Bonham Carter, V.

Assisi (Italy), {iii}712, 721, 730, {v}410, 413–14, 421, {vi}75, 250, 262 DHL impressed by, {v}426; 'didn't even like', {v}441; 'too museumish', {v}442

At the Harlot's Burial: Poems, see Powys L.

Atalanta in Calydon, see Swinburne, A. C.

Atenasios, Ciccio, {iv}101, {viii}48

Athena, {i}550, {vi}96

Athenæum, The, {iii}349, 387, 407, {v}87 Weekley favourably reviewed in, {i}384; *Trespasser* reviewed in, {i}415, 420; 'Whistling of Birds' in, {iii}100, {v}103–4; Murry edits, {iii}321,332, 335, 344; DHL invited to contribute to, {iii}335–7, 346, 350; 'the messiest' of 'all the wet and be-snivelled rags', {iii}350 *see also Nation and Athenæum*

Athens (Greece), {i}29, {ii}320, {v}484, 519, 530, 560–1, 573, 613, {vii}506, 508

Atherton, Constance Crowninshield Coolidge, *see* Jumilhac, Comtesse de

Athos, see Byron, R.

Atina (Italy), {iii}432–3, 442

Atkin, Dorothy, {vii}127

ATKINS (AIKEN), ROBERT, expected to produce *David*, {v}524, 529, 543, 555, {viii}96–7; DHL sends music for play to, {v}557; 'funked' *David*, {v}576–7, {vi}26, {viii}98 *Letters to* {v}557

ATKINSON, FREDERICK MACCURDY, Heinemann's reader for *White Peacock*, {i}152; literary taste of, {i}162, 222; asked DHL to name novel, {i}166–7, 169; copies of *White Peacock* from, {i}220–2; *Trespasser* submitted to, {i}229–30; return of *Trespasser* request-ed from, {i}240, 339; DHL hates,

{i}310, 348, 355; ignores DHL's poems, {i}340; 'very warm about the poetry', {i}442 *Letters to* {i}162–3, 166–7, 169–70, 220–2, 229–30, 240–1

Atlantic Monthly, The, {iii}401, 405, 644, {v}521, 542, {vii}28, 496

Atlantic Ocean, {ii}223, 612, 651, {iii}13, 565, {iv}7, 95, 177, 462, 559, {v}167, 211, {vi}553, {vii}96, 263 'all peacock-mingled colours', {ii}550; 'an unsympathetic ocean,' {v}305; 'good crossing of', {v}307

Atlixco (Mexico), {iv}425

Attila, {i}114

Aucassin and Nicolette, {i}213, {viii}5

Augsburg (Germany), {iv}73, {vi}144–6

Augustan Books of English Poetry, {v}2, 521, 626, {vi}305, 464

Augustine, St, (i)38, {ii}572

Aulla (Italy), {ii}116, 120, 126–9, 172–3, 178, {vi}371

Aunt Ada, *see* Krenkow, A.

Aunt Barbara, *see* Low, B.

Aunt Perdy, *see* Carswell, C.

Auserlesene Griechische Vasenbilder, see Gerhard, E.

Austen, Jane, {ii}188

Austin, Mary, {iii}654, 657, {v}280

Australia, {i}44, 48, 69, 324, 499, {ii}208, 321, {iv}1, 9–12, 199, 213, 218, 220–34, 248, 294–5, 313, 319, 387, {v}67, 71, 95, 113–14, 171, {vii}66, 74, 117, 180, {viii}54, 78 'new country, new morals . . . new nation', {i}425; 'I'm doubting if I shall be long in', {iv}235; *too* new...too vast', {iv}238; '*so* democratic', {iv}239, 263; 'strange and empty and *unready*', {iv}240, 249; 'doubt if I shall ever like', {iv}245; 'liberty gone senile' in, {iv}246, 251; 'hateful newness, the democratic conceit', {iv}247, 260; people 'crude in their feelings', {iv}249–50; DHL feels 'awfully foreign' in, {iv}253, 256; as a country 'awfully nice', {iv}254; writing 'weird novel of', {iv}255, 257–9; DHL incognito in, {iv}259, 262, 269, 275, 280;

Australia (*cont.*)
     'weird country...humanly non-existent',
         {iv}, 261, 271–3; afraid of Japanese,
         {iv}263; 'I *can not* bear it', {iv}268; 'no
         inside life of any sort', {iv}271; 'weird
         and wonderful fascination' of,
         {iv}279–80; dark, 'sad country, under-
         neath – like an abyss', {iv}282; contin-
         ued influence of, {iv}303; sales of
         Aaron's Rod in, {iv}316; question of
         apology over *Kangaroo* to, {iv}323;
         publication of *Kangaroo*, {iv}428, {v}20;
         'new public' for DHL in, {v}161, 184;
         Kangaroo not last word on, {vii}322;
         mimosa flowers recall, {vii}646
         see also New South Wales; Western
         Australia
Austria, {ii}373, {iv}36, 44–52, 54–60,
         {vi}97–137 *passim*, {vi}220, 553,
         {vii}415, 504, 512, 623, {viii}44,
         104–5
     DHL longs for peace in, {i}430; train
         waits for DHL in, {i}456; wants to
         separate from Germany, {iii}116; made
         attractive by exchange rate, {iii}721,
         {iv}67; DHL arrives in, {iv}53, {vi}122;
         happy in, {iv}71; not sorry to leave,
         {iv}74; Catholic Church politically
         active in, {iv}124, 133; DHL depressed
         in, {iv}189; 'Captain's Doll' and,
         {iv}398; poor but happy-go-lucky,
         {vi}127, 136; 'centre of a vital vacuum',
         {vi}136; Germany more cheerful than,
         {vi}141–3; 'awful', {vi}182
         see also Bad Fusch; Tyrol
Author, The, see Society of Authors
Authors Society, *see* Society of Authors
Authors' Publishing Company, {vi}322, 342
Autobiography, see Gibbon E.
Autobiography of Countess Sophie Tolstoi, The,
     see Tolstoy, S.
AUTOBIOGRAPHY/BIOGRAPHY,
     'awful..to write a biography of my
     mother', {i}195; DHL can write 'Burns
     Novel' 'almost like an autobiography',
     {i}487; 'my novel - *S and L* - autobiog-
     raphy', {i}490; biographical note for
     Kennerley, {ii}26; (spiritual) 'autobiog-

raphy' for Cynthia Asquith, {ii}269;
     Maria Chambers advised to write
     autobiography not fiction, {vi}296, 418;
     'I ..can't write biographical facts about
     myself', {vi}391; reluctantly writes
     autobiographical sketch, {vi}465
Avernus, Lake (Italy), {i}529
Avignon (France), {iv}565, {vii}245
Avon, River (Hampshire), {i}349
Aylesbury (Buckinghamshire), {viii}13
Aylwin, Robert Henry, {i}194, 246, 250, 355,
         368, 407, 465, 552, {ii}91, {v}640
     'afraid to risk himself', {i}418; leaves
         Davidson Road School, {i}524; enlists,
         {iii}61
Azores, {iii}673, 678, {v}299
Azrael, {vi}169
Aztecs, {iv}310, 431, 541, {v}174
     DHL fascinated by, {v}125; does not
         like 'gruesome' carvings of, {iv}416;
         wonderful feather-work of, {iv}509;
         fertility ritual, {iv}527; DHL studies
         religion of, {v}7; god of war, {v}160;
         'cloud-tower' motif of, {vi}404
Azul (horse), {v}50, 149, 159, 164, 182, 212,
         218, 234, 296, 299, 425, 466, 478, 492,
         504, 531, 537
     Frieda's grey horse, {v}59, 111, 114,
         191, {vi}212, {vii}475; Frieda proud of,
         {v}62; DHL dreams of, {v}453; runs
         away, {v}477, 480

Bab-el-Mandeb, Straits of, {iv}212
Babe Unborn, A, see Oldmeadow, E. J.
Babylon, {ii}528, 660–1, {vii}507, 545, 547
Bacchae, see Euripides
Bacchelli, Riccardo, *Lo Sa il Tonno*, 'utter
     boredom' of, {v}562–3; 'silly book',
     {vi}295, 305
Bach, Johann Sebastian, {i}324, {iii}514,
     {vi}353
Bacon, Francis, {i}5, 321
Bad End, A, see Gerhardie, W. A.
Bad Fusch (Austria), {iv}56
Baddeley, Angela, {v}8, {viii}103
     'acted very, very well' as Michal, {vi}66
Baden, Grand Duchess Louise of, {iii}571

Baden, Grand Duke Frederick of, {iii}571

Baden-Baden (Germany), {ii}72, 184–6, {iii}344, 420, 422–3, 441, 452, 539, 579, 581, 603, 703–33 *passim*, {iv}23–52 *passim*, 56–7, 78, 561–88 *passim*, {v}266, 282, 313–14, 321–36 *passim*, 450, 465, 468–503 *passim*, 542, {vi}142–4, 151, 155, 158–92 *passim*, 398, 473–513 *passim*, 527, 529, 553–7, 562–7, {vii}241, 359–76 *passim*, 460–1, 464, 466, 474, 478–9, {viii} 43–4, 81, 83, 105–6 Frieda's parents' home, {i}542, {ii}19, 52, 61, 67, 70, 74–6, 88, 175, 177, 179; her mother's home, {iii}311, 331, 370, 392, 413, 435, 505, 571, 587–9, 601, 542, 714, {iv}132, 161–2, 238, {v}9, 277–8, 304, 366, {vi}104; Frieda's mother ill in, {iii}678–702 *passim*; severe shortages in, {iii}450, 620–1; DHL in, {iii}706, {iv}572, {v}494, {vi}173, 571–83, {vii}377–449; DHL moves to inn nearby, {iii}710; 'a lovely little town', {iii}710; Frieda going to, {iv}479, 488, 531, {v}417, 427–8, 651–7, {vi}30, 44, 301–11, 426–39, {vii}208–16, 227, 356; 'departed grandeur' of, {v}329, {vi}184; DHL fond of, {v}489; DHL takes 'inhalation cure' in, {vi}177ff, 221; his memories of, {vi}207; 'easy to loaf in', {vi}538; DHL 'not very keen on', {vii}366; 'had enough of', {vii}431; 'no place for a man', {vii}611

Bader, Fräulein, {iv}72, 120, 122, 135–6

Baedeker, {i}322, {iii}45, 481, 499, 622, {iv}195, {v}243, {vii}183 DHL loves 'its plans and maps and panoramas', {iii}35 *Southern France*, {vi}537

Bagh Caves in the Gwalior State, The, see Marshall, Sir J. H.

Bailabhadan (Newtonmore), {v}474, 506–12, 517

Baillot, Marie Juliette ('Cendrella'), *see* Huxley (Lady), M. J.

Baillot, Mélanie Antonia, {vi}311, 314, 316, 345, 373–5, 386, 460, {vii}79, 104

Bain, Francis William, {v}180

Baker, Harold Trevor, {ii}369, 398

Baker, Ida Constance, {iii}301

BAKER, JACOB, {vi}527, 538, 568, 572, {vii}35 'a twisty customer', {vi}539 *Letters to* {viii}115

Baker, Karle Wilson, {ii}232

Bakewell (Derbyshire), {i}24, 259, 368

Balaam's Ass, {iv}177, 180–1, 479

Baldwin, *see* Bowdwin, Mr

Baldwin, Stanley, {vii}325 'mealy-mouthed' nonentity, {vii}327

Bale, Edwin, {ii}384

Balestri, *see* Pensione Balestri

Balfour, Arthur James, {ii}91, 399, {iii}260 DHL due to meet, {ii}402; 'old poodle', {iii}118; 'hopeless', {iii}283 'Creative Evolution and Philosophic Doubt', {i}359, {ii}398

Balfour, Hilda ('Bal'), {vi}22

Balkan War, {i}473, 475

'Ball, Thomas', possible nom de plume for DHL, {iii}381

Ballantyne, Robert Michael, {ii}588 *Ungava*, {iii}340

Baltic (USA), {iii}659, 668, 672

Balzac, Honoré de, {i}59, 96, 98, {v}642, 646, {vi}37, 68 *The Atheist's Mass*, {i}98; *Les Contes Drolatiques*, {iv}40, 151; *Le Cousin Pons*, {iii}38; *Eugénie Grandet*, {i}89, 91–2, 99, 102; *Old Goriot*, {i}98; *Wild Ass's Skin*, {i}98

Banca Commerciale, {iv}89

Banca di Sconto, {iii}497 fails, {iv}156–7, 160, 162, 179, 203, 312

Bandelier, Adolph Francis Alphonse, *The Delight Makers*, {v}42

Bandelli family, {vi}361, 392

Bandelli, Dino, {vi}243, 251

Bandello, Matteo, {vii}21–2, 141

Bandinelli, Bartolommeo, {vi}79

Bandol (France), {vi}608–11, {vii}18, 20, 31, 48, 67, 104, 643 'little place on the coast', {vi}615; 'very pretty', {vii}22, 46; 'everybody spells it wrong', {vii}65, 184; dull but friendly,

Bandol (France) (*cont.*)
{vii}87, 585; DHL ready to leave,
{vii}169; philharmonic concert in,
{vii}171; palm trees frozen in, {vii}185,
501; DHL feels well and content in,
{vii}203, 230, 379, 453, 482; DHL
leaving, {vii}205, 209; returning to,
{vii}480–6, 500; 'sun shines and the sea
sparkles' at, {vii}552, 605; 'not much
help', {vii}633; almond blossom lovely
around, {vii}646
Banfield, Mr, {ii}631, 648, 652
Bank of California, {iv}501
Bank of Hong Kong, {iv}227
Bank of India, {iv}221
Bannerman, John Sholto, *see* Carswell, C.
Barbara, *see* Low, B.
Barber, Walker and Co., {i}9, 82
Barbusse, Henri, founder-member of Clarté,
{iii}5, 379; link with Goldring, {iii}441,
467, 483; link with Seltzers, {iii}467, 662
Le Feu, {iii}483
'Barby', *see* Weekley, B.
Barca, Frances Erskine Calderón de la, *Life in
Mexico*, {iv}449
Barcelona (Spain), {vi}65, {vii}53–4, 86,
205, 242–3, 252, 246–55 *passim*, 275,
284, 286, 291–2, 523, 536
DHL going to, {vii}195, 234, 238; DHL
arrives in, {vii}249; described,
{vii}250–1; revolution in, {vii}265, 267;
international exhibition in, {vii}334
Barclay, Florence Louisa, *The Rosary*,
{ii}285
Barclay, R. A., {vii}12, 582
Barezzi, Giuseppe ('Joseph'), general
factotum on Ile de Port-Cros, {vi}18,
590, 592–3, 596, 599, 604, 614, {vii}152,
183
Baring, Maurice, DHL reviews *Comfortless
Memory* by, {vi}463
Baring-Gould, Sabine, {v}634
Barjansky, Alexander, {iii}514
Barker, *see* Granville-Barker, H.
Barker, Misses, {vi}498, 506, 510
Barker, Mrs, {i}342
Barlow, Alpha, {iv}90, 108, {v}419, 421,
{vi}24, 124

BARLOW, ROBERT PRATT, {iv}8, 218
Letters to {iv}218–19
Barmby, Arthur William, {v}21, 26, 31–2,
45, 58, 105, 149, 161,165, 179, 193, 207,
211, 243–4, 317, 329, 333, 342–3, 361,
370, 393, 435, 509, 636, 654, {vi}29, 31,
40, 48, {vii}375
manager of Curtis Brown, New York,
{iv}597, {v}2, 33, 186, 188, 241, 304,
308, 458; 'decent and reliable',
{v}16–17; DHL gets on well with,
{v}19, {vii}439, 463; responsible for
DHL's MSS in USA, {v}127–8, 255;
dislikes 'Quetzalcoatl' as title, {v}250; in
England, {v}268, 271; leaves Curtis
Brown, N.Y., {vi}222, {vii}27
Letters from {v}128
Barmouth (Wales), {i}59, 281
Barnes Foundation, {v}295–6
Barnes, Dr Albert Coombs, {v}296
Barnes, James Thomas Strachey, {ii}154, 195
'rum chap', {ii}91; has appendicitis,
{ii}119, 131; visits DHL in Lerici,
{ii}136, 142
Barnes, Miss, {v}331
Barnes, William, dialect in his poetry,
{viii}15
Baroja y Nessi, Pio, *César o Nada*, {iv}452
Barrie, Sir James Matthew, {ii}208, 213,
{iii}28,77, 449, 575, 678, {v}141,
{vi}276, {viii}13
DHL writes to, {ii}120, 128, 195; praises
S and L, {ii}224–5; Cynthia Asquith
secretary to, {iii}272, 287, 293, {iv}32,
312, 353, {vi}358; a 'commercial
proposition', {iii}547; might approve of
W in L, {iii}693; deaths of friends of,
{iv}48; a 'suburbanian', {v}94; pornographic, {vii}503; good on Scottish life,
{viii}19
Dear Brutus, {iii}188;
Little Mary, {i}60;
Sentimental Tommy, {i}175, {viii}19;
A Window in Thrums, {viii}19
Barrow-in-Furness (Lancashire), {i}131–3,
172, {ii}204–5, {iii}228
when war declared DHL at, {ii}268,
276, {v}355

Barth, Arthur, J., {vi}158
Basel (Switzerland), {i}465, {ii}74–7,
  {iii}523, 698, {iv}78, {vi}108, 556, 562,
  {vi}564, {vii}377
Bastia (Corsica), {vii}184
Bastien-Lepage, Jules, paintings 'sad',
  'haunting', {i}113, 116, 120–1, 124
  Pauvre Fauvette, {i}113, 116, 120
Bates, Henry W., *The Naturalist on the
  Amazon*, {iii}315, 317, 340
'Bath', *see* Lowell, A.
Bathers, The, see Gertler, M.
Batouala, see Maran, R.
Baudelaire, Charles, {i}5, 179, {ii}101,
  {vi}342
  Fleurs du Mal, {i}179, {iii}679
  see also Huxley, A.
Bavaria (Germany), {i}411, 428, 464, 542,
  {ii}29, 42, 47, 84, {iii}311, 314–48
  passim, 459, 711–12, 728, {v}499–503,
  512, 526, 635, {vi}38, 43, 46, 55–6, 67,
  70–2, 86, 100, 122–8, 171, 221, 282, 286,
  350, {vii}74, 355, 363–6, 375, 391–6,
  422–3, 433–40, {viii}6
  villages and flowers of, {i}415; shrines,
  {i}417; tidy, {i}547; humid and moun-
  tainous, {i}552; DHL happy to be in,
  {ii}59; beauty of highlands in, {ii}65;
  DHL prefers to England, {ii}173; DHL
  in highlands of, {vi}139–68; in mountains of Upper, {vii}449–80
Bavarian Tyrol, *see* Tyrol
Bax, (Sir) Arnold, {ii}548
BAX, CLIFFORD, {ii}407, {iii}368
  attitude to DHL, {iii}542
  Twenty Chinese Poems, Paraphrased,
  {i}405
  Letters to {iii}368
Bay of Biscay, {iv}249
Bayard, Pierre du Terrail, {i}114
Bayly, Thomas Haynes, {i}48
Baynes, Bridget, {iii}416, 432, 449, 463, 488,
  521, 542, 623, 642, 677, {iv}66–7,
  189–190
Baynes, Chlöe, {iii}416, 432, 449, 463, 488,
  521, 542, 623, 642, 677, {iv}67, 189
BAYNES, HELTON GODWIN, {i}475,
  {ii}322, {iii}377, 385, 414, 521, 542,

  {v}475, {vi}440
  marriage breakdown, {iii}412; separated
  from wife, {iii}463; divorce proceedings,
  {iii}478, 488, 677; Jung's assistant,
  {iii}623; divorced, {iv}66–7; remarried,
  {iv}189
  Letters to, {iii}478
Baynes, Jennifer Nan, {iii}416, 432, 449, 463,
  488, 521, 542, 623, 642, 677, {iv}67, 189
BAYNES, ROSALIND, {iii}393, 422, 449,
  633, 649, {iv}3, 7, 193
  DHL first meets, {i}475; house loaned
  by, {iii}382–3; marriage breakdown,
  {iii}412, 478; DHL's travel instructions
  for, {iii}414–16, 423–4, 431–2,
  {iv}189–90; DHL worried for, {iii}463;
  divorce proceedings against, {iii}488;
  DHL wants to meet, {iii}520–1, 585;
  DHL stays with, {iii}602–3; divorced,
  {iv}66; marries A. E. Popham, {v}475
  see also Popham, R.
  Letters to {iii}377–8, 413–16, 423–4, 431–2,
  487–8, 520–1, 542, 574–5, 585, 604, 609,
  622–3, 641–2, 676–7 {iv}66–7, 189–90,
  202, 213, 223, 230, 532
Baynes, Ruth, {ii}322
BBC, {vi}7, 552
BEACH, SYLVIA WOODBRIDGE,
  {v}450, {vii}7, 58, 159, 177, 219, 229
  publishes *Ulysses*, {iv}19, 275, {v}457,
  {vi}545; famous Paris bookshop,
  {iv}569; DHL does not trust, {vi}489;
  DHL doesn't like, {vii}62, 64; 'absorbed
  in Joyce', {vii}67; is asked to sell *LCL*,
  {vii}75–7; buys two copies of *LCL*,
  {vii}90–1, 97–8, 134, 140, 142–3, 146,
  150, 153; declines to distribute Paris edn
  of *LCL*, {vii}109–10, 115, 118, 125, 131
  Letters to {vii}75, 89, 131–2
Beacon, The, {v}49–50
Beacroft, Thomas Alfred, {i}26
Beakbane, Ellen ('Nellie'), {iv}236, 558,
  {v}291, {vii}36–7
Beardsall, George, {ii}257–8
Beardsall, Maud, {v}530
Beardsley, Aubrey, {ii}157, {vi}169
  DHL hates illustrations to Dowson's
  Poems by, {ii}118

Bearne, Catherine Mary, {ii}68
Beasts, Men and Gods, see Ossendowski, F. A.
Beatrice, *see* Campbell, B.
Beau Séjour (Hotel, Taormina), {iv}138, 140, 143
Beau-Sejour (Hotel, Monaco) {vi}397, 417
Beauchamp, Leslie Heron, {ii}409, 481, 658
BEAUMONT, CYRIL WILLIAM, {iii}12, 338, {v}120
    edited and published *New Paths*, {iii}202, 263, {iv}31; considers publishing *W in L* but refuses, {iii}206–7, 212, 214, 216, 219–20; requests poems for publication, {iii}221, 229, 232, 234; publishes *Bay*, {iii}233, 237–8, 241–3, 246, 249, 261, 287, 331, 362, 366, 395, 462, 494, 547, 568, 595, {iv}429, {vi}167, {viii}28–9; omits dedication and some poems from *Bay*, {iii}465, 469; 'not very responsible', {iii}475, 487, 535; 'bewildered chicken', {iii}494; 'slip-shod imbecile', {iii}585–6
    First Score, {iii}465
    Letters to {iii}212, 218, 228, 233, 237, 241, 263, 360–1, 365, 390, 429, 446, 465, 584–5, 592, 614, {iv}242, {vi}76, {viii}28–9
Beaumont, Francis, {iii}502
Beauvale (Nottinghamshire), {i}23; Abbey, {i}38, 68; Board School, {i}34, 386
Beaverbrook, Lord, *see* Aitken, W.
Beazley, H. K., & Co., {vi}514, 573, 603
    Letters from {vi}603
Beckenham (Kent), {i}77, {vii}193
Becker, Carl Heinrich, {vi}259
BECKER, CHARLOTTE,
    Letters to {viii}83
Becker, Lady Delphine Therese, {iii}417, {vii}262
Becker, Sir Walter Frederick, {iii}417, {vii}262
Becket, Edith Mary, {i}30–2, 49
Beckett, Lucy ('Lucile', 'Lucille') Katherine, {v}406, {vi}124, 211, 367, 435, 522
    Carcere convent, Assisi, and, {iii}712, 719; DHL wrote to, {vi}36; friend of Brewsters, {vi}435, 447

Beckett, Ralph William Ernest, 3rd Baron Grimthorpe, {v}651, 655, {vi}22–3, 43, {viii}100
Beckford, William, *Vathek*, {i}166
Bed of Feathers, see Davies, R.
Bed of Roses, A, see George, W. L.
Beddington-Behrens, (Sir) Edward, {vi}11, 375
'Bee, The', *see* Rolfe, B.
Beecham, (Sir) Thomas, {i}157, {iii}178
Beerbohm, Max, {v}18, 570, {vii}85
Beethoven, Ludwig Van, {i}279
    Letters, {vi}213–15, 217–8;
    'Pastoral Symphony', {i}101
Beeton, Isabella Mary, {vi}202
Belgium, {ii}69, 215, 325, 557, 604, 626, {vii}58, 110
Bell, Arthur Clive Heward, {ii}451, 612
    opposed prosecution of *Rainbow*, {ii}16; DHL likes but 'not deeply', {ii}435; 'very wearing', {v}651; no order for *LCL* from, {vi}11, 383; 'What a fool', {vii}125
    Art, {ii}435, {vii}117, 125
Bell, Enid, {v}18
Bell, Ethel, {v}18
Bell, John Keble, pseud. Keble Howard, *The Smiths of Surbiton*, {ii}670
Bell, Selma, *see* McElligott, S.
Bell, Vanessa, {ii}320, {vii}8
Bellagio (Italy), {vii}416
Bellingdon (Buckinghamshire), {ii}210–11, 213, 222, 231, 237, 241–2, 246, 252, 258, 260, {iii}209
Bellinzona (Switzerland), {ii}79, {iii}344, {viii}9
Belloc, Joseph Hilaire, {i}381, {ii}28, 226, {iv}134, {v}3, 570, {vii}85
    founded *The Eyewitness*, {i}379;
    'conceited', {ii}146; journalism in *Land and Water*, {ii}352–3
Beloved Stranger, see Bynner, H.W.
Belper (Derbyshire), {i}508
Bemax, {vii}286, 501
Benally (Bennerley), {i}206
Benares (India), {v}519, 561, 608, 613
Bendex, Daisy, {vi}512
Benét, William Rose, {iii}576, {iv}16

Benn, Ernest, *Augustan Books of English Poetry* series by, {v}521, {vi}305; DHL's *Glad Ghosts* in 'Yellow Books' series by, {v}2, 521, 523–4, 528, 535–6, 539, 543, 575, 596, 607, {v}626, {viii}100

Bennett, Enoch Arnold, {i}12, 16, 138, 318, {ii}417, {iii}27, 183, 573, {vii}85, 117, 206
  DHL hates 'resignation' of, {i}459; recommends DHL to Stage Society, {ii}127, 136; thinks highly of *Rainbow*, {ii}446–7, 479, {iii}692; DHL reluctant to write about, {iii}166; willing to contribute to DHL's income, {iii}205; DHL bitter about lack of support from, {iii}14, 213, 281; DHL ready to meet, {iii}289; self-regarding, {iii}316; anonymous gift to DHL from, {iii}472; 'sort of pig in clover', {vi}342; regarded DHL as 'strongest novelist writing today', {vi}438; 'journalist' and 'time-server', {viii}19; 'a cad', praises DHL in private not publicly, {viii}41
  Anna of the Five Towns, {i}459;
  Clayhanger, {i}456;
  The Old Wives' Tale, {i}142
  Letters from, {iii}205

Bennetto, R. M., {i}355, 368, 373

Benney, Mr, {iii}222
  DHL buys furniture from, {ii}585, 590, 631; sells furniture to, {iii}225, 314, 317, 320

Benson, (Sir) Francis (Frank) R., {i}149, 384, {ii}187

Beowulf, {ii}495

Ber, Mrs, {v}415

Béranger, Pierre Jean de, {i}5, {iii}136

Beresford, Aden Noel, {ii}641

BERESFORD, BEATRICE ('TRISSIE'), {ii}482, 484–5, 496, 521, 523, 525, 533, 541, 553, 641
  Letters to {ii}559–60

Beresford, John Tristram, {ii}496, 521, 525, 559

BERESFORD, JOHN DAVYS, {ii}13, 435, 472, 559, 631, {iii}166, 359
  house loaned to DHL by, {ii}482, 484–5, 487, 490, 494–7; DHL prefers the man

to his books, {ii}497; returning to his house {ii}519–21, 523–4, 525, 533, 541, 551–2; should ignore reviewers, {ii}560; little in common between DHL and, {iii}160; wrote to Royal Literary Fund on DHL's behalf, {iii}249; benefactor to DHL, {iii}309–10; DHL invites collaboration from, {iv}31
  The House in Demetrius Road, {ii}497;
  Howard and Son, {ii}640;
  These Lynnekers, {ii}560
  Letters to {ii}484–5, 495–6, 519–21, 525, 551–3, 640–1, {iii}309–10
  Letters from, {iii}249

BERGMAN, MRS,
  Letters to {iv}370

Bergson, Henri, {i}544

Berkshire, {i}242, 528, {ii}476, 478, 480–1, {iii}96, 356, {vii}529
  'a dozy country', {iv}98

Berlin (Germany), {i}395, 413, 514, {iii}5, 314, 331, 334, 505, 714, 730, {iv}52, 74–6, 91, 380, 383, 390, 595, {v}343, 469, 488–9, 491, 555, {vi}26, 98, 130, 137, 178, 204, 226, 238, 248, 259, 284, 302, 304, 338, 341, 417, 434, 524, 582, {vii}137, 141, 143, 255, 341, 383, 392, 507, 517, 535, 548, 572, 596, 604, 611

Berliner Tageblatt, {ii}609

Berman, Louis, *The Glands Regulating Personality*, {iv}243, 252, 265–6, 268–9

Bern(e) (Switzerland), {i}374, {ii}186, {iii}441, {vi}443, 473, 488

Bernadine, see Filippi, R.

Bernarda, *see* Villa Bernarda

Berne Convention, {vii}239–40, 323, 643

Berners, Lord (Gerald Tyrwhitt-Wilson), {v}12, 650
  'very nice...too rich: RollsRoycey', {v}491, 648

Bernhardt, Sarah, {iii}196
  in *La Dame aux Camelias* {i}5–6, 55–6; 'wonderful and terrible', {i}59

Berni, Francesco, {vii}433

BERRINGTON, ADRIAN {i}14
  Rose and Vine borrowed from, {i}185, 188–9
  Letters to {i}188–9

Berry, Hedley, {iii}291
BERRY, LETTICE ADA, {i}132, {iii}290
    Letters to {iii}290–1
'Berry, Matilda', *see* Mansfield, K.
Berry, Meta, {iv}332, 434
Berryman, Katie, {ii}624, 632, {iii}51, 66,
    181, 197, 200, 261
Berryman, Tom, {ii}624
Berryman, Willie, {iii}122
Bertie (Bertram), *see* Clarke, W. H.
Besançon (France), {vii}208
Besant, Annie, {iv}235, {vi}307
Besier, Rudolf, *Don*, {i}141, 143
Bessie, *see* Freeman, E. W.
Best British Stories, The, see O'Brien,
    E. J. H.
Best, Marshall Ayres, {vii}130
Bet, The, see Chekhov, A.
Bettina, *see* Humes, E.
Betts, Thomas, ('Tom'), {v}476
Betty, *see* Cottam, E. M.
Beuerberg (Germany), {i}18, 411–14,
    417–18, {vi}76, {vii}438
BEVERIDGE, ANNE MILLICENT,
    {v}12, 407, 412, 501, 578, 583, 599,
    653, {vi}11, 47, 62, 66, 82, 102, 371,
    {vii}453
    paints 'in a certain one-line modern
    Parissy way', {iii}671; portrait of DHL
    by, {iii}683, 686, 694–5, 701, {v}402–3;
    invites DHL to Scotland, {v}499,
    506–7; TS of 'Sun' sent to, {v}533;
    DHL sends Christmas present to,
    {v}598; in Villa la Massa, {v}616–17,
    643–6, {vi}39, 78, {viii}103; *Etruscan
    Places* essays sent to, {vi}93; on list for
    order-forms for *LCL*, {vi}334–5;
    WWRA sent to, {vi}396; *LCL* sent to,
    {vi}448; *Pansies* for, {vii}347; in
    Florence, {viii}107
    Letters to {v}473–4, 532–3, {viii}100–1, 103
BEVERIDGE, MARY, {v}12, 474, 517, 653
    DHL gives Christmas present to,
    {v}598; in Villa la Massa, {v}616–17,
    643, 645–6, {vi}93; returns to Scotland,
    {vi}39; in Florence, {vi}367, {viii}107;
    copy of *LCL* for, {vi}448
    Letters to {viii}100–1

Biagi, Guido, {vii}415, 432
Biarritz (France), {vi}608, {vii}558, 561, 571
BIART-BELLENS, GUSTAV,
    Letters to {ii}463
Bibbles, *see* Pips
Bibesco, Elizabeth, {ii}63, 453, {iii}220,
    {iv}495, {vii}303
BIBESCO, PRINCE ANTOINE, {ii}17, 63,
    629–30, {iii}12, 14, {vii}303
    proposes publication of *Rainbow* in Paris,
    {ii}453, 458, 462–4; 'rather nice...but
    not deep', {ii}462; unsympathetic to
    publication of *W in L*, {iii}220–1, 228,
    242; 'buffoon-prince' refuses financial
    support for DHL, {iii}315–18; 'Don't
    care for him much', {iv}495; orders copy
    of *LCL*, {vi}544
    Letters to {ii}458
BIBLE, THE, {i}75, 357, {ii}129, {iv}461,
    {v}74, 257, {vii}71, 560
    for DHL 'flesh and blood are the
    Scriptures', {i}244; truth established by
    comparing Gospel narratives, {i}475;
    Frieda reading, {i}506; among DHL's
    'books of reference', {iii}236; Joyce's
    prose pot-pourri of, {vi}507, {vii}7;
    Moffat translation of New Testament
    approved, {vii}550

    Allusions to/quotations from:
    Acts, {i}39, 341, {ii}248, {iv}57, 246,
    317, {v}322, {vi}308, {vii}309;
    1 Chronicles, {iii}98;
    1 Corinthians, {i}363, {ii}161, 347,
    {iv}250;
    Daniel, {ii}640, {vii}309, 411;
    Deuteronomy, {i}62, {iv}90, 290,
    {vii}556;
    Ecclesiastes, {i}301, {ii}62, 478, {v}262,
    496;
    Exodus, {i}82, 511, {iii}24, 46, 59, 133,
    214, {v}587, {vi}100, {viii}13;
    Ezekiel, {iii}93;
    Genesis, {i}98, 208, 450, {ii}9–10, 16,
    295, 330, 524, 627, 650, {iii}118, 143,
    207, {iv}90, 198, 365, 580, {v}52, 209,
    229, {vi}159, 307, 345;
    Hebrews, {iv}239;

Hezekiah, {iii}93;
Isaiah, {i}81, {iii}134, {iv}514, {v}157, {viii}24;
Jeremiah, {i}200, {iii}19, {vi}75;
Job, {i}232, {ii}247, {v}54, 629;
John, {ii}526, 658, {iii}97, 116, 124, 157, 176, {iv}491, {v}423, {vi}151;
Jonah, {iii}131, {iv}219, {vi}298 ;
Judges, {i}250, {ii}247, 312, 437, {iv}516, {v}495, {vi}283, {vii}79;
1 Kings, {ii}85, 219, 389, {iii}47, 481, {v}65;
2 Kings, {iii}93;
Lamentations, {i}200, 222;
Leviticus, {iii}53;
Luke, {i}47, 60, 73, 81, 188, 391, 449, {ii}107, 109, 271, 362, 544, 625, {iii}58, 80, 179, 339, 395, {iv}352, {v}456, 627, {vi}43, 304, {vii}106;
Mark, {i}86, 462, {ii}192, 274, 277, 318, 379, 592, {iii}39, 179, 341, {v}627, {vi}109, 132, 240;
Matthew, {i}51, 52, 62, 97, 119, 337, 340,394, 496, 536, 549, {ii}37, 92, 169, 223, 271, 277, 381, 404, 408, 414, 544, 571, 575, 600, 627, 638, 656, 662, {iii}34, 45, 72, 74, 84, 143, 158, 327, 394, 617, {iv}419, 494, 500, {v}94, 157, 291, 344, 368, 437, 490, 530, 638, {vi}241, 484, {vii}519, 574;
Numbers, {i}97, {iii}293, {iv}177, 516, 537, {vi}508, {vii}177, {viii}13;
1 Peter, {ii}594;
Philippians, {iii}595, 720;
Proverbs, {ii}616, {iii}321, 454;
Psalms, {i}86, 211,347, 357, 391, 395, 503, {ii}101, 125, 252, 660–1, {iii}42, 56, 92–3, 449, 475, 574, 621, 728, {iv}165, 250, 317, {v}157, 552, 557, 629, {vi}159, 283;
Revelation, {ii}10, 254, 390, {iii}70, 124, 395, {iv}19, 124, 460–1, 583, {vii}12, 456, 506, 508, 519, 524, 544, 555–6, 570, 599, 610, 613, 640;
Romans, {iii}145;
Ruth, {vi}87;
1 Samuel, {ii}105, {iv}317, 584, {vi}133, 344, {vii}189;

2 Samuel, {i}66, 100, {iii}98;
Song of Songs, {i}227, {ii}262, {v}629;
Zechariah, {i}76
Bibliography of the Writings of D. H. Lawrence, A, see McDonald, E. D.
Bibliography of the Writings of James Branch Cabell, A, see Holt, G.
Biblioteca Mundi, {iii}679–81, 715, {iv}117–18
Bickersteth, Edward Henry, {iii}366, {vi}148
'Biddie', *see* Campbell, B. C.
'Biddy', *see* Dunlop, M.D.L.
Bieda (Italy), {vi}89, 508, 566
Bierbaum, Otto Julius, *The Snake Charmer,* {iii}532
BIERSTADT, EDWARD HALE,
    Letters to {vi}83
Bigelow, Josephine Rotch, {vi}504, {vii}600, 604, 606–7
Bigham, Hon. Frank, {iii}177
Bill, *see* Holbrook, W.
Billing, Noel Pemberton, {iii}248
'Bim', *see* Wilkinson, F.
'Bimsey', *see* Pips
Bindo, *see* Medici, B. P. de
Bingham (Nottinghamshire), {i}357
'Bingham man', *see* Bigham, F.
'Binky', *see* Cannan, F.
Binyon, Laurence, {viii}15
Bird, Annie Florence, {i}32, 49
Bird, Mrs, {i}322
Birds and Beasts of the Greek Anthology, see Douglas, G. N.
BIRDS, DHL juggles with words and gets 'turtle dove out of a black saucepan', {i}87; composers 'mostly birds who sing up in the air', {i}101; child laughs 'like a blackbird in a bush', {i}102; friend 'mum as a sulky crow'..birds 'like black rags', {i}104; Jones paints 'like a bird pecking crumbs off the doorstep', {i}207; Louie Burrows 'dark dove - little pigeon of my breast', {i}219; Hueffer's 'dove-grey kindliness..hops forth a very rook among rooks', {i}227; 'three rooks strutting like mad old maids in black', {i}253; 'lightning beat about in the sky like a frightened bird', {i}274; DHL

BIRDS (*cont.*)

sticks to writing book 'like a broody hen
at her eggs', {i}276; Italians 'perch like
queer birds on a ladder', {i}474; poetic
metre like 'bird with broad wings flying
and lapsing through the air', {ii}103; like
Prometheus, world suffers from 'birds of
foul desire which gnaw its liver', {ii}283;
from dark despair 'one rises like the dove
from the ark: but there is no olive
branch', {ii}330, {vi}2, 159; poetic muse
gone 'like swallows in winter', {ii}393;
for Christ Holy Spirit is Dove but 'in
supreme moments he includes the
Eagle', {ii}408; 'peacock-mingled
colours' of Atlantic, {ii}550; 'go rustling
by', {ii}574; visitors 'such stray, blown,
sooty birds they seem', {ii}639; turtle-
dove innocence 'ridiculous', time for
'wisdom of the serpent', {ii}656; 'doves
cooed all day', {iii}97; 'money is a shy
bird', {iii}163; dead owl, throat eaten by
weasels, seems 'important', {iii}240;
pheasant's 'straight advance', wood-
pigeons' clumsiness, in snow, {iii}328;
Shestov's '"flying in the face of Reason"
like a cross hen', {iii}387; 'Every
hen..occupied with her own tail-
feathers', {iii}434; Beaumont a 'bewildered chicken', {iii}494; 'stream
dabbling', {iii}580; Buddhists 'dark
birds' hardly knowing what nests built
of, {iii}718; Murry 'renewing..bald
youth like the vulture', {iii}728; 'shriek
and pop and cackle out of the jungle',
{iv}221; in Mexico 'clouds of birds
passing, the zopilotes like flies', {iv}506;
because of cacciatori 'robins and finches
fly about in perfect bewilderment..occa-
sionally in bits', {v}379; Secker 'one of
those slow little', {v}460; nightingales
'like a dancing chorus..very inquisitive',
{vi}43, 45; DHL 'as miserable as a wet
hen', {vi}64; Huxley 'like a long stalky
bird, all stalk and claw', {vi}275; US
postal inspectors 'timid and dove-like'
(Mason), {vi}450; engaged couple 'like
two birds of Paradise', {vii}207; blue sea

'not hard like peacocks..but soft like blue
feathers of the tit', {vii}275; DHL 'a
tough and stringy bird', {vii}293;
Trotters 'hardest birds to lay hold of',
{vii}479; 'I'd hop over like a bird',
{viii}98

Birge, Mrs, {iv}504–5, 537, {viii}86
Birkenhead, Earl of, *see* Smith, F. E.
Birkindele (New Jersey), Seltzers' country
cottage, {iv}16, 471–3, 476–8, 488, 495,
501, 503, 522
Birmingham (England), {i}508, {ii}92,
{iii}252, 257, 353, {v}177, 362, {vi}496,
515, 519, 545, (vii}28, {viii}1
'Brum', {viii}1;
University, {ii}16, 440
Birrell & Garnett Ltd., {iv}100, {vi}520,
533, 567, 574
Birrell, Augustine, {ii}238
Birrell, Francis Frederick Locker, {i}238,
{ii}230, 238–9, 353, {iv}100, {vi}520
DHL comes to detest, {ii}319–23
Bischoff-Collins, V. H., *see* Collins, V. H. G.
Bithell, Jethro, {i}324–5, 331
Bizet, George, *Carmen*, {i}247
Bjerre, Poul Carl, *The History and Practice of
Psychoanalysis*, {iv}142
Björkman, Edwin August, {ii}80–2, 144, 174,
{v}35
Björnson, Björnstjerne, {i}5, 118, {ii}80
'Black Bread', *see* Verga, G.
Black Cap, The, see Asquith, Lady C.
Black Curtain, The, see Goldring, D.
Black Diamond, The, see Young, F. B.
Black Forest (Schwarzwald, Germany),
{i}385, {iii}533, 536, 539, 615, 685, 697,
707, 713, 723, 732, {iv}28, 33, 38, 44,
48–52, 575–6, {v}327–9, 491, 494, 502,
{vii}388–9, 403, {viii}40
described, {iii}720, 725–6, 728; made 'a
big impression' on DHL, {iv}67; DHL
'very fond of', {v}489, 498; 'as black as
its name', {vii}415
Black Opal, The, see Throssell, K.
Black Sun Press, {v}352, {vi}40, 300–1, 388,
503, 570, {vii}4, 115, 119, 233, 240, 243,
322, 334, 340, 412, 429, 496, 499, 504,
516, 531, 538, 577, 634

Black Swans, see Skinner, M.

Black, James Tait, {iv}146
   see also James Tait Black Memorial Prize

'Blackbird', *see* Lowell, A.

Blackie & Son Ltd, {iv}27

Blackie (horse), {v}59

Blackmore, Richard Doddridge, *Lorna Doone*, {viii}3

Blackpool (Lancashire), {i}172, 175, {ii}213

BLACKWELL, BASIL, {iii}149, 474, {v}49
   'good publisher for getting at the young life in England', {iii}475; publishes DHL's stories in *New Decameron*, {iv}31, 36, 68, 103, 117, 169, 262, {v}20, 26, 57, 606, {vi}176; requests book of short stories, {iv}159; publishes *Little Novels*, {iv}300,302, {v}93, 165, 247, 260, {vi}53, 152; considers *Gesualdo*, {iv}394, 401, 447, 549, {viii}88
   Letters to {v}247
   Letters from {v}260

Blackwood's Magazine, {iii}187, {v}387

Blackwood, Frederick Temple, Marquess of Dufferin and Ava, *Letters from High Latitudes*, {v}383

Blackwood, Lord Basil, {ii}431

Blake, William, {iii}393, {iv}456, 556, {v}356, {vi}174, 421, {vii}78, 419
   DHL's paintings recall, {vii}235;
   'solidity' of paintings by, {vii}508
   'Infant Joy', {i}109;
   Pencil Drawings, {vii}8

Blanca (Colorado), {v}297

Blanchard, Agnes, *see* Holt, A.

Blanchard, M., *see* Luhan, M.

Blanchard, Walter E., {i}139, 313, 526

BLAND, EMILY BEATRICE, {iii}654
   Letters to {iii}654, 671

Blatchford, Robert Peel, {i}36–7, 39, 41, 103
   God and My Neighbour, {i}37, 39

Blavatsky, Helena Petrovna, {iii}150, 298, {iv}461
   Isis Unveiled, {iii}299;
   The Secret Doctrine, {iii}150, 299, 526

Blaylock, Mary, {i}302

Blind Mice, see Scott, C. K.

Bliss and Other Stories, see Mansfield, K.

Blithedale Romance, see Hawthorne, N.

BLOOD, some in DHL's verses, {i}63; Wagner's operas 'run a knowledge of music into your', {i}99; Louie Burrows 'will never plunge her hands through my blood and feel for my soul', {i}191; for DHL 'flesh and blood are the Scriptures', {i}244; beats 'tiresomely and rebelliously in spring', {i}258; 'withered beech as red as', {i}362; 'in life one's own flesh and blood goes through the mill', {i}410; *S and L* contains 'heap of warmth and blood and tissue', {i}462, 476; rhythm and sound of Collings' verse 'don't penetrate the', {i}471; DHL's 'religion..belief in the blood, the flesh..what our blood feels..always true', {i}503; in pregnancy 'the mother's blood ought to run in the womb sweet like sunshine', {ii}43; 'dark-crimson fig-trees hang like blood on the grey rocks', {ii}69; 'flesh and blood must go its own road' and not be turned into 'an idea', {ii}129; Russell full of 'mental blood-lust', {ii}392–3; 'we have a blood-being, a blood-consciousness, a blood-soul', {ii}470–1; Cornish people ought to be living in 'the passionateness of the', {ii}520; Heseltine desires 'blood-connection..consciousness of the senses' with Puma, {ii}539; 'blood-pudding of *passion*' in *Cavalleria Rusticana*, {iii}53; 'prejudices..rarely in the very blood, only in the mind', {iii}369; 'Money is the blood of an Italian', {iv}162; 'Mount Sinai like a vengeful dagger..dipped in', {iv}208, 211; 'tropical sweetness..suggests an undertang of', {iv}225; 'vastness of the blood streams' felt in Ceylon, {iv}234; in USA 'no life of the', {iv}406; in Mexico flows freely in veins, {iv}415; Mexicans 'follow the stream of the', {iv}522; life is 'living' that 'rises from the blood itself', {iv}573; not 'sullied' on ranch, {v}211; in Jewish consciousness nothing 'alive and new from the', {v}262; forms almost unbreakable habits of 'hostility or

BLOOD (*cont*.)

sympathy', {v}647; hemorrhages perhaps take 'bad blood out of the system', {vi}109; 'whole chemical and dynamic condition of the blood and body' changes in time of plague, {vii}179; 'intermingled play and blood-destruction, all through life..the core of the mystery', {viii}21; boy washes carpet in Arno, 'colour streams out like', {viii}46
see also Blutbrüderschaft

Bloomsbury group, {ii}203, 263, 435, {v}286, {vi}220, 506, {vii}82, 117

Blue Flowers, see Gertler, M.

Blue Guide, {vii}86

Blue Jade Library, {v}301, 320, 393, 446

Blue Review, {ii}31, 112
DHL reviews in, {i}546; 'that scoundrel', {i}548; 'dead', {ii}47; 'Soiled Rose' in, {ii}197

Blunden, Edmund, {iii}212, {iv}38, {vii}85

Blutbrüderschaft, {ii}363, 570, 576, 645

Bobbie, Bobby, *see* Gillette, B.

Boccaccio, Giovanni, {ii}116, {vi}343, {vii}141, 608
The Decameron, {ii}359, {vi}401, {vii}503
see also Lawrence, D. H., *Boccaccio Story*

Böcklin, Arnold, {i}503

Bodenheim, Maxwell, {ii}233

Bodley Head Ltd, {ii}519

Bodmin (Cornwall), DHL's military medical examinations at, {ii}14, 618–20, 625, 644, 648, {iii}1, 130, 134; has 'a bad feeling about', {iii}132; rejected again at, {iii}136

Boehme, Jakob, {iv}460

Bogliaco (Italy), {i}460, 500, 508, 520

Bognor Regis (Sussex), {ii}342

Bohème, La, see Puccini, G.

Bohn Library Edition, {vii}560, 589

Bois de Boulogne (Paris), {vii}241

Boissière, Jules, *Fumeurs d'Opium,* {ii}114

Bokhara, {vii}576

Boldrewood, Rolf, pseud. of Thomas Alexander Browne, {ii}588

Bole Hill (Derbyshire), {iii}222, {v}393

Bologna (Italy), {v}427, 447, 449, 465

Bolseno (Italy), {vi}43

Bolshevism, {iv}433, {vii}179
'some sort' inevitable, {iii}728

Bolshevists, {iii}570, {iv}468, {vi}102, 282
Mountsier detests, {iv}113; 'loutish and common', {v}455; 'English are not', {vi}215

Bolton, Sarah Jane ('Jinny'), {v}633

Bonaparte, Josephine, {iv}567–8, 588

Bonaparte, Napoleon, {iii}30, {iv}99, 568

Bond, Frank, {iv}347, 354, {v}51

Bond, George, {vi}10, 335

Bondfield, Margaret Grace, {iii}5, 284

Bone, Gertrude, *Provincial Tales,* {i}353

Bonham Carter, Sir Maurice, {ii}63

Bonham Carter, Violet, {ii}63, 606

Boni & Liveright, {iii}390, 678, 733, 735, {iv}318–19, 324, 417–18, 445, {vi}92, 538–9, {vii}84, 626

Boni, Alfred, {iv}544, {vii}38, 84–5, 111, 222, 242–3, 257, 468, 533, 536, 568–9, 584, 601–2
'brute', {iv}446; 'beastly', {vii}122; DHL will meet, {vii}231; 'rather repulsive' but offers 'uniform edition' of DHL's works, {vii}236, 238, 440, 520–1; perhaps treated 'shabbily', {vii}265; 'tête de veau truffée', {vii}375; 'artful', {vii}445; probably 'too smart' for DHL's agent, {vii}496; 'tough nut', {vii}503; 'a little Jew in a big overcoat', {vii}521; 'rat in a corner, not so easy to handle', {vii}522–3, 526–7; legal action against, {vii}612, 624, 625–6, 637, 649

Bonn (Germany), {i}8, 77, 385, 408, 410, 413
'beautiful town', {i}407

Bonner, Mr, {iii}634, 636, 640, 644, 650, 668, 674, {iv}187, {v}419

Bonsal(l) (Derbyshire), {i}24

Bonsels, Waldemar, *The Adventures of Maya, The Bee,* {iv}342, 359

Book of Common Prayer, The, {i}347, {ii}271, 661, {v}552, {vi}179, 315

Book of Friendship, The, see Ransome, A. M.

Book of Hours, {iv}124

Book of Italy, The, see Piccoli, R.

Book of Love, The, see Ransome, A. M.
Book of Marriage, The, see Keyserling, H.
Book of Revelation, see Oman, J. W.
'Booklovers, The' (bookshop, Perth), {iv}9, 237, 241, 309
Bookman (London) {i}548, {ii}135
   article on DHL by W.L.George in, {ii}28, 99–100, 108, 127, 136, 139, 144, 150, 152
Bookman (New York), {iv}61, {vi}115, 189, 562 {vii}252, 513
Boot, Sir Jesse (Baron Trent), {ii}2, 257, {vi}474
Booth, Elizabeth ('Lizzie'), {v}10, 377, 388, 390–2, 399–400, 609, {vi}245
Booth, Harold, {ii}488, {v}377, {vi}245
Boots Lending Library, {ii}257, {iii}621–2, 624, {iv}262
Boots Pure Drug Co. Ltd, {i}282–3
Bordeaux (France), {i}452, {iv}152, 154, 156–8, 163, 165
BORG, MICHAEL ('MAZZAIBA'), {iv}278, {v}141, 173
   Magnus MS delivered to, {iv}178; 'timid fool', {iv}257; DHL's memoir of Magnus to recover money for, {v}31–3, 240, 348, {viii}48–50; receives half royalties from *Foreign Legion*, {v}54, 361; refuses MS of *Foreign Legion* to Douglas but gives to DHL, {v}395–7, {viii}48–50
   Letters to {iv}188, {v}33
Boris, *see* Croustchoff, B. de
Bormes (France), {v}400, 417, {vii}132
Bormio (Italy), {vii}480
Borrow, George, {iii}562
Borzoi, The, {v}243, 251, 256, 383, 392, 303, 416
Boshi, *see* Sen, B.
Boshier, Walter Edward, {iii}411, 454, 581
Bosigran (Cornwall), {iii}128–30, 133–4, 138, 197–9, 223, 265–6, {viii}25
Bosis, Lauro de, {vi}40
Boston (Lincolnshire), {vi}371
Boston (USA), {ii}26, 246, {iii}12, 129, 362, 506–7, 515, 519, 527, 538, 540, 545–7, 549, 555, 557, 560, 563–4, 571, 636, 664, 670, 690, 709, {iv}4, 276, 364, 410, 464,

{v}255, 272, 299, 429–30, 435, 437–8, 655, {vi}404, {vii}314, 636
BÓTTERN, ANNA, {iv}507, 509, 526, {v}188, 232, 261, {viii}85
   Letters to {v}188, 231–2
BÓTTERN, J. WINCHELL, {iv}507, 526, {v}188, 231, {viii}85
   Letters to {v}188
Bóttern, Simone, {v}188, 232
Botticelli, Alessandro di Mariano dei Filipepi, {ii}120, {iv}92, {vi}79
   'vulgar' beside Ajanta frescoes, {ii}489
Bottom Dogs, see Dahlberg, E.
Bottomley, Horatio William, DHL's bête-noire, {ii}371, 380, {iii}4, 60, {iv}219
   tried to effect prosecution of *W in L*, {iv}126
   see also John Bull
Boucher, François, {ii}68, 549, {vi}543
Boulogne (France), {iii}569, {v}545, {viii}36
Bourgeois Gentilhomme, Le, see Molière, J. B.P.
Bourges (France), {vii}571
Bournemouth (Hampshire), {i}17, 331–62, 498, {iii}138, 147, 164, {iv}135, 137, {v}556, 589, {vii}210, {viii}6
Bourse Gazette, {iii}273, 398, 408, 410, {iv}24, 39, {vi}488, {vii}84
Boutrit, Marc, {i}452
Bowden, George, {i}507, {ii}32, {iii}82
Bowden, Katherine, *see* Mansfield, K.
Bowdwin ('Baldwin'), Mr, {iii}526, 533, 552–3, 606, 636, {iv}101
   owner of Rocca Bella, Taormina, {iii}10, 506, 580, 637, 639, 658, 666, 670, 686; in Rome, {iii}620; suffers brutal assault, {iv}102, 140–1
Bowen, M. Thompson, {vi}433
BOWEN-DAVIES, OLWEN, {v}544
   Letters to {v}544–5
Boy in the Bush, The, see Lawrence, D.H. *and* Skinner, M.
Boyle, Kay, *Short Stories*, {vii}340
Bozen (Austria), {i}444–7, 450, 452–3, 465, {iv}64, 189
Brackenbury, A., {ii}407, 509
Bracknels, The, see Reid, F.
Bradbury, Sir John, {iii}395

Bradley, Frederick James, {i}388

Bradley, Gladys, {i}388, {iii}109

Bradley, Madge, {i}388, {iii}109

BRADLEY, WILLIAM ASPENWALL,
{vii}222, 225, 232
acts as DHL's agent in Paris, {vii}272;
negotiates with Gallimard over *LCL*,
{vii}297, 390, 452, 488
Letters to {vii}229, 245–6, 261, 273

Bradnop (Staffordshire), {i}64, 373, 377

Brahmin, {v}613, {vii}465
see also Mukhopadhyaya, D.–G.

Brahms, Johannes, {i}277, {iii}514

Brailsford, Henry Noel, {ii}315, 320

Bramanti, {vi}329

BRAMBLE, HELEN, {vi}370
Letters to {vi}370

Brand's Essence, {ii}557

Branford, Martha, {v}356

Branford, Flight-Lieut. Frederick Victor,
{iii}342, {v}356
Titans and Gods, {v}356–7;
The White Stallion, {v}356

Brangwyn, Frank, {i}8, 199
DHL copies *The Orange Market* by,
{i}196; 'a joy' to copy picture by, {i}491;
designed room in house in Taormina,
{iii}10; to illustrate DHL's putative
book on Venice, {iii}620, {viii}37

Branksome Chine (Dorset), {i}357

Brazil, {i}308, {iii}174

Breaking Point, The, see Garnett, E.

Bregenz (Austria), {iv}44–6, 48, 53

Bremen, S. S., {vii}539

Brendon, William, & Son Ltd, {ii}221

Brenner Pass, {i}438, 441, 443, 445, {iv}48,
73, {vii}335, 391

Brentano's bookstore, {iv}372, {vii}115, 159,
185, 202, 261

Brentford, Lord, *see* Hicks, Sir W.

Brescia (Italy), {i}165, 453, 464, 475

Brett, Antoine Heckscher, {iv}580–1, {v}425

BRETT, HON. DOROTHY EUGENIE,
{ii}208, 214, 508–9, 655, {iv}20, 555–6,
559, 572, {v}3–4, 6–10, 12, 22–4, 36, 47,
49, 51, 53, 57, 68–9, 95, 138, 168–9, 172,
176, 185, 224, 228, 244, 252, 254, 257,
280–2, 287, 306–6, 308, 312, 323, 329,
356, 369, 391, 413, 541, 562, 597, 600,
625, 647, 653, {vi}3, 10–11, 17, 36, 69,
101, 135–6, 223, 283, 319, 432–3, 459,
506, 522, 604, 607, {vii}54, 71, 94, 96,
387, 414, 533, 616, 624, 629, {viii}87,
104
DHL meets, {ii}427–8, 468; 'her rôle is
always to be a sister,'{ii}474; 'paints, is
deaf, forty, very nice, and daughter of
Viscount Esher', {iv}546, 550, 596,
{v}50, 155, 283; preparations for move
to USA, {iv}581, 592–3; 'insatiably
curious', {iv}600; arrives in New York,
{iv}600–1; 'calm' and 'detached', {v}15,
17–18; 'blissfully happy', {v}27–9;
designs book jacket, {v}32, 37; 'terrible
sloven', {v}42; has one-room cabin on
ranch, {v}43, 45–6, 75; her horse,
Bessie, {v}59, 62; 'a bit simple, but
harmless. and always likes helping',
{v}63; paints, shoots, fishes, rides,
{v}117, 121, 277–8; Toby, her hearing
aid, {v}129, 132, 164–5, 199, 302,
{vii}144; model for DHL's 'The
Princess', {v}136; photography by,
{v}179–80, 183, 594, 629; loves Del
Monte ranch, {v}191, 196–9; her horse,
Ambrose, {v}192; strained relationship
between DHL, Frieda and, {v}192, 239;
leaves Mexico for Del Monte, {v}198–9,
208–9, 211; 'no sensual correspondence'
between DHL and, {v}203; her 'loyalty
fatal', {v}204; 'a born separator',
{v}234; does typing for DHL, {v}236,
248, 343–4, 348, 351–2, 362, 365, 370,
380, 382, 584, {vi}293; designed jacket
for *Plumed Serpent*, {v}250, 342; stays in
USA while DHL to England, {v}310; in
England, {v}326; in Capri, {v}345, 347,
358, 364, 366, 379, 395; paints
Crucifixion picture with DHL's head as
Christ's and Pan's, {v}348–9, 390,
{vi}23–4; Frieda 'implacably' opposed
to, {v}390, 470–1, 537, {vi}1, 49, 278;
sends DHL's typewriter, {v}392; DHL
in Capri and Ravello with, {v}400–4,
407, 421; returns to ranch, {v}417, 421,
426, 429–30, 437–8, 440–1, 453, 455,

457, 463, 465–8, 470, 475–8, 480, 485–6, 491; DHL offers financial help to, {v}435, 509, {vi}5, 293, 310, 357, 469, {vii}26, 263; spinsterish reaction to children, {v}506; as car-owner, {v}530, 546, 550, 559, 630, {vi}82, 293; Mabel Luhan friendly towards, {v}594–5, {vii}547; her horse, Prince, {vi}22–3; urges DHL's return to ranch, {vi}30, 38, 49, 54–6, 58, 75, 82; her preaching about 'faith' rejected, {vi}73, 91; custodian of ranch, {vi}175–6, 536, 55, {vii}203–4, 287–8, 506; arranges for exhibition of DHL's paintings in New York, {vi}340, 343, 357, 380–1, 383–4, 393, 437, 445, 469; mistrusted over alleged disappearance of DHL's MSS, {vii}10, 205, 263, 276–7, 289, 342–6, 360, 385, 472, 474–5, 490, 505; exhibition of paintings by, {vii}24, 36, 55, 138–9, 155, 170, 206, 214, 224, 317–18; Frieda's hostility abating towards, {vii}617, 628, 636

Trinidad, {vi}223

Letters to {iv}562, 565, 568–9, 580–1, 587, 591–3, 599, {v}96–8, 101, 152, 174–5, 180–1, 192, 200, 202–6, 210–15, 218–20, 222, 233–4, 253–4, 265, 269, 297–300, 302–3, 306–7, 313–14, 326, 332–3, 335, 338–9, 342–52, 355–6, 362–5, 370, 373, 380–3, 389–93, 398, 400, 405–12, 417–18, 420–1, 425–6, 433–5, 440–2, 453–4, 469–71, 477–8, 491–2, 494, 503–4, 509–11, 514, 530–1, 546, 559–60, 584–6, 594–5, 605–6, 608–9, 629–30, 639–40, 650–2, {vi}22–4, 27, 54–5, 85–6, 127–8, 154–5, 175–6, 211–12, 254–5, 263, 276, 292–4, 310–11, 357–8, 380–2, 436–7, 444–5, 468–9, 550–1, {vii}24–7, 55–6, 137–9, 205–6, 263, 288–9, 307, 342–3, 385, 472–5, 490, 505–6, 594–5, 617–18, 627–28

Letters from {v}101–2, {vii}138, 342

Brett, Maurice Vyner Baliol, {v}204, {vi}381

Brett, Oliver Sylvain Baliol, {iv}581, {v}204, 344, {vi}381

Brett, Reginald Baliol, *see* Esher, 2nd Viscount,

Brewis, Joseph, {iv}390, 491

Brewis, Mrs Joseph, {iv}390, 491

BREWSTER, ACHSAH, {iii}711–12, {iv}3–4, 89, 93, 96, 110, 125, 231, 294, 304–5, 444, 466, 485, 512–13, {v}75, 307, 323, 326, 333, 343–4, 348, 362, 370, 391, 421, 426, 456, 470, 518–20, 618, 625, {vi}17, 56, 72, 80, 124, 208, 284, 310, 319–20, 392, 414–15, 514, 547, {vii}5, 11–12, 423, 427, 465, 501, 510–11, 591, 601, 621–2, 634, 653, {viii}51, 101

DHL declares long-term friendship with, {iv}90, 95; Taormina friends deplore departure to Ceylon of, {iv}101–2; DHL determined to join in Ceylon, {iv}155, 175, 180, 192; domestic life in Ceylon of, {iv}214, 216, 222; gifts from, {iv}266, 280; Frieda requests painting by, {iv}592, {v}350; DHL proposes to share boat with, {v}372–3; snubs Brett's Crucifixion painting, {v}390; DHL stays on Capri with, {v}401; left Capri for India, {v}422; leaving India where went 'to be Buddhist', {v}573; goes to Greece, {v}595; seeking house in Italy, {v}626–7, 629, 635, 649–51, 653; in Ravello, {v}653, 655; on Capri, {vi}38, 91, 150, 234–5, 241, 336; leaving Ravello, {vi}155; 'her long white robes and floating veils', {vi}223; *LCL* not in her 'line', {vi}317, 340, {vii}54; DHL muses on joint exhibition of paintings with, {vi}381, 383; at the Mirenda, {vi}420; in Grenoble, {vi}422–4; in Chexbres, {vi}426, 428–9, 431, 433–4, 436–7, 439–42, 453; in Gsteig, {vi}455–9, 462–4, 468, 483–5, 487, 498, 507, 509–10; 'always in white and her soul is so white too', {vi}487; to Geneva, {vi}529, 533; hates Switzerland, {vi}542; is vegetarian, {vi}556; buys birthday gift for DHL, {vi}562; with DHL in Baden, {vi}568, 570–1; returns to Capri, {vi}599, 616, {vii}22, 25, 34, 52–3, 314; DHL's present for, {vii}104–5; exhibits paintings in New

BREWSTER, ACHSAH (*cont.*)

York, {vii}170, 214, 224; DHL gives MS to, {vii}306; copy of *Pansies* for, {vii}362, 379; in Stratford-on-Avon, {vii}436; only person to remember DHL's birthday, {vii}478, 493; in Totnes, {vii}483; with DHL in Bandol, {vii}532, 534, 537–8, 541, 543–4, 547–8, 552, 558–65, 588, 598, 604; happy to own chateau and 'be a châtelaine', {vii}566, 570, 577, 579, 613, 645; slight pretentiousness of, {vii}576, 581, 593–4

L'oeuvre de E. H. Brewster et Achsah Barlow Brewster, {iv}466, {vii}379

see also Brewster, Earl Henry

Letters to {iii}718–21, {iv}90, 101–2, 243, 279–80, 421–2, 471, 581–2, {v}135, 179, 282–3, 305, 345, 356–7, 372–3, 421–2, 492, 502, 561–2, 626–7, 637–8, {vi}27, 60–2, 150–1, 195–6, 264, 301–2, 367–8, 452–3, 537–8, 587–8, 593, 608–9, {vii}19–20, 28–9, 53–4, 56, 68, 104–5, 155–6, 169–71, 213–14, 224, 250–1, 283–4, 316–18, 378–9, 463–4, 478–9, 482–3, 580, 644–5

Letters from {vi}22–4

Brewster, Ara, {vii}316

BREWSTER, EARL HENRY, {iii}711–12, {iv}3–4, 89, 93, 96, 214, 231, 243, 279–80, 421, {v}307, 326, 333, 338, 343, 365, 421, 426, 454, 560, {vi}10, 17, 61, 223, 310, 319, 336, 414, 543, 564, {vii}11, 14, 22, 28, 250–1, 427, 436, 463, 495, 501, 601, 617, 627, 634, 645, {viii}101

Nirvana and, {iii}712, 718–19; DHL declares long-term friendship with, {iv}90, 95; Taormina friends deplore departure for Ceylon of, {iv}101–2; DHL determined to join in Ceylon, {iv}155, 175, 180, 192; domestic life in Ceylon of, {iv}214, 216, 222; learns sacred language of Buddhists, {iv}216; *Aaron's Rod* to, {iv}259; Frieda requests painting by, {iv}592, {v}350; *Foreign Legion* to, {v}184; *Little Novels* to, {v}247; *Plumed Serpent* to, {v}371;

DHL proposes to share boat with, {v}372–3; 'old-maidish' letter from, {v}380; snubs Brett's Crucifixion painting, {v}390; DHL stays on Capri with, {v}401; left Capri for India, {v}422; 'doesn't really like' India, {v}470, 530, 586; leaving India where went 'to be Buddhist', {v}573, 632; goes to Greece, {v}595, 608; seeking house in Italy, {v}625–7, 629, 635, 649–51, 653; 'a bit down in the mouth', {v}635; in Ravello, {v}653, 655, 657; with DHL visiting Etruscan sites, {vi}25–8, 33, 38, 43, {vii}19, {viii}101; on Capri, {vi}38, 91, 150, 234–5, 241, 336; 'won't face America', {vi}55; *Mornings* to, {vi}69; leaving Ravello, {vi}155, 211–12; *LCL* not in his 'line', {vi}317, 340, {vii}54; DHL muses on joint exhibition of paintings with, {vi}381, 383; at the Mirenda, {vi}420; in Grenoble, {vi}422–4; in Chexbres, {vi}426, 428–9, 431, 433–4, 436–7, 439–42, 453; in Gsteig, {vi}455–9, 462–4, 468, 483–5, 487, 498, 509–10; to Geneva, {vi}529, 533; hates Switzerland, {vi}542; is vegetarian, {vi}556; with DHL in Baden, {vi}568, 570–1; returns to Capri, {vi}599, 616, {vii}22, 25, 34, 52–3, 314; *LCL* to, {vii}48; DHL's present for, {vii}105; *Pansies* to, {vii}362, 379; birthday remembered by DHL, {vii}493; with DHL in Bandol, {vii}510–11, 532, 537–8, 541, 543–4, 547–8, 552, 558–65, 588, 598, 604; in Chateau Brun, {vii}566, 570, 577, 579, 613, 621–2, 645; slight pretentiousness of, {vii}576, 581, 591, 593–4; DHL expects to visit in Ceylon, {viii}51

Life of Gotama the Buddha, {v}391, 562; *L'oeuvre de E. H. Brewster et Achsah Barlow Brewster*, {iv}466, {vii}379

Letters to {iii}711–12, 718–21, {iv}90, 95, 102–3, 108–10, 124–6, 154–5, 170–1, 238–9, 253, 265–6, 284, 294, 304–5, 444, 466, 471, 484–5, 512–13, 581–2, 592, {v}75, 135, 183–4, 282–3, 305, 322–3, 345, 356–7, 372–3, 391, 421–2, 436–8,

455–6, 484–5, 517–20, 561–2, 613,
617–18, 624, 636–7, 648–50, {vi}35–6,
44, 49–50, 55–6, 71–3, 78–80, 85, 89–92,
107, 123–4, 132–3, 150–1, 195–6, 208–9,
264, 284, 301–2, 317–18, 339–40, 367–8,
382–3, 392, 407–8, 415, 451–4, 506–7,
529, 537–8, 557, 562–3, 584–9, 593,
608–9, {vii}53–4, 56, 104–5, 155–6,
169–71, 213–14, 224, 250–1, 283–4,
316–18, 378–9, 423–4, 464–5, 481–2,
493–4, 511, 580, 650, 653, {viii}51
Letters from {vi}22–4
BREWSTER, HARWOOD, {iii}712, 720,
{iv}3, 95, 155, 175, 266, 466, 466, 513,
582, 592, {v}437, 625 629, {vi}27, 71,
90, 151, 196, 284, 302, 382, 415, 562,
{vii}19, 171, 593
'will soon be a Mademoiselle', {iv}305,
{v}283, 305; 'must be growing a big
girl', {v}179; expected to be 'a gentle
oriental angel', {v}422, 456; 'a real
whopper', {v}627; close friend of
Reynolds girls, {v}627, {vi}22, 367, 609;
should read *Glad Ghosts*, {v}637;
'imperturbable', {v}650; DHL buys
ribbons for, {vi}36, 44, 50, 57, 61, 126;
DHL is 'Uncle' to, {vi}22–4, 57, 126,
241, {vii}214; DHL's generosity to,
{vi}132, 241, {vii}105, 155, 427; in
Florence, {vi}422; in Grenoble,
{vi}423–4; in Chexbres, {vi}426ff, 453;
in Gsteig, {vi}455ff, 483, 487, 498, 509;
in Geneva, {vi}533, 538, 556; in Baden,
{vi}568ff; at Dartington Hall School,
Devon, {vi}588, {vii}317, 436, 479, 483,
495, 501, 510–11, 547, 581, 592, 621–2;
DHL's concern for personal independence and future of, {vii}2, 251, 427,
463, 495, 621; on Capri, {vii}22, 25, 34,
316–17; poem about DHL by,
{vii}378–9; in Stratford-on-Avon,
{vii}436; birthday gift for DHL from,
{vii}493–4; to Bandol, {vii}599
Letters to {vi}57, 126, 240–1, 537–8,
{vii}104–5, 378–9, 426–7, 463–4,
494–5
Letters from {vi}22–4
Briand, Aristide, {iv}133

Bridge of San Luis Rey, The, see Wilder, T.
'Bridge of Sighs, The', *see* Hood, T.
Bridgefoot, (Iver, Buckinghamshire),
Secker's home, {v}24, 34, 312, 318, 346,
529, 556, 656, {vi}77, 111, 130, 472,
{vii}41, 72, 85, 171, 563, 611
Bridges, Robert, {i}12, {viii}15
possible author of introduction for
DHL's *Collected Poems*, {vi}269, 305,
330; possibility rejected, {vi}395
Bridget, *see* Baynes, B.
Bridlington (Yorkshire), {i}70, {vii}397
Brierley Hill (Staffordshire), {i}23
Bright, Henry, {i}88
Brighton (Sussex), {i}115, 216, 219, {iii}26,
91, {iv}377, {v}589, {vi}481
'splendid – big, stately, magnificent',
{i}127; holiday in, {i}198, 202–3, 205,
210–12, 214, {viii}113; DHL stays with
Cynthia Asquith in, {ii}335, 338–9
Brighton Gazette, {i}219
Brill, Dr Abraham Arden, translates Freud's
Die Traumdeutung, {iii}716; Mabel
Luhan's psychiatrist should be sent 'to
hell', {iv}182, {v}125; subscribed to
LCL, {vi}12, 381; Mabel Luhan gives
MS of *S and L* to, {vi}365
Brinsley (Nottinghamshire), {i}374, {v}583,
593
BRINTON, IRENE, {i}350
Letters to {viii}6
Brinton, Margaret ('Peg' or 'Meg'), {i}350,
{viii}6
Brisbane, Arthur, {vii}636
Bristol (Gloucestershire) {i}323, {iii}126,
{vi}11, 369
Bristol Art Gallery, {i}107
Bristol Hotel (Taormina), {iii}479–81, 496,
506, 515, 517, 535, 549, 551–2, 554, 557,
648, {iv}138
Bristowe, Charles John, {i}78
British Columbia (Canada), {iv}95,
{v}229
British Government, *see* Parliament
British Institute, Florence, {iii}575, 591,
{iv}41, {v}472, {vi}328, {vii}48, 363,
493
British League/*Legion Book, see* Minchin, H.

British Museum, {i}168, 297, {ii}205,
{iii}71, {iv}599, {v}121, 475, {vi}93,
105, {viii}104–5
  DHL might wish to read for next novel
  in, {ii}175; studied Egyptian and
  Assyrian sculpture in, {ii}218; 'that
  imposing place', {v}117
BRITNELL, ROY, {vi}574, {vii}218, 320
  Letters to {vii}306–7
  Letters from {vii}306–7
Brittany (France), {i}254, 449, {vi}395, 403
BROADBENT, NURSE,
  Letters to {viii}113
Broadstairs (Kent), {ii}3, 31–53, {viii}6
Broch, Hermann, {viii}106
Brogi, Giacomo, {vi}48, 85, {viii}104
Brontë, Charlotte ('Carlotta'), {i}105–6
  Jane Eyre, {i}59, 88, 159, 191,
  {viii}4;
  Shirley, {i}88
Brontë, Duca di, *see* Hood, Hon. A. N.
Brooke, Lady Sylvia, {vi}239
Brooke, Rupert, {ii}2, 36, 136, 155, 186, 195,
535, {iii}358, {viii}15
  'slain by bright Phoebus shaft',
  {ii}330–1; 'one can smell death in',
  {iii}38; DHL respects death of, {iii}77
  'The Old Vicarage, Grantchester',
  {ii}330–1;
  'The Soldier', {iii}33
Brooke, Sir Charles Vyner de Windt, {vi}239
Brooke-Pechell, Sir Alexander, {vi}205
Brookline (Mass.), Amy Lowell's home in,
{ii}515, {iii}281, 290, 485, 619, 629,
634, 657, {v}198
Brooklyn Eagle, The, {iv}68
Brooklyn Institute (New York), {iii}253
Brooklyn Library (New York), {iv}442
BROOKS, JOHN ELLINGHAM, {iii}490,
{v}390, {vii}170
  'nice man', {iii}443; *New Poems* sent to,
  {iii}470; *Lost Girl* sent to, {iii}703;
  'quite brisk, but looks older', {v}401;
  Douglas 'very mean' to, {vi}545; dies,
  {vii}340
  Letters to {iii}481, 497–9, 599, 706, {iv}54
Brooks, Philip, {vi}559–60
  Letters from {vi}559

Brooks, Romaine, {iii}443, 497
Brooks, Van Wyck, *The Second American
  Carvan*, {vii}139, 157
Brother Scots, see Carswell, D.
Brothers Karamazov, The, see Dostoievsky, F.
BROWN, ALBERT CURTIS, {i}482,
{ii}135, {iii}723, {iv}6, 15, 18, 29, 80,
96, 134, 153, 169, 173, 178, 194, 196,
219–20, 224, 226, 296, 298, 391, 401,
432, 442, 447, 474, 519, 524, 562, 569,
592–3, 600, {v}66, 122–3, 140–1, 186,
188, 197–8, 201, 211, 218, 220, 241, 252,
283, 285–92, 296, 298, 302–25 *passim*,
347, 393, 419–20, 422, 424–31 *passim*,
438–9, 450, 459, 470–1, 484, 486, 493,
495–6, 518–20, 523, 558, 561, 581,
595–6, 621, {vi}21, 41, 46, 53, 76, 199,
228–9, 277, 297, 299, 310–11, 358–9,
373, 391, 394–6, 416, 421, 429, 448, 462,
501, 539, 568, 607, 614, 617, {vii}1, 3,
23, 35, 37, 39, 48, 51, 112–13, 128–9,
144, 192, 200, 255, 258, 267, 288, 292,
343, 395, 444, 483, 502, 515, 525, 531,
547, 551, 559, 569, 575, 585, 609, 613,
622, {viii}87–8, 94, 106, 114
  approaches DHL, {ii}98, 165; DHL's
  English agent, {iii}16, 566, 651, 692,
  697, 699, 714, {iv}24, 32, 68, 187, 200–1,
  242; DHL sends MSS to, {iii}702, 708;
  wants to be DHL's agent in USA,
  {iii}709; tone 'familiar, and a bit
  impertinent', {iii}710; told to act
  'friendlily' to Secker, {iii}722; some
  details secret from, {iii}725, {iv}35–6;
  DHL's enduring relationship with,
  {iv}1; negotiates about *S and S*, {iv}34,
  39, 47, 52, 58, 60, 69, 73, 108, 163, 183,
  199, 328, {v}460, 481; *Aaron's Rod*
  handled by, {iv}55, 65–6, 69, 85–6, 116,
  127, 129–30, 138, 159, 177, 258; *EME*
  stories to, {iv}143–4, 148, 156, 159, 164,
  177, 183; signed sheets of *W in L* to,
  {iv}173–4, 200; *SCAL* to, {iv}197, 399,
  454; Verga translations to, {iv}232–3,
  235, 277, 300; handles *Kangaroo*,
  {iv}299, 302, 343, 369, 380, 394, 399,
  428, 475, 486, 490; 'hates' playing
  'second fiddle to American publication',

{iv}324; *BBF* to, {iv}378, 380, 407, 409, 428, 454, 475, 481, 486, 490; offers to handle DHL's American business, {iv}419, 437, 544; *B in B* to, {iv}533, 543, 549, 557, 560, 563, 566, 588, {v}35–6, 55, 78, 95–6; son has 'lung trouble', {iv}546–7, {v}20; to act for DHL in America through New York branch, {iv}559, 584, 588, {v}2, 127; DHL admires Barmby, New York branch manager for, {v}17–21,147, {vi}222; negotiates over *Foreign Legion*, {v}30–3, 54, 165, 240, 256–7, 340; 'Hopi Snake Dance' article to, {v}109, 116, 170, 173; *St Mawr* to, {v}136, 147, 161, 173, 207, 213–14, 230; 'Epilogue' for *Movements* to, {v}136; handles *Plumed Serpent*, {v}267, 270–1, 286, 297–8, 342; negotiates over *David*, {v}268, 274–6, 281, 285–6, 336, 415, 460, 481, 623; expected to join DHL in Italy, {v}361–5, 369–70, 372, 386; irritated by Cynthia Asquith, {v}590; handling *Mornings*, {v}636; DHL sends *Etruscan Places* to, {vi}83–4, 105, 111, 130, 151, 182; charges DHL 10% on earnings, {vi}169, 176, 232, {vii}26; angered by unexpurgated *LCL*, {vi}261, 295, 352, 356, 360, 371, 373, 526; copy for *Collected Poems* to, {vi}291; expurgated *LCL* to, {vi}309, 315, 354, 384; purchases copy of unexpurgated *LCL*, {vi}345; DHL refuses to negotiate behind back of, {vi}471; defends DHL's financial interests, {vi}516, 524; essay 'New Mexico' sent to, {vii}94; *Pansies* sent to, {vii}120, 320; 'Introduction to These Paintings' sent to, {vii}135; *Pansies* MS seized by police from mail to, {vii}143, 147–154, 157, 163, 167, 171, 174, 293; police appear to be persecuting, {vii}154, 161, 165; 'fuddled' arrangement between Kra and, {vii}245; in negotiations with Parisian publishers DHL wants Bradley to replace, {vii}261, 273; tries to prevent publication of *Escaped Cock*, {vii}285, 290, 322; Rich replaced Barmby in New York

office of, {vii}308; to negotiate with Titus over *LCL*, {vii}392, 396, 410, 429, 451–2, 464, 476; DHL critical of New York office but generally loyal to, 439–40, 522; DHL's MSS in New York office of, {vii}490, 505; Boni probably too smart for, {vii}496, 520–2, 533, 612; 'huffed with' DHL over private editions, {vii}518, 522; DHL doesn't trust, {viii}57; DHL cables about US edn of *Captain's Doll [The Ladybird]*, {viii}74; Maria Chambers anxious to be DHL's American agent in place of, {viii}108 *see also* Barmby, A. W., Pearn, A. R., Pollinger, L., Rich, E .G. and Watson, J.
Letters to {iii}700–1,705, 707, 717, 731–2, {iv}26–7, 34, 46–8, 52, 54–5, 65–6, 69, 79, 88, 129, 133–4, 143–4, 159, 163–4,167–8, 174, 176–7, 183, 187–8 197, 199–200, 232–3, 239–40, 301–2, 371, 379–80, 389–90, 398–9, 427–9, 448, 454, 475–6, 486, 490, 533, 543, 560, 563, 571, 583–4, 591, {v}19–20, 26, 30–2, 36, 54–5, 71, 136, 146–7, 161, 165–6, 173–4, 179–80, 193–4, 207, 213–14, 217, 223–4, 232, 240, 256–7, 260, 270–1, 283, 286, 297–8, 334, 336, 361, 369, 373, 415, 460, 481, 553–4, 555, 571, 575, 596, {vi}221–2, 326–7, 345–6, 418, {vii}121, 130, 148–9, {viii}74
Letters from {iv}69–70, {v}270
Brown, Beatrice Curtis, {v}361
Brown, Caroline Louise, {v}19, 283, 373
Brown, Ford Madox, {i}138
Brown, George Douglas, *The House with the Green Shutters*, by 'George Douglas', {i}172, {viii}19
BROWN, HILDA, {iii}120, 382
Letters to {iii}420, 431, 548, 580–2, 610, {iv}223
Brown, Ivor, {v}614
Brown, M. L. Curtis, {iv}546–7, 584, {v}20
Brown, Montagu, {ii}172
Brown, Mr, {iii}120, 449, 581–2
Brown, Mrs, {iii}120, 361, 449, 581
Brown, Oliver, {vi}16, 522
Brown, Shipley & Co., {iv}58, 74, 78

BROWN, SPENCER CURTIS, {vi}257, 262, {vii}32, 596
Letters to {vi}257
Browne, Frances, *Granny's Wonderful Chair*, {v}388
Browne, Professor Edward Granville, {i}13, 469
Browne, Sir Thomas, {i}205
Browne, Thomas Alexander, *see* Boldrewood, R.
Browning, Oscar, {vi}223
Browning, Robert, {i}3, 5, {ii}4, 147
'Hervé Riel', {i}484 ;
'Last Ride Together', {i}271;
'Pippa Passes', {iii}156;
'A Woman's Last Word', {vi}114
Bruck (Austria), {iv}72
Brummagem, *see* Birmingham
Brussels (Belgium), {i}315, {v}110, 324, 502–3
Bubastis, *see* Pips
Buckesfeld, F., {iii}620
Bucklebury Common (Berkshire), {iii}304, 378, 449
Budapest (Hungary), {iv}69; {viii}44
Buddhism, {iii}718–20, {iv}8, 110, 177, 180, 184, 189, 191, 207, 216, 246, 266, {v}456, {vi}22, 512, {vii}314, 316–17, 570
DHL has 'no deep hope' of Buddha, {iv}95, 125, 154; Taormina residents on, {iv}101; DHL 'can't help rather hating Buddha, the cross-legged pigeon', {iv}126, 234; admits he may have been wrong about, {iv}170–1; 'Buddhistic peace' preferable to 'strident fretting and squabbling', {iv}175; substratum 'barbaric', {iv}218; temples 'like decked up pigsties', {iv}221, 225, 228, 234; 'a vulgar temple of serenity built over an empty hole in space', {iv}226; 'a barren, dead affair', {iv}227; DHL likes Buddha '*much less* than ever on closer acquaintance', {iv}231, 301; 'the vast lotus-pool of', {v}519; Brewster disenchanted with, {v}631–2, 635; Buddha fosters 'paresse de l'âme', {vi}90; 'standing Buddha has still a phallic quality', {vi}208

Buffalo (USA), {iv}4, 332,351, 450, 498, 505, {v}625, {vii}318
DHL visits, {iv}490–3
Buffalo Bill (William Cody), {i}166, {iv}359
Bulfinch, Thomas, *Legends of Charlemagne*, {iii}304
Bull, Harry Adsit, {iv}332, {vi}209
Bull, Harry Adsit Jr, {v}306
Bull, Marion, {v}302, 306, 309
Bull, Rosalie, {iii}10, 636–7, 639, 720, {iv}101–2, 125
Bulwer-Lytton, Edward George Earle, {vi}506
Bumpus, J. & E., Ltd, {ii}497, 506, 511, {vii}125, {viii}16
Bunbury, Mr, *see* Wilde, O.
Bünde, {vi}257–8, 307
Bunin, Ivan, {ii}205, {iv}7, 23, 37, 58, 114, 168, 274–5, {v}347
'The Gentleman from San Francisco', {iv}7, 23, 37, 58, 73, 78–9, 87, 91, 98, 108, 165, 168, 275;
The Gentleman from San Francisco and Other Stories, {iv}23, 37, 275, 322, {v}347
Bunn, Alfred, {vii}126
Bunny, *see* Garnett, D.
Bunty Pulls the Strings, see Moffat, G.
Bunyan, John, {i}40
Pilgrim's Progress, {ii}544
Buonaparte, Napoleon, {vi}114
Bureau, The, *see* Russian Law Bureau
Burgess, Evie, {iv}99
Burgess, Percy, {i}325
Burgos (Spain), {vii}276, 282–3
Burke, Edmund, {ii}4
Burke, Thomas, {vii}531
Burma, {viii}50
Burne-Jones, Sir Edward, {i}86
Burnet, John, *Early Greek Philosophy*, {ii}364–5, 367, 652, {v}505, {vii}518
Burnett, Frances Eliza Hodgson, *Little Lord Fauntleroy*, {i}510, {ii}588
Burnett, Mrs Effingham, {iv}493
Burns, Robert, {i}3, 151, {vi}261, 303, {vii}293, 419
DHL's 'Burns Novel', {i}487, 489, 491, 504–5; DHL loves, {ii}34; among the poets who 'died of sex', {ii}101; DHL

despises bourgeois view of, {vi}231–2
'For a' that and a' that', {vi}231–2;
Merry Muses of Caledonia, {vi}287–8,
  291, 337;
'Tam o'Shanter', {v}446;
'To a Louse', {i}164, {vi}399;
'To a Mouse', {i}5, 305;
'Twa Dogs', {v}633
see also Carswell, C.R.
Burr, *see* Humes, E.
Burr, Jane, pseud. for Rosalind Mae
  Guggenheim Winslow, {iii}430, 675
  The Glorious Hope, {iii}400
Burridge, {i}192
BURROW, DR TRIGANT, {vi}6
  DHL accepts 'idea of social images' of,
  {v}262; critical of syntax of, {v}611;
  'more a philosopher, or artist, than a
  scientist', {vi}113
  'Genesis and Meaning of
  Homosexuality', {vi}100;
  'Psychoanalysis in Theory and in Life',
  {v}611, {vi}4, 99;
  'A Relative Concept of Consciousness',
  {v}261;
  The Social Basis of Consciousness, DHL
  reviews, {v}262, {vi}4, 113–15, 120,
  189;
  'Social Images versus Reality', {v}261;
  'Speaking of Resistances', {vi}99
  Letters to {v}261–2, 611–12, {vi}99–100,
  113–15, 324–5
  Letters from {v}261, 612, {vi}115
Burrows, Alfred (Louie's brother), {i}329
Burrows, Alfred, (father), {i}35, 112, 122,
  179, 209, 215, 251, 258, 271, 326, 341
  DHL wrote to, {i}191, 193, 197; skilled
  wood-carver, {i}299
BURROWS, CONSTANCE (cousin),
  Letters to {i}28
Burrows, Etheldreda ('Ethel') Helen (sister),
  {i}34–5, 70–1, 74, 231, 258, 280, 289,
  303, 305, 331, 354, 367
Burrows, George Campbell (uncle), {i}28,
  296, 325
Burrows, Helen ('Nell') (aunt), {i}321
Burrows, Louisa Ann (mother), {i}35, 112,
  136, 197, 207, 209, 215, 270, 284, 286,
  289–91, 326, 328, 336

BURROWS, LOUISA ('LOUIE'), {i}2, 6,
  11, 13, 15–17, 19, 28, 164, 256, 313, 364,
  403, 487, 527, {ii}142, {iii}38
  prose-style 'wordy', {i}29–30; entered
  'The White Stocking' in competition,
  for DHL, {i}38, 42; begins teaching,
  {i}60; 'big, dark, laughing girl', {i}68;
  writes short stories, {i}78–9, 130–2, 136,
  139–40, 152; unhappy in teaching,
  {i}93–5; DHL gives books to,
  {i}112–14, 209, 242; sends snowdrops,
  {i}117, 121–2, 203, 225; joint authorship
  with DHL of 'Goose Fair', {ii}136,
  139–40, 144, 147, 156; sends birthday
  present, {i}137, 302; recognition of
  mutual love, {i}181; sends flowers to
  DHL's mother, {i}189; DHL proposes
  marriage to, {i}190–1, 193–4, 197; DHL
  declares love for, {i}195–219; he begins
  to retreat from, {i}223–4, 236–7, 249,
  251, 281, 292–3, 326; 'more *real*
  strength' in affection for sister than for,
  {i}231, 243; loved by 'the common
  everyday.. superficial side' of DHL,
  {i}240; *Idyll* painted for, {i}243, 245;
  'Odour of Chrysanthemums' sent to,
  {i}249, 252, 258; in London with DHL,
  {i}266–8; 'Paul Morel' MS sent to,
  {i}273; holiday in N. Wales with DHL
  and sister, {i}280, 284, 290, 295; new
  teaching post, {i}281; hostility to
  engagement from parents of, {i}291–2;
  'big..swarthy..passionate as a gipsy – but
  good..churchy', {i}343; DHL breaks
  engagement to, {i}361, 363; 'angry and
  disgusted', {i}366; hopes for reconciliation, {i}369; DHL admits being 'a rotter
  to', {i}479; 'painful' for DHL to see
  again, {iii}353
  'The Chimney Sweeper', {i}152;
  'Cupid and the Puppy', {i}132–3, 135,
  136, 138
  Letters to {i}29–35, 38, 42, 46–7, 60–1,
  64–5, 70–1, 73–9, 83–4, 90, 93–5, 98,
  105, 112–14, 117–18, 121–5, 128–40,
  142–5, 147, 149, 151–3, 156, 161, 171–2,
  176–9, 181, 189, 195–219, 223–6, 234–5,
  237–8, 241–2, 245–55, 257–60, 262–82,
  284–96, 298–306, 308–11, 314–16,

BURROWS, LOUISA ('LOUIE') (*cont.*)
319–22, 325–9, 331–3, 336–8, 340–2,
347–52, 354–5, 357–8, 361, 363, 365,
367, 369–70, 379–80, 387, 397, 426, 452,
479–81
Letters from {i}181, 197, 291, 294
Burrows, Marguerite (cousin), {i}325, 328
Burrows, Nora (sister), {i}267
Burrows, William (uncle), {i}178
Burrows, William Ralph (grandfather),
{i}270
Burrows, William Ralph (brother), {i}267,
329
Bursum Land Bill, {iv}14, 329, 332–4,
338–9
Burton, Alfred E., {iv}505
Burton, Jeanne, {iv}505
Burton, Robert, *The Anatomy of Melancholy*,
{v}646
Busby, George, {vi}362
Busch, Wilhelm, {vi}144, 157–8, 170
Die Fromme Helene, {vi}170;
Plisch und Plum, {vi}144, 153, 157
Buschbach (Germany), {i}405
Bushwhackers, The, see Stephensen, P. R.
Butler, Samuel, {i}100, {iii}21
Erewhon, {i}100, {iii}21;
The Way of All Flesh, {vi}14, 561,
{vii}609
Butterley (Derbyshire), {iii}302
Buzzi, Paolo, {ii}180
Byles, Réné Boileau, {i}167
BYNNER, HAROLD ('HAL') WITTER,
{iv}12, 15, 17, 316, 321, 331, 359, 367,
385–9, 405–6, 409–10, 417, 429, 473,
497, 536–7, 555, 567, {v}27, 40, 53,
55–6, 60, 89, 100, 127, 132, 156, 158,
169, 191, 199, 219, 228, 235, 250, 261,
285, 424, 600, {vi}12, 319,357, {vii}138,
505, {viii}76–7, 79
alleged 'enemy' of Amy Lowell, {iv}326;
poem from, {iv}368; with DHL in
Mexico City, {iv}416–18, 420–4, 434;
'very companiable and nice', {iv}432; in
Chapala with DHL, {iv}443–6, 453,
455, 457, 467; invited to ranch, {v}54,
65, 81–2; sends jade necklace for Frieda,
poem for DHL, {v}259–60; DHL in

feline imagery in poem by, {v}384,
{vii}575; presented as Owen Rhys in
Plumed Serpent, {v}384, {viii}88; pen
and ink portrait of DHL by, {v}472;
'belated sort of mosquito', {v}580; copy
of *David* for, {vi}278, 295; rejects
concept of 'hero' in *Plumed Serpent*,
{vi}321; buys copy of *LCL*, {vi}448;
Collected Poems for, {vii}387
The Beloved Stranger, {iv}484;
A Book of Plays, {iv}484;
Cake, {v}259, {vi}365;
'Calendar', {vi}278;
Caravan, {v}84, 384;
'Chapala poems', {v}84, {vi}278;
Indian Earth, {v}84, 185, {vii}574;
The Jade Mountain, {vi}278, {vii}649;
Witter Bynner (Pamphlet Poets),
{vi}278
Letters to {iv}316, 368, 404, 408, 412,
415–16, 436, 441, 467–8, 483–4, 505–6,
534–5, 546–7, 595–6, {v}48, 54, 65–6,
81, 84, 151, 157–8, 185, 259–60, 384,
{vi}278–9, 321–2, 365–6, {vii}574–5
Letters from {iv}467
Byrne, Algernon M. {i}194, 246, 368, 465,
524, {iii}62
Byrne, James, *see* Garnett, E.
Byron, George Gordon, Lord, {i}523,
{ii}63, 625, {iii}679, {vi}141, 342
Byron, Robert, DHL reviews *The Station:
Athos, Treasures and Men* by, {vi}463
Bystander, The, {v}56

Cabell, James Branch, *see* Holt, G.
Cacópardo, Carmelo, {iii}506, 551, 602, 606,
686, {iv}109, 139–41, 192, {viii}47, 52
wants to go to USA, {iii}620, 640,
{iv}141
Cacópardo, Emma ('Gemma'), {iii}507, 538,
540, 557
Cacópardo, Francesca ('Ciccia'), {iii}606,
661, 664–6, 668–9, {iv}109, 141,
{viii}47
Cacópardo, Francesco ('Ciccio'), {iii}506,
526, 620, 640, {iv}109,
DHL's landlord at Fontana Vecchia,
{iii}481, 486–7, {viii}47; going to

Boston, USA, {iii}507, 515, 519, 528–9, 533, 538, 557, 709; takes TS of *Lost Girl* to USA, {iii}535, 540, 544, 549, 551, 560, 563–4, 572, 575

Cacópardo, Giovanna, {iv}141

Cacópardo, Grazia, {iii}551, 640, {iv}109, 14, {viii}47

Cacópardo, Vincenzo, {iii}606, 661, 664–6, 668–9, 672–3, 678, {iv}141

Caesar, Julius, {i}114, {ii}371, {v}635

Cagliari (Sardinia), {iii}656, 662, 667, 675, {iv}34, 43

Cagnes (France), {vii}646–7

Cairo (Egypt), {v}558–9, 577, 630, {vi}41, 175, 179, 204, 301, 379, 513, {viii}99

Cake, see Bynner, H. W.

Cala Ratjada (Mallorca), {vii}286, 326

Calabria (Italy), {iii}487–9, 671, {iv}114, 116, 119, 122, 124, {v}184, 357, 370, 373 'glimmering' {iii}507, 552; 'blue morning-jewel', {iii}629; twinkles 'like seven jewels', {iv}109

Calais (France), {v}378, {vi}473, 493

'Calamus. A Song', *see* Whitman, W.

'Calendar', *see* Bynner, H. W.

Calendar, The, {v}601, 649 DHL reviews in, {v}513, 570–1, 590, 647, {vi}41, 54, 280, {viii}99, 107; two poems in, {v}617, 626; demise of, {vi}83–4 *see also Calendar of Modern Letters*

Calendar of Modern Letters, The, {v}311, 367, 601 'Princess' in, {v}180, 227, 231–2, 241, 331; 'Art and Morality' and 'Morality and the Novel' in, {v}275; re-named *Calendar,* {v}367 *see also Calendar, The*

Calhouse, W. J., {ii}412

California (USA), {iii}83, {iv}93, 224, 256, 261, 343, 410, 478–80, 482, 485–8, 527, 562, 585, {vi}136, 319, {vii}120, 124, 127–8, 132, 135, 137, 264, {viii}59 possible site for 'Rananim', {iii}8, 70; DHL in, {iv}496–7, 499; 'Drunk with trivial externalities', {iv}501–3; Taos far better than, {iv}539; US mail confiscates

LCL announced in, {vi}14, 530–1; 'mystic' from, {viii}57; 'all so on the outside, and *so* empty inside', {viii}85

'California Limited' (train), {viii}55

Calle Zaragoza (Chapala, Mexico), {iv}436–62 *passim,* {v}55

Calles, Plutarco Elías, {iv}465, 536, {v}59, 156, 161, 182, 185, 187

Camàldoli (Italy), {vi}605, {vii}432–3

Cambridge, {i}4, 13, 77, {ii}11–12, 331, {iii}10, 376, 496, {vii}165, 376, {viii}27 Weekley 'worships', {ii}281; DHL to visit Russell in, {ii}289, 291–2, 295, 297, 303–4; feels 'frightfully important' going to, {ii}300; 'hated it beyond expression', {ii}305; 'its smell of rottenness, marsh-stagnancy', {ii}309, 320–1; needs 'surgery', {ii}318, {iii}49; DHL urges Russell to leave, {ii}348

Cambridge, Ada, *Sisters,* {iii}391

Cambridge Review, The, {ii}286, 389

Cambridge University Press, {iv}583, {vi}607

Cameron, Miss, {i}122–3

Cameronian, S. S., {vii}586

Camille, *see* Martens, C.

Camomile, The, see Carswell, C. R.

CAMPBELL, BEATRICE MOSS, {ii}187, 218, 249–50, 274, 303, 427, 482, {iii}81, 117, 330, 336, {iv}29, {vi}17, 191, 335 DHL contemplates visiting Ireland to see, (vi}194–5, 219–20, 282–4 *Letters to* {iii}334–5, {vi}194–5, 219–20, 282–4, {viii}635

Campbell, Brigid ('Biddie') Columbine, {iii}125, {vi}195, 283, 335

Campbell, Capt. Patrick, {iii}305

CAMPBELL, CHARLES HENRY GORDON, {ii}167–8, 240, 252, 260–1, 264, 272, 359, 482, 551, 571, 616, {iii}90, 108, 112, 125, 175, 183, 284, 318, 321, 335–6, {iv}28, 38, {v}355, {vi}10, 17, 191, 283–4, {viii}8–9 'a most delightful man', {ii}50–1, 178; 'a perverse devil', {ii}161; DHL to stay in house of, {ii}175, 178, 185, 187; witness at DHL's wedding, {ii}195, 198; 'his

CAMPBELL, CHARLES HENRY
GORDON, (*cont.*)
  belief in evil', {ii}282; too uncertain
  'ever to feel anything like religious
  passion', {ii}288; Frieda's guarantor for
  passport, {ii}418; works in Ministry of
  Munitions, {ii}570, {iii}307; needs 'a
  fresh start', {iii}54; DHL seeks help
  over passport, {iii}78, 81–2, 96; exasper-
  ating but likeable, {iii}83; possible
  recruit for 'Rananim' in Italy,
  {iii}214–16; DHL 'a bit disgusted with
  him', {iii}285; 'like a strip of litmus
  paper': in Dublin, 'bright British red', in
  London 'emerald green', {iii}334; DHL
  contemplates visiting Ireland to see,
  {vi}194–5, 219–20; did not order copy of
  LCL, {vii}635; Frieda to stay with,
  {viii}20
  Letters to {ii}217–19, 246–50, 273–4,
  300–3, {iii}48–9, 62–4, 80–3, 96, {iv}29,
  {vi}194–5, 219–20, 334–5
Campbell, Mary, 'Highland Mary', {i}487
Campbell, Michael Mussen, {vi}195, 283,
  335
Campbell, Mrs Patrick, *see* Cornwallis-West,
  B. S.
Campbell, Nancy, 'The Monkey', {ii}416–17
Campbell, Patrick Gordon, {iii}63, {vi}195,
  283, 335
Campbell, Reginald John, {i}37, 310
Campbell, Sir James Henry Mussen, {iii}63,
  {iv}28
Campbell, Thomas, {i}540
Campbell, Violet Lilian, {vi}220
Campione (Italy), {i}515
Campkin, Hugh T., {ii}233, 236, 241, 427
Campo di Marte (Italy), {iii}592
Canada, {iii}383, 576, {iv}142, {v}229, 479,
  {vi}323
  emigrants to, {i}34, 91, 499, 553,
  {ii}148; DHL dreams of, {vi}82; two
  copies of *LCL* to, {vi}520; meagre
  royalty on *Twilight* sold in, {vii}266
CANBY, HENRY SEIDEL, {iv}16
  Letters to {iv}494–5
Cannan, Felix ('Binky'), {iii}251

Cannan, Gilbert, {ii}2–4, 17, 33, 205, 208,
  214, 229, 238–9, 252, 255–6, 292–3, 303,
  345–6, 351, 359, 363, 367, 435, 427, 485,
  531, 657, {iii}10, 28, 77–8, 166, 209, 486,
  492, 534, 560, 632, 664, 678, {iv}32, 312,
  374, 385, 442, {viii}13
  DHL bored by *Devious Ways*, {i}162–3;
  liked by DHL, {ii}212; supported
  DHL's application to Royal Literary
  Fund, {ii}225; DHL very friendly with,
  {ii}254; DHL disparaging about *Young
  Earnest*, {ii}284–5; 'power for Good',
  {ii}310–11; DHL praises *Windmills*,
  {ii}334, {iii}78; possible contributor to
  Signature, {ii}385–7; belongs only to the
  past, {ii}482; attitude to military service
  unclear, {ii}602, 623, 647; *Mendel*
  'statement without creation – really
  journalism', {iii}44, 50, 52; working on
  a farm, {iii}71; nervous breakdown and
  marriage disintegrating, {iii}90, 96,
  103, 251–2, {viii}20; broke with
  agent, Pinker, {iii}439; raises funds in
  USA and treats DHL like 'charity-boy
  of literature', {iii}475, 493, 500–3,
  506, 508, 511, {viii}79; 'a soap pill',
  {iii}502; 'imbecile', {iii}516; in South
  Africa, {iv}159; DHL scathing about,
  {iv}349, 352–3; certified insane, {v}141,
  185
  'A Defense of Lawrence', {iii}475;
  Devious Ways, {i}162–3;
  'Gynecologia', {iii}78–9;
  Mendel, {ii}208, {iii}35, 44, 50, 52, 352,
  471;
  Pug and Peacocks, {iii}670;
  Windmills, {ii}334, {iii}78;
  Young Earnest, {ii}284–5
CANNAN, MARY, {ii}208, 238–9, 252,
  254–6, 310, 345–6, 351, 363, 367, 412,
  451, 494, 531, {iii}10, 28, 77, 209, 492,
  535, 601, 667, 675, {iv}6, 20, 32, 66, 261,
  478, 480–1, 485, 548
  obtained financial help for DHL,
  {ii}213, 225, {iii}251, {viii}13; 'a dear:
  but shallow', {ii}311; belongs only to the
  past, {ii}482; marriage to Cannan

disintegrating, {iii}90; DHL sympathetic towards, {iii}251–2; on Capri, {iii}442, 446–8, 451, 462; source of local scandal, {iii}444; 'Very much afraid of death', {iii}471; in Taormina, {iii}479–82, 496–8, 506–7, 514–15, 526, 551, 553, 557–8; 'seems to get old', {iii}500; waspish humour, {iii}503; to Malta with DHL, {iii}522, 525, 533; 'flutters round in her bits of ninon and fringe', {iii}532; threatens to write a novel, {iii}537, 551–2; intends going to Vallombrosa, {iii}567–8, 575; in Monaco, {iii}609, 614, 624, 632, 636, 658; DHL seeks and secures loan from, {iii}664, 669, 673, 678, 683, {iv}224; in Florence, {iv}80–1; goes off 'like a wickwack' about Cannan, {iv}159; copy of *S and S* for, {iv}162, 179; *EME* to, {iv}352; *Foreign Legion* to, {v}141; sought financial help for DHL from Sutro, {viii}13

Letters to {ii}292–3, 485, {iii}251–2, 624, 636–7, 663–5, 669–70, 683, 694–5, 710–11, {iv}48–9, 142–3, 162–3, 179–80, 190–1, 203, 221–2, 224, 286–7, 311–12, 352–3, 424

Cannes (France), {iii}526, 553, 558, 640, 665, 679–80, {iv}49, {v}378, {vii}332, 339, 399, 405, 488, 530, 544, 575, 641, 653

Canovaia, *see* Villa Canovaia

Canute, King, {ii}375

Cape Socotra (Socotra, Indian Ocean), {iv}210, 212

Cape Town (South Africa), {iv}139, {v}448

CAPE, JONATHAN, {i}297, {iv}99, 401, 464, {v}171, 292, 331, 542, {vi}54, {vii}242, 257, 521–2, 533, 595
asked DHL for 'book of short things', {iv}129; favoured for *SCAL*, {iv}177, 196–8; publishes *Gesualdo*, {v}165, {vi}40, 53, 68, 130, 516–17; *Twilight* published by, {v}460, 555–6, {vi}281, {vii}158, 265–6, 297–8; *Cavalleria Rusticana* to be published by, {vi}68, 70, 110, 130, 137, 152, 168, 343, 517; DHL's introduction to *The Mother* for, {vi}254;

LCL offered to but refused by, {vi}333, 352, 371; US edn of *Collected Poems* by, {vi}610, {vii}65–6, 221, 236, 243, 266, 272, 297–8, 315, 320, 324, 328, 336, 387, 396, 413, 445, 485, 526; asked DHL for book of critical pieces, {vii}218, 231–2; 'eager to get your books', {viii}70

Letters to {vi}53–4

Capek, Karel, {vi}239

Capellero, Caterina, {v}24, 352, {vi}377

Capellero, Luigi, {v}24, 336, 352, {vi}377

Capellero, Rina *see* Secker, C. M.

Capelli family, {i}535

Capelli, Maria, {iv}189

Capelli, Paolo, {iv}189

CAPITALISM, Jaffe on, {ii}63; war is struggle between Labour and, {ii}366–7; must not gain power, {ii}368; detestable, {ii}593; 'limb' of body of 'destructive evil', {iii}123; DHL hates, {iii}561; liberalism perhaps worse than, {iv}419; miners should favour neither bolshevism nor, {vi}267

Capri, {iii}9, 401, 407, 420, 432–522 *passim,*, 558, 562, 567, 575, 594, 599, 602, 624, 664, 706, 721, {iv}3–4, 80, 89–90, 96, 105, 110, 121, 207, 266, 444, {v}3, 6, 10, 31, 75, 179, 208, 282, 305, 313–442 *passim*, 573, 625, 629, 631, 635, 637, {vi}1, 23, 35, 38, 71–2, 91, 150, 212, 234–5, 240–1, 284, 302, 317, 329, 336, 350–1, 353, 361, 366, 383, 414, 428, 433, 448, 458–9, 593, 599, 616, {vii}22, 25, 28, 34, 53, 56–7, 68, 170, 224, 226, 250, 253, 263, 314, 340, 379, 465, 482–3, 494, 538, 541, 552, 588, 591, 593–4, 598–9, {viii}46, 51
'Morgano's cafe - the centre of', {iii}443; town 'about as big as Eastwood', {iii}451; 'gossipy, villa-stricken, two-humped chunk of limestone', {iii}462; 'stewpot of semi-literary cats', {iii}469, 471; 'too dry and small', {iii}482; 'unhatched egg' compared to Sicily, {iii}498; DHL doesn't 'feel *at all* drawn to', {iii}616; 'Gentleman from San Francisco'

Capri (*cont.*)
    'screamingly good..so comically like the
    reality' of, {iv}37, 58; preferred to Santa
    Fe, {v}184; DHL in, {v}400–4; 'too
    small' for DHL to live in, {vii}436, 463
'Captain Blackbird', {iv}287
Carcassonne (France), {vii}251
Carco, Francis, {ii}270, 289
Cardiff (Wales), {ii}575, {iii}334, {vii}98
Careggi (Italy), {vii}432
Caresse, *see* Crosby, M. J.
Carinthia (Austria), {v}480, {vi}96–7
Carl, *see* Seelig, K.
Carletto, *see* Zanotti, C.
Carlotta, *see* Brontë, C.
Carlyle, Thomas, {i}49, 504, {vi}342
Carman, Bliss, {i}5, 546
Carmel (USA), {iv}505, {v}23
Carmelo, *see* Cacópardo, C.
Carmen, *see* Bizet, G.
Carmichael, Joseph, {ii}497
Carmichael, Mrs, DHL's typist in Florence,
    {iv}107, 144, 196–7, 200, 214–15, 220
Carmina, *see* Catullus
Carossa, Hans, {vi}4, 154–5, 350, {viii}18
    DHL meets and consults, {vi}154–7,
    163, 167, 172, 185, 189; thinks DHL 'the
    greatest living novelist', {vi}157;
    'Hymns in a Man's Life' written in
    honour of, {vi}524, 540–1
Carpenter, Edward, {ii}391, 401
Carpenter, Joseph Edwards, {ii}62, {iii}278
Carrara (Italy), {ii}123, 138, 153, 156,
    {iv}84, {v}633, {vi}86, {vii}339
Carrie, {vii}39
Carrington, Dora de Houghton, {ii}208, 214,
    508–9, 515, {iii}35, 103, 109, 112, 194,
    304, {vi}70
Carroll, Lewis (Dodgson, Charles
    Lutwidge), *Alice's Adventures in
    Wonderland*, {i}61, 228;
    Through the Looking Glass, {i}269
Carson, (Sir) Edward, {iii}39
CARSWELL, CATHERINE ROXBURGH
    (JACKSON), {ii}1–2, 7, 9, 14, 160, 187,
    204–6, 227, 504, 567–8, 652, 659, {iii}1,
    4, 8–9, 14–15, 17, 52, 73, 275, 277–9,
    300, 324, 329, 354, 363, 406, 428, {iv}3,

8, 14, 17–18, 20, 70, 92, 122–4, {v}2, 9,
    123, 311, 346, {vi}10–11, {vii}239,
    {viii}28, 98
DHL reads draft of her novel,
    {ii}187–8; hers is 'often a simply *beastly*
    style', {ii}188; to marry Carswell,
    {ii}225; reviews *Rainbow*, {ii}456, 502;
    poems by, {ii}493, 502–3, 532; TS
    of *W in L* sent to, {iii}36, 41; MS of
    LWHCT sent to, {iii}93–4; 'Reality of
    Peace' essays sent to, {iii}102; in car-
    accident, {iii}146; DHL compliments
    on *Open the Door!*, {iii}173, 536–7; 'War
    Baby' poem celebrates arrival of son to,
    {iii}246; sends DHL cheque, {iii}274;
    sends wine, {iii}330, 336–7; DHL sends
    £1, {iii}359; sells typewriter for DHL,
    {iii}365; DHL gives De Quincey
    volumes to, {iii}407; at production of
    Widowing and reviews, {iii}428, 477,
    487, 495; offers DHL £50, {iii}495,
    524–5, 537; *Open the Door!* selected as
    'Melrose's £250 Prize Novel', {iii}525;
    DHL sends *Tortoises*, {iv}153, 174;
    sends *S and S*, {iv}193; *Camomile*
    'slighter than *Open the Door* but better
    made', {iv}270, 275; *EME* ordered for,
    {iv}362; *B in B* for, {v}81, 148; *Foreign
    Legion* for, {v}141, 148; *Little Novels* for,
    {v}247; 'buried alive...in damp and
    dismal Bucks', {v}313; *Plumed Serpent*
    for, {v}401–2; 'very poor', {v}475;
    proposes book on Burns and receives
    advice, {vi}231–2, 291, 303; shared
    typing of *LCL*, {vi}260, 274, 290–1, 294,
    303, 306; subscribed early for *LCL*,
    {vi}385; felt maligned, {vi}385, 430,
    {vii}293; *WWRA* for, {vi}430, 432;
    'nervous and irritable', {vi}439; likes
    DHL's paintings, {vii}418; Frieda finds
    'certain scotch impudence about her at
    times', {viii}20
The Camomile, {iv}52–3, 64, 104, 106,
    124, 175, 195, 270, 275, 485; {v}123;
    Open the Door! ('Joanna'), {ii}187–9,
    532, 556, 595, 617, 638–40, 643, {iii}26,
    33, 44–5, 58, 72, 87, 93, 125, 131, 147,
    153, 171, 173, 179, 210, 231, 297, 445,

468, 495, 525, 536–7, 608, {iv}52, 270, 485, {v}123; fictional characters: John Sholto Bannerman, {iii}44, Louis Pender, {iii}173, Aunt Perdy, {iii}173, Lawrence Urquhart, {iii}173;
Robert Burns, {vi}231, 261, 290–1, 303, {vii}293, 419
Letters to {ii}187–9, 196, 225–6, 228–9, 261, 456–7, 463, 485–6, 492–3, 502–3, 532–3, 555–6, 560, 578, 594–5, 616–17, 625–8, 633–40, 643, 662–3, {iii}24–6, 33–4, 36, 41–2, 44–5, 57–8, 64, 71–2, 75, 86–7, 92–4, 97–8, 100, 102, 105–7, 112–14, 119, 125–6, 130–2,146–7, 152–3, 159, 161, 164–5, 169, 171–4, 179, 192, 210, 231–2, 240–1, 245–6, 248, 258–9, 270–1, 273–5, 288, 297–8, 306, 322–3, 330, 336–7, 351, 359, 361–2, 365, 383–4, 407, 419, 442–5, 468–70, 477, 479, 487, 495, 524–5, 533–4, 536–7, 607–8, 701–2, 704, 726, {iv}52–3, 55–6, 61, 63–5, 70, 89, 91, 104–6, 151, 153–4, 174–6, 195, 202, 217, 222, 230, 270–1, 283, 285, 291, 312–14, 362–3, 422–3, 425, 440, 453–4, 470, 485, 513, 561, 563–4, 570–1, 580, 588, {v}17–19, 36–7, 46–7, 97,147–8, 152, 269–70, 289, 309–10, 315–19, 325, 330, 402, 435–6, 458–9, 493, 498, 538, {vi}187–8, 260–1, 265–6, 274–5, 287–8, 290–1, 294, 303, 306, 336–7, 385–6, 395, 430, {vii}293, 418–19
CARSWELL, DONALD, {ii}7, 17, 226, 261, 456, 493, 503, 532, 556, 560, 616–17, 627–8, 639, 663, {iii}24–5, 38, 41, 44, 57–8, 75, 86–7, 94, 105, 126, 131, 172–4, 179, 192, 231, 240, 245–6, 259, 288, 297, 330, 336, 361, 407, 443, 445, 468–9, 487, 537, 608, 702, {iv}18, 20, 53, 89, 106, 176, 195, 222, 271, 314, 513, {v}9, 17, 37, 46–7, 148, 270, 316, 319, 402, {vi}187, 261, 275, 303, {vii}293, {viii}20

   to marry Catherine Jackson, {ii}225; advises libel action against Clement Shorter and James Douglas, {ii}462–3; liable to conscription, {iii}34, 45, 64; must develop 'faith in the creative unknown', {iii}97–8; ill in military

hospital, {iii}161, 169; assists over DHL's passport, {iii}383, {iv}56, 61, 64; DHL seeks legal advice from, {iii}525; is too conventional, {iii}534; advice sought about regimental dress, {iv}105, 122; applies for Guernsey magistracy, {v}289; has no work, {v}332; admires English detachment 'a little overmuch', {vi}231; *Brother Scots* 'a bit *slow*,' {vi}439
Brother Scots, {vi}187–8, 232, 265, 439;
Count Albany, {vi}386
Letters to {iii}278–9, 298, {iv}122–4, {vi}231–2
Carswell, Isabel Macquarie, {ii}404, 617, {iii}57
Carswell, John Jamieson, {ii}617
Carswell, John Patrick ('Johannes'), {iii}240, 297, 306, 336, 365, 383, 444, 524, 608, {iv}124, 176, 271, 314, 513, {v}19, 148, 270, 289, 319, 402, 459, {vi}187, 232, 261, 288, 291, 303
   birth of, {iii}245; 'Johannes', {iii}273, 359; 'little J.P.', {iii}278; 'teeth already', {iii}323; 'runs about', {iii}470, 702; DHL sends toys for, {iii}726; at school in France, {v}435, 475
CARTER, FREDERICK, {iv}18–20, {vii}538, 562, 569, 587, 589–90
   DHL very interested in *Dragon of the Alechemists* MS, {iv}365, 405, 430–1, 459–61, 475; drawings 'beautifully executed', {iv}456; DHL considers writing introduction to *Dragon*, {iv}497; style 'sometimes odd and obscure', {iv}556; 'a vulgar side' to his drawings, {vii}508; *Pansies* for, {vii}561; visits DHL in Bandol, {vii}570, 575–81, 583; 'No fire, no courage, no spunk', {vii}577
'The Ancient Science of Astrology', {iv}556, 593;
'Antique Heavens', {vii}622, 640;
D. H. Lawrence and the Body Mystical, {iv}19;
The Dragon of the Alchemists, {iv}18–19, 365, 405, 430–1, 456–7, 459–61, 475, 497, 547, 557, 575, {vii}432, 444, 456,

CARTER, FREDERICK (*cont.*)
506, 519, 528, 545;
'The Dragon of the Apocalypse',
{vii}455–6, 506–7, 562, 613–14, 622,
640;
The Dragon of Revelation, {iv}19,
{vii}506, 544, 554–5, 613, 618, 640;
'Revelation of St. John the Divine',
{vii}599;
'Silence in Heaven', {vii}508;
'The Visionary Way', {vii}544, 554–5
Letters to {iv}365, 405, 430–1, 456–7,
459–61, 475, 497–8, 542, 547, 553–4,
556–7, 568, 575, 583, 593, {v}49–51,
{vii}444, 455–6, 507–9, 518–19, 544–5,
554–6, 562, 599, 613, 622, 640
CARTER, MARY HAMILTON, {iv}557,
583, 593, {v}50–1, {vii} 444, 455,
570
Letters to {iv}554
Carter, Vivian, {iii}373
Carter Paterson, {ii}579, 584
Carter's Little Liver Pills, {vii}346
Carthage, {ii}650, {iii}233, {vii}422
Caruso, Enrico, {i}155, 505
Casa dei Sogni (Cagnes), {vii}645–6
Casa Melcher (Mazatlan), {iv}518–19
Casa Petrarca (Venice), {iv}195
Casa Solitaria (Capri), {iii}428, 436–7, 494,
599
Casanova de Seingalt, Giacomo, {ii}42, 100,
{iv}81
Casanova's Homecoming, see Schnitzler, A.
Casardi, *see* Haskard & Casardi Ltd
Case of Sergeant Grischa, The, see Zweig, A.
Casement, Roger David, {ii}656
Cassandra, {ii}297–8, {iv}307
Cassino (Italy), {iii}442
Cassis (France), {vii}379, 465, 480–3, 486
Castellammare (Italy), {iii}448
Castellano, Cavaliere, {i}247
Castello di Maniace (Sicily), {iii}10, 509–10,
637
Castello di Montegufoni (Italy), {v}12, 468,
{vi}60, {viii}103
Castello Ruggero (Italy), {iv}84–5
Castle Donington (Leicestershire), {i}426
Castle Rising (Norfolk), {i}27

Castrogiovanni (Sicily), {iii}695
Catallus, *Carmina*, {iii}161
Catalogue, Gérard de, {vi}600
Catania (Sicily), {iii}479, 506, {iv}127, 175,
186, 188, 200, {viii}31
Cathay, {ii{608, {vii}577
Cather, Willa, {v}249, 567, {vi}269, 340
DHL sees in New York, {iv}592;
Kangaroo and *Captain's Doll* sent to,
{v}23; possible tenant for the ranch,
{v}216, 218; 'steam-roller', {v}277, 280,
283
Cato the Elder, {ii}650, {vii}422
Cavalleria Rusticana, see Mascagni, P. *and*
Verga, G.
Cave/cavern, the (Koteliansky's home),
{iii}376, 640, {iv}282, 296, 349, 478,
{v}81, 355, 366, 418, 601, {vi}135, 233,
323, 356, 458, 546, {vii}282, 302
'the house is like a cave', {iii}250;
description of, {iv}171–2, 184–5
Cearne, The, {i}16, 17–18, 297, 309, 311,
326–8, 330, 340, 345, 354, 362, 364, 384,
423, 430, 444, 447–8, 467, 517, 520, 523,
527, 535, 537, 539, 543, {ii}20–4, 26–7,
37, 41, 44, 46–7, 52, 54, 59–60, 83, 99,
127, 168, 175, 187, 190, 202, 208,
{iv}116, {vi}520
'one of these new, ancient cottages',
{i}314–15; 'built in the 15th Century
style', {i}316; DHL visits with Frieda,
{i}386, 400, 409; 'beer, apples, a big fire,
and a jaw till midnight' at, {i}485; 'the
only place in England' open to DHL and
Frieda, {i}510; 'the nearest place to
home that I've got', {i}530, {ii}51; 'I
could live for ages...and be happy' at,
{ii}33
Celestial Omnibus, The, see Forster, E. M.
Cellini, Benvenuto, {i}448, 450
Cendrella, *see* Huxley, (Lady) M. J.
CENSORSHIP, Garnett cuts *Sand L*,
{i}481–2, 489, 496, 501, 517; suppression of *Rainbow*, {ii}428, 431, 439, 441,
456–7, {iii}459; *Rainbow* might do well
in USA 'since their postal-censor man is
dead', {ii}446; in USA 'keener than.. for
a generation', {ii}561; DHL's letter

opened by censor, {iii}324, 364;
Huebsch lets *W in L* 'dribble out' to
avoid US, {iii}457; Secker fears,
{iii}517, {vii}296; lending libraries
compel textual change in *Lost Girl*,
{iii}619, 621; over *LCL* DHL fearful of
'damned interfering censorship' in USA,
{vi}242, 444; edn of Rabelais seized as
obscene in USA, {vi}288; Mason fears
'censor and smut-hunting authorities',
{vi}314; methods to outwit US,
{vi}362–3, 531; booksellers impose form
of censorship on *LCL*, {vi}476–7, 481,
484, 518; US postal officials seize *LCL* as
'grossly obscene', {vi}531; Mason's view
of US 'Customs authorities', {vi}548;
US authorities 'ought to censor eggs, as
revealing the intimate relation of cock
and hen', {vi}559; DHL invited to write
on 'film he would write or produce if
there were no censor', {vi}601; 'the
ageless censor-animal..civilisation
cannot afford to let the censor-moron
loose', {vi}613–14; official Government
policy on, {vii}5–6; Paris free of,
{vii}58; police seize *Pansies* MS and
copies of *LCL*, {vii}148–50; DHL's
paintings seized by police, {vii}361;
paintings not to be sacrificed to prove
'censorship law' faulty, {vii}371; subject
of *P and O*, {vii}468, 582; private edn is
answer to, {vii}504; Home Secretary on,
{vii}584

Centaur Book Shop and Press, {v}133, 176,
263, 284, 290, 295, 319, 580, 615, {vi}11,
296, 315, 363, 408, 450, 470, 475–6, 487,
{vii}20, 35, 159, 161–2, 240, 297–8, 308,
400–1
see also Mason, H. T.

Centre, *see* Ilkeston, Pupil-Teacher

Century Co., {i}298, 301

Century, The, {i}299, 301–2, 304, 307–8, 321,
345, {iii}528–9, 538, 540, 545, 555, 560,
562, 564, 571–2, 575, 582, 584, 586, 602,
644, {vi}296, {viii}35

Century Illustrated Monthly Magazine, The,
{ii}27, 373

Certificate, *see* Teacher's Certificate

Cervantes Saavedra, Miguel de, *Don Quixote*,
{i}151, {vi}146, 400

Cerveteri (Cervetri) (Italy), {v}650–1,
{vi}28, 30–1, 33, 36, 39, 42–3, 48, 77, 89,
{vii}19, 508
see also Lawrence, D. H., *Etruscan Places*

Cervi, Orazio ('Grazio'), {iii}422, 425–31,
433–7
model for Pancrazio in *Lost Girl*,
{iii}414

Cervo Inn, *see* Hotel del Cervo (Gargnano)

César o Nada, see Baroja y Nessi, P.

Ceylon, {iv}4–8, 11, 236, 242, 252, 257–8,
266, 269–70, 452, {v}7, 67, 211, {vi}10,
458–9, {viii}76
Brewsters urge DHL to visit, {iv}93,
95–6, 102–3, 107–10, 124–6; DHL
deciding to go to USA via, {iv}168,
170–3, 175, 179–80, 184–208; DHL
arrives in, {iv}214; account of life in,
{iv}215ff; 'I feel I don't belong, and
never should', {iv}218; 'interesting to
look at, but...deadly to live in', {iv}227,
230, 244; DHL leaves, {iv}233; DHL
hated much of time in, {iv}239; mystery
and beauty of 'devil dance' in, {vi}80

Cézanne, see Fry, R.

Chaldea, {iv}461, {vii}507, 545

Chalet Beau Site (Les Diablerets), rented by
DHL, {vi}270–92, 294–7, 300–7, 527,
{vii}79–80
like 'wooden cigar-box', {vi}344

Chalet des Aroles (Les Diablerets), rented by
Huxleys, {vi}246, 261–2, 264, 314, 374,
527, {vii}79

Chalet Kesselmatte (Gsteig), rented by
DHL, {vi}451–568 *passim*, 593,
{vii}105, 155

Chamberlain, Joseph, {viii}1
Highbury, his Birmingham home,
{viii}1

Chamberlain, Mr, {iv}462

Chambers family, {i}196, 412, 500, {vi}18

Chambers, Alan Aubrey, {i}34, 36, 38, 53,
64, 70–1, 135, {v}634
'original' of George Saxton in *White
Peacock*, {i}65, 68; infatuated with
Alvina Reeve, {i}74, 104

Chambers, Alvina, *see* Lawrence, A.

Chambers, Henry Kellett, {vi}210, 290, 296, 335, {vii}55, 137, 446, {viii}108

CHAMBERS, JESSIE, {i}1–4, 6, 9, 13, 15–16, 19–20, 32–6, 42, 49, 64, 74, 79, 114, 136, 140, 146, 154, 164, 172, 225–6, 252, 269, 311, 359, 373–4, 377, 397, 452, {ii}77, 150, 401, {vi}18

prototype for Miriam in *Sons and Lovers*, {i}22; DHL proposes engagement to, {i}26; still-life painting for, {i}28; 'A Prelude' submitted in short-story competition by, {i}38, 41, {v}86; loves DHL but not loved by him, {i}50; member of group discussing social problems, {i}53; Emily in *White Peacock*, {i}68, 131; DHL sends books to, {i}95, 151; Teacher's Certificate results, {i}111; visits DHL in Croydon, {i}129–30, 158–9; sends DHL's poems to Hueffer, {i}137; known as 'Muriel', {i}159, 164, 173; moves DHL's 'sex fire', {i}173; DHL breaks engagement to, {i}187, 208; Lydia Lawrence 'hated', {i}197; reaction to DHL-Louie Burrows engagement, {i}198, 205; writes occasionally to DHL, {i}243; described by DHL as 'love of my life', {i}268; 'Paul Morel' MS sent for comment to, {i}317; hears from DHL about Frieda, {i}412, 440, 499, 553; autobiographical novel by, {i}525–6, 532, 545, 550–1; proofs of *S and L* sent to, {i}527; asserts 'the Miriam part of ..novel..a slander', {i}531

'Eunice Temple', {i}525;

'The Rathe Primrose', {i}525

Letters to {i}22, 26–30, 42–3, 47, 56, 82, 87, 95, 104, 111–12, 125, 131, 135, 138–9, 143, 151, 155, 157–8, 161, 175, 177, 191, 212, 219, 221–2, 235, 238, 267–8, 317, 322, 328, 360, 363, 408, 412, 527–8

Letters from {i}527, 531, 553

CHAMBERS, JONATHAN DAVID, {vi}18

Letters to {vi}618

CHAMBERS, MARIA CRISTINA, {vi}14, 210, {vii}55, 68, 137–8, 204, 277, 334–5, 348, 446, 473, 512

her story 'so well written', {vi}211; not destined to be writer 'at least of fiction', {vi}296; turns like DHL to 'the life implicit instead of the life explicit', {vi}378, {viii}110; subscribes for *LCL*, {vi}419, 521, 532, 555, 575, 598, {vii}145; 'mad', {vi}518; *Collected Poems* sent to, {vi}602–3, {vii}96; at Forte dei Marmi, {vii}351, 353–7; 'awful..poor pathetic thing', {vii}360; keen to be DHL's US agent, {vii}439–40, 495–6, 524–5, 547, 550–1, 586, {viii}108; *Escaped Cock* for, {vii}496, 498, 530; 'Men and Women'and 'Mother and Daughter' sent to, {vii}499–500; slaves for but not liked by DHL, {vii}617 'John of God, the Water Carrier', {vi}211

Letters to {vi}210–11, 296–7, 377–9, 418–19, 521–2, 555, 575–6, {vii}96, 144–5, 351, 357–9, 363–4, 366–7, 377, 385–6, 438–41, 495–7, 524–5, 538–9, 550–2, 586, 623–4

Letters from {vii}357, 367, {viii}108–10

Chambers, Muriel May, *see* Holbrook, M. M.

CHAMBERS, SARAH ANN, {i}22, 191, {vi}618

Letters to {i}22, 36

CHAMBERS, EDMUND, {i}28, 67, 191, {vi}618

Letters to {i}22, 36

Champlain, Lake (USA), {iv}543

Channel Isles, {v}289, 310, 413

Mackenzie leases Herm and Jethou, {iii}594, 600–1, 603, 628, 653, 656, {iv}36

Channing, Minnie Lucy ('Puma'), {ii}524–5, 530, 540

Heseltine's relationship with, {ii}481, 501, 504, 517, 539, 546, 557, 598; 'Pussum' in *W in L*, {iii}36, {iv}87, 93–4, 114, 116, 123; in Zennor, {viii}25

CHANSLOR, ROY

Letters to {iv}331

Chapala (Mexico), {iv}15, 17, 433–67, 474, 484, 505, 508–9, 511, 519–20, {v}24, 55, 84, 163, 219, 235, 273, 281, {vi}213, 278, {vii}574, {viii}80

Chapala, Lake (Mexico), {iv}433–40, 443–6, 449–50, 45–5, 467, 474, 519

Chapel Farm Cottage, *see* Hermitage

CHAPMAN & HALL, {iii}441, 537, {iv}133, 248
Letters to {iv}247

Chapman, George, {ii}253
see also Homer

CHAPTER, SONIA K., {v}110, {vii}430
Letters to {vii}453
Letters from {v}110, 118

Chardin, Jean-Baptiste-Siméon, {iv}47; figurines, {iv}75–6, 78, 86

'Charge of the Light Brigade, The', *see* Tennyson, A.

Chariot of the Sun, see Crosby, H.

Charlemagne, {i}114
see also Bulfinch, T.

Charleroi (Belgium), {i}404

Charleroi (Pennsylvania), {iv}103, 214, 409

Charleroi Savings & Trust Co., DHL's account with, {iv}103, 268, 295, 374, 384, 390, 401, 409, 419, 521, {viii}69, 79

Charles Auchester: a Memorial, see Sheppard, E.S.

Charles I, {i}124

Charles II, {i}124

Charles IX of Sweden, {i}114

Charles, Robert Henry, {vii}519, 528

Charles Stewart Parnell, see O'Shea, K.

Charlesworth, May ('Violet Gordon'), {i}127

Charman, John George, {ii}374

Chart (Kent), {i}317, 362–3

Charteris, Hon. Yvo, {ii}414, {iii}212

Charteris, Hugo, *see* Wemyss, 11th Earl of

Chartres (France), {iv}568, 590–1, {vi}78

Chartreuse de Parme, La, see Stendhal, H.B.

Charwoman's Daughter, The, see Stephens, J.

Chase National Bank, DHL's account with, {iv}401, 521, 588, {v}18, {viii}69, 88

Château Brun (St. Cyr), rented by Brewsters, {vii}560, 566, 570, 577, 579, 581, 591, 594, 599, 610, 613, 621–2, 645

Château des Aroles (Les Diablerets), *see* Chalet des Aroles

Chatterji, Jagadish Chandra, {vi}562

Chatterton, Thomas, {i}501

CHATTO & WINDUS LTD, {iii}13, 211, 379, {iv}183, {vi}203, {vii}261, 350, 577, 613, 622
publishers of *LWHCT*, {iii}144ff, 547, {vi}607, {viii}27; object to inclusion of some poems in *LWHCT*, {iii}145–6, 148, 152, 164, 513, {iv}429; DHL signs agreement with, {iii}155–6, 158; proofs of poems, {iii}162–5; publication of volume, {iii}172, 175, 182, 184–6; *LWHCT* in USA, {iii}238, 254; *New Poems* offered to, {iii}265–6; *LWHCT* not reprinted by, {iv}153, 176–7, 181, {vi}168; *LCL* offered to, {vi}343, 352, 372, 375, 384
Letters to {iii}182, 184, 186
Letters from {iii}145, 148, 162, 172, 184, 186, {iv}176

Chekhov, Anton, {i}12, 509, {ii}205, {iii}392–3, {iv}14
DHL receives plays by, {i}385; tired of, {vi}41; 'second-rate writer', {vii}94
The Bet and Other Stories, {ii}447, {iii}183;
The House with the Mezzanine (My Life), {ii}623;
Literary and Theatrical Reminiscences, {vi}42

Cherbourg (France), {iv}483

Cherry Blossom Boot Polish Co., {i}300

Chesham (Buckinghamshire), {ii}208–60 *passim*, {iii}163, 398, {iv}33, 165, 180, 487, {v}141, {vi}219, {viii}12–14

Chesterfield (Derbyshire), {v}468, 551

CHESTERTON, GILBERT KEITH, {i}43, 530, {ii}28, 97, 384, {v}3, 570, {vii}85
Letters to {i}43

Chexbres-sur-Vevey (Switzerland), {iv}279, {vi}7, 425–50, 457–9, {vii}28, 109

Chiara, Anna di, {iii}594, 599, 602, 721, {v}349, 426, {vi}73, 89, 107, 302, 335, {vii}12, 591, 598–600, 604, 646
DHL meets in Capri, {iii}559, {vii}22; 'perfect hostess', {iii}703; owns Villa Giulia, Anacapri, {v}629, {vii}22, 25, 250; orders five copies of *LCL*, {vi}340,

Chiara, Anna di (*cont.*)
    448, {vii}588; 'smaller and older',
    {vii}593–4
Chiara, Ferdinando di, {iii}599, 602, {v}349,
    {vi}73, {vii}12, 22, 250, 588, 591, 593–4,
    598–600, 604, 646
Chiasso (Switzerland), {iii}523
Chiavacci, Giorgio, {v}12, 483
Chicago (USA), {iii}140, 305, 325, 331, 586,
    597, 657, {iv}12, 17, 101, 317, 364,
    492–3, 540, {v}17, 28, 119, 277, 285,
    297–8, {vi}320, {viii}60
    'Something queer and terrifying' about,
    {vi}328
Chihuahua (Mexico), {iv}526–7, {v}153
Child of the Deep, see Lowell, J.
Child, Harold Hannyngton, {viii}90
CHILDHOOD, 'sunny paradise of', {i}195;
    DHL may cut 'childhood part' from
    'Paul Morel', {i}417; 'Odour of
    Chrysanthemums' 'full of my child-
    hood's atmosphere', {i}471; painful to
    be plunged back into world of, {ii}487;
    mind 'dark and without understanding'
    and 'senses violently active' in, {ii}489;
    Americans older than Europeans, 'a
    second childhood', {iii}25; German
    children 'playing so childlike, not Italian
    adult-infant', {iii}720; Carossa associat-
    ed with hymns and, {vi}541; Harwood
    Brewster impressed by DHL's recall of,
    {vii}379
Children of the Bush, see Lawson, H. H.
Chile, {i}228, {ii}178
Chillon, Castle of, (Switzerland),
    {vi}437–41, 445–6, 474
China, {i}4, 168, {iv}141, 182, 316, 361,
    {v}259, {vi}1
    DHL would like to visit, {iv}180, 239,
    279, 458, {v}75, {vi}208
Chinese Poems, see Bax, C.
Chipstead Valley (Surrey), {i}319
Chiusi (Italy), Etruscan remains in, {v}449,
    453, 461, 650, {vi}42–3, 48, 75, 79, 86,
    88–9, 93–4, 182, 302, 317, 508, 538, 566
Chocolate Soldier, The, see Straus, O.
Cholesbury (Buckinghamshire), {ii}238, 254,
    {iii}209, 251–2, {iv}180

Cholmondeley, Mary, {i}14, 144
Chopin, Frédéric François, {i}9, 253, 308,
    {iv}233, {vii}275
Christ, Jesus, *see* Jesus Christ
Christchurch (Hampshire), {i}349, 352
Christian Symbolism, see Jenner, Mrs H.
Christian, Bertram, {ii}193, 199, 222
Christian, Gilbert A., {i}26
Christiania, *see* Kristiania
CHRISTIANITY, writers against, {i}37,
    39, 41; DHL doubts but disapproves of
    uncompromising hostility towards,
    {i}41, 98–9, 101, 215; resurrection
    essential as well as crucifixion in,
    {ii}248–9; phoenix in, {ii}252–3;
    Solovyov and Dostoievsky made mess
    'fiddling about with orthodox', {ii}343,
    345; 'christian religiosity' abandoned,
    {ii}364–5, 367; 'eternal opposition'
    central to Christian theology, {ii}408;
    end of Christian era in sight, {ii}433;
    Cornwall 'belongs still to the days
    before', {ii}493, 496, 499, 503; Cornish
    attachment to 'self-fulfilment and social
    destruction' not Christian principles of
    'social love and self-sacrifice', {ii}505;
    'original self in man' modified by
    'universal idea' of, {ii}538; in
    Dostoievsky, {ii}543–4; time to leave
    'our Christian-democratic epoch',
    {ii}592, 600, 604; 'based on the love of
    self, the love of property, one degree
    removed', {ii}626–7; Forster 'one of the
    last products of', {iii}22; DHL detests
    lambs, 'symbols of Christian meekness',
    {iii}124; 'pure understanding' between
    Christ and Magdalen 'deeper than the
    knowledge of', {iii}180; Christian
    ascetics in Egyptian desert, {iii}669–70;
    Murry's (Frieda), {v}344; every Jew a
    Jehovah, every Christian a Jesus,
    {vi}100; 'forgiving' has 'humble
    christian apology sound', {vi}113; for
    Italian peasant children Christmas a
    fairy-tale, 'not Christian a bit', {vi}243;
    DHL loves 'pre-Christian heavens',
    {vii}544; impossible to fit 'Christian
    religion to the State', {vii}618; DHL

assumes 'forbearance of a Christian
martyr', {viii}7
see also Jenner, Mrs. H.
Christine, *see* Hughes, C.
Chrustchoff, *see* Croustchoff, B.
Church of England Society for Providing
Homes for Waifs and Strays, {i}97
Church Times, The, {vi}603
Churchill, (Sir) Winston Spencer, {i}459,
{ii}41, 48, 371, 609, {iii}55
Churchill, Lord Ivor, *see* Spencer-Churchill,
Lord I.C.
Ciccia, *see* Falanga, F.
Ciccio, *see* Cacópardo, Francesco
Cicero, {ii}91
Cimabue, Giovanni, {ii}275, 296
Cimbrone, *see* Palazzo Cimbrone
Cities and Cemeteries of Etruria, see Dennis,
G.
City of the Soul, The, see Douglas, Lord A.
Ciudad Juarez (Mexico), {iv}412, 525–7
CIVILISATION, freedom incompatible
with 'town and', {i}427; interchange and
mingling of man and woman essential to
give new start to, {ii}181; DHL disputes
greatness of present, {ii}380; 'living
organism of the soul of Europe' has
potential for growth into new 'epoch of',
{ii}425; collapse of present 'wave of',
{ii}431, 441; Ajanta frescoes 'the zenith
of a very lovely', {ii}489; Cornwall has
remains of pre-Christian Celtic,
{ii}495–6, 499; European 'far higher'
than Eastern, {ii}608; New York more
awful than savage jungle because of
'overweening mechanical', {iii}357;
'million curses on European', {iii}566;
'beautiful and fine' so long as alive and
not 'ennuyée', {iv}206; DHL's nostalgia
for 'old', {iv}250; Indians opposed to
but influenced by American, {iv}310;
DHL sickened by 'so-called white',
{iv}481, {v}147; 'Sundays better away
from', {v}56; to lack 'any centre, any
centrifugal I' is 'central malady' of
present, {v}431; 'It's all such a mess',
{vi}304; 'censor-moron' dangerous to,
{vi}613; hateful 'machine civilisation'

wants to 'destroy real humanness',
{vii}179; in 'S of France..old civilisation
jogging along on its income', {vii}594
Civita Castellana (Italy), {v}649, {vi}89
Clairouin, Denyse, {vii}223, 228
Clapps, *see* Klapps
Clarence, *see* Thompson, C.
Claridge Gallery, {vi}16, 433–4, 437, 440,
446
Clarissa Harlowe, see Richardson, S.
CLARK, JOHN, {vi}518
   Letters to {vi}617–18
   Letters from {vi}520
Clark, R. & R., Ltd, {ii}532, 601, 605
Clark, Rose ('Tante'), {v}642, {vi}435
CLARKE, JOHN LAWRENCE ('JACK'),
{ii}486, 488, {iii}245–7, 259–60, 340,
350–1, 550, 618, 647, {iv}70, 137, 377,
423, {v}9, 259, 279, 366, 468, 566, 579,
617, 631–2, 643, {vi}5, 63, 69, 121, 143,
180, 201–2, 227, 336, 350–1, 510,
{vii}107, 181, 212, 398, 459, 621
DHL sends present to, {iv}164, {v}181,
359, {vi}107, 235, {vii}76, 127, 592; gift
for DHL from, {vi}255
   Letters to {iii}703–4, {iv}164, {v}30,
359–60, {vi}83, 250, {vii}254
CLARKE, LETTICE ADA (LAWRENCE),
{i}15, 17–18, 23, 27, 33–4, 36, 39, 42,
85, 143, 147, 174, 189, 194–5, 197–8,
202–3, 205, 209, 211–13, 215–16, 225,
263, 267, 270–1, 275, 277–8, 280–1,
287–9, 293, 295–6, 302, 306, 319–20,
328–43 *passim,* 365, 369, 379–80, 398,
401, 416, 442, 480, 490, 493, 527, {ii}7,
11, 38, 194, 199–200, 216, 244, 355, 472,
474, 476, 482–8, 654, {iii}50, 112–13,
179, 191–3, 222, 232, 242, 245–6,
258–60, 300, 307–12, 316–17, 320, 333,
339–40, 351, 378, 383, 407, 434, 440,
452–3, 461, 477–8, 574, 579, 595, 603,
609, 616, 670, 677, 682–3, 697, 721,
723–4, {iv}28, 39, 64, 137, 174, 311, 327,
493, 497, 542, 554, {v}1, 9–10, 13, 112,
124, 184, 193, 206, 227, 257, 266, 304,
309–12, 315–20, 332, 343, 359, 362–3,
369, 372, 405, 474, 483, 489–90, 498–9,
501, 506, 514, 517, 521, 524–8, 534, 538,

CLARKE, LETTICE ADA
(LAWRENCE) (*cont.*)
545, 566, 582–3, 609–10, 618, 653, {vi}3,
5, 10, 63, 83, 87, 110, 177, 191, 215, 245,
250, 285, {vii}5, 10–11, 180, 195, 262,
309,360, 418, 489, 510, 513, 559, 588,
591, 593, 598, 602, 604, 622, 630, 633,
647, {viii}113
spends slender earnings on father,
{i}219–20, 230, 232; DHL's 'one, *real*
relative', {i}231; DHL paints *Idyll* for,
{i}243; 'dipped into disbelief', {i}248,
255–6, 261–2; DHL sends music to,
{i}324; approves DHL's breaking
engagement, {i}361; DHL's attachment
to Frieda known only to, {i}412, 446;
'very bitter' about Frieda, {i}440; to be
married, {i}440, 452, 457, 497, 544;
marriage, {ii}38, 41, 55; offers present
for DHL, {i}454, 461, 463; writes to
Frieda {i}538; copies of DHL's
publications for, {ii}19, {iii}494, 729,
{iv}261, 299, 342, {v}80, 100, 114,
141–2, 150, 189, 226, 247, 329, 413, 607,
{vi}69, 396, {vii}68, 95, 97, 232, 318,
347, 380, 422, 530, 557, 573; source of
financial help for DHL, {iii}207, 240,
427; friction between DHL and,
{iii}223; arranges Mountain Cottage for
DHL, {iii}234–6, 251; nurses DHL,
{iii}335, 337; sends coat for DHL,
{iv}50; DHL sends presents to, {iv}92,
233, 254, 423, {v}85, 139, 181, 476,
598–9, {vi}81, 107, 228, 235, 256, 458,
482, {vii}330, 592; visits DHL in
Spotorno, {v}382–3, 388–94; in Monaco
with DHL, {v}397–9; 'bust-up' with
Frieda spoiled holiday, {v}401; sends
shirts etc for DHL, {vi}143, 178–9, 202,
{vii}330–1, 397, 581; orders
Umckaloaba medicine for DHL,
{vi}325, 350, 360–1, 366, 387; ignorant
about *LCL*, {vi}486, 489, 492; DHL's
birthday remembered by, {vi}562; and
LCL, {vii}68, 76, 107, 112, 125, 127,
142; in Bandol, {vii}173, 176, 178, 181,
183–5; unhappy and dissatisfied,
{vii}186–7, 190, 197, 210, 213–14;

reimbursed for rent on Mountain
Cottage, {vii}193–4, 211; transports two
paintings to England, {vii}199; MS of
Pansies to, {vii}238, 259, 278, 318;
exhibition of paintings and, {vii}319,
321–2, 329–30, 337–8, 364, 395, 419,
425, 632, 652–3; finds *Rainbow* MS,
{vii}458–9, 515, 541; forgets DHL's
birthday, {vii}478, 494; has DHL's
notebook with early poems, {vii}532
Letters to {i}228–31, 233–4, 236–7, 242–4,
255–7, 261–2, 282–4, 313–14, 316,
324–5, 407, 411, 433, 443–4, 454, 457,
461, 463, 484, 502, 531–3, 537–8, 540–2,
{ii}100, 184–5, {iii}421, 426–8, 431,
437, 464, 479, 499, 508–9, 550, 583, 589,
618, 626, 647, {iv}50, 53, 59, 70, 203,
233, 254, 283–5, 303, 377, 384, 411,
413–14, 423, 427, 439–40, 535, 552, 591,
{v}85, 98, 113–15, 126, 142, 168–9, 176,
181, 197, 258–9, 278–9, 296–7, 324–5,
352–3, 365–6, 377–8, 399–403, 408, 410,
413–14, 432, 448–9, 467–9, 475–6, 492,
511, 525–6, 546, 551–2, 565–6, 578–9,
598–9, 616–17, 630–2, 642–3, 657,
{vi}25–7, 38–9, 48–9, 62–3, 69–70, 80–1,
97–8, 106–7, 117, 121, 134, 137–8, 140,
143, 178–80, 201–2, 227–8, 235–6,
255–6, 263, 272, 286–7, 350–1, 360–1,
387, 412–13, 422–3, 425–6, 439, 455,
457–8, 482, 509–10, 553–4, 571, 577,
586, 596–7, 612, {vii}17, 76, 107, 126–7,
186–7, 192–3, 211–12, 221, 247, 259,
299, 318–19, 330–1, 338, 352, 364, 366,
378, 393, 397–8, 421–2, 449, 458–60,
480, 492, 531–2, 579–80, 591–2, 621,
631–2, 639, 641, 652–3
Letters from {i}328–9, 337, 341, 361, 527,
{v}394
Clarke, Stanley, {v}448, 469, 566
Clarke, William, {iii}259, {v}279,
{vii}192–5, 212
CLARKE, WILLIAM EDWIN ('EDDIE')
{i}27, 174, 216, 244, 278, 333, 336,
340–1, 343, 444, 461, 541, {ii}38,
{iii}307–8, 378, {v}259, 353, 448, 469,
545, 610, 632, {vi}25, 81, 180, {vii}17,
261, 338, 513

doesn't understand tragedy of life, {i}261; to be married, {i}440, {ii}38; to be discharged from navy, {iii}339; makes suit for DHL, {v}324; tailor's shop, {v}592, 643; death of father, {vii}193
Letters to {vii}193–4

Clarke, William Herbert ('Bertie', 'Bertram') {iv}493, 497, {v}9, 85, 209, 259, 324, 330, 366, 552, 610, 617, 631, 643, {vi}5, 63, 69, 121, 143, 179–80, 510, {vii}212, 319, 459
DHL sends present for, {v}181, {vi}107, 202, 215, 217, 235, 256, 458, {vii}76, 592; already 'prisoner' in school, {vi}554, 571, 597

'Clarté' movement, {iii}5, 371, 379, 484

Clayhanger, see Bennett, E. A.

CLAYTON, DOUGLAS, {ii}7, 15, 67, 370, 398, 414, 524, 583, 666, {iii}34, 135 typing short stories for DHL, {ii}30, 52, 64–5, 190, 194, 201; types poems, {ii}55–6, 87; DHL pays for typing, {ii}59, 125, 395, 416, 581; types 'sketches', {ii}202, 204–5, 236, 381–3, 385, 387, 390, 408, 410, 413, 416; 'excellent typist, and perfect in reliability', {ii}446; 'honest', {vii}614; return of MSS requested from, {vii}632
Letters to {ii}45, 52, 59, 64, 190, 194, 201–2, 204–5, 356, 381–3, 385, 387, 390, 395, 397, 408, 410, 413, 416, {vii}632
Letters from {ii}381, {viii}11–12

CLAYTON, KATHARINE ('Katie'), {vii}632
acts as intermediary for Douglas Clayton, {ii}30, 37–8, 40, 55–6, 370, 413–14, 581; cottage at Lerici described for, {ii}125–6
Letters to {ii}30, 37–8, 40, 55–6, 87, 125–6, 370, 413–14, 524, 581–3, 666, 668

Clayton, Patrick ('Pat') Andrew, {ii}87, 125, 370, 408, 524, 666

Clemenceau, Georges, {iii}318
'that old scoundrel', {iii}294

Clifton, Selma, *see* McElligot, S.

Clive, {iii}521, 542

Cloister and the Hearth, The, see Reade, C.

Clutton-Brock, Alan Francis, {vii}362

Clydeside, {ii}371, {vii}468

Clynes, John Robert, {vii}328

COBDEN-SANDERSON, RICHARD, {i}86
Letters to {v}180–1
see also Criterion

Coblenz (Germany), {i}398

Cochranes, the, rich English expatriates in Italy, {ii}3, 133, 139, 149, 168, 173, 175, 178, 629

Codnor Castle (Derbyshire), {i}68

Codrington, Kenneth de Burgh, *An Introduction to the Study of Medieval Indian Sculpture*, {vii}270

Coeur De Lion, *see* Richard I

Coffin, Mr, {iv}476

Colacicchi, Giovanni, {vi}62

Colchester (Essex), {iii}273

Colefax, Sybil, Lady, {vi}6, 353, 371–2, 374–5, 383–4

Coleridge, Samuel Taylor, {ii}223, {vii}615
Christabel, {iii}502;
Rime of the Ancient Mariner, {i}55, 294, {vi}150;
'Youth and Age', {i}132

Colet Court School (West Kensington), {viii}6

Colette (Sidonie-Gabrielle Willy), {ii}39, 41
La Vagabonde, {ii}39

Coll., *see* Nottingham University College

Collar, George, {i}26

Collard, Mr, {iii}266, 269

Collard, Mrs, {iii}266

Collier, John, {iv}332, 527, 577
'always was a worm', {vi}551

Collier, Lucy Wood, {vi}551

COLLINGS, ERNEST HENRY ROBERTS, {i}19, 543, {iii}5, 13, 135, 556
sends *Sappho* to DHL, {i}468, 481–3, 491; DHL's critical assessment of poetry by, {i}471–3; DHL declares his 'great religion' to, {i}503–4; *Love Poems* sent to, {i}519; jacket-design for *S and L* requested from, {i}528–9, 535–6, 538, 539–40; design rejected, {i}547; exhibits in London, {ii}46–7; Boucher cover

COLLINGS, ERNEST HENRY
ROBERTS (*cont.*)
design by, {ii}68–9; on *Outlines* (dedicated to DHL), {ii}156–9; subscribes to
Signature, {ii}400, 404
Outlines, {i}468, 503, 518–19, {ii}134,
156–60;
Sappho, {i}468, 473, 481–3, 503
Letters to {i}468, 471–3, 490–2, 502–4,
518–19, 528–9, 535, 539–40, 547–9
{ii}46–7, 53, 68–9, 134, 156–60, 360,
395, 400, {iii}99–100, 128–9, 137–8, 153
Letters from {i}547
Collingwood, Harry, *see* Lancaster, W. J. C.
COLLINS, VERE HENRY GRATZ,
{ii}447, 463, 483, 653, {iii}121, 194,
219–20, 242, 269, 286, 299, {v}26,
{vii}485
prompts writing of *Movements*, {iii}261,
{v}32, 117; introduces DHL to Helen
Thomas, {iii}372; DHL writes Epilogue
for *Movements* for, {v}136; *Movements*
'mauled' by Irish censor sent to, {v}336,
495; *Glad Ghosts* for, {v}588; subscribes
for *LCL*, {vii}90–1, 124
Lord Byron in his Letters, {v}588
Letters to {v}136, 336–7, 495, 588
Letters from {v}136–7, {vii}90
Collins, William Wilkie, {i}166
Collins, William, Sons & Co., {iii}121, 135
Collodi, C., *see* Lorenzini, C.
COLMAN, MR, *see also* Gilman, C.
Letters to {vi}48
Colocicchi, *see* Colacicchi, G.
Cologne (Germany), {i}350, {iii}46, {iv}78,
{vi}142–3, 148 {vii}392
Colombia, {iii}173–4
Colombo (Ceylon), {iv}7–8, 171–238 *passim*,
{v}80
Colonna, Vittoria, {ii}592
Colorado (USA), {iv}336, 338, 354, 356–7,
389, 567, {v}297, 304
Columbus, see Irving, W.
Columbus, Christopher, {i}114, {ii}162, 362,
556, {iii}66, {vii}14
Colwyn Bay (Wales), {i}295
Comfort, Will Levington, {iv}430, 434, 439,
444, 499
The Public Square, {iv}499

Comfortless Memory, see Baring, M.
Commando, see Reitz, D.
'Common Sense About the War', *see* Shaw,
G. B.
COMMUNISM, {ii}11, {iii}5, 379, 450,
{v}13, {vii}3, 146
Rananim 'a sort of', {ii}259, 273; Roman
Catholic Church seemingly sympathetic
to, {iv}124, 133; despite economic
depression in Derbyshire little sign of,
{v}315
Como (Italy) {ii}79, 384, {v}140, {viii}9
Como, Lake (Italy), {iii}568–9, 574, 585,
587–8, 592–3, 599, 602, {iv}167, 190,
194–5, {vii}11, 351, 354–5, 359, 396,
398–400, 402, 410, 416
Compton (Berkshire), {iii}382
Compton House (Bournemouth), {i}344–61,
{viii}6
Comstock, Anthony, {ii}446
Comte, Auguste, {iii}381
Conard, Editions, {ii}453, 458–9, 464
Concerning Corsica, see Juta, R.
Concha, Agapeto, {vi}211
Concha, John, {iv}325, 332, {v}38, 42
Conduct of Life, see Emerson, R. W.
Cone, William, {iii}668, 672
Confessions, see St Augustine; Rousseau, J.-J
CONFLICT, 'School is a', {i}85; 'machinery
of soul..deranged by..shocks of', {i}93;
'of unaccomplished passion', {i}300; in
Garnett's *Jeanne D'Arc*, {i}470; life 'a
knot of conflicts' (Frieda), {ii}288;
maturity involves experience of, {ii}366;
essential to have 'give and take of love
and', {ii}376; DHL finds 'peace beyond
understanding' in, {iii}595; in Burrow
'unresolved conflict between science and
art', {vi}115; ill-health denotes conflict
with 'present system', {vii}464; to be in
conflict wtih the self creates difficulties
in living, {vii}542
Congregational Literary Society, *see*
Eastwood 11
Conibear, *see* Conybear, Mrs
Connecticut (USA), {iii}17, 166, 178, 600,
603, 628, 668, 672, {iv}326, {viii}39
Conrad, Joseph, {i}12, 15, 104, 118, 138,
278, 381, 488, {iii}167, 693

Twixt Land and Sea: Tales, {i}465;
  Under Western Eyes, {i}456, 465, 467,
  {iii}167
Conscription (Military Service Bill), {ii}10,
  14, 343, 463, 502, 522, 551, 556, 597,
  599, 600–2, 605–7, 611–12, 614–16, 650,
  656, {iii}250
    DHL ordered to enlist, {ii}616; 'final
    fall.. when England chose general
    compulsion to military service', {ii}618;
    'I hated my Conscription experience',
    {ii}622; Cornishmen unwarlike but
    accepted, {ii}625
CONSERVATIVE(S), committed to
  'old..glorious national ideal', {ii}378;
  want 'to bully or..be bullied', {ii}378;
  aim is 'retrogressive "equal distribution
  of burden"', {ii}629; Europe swinging
  back to, {iii}728; socialists more hostile
  to DHL than, {vii}460
Constable and Co., {ii}180, 296, 610,
  {iii}202, 421, {iv}345, {vi}265, 471,
  480, {viii}16
    '"New Poetry Series"..looks so
    mediocre', {ii}519; 'a bit cheap', {ii}525;
    refuse *Amores*, {ii}535, 558, 560, 562,
    {iii}147; 'too timid and niggardly',
    {iii}153
    Letters from {ii}535
Constance (Germany), {i}429, {ii}74,
  {iv}44–52, {vi}95, 103, 382–3, {viii}40,
  42
Constance, Lake (Germany), {ii}76, {iv}38,
  44–5, 49–50
Constant Nymph, The, see Kennedy, M.
Constantine Bay (Cornwall), {ii}525, 551
Constantine, Emperor, {i}114
Constantinople (Turkey), {v}343, 345
Co(n)sulich Line, {v}299
Contemporary Belgian Poetry, see Bithell, J.
Contes Drolatiques, Les, see Balzac, H. de
CONWAY, ANNE ELIZABETH, {v}228,
  254, 262–4, 399, {vi}323–4, {vii}108
    S and S sent to, {v}264
    Letters to {v}228–9, 290–1
CONWAY, GEORGE ROBERT GRAHAM,
  {v}219, 228–229, 268, 287, 291, {vi}10
    WWRA sent to, {vi}432; subscribed for
    LCL, {vii}108, 184, 202, 246

*An Englishman and the Mexican
  Inquisition*, {vi}323
Letters to {v}262–4, 399, {vi}323–4,
  {vii}108
Letters from {vii}184
Conybear, Mrs, {vi}220, 335
Cook, James, *Voyages of Discovery*, {v}321
Cook, Thomas, Ltd {ii}464, {iii}383,
  414–15, 424, 452, 524, 590, 639, 721,
  725, {iv}56, 166, 172, 177, 180, 257, 259,
  487, {v}299–300, 327, 330, 333, 560,
  {vi}112, 170–1, 473, 588, {vii}185, 498
    DHL uses as poste restante, {iii}418,
    585–7, 591, 600, 603–4, 611, 627, 693,
    696–7, 700, 702, {iv}80, 184, 220, 236,
    265, {vii}226, 242–3, 246–50, 255, 275,
    452, 482, 488, 490; 'isn't very good
    nowadays', {iii}569; 'at all big stations'
    in Italy is agent from, {iv}195; 'tells you
    every mortal thing', {vi}419; 'most
    unreliable', {vii}292
COOPER, ETHEL,
  Letters to {i}23
Cooper, Florence ('Florrie'), {v}115,
  583
COOPER, FRANCES ('FRANKIE')
  AMELIA, {i}34, 36, 83, 198, 215–16,
  243, 278, 280, 314, 432, 539, {vi}88
    dies of TB, {iii}307, 310, {v}115, 633–4,
    {vi}63
    Letters to {i}90, 93
COOPER, GERTRUDE ('GERTIE'), {i}23,
  34, 93, 243, 278, 280, 283–4, {iv}254,
  {v}9, 115, 259, 279, 325, 366, 589, 599,
  {vi}2, 5, 69–70, 80, 256, 287, 350, 439,
  554, 597, 612, {vii}259, 418, 459, 538
    in hospital, {v}359; present for, {v}359,
    {vi}235, {vii}76; collects medical
    insurance monies, {v}468, 541; DHL's
    anxiety about tubercular condition of,
    {v}516, 521, 524–6, 530, 536, 538, 541,
    545, 552, 557, 564–5, 578–9, 607, 617;
    threatened with operation, {v}630,
    632–3, 635, 641–3, 643–4, 645, 654,
    {vi}25, 27, 38; recovers after operation,
    {vi}42, 47–8, 60, 62–3, 87–8, 125, 140,
    215, 227, 481, 510, 577; DHL offers
    financial support for, {vi}137, 245; lives
    with Ada Clarke, {vi}143, 177–80, 201

COOPER, GERTRUDE ('GERTIE') (*cont.*)
  Letters to {i}23–4, 36, 83, 90, 268, 432,
    538–9, {iii}419, 477–8, 588–9, 603, 611,
    {iv}53, 60, {v}330–1, 360, 541, 545,
    547–8, 560–1, 566–7, 582–3, 609–10,
    632–4, 643–4, {vi}63–4, 87–8, 125,
    244–5, 335–6, 481–2, {vii}210–11
Cooper, Gussie, {i}286
Cooper, James Fenimore, {ii}615, {iii}40–1,
    324, {iv}543
  The Deerslayer, {ii}615, {iii}41, 54, 65;
  The Last of the Mohicans, {ii}615,
    {iii}40;
  The Pathfinder, {iii}40;
  The Pioneers, {iii}65;
  The Prairie, {iii}65
Copenhagen (Denmark), {iv}345
Coppard, Alfred Edgar, {v}284, {vi}180,
    198, 203
  Yokohama, Garland, and Other Poems,
    {v}641
Corbin, Alice, *see* Henderson, A. C.
Corbinetta, *see* Evans, A. O.
Cordoba (Spain), {vii}276, 283
Coréine, {vii}642, 651
Corfu (Greece), {v}427, 573
Corke, Alfred E., {i}411
Corke, Annie ('Nance'), {i}225
Corke, Arthur Stanley, {i}168, 175
    requests loan, {i}225, 390; unreliable
    typist for DHL, {i}309, 311, 321, 323,
    326, 328, {ii}44
CORKE, HELEN, {i}5, 9–11, 16–17, 19–20,
    136, 225, 236, 253, 412, 527, 531, {ii}91
  '*interests*' DHL, {i}154, 158; DHL
    tormented by relationship with,
    {i}159–64, 238–40, 245; DHL will never
    ask for extra-marital sex again, {i}286;
  Trespasser 'a work of fiction on a frame of
    [her] actual experience', {i}359; DHL
    proposes night together at Garnett's
    house, {i}362; offers 'The Cornwall
    Writing' to Garnett, {i}373; copy of
    Trespasser for, {i}411, 419–20; DHL
    questions wisdom of maintaining link
    with, {i}553
  'The Cornwall Writing'{i}373;
  The Freshwater Diary', {i}129;

  Neutral Ground, {i}129, 136, 157, 160,
    163
  Letters to {i}129, 157, 159–64, 173, 175,
    238–40, 245, 285–6, 303, 357, 359–60,
    362, 411, 553–4
  Letters from {i}353, 373
Corke, Louisa, {i}411
Corn of Wheat, see Young, E. M.
Corneille, Pierre, {i}217
Cornell University (USA), {viii}106
Corneto (Italy), {v}650–1, {vi}51,
    {vii}508
Cornish Bros (Birmingham), 'Dirty swine'
    order two copies of *LCL*, then cancel,
    {vi}496, 500–1, 510, 515, 517, 519;
    cheque stopped by, {vi}529; cheque
    received from, {vi}545
Cornish, J. E., Ltd (Manchester), three
    copies of *LCL* ordered by, {vi}503
Cornwall, {ii}13, 515, 523–4, 528–9, 539–41,
    584–5, 624, {iii}1–2, 4, 14, 16, 47–9, 62,
    115–17, 134, 193, 197–9, 250, 266, 269,
    280, 321, 327, 343, 363, 365, 435, 587,
    697, 712, 714, {iv}25, 249, 313, {v}450,
    475
    teaching post available in, {i}207, 210,
    213–14, 216, 218; DHL at Beresford's
    cottage in, {ii}482, 484–5, 487–8,
    491–559; 'bare..dark..elemental',
    {ii}503, 514; 'flicker of Celtic conscious-
    ness' in, {ii}505, 507–8; 'sense
    of..primeval darkness' in, {ii}519, 526;
    people '*anti-social* and unchristian',
    {ii}520; DHL at Tinners Arms,
    {ii}560–81; moves to Higher
    Tregerthen, {ii}582; Cornishmen
    unwarlike but accepted conscription,
    {ii}625; Cornish people depressed over
    war, {iii}49, 52; people limited and
    'horrible', {iii}82; DHL excluded from,
    {iii}167–9, 171–9, 182, 186, 188–90,
    193, 197–9, 207, 221–2, 242, 251; feels
    persecuted by people of, {iii}188; 'a
    malicious place', {iii}344; 'I loved
    Cornwall', {vi}517
  see also Higher Tregerthen, Porthcothan,
    Zennor
'Cornwall Writing, The', *see* Corke, H.

Cornwallis-West, Beatrice Stella, {iii}69, 305

Corot, Jean Baptiste Camille, {i}130, 266–7, 282, {ii}263

Corriere della Sera, {ii}135, {v}90, 92, 200

Corsica (France), {v}436, {vi}584, {vii}176, 183–7, 191–2, 194–6, 202, 213, 339

Cortina d'Ampezzo (Italy), {iv}48, {vi}133, 204, 207, 218, 221, 227

    Huxleys in, {v}532, 560, 563, 574, 585–6, 595, 597, 647, {vi}155, 201, 214

Cortona (Italy), Etruscan remains in, {v}413, 415–16, 427, 447, 449, 461, 464, {vi}42–3, 48, 75, 79, 86, 88–9, 93, 508, 538, 566

Corvo, Baron, (Frederick Rolfe), DHL reviews *Hadrian the Seventh* by, {v}301, 317, 320, 325

    In His Own Image, {v}315

Corydon, see Gide, A. P. G.

Cosa (Italy), {vi}89

Cosmopolitan, {iii}355, 360, {v}312, {viii}61

Cossall (Nottinghamshire), {i}35, 117, 161, 206, {v}243

Costanza, *see* Peterich, C.

Côte d'Azur (France), {vii}17–18, 20, 94, 158, 185–6, 211, 490–2, 567

Coterie, see New Coterie

Coteshael (Quorn), {i}171, 215, 254, 280, 291–2, 325, 336, 340, 342, 348, 350, 369

Cottam, Barbara, {v}57

Cottam, Brooke, {v}57

Cottam, Elisabeth ('Betty') Moore, {iv}525, {v}39, 57, 467, 492, 530, 537, {vi}155

Cottam, Louis Francis, {v}57, 159, 164

Coulton, George Gordon, *From St Francis to Dante*, {ii}538, 572, 580

Count Albany, see Carswell, D.

Counterpane, see Huxley, A., *Point Counter Point*

Country Life, {iv}55

'Country of the Blind, The', *see* Wells, H. G.

COURNOS, HELEN, {v}410, 434, 450, {vi}221, {vii}394–5

    Letters to {v}410

COURNOS, JOHN, {iii}173, 190, {iv}296, 464–5, {v}87, 270

St Mawr for, {v}410; 'pious and Jesusy', {vi}221; *LCL* for, {vii}395, 452–3; 'in some respects *awful* - in some respects, nice', {vii}482

    Best British Short Stories, {iv}296, 464, {v}87, 270;

    Miranda Masters, {iii}173, {v}433;

    O'Flaherty the Great, {vii}394, 453

    Letters to {v}410, 433–4, 450, {vii}394–5, 453–4, 483

    Letters from {iv}464–5

Court, Ernest, {i}208, 214, 238

Cousin Pons, Le, see Balzac, H. de

Covarrubias, Miguel, {iv}534

Coventry (Warwickshire), {viii}1

Coventry, Camilla, {v}93

Covici, Friede, Inc., {vi}560–1

Covici, Pascal, {vi}14, 560–1

    Letters from {vi}560

Coward, Ralph, {vi}298, 308

Cowes (Isle of Wight), {i}134, 278

Cox, Sarah Elizabeth, {i}242, 250, 269

Coyoacán (Mexico City), {iv}421–3, {v}155–7, 236, 263

Cradle of the Deep, see Lowell, J.

Craig, Gordon, {iii}262, {v}579

Craig, Mary A., {iv}188

    The House by the Medlar-Tree, {iv}196, 200, 219

Cramb, John Adam (J. A. Revermort), *Cuthbert Learmont*, {ii}609;

    Lucius Scarfield, {ii}609;

    The Marrying of Hester Rainsbrook, {ii}609

Cramb, Meyrick, {ii}609, 631–2

Cramb, Mrs Meyrick, {ii}609, 631–2

Crambseys, {iv}501

Crane, Nathalia, *see* Abarbanel, N. C. R.

Cranford, see Gaskell, E.

Cranmer-Byng, Launcelot, *A Lute of Jade*, {i}168

Crawford, Clare, {i}169–70

Crawford, Dorothy, {i}169

CRAWFORD, GRACE, {i}14, 226

    MS copy of Francis Thompson's 'Absence' sent to, {i}145; DHL dreams about, {i}147–8; Christmas card and poem for, {i}149–50; *Elga* returned to,

CRAWFORD, GRACE (*cont.*)
{i}164; *Lute of Jade* sent to, {i}168;
Scarlatti's 'O Cessate' signature-tune of
friendship with, {i}171, 335; DHL's
home described for, {i}174; MS of
Widowing sent to, {i}188
Letters to {i}145–50, 164–71, 174–5, 182–3,
186, 188, 334–5
Crawford, Inez Randall, {i}166, 171, 183,
188, 226, 335
Crawford, Jack Randall, {i}169
Crawford, Theron Clark, {i}166, 171, 335
Creative Art, {vi}81, {vii}249, 536
Crécy, Battle of, {i}86
Credito Italiano, {iii}482–3, {iii}539–40,
{vi}410
Creel, George Edward, {v}59, 83
Cresset Press, {ii}205, {vi}411, {vii}457,
503, 549, 563, 573
Creswell, Peter, {viii}103
Crete, {iv}108, 203–6, {vii}290, 507–8
Crèvecœur, Michel Guillaume Jean de
('Hector St. John'), {iii}66, 160, 299,
324
Letters from an American Farmer,
{ii}645, {iii}65–6
Craigie, Pearl Mary Teresa, pseud. John
Oliver Hobbes, {i}163
Crich (Derbyshire), {i}34, 57, {ii}57,
{v}592–3
Crichton, Andrew Sanquar, {v}308
CRICHTON, KYLE SAMUEL, {v}200,
202, 506
critical report on story by, {v}293–4;
lacks courage to be creative writer,
{v}307–8; wrote article on DHL at
ranch, {v}343–4
Law and Order, Ltd., {v}289;
'The Tipple', {v}293
Letters to {v}288–9, 293–4, 307–8
Crichton, Mary ('Mae') C., {v}200, 202,
288–9, 294, 308, 506
Crichton, Robert Collier, {v}308
Crichton, Vivienne Ann, {v}308
Crime and Punishment, see Dostoievsky, F.
Criminal Investigation Department, *see*
Scotland Yard
Crippen, Hawley H., {i}505, {vi}218

Criterion Miscellany, see Faber & Faber
Criterion, {v}71, 85–6, 180–1, 193, 205, 331,
432, 459, 514, {vi}76, 270–1, 421, 503,
{vii}170, 272, 439, 500, 507
see also New Criterion
CRITICISM/CRITICS, 'ointment
of..sincere', {i}50; too much approval
valueless as, {i}50; 'insolent', {i}230;
DHL would 'go with surer feet' after
Garnett's, {i}301; *S and L* 'so great it
needs sharp', {ii}1; DHL 'rotten critic',
{ii}74; from Garnett DHL seeks frank,
{ii}142, 151; Murry 'the best critic in
England', {ii}171; 'no critic can admit
anything bigger than himself', {ii}243;
'I really do like', {ii}314; fundamental
human impulse towards construction,
'the rest is criticism, destruction',
{ii}361, 366; 'Criticism..introspection..
analysis' hostile to 'new life', {ii}485;
Sidgwick refuses *Amores*, gives 'very
impertinent criticism of MS', {ii}558;
SCAL 'very keen essays in', {iii}156;
Moore on DHL, {iii}196; DHL '*never*
reads' his critics (Frieda), {v}190; critic
describes DHL as 'the best of the little
writers', {v}387; critics on *Widowing*,
{v}604; Burrow's criticism of psychoanalysis 'is to the quick', {vi}113;
'feelings..less susceptible [than thoughts]
to', {vi}230; DHL on Burns and
Lockhart, {vi}231–2; some sympathy for
Hargrave so DHL 'wouldn't write a
criticism in a paper against him',
{vi}267; 'self-criticism' suggested to
Mabel Luhan, {vi}393; DHL enjoys
'slanging a book', Dobrée avoids 'first-
hand feeling' and writes boring, {vi}502;
I. A. Richards' critique of 'Piano',
{vii}376; 'literary critic' in poem
'Editorial Office', {vii}442; critic 'can
neither paint or write, ..can only put
other people right', {vii}447; function of
critic in 'The Squib', {vii}484–5; 'higher
criticism' scholastic, not for 'great
public', {vii}519; Del Monte not
conducive to 'creative work: only
critical', {viii}59

Crock of Gold, The, see Stephens, J.

Croesus, {vi}81, 410

Croft-Cooke, Rupert, *Natal Verses for Sheila*,
{vii}121

Cromer (Norfolk), {iii}334

Cromford (Derbyshire), {i}24, {iii}232, 243,
253, 264, 300, 312, 343
Hermione in *W in L* 'supposed to live
not far from', {v}243

Cromwell, Oliver, {i}114, {iii}282,
{vii}179

CROSBY, HENRY GREW ('HARRY'),
{v}352, {vi}4, 6, 391, {vii}2, 4, 7, 9,
119, 233, 408, 418, 433, 472, 488, 530,
548
wishes to buy MS, {vi}301; offers $100
for *Sun* MS, {vi}347; sends gold pieces,
{vi}348, 410, {vii}342; DHL writes
'Chaos in Poetry' as introduction for
poems by, {vi}372, 389, 404, 461; DHL
sends MSS to, {vi}388, {vii}306; invited
to publish edn of *Sun*, {vi}404, 462,
504–5, 548, 570, 580, 591, {vii}239;
WWRA sent to, {vi}432; DHL's picture
for, {vi}549; *Collected Poems* for,
{vi}591; *Escaped Cock* for publication by,
{vii}255, 290, 322–3, 339, 398–9, 412,
429, 577, 606–7, 634, 647; commits
suicide, {vii}600–7; 'very very *spoilt*',
{vii}623
Chariot of the Sun, {vi}300, 372, 389–90,
404, {vii}115, 634;
Sleeping Together, {vii}634
see also Lawrence, D. H., *Sun*
Letters to {vi}300–1, 348–9, 372, 388–90,
404–5, 410–11, 429, 461–2, 503–4,
548–9, 570, 580, 590–1, {vii}115–16,
216–17, 220, 231, 239–40, 246–7, 255,
290–1, 322–4, 332, 339, 398–9, 405

CROSBY, MARY JACOB ('CARESSE'),
{v}352, {vi}300, 390, 405, 591, {vii}2,
4, 7, 9, 116, 246, 291, 408, 429, 433, 498,
538, 550, 565, 577–8
sends cheque for *Sun*, {vii}119;
Rawdon's Roof for, {vii}232; DHL
sculpted by, {vii}233; MS of *Escaped
Cock* sent to, {vii}236, 267, 285, 290,
292, 296–7, 322–3; sends proofs of

Escaped Cock, {vii}411; decorations for
Escaped Cock sent to, {vii}417, 426;
Doctor Manente for, {vii}557; business
manager of Black Sun Press, {vii}557–8;
husband's suicide, {vii}600–1, 604, 606,
623; DHL's sympathy for, {vii}634,
647
Letters to {vi}410–11, 614, {vii}119, 216,
220, 231, 239–40, 255, 284–5, 322–4,
332, 339, 398–9, 405, 411–12, 417–18,
426, 450, 471–2, 487–8, 491, 497–8, 530,
536, 548, 557, 634, 647
Letters from {vii}471, 497

Crosby, Stephen van Rensselaer, {vii}240,
255

Crosland, Thomas William Hodgson,
Sonnets, {ii}146

CROSS, WILBUR LUCIUS, {iii}13, 166
invites DHL to write article for *Yale
Review*, {iii}166–7; article rejected,
{iii}177
Letters to {iii}166–7, 177
Letters from {iii}166–7, 177–8

Croton, {i}181, 505

Croton-on-the-Hudson (New York), *see*
Finney Farm

Croustchoff, Boris de, {ii}448, {iii}138, 151,
172, {v}532, {vi}480, 490, 501–2,
{vii}78, 541

Crowley, Edward Alexander ('Aleister'),
{vii}533, 558, 564
DHL disapproves of, {i}169, 171,
{vii}469, 573
Ambergris {i}169, 171

Crown de Leon, {ii}456, 462, 464–6

Crown of Hinduism, The, see Farquhar, J. N.

Crowninshield, Francis Welch ('Frank'),
{v}185, {vii}503–4, 525

Crowthers, the, {ii}632

Croydon I General, {i}8–11, 15, 19, 52, 91,
95, 97, 103, 116, 122, 129, 154–76
passim, 187–214 *passim*, 235–6, 260–1,
278–9, 291–307 *passim*, 322, 345, 357,
361, 373, 512, 553, {ii}7, 22, 188, 404,
589, {iii}60, 62, {v}3, 582, 640, {vii}228
'socialists...stupid, ... Fabians so flat' in,
{i}176; DHL doesn't want to visit,
{ii}27

Croydon II Localities etc.
  Actors' Orphanage, {i}97, 314
  Colworth Road {i}115, 245, 298, 300,
    302–5, 326, 332, 336, {iii}62, {v}640
  Davidson Road School, {i}10, 17, 129,
    136, 146, 186, 210, 231, 252, 260, 268,
    270, 282–3, 293, 298–300, 319, 357, 373,
    513, {ii}19–20. 22, 91, {iii}60–1, {v}3
  DHL appointed to, salary £95,
    {i}79–80; described, {i}83–4, 96–7;
    headmaster of, {i}84, 243, 265, 303, 455,
    506, 523, {ii}48, {v}640–1; DHL as
    disciplinarian in, {i}85, 87, 89, 93, 100,
    117, 321; 'quite decent', {i}92; poverty
    among children at, {i}124; DHL
    becoming tired of, {i}156; concert at,
    {i}193; DHL paints water-colour in,
    {i}201; teaches *As You Like It*, {i}242,
    245; is librarian at, {i}254, {ii}589;
    teaches *Under the Red Robe*, {i}258; visit
    by inspectors to, {i}303; DHL wants to
    leave, {i}324, 326; illness threatens
    DHL's teaching career, {i}337; eager for
    news of, {i}355; DHL determined to
    resign from, {i}367–9; colleagues
    present DHL with books, {i}382, 385–6;
    DHL's judgment on, {i}395, 446, 455,
    483, 506, 523; nostalgic view of,
    {v}640–1
  Dering Place School, {i}84, 129, 254
  Everton Road, {i}326
  Grand Theatre, {i}140, 306
  Greyhound Hotel, {i}162
  Morland Road, {i}314
  Public Hall, {i}204, 322
  Selhurst Grammar School, {i}97
  String-Players' Club, {i}204,
  Sydenham Road School, {i}483
  Symphony Orchestra, {i}322
CROYDON EDUCATION COMMITTEE
  Letters to {i}207, 369
  Letters from {i}207
CRUELTY, 'cruel, stultifying shame' when
    married folk abandon friends, {i}67;
    DHL could be cruel, not stern, as
    teacher, {i}85; at political meeting mob
    'lusted with', {i}124; Helen Corke has
    'cruel blindness', {i}164; not 'cold clear

diamond' for DHL, {i}182; DHL cruel
    to Jessie Chambers, {i}190; Lydia
    Lawrence had worn 'a mask of bitter
    cruel suffering', {i}192; 'the hard, cruel
    if need be' writer in DHL, {i}214; Life
    'so ugly and cruel', {i}230, {vii}289; 'a
    form of perverted sex', {i}469; 'moral
    folk [in Germany] have such a cruel feel
    about them', {i}543; poets 'go on the
    loose in cruelty against themselves',
    {ii}95; Abercrombie's 'rather nasty
    efforts at', {ii}176; German 'rapine and
    cruelty' preferable to Russell's 'devilish
    repressions', {ii}392; 'cruel thing' to
    return to one's past, {ii}489; Scott's
    Blind Mice 'wee bit too cruel', {iii}691;
    shores of Red Sea 'Semitic and cruel',
    {iv}212; spirit of South America 'sub-
    cruel, a bit ghastly', {iv}416; from
    landscape near ranch DHL derives
    'something wild and untamed, cruel and
    proud', {v}63; mystery, cruelty, deathli-
    ness of steel compared to 'naturalness of
    coal', {v}294; cruel to take Tony Luhan
    to Europe, {v}540; animal-man has to be
    sly, cruel and horrible, {vi}161; 'primal
    cruelty..belongs to all life', {viii}21
Cruise of the Dream Ship, see Stock, R.
Cuba, {iv}541, {vii}146, 154, 341
Cuernavaca (Mexico), {iv}15, 418–19, 421,
    429, 431, 435, {v}200, {viii}79
  Somerset Maugham at, {v}155,157–8,
    160
Cull, A. Tulloch, {i}519, {ii}68
CULLEN, FLORENCE ('FLOSSIE'),
    {i}244, 278, 283–4, 325
  prototype for Alvina in *Lost Girl*,
    {i}234
  Letters to {i}398
Cullen, George Henry, {i}234
*Culture of Profitable Vegetables in Small
    Gardens,* {iii}103, 108
Cummings, Albert, A., {v}64, {viii}93
Cummings, Edward Estlin ('e.e.'), *The
    Enormous Room*, {vi}301
Cunard, Nancy, {vii}167, 169, 183, 190
Cunard, Victor, {iv}218, {vii}367–8, 395,
    477

Cunningham, {i}116

Cunninghame Graham, Robert B., {i}12
DHL reviews *Pedro de Valdivia* by,
(v}590, 601, {viii}99

'Cupid and the Puppy', *see* Burrows, L.

Curonia, *see* Villa Curonia

Curtin, Frank, A., US customs confiscate
copy of *LCL* sent to, {vi}531–2, {vii}98,
177, 246
Letters from {vi}531, {vii}97, 177

Curtis Brown, *see* Brown, A. C.

Curtis, *see* Brown, A. C.

Curtis, Phyllis, {iv}309

Curtius, Julius, {vii}567

Curwood, James Oliver, *The Glory of Living*,
{vii}147

Curzon, Lord Robert, *Visits to Monasteries in
the Levant*, {ii}572, 580, 648

Cuthbert Learmont, *see* Cramb, J. A.

Cuyp, Albert, {i}124

Cyprian, Brother, {iii}388, 399

Cyprus, {vi}56, 71, 91, 383, {vii}290

Cyriax, (Tony), Antonia, *see* Almgren, A.

Cythera, {i}343

Czernin, Count Otto, {iii}712, {vi}211, 367

Czernin, Manfred, {vi}367

Czolgosz, Leon F., {ii}332

D'Aurevilly, Jules Amédée Barbey, *Les
Diaboliques*, {v}321

D. H. Lawrence: A First Study, *see* Potter, S.

D. H. Lawrence: An Indiscretion, *see*
Aldington, R.

*D.H. Lawrence and Maurice Magnus: A Plea
for Better Manners*, *see* Douglas, G. N.

D. H. Lawrence and the Body Mystical, *see*
Carter, F.

Daft, Mr, {i}541

DAHLBERG, EDWARD, {vii}5, 151, 232,
569
DHL asked to read MS by, {vii}65, 69;
critique of MS, {vii}83–4; wants copy of
LCL, {vii}112, 160, 182, 224, 226, 231;
DHL gives advice on publishing,
{vii}129; DHL and foreword for *Bottom
Dogs*, {vii}156–7, 160, 182, 191, 201,
218, 226, 272, 526, 618; 'a poor under-
dog', {vii}218

Letters to {vii}65, 69, 83–4, 112, 129,
156–7, 160, 182, 217–18, 224, 226, 231,
271–2

Daily Chronicle, {i}227–8, 230, {ii}1, 47,
{vi}7, 403

Daily Express, {i}228, {iii}373, {vi}271,
{vi}616, {vii}424
DHL writes for, {vi}7, 602, 606,
{vii}26, 51; attack on DHL's paintings
in, {vii}348

Daily Herald, {iii}213, {vi}422

Daily Mail, {i}142, {ii}67, 135, {iv}599
favourable notice of *White Peacock* in,
{i}230

Daily News, {i}16, 299, 324, 326–7, 469, 474,
{ii}47, {iii}237, {viii}7
DHL keen reader of, {i}43; reviews of
DHL in, {i}231, 240, 318, 419, 528,
{vii}361–2; rejects article, {i}379;
'enough to break one's heart nowadays',
{i}380

Daily Telegraph, {iii}101
attacks DHL's paintings, {vii}424

Dalmatia, {iii}699, {v}321, 323, 343, 345,
373

Damascus (Syria), {iii}346, {v}343, 363

Dan, *see* Eastman, D.

Dana, Richard Henry, *Two Years before the
Mast*, {ii}614, 615, 645, {iii}83; DHL's
essay on, {iii}401, 405, 565, {iv}197, 348

Dance, Herbert, {i}450

Danes, the, *see* Götzsche, K. and Merrild, K.

'Danger to Civilization, The', *see* Russell B.
A. W.

Daniel, C. W., {iii}411, 423, {iv}146
T and G published by, {iii}6–7, 375, 385,
400, 427, 441, 469, 471, 482, 510, 513,
545

Daniel, Evan, {i}26

D'Annunzio, Gabriele, {ii}26, 247, {iii}733
'cruder and stupider' than *Trespasser*,
{iii}41; 'sensationalist, nearly always in
bad taste', {v}276
*La Fiacola sotto il Moggio (The Light
under the Bushel)*, {i}505;
Il Fuoco (The Flame of Life), {ii}595,
{iii}43, {v}175, 276;
L'Innocente, {iii}40;

D'Annunzio, Gabriele (*cont.*)
  Trionfo della Morte (The Triumph of Death), {iii}43, {v}276;
  Vergine Della Roche (Virgins of the Rocks), {iii}43, {iv}492, {viii}36
Dante, Alighieri, {ii}538, {iii}295, 335, 679, {iv}84–5, 87–8, {vi}421
  Divine Comedy, {iv}235;
  Inferno {iv}340;
  Vita Nuova, {iv}89
  see also Eliot, T.S.
Danton, Georges Jacques, {i}114
Danube, River, {i}540, {ii}62, {vi}204
Darley, Cumberland & Co., {i}516
Darlington (Australia), {iv}9–10, 236–40, 250–1, 270, 467, 533, {v}20, 23–4, 55
Dartington Hall School (Devon), {vi}588, {vii}2
  Harwood Brewster attended, {vii}317, 436, 479, 483, 495, 501, 510–11, 547, 581, 592, 622
Darwin, Charles Robert, {i}9, 36, {iii}489
  The Origin of Species, {i}37;
  The Voyage of the Beagle, {vi}214
DASBURG, ANDREW MICHAEL, {v}28, 159, 174, 185, 199, 218, 224, 226–8, 233, 236–7, 252, 269, 277, 282, 639, {vi}224, 365, {vii}24, 345
  Letters to {v}159–60, 248
Dasburg, Mrs, see Rauh, I.
Dashwood, Mrs, {iii}620, {iv}138, 141
Daudet, Alphonse, *Tartarin de Tarascon*, {ii}85, 537
Daudet, Leon, *Le partage de l'enfant*, {i}212
Davey, Norman, {iv}31
David, see Garnett, D.
Davids, Caroline A. F. Rhys, {vi}50, 56, 340, 512, 534
Davidson, Jo, {vii}14, 653
Davidson, Yvonne, {vii}14
Davies, Michael Llewelyn, {iv}48
Davies, R. H., see Davis, R. H.
DAVIES, RHYS, {vi}512, {vii}3, 5, 7, 23, 47, 53, 60, 74, 76, 85, 88, 107, 154, 172, 193, 198, 207, 233–4, 247, 256, 278, 346, 434, 458, 559, 569, 579–80, 589, 599, 627
  'good, and real' novel by, {vi}533–4;
  invited to Bandol by DHL, {vii}31, 67;

'nice fellow', {vii}49, 72; 'quiet and not tiring', {vii}69, 209; Christmas present from, {vii}93, 116; critique of story by, {vii}152, 162, 173; accompanies DHL to Paris, {vii}208–12, 216; proofs of *Pansies* for, {vii}325–6, 328, 334, 361, 365; copy of *Pansies* for, {vii}380; invited to contribute to 'The Squib', {vii}448–9, 501, 516; DHL gives £10 to, {vii}461, 499, 516, 528, 550; copy of *P and O* for, {vii}573
  Bed of Feathers, {vii}30, 531;
  'Interlude', {vii}128, 152, 162, 173;
  'A Pig in a Poke', {vii}265, 278;
  Print of a Hare's Foot, {vii}86, 607;
  'Revelation', {vii}607;
  Rings on Her Fingers, {vii}43;
  The Withered Root, {vi}512, 533–4
  Letters to {vii}31, 43, 49–50, 67, 88–9, 93–4, 116, 128–9, 152, 173, 185, 191, 194, 196, 220, 260–1, 308–10, 447–9, 606–7
Davies, Turner & Cocquyt, {vii}175, 181, 274
DAVIES, WILLIAM HENRY, {i}12, 106, {ii}51, 61, 85–6, 118, 341, {iii}261
  'feels so nice in all his work', {ii}39;
  DHL meets, {ii}54; DHL 'so furious, and so sorry' about, {ii}92; apologises to, {ii}124
  Nature Poems and Others, {ii}136
  Letters to {ii}124
Davis & Orioli Ltd, {vi}564, 566–8, 575, {vii}177, 539, 541
Davis, J. I., {vii}124
Davis, R. N. {iv}388, 405, 413
Davis, Robert Hobart, {vii}134, 242, 324
Davison, Lawrence H., see Lawrence, D. H., *Movements in European History*
Dawn, The, see Nietzsche, F. W.
DAX, ALICE MARY, {i}2, 4, 6, 43, 54, 58, 72, 87, 100, 104, 126, 128, 256, 295–6, 365, 461, {ii}42
  DHL 'sensitive..on her score', {i}44–5;
  'Laetitia' MS on loan to, {i}48–50, 52–3, 55–6, 61, 69; 'no judge of style', {i}88;
  'all finished now' between DHL and, {i}157; Balfour article for, {i}359; DHL

concerned for health of, {i}440, 457;
subscribes to *Signature*, {ii}18, 391;
reaction to *LCL* queried, {vi}558
Letters to {i}137, 457
Letters from {ii}391

Dax, Eric Cunningham, {i}48, 69, 72

Dax, Henry Richard, {i}4, 44, 53, 69, 85,
104, 295, 296, 457

Dax, Phyllis Maude, {i}48, 52, 137, 461

Day, Sam, {v}99

De Goncourt, Edmond Louis Antoine, *Soeur
Philomène*, {iv}452

De Goncourt, Jules Alfred Huot, *Soeur
Philomène*, {iv}452

De Gourmont, Rémy, 'Dust for Sparrows',
{iv}59

De Grey, Nigel, proposes book of 'Art
Pictures for Children', {iii}723, 730,
{iv}24, 26–7, 34, 47–8; DHL rejects
proposal, {iv}66

De Haulleville, Baron Eric, {vii}487

De l'Amour, see Stendhal, H. B.

De la Feld, Count, {ii}412

De la Huerta, Adolfo, {iv}536

DE LA MARE, RICHARD HERBERT
INGPEN, 'such a wet rag', {vii}589
Letters to {vii}585

DE LA MARE, WALTER JOHN, {i}12, 14,
19–20, 459, {ii}131, 341, 435, {vii}585,
589, {viii}15
reader for Heinemann, {i}348, 355;
DHL's poems and, {i}370–1, 375, 378,
382–5, 442, 444–6, 522; DHL's sketches
and, {i}383, 405, 422, 430–2, 443, 447,
{ii}56, 83; DHL commends 'Paul
Morel' to, {i}416–17, 423; 'a bit funky',
{i}424; a 'friend in the field' of poetry,
{i}526; 'very cautious' as reviewer,
{i}530
The Listeners, {i}417;
Peacock Pie, {ii}54;
The Return, {i}348, 370;
Songs of Childhood by 'Walter Ramal',
{i}348, 370
Letters to {i}370–1, 375, 382–5, 387, 405–6,
416–17, 422–3, 431–2, 447, {ii}54, 56,
83–4
Letters from {i}423–4

De Morgan, William Frend, {viii}3

De Quincey, Thomas, {iii}407, {vii}615
'Goethe', {iii}407;
Reminiscences of the English Lake Poets,
{ii}633

De Selincourt, Basil, {i}19, 420

De Wint, Peter, {i}8, 88–9
'most soothing' to copy picture by,
{i}491

DE WIT, ANNA AUGUSTA
HENRIETTE, enquires about English
writings on working-class life,
{viii}18–19; reviews *Widowing*, {viii}19;
DHL agreeable to her translating him
into Dutch, {iii}95, {viii}21;
'The Hunter', {iii}166–7, {viii}21;
'Orpheus in a Malay Village', {viii}18
Letters to {viii}18–19, 21

DEATH, those who endure great suffering
should not be 'punished' after, {i}40;
Bernhardt sighs 'like a deer sobs,
wounded to', {i}59; 'filched the pride
out of [Housman's] blood..conceit of
death..in his voice', {i}103; Douglas's
false images of, {i}107; Watts' figure of,
{i}107; 'desolation of', {i}169; many
'degrees of', {i}194; of Lydia Lawrence,
{i}198, 202, 234, 243; DHL in 'one of
the kingdoms of death' after his
mother's, {i}199; 'the one beautiful and
generous adventure left', {i}245;
Wagner's 'bellowings' at, {i}247; 'You
[Jessie Chambers] say you died a death
of me..I must have died also', {i}268;
Campbell's sermon on 'the positivity
of', {i}310; Paul in *S and L* 'left in the
end..with the drift towards', {i}477; 'all
right in its way', {ii}28; Good Friday
procession creates impression of 'Death
itself, robbed of its horrors', {ii}164;
mob will not 'crush..starve nor cry us
to', {ii}273; each person should have
wage till, {ii}286; fighting false gods
'matter of life and', {ii}319; of Rupert
Brooke, {ii}330–1, {iii}38; fear of
conscription brings 'touch of death..very
cold and horrible on us all', {ii}343;
'must be accomplished' before

DEATH (*cont.*)
resurrection, {ii}348; in 1915 DHL sees
'only death and more death, till we are
black and swollen with', {ii}352–3; 'sick
in my soul, sick to', {ii}414; 'kingdom of
death endures and is real', {ii}416;
'whole tree of life is dying', {ii}417; 'the
gossamer..serried ecstasy of prevalent',
{ii}423; 'further destruction only means
death, universal', {ii}425; 'most
wretched form of undying', {ii}426; to
leave native country 'a form of', {ii}428;
courage to die has become a vice', {ii}443,
445; Murry's death and rebirth,
{ii}481–2; since 'life such a mean
paucity..how can death be great',
{ii}500; 'confident faith' born out of
'very depths of one's despair and',
{ii}532; Michael Angelo felt most 'the
death of the God', {ii}592; Irish rebels
'tragically significant in', {ii}611;
manliness of conscripts 'in accepting
calmly this death, this loss of..integrity',
{ii}625; procreation is 'throwing life on
to the bonfire of', {ii}635–6; 'sheer
tension of life' should be 'stubborn
against', {ii}638; 'spirit of militarism is
sheer death' to creative man, {ii}644;
destruction of mankind 'with invisible
arrows of death' is righteous, {ii}650;
'fury of strident lies and foul', {ii}657; 'a
death to die, for us all', {ii}658; Jews to
utter 'final and great death-cry of this
epoch', {ii}661; 'plenty of the slave
courage of death..slow flood of death
will drown them all', {iii}21; seems 'a
good clean unknown', {iii}22; England
has 'awful process of corruption and
death to go through', {iii}25, 116;
'soldier-spirit..means endless process
of', {iii}27; unlike war, death 'no
violation nor ignominy', {iii}32; a 'seal
of truth', {iii}33; in 'tearing asunder of
the sexes lies the universal', {iii}78; not
a calamity, {iii}88–9; of Herbert Watson,
{iii}101; principle of life stronger than,
{iii}118; consummation possible in

death but war leads to extinction,
{iii}143; in Midlands fear of death from
flu, {iii}302, 304, 306; 'death struggle'
of revolution DHL's sole concern,
{iii}649; US will, England will not face
death before resurrection, {iii}694;
better than 'ignominious living on',
{iii}717; in San Francisco 'steel rails in
ribbons like the path of death itself',
{iv}290; of Sallie Hopkin, {iv}327; of
Katherine Mansfield, {iv}375, 385; New
York free of 'sense of', {v}15; 'not sad
when one has lived', {v}293; 'deathli-
ness of steel' against 'silkiness' of coal,
{v}294; Villa Curonia 'sad as', {v}623;
DHL feels 'angel of death waving his
wings' over central Europe, {vi}169;
'even Leadership must die and be born
different', {vi}307; 'of phallic consciousness', {vi}355; DHL's cough a nuisance
'not a death cough', {vi}522; 'so *easy* in
novels. It never kills the novelist',
{vi}533; newspapers 'pining to
announce one's', {vii}318; 'narcissus
image..real death of all joy', {vii}469;
'the north..full of', {vii}494, 502; 'what
the mystics call the little', {vii}605; in
last Act of *Widowing* 'too much
death..life not given a look in', {viii}99
Death of a Hero, see Aldington, R.
Débâcle, La, see Zola, E.
Debussy, Claude Achille, {i}9, 205, 247,
308–9.
Decameron, see Boccaccio, G.
Decline and Fall of the Roman Empire, The, see
Gibbon, E.
Deerslayer, The, see Cooper, J. F.
'Defense of Lawrence, A', *see* Cannan, G.
Defoe, Daniel, *Robinson Crusoe*, {ii}107,
588
Dehan, Richard, *see* Graves, C. I. M.
Dehmel, Richard, {i}513
Dekker, Eduard Douwes (Multatuli),
{iv}240, 496, 518, {v}493, {viii}56
Max Havelaar, {iv}9, 240, {v}32; DHL
encourages publication of, {iv}270, 281,
309, 326–9, 386, 435, 449, {v}34, 393;

DHL's introduction to, {v}320, 446, 452, 458, 527
see also Siebenhaar, W.

Del Monte Ranch, Valdez (USA), {iv}13, 336, 346–76 *passim*, 494, 506, {v}39, 50–1, 61–2, 75, 82, 88, 95, 114, 122, 135, 137–9, 157–8, 164, 185, 192, 199, 211–12, 219–28, 233, 264, 278, 282, 364, 429–30, 438, 466, 477, 491, 537, 586, 652–3, {vi}293, {vii}475, {viii}75, 85, 110
'very splendid landscape..But humanly nothing', {iv}366; Frieda owns Kiowa, {v}111, {viii}90; '*far* better' than Oaxaca, {v}191; Brett longing to return to, {v}196–7, 208–9; DHL glad to see again, {v}224; described, {v}239, 244

Deledda, Grazia Cosima, {iii}43, 338, {vi}254

Delhi (India), {iv}582, {v}561, {vii}529

Delight Makers, The, see Bandelier, A.

Delius, Frederick, {ii}548, 598, 605
owned 'forsaken estate in Florida', {ii}444, 446, 450

Demian, see Hesse, H.

DEMOCRACY, 'drop all your [Russell's] democracy. You must not believe in "the people"..no Presidents and democracies', {ii}364; 'our enemy' is 'the extant', {ii}365; DHL scorns 'idea of democratic control', {ii}378–9; 'false', {ii}421; art trampled under 'choice of a free democracy, a public opinion..I hate democracy so much', {ii}593; 'poor dear old ship of christian democracy is scuttled at last', {ii}600; comes to an end 'so despicably', {ii}603; 'I hate a vulgar', {iii}345; DHL's essays on, {iii}404–5; era of love, peace, democracy in Germany gone, {iii}732; DHL believes in 'natural aristocacy' not in American 'negative creed' of, {iv}226; 'the more I see of democracy the more I dislike it', {iv}263; Australia 'the most democratic place' DHL knew..really democratic but 'slovenly, slip-shod', {iv}263–4; 'democracy of decadence' in the world, {v}218

Denmark, {i}504, {ii}69, 623, 628, {iv}525–7, 534, 548, {v}232, 656, {vi}532

Dennis, Geoffrey Pomeroy, *Harvest in Poland*, {v}256

Dennis, George, {vi}105
The Cities and Cemeteries of Etruria, {v}413, {vi}45

Dent, J. M. and Sons Ltd, {i}144, 306

Dentist, *see* Campkin, H. T.

Denver (USA), {iv}338, 348, 354, 373, {v}276, 295–6, 298

Denver and Rio Grande Railway, {iv}338, 354

Denver Post, {iv}350

Derby (Derbyshire), {i}296, {iii}126, 252, 257, 264, 271, 273, 278, 300, 723–4, {iv}542, 547, 553–4, {v}499, 536, {vii}261, 580
railway strike at, {i}296, {iii}327; DHL medically examined at, {iii}1, 250, 283

Derby, Earl of, *see* Stanley, E. G.

Derby, Lola, {vii}251

Derby, Rachel, {vii}251

'Derby, The', {i}129

'Derby Scheme', {ii}495–6

Derbyshire, {i}24, 35, 91, 373, 377, 397, 487, 489, {iii}3, 95, 112, 199, 222–3, 228, 234–5, 254, 274, 291, 309, 322, 467, {iv}18, {v}243, 321, 324, 476, 534, 551
'beautiful', {iii}193; location of some novels, {v}243, 576, 596; 'one of the most interesting counties in England', {v}318, 320

Derwent, River, {i}259, 397, {iii}307

Desenzano (Italy), {i}520, 522, {iv}189, 195

Desgrand, Gabrielle, {v}444

Desire under the Elms, see O'Neill, E.

Devious Ways, see Cannan, G.

Devon(shire), {i}95, 136, {ii}472, 474, {v}, 202, 214–17, 219, 294, 447, 640, {vi}1, 68, 202, 588, {vii}436, 511, 581

Dewar, George A. B., {ii}47

Di Rescis, Baroness, {ii}166, 168

Diablerets, *see* Les Diablerets

Diaboliques, Les, see D'Auréuilly, J.A.B.

Dial, The, {ii}653, {iv}7, 10, 14–16, 66, 127,
  149, 151, 232, 329, 334, 379, 384, 406–7,
  478, 482, 487, 560, {v}92, 459, 500
  DHL's stories in, {ii}212, {iii}13, 536,
  562, 597, 627, 634, {iv}23, 37, 39, 78, 87,
  123, 144, 168, {v}71, 103–5, 180, 255,
  260, 416, 442, 451, 482, 504, 521, 523,
  571, {vi}46, 52, 69, 76, 103, 152, 176,
  189, 270, 348, {viii}36; doesn't serialise
  Lost Girl, {iii}564, 571, 576, 582; DHL's
  poetry in, {iii}644, {iv}59, 297,
  {vii}173, 257–8, 296, 305, 396; review of
  W in L in, {iii}694, 734; selection from *S
  and S* in, {iv}58, 73–4, 107, 126, 130;
  extract from *Aaron's Rod* in, {iv}74, 187,
  388; 'impudent people' at, {iv}165;
  DHL's essays in, {iv}298, 332, 340, 369,
  372, 380–1, 383, 392, 404, 432; review by
  DHL in, {iv}355, {viii}59; 'bores'
  DHL, {v}255; 'doesn't like [DHL]
  much', {vii}174
DIALECT, Hauptmann's play 'horribly
  tiresome', with, {i}171; DHL could not
  understand foreign, {i}433, 515,
  {iii}432, 435, {v}610; in Bennett's novel
  dialect almost like DHL's own, {i}459;
  Verga's dialect made translation difficult,
  {iv}115; dialect in *LCL* problem for
  translator, {vii}114; 'difficult, even
  painful' to read, as in Barnes' poetry,
  {viii}15
  DHL uses dialectal words: {i}98, 201,
  231, 257, 364, 371, 494, {ii}353, 451,
  648, {iii}487, 618, 657, {iv}139, 492,
  {v}346, 359, 548, 614, 633, {vi}237, 313,
  {vii}577, 584
Díaz del Castillo, Bernal, *The True History of
  the Conquest of New Spain*, {iv}383,
  445–6, 452
Díaz, Porfirio, {iv}394
DIBDIN (DIBBEN?), WILLIAM H.,
  {vi}11
  Letters to {vi}369–70
  Letters from {vi}369
Dickens, Charles, {i}165, {ii}74
  'so governessy towards life', {ii}95
  Bleak House, {i}127;
  David Copperfield, {i}532, {vi}315, 553;
  Dombey and Son, {ii}62;
  Great Expectations, {iii}131;
  Martin Chuzzlewit, {iv}470, {v}313;
  Nicholas Nickleby, {i}474;
  Pickwick Papers, {ii}614
Dickinson, Goldsworthy ('Goldie') Lowes,
  {i}12
  DHL wants to meet, {ii}286, 295;
  president of Union of Democratic
  Control {ii}309, {iii}71; one of 'old
  "advanced" crowd', {iii}49
Dictionnaire Universel d'Histoire Naturelle, see
  D'Orbigny, C. D.
Didcot (Berkshire), {iii}275
'Diddler', see Neville, G. H.
'Diddy', see Wilkinson, L.
Didier, M., {i}215, 217
Dieppe (France), {iii}415, 569, {vi}60, 62,
  64
Dieu des Corps, Le, see Romains, J.
Dina, {vii}82
Diodoro Hotel (Taormina), {iii}620, 637,
  639–40, {iv}138, 141
Dionyso(u)s, {iii}179, 562, {vii}519
Dionysos: Nietzsche contra Nietzsche, see
  Lindsay, J.
'Dionysus Crossing the Sea', see Gerhard, E.
  see also Hesiod, *The Homeric Hymns and
  Homerica*
Discursions on Travel, Art and Life, see
  Sitwell, O.
Discus-Thrower, see Myron
'District Visitor, The', see Middleton, R. B.
Dives, {i}73
Divine Comedy, see Dante, A.
Dixon, Campbell, {vii}626
Dixon, 'Ma', {iii}608
Do We Need a Censor?, see Hicks, Sir W.J.
Do What You Will, see Huxley, A.
DOBRÉE, BONAMY, {v}558–9, 628, {vi}1,
  10, 47, 67, 171, 205, 458, {viii}99–100
  DHL might visit in Cairo, {v}577,
  {vi}41, 169–70, 175, 177, 179, 201, 379,
  502, 513; offers DHL use of London
  flat, {v}597, 628, 630; seeming rupture
  in relationship with, {vi}221, 233,

299–300; bought *LCL*, {vi}502; reviews
WWRA, {vi}502–3
Histriophone, {v}596
Letters to {v}577, 596–7, {vi}170, 299–300,
337–8, 379, 502–3
DOBRÉE, VALENTINE GLADYS,
{v}558–9, 577, {vi}1, 41, 47, 169, 175,
177, 179, 201, 233, 299–300, 337, 513
invited to Villa Mirenda, {vi}170–1
Your Cuckoo Sings By Kind, {vi}41
Letters to {vi}171, 205
Dobson, Mr, {i}483
Doctor Transit, see Schneider, I.
Dodge, Edwin, {iv}4, 13, 110, 313, 350–1,
{vi}230
and Villa Curonia, {v}5, 407, 423–4,
458, 487, 580, 608, 625, 642
Dodge, Mabel, *see* Luhan, M. D.
'Dolittle, David', DHL's possible *nom de
plume* in 'The Squib', {vii}448
Dollar (Shipping) Line, {vii}138, 144, 617,
628–9, 637
Dolomites, {i}465, {iv}48, {vi}100, 201
Dombey and Son, see Dickens, C.
Domela, Harry, *The False Prince*, {vi}495,
504–5
Dominicushütte (Austria), {i}443, 445
Domleo, Mary B., {i}79
Don Juan in Hell, see Shaw, G. B.
Don Quixote, see Cervantes Saavedra, M. de
Don, see Besier, R.
Don, *see* Carswell, D.
Donald, Mrs {iii}219
Donizetti, Gaetano, *Lucia di Lammermoor*,
{i}130
Doolittle, Charles Leander, {v}104
Doolittle, Hilda, *see,* Aldington, H.
Doorn (Holland), {iii}489, 533, 607, 621,
667, 687, 726–7, 730, {iv}51, 87,
193
Dop Doctor, see Graves, C. I. M.
Doran, George H., Co. (New York), {ii}560,
{iii}635, 674, 689–90, {iv}178, 187, 220,
276, 376, {vi}345
interested in publishing DHL, {ii}223,
417; refuses *Rainbow* but copyrights it in
USA {ii}419; arranges for Huebsch to

publish DHL titles, {ii}420, 426, 453,
475, 561, 605, 610–11, 645, {iii}612, 627,
643, 651, 661, 693, {iv}182, 229, 403;
DHL has control of Doran contracts,
{iv}169; 'makes the creative truth serve
him, for money', {v}79
Letters from {ii}419, 610–11, {iv}170
D'Orbigny, Charles Dessalines, *Dictionnaire
Universel d'Histoire Naturelle*, {vii}154
Doren, Carl van, *see* van Doren, C.
Doren, Irita van, *see* van Doren, I.
Doris, *see* Smith, D. E.
Dorking (Surrey), {i}90–1
Dorothea, a Lyrical Romance in Verse, see
Siebenhaar, W.
Dorothy, *see* Warren, D.
Dorset, {ii}655, {v}43, 66, 142, 313, 326,
483, {vii}87, 200, 256, {viii}15
Dos Passos, John, {vi}17, 180
Manhattan Transfer reviewed by DHL,
{v}647;
Three Soldiers, {iv}151, 178
Dostoievsky, Feodor, {i}199, 314, 380, 547,
{ii}21
'so much *statement*' in, {ii}155; DHL
objects to 'moral scheme' in writings by,
{ii}182; DHL dislikes, {ii}311, 521,
{viii}17; 'lost his spell' over DHL,
{ii}537; his novels 'great parables..but
false art', {ii}542–4; 'Dream of a Queer
Fellow' is 'offal, putrid stuff', {iii}53;
brought 'dismal time...upon himself',
{iv}462
The Brothers Karamazov, {ii}315, 331,
367, 537, 543–4, {v}374, 379, 383,
{vii}518, 618, 643;
Crime and Punishment, {i}126–7;
The Grand Inquisitor, {vii}618, 620, 629;
The House of the Dead, {ii}155, 579;
The Idiot, {ii}311, 313, 537, 543–4;
Letters and Reminiscences, {iv}462;
Letters from the Underworld, {ii}247;
Pages from the Journal of an Author,
{ii}545, {iii}53, 183;
The Possessed, {ii}510, 521, 537, 542–5,
{viii}17
see also Murry, J. M., *Fyodor Dostoevsky*

Doubleday, Nelson, {vii}520, 522, 534
Doughty, Charles Montagu {iv}134
  Adam Cast Forth, {i}95;
  Travels in Arabia Deserta, {iv}586,
  {v}89, 246
Douglas, Archibald, {vi}516
DOUGLAS, GEORGE NORMAN,
  {iii}409, 420, 480, 492, 594, {iv}189,
  {v}11, 260, 346, 444, 462, 472, 549, 602,
  {vi}9, 17, 135, 180, 187, 202–4, 253, 273,
  289, 316, 466, 605, {vii}3, 62, 162, 253,
  265, 274, 340, 363, 376, 384, 478, 493,
  498, 573, 578, 586
  'I like him', {ii}31; publishes DHL's
  stories in *English Review*, {ii}44, 82;
  '*loathes* the French', {iii}636; *Lost Girl*
  sent to, {iii}639, 648; *W in L* for, {iv}54;
  portrayed as James Argyle in *Aaron's
  Rod*, {iv}54, 129, 131, 167; Magnus's
  literary executor, {iv}178–9; *Foreign
  Legion* and, {v}184, 231–2, 240, 244,
  255–6, {viii}48–50; 'really terrible',
  {v}231–2; DHL's public response to,
  {v}395–7; DHL reconciled with,
  {vi}45, 342; 'irritable and nervy',
  {vi}191; favours private publication,
  {vi}222. 225, 242, 415; in Orioli's inner
  circle, {vii}496, 614–15, 629–30; *Pansies*
  for, {vii}561
  Birds and Beasts of the Greek Anthology,
  {v}444, {vi}545;
  *D.H. Lawrence and Maurice Magnus: A
  Plea for Better Manners*, {iv}6, {v}185,
  242, 340;
  Experiments, {v}340, 395;
  How about Europe, {vii}577, 579;
  In the Beginning, {vi}241, 249, 408,
  {vii}62;
  Nerinda, {vii}62, 141, 178, 246, 252,
  274;
  Siren Land, {vi}45;
  Some Limericks, {vi}591, 598, {vii}62,
  91, 134, 142–4;
  Venus in the Kitchen, {vii}124, 134, 565
  Letters to {iii}409, {iv}207–8, {vi}111,
  197–8, {viii}38–9, 48–50
  Letters from {v}184–5, 396, {vi}203,
  {viii}49–50

Douglas, George, *see* Brown, G. D.
Douglas, James, {ii}462, {iii}459
Douglas, Lord Alfred, 'a louse', {iii}708
  City of the Soul, {i}107;
  'Silence', {i}180, {ii}101
DOUILLET, MADAME, owner of Hotel
  Beau Rivage, Bandol, {vii}171, 183, 185,
  483, 501, 553, 562, 570–1, 619
  Letters to {vii}590
Dover (Kent), {i}285–6, {v}390–1, {vi}527,
  {vii}353
Dover (New Jersey,USA), {iv}16, 472, 476,
  478, 589
Dove's Nest, see Mansfield, K.
Dowling, Albert, {vi}574
Downland Man, see Massingham, H.J.
Downs,The (Berkshire, Kent, Sussex)
  {i}127–8, 162, 215, 218, 314–15,
  {ii}259, 269, 273, 282, 296, 346, 478,
  495–6, {iii}9, 382, {iv}301
Dowson, Ernest, {ii}91, 117–18
  'Non sum qualis', {ii}103–5, 118;
  The Pierrot of the Minute, {ii}118;
  Poems, {ii}117–18
Dowson, Will, {i}409
Doxey, Mrs, {iii}300–1
Drachenfels (Germany), {i}407–8, 410
Dracott, E., {vi}567
Dragon of Revelation, The, see Carter, F.
Dragon of the Alchemists, The, see Carter, F.
'Dragon of the Apocalypse, The', *see* Carter,
  F.
Drake, Mr, {v}199, 206, 212
Drake, Sir Francis, {iii}561
Drave, River (Austria), {vi}117, 120–1,
  123–4, 127
Dreadnought, HMS, {i}134
'Dream Ship, The', *see* Stock, R.
Dream-Songs for the Beloved, see Farjeon, E.
'Dregs', *see* Magnus, M.
Dresden (Germany), {iv}138
Drexel Institute (Philadelphia, USA), {v}65,
  92, 122, 338, 376, {vi}28, 548, {vii}35
  see also McDonald, E. D.
Drey, O. Raymond, {ii}404, {iii}331, 362
Dreyfus, Louis Goethe, {iv}138
DRINK, women in slums 'drunk, with
  breasts half bare', {i}40; home-made

elderberry wine, 'turbid, inky, flat, with a rough medicinal flavour suggestive of colds on the chest', {i}102; DHL's father drinking beer with 'money he begged from me', {i}174; DHL 'one degree from sober', {i}181; Louie Burrows 'bright and vital as a pitcher of wine', {i}193; DHL prefers Scotch to Irish whiskey, 'too much whiskey is better than too much melancholies', {i}218; child 'sneaks off and drinks my beer', {i}253; DHL does 'nothing in excess' including drinking, {i}272; 'a brew of fermented honey', {i}295; at the Cearne drinks 'wine in the ingle nook', {i}315; in convalesence DHL drinks hot milk, {i}351; DHL drinking Scotch 'till the small hours - so..as dull as cold tea', {i}356; 'drinking my third pint of German beer', {i}390; 'wine is only 7d a litre', {i}463; DHL drinks 'a little wine, to assert..masculine and marital independence', {i}474; Vermouth in 'pub in Bogliaco', {i}508; DHL has 'wine and brandy..and devil a fellow to drink with', {i}509; 'moscato - Asti Spumanti..muscadine - lovely white fizzy wine', {i}516; Munich 'puffed under the eyes with beer and bohemianism', {i}548; 'dawn comes up green like wine', {ii}70, {iii}499; 'well done to call a good wine Lachrimae Christi', {ii}105; DHL gloats over his 'rush-wrapped fat bottles' of wine, {ii}106; books and genius 'the cake and wine of life', {ii}130; 'drinking Chianti in memory of Italy', {ii}243; DHL feels like 'enjoying..a mild drunk and a great and rowdy spree', {ii}245; Kot asked to 'bring two flasks of Chianti' costing 10/-, {ii}250-1, 312; DHL and Heseltine drank bottle of Beresford's sloe gin, {ii}552; whisky taken for 'self-indulgence', {iii}137; Christmas celebrated with 'whiskey, gin, port-wine, burgundy, muscatel', {iii}313; DHL toasts New Year in gin, {iii}316; Kot's brandy 'good and soft', {iii}330; Frieda 'drank so much wine that her pancia..went on

strike', {iii}435; Mackenzie's drunken escapade, {iii}443; 'Have drunk a bottle of wine lunching out, so am not to be trusted', {iii}505; 'two huge bottiglione of dark and powerful wine..See me bibbing away', {iii}558; DHL 'supplied the wine' for Falanga wedding, {iii}665; 'bottle of beautiful Moselle' drunk to luck of *W in L*, {iv}35; DHL doesn't like 'new Fontana Vecchia wine..it's going to be *rough*', {iv}108; DHL wants 'peace like a river: not this whiskey and soda, bad whiskey too, of life so-called', {iv}175; 'a new land is like sharp wine in which floats a pearl the soul of an incoming people', {iv}238; several of 'cinema crowd..drunk all the trip', {iv}303; Taos nice 'but so much artistic small beer', {iv}366; 'good to have a flask of Chianti at one's elbow again', {iv}414; 'At Minas Nuevas we did nothing but drink beer and whiskey cocktails', {iv}507; 'flask of *very* good chianti for lunch', {iv}534; 'quite tipsy with a flask of very good chianti', {iv}536; to ranch 'with 12 bottles of smuggled whiskey', {v}60; 'Dinner at Coyoacan, and drank Absinthe, gin, bouilly, Chablis, Beaune, port, and whiskey', {v}157; Brett made 'dandy beer', {v}234; in Baden 'we'll drink Moselle', {v}267; 1924 wine at Villa Bernarda 'quite good', {v}376; DHL has '30 bottles of the red, and 20 of the white, 1920 vintage' at Bernarda, {v}388; DHL drinks hot water at Baden for his 'miserable bronchi', {v}502-3; peasants given sweet wine at Mirenda Christmas, {v}610; 'home-brewed black beer sounds A. 1.' {vi}28; Turner is 'small beer', {vi}82; DHL drinks 'fresh mountain water', {vi}118-19, 123; drinks goat's milk, {vi}141-3; Krug sends '*30 bottles* of malt beer', {vi}146-7, 166, 178; DHL seeks inn where peasants drink in the evening, {vi}380, 382, 384; 'wine spilled to Phoebus Apollo', {vi}404; drink 'only a

DRINK (*cont.*)

    form of evasion', {vii}79; Orioli warned against excessive drinking, {vii}90, 629; Ottoline Morrell advised to 'drink a little burgundy', {vii}164; Spanish wine 'foul, cat-piss is champagne compared..the sulphureous urination of some aged horse', {vii}260; 'canary be-pissed beer', {vii}310; 'peach Bowle made with champagne and Gauwinkelheimer', {vii}427; 'headache after drinking Chablis', {vii}604; 'a bottle of wine in its rush singlet', {viii}9; 'drinking Meersburg red wine', {viii}42

Drinkwater, John, {ii}16, 136, 155, 447, {iii}212, 363

Driscoll, Louise, {ii}219, 232

DRUMMOND, ANNIE MAUD, {v}110

    Letters to {v}92–3

Dubberke Farm/Mills (Connecticut, USA), {iii}659, 668, 672

Dublin (Ireland), {ii}10, 187, 211, 603, {iii}5, 12, 183, 185, 187, 196, 334, 371, 594, {iv}28, {v}555, {vi}219, 283, 334

Duca, *see* Hood, Hon. A. N.

Duca's sister, *see* Evans, Mrs

Ducati, Pericle, *Etruria Antica*, {v}465

Duckworth & Co., {i}15, 19, 297, 306, 319, 415, 542, {ii}6, 29, 98, 133, 152, 174, 184, 203, 221, 240, 243, 246, 279, 527, 561, 623, 644, 665, {iii}20, 356, 650, 652, {iv}181, 183, 427, {v}66, 481, {vi}68, 305

    Garnett at, {i}307, 323, 339; publishes *Love Poems*, {i}309, 442–3, 445, 447, 455, 457, 461–2, 513, 519–20, {ii}43, 131, {v}626, {vi}168, 264, 369, 607, {vii}52, 66; *Trespasser* and, {i}351, 356, 367, 369, 373, 378–9, 381, 388–9, 408–9, 417, {iii}692; accepts *S and L*, {i}423, 427, 431, 434, 445, 455, 476, 518, 522, 536, {ii}117, 165–6; royalties from, {i}448, 454, 482, 486, 511, 527, 529, 531, {ii}26, 178; 'damned dilatory', {i}544–8; *Widowing* sent to, {ii}65, 135, 144, {iii}374, {v}87, {vi}229; *Sisters* to, {ii}132, 166–7; Methuen to have

Rainbow instead of, {ii}186–7; *Prussian Officer* published by, {ii}223–4, 589; DHL feels 'a sort of gratitude to', {ii}372–3; *Twilight* published by, {ii}398, 405–6, 417, 484, 494, 513, 524, {v}460; 'doesn't make things go', {ii}519; 'unimpressive', {ii}525; publishes *Amores*, {ii}576, 589, 605–7, 612, {v}626, {vi}168, 264; Curtis Brown assumes responsibility for DHL books by, {iv}187, 200–1, 302, 428, 592; published all DHL's early works, {viii}18

    see also Duckworth, G. de l'E.

DUCKWORTH, GERALD DE L'ETANG, {ii}5, 31, 71, 198, {iii}74, 210, 231, 262, 379, 398, 510, 547, 612, 627, 630, 644–5, 651, 653, 656, 661, {iv}134, 247

    'jolly nice', {i}372; 'tone peremptory', {ii}189; refuses *Rainbow*, {ii}189–90, {iii}13–14; 'so decent...treats my books so well', {ii}619–20; refuses *W in L*, {iii}80, 84; DHL in negotiation with, {iii}458–60, 468, 470–2, 474, 477, 484, 490–1, 497, 544; 'an old woman', {iii}561

    see also Duckworth & Co.

    Letters to {iv}592

Duclaux, Mary, {vii}223

Duddington, Iris, {i}451

Duddington, Rev. John Nightingale, {i}451

Dudley, Dr Emelius C., {ii}229–30, 449

Dudley, Helen, {ii}229–30

Dufferin, Lord, *see* Blackwood, F. T.

Duffield & Co. (New York), {i}184, {iii}547, 652, 653, 661, 674, {iv}372, 403, {v}146

Duke of Brontë, *see* Hood, Hon. A. N.

Dulac, Edmund, {iii}414

Dulau's Ltd, {vi}12, 346, 448

Dulwich College Art Gallery, {i}11, 124, {iii}342

Dumas, Alexandre, fils, {i}5, 55

Dunbar, William, {vii}419

'Duneville' (Sutton-on-Sea), {v}515–18, 520–2, 525–30

Dunlop, John Dacre, {ii}191, 477, 498, 628, {iii}19

DUNLOP, MARGARET ANNIE JESSIE
('MADGE'), {ii}152, 191–2, 477–8, 497,
628, 630, {iii}11, 19, 414
Letters to {iii}19–20
Dunlop, Margaret Dorothea Leda ('Biddy'),
{ii}477, 498, 628, {iii}19
Dunlop, Maurice Hamilton ('Paddy'),
{ii}192, 477, 498, 628, {iii}19
DUNLOP, (SIR) THOMAS DACRE, {ii}4,
168, {iii}19–20, 229, 411, 414
typed *Rainbow*, {ii}152, 164, 173;
Trespasser and *S and L* for, {ii}175–6,
182; DHL offers marital advice to,
{ii}191–2; advised not to become Roman
Catholic, {ii}497–8
Letters to {ii}191–2, 477–8, 497–8, 506,
511, 628–30
Dunn, John Harris ('Long John'), {iv}338,
444, {v}159
Dunn, William, {ii}124
Dunning, Millar, {v}313, 326
Dunning, Mrs, {v}313, 326
Duomo (Capri), {iii}439, 442
Duomo (Florence), {iv}41, 82, {v}459, 464,
{vi}128, 330–1
Duplessis, Marie, {i}55
Duport, James, *Homeri Gnomologia*, {iii}48
Dürer, Albrecht, {ii}63, {iii}422, {iv}47
Durham (city and county), {iv}458, {vi}18,
229–30, 247, 281, 428, 430, 476,
{vii}137, 161
Duse, Eleonora, {ii}595, {iii}660, {iv}485,
543, {v}423, 568, {vi}418
'Dust for Sparrows', *see* de Gourmont, R.
Dutton & Co., {v}391
Dyer, Sir Edward, {vi}91
Dymchurch (Kent), {ii}70

Eakring (Nottinghamshire), {i}24–5, 295,
369
Eames, Emma, {vi}209, 327
Eames, Hamilton, {v}302, {vi}209–10, 327
EAMES, MARIAN, {v}302, {vi}209
Letters to {vi}209–10, 327
Earl, *see* Brewster, E. H.
Early Greek Philosophy, see Burnet, J.
Earp, Thomas Wade, {vii}447
East Croydon, {i}260, 293, 330

East Lynne, *see* Wood, Mrs H.
Eastbourne (Sussex), {i}261, {iii}256
EASTERBROOK, ANGELA, {iv}153, 159,
176–7
Letters to {iv}153, 155, 164
Eastman, Daniel ('Dan'), {v}199, 224, 282,
{vii}604
Eastman, Max Forrester, {v}28
Eastman, Mrs Max, *see* Rauh, I.
'Easton Glebe' (Kent), {vi}373
Eastwood (Nottinghamshire) I General, {i}2,
5, 8, 9, 11, 15, 16, 24–5, 31, 35, 57, 64,
69, 77, 82, 86, 104, 116, 149, 161, 169,
174, 176, 203, 206, 211, 229, 235, 244,
252, 263, 266, 278, 281, 285–7, 293, 301,
312, 320, 325, 328, 354, 359–60, 363–4,
368, 371, 378, 388, 539, {ii}7, 42, 44,
54–5, 57–8, 124, 149, 196, {iii}3, 246,
281, 284, 300, 307, 310, 451, {iv}231,
327, {v}9, 13, 645, {vi}18, 47, 248,
{vii}193, 610, {viii}6
'miserable cacklers in', {i}41; 'one does
seem buried in', {i}96; DHL begins to
'hate', {i}134, 233; 'the insipid Sodom
of', {i}232; DHL reluctant to visit,
{i}243, 257, 270; enjoys 'crusty.. gossip'
from, {ii}122; feels 'quite aimiably
towards', {iii}250; 'hates to think of',
{v}126; in novels centrality of, {v}243;
vivid memory of, {v}592–3; 'a dreary
place now', {vii}451; Stephensen's view
of, {vii}460, 468; 'charming', {viii}2
Eastwood II Localities etc.
Albert Street, {i}24;
British School, {i}24–6;
Congregational Chapel, {i}24;
Congregational Literary Society, {i}3–4,
31, 44, 176;
Lynn Croft, {i}22–79 *passim*, 102,
135–6, 149, 169, 174–6, 189–98, 220,
229, 268, {iv}53, {v}115, 582, 631, 633,
645, {viii}1–2;
Mechanics' Institute, {i}6;
Nethergreen, {i}82;
Percy Street, {i}35, 442;
Queen's Square, {i}233, 280, 363, 369,
374, 376, 378, 381;
Walker Street, {v}592

Eastwood and Kimberley Advertiser, The,
    {i}3–4, 176, 233, {ii}57
Eaton, Mrs, {iv}498
Ebenhausen (Germany), {i}431, 540–53,
    {ii}19–23, 55–9, 61–74, {vi}132–67, 179,
    {vii}408–9, {viii}7, 106
Ebers, George Moritz, {i}180
Ebersteinberg (Germany), {iii}710, 714,
    723–9, {iv}2–3, 6, 24, 28–51, 72, 118–19,
    121, 254–5, 433–4, 451–2, {v}401,
    {vii}360
Ecce Homo, see Grosz, G.
Echanges, {vi}422, 438, 461, {vii}291
Ecuador, {iii}315
Eddie, *see* Clarke, W.; Marsh, E.
Eddy, Dr James {i}176, 283
Ede, Harold Stanley, ('Jim'), {v}525
Edenbridge (Kent), {i}309, 327, 358, 447
EDER, DR MONTAGU DAVID, {ii}1,
    260, 279, 317, 483, 643, 652–3, {iii}8, 42,
    161, 173–4, 178, 242–3, 245, 299, 316,
    400, 511, {iv}23, {v}311, {vii}380
    DHL stays with, {ii}258; candidate for
    Andes, {iii}173; DHL wishes to visit
    Palestine with, {iii}214, 285, 332, 335–6,
    340, 353–4, 687, 689; translates Freud's
    Über den Traum, {iii}716; *Psychoanalysis*
    for, {iv}37; *'nice* man, not a liar', {v}333;
    Porcupine for, {v}375
    Letters to {iii}149–50, 353–4, 687–8,
    {vii}377
EDER, EDITH, {ii}258, 260, 280, 483, 614,
    642, 652, {iii}42, 161, 173, 179, 181,
    226–7, 229, 273–4, 299, 340, 400, 511,
    688, 716, {v}311, {vii}377
    Letters to {ii}491–2, {iii}242–5, 277, 316
Edgar, *see* Jaffe, E.
Edinburgh (Scotland), {ii}17, 382, 384, 601,
    605, {iii}169, 171, 252, 258, 264, 306,
    313, 599, {v}505, 507
Edinburgh University, {iv}146–7, 150, 157,
    186, 304
EDITOR, *NEW STATESMAN, THE,*
    Letters to {ii}52, {v}395–7
EDITOR, *POETRY* (Chicago)
    Letters to {iv}337
EDITOR, *TEACHER, THE,*
    Letters to {i}25–6

Edler, John, {viii}19
Fanciulla Del West, La, see Puccini, G.
Edna, {v}366, 383, 633, {vi}88, 245
Edson, Charles Leroy, *The Great American
    Ass,* {vi}28
EDUCATION, value of *The Teacher* in,
    {i}25; '*Never* advise anyone to be a
    teacher', {i}54, {vii}563; DHL's
    disillusionment over College teachers,
    {i}72; 'School is a conflict', {i}85;
    teaching best when students known
    individually, {i}89; poverty-stricken
    boys at school, {i}124; 'school is hard
    work, anywhere', {i}385; Herakleitos on,
    {ii}364–5; 'One must be an outlaw..not a
    teacher or preacher', {ii}546; Hesiod's
    'virtue is so school-masterish', {ii}572;
    'I'd rather be a soldier than a school-
    teacher', {ii}616; 'introduce the deep,
    philosophic note into education: deep,
    philosophic reverence', {iii}269; in
    wartime DHL seeks job in Ministry of,
    {iii}287–8; 'schools and education will
    finish' American Indians, {v}47; 'I hate
    exams. and exam. fiends', {v}139–40;
    degree valuable mainly for teaching,
    {v}326; 'School-masters are terribly
    important to themselves: have to be',
    {v}533; 'horrible thing' to dabble in
    school-teaching, {vii}88; DHL thinks
    little of school prizes, {vii}398; voca-
    tional purpose important in, {vii}463;
    essential qualities in child's book on art,
    {viii}41
Edward, *see* Clarke, W. E.
Edward VII, {i}133, {iii}733, {v}328,
    {vi}61, 180
Edward VIII, {iv}215
    see also Wales, Prince of,
Edwards, Agustin, {ii}178
EDWARDS, GERALD BASIL,
    Letters to {vii}201
Edwin, *see* Dodge, E.
Eekhoud, George, {ii}100
Eel Pie Island (Middlesex), {i}292
Egadi (Sicily), {iii}688
Egidi, G., general shipping agent,
    {v}618–19, 646, {vi}101, 412, 431–3,

443, 559, 561, {vii}147, 493, 526, 558,
561, 565, 577

Egoist, The, {ii}203, {iii}31, 84
DHL's poems in, {i}109, 149, {ii}154,
156, 162, 232–4, {iii}29; originally *New
Freewoman,* {ii}131; story refused by,
{ii}132, {iii}135

Egypt, {i}52, 86, 337, {ii}87, 152, 454, 511,
611, 648, {iii}168, 233, 637, 640,
669–70, {iv}272, 461, 584, {v}287, 343,
345, 496, 577, 587, 596, {vi}1, 56 67,
378, {vii}544–5
DHL seeks job in, {i}69; interested in
early history of, {ii}529, 538, 556,
{iv}240; DHL read 'many fat books' on,
{iii}338, {vi}302; DHL might visit,
{vi}41, 58, 169–71, 175, 177, 179, 181,
189, 195, 200–1, 204–5, 208, 338, 437,
502, 513, 551; DHL not going to,
{vi}218, 221, 227, 233–4, 237, 299;
would like to see ancient, {vi}300

Egypt, S.S., {iv}249, 261
Egypte, see Maspéro, Sir G. C. C.
Ehrenstein, Albert, {vii}141
Ehrenstein, Carl, {vii}141
Einsame Menschen, see Hauptmann, G.
Einstein, Albert, {vii}653, {viii}106
Relativity, {iv}23, 30, 36–8, 128
Eisler, Robert, *Orpheus the Fisher,*
{vii}545
Ejutla (Mexico), {v}163
Ekkehard, see Scheffel, J. V. von
Ekkie, *see* Peterich, E.
El Greco, *see* Greco, El
El Paso (USA), {iv}112, 368–9, 378, 381,
388–9, 392, 405, 408, 412–13, 443, 525,
527, {v}144, 150–1, 153, 196, 211–12,
223–4, 235, {viii}75–8
'most insulting and hateful' Emigration
officials in, {v}229–30, {vii}144, 636
Elcho, Lord (Hugo Charteris), *see* Wemyss,
11th Earl of
Elcho, Lord Hugo, {ii}649
Eleanor, *see* Farjeon, E.
Elektra, see Strauss, R.
Elen, Ernest Augustus ('Gus'), {iii}446
Eleven Billion Dollars, see Mountsier, R.
Elga, see Hauptmann, G.

Elgin (Scotland), {v}500
Elide, *see* Fiori, E.
Eliot, George, {i}5, 88, 98
DHL 'very fond of', {i}101
Adam Bede, {ii}101;
The Mill on the Floss, {i}88, {ii}101
Eliot, Thomas Stearns, {ii}53, {iii}187
shares DHL's view of 'essence of
poetry', {ii}503; edits *Criterion,* {v}180,
514, {vii}170; 'instinctively' dislikes
DHL, {vii}294
Dante, {vii}589;
A Song for Simeon, {vii}585;
The Waste Land, {ii}12
Elizabeth (Pennsylvania, USA), {iv}276, 324
Elizabeth, *see* Hawk, E. M.
Elizabeth I, {vii}168
Elizabeth Barrett Browning, see Huxley, L.
Elizabeth, Betsy and Bess, see Schofield, L.
Ellesina, *see* Santoro, E.
Ellide, *see* Fiori, E.
Ellis Island (USA), {v}18, {vii}438, 446
Ellis, Havelock, {v}231, 330, 378, 423, 430,
{vii}115
Ellsworth, William Webster, *Readings from
the New Poets,* {vi}320
Elsa, *see* Weekley, E.
Else, *see* Jaffe, E.
Elstob, Ivy Turner, {vi}260
Elvery, Marjorie, {vi}220
Ely (Cambridgeshire), {i}80
Ely, George Herbert, {iii}276, 326, 713, 724,
730, {iv}26
Emblems of Love, see Abercrombie, L.
Emergency Committee (for the Assistance of
Germans, Austrians and Hungarians in
Distress) {iii}373, 375
Emerson, Ralph Waldo, {i}5
Conduct of Life, {iii}66;
Essays, {iii}66;
Nature, {iii}66;
Society and Solitude, {iii}66
Emil, *see* Krug, E. von
Emile, see Rousseau, J. J.
Emily, *see* King, E. U.
Emmerich (Germany), {iii}721, 723, 725
Emmie, *see* Limb, E.
Empedocles, {iii}551, {vii}573

Encyclopaedia Britannica, {vii}501
England and the Octopus, see William-Ellis, C.
England, {i}20, 81, 175, 253, 274, 315, 378,
   398–9, 401, 410, 419, 425–6, 438–9, 443,
   452, 463–554 *passim*, {ii}12, 19, 331, 337,
   340, 360, 373, 414, 420, 461, 491, 494,
   505, 508, 512, 600, 644–5, 650, 656, 663,
   {iii}1, 7–9, 11, 16, 76, 91–2, 95–6, 155,
   158, 190, 254, 270, 285, 344–6, 352,
   357–8, 365–7, 369, 372, 405, 416–587
   passim, 601, 619–24, 628, 639, 645, 658,
   663, 667, 670, 674–6, 683, 704–15, 723,
   728–9, {iv}1–20 *passim*, 31, 33, 35, 42,
   45–57, 67, 83, 85–9, 93, 99–100, 105–10,
   117–31 *passim*, 142, 145, 148–9, 153, 165,
   167, 178–9, 188, 213, 224, 228, 238, 242,
   253, 263, 275, 277, 282, 284, 287, 324,
   350, 352–3, 361–5, 370, 373, 375, 377,
   380, 394, 405, 416–99 *passim*, 501,
   519–20, 537–41, 574–5, 598, {v}1, 8, 10,
   13, 19, 29–30, 36, 43–4, 58, 67, 77, 91, 93,
   122, 126, 141, 189–242 *passim*, 252–3,
   268–348 *passim*, 367, 374, 376, 379,
   381–2, 390–405, 417–55 *passim*, 463–8,
   471–8, 481–5, 490, 492–7, 503, 510–24,
   538, 542, 549, 552–6, 565, 569, 573,
   576–8, 582–6, 591–5, 608–56 *passim*,
   {vi}1, 9–14, 49, 51, 67–74, 80, 84, 87, 96,
   106, 109, 122–5, 131, 138, 142, 147,
   153–8, 173, 191, 215, 231, 240, 247, 264,
   280, 286–7, 293, 297–8, 302–3, 322–407
   passim, 412–13, 418–20, 428, 436–40,
   457–8, 473–5, 507–13, 527, 532, 536–7,
   546, 567–78, 595, 607, {vii}6–8, 47, 53,
   58, 98–9, 117, 141, 180, 187, 199, 202,
   210–15, 235, 238, 240–3, 252, 262, 268,
   285–6, 304, 316–17, 323, 329–34, 339,
   343–4, 347, 351–2, 369, 384, 394, 399,
   401, 412, 436, 445–6, 451, 462–4, 483,
   496–8, 501, 504, 510, 524, 532, 547–8,
   569, 576–9, 586–8, 593, 615, 621–4,
   627, 630, 634, 637, 644, {viii}14, 44,
   78, 88
   Frieda 'the most wonderful woman in',
   {i}376; DHL 'can't breathe while we're
   in', {i}389; DHL loves, {i}417; 'storms
   of letters from', {i}420; DHL doesn't
   'want to come back to, {i}424–5, 446,
   515, 524, 538, 553–4, {ii}23, {v}506,
   {vi}41; 'I loathe the idea of', {i}427, 459,
   {ii}504; *S and L* 'the tragedy of thousands of young men in', {i}477; McLeod
   'the decentest man' to DHL in, {i}482;
   'looks cold and inhospitable', {i}512;
   DHL 'can write bigger stuff than any
   man in', {i}546; 'makes one so melancholy', {ii}25; 'big change in', {ii}47;
   'dull and woolly', {ii}58; uptight, {ii}73;
   'blue-grey, wistful-tender', {ii}96; DHL
   not considered a poet in, {ii}146; '*I* am
   the English nation', {ii}301; needs
   'surgery', {ii}318; DHL hates 'whole
   constitution of', {ii}328, 597; socio-
   political revolution needed in, {ii}365–8;
   'winter of the spirit in', {ii}393; 'living
   organism' of Europe dependent on,
   {ii}425; Garsington symbolic of,
   {ii}431–2, 459–60; 'collapsing civilisation' of, {ii}441; 'hopeless to stay in',
   {ii}490; 'banquet of vomit', {ii}500;
   represents 'the great christian-democrat-
   ic principle', {ii}604; 'striving to degrade
   and defile itself', {ii}629; 'terrible
   moisture' of, {iii}19; DHL wants to leave
   for ever, {iii}25, 74, 80, 144, 215, 312,
   316, 318, 322–3, 332, 335–7, 495; its art
   'subtlest...and most perfect in the world',
   {iii}41; Lloyd George 'a bad look-out
   for', {iii}48; 'disaster impending for',
   {iii}69; DHL unable to write any more
   for, {iii}87; 'country of the damned',
   {iii}92; 'bound to be labour insurrec-
   tions' in, {iii}116; reluctant to bring
   about peace, {iii}123; 'quite hopeless',
   {iii}136; *W in L* regarded as 'too strong
   for', {iii}156; Midlands 'the navel of',
   {iii}240; 'gloomy', {iii}305, 314; DHL
   hates 'dear old régime of happy industrial', {iii}339; literature of no consequence
   in, {iii}348; never to be forgiven for
   Rainbow, {iii}391; Italy '*much* better
   than', {iii}425; DHL enjoys Sicily better
   than, {iii}534; 'a mud-bathos', {iii}677;
   attack on *W in L* not expected in,
   {iii}678; 'moulders', {iii}694; DHL
   'can't work in', {iii}730; 'makes every-

thing feel barren,' {iii}733; 'in a bad way', {iv}26; 'deserves to have her coal strike', {iv}40; 'gone all thick and fuzzy in the head', {iv}97; 'a dead dog', {iv}114; 'European ring' possible, excluding, {iv}124; 'drifting to' alliance with Germany, {iv}132; 'no strict copyright law' between USA and, {iv}196–7; 'the most living clue of life is in us Englishmen in', {iv}219; DHL English despite, {iv}234, 314; homesick for, {iv}249, 312; cost of living in Australia compared with, {iv}263, 271; 'pettyfogging narrowness of', {iv}296; royalty income from, {iv}299, 302, 367, 383, 596; 'seems full of graves', {iv}327; DHL has 'such a deep mistrust of', {iv}397, 432; DHL reluctant to visit, {iv}418, 420, 422, 424, 446, 470, 474, 479–80, 485–8, {vi}564; Frieda insists on DHL's return to, {iv}512–18, 524–32; 'hateful', {iv}542, 546. 548–50, 552, 558, 560; 'a tomb', {iv}545; 'like an unboiled pudding' (Frieda), {iv}578; 'tight...like a box', {v}116, {vi}91; serious unemployment in, {v}259; 'fantastic *Alice-in-Wonderland* country', {v}311; 'almost gruesome', {v}313; people 'about as active as seaweed', {v}321; 'rain, bad trade, general gloom' in, {v}323, 329, 332; coal the making and breaking of, {v}479, 499, 518, 565, {vi}180; DHL dreads thought of, {v}498, {vi}554, 558; 'class hatred' dangerous in, {v}515; DHL 'glad to be at home in', {v}521; 'not so scratchy as' USA, {v}530; safe, kindly but ruthless, {v}535; 'they've pushed the spear through the side of *my*', {v}592; Italy dearer than, {vi}62, 64, 81; inclement weather in, {vi}200, 248; people 'wofully disembodied' in, {vi}258, {vii}275; copies of *LCL* for, {vi}265, 282, 288, 371, 375, 401, 408, 416, 432, 436, 448, 461–505 *passim*, 517–21, 530, 561, {vii}39, 89, 131, 134, 143, 145; materialism of, {vi}542, 547–9; *LCL* attacked in, {vi}609, {vii}155–7, 160–1; royalties of expatriates taxed in,

{vii}26; DHL fears arrest in, {vii}166, 222, 293; would vote Labour in, {vii}327; shrinks from journey to, {vii}353–4; hypocrisy of, {vii}379, 518; DHL 'out of temper with', {vii}405, 415; 'lily-livered', {vii}419, 421–5; *P and O* intensified distaste for DHL in, {vii}604; evil destructiveness in, {viii}21; Frieda doesn't much like, {viii}84

English Association, The, {i}84, 179, 187, 189, 191

English Authors' Society, *see* Society of Authors

English Channel, {i}341, {ii}373, 588, {iii}9, 239,608, 677, {vi}105
see also Channel Isles

English Review, The, {i}11–15, 104, 145, 157, 167, 277, 281–4, 304–5, 310, 327, 372, 378, 380, 405, 456, 469, 505, 512–14, 533, {ii}6, 26–7, 29, 31, 67, 92, 98, 115, 225, 262, {iii}4, 15, 102, 135, 142, 161, 166, 178, 234, 310, 330, 342, 398–9, 576, 643–4, 708, {iv}7–8, 11, 15, 54, {v}184, {vi}45, {viii}2, 33, 38
DHL's poems in, {i}94, 137–9, 141, 143, 149, 156, 179, 254, 375, 407, 459, 471, {ii}90, 93, 120, 129, 136, 139, 146, 209, 446, 670, {iii}115, 246, 361, {iv}69, 71, 83, 177, 378, 380, {v}86, {vi}541; *Tono Bungay* in, {i}119, 128; 'very fine, and very "new"', {i}139; Harrison becomes editor, {i}152; DHL's stories in, {i}153, 156, 162, 172, 245–6, 275, 292, 313, 335, 345, 348, 351, 510, {ii}44–5, 81–2, 86–7, 90, 99, 175, 187, 196–7, 216, 354, 372, 386, 391, 395, 406, 493, {iii}22, 74, 79, 100, 298, 633, 635, 650, 690, {iv}32, 134, 143–4, 156, 159, 177, 226, {viii}40; *White Peacock* reviewed in, {i}240; DHL reviews for, {i}324, 331; 'so piffling now', {ii}21–2; Douglas and, {ii}44, 82; DHL's sketches in, {ii}58, 66, 70, 127; DHL's essays in, {iii}104–13, 146, 164–5, 217, 270, 292–3, 324–5, 346, 357, 369, 407, 565, 577, {iv}197, {v}103–4, {viii}32; DHL doesn't really like at all, {iv}55

English, The, *see English Review*,
English Water-Colour, see Holme, C.
Englishman and the Mexican Inquisition, An,
 see Conway, G. R. G.
Enid, *see* Hopkin, E.
Ennis, Ethel, {iv}232–3
Ennis, Hon. George Francis Macdaniel,
 {iv}232–3
Enoch, {vii}599, 640
Enormous Room, The, see Cummings, E.E.
Enquiry concerning Human Understanding, see
 Hume, D.
Eplett, Frederick, {iii}446
Epsom (Surrey), {i}90–1, 129
Epstein, (Sir) Jacob, {ii}661, {iii}158, {vii}8
Erewhon, see Butler, S.
ERFFA, HELMUTH HARTMANN VON,
 Letters to {v}287–8
Erie, Lake (USA), {iv}350–1
Ermengarde, see Legend of Ermengarde, The
Ermenonville, *see* Moulin du Soleil, Le
Ern(e)st, *see* Weekley, E.
Ernie, see Humphreys, E. A.; Prior, E.
ERNST, MORRIS LEOPOLD,
 To the Pure, {vi}548, 613
 Letters to {vi}613–14
Erskine of Marr, Hon. Ruaraidh, {vii}531
Ertel, Lola, {i}521, 533
Ertel, Natasha, {i}451
Erzberger, Matthias, {iv}83
Escapes and Escapades, see Savage, H.
Esher, Eleanor, Viscountess, {vi}227
Esher, 2nd Viscount (Reginald Baliol Brett),
 {iv}546, 550, 593, 596, {v}3, 24, 50, 155,
 283, 329, 333, 342, 504, {vi}22, {vii}24,
 627–9
Esperanza (Mexico), {v}162–3
Essays in Popular Science, see Huxley, J.
Esson, Louis, {iv}281
Esther Waters, see Moore, G.
Esthwaite Lodge (Lancashire), {vii}615
Estrada, Genaro, {v}124, 155, 157, 162, 182,
 221, {vi}10, 335
Esty, Alice, {i}322
Eth, *see* Burrows, E. H.
Etienne, Charles-Guillaume, *Joconde ou les*
 Coureurs d'Aventures, {ii}561

Etna, Mt. (Sicily), {iii}497–8, 505–7, 509,
 514, 516, 533, 553, 639, {iv}7, 100,
 157–8
 'snowy silent', {iii}485, 672, 676, 695,
 {iv}116, 122, 139; 'beautiful', {iii}488;
 Mary Cannan climbs, {iii}551, 557;
 'smokes a lot of black smoke', {iv}137;
 'like a white queen, or a white witch',
 {iv}205, 207
Etruria and Rome, see Fell, R. A. L.
Etruria Antica, see Ducati, P.
Etruria, {v}413, 465
 see also Lawrence, D. H., *Etruscan*
 Places
Etruscan(s), {vi}1, 17, 95, 150, 575, {vii}5,
 195, 508, 569–70
 DHL 'looking at Etruscan things',
 {vi}25–31, 33–6, 38–40, 43, 88–90;
 wants 'to go etruscanising', {vi}92; plans
 further visit, {vi}508, 538, 542, 546, 575,
 {vii}19, 21, 25–6; DHL 'scared of tombs
 in winter', {vii}40, 49, 72
Etruskische Malerei, see Weege, F.
Etruskische Frühgeschichte, see Schachermeyr,
 F.
Etzatlan (Mexico), {iv}17, 513, 515–16
Euclid, {vii}507
Eugénie Grandet, see Balzac, H. de
'Eunice Temple', *see* Chambers, J.
Euripides, {i}5, 525, {ii}130, {vi}24
 Bacchae, {i}160, 261, {vi}24;
 Medea, {i}543, {iii}24;
 Rhesus. {ii}136;
 Trojan Women, {i}261
Europe, {i}5, 8, {iii}6, }8, 10, 17, 160, 318,
 326, 347–8, 487–8, 491, 494, 501, 504,
 544, 580, 634, 689, 707, 734, {iv}1–4,
 7–8, 11–14, 18–20, 59, 83, 100, 107, 212,
 225, 228, 244, 256, 258, 260, 275, 340,
 351, 366, 373, 380, 398, 404, 421, 423,
 426, 464, 478, 492, 502–3, 517, 545–8,
 566, 572, 586, {v}1, 6, 9, 12, 24, 90, 135,
 184–5, 190, 201, 208, 235, 241, 244–5,
 253, 264, 277–8, 281–2, 294, 298, 305,
 309, 342, 350, 375, 381, 388, 412, 420,
 438, 468, 471, 473, 519, 540, 562, 568,
 585, 629, 635, {vi}1, 73–4, 99–100, 154,

175, 182, 209, 278, 310, 315, 323, 358, 378, 393, 419, 437, 547–51, 567–8, 604, {vii}25, 54, 108, 116, 131, 263–4, 284, 290, 343–4, 418, 429, 471, 483, 552, 594, 602, 624, {viii}48, 79, 92

'no hope in', {iii}69; 'courage of ultimate truth' not in, {iii}141; like 'Gadarene swine' in, {iii}143; 'mass of ruins from the past', {iii}144; DHL wants to leave, {iii}312–13, 316, 322, 439, 460, 522, 563, 524, 626, 655–6, 664, 693, {iv}67, 80, 90–3, 97, 111, 114, 151, 155, 165, 180, 182, 196; 'bored with', {iii}323; 'stupid, wearisome', {iii}334; feels 'insecure', {iii}483; collapsing civilisation of, {iii}566; 'no good', {iii}678; 'new wave of idealism in', {iii}680; 'having a slight reactionary swing, back to conservatism', {iii}728; 'like a bad meal of various courses', {iv}49; is 'the world to *feel* in', {iv}103; 'hopeless place', {iv}117, 121, 133, 141, 143, {v}93–4; 'takes the heart out of one', {iv}149, 157; 'nothing new' can come in, {iv}162; DHL glad to leave, {iv}201, 213; Roman Catholic Church might save, {iv}219; 'most satisfactory place in the end', {iv}222; in Australia DHL longs for, {iv}247, 249–50, 266, 325; Australia free from tension of, {iv}260, 264; 'stiflingness' of, {iv}305; DHL wants to return to, {iv}311, 388, {v}172, 174; prefers to New Mexico, {iv}362; DHL hesitates to leave Mexico for, {iv}430, 433–4, 437–40, 444. 451, 453, 458–9, {viii}81; 'I know I am European', {iv}463, {v}304, 651, {vii}287, 424; USA makes DHL long for, {iv}471; reluctant to return to, {iv}479, 481, 483, 485, 488; DHL's 'destiny' may be in, {iv}513; time for DHL to return to, {iv}519–20, 534, 536; returns hesitantly to, {iv}539–41; 'unspeakably dreary', {iv}550, 562–3, 569; 'wearying', {iv}579–82, 593–4, 596–7; DHL glad to leave 'the doom of', {iv}600; New York 'more stimulating' than, {v}15; 'depression' felt in, {v}23, 26, 28, 34, 50; 'the mushiness of', {v}170; DHL *'really'* wants to get back to, {v}219, 229–31, 266, 269, 307; DHL needs to be 'softened…with a little oil of', {v}272–4; 'nice to be in' after strain of USA, {v}364, 600; 'is easy', {v}379; viewed from USA 'seems unreal', {v}457; 'strange psychical gulf' between USA and, {v}491–2; Skye 'like the very beginning of', {v}512; 'no spunk in', {vi}72; 'like a dying pig', {vi}82; a 'queer vacuum is the centre of', {vi}136; 'angel of death..waving his wings over the middle of', {vi}169; 'awfully dead', {vi}212, 229, 508; DHL gets sick of, {vi}219, 221, 232; *'energyless'*, {vi}242; DHL can't digest his 'inward spleen' in, {vii}574; is 'reesty', {vii}577, 579; slowly killing DHL, {vii}616–17; its cup 'drunk empty', {viii}24; 'smell of its misery in the air', {viii}75; 'lost its courage to live', {viii}84; DHL doesn't think he will ever return to, {viii}85

Eva, {ii}435, 507, 510, 512

Evans, Alice ('Corbinetta') Oliver, {iv}308, {v}103, {vi}228

Evans, Carl, {iv}110, 313

Evans, John Ganson, {iv}308, 317, 329, 332–3, 337, 339, 348, 358, 360, 372, 514, {v}23, 103, 132, 187, {vi}228, {vii}276

Evans, Mrs, {iv}125, 139, 231, 365

Evans, Natalie Sarah, {v}103

Evans, Powys Arthur Lenthall, {vii}118

Evans, Rosalie, {v}155

Evans, Sir Arthur John, *The Mycenaean Tree and Pillar Cult and its Mediterranean Relations*, {vii}507

Evans, Sir Samuel Thomas, {i}516

'Eve in the Land of Nod', *see* Skinner, M. L.

Eve, {vi}313, 316, 334, 460

Eve, *see* Young-Hunter, E.

Eve, {v}3, 416

Eve: The Ladies Pictorial, {vi}4, 438, 454, 475, 606, 609, {vii}507

Evelyn Innes, *see* Moore, G.

Evening News (London), {iii}576, {vi}6
  DHL's articles for, {iii}564, {vi}401,
  403, 438, 441, 454, 460–1, 541, 563, 602,
  610, {vii}28, 117; articles prompt
  invitation from BBC, {vi}552; valuable
  income from, {vii}26
  see also Olley, A. E.
Evening Standard, {vi}271, 595
  WWRA reviewed in, {vi}438; DHL in
  Low cartoon in, {vii}198–9, 202,
  206–7
Everybody's Magazine, {iv}406
Everyman, DHL's 'The Risen Lord' in,
  {vii}10, 401, 500, 512, 525, 532; review
  by DHL in, {vii}82, 556; 'a cringing
  mongrel', {vii}334; Hicks on DHL in,
  {vii}584
Everyman's Library, {i}89, 98, 144, 213,
  {ii}155, 253, 572, 614–15, 633, {iii}40,
  213, 304, 315, 340, {iv}449, {vi}45
EVIL, 'good and evil flowing from God
  through humanity as through a filter',
  {ii}266; DHL 'depressed by the sense of
  evil in the world', {ii}310; 'a principle of
  evil' seen 'plainly in Keynes..prevalence
  of evil, as if it were some insidious
  disease', {ii}311; in Dostoievsky 'all the
  passion of hate, of evil', {ii}314; Shelley
  rightly believed in 'principle of Evil,
  coeval with the Principle of Good',
  {ii}315; 'evil, bad, separating spirit',
  {ii}378; 'disintegrating process of the
  war..an internal evil' leading to 'brink of
  oblivion', {ii}424–5; destruction follows
  from 'evil mood' in child provoked by
  evil intent, but 'no child..all evil',
  {ii}425; 'loving forces of life' exist
  though 'evil predominates', {ii}443; in
  London neither good nor evil 'ripens',
  {ii}452; 'evil face' of world only threat to
  happiness at Tregerthen, {ii}566;
  democracy and aristocracy both, {ii}593,
  {iii}123; analysis is, {iii}42; war is
  'maximum of', {iii}88; 'acid fumes of a
  world's accumulated evil..evil destructive process', {iii}93; 'evil ones, the
  death-makers', {iii}101; DHL's illness
  from 'evil influence of aggreggate

London', {iii}117; 'man with his evil
  stupidity is after all nothing', {iii}118;
  John Asquith 'possessed by an evil
  spirit', {iii}118; people have become
  'evil spirits of the dead', {iii}170; 'I am
  all things evil' according to *John Bull*,
  {iv}90, {vi}598; everywhere, {iv}151;
  Mabel Luhan's 'will' evil masquerading
  as good, {iv}528; 'sex in the head..an evil
  and destructive thing', {v}204; 'gods of
  evil, even Mammon, to be placated',
  {v}456; real principle of evil is 'anti-life',
  {vii}239, 332; 'evil world-soul..some-
  times overpowers one', {vii}546; 'a
  morbid evil destructiveness in the soul
  and will of people',
  {viii}21
Evin/Evna, {i}343
Ewald, Francisca, {vii}507, 510, 536, 572
Ewart, Wilfrid Herbert Gore, {iv}368–9
Ewing, Juliana Horatia, *Lob Lie-by-the-Fire*,
  {ii}588
Exeter (Devon), {ii}511, {iii}346
Experiments, see Douglas, G. N.
Eyam (Derbyshire), {i}259
Eyes of Vigilance, see Wilmot, F. L. T.
Eyewitness, The, {i}379
Eyre & Spottiswood, {vii}583
Eyre, Charles, {v}487
Eyre, Eva, {v}487
Ezzechiele, *see* Azzarini, E.

Faakersee (Austria), {vi}129–30
Faber & Faber, {vii}467–8, 470, 503, 509,
  526, 554, 560, 569, 589, 606
  Ariel Poems, {vii}585, 619;
  Criterion Miscellany, *P and O* in,
  {vii}468, 470–1, 503, 509, 526, 554, 560,
  569, 588–9;
  Poets on Poets, {vii}589
Fabians, {i}176, {iii}49–50
Faerie Queene, The, see Spenser, E.
Fagan, James Bernard, {iii}6, 374–5
Fairfield, the Misses, {ii}407
'Fairy-Tale', *see* Luhan, M. D. S.
Falanga, Francesca ('Ciccia'), {iii}606, 620,
  640, 661, 664–6, 668–9, 672–3, 696, 709,
  {iv}141

Falanga, Vincenzo, {iii}606, 620, 640, 661,
  664–6, 668–9, 672–3, 678, 696, 709,
  {iv}141
FALK, BERNARD, {vii}188, 201
  Letters to {vii}189
Fallen Leaves, see Rozanov, V. V.
Falmouth (Cornwall), {ii}613, {iii}66, 76,
  85, 127, {vi}510–11
False Prince, The, see Dolmela, H.
Fanfrolico Press, The, {vii}31, 95, 98, 123,
  508
  DHL's *Paintings* and, {vii}48–50, 60, 66,
  70–1, 77, 82–3, 85–6, 124–5, 130, 170,
  253
  see also Mandrake Press
Fantazius Mallare, see Hecht, B.
Fantin-Latour, Ignace H. J. T., {i}146
Far Off Things, see Machen, A. L. J.
Farbman, Ghita, {ii}570, {iii}124, 163, 275,
  310, 318, 327, 336, 340, 347, 349, 363,
  387, 397, 433, 486, 511, 676, 728, {iv}30,
  87, 114, 166, 276, 350, 574, {v}347, 355,
  367, 374, 377, 419, 455, 483, 558, 559,
  {vi}30, 233, 247, 271, 323, 458, 604,
  {vii}40
Farbman, Michael S. ('Grisha'), {ii}268, 570,
  615, {iii}114, 121, 136, 163, 191, 193–5,
  198, 208, 235, 256, 272, 284, 318, 321,
  327, 347, 349, 401, 486, 501, 511–12,
  515–16, 632, 658, 676, {iv}23–4, 87, 114,
  166, 276, 350, 566, 574, 595, {v}81, 347,
  367, 374, 418–19, 455, 483, {vi}30, 323,
  346, 458, 604, {vii}40, 49
  After Lenin, {v}366, 371, {vii}84
Farbman, Sonia Issayevna ('Sonya', 'Sophie'),
  {ii}570, {iii}114, 121, 124, 163, 191,
  193–5, 198, 235, 256, 272, 275, 284, 292,
  310, 318, 321, 327, 330, 336, 347,
  349–52, 354–5, 363, 367–8, 376, 387,
  397, 408, 428, 433, 471, 482, 486,
  511–12, 632, 676, 725, 728, {iv}23, 30,
  37, 87, 114, 149, 166, 171–2, 208, 276,
  350, 566, 570, 574, {v}81, 347, 355, 367,
  374, 419, 455, 483, 506, 508, 513, 529,
  536, 558–9, 601–2, 628, {vi}30, 42, 67,
  271, 458, 604, {vii}40, 49, 618
Farjeon, Annabel, {iii}677, {iv}67
Farjeon, Benjamin Leopold, {ii}321

FARJEON, ELEANOR, {ii}321, {iii}279,
  623, 641–2, 677, {iv}67
  DHL sends words of song to, {ii}332;
  critique of poems by, {ii}340–1; writes
  'nice letter' about *Rainbow*, {ii}566
  Dream-Songs for the Beloved, {ii}341;
  First & Second Love: Sonnets, {ii}341;
  The Soul of Kol Nikon, {ii}341
  Letters to {ii}332–3, 338, 340–2, 407–8,
  {iii}372–3, 375, 633, 649
Farjeon, Gervase, {iii}677, {iv}67
FARJEON, HERBERT ('BERTIE') {ii}321,
  {iii}279, 378, 520, 677, {iv}67
  Letters to {iii}304
Farjeon, Joan, {iii}304, 378, 411, 413, 520,
  677, {iv}67
Farjeon, Joscelyn, {iii}304, 677, {iv}67
Farley (Surrey), {i}250
Farm of the Dagger, The, see Phillpotts, E.
Farquhar, John N., *The Crown of Hinduism*,
  {ii}351
Farrand, Frederick George, {viii}98
FARRAND, GRACE,
  Letters to {viii}98
FASCISM, {ii}91, 180, {iv}353, {v}67, 301,
  433, 472, 620, {vi}258, 307, {vii}196
  in Mexico, {iv}433; not 'natural' to
  Italians but Florence 'irritable' with,
  {v}496, 499; 'spreads the grand blight of
  boredom', {v}550; 'bossiness' of,
  {vi}121; 'false power', {vi}308
Fasola, Costanza, *see* Peterich, C.
Faux-Monnayeurs, Les, see Gide, A. P. G.
Favre Shipping Line, {iii}673, 678
Fay, Mrs Stanley, {v}504
Federalist, The, see Hamilton, A.
FEIPEL, LOUIS N., sends 'massive list' of
  textual errors in *Captain's Doll* and
  Fantasia, {iv}442
  Letters to {iv}443
Feldberg (Germany), {iv}46
Felice, *see* Fiori, F.
Fell, Roland Arthur Lonsdale, *Etruria and
  Rome*, {v}473
Fellah Songs, DHL's translations of, {i}8,
  196, 200–1, 203–6, 230, 248
Feltrelline, Signorina, {i}474, 483, 500
Ferdinando, *see* Chiara, F. di

Ferdinando, Paul, {ii}561, 571
Ferguson, Edna, {iv}442
Ferguson, Rev. Joseph, {i}23
Ferleiten (Austria), {iv}56, 59–60
Fernandez, Ramon, {v}180
Feroze, Dr, *see* Mullan-Feroze, Dr D. F.
Feu, Le, see Barbusse, H.
Feuchtwanger, Lion, {v}388, {vii}563
  Jud Süss, 'a vulgar affair', {v}388; its
    commercial success, {vi}46, 152, 173,
    {vii}197
Feud, The, see Garnett, E.
Fiammetta (The Hours of), see Taylor, R. A.
Fiascherino (Italy), {ii}3, 63, 78, 122, 140,
  175, 190, 478, 497, 550, {vi}417
Fiedler, Dr Kurt, {vii}596, 598
Fiedler, H. G., {i}331
Field, Louise Maunsell, {ii}82
Field, Roscoe & Co., {vii}163, 257
Fielding, Henry, {iii}166
  Tom Jones {i}484, 487, {ii}33
Fiesole (Italy), {iii}594, {iv}83–4, 193, 594,
  {v}459, 656, (vi}93, {vii}305, 359,
Fight for Freedom, see Goldring, D.
Fiji, {iv}239, {vi}83
Filey (Yorkshire), {i}70
Filiberto, {v}616
Filippi, Rosina, *Bernadine*, {i}496, 512
FILM (including CINEMA), DHL dreams
  of Cynthia Asquith as 'sort of..cinema
  star', {iii}195; DHL unwilling 'to be
  ravelled up in a film' by Mackenzie,
  {iii}504; *Lost Girl* 'such a film title',
  {iii}528; DHL accepts Revnes' offer to
  represent him in USA for film rights,
  {iii}546–7; rumour of Mackenzie's film
  studio on Herm, {iii}608, 628; Buddhist
  temples 'better..on the cinema' than in
  reality, {iv}221; DHL meets 'Utterly
  undistinguished' film actors and crew,
  {iv}287; DHL visits San Francisco
  cinema 'with jazz orchestra..and
  voluminous organ', {iv}290; offer of
  $5000 for film rights of *W in L* accepted,
  {iv}558, 589, {viii}87; Skinner's *Black
  Swans* 'too much of a cinema piece',
  {v}419; production of *David* alleged to
  be like 'bad film', {vi}66, 75; DHL
  refuses invitation to write for *Film*

Weekly about 'uncensored Film',
  {vi}601
Film Weekly, {vi}7, 601
Filsinger, Ernst B., {viii}39
Finland, {i}355, {iv}175, {vi}302
Finney Farm (New York, USA), {v}83, 159,
  237, 406, 417, 434
Fiori, Elide, {ii}87–9, 119, 123, 125, 140–2,
  158, 163, 478, {iii}19
Fiori, Felice, {ii}80–2, 84–5, 87, 122–3,
  141–2, 163, 478, 629, {iii}19
Fir-Flower Tablets, see Lowell, A.
Firenze (Italy), *see* Florence
First & Second Love, see Farjeon, E.
First Novel Library, {iii}210
Fischer Verlag, {vi}421, 465, 524, 582, 616,
  {vii}51, 333, 536, 543, 567, 572
'Fish, The', *see* Fisher, Mrs
Fisher Unwin, Ltd, {i}154, 297, {ii}384,
  {iii}12, 184–5, 187, 191, 195, 210,
  {iv}27
  see also Unwin, T. F.
FISHER, BESSIE, {iv}101–2, 108, 110, 125,
  190
  Letters to {iv}231, 285
Fisher, Herbert Albert Laurens, {iii}287
Fisher, Mrs, {iii}197, 199, 261, 266
'Fisher, the', *see* Fisher, B.
Fitness of the Environment, The, see
  Henderson, L. J.
Fiume (Croatia), {iii}462
Flamborough (Yorkshire), {i}62, 68, 70–1,
  {vii}421
Flame and Shadow, see Teasdale, S.
Flaubert, Gustave, {i}9, 14, 459, {ii}654,
  {iii}197
  'accurate-impersonal school of', {i}169,
  178, 417; his is 'art of self-hate', {ii}101;
  'obvious and coarse' beside Fenimore
  Cooper or Hardy, {iii}41
  Sentimental Education, {i}174
Flecker, James Elroy, {ii}61–2, {iii}212
  The Golden Journey to Samarkand,
    {ii}61–2, 104
Fletcher, John Gould, {iii}190, {v}450,
  {vii}395
  reviewed *LWHCT*, {iii}280
Fleurs du Mal, Les, see Baudelaire, C.
Flewins, Alice M., {vi}513

Flight, see White, W.

Flint, Frank Stewart, {ii}427, {iii}253, 261, {v}450, {vii}86
  'Fluff' a better name for, {vi}43

Flitter, Louie, {iii}411–12

Florence (Firenze) (Italy), {i}530–1, 535, {iii}9, 409, 413–18, 435, 450, 452, 455, 463, 476, 542, 553, 558, 567, 572, 585, 587, 589–90, 606–11, 614, 632, 648, 651, 669, 679, 687, 692–3, 696–8, 715, 721–4, 730, 733, {iv}3–6, 13, 25–9, 41–6, 48, 59, 61–7, 111, 151, 179, 212, 254, 351, 532, {v}10–12, 31, 361–432 *passim*, 540, 557–656 *passim*, {vi}1–5, 9, 34, 39–109 *passim*, 124, 128, 130, 170–1, 180, 186–91, 196–7, 201–2, 250, 255–6, 272, 307, 360–1, 367–8, 380, 392, 398, 407, 410, 413, 417, 427–9, 434, 522, 524, 563, 574–616 *passim*, {vii}8–9, 19, 21, 28, 30, 32–5, 39–41, 49–58, 77, 88, 91, 98, 141, 151, 155, 159, 167, 171, 181–4, 186, 200, 236, 255, 274, 281–2, 305, 341, 351–8, 379, 381, 396, 410–11, 416, 425, 428, 432, 435, 444, 453–4, 456, 463–5, 467–71, 479–80, 483, 490, 494, 496, 514, 530, 559, 566, 578–80, 585, {viii}37, 44, 49, 98, 103, 105, 107
  DHL in, {iii}418–29, 591–604, 704–5, {iv}79–89, 409–10, 433–49, {vii}358–76; DHL banks with Haskard & Co in, {iii}482, 519, {iv}91, 179, 201, {vii}63; poems written near, {iii}657; Rebecca West in, {iii}709; for access to library DHL prefers, {iii}714, 717, 726; DHL's typist (Mrs Carmichael) in, {iv}107, 129, 131, 144, 196–7, 215, {vi}245; Villa Mirenda near, {v}450–1, {vi}422; DHL rarely in, {v}588, 593, 598, 601, 603, {vi}207–9, 213–15, 217, 220; very expensive, {v}615; DHL treated by 'best doctor' (Giglioli) in, {vi}95, 98, 106, 109, 177; *LCL* published in, {vi}222–5, 237–9, 253, 260–388 *passim*, 415, 431, 437, 466–82 *passim*, 493–4, 505, 510–52 *passim*, 566, 570, {vii}23, 43–7, 63, 76, 113, 120, 134, 186, 208, 631; 'very social', {vii}314; its *noise* ..real torture', {vii}363–4, {viii}46; MS of *LCL* in, {vii}391

Flores, General Angel, {v}164

Florida (USA), {ii}12
  DHL hopes to go to, {ii}428–32, 448–9, 452–4, 459, 463–7, 472, 475–8, 482–92, 497; Delius's estate in, {ii}444, 446, 450; Fort Myers, {ii}449–50, 452, 454, 464, 466; Jacksonville, {ii}449–50; Susquehanna, {ii}450; wild turkeys in, {ii}458, 461; DHL despairs of going to, {ii}498, 500; 'Florida idea' right, {iii}23, 25, 70
  see also Rananim

Floss(ie), *see* Cullen, F.

Flower, Fruit and Thorn Pieces, see Richter, J. P.

'Flowers of the Greek Anthology, The', *see* Douglas, G. N., *Birds and Beasts of the Greek Anthology*

FLOWERS, with Bernhardt 'Intellect is shed as flowers shed..petals', {i}59; 'scarlet coated golfers moving like vivid', {i}118; mustard and cress are flowers if 'run to seed', {i}126; 'wonderful silken bravery of green and crocus', {i}156; 'I cannot slowly gather flowers..I love my rose and no other', {i}237; McLeod's blood 'as blue as a cornflower', {i}277; Louie Burrows a 'flagging hollyhock', {i}285; 'bachelor's buttons - pale gold great bubbles', primulas, violets, orchids, harebells, 'stuff like larkspur': 'flowers, great wild profusion of them', {i}413–16; harebells ('hairy strange creatures'), gentian and 'flowers like monkey-musk', {i}441; in spring snowdrops, violets and primroses, {i}493; primroses, Leber Blumen ('lovely little blue things'), 'lilac-coloured crocuses', {i}514; 'autumn crocuses stand slim..each standing single..lovely slender mauve-pink things, balancing their gold in the centre', {ii}65; 'Herbst Zeitlosen..exquisite autumn crocuses', {ii}66, {viii}7–8; 'like bulbs in the ground, only shadowy flowers..for another spring', {ii}143; 'gay and fluttering' anemones, rananculi in bud, gladioli 'long spears'. {ii}172; feeling emerging from letter 'like a scent

FLOWERS (*cont.*)

of flowers, so generous and reassuring',
{ii}311; turkeys 'ruffled themselves like
flowers suddenly ruffled into blossom',
{ii}460; 'gorse is sunshine itself',
{ii}550; 'blue, graceful little companies
of bluebells..gorse in flame..primroses
like settling butterflies..sea-pinks like a
hover of pink bees', {ii}609; roses as
likely to 'bloom in January' as 'living
work' to be published, {iii}100; yellow
rock-roses ('pure flowers of light'),
milkworts, 'wild columbines are wood-
avens', yellow pansies, wood-ruff 'we call
it new-mown-hay', {iii}248; 'wild
crocuses..like great lavender stars',
Amalfi coast full of, {iii}464; parterre of
weeds and (Swinburnian) flowers,
{iii}494; 'no flowers like English',
{iii}536; 'Almond Blossom in clouds',
{iii}656; 'hibiscus flowers coming again',
{iv}97; 'hairy, pale mauve anemones that
the Indians call Owl', {v}236; *Porcupine*
'gayer than a geranium in a pot', {v}376;
'nuns in frocks like lavender crocuses',
{v}606; 'I love cowslips', {vi}43; DHL
discovers 'rare white orchid..and a dark
purple and yellow wild gladiolus',
{vi}56; 'middle-class Lockharts grew
lilies of the valley up their arses',
{vi}231; Frieda flourishes 'like a
dandelion in the sun' from furore over
LCL, {vi}487; crocuses 'very lovely, long
pale bubbles', {vi}562; chicory 'blue as
blue', {viii}7; 'white flutter with cistus',
'queer perfume' of broom, {viii}103

Fluelen (Switzerland), {ii}77

Flying Carpet, The, see Asquith, Lady C.

Flying Heart, The, *see* Kiowa ranch

Folkestone (Kent), {iii}9, 569, {v}545

Fonda, *see* La Fonda Hotel

Font, Leopold, {iv}445

Fontainebleau (France), {iv}365, 375, 555,
567–8, 573, 578, {v}422, 441, 486,
{vi}57, 258, 609, {vii}175
see also Gurdjieff, G.

Fontana Vecchia (Taormina, Sicily), {iii}10,
17, 500, 506, 526, 529–30, 552, 613, 640,
647–8, 657, 670, 682–8, 693, 695–7, 705,
711, 714, {iv}3–6, 25, 86–9, 108, 199,
434, 483, {viii}52
'charming house..in a big garden',
{iii}479–85, 488–91, 517–18, {viii}29,
47; 'a watch-tower of the sea', {iii}492;
DHL loves, {iii}539, 619, 676, {iv}90,
385; garden described in 'Sun', {v}533
see also Taormina (Sicily)

FOOD, 'copious' from Mrs Jones, {i}83; free
for poor schoolboys, {i}97; 'custard
pudding' during convalescence, {i}330;
'heaps of butter and toast and biscuits
about' in convalescent home, {i}350;
'spaghetti and risotto..of our own
making', {i}458; 'I've cooked cart-loads
of', {i}523; 'nice little steak.. carrots in
butter', {ii}105; at Lerici diet of soup,
polenta, pasta, 'queer vegetables', fresh
sardines, {ii}125; 'Jewish Cosher
Supper' with Kot, {ii}251; a universal
birthright, {ii}292, {iii}353, {vii}103–4;
details of 'masses of [Christmas] food' at
Ripley, {iii}313; after flu DHL has food
(especially grapefruit), 'not only
accursed milk', {iii}329; needed in post-
war Germany, {iii}373; in Picinisco
house, {iii}432; lunch of 'poached eggs'
at Timeo Hotel, {iii}496; at Maltese
hotel, {iii}522, 531; 'wonderful aspara-
gus' in Baden, {iii}710, 721; 'No
sausageless Nirvana' in Baden, {iii}721;
'monotonous' in Austria, {iv}64; no
milk, only tinned butter and 'rather bad
bread' in Taormina, {iv}92; aboard ship
'one is always eating', {iv}205–6; 'quite
cheap' in Thirroul, {iv}249; supper of
small trout at ranch, {v}278; 'cake
and..Kümmel' after supper, {v}460; in
Italian village inn 'always beef-tea and
macaroni, and boiled beef, on Sundays',
{v}633; 'little orange-yellow' mush-
rooms eaten 'fried in butter', {vi}158;
'Michaelmas goose, superb..potatoes and
cutlets big as carpets', {vi}172–3; 'Nice
little artichokes for lunch', {vi}221; at
Haggs Farm 'stewed figs for tea in
winter..in August green stewed apples',

{vi}618; at Bandol 'nice fishes which I like so much', {vii}22; DHL eats 'Bemax for breakfast', {vii}286, 501; 'so abundant' in Mallorcan hotel ..'I never want to see roast..or fried chicken again', {vii}309; diet specified by German doctor, {vii}466, 474; DHL 'becoming by choice rather a vegetarian', {vii}478; 'good yogurt' in Bandol, {vii}511; 'special octopus for supper', {vii}566;'plum-pudding..cake..mince-meat' for Christmas, {vii}604; 'good Kringels and cakes', {viii}8

FOOTE, MARY, {v}107, 597, 603, {vi}17, 371
  impressed by DHL's paintings, {vi}381; 'handsome Louis XV sort' of woman, {vi}391; views on Mabel Luhan from, {vi}393; subscribed to *LCL*, {vi}579–80
  Letters to {vi}363–4, 368

Forbes-Robertson, Sir Johnston, {v}274

Ford, Ford Madox, {vii}394–5
  see also Hueffer, F. M.

Ford, Henry, {ii}475, {vi}132

Ford, Judge John, {iv}382, 386
  tried to suppress *W in L*, {iv}379, 406, 409, 437, 501, {viii}71, 73

Foreign Office, {i}524, {ii}31, {iii}92, 103, 189, {v}187, 435
  Cynthia Asquith's friend in, {ii}418, 420, 466

Forest of Dean (Gloucestershire), {iii}271, 277

Forest Row (Sussex), {i}526, 536

Form: A Quarterly of the Arts, {ii}395, 400

Forman, Henry James, {iv}187–8, {vi}335

Fornaciari, Raffaello, {vii}415, 432

Forrest, John, *see* Skinner, M.

Forrester, Arthur Denis, {viii}55

FORRESTER, LAURA,
  Letters to {viii}55–6, 78

FORSTER, EDWARD MORGAN, {i}138, {ii}4, 9–11, 18, 257, 263, 281, 302, 308, 402, 425–6, 435, {iii}1, {v}189, {vi}11, 17, 180, 198, {vii}468
  Howards End 'exceedingly good', {i}278; invited to visit DHL, {ii}262, 267,

275–6, 278, 388, 612; some writings 'perverse and not vitally interesting', {ii}276; 'very nice', {ii}280; ethical and sexual dilemma of, {ii}282–5, 292; 'dying of inanition', {ii}293; DHL sends 'philosophy' to, {ii}355; 'still annulled and inconclusive', {ii}390; subscribes to *Signature*, {ii}404; 'the last Englishman', {iv}584; *SCAL* and *B in B* for, {v}80–1; *St Mawr* to, {v}226; 'The Crown' admired by, {v}255; DHL finished with, {v}286; 'not dependable', {vi}191; 'rather a piffler', {vi}225; did not order *LCL*, {vi}375, 383; admires but doesn't read DHL, {vii}165
  Alexandria, {iv}420;
  Aspects of the Novel, {vi}225;
  The Celestial Omnibus, {ii}262, 267, 275, {vi}225;
  Howards End, {i}278, {ii}266, 275, 277–8, {iv}301;
  A Passage to India, {v}74, 77, 81, 91, 142–3;
  Pharos and Pharillon, {iv}584;
  Where Angels Fear to Tread, {ii}267
  Letters to {ii}262, 265–7, 275–9, 291–2, 347, 351, 355, 360–1, 388, 403–4, 611–12, {iii}20–2, {iv}301, 420, 584, {v}74, 77, 116

Forsyth, James, {iv}498, 505, {viii}86

Forsyth, Mrs James, {iv}498, 505, {vi}335, {viii}86

Forte dei Marmi (Italy), {vi}5, 77, 81–7, 106, 202, 246, 384, 443–6, 459, 533, 543, 545, {vii}7–8 274, 276, 314, 334–59, 385, 417–18, 433, 435–6, 500, 527
  'beastly', {vi}89; sea-bathing harmful at, {vi}97–8, 109, {vii}367; DHL would 'never love', {vii}362

Fortes family, {iv}414

Fortune, The, see Goldring, D.

Forty Drawings of Roman Scenes by British Artists, see Ashby, T.

Forum, The, {i}546, {ii}27, 44, 67, 80, 197
  DHL's writings in, {i}372, 378, 380, 489, 507, 510, 524, 528, {v}482, 584, {vi}52, 176, 196, 224, 226, 310, 326, 521, 609, {vii}239, 290, 426; fee from,

Forum, The (cont.)
  {i}522, {v}625 ; Kennerley and, {ii}80,
  243; *Escaped Cock* scandalised readers of,
  {vi}370–1, 378, 382, 539
Forward from Babylon, see Golding, L.
Forza, Mt. (Sicily), {iv}158
Foss Way, {i}76
FOSS, HUBERT JAMES, {iii}572, 586
  '*Land and Water* man', {iii}480, 555,
  559; DHL sends TS of *Lost Girl* for
  possible serialisation, {viii}33
  Letters to {viii}33–5
FOSTER, JOSEPH O'KANE, {v}90, 280,
  {vi}416
  Letters to {v}295, 321, {viii}93, 95
Foster, Wilson, {i}366
Fottrell, Netty, {iii}125
Fountain Press, The, {vii}285
Fouqué, Friedrich de la Motte, *Undine*,
  {i}213
'Four Marys (Maries), The', {vi}507
Four Stages of Greek Religion, The, see
  Murray, G. G. A.
Fox (dog), {v}347
Fox, George, {ii}652
Foyle, W. and G. Ltd, *LCL* and, {vi}12, 479,
  481, 490, 501–2, 511, 514, 518
Fracastoro, Girolamo, *Syphilis, Sive Morbus
  Gallicus*, {vii}564
Fraita, *see* Villa Fraita
France, Anatole, {i}12, {v}201, 207
  'delicate irony of', {i}104; 'very graceful
  piffler', {iii}350
  L'Ile des Pingouins, {i}104, {v}201;
  Le Petit Pierre, {iii}341, 348–50, {v}201;
  Thaïs, {iii}670
France/French, {i}186, 406, {iii}56, 91, 101,
  146, 174, 233, 280, 294, 318, 344, 401,
  412, 415, 524, 534, 553, 624, 663, {iv}20,
  47, 66, 81, 124, 150, 182, 381, 521, 574,
  {v}1, 202, 237, 289, 347, 392, 417, 475,
  497, {vi}1, 3, 354, 405–7, 416–22, 456–8,
  465, 490, 516, 519, 551–93 *passim*, 612,
  {vii}12, 40, 116, 241, 283, 370, 379, 419,
  465, 480–94, 588, 594, 646, {viii}18–19,
  31, 55
  DHL wants to visit, {i}140, 215, 254,
  259, 274, 280, 287, 289; 'that great

holocaust of atonement for the wrongs of
  mankind' (Aldington), {iii}197; books
  'always trivial' in, {iii}679; Italy hates,
  {iii}680, {iv}133; England hated in,
  {iv}132; 'beastly', {iv}180; Italy dearer
  than, {v}459, {vi}60, 64;
  'insolent..people' at St Nizier, {vi}428;
  'Frenchy mind' become feeble, {vi}508,
  549; 'rather self-centred smallish people'
  but nice, {vii}53–5, 611, 623; 'a ghastly
  slummy nowhereness', {vii}64, 107;
  people very friendly, {vii}74, 79; edn of
  LCL in, {vii}89–90, 110, 119, 131, 137,
  143, 159, 245; DHL at 'literary tea' in,
  {vii}225, 228; translation of *LCL* in,
  {vii}261,382, 401, 452–4, 517; publishers 'difficult' in, {vii}273, 517; *LCL*
  pirated in, {vii}335
Frances, *see* Cooper, F. A.
Francesca, Piero della, {iii}422, {v}409, 597
Franceschina, *see* Wilkinson, F.
Franceschini, L., {vi}7, 314, 415, {vii}432
Franchetti, Baron Luigi, {vi}81, 187,
  {vii}293, 346, 359
Franchetti, Baroness, {vii}346
Franchetti, Countess Yvonne, {vi}81, 385–6,
  430, {vii}293, 356, 615
  'spoilt little girl par excellence', {vi}187
Francis, *see* Young, F. B.
Franco-Prussian War, {i}399
François le Champi, see Sand, G.
Franconia (USA), {iv}466, {viii}81
Frank, Nino, {vii}7
FRANK, WALDO, {iii}142, {iv}407
  The Unwelcome Man, {iii}142, 159
  Letters to {iii}142–4, 159–61
Frankau, Gilbert, {v}301
Frankfurt-on-Oder (Germany), {vi}259
Frankfurter Zeitung, {vi}391, 429–30
Frankie, *see* Cooper, F. A.
Franklin, Benjamin, {iii}66
Franklin, Edgar James, {i}308
Franz Ferdinand, Archduke, {i}432
Franzius, Franz, {v}38, {v}332
  his 'pompous and heavy translations',
  {v}558, 561, {vii}572; turned '*Plumed
  Serpent* into a ponderous boa-constric-
  tor!', {v}559

Fraser, Claud Lovat, {i}145, {ii}427

Fraser, John Foster, {i}40

Fraser, Major, {iv}155

Fratelli Treves (Milan), {iv}188, 196–7, 200, {vi}516, {vii}386

'Frau auf dem Southern Cross, Die', *see* Nylander, J. W.

Frau, Die, {i}514

Frayne, Mr, {v}70, 183, 594–5, 630, {vii}343–4

Frazer, Sir James George, {ii}384, 470, 511
The Golden Bough, {ii}470, 593, 630, {iii}526;
Totemism and Exogamy, {ii}470

Freedom Association, {vii}4, 405

Freeman, Donald, {vii}4, 614
see also Vanity Fair

FREEMAN, ELIZABETH ('BESSIE') WILKESON, {iv}17, 331, 409, 430, 434, {vi}101, {viii}76, 85
EME sent to, {iv}361, 372, 392, 403;
Captain's Doll for, {iv}390, 392; DHL visits in Buffalo, {iv}491–4; DHL tries to visit in Palm Springs, {iv}504–5, {viii}86; travelling to Baghdad and Teheran, {vi}299
Letters to {iv}331–4, 339, 360–1, 372–3, 381, 392–3, 413, 415, 421, 443, 450, 462, 471–3, 476, 484, 489–90, 493–4, 498, 504–5, 537, 567, 594–5, {v}302, {vi}104, 108, 298–9

Freeman, George Sydney, DHL visits at *Times*, {iii}291; invites DHL to write for *Educational Supplement*, {iii}303, 306; rejects 'Education of the People', {iii}323, {viii}30

Freeman, Helen, {vii}309

Freeman, John Knox, {iv}331, {v}302

Freeman, Mr, {iv}484, 490, {vi}101, 104

Freeman, The, {iii}473, 493, 508, 510–12, {iv}183, 229
extracts from Shestov translation in, {iii}516, 520, 543, 553, {v}624

Freer, Mrs, {v}28

Freiburg (Germany), {iv}45–6, 48–50

Fremantle (Australia), {iv}8–11, 222, 224–5, 232–9, 241, 267, {viii}55

French Literature, see Strachey, L.

French Song and Verse for Children, {i}242

French, Jared B., {vii}159
Letters from {vii}70–1

Frere-Reeves, Mr, 'one of the big men at Heinemann's', {vii}520, 533, 540, 602

Freshwater (Isle of Wight), {i}173

'Freshwater Diary, The', *see* Corke, H.

Fresno Morning Republican, {vi}14, 530–1

Freud, Sigmund, {ii}305–6, {iii}42, 343
'I never did read Freud, but have heard about him..in Germany', {ii}80; DHL's ideas on psychology grafted on to theory of unconscious of, {iii}400; 'I..detest him', {iii}526
Die Traumdeutung, {iii}716;
Über den Traum, {iii}716

Freudianism, {ii}1, 305, 655, {iii}400, 716
'I am not Freudian...Freudianism is only a branch of medical science', {ii}218

Friedel, *see* Jaffe, F.

FRIENDSHIP, 'I value the friendship of men more than that of women', {i}65; 'I do not need the friendship of the folks here' [Croydon], {i}119; 'real friends in the deep, honorable, permanent sense..our permanent friendship, something not temporal', {ii}388; with Heseltine will not hurt that with Murrys, {ii}549; apologies not 'fair to our old', {iii}291; 'I believe tremendously in friendship between man and man..men and women..women and women, sworn, pledged..as eternal as the marriage bond, and as deep', {iii}302; for Mountsier no longer felt, {iv}374; modification of, {iv}548; 'between a man and a woman, as a thing of first importance..is impossible', {v}203; Brett's for DHL 'betrays the essential man and male' in him, {v}204; if Brett recovers 'wholeness..friendship is possible', {v}205; with Brett DHL lost 'all desire for intense or intimate', {v}234; people used by Murry to attack DHL and DHL doesn't 'like that kind of', {v}242; incurs obligations, {v}551, {vi}259; 'today friendship is a difficult thing..one has to be sadly disembodied', {v}585;

FRIENDSHIP (*cont.*)
　'that stillness in friendship which is the
　best', {vii}235; Mason 'professes the
　greatest friendship' but is suspected
　source of *LCL* piracies, {vii}297
Fritz, *see* Krenkow, F. J. H.
Frobenius, Leo, *The Voice of Africa*, {iii}233
Froebel, Friedrich, {ii}486
Fröhliche Wissenschaft, Die, see Nietzsche, F.
From an Old House, see Hergesheimer, J.
'From Greenland's Icy Mountains', *see*
　Heber, Bishop R.
From St Francis to Dante, see Coulton, G. G.
Fromme Helene, Die, see Busch, W.
Frost, Lucil(l)e, *see* Beckett, L.
Frost, Oliver Harry, {vi}211
Frost, Robert, {iii}141
Fry, Roger Eliot, {vii}8
　'literary gentleman, or a painter?',
　{vi}506; DHL's paintings 'ten times
　better' than those by, {vi}564;
　'significant form piffle', {vii}82
　Cézanne, {vii}82, 125
Fuchs, Der, {v}554, 561
　see also Jaffe, E. *and* Lawrence, D. H.
Fueloep-Miller, René, *Rasputin, The Holy
　Devil,* {vii}86
Fumeurs d'Opium, see Boissière, J.
Fuoco, Il, see D'Annunzio, G.
FURLONG, MISS, {iii}413, 417, {iv}99
　Letters to {iv}166–7
Futurists, {ii}183, {iii}413, {v}627
　'very young, infantile...But I like them',
　{ii}180–1
Fyodor Dostoevsky, see Murry, J. M.

Gabli, {vi}85
Gabriel, Archangel, {vii}331
Gaddesby (Leicestershire), {i}197, 202, 211,
　218, 242, 250–1, 258, 265, 271, 279–81,
　291, 299
Gade, Niels Wilhelm, {i}324
Gadfly, The, see Voynich, E. L.
Gage, Thomas, {v}264
Gaiety Theatre (Manchester), {i}344,
　384
Gaige, Crosby, {vi}344–5, {vii}239
　wanted (but failed) to publish *Escaped*

Cock, {vi}326, 358, 416, 418, 442, 469,
　526, 552, 572, 576, {vii}111, 121, 202,
　236
Gainsborough, Thomas, {i}277
Galata, Gwen, {iii}444, 484
Galignani, {vi}574, 579, {vii}30, 44, 47–8,
　56–7, 61–2, 67, 154, 194, 200–2, 208–9,
　219, 489
Gall, Alice, *see* Hall, A. B.
Gallardo, {iv}452
Gallimard, wants to publish French transla-
　tion of *LCL,* {vii}261, 297, 396, 401,
　429–30, 515, 539–40; offers to publish all
　DHL's works in translation, {vii}272;
　agreement signed for *LCL,* {vii}451–3,
　464, 515
Gallina Canyon (New Mexico, USA), {v}57,
　111, 209, 244, 248, 258, 268–9
Gallup (USA), {v}98–101
Galsworthy, John, {i}12, 16, 20, 62, 277, 297,
　{ii}97, 384, {iii}693, {vii}85
　'bloodless drama' by, {i}509; DHL
　bored by, {iii}166, 183; 'out-of-date',
　{iii}184–5; probably 'loathed' *W in L,*
　{iii}187; DHL's critical 'Scrutiny' on,
　{v}649, {vi}67, 136, {vii}23, {viii}107;
　disparaged in *P and O,* {vii}503
　Joy, {ii}98;
　The Little Dream, {i}326;
　The Man of Property, {i}142;
　Strife, {i}138, 140
Galuzzo (Italy), {v}614
Galveston (USA), {iv}112, 114, 123, 125,
　151, 156, 600, {v}646, {vi}11, 408
Gamio, Manuel, {v}23, 45, 55, 59, 155,
　158
Gandhi, Mahatma, {iv}234, 577, 582,
　{vi}307, {vii}424, 653
Gannet, Lewis, {iv}16
Ganson, Sara Cook, {iv}492, {viii}82
Gaona, Rodolfo, {vi}70
Garborg, Arne, {i}174
Garcia, José, {v}182–3
Garda, Lake, *see* Lago di Garda
'Garden of Proserpine, The', *see* Swinburne,
　A. C.
Garden of the Hesperides, see Leighton, Lord
　F.

GARDINER, MARGARET EMILIA,
{vi}17, 308, 369, 431, {vii}88
invited to Villa Mirenda, {vi}331, 360
Letters to {vi}360
GARDINER, ROLF, {v}1, 66, 503, 604–5,
{vi}10, 17, 360
told to be aggressive against what is
'rotten', {v}93–4; DHL's fundamental
sympathy with supposed aims of,
{v}552–3, 591, {vi}240, 258–9; 'country
of my heart' described for, {v}592–3;
invited to visit Diablerets, {vi}279, 282,
293; 'very nice but not much in my line',
{vi}293–4; asked to recruit subscribers
for *LCL*, {vi}331–2, 334; disapproves of
LCL, {vii}88
Youth, {v}93–4, 497
Letters to {v}66–8, 93–4, 497, 501–2, 504,
508–9, 533–4, 552–3, 591–3, {vi}96,
239–40, 257–9, 262, 267–8, 279, 281–2,
297–8, 307–8, 331–2, 431, {vii}87–8
Gardiner, Samuel Rawson, {i}26
Gardola di Tignale (Italy), {i}512, 515, 535
Gardone (Italy), {i}453
Gargnano (Italy), {i}452–6, 473, 485–7, 520,
531, 538, 551, (ii)139, {iv}189, 195, 202
'rather tumble-downish place on the
lake', {i}453
Garibaldi, Giuseppe, {i}114, {iii}622,
{v}434
Garman, Douglas Mavin, {viii}107
Garnett, Arthur, {i}539
GARNETT, CONSTANCE, {i}16, 334,
534, {ii}22, 26–7, 30, 32, 44, 55, 59, 61,
75, 78–9, 82–3, 87, 166, 184, 186, 222,
258, 321, 414, {iii}392, {iv}99–100, 116
'content to be a good deal apart' from
Garnett, {i}315; translations by, {i}334,
{ii}311, 315, 331, 510, 579, {iii}41;
'awfully good' to DHL, {ii}51; visits
Lerici, {ii}139–53 *passim*; regards DHL
as without 'true nobility', {ii}165; 'like
an old fighter', {ii}524, 666; would
disapprove of *LCL*, {vi}520
Letters to {ii}31–4, 36–7, 42, 139–40,
167–8, 441
GARNETT, DAVID ('BUNNY'), {i}18, 20,
315, 433–4, 440, 444, 446, 448, 457–8,

463, 466–7, 478, 511, 526–7, 530, 539,
549, 551, {ii}12, 23, 26, 33, 36–7, 44, 46,
54, 58, 75, 78–9, 168, 186, 222, 258, 263,
323, 367, {vi}174, 567
invited to meet DHL, {i}427–8; *S and L*
may reflect 'tragedy' of, {i}477; 'rag-bag
letters' from, {i}494; invited to
Gargnano, {i}516; 'varied and boldly-
coloured person', {i}535; his ARCS
exam, {ii}27–8; to see and understand
Rainbow, {ii}184; 'scanty letter-writer',
{ii}237; 'something wrong with him',
{ii}319; sternly rebuked for homosexual
friends, {ii}320–2; congratulated on
marriage, {iv}100, 115; likes *LCL*,
{vi}13, 520
Lady into Fox, {iv}500, 575; 'childish',
{v}90
Letters to {i}427–8, 431, 438, 445, 450–1,
473–6, 484–5, 493–5, 515–16, 520–1,
533–7, {ii}28, 32–3, 59–61, 185, 208,
229–30, 237–9, 242, 320–2, 353, {iv}575,
{vi}520
GARNETT, EDWARD, {i}13, 15–20, 305,
309–10, 313, 326, 329, 341, 390, 446,
451, 455, 464, 532, {ii}2–7, 15–16, 80,
87, 167, 348, 373, 441, 477, {iii}16–17,
612, {vi}13, {vii}3, 614, {viii}11
stories submitted to, {i}297–9, 301–2,
304, 307–8, 327–8, 343, 345, 366; DHL
sends play to, {i}309; DHL at the
Cearne, {i}314–16, 354, 358, 360, 362,
{ii}26, 52–4; verses submitted to,
{i}316–18, 323, 325; *Trespasser* sent to,
{i}330, 337, 339–40, 343–5, 349, 351–3,
358; loan from, {i}337, 364–5; pseudonym, 'James Byrne', {i}344, 467; DHL
reports on Louie Burrows to, {i}365–6;
MS of *S and L* offered to, {i}372;
sketches sent to, {i}375–6; acts for
DHL, {i}377–8, 380; advises on books
for review, {i}381; DHL describes
Frieda to, {i}384; her family {i}394–5,
409; Frieda's affection for, {i}410, 415,
439; MS of *S and L* sent to, {i}423;
advises on *S and L*, {i}426–7 ; DHL's
feeling of affinity with, {i}448; 'Fight for
Barbara' sent to, {i}466, 468, 475, 477–8;

GARNETT, EDWARD (*cont.*)
'a curious monk', {i}470; *S and L*
defended against, {i}476–9; *S and L*
dedicated to, {i}477, 520; cuts *S and L*,
{i}481–2, 489, 496, 517, 520; 'Daughter-
in-Law' sent to, {i}500–1; returns three
plays, {i}509; requests dust-jacket
design for *S and L*, {i}528–30, 535–6,
539; comments on 'Sisters', {i}549–51,
{ii}20; *Widowing* two years with, {ii}71;
MS of 'Primrose Path', requested from,
{ii}127, 133, {iv}100, 115; 'Wedding
Ring' sent to, {ii}134, 142–3, 164–6;
DHL challenges unsympathetic attitude
to his writing from, {ii}164–6, 182–4;
Rainbow sent to, {ii}174; DHL sends
stories for *Prussian Officer* to, {ii}196–9;
'a devil to call my book of stories *The
Prussian Officer*', {ii}241, 258; 'shame-
fully treated at the hands of life', {ii}321;
supports action against suppression of
Rainbow, {ii}464; 'a humming wasp',
{iv}100; 'tiresome old pontiff', {iv}115;
'very good friend' to DHL, {v}171;
'conventional as the King', {vi}343;
LCL sent to, {vi}520, 573
The Breaking Point, {i}317, 325;
The Feud, {i}317;
Jeanne d'Arc, {i}467, 469–71, 478, 487,
{ii}98–9;
Lords and Masters, {i}344–5, 467,
469–70;
The Spanish Lovers, {i}414, 417, 420;
Tolstoy, {i}536
Letters to {i}297–8, 301, 307, 309, 311,
317–19, 322–4, 326–8, 330, 334, 337,
339–40, 342–5, 348–9, 351–4, 358–9,
363–6, 368–9, 371–6, 378–84, 386,
388–9, 394–5, 400, 408–10, 414–15,
419–27, 429–31, 433–40, 442–4, 447–9,
453–4, 457–9, 461–3, 465–71, 476–9,
481–2, 488–9, 495–8, 500–2, 507,
509–12, 516–20, 522–3, 525–7, 529–31,
539–40, 542–3, 545–7, 549–51,
{ii}19–24, 26–7, 29, 31, 38–41, 44, 50–1,
55, 58–9, 65–8, 74–9, 81–3, 98–100,
126–7, 132–5, 142–3, 150–2, 164–6,
173–6, 178, 182–6, 189, 196–9, 221–2,

257–8, 260, 451, 453, {iv}99–100,
115–16
Garnett, Rachel, {iv}100
Garnett, Richard, {i}4–6, 15, 297, 539
  *The International Library of Famous
  Literature*, {i}4–6, 50, 99, 160, 180, 192,
  256, 305, {ii}217, 537
GARNETT, ROBERT SINGLETON,
  {i}15, 516, 522, 526, 551, {ii}20, 27, 42,
  328, 348–9, 354, 356–7
Letters to {ii}333–4
Garsington Manor (Oxfordshire), {ii}253,
  264, 291, 308–26 *passim*, 344–72 *passim*,
  431–4, 448, 450, 465–6, 476, 504, 521,
  656, {iii}23, 112, 226, 228, 257, 318, 570,
  {v}519, {vi}127, 246, 409, {viii}14
  'so pefectly a small world to itself',
  {ii}359; DHL's vision of, {ii}459–61;
  'very bad, really', {ii}651; 'beware of',
  {iii}216
Garvice, Charles, {i}294
Gaskell, Elizabeth, *Cranford*, {iii}227,
  {iv}492–3;
  Life of Charlotte Bronte, {i}105
Gaspard, Evelyn Adell, {iv}361, {v}89–90
Gaspard, Leon, {iv}361, {v}89–90
Gasthaus Zur Post (Beuerberg), {i}411, 413,
  415
Gastone de' Medici, {vi}470, 591
Gauguin, Eugene Henri Paul, *Noa Noa*,
  {iii}505, 563, 566
Gautier, Théophile, *Mademoiselle de Maupin*,
  {vii}179
Gawler, Douglas George, {iv}251
Gawler, May Eva, {iv}251
Gebhard, {vii}48
Gemma, {v}655, {vi}32
General Election (1929) {vii}218, 303, 308,
  328
  DHL 'pining to know the..results',
  {vii}314–15; interested in 'election-govt.
  news', {vii}320; 'Hope they won't be a
  lot of Willy wet-legs, the Laborites',
  {vii}325
Geneva (Switzerland), {iv}265, 279, {v}351,
  603, {vi}402, 406–7, 529, 533, 538, 542,
  556, {vii}547, 551, 574, 604
  see also Lake Geneva

Genoa (Italy), {ii}78, 93, 123–4, 139–40, 175, {iii}414, 415, 523, 541, {iv}142, 167, 351, {vi}420, 593, {vii}169, 286, 289, 291–3, 298, {viii}9

'Gentleman' *see* Bunin, I.

Gentleman from San Francisco and Other Stories, The, see Bunin, I.

Gentlemen Prefer Blondes, see Loos, A.

Geography of the World, *see World of Today, The,*

George V, {i}271, 276, 278, {ii}379, {iii}56, {vi}474, {vii}70

George, *see* Lawrence, G. A.

George, Lake (USA), {iv}543

George, Samuel, {iii}138, 147

George, Stefan, {i}513

George, Walter Lionel, {ii}51, 98, 428, 433, 440

    congratulates DHL on *S and L*, {ii}26; article on DHL by, {ii}28, 99–100, 108, 127, 135,144, 152 ; 'one of the funniest men in London', {ii}108; strongly disliked, {viii}41

    A Bed of Roses, {ii}108

Georgian Poetry, {ii}2–3, 61, 85, 92, 406, {iii}84, {iv}33, 133

    royalty from, {ii}35, 39, 140, 211, 565, 668, {iii}135, 486, 611, {iv}297, 430; DHL's poetry in, {ii}35, 106, 154, 518, 521, {iii}146, 371, {viii}17; Marsh edits, {ii}43, 48, 136, 384, 400–1, 429

    see also Marsh, (Sir) E.

Georgian Stories, {iv}11, 133, 248

Georgics, see Virgil

Gerhard, Edward, *Auserlesene Griechische Vasenbilder*, {ii}517

GERHARDIE, WILLIAM ALEXANDER, {v}322, 324, 326, 332, {vi}180, 191, {vii}447

    A Bad End, {v}536; *The Polyglots*, {v}322, 523

    Letters to {vi}616–17

Germany, {i}6, 17, 182, 186, 200, 226, 228, 298, 301, 313–16, 327, 350, 352, 366–412 *passim*, 424, 432, 446, 551, 553, {iii}7, 9, 26, 39, 51–2, 57, 116, 175, 224, 282, 314–16, 331–4, 337, 340, 344–7, 351, 359, 367–70, 375, 383, 392, 397, 404–5, 414, 427, 430, 435, 439, 441, 453–4, 459, 476, 520–733 *passim*, {iv}2–5, 20, 30–74 *passim*, 113, 121, 161, 182, 238, 242, 249, 259, 294–5, 326, 352, 373, 384, 422, 431–4, 451, 478, 485, 488, 451, 478, 485, 488, 512, 520–1, 531, 560, 570, 582, 596, {v}8, 173, 191, 195, 197, 199, 239, 241, 244, 266, 278, 288, 309, 312, 333–4, 339, 405, 407, 412–514 *passim*, 623, 648–9, 653, 656, {vi}1, 37, 61, 69, 80, 87–8, 96, 120, 123, 125, 133, 136, 146, 176–302 *passim*, 329, 359, 368, 419, 456–7, 467–8, 485, 516, 524, 538, 541, 612, {vii}9, 11, 53, 78, 123, 141–4, 243, 262, 273, 297, 312, 327, 350–2, 355, 362–3, 369, 372, 377–9,392, 428, 434–5, 446, 449–51, 466, 481, 486, 536–7, 621, {viii}20, 83–4, 86

    after Italy DHL hates, {i}543, 546–7; 'gloom of the dark moral judgment' lies over, {i}544; 'a bit of a fool's paradise now', {iii}680; 'quiet and empty-feeling', {iii}708, 725–8, 732, {iv}33, 38; 'cut off', {iv}25; 'has an almost feminine power of passive resistance and stubbornness', {iv}41; 'Nobody swindles' in, {iv}51; DHL's 'absolute belief in Germany's power to save herself', {iv}117; 'will survive as a great and leading nation', {iv}133; people getting their back up again despite poverty, {iv}574–6, 579–80, {viii}87; 'fat and foody', {v}496; 'not so nervoso as Italy', {v}500; 'busy' and 'flourishing', {vi}141–3; much revived but hopelessness underneath, {vi}168–9, 182, 240; youth prepared to 'fuse into a new sort of fighting unity', {vi}259; 'prosperous and alive' but chilling to the soul, {vi}568, 575–6; translation of *LCL* for, {vii}113–14, 139, 178, 202, 245, 304, 333, 335, 375, 383, 567, 571–2, 596–8, 609; pirate edn of *LCL* alleged in, {vii}209–10, 215, 219; quiet, prosperous and not so assertive, {vii}382; people never 'live direct from their spontaneous feeling', {vii}384; 'depressing', {vii}398–400, 402–3, 408, 410, 412,

Germany (*cont.*)
  416–17, 419–21, 437, 481, 486, 494–5,
  500–1; DHL 'lost a lot of strength in',
  {vii}509–13, 518, 530–2, 541, 546,
  552–3, 558
Germinal, see Zola, E.
Geroldsan (Germany), {vii}427
Geronimo, {v}38, 40, 43, 51, 53, 57, 59, 94,
  96, 108, 111
Gerould, Katharine Fullerton, 'British
  Novelists Ltd.', {iii}166, 177
Gersons, see Gusdorf, G.
Gert(ie), *see* Cooper, G.
Gertler, Kate, {iii}89
Gertler, Louis, {iii}89
GERTLER, MARK, {ii}4, 13, 18, 205, 214,
  221, 236, 251–2, 427, 468, 504, 549, 551,
  555, 568, 577–8, 589, 591, 607, 647,
  {iii}12, 36, 52, 71, 90, 96, 103, 108, 112,
  163, 175, 181, 195, 220, 228–9, 235, 261,
  270, 285, 315–16, 318, 335, 342, 354,
  570, 658, 728, {iv}20–1, {v}9, 213, 522,
  524–5, 531, 533, 538, 548, 565, 601–2,
  606, 628, {vi}11, 42, 171, 323, 402, 522,
  {vii}12–13, 538
  principal character in Cannan's *Mendel*,
  {ii}208, {iii}35, 40, 44, 50, 352; 'may do
  something valuable', {ii}215; subscribes
  to *Signature*, {ii}407; having a 'bad time'
  financially, {ii}515; painted 'the best
  modern picture' DHL had seen,
  {ii}660–1; 'real friend' for Frieda,
  {ii}668; offers financial help to DHL,
  {iii}46; possible recruit for liberated
  group, {iii}214–16; invited to visit DHL,
  {iii}226, 257, 341, 352; intermediary
  with Lady Ottoline, {iii}257, 260; suffers
  from tuberculosis, {iii}632, {v}311, 313,
  516, {vi}155; admires Valentine Dobrée,
  {v}559; *M in M* ordered for, {vi}67, 69;
  intermediary with Dobrée, {vi}233;
  DHL seeks advice about paintings from,
  {vi}406; 'one of the modern painters',
  {vi}417; says 'nasty things' about DHL's
  paintings, {vi}558; persuades Dr
  Morland to examine DHL, {vii}575,
  619

Abraham and the Angels, {ii}215;
The Acrobats, {iii}28, 109;
Agapanthus, {ii}215;
The Bathers, {iii}109, 261;
Blue Flowers, {ii}214–15;
Mark Gertler, {v}628, {vi}110;
The Merry-Go-Round, {ii}10, 515, 531,
  657, 660–1, 668, {iii}28, 46, {v}630;
Reclining Nude, {vi}406
Letters to {ii}508–9, 530–1, 562–3, 566–7,
  584, 598–600, 601–2, 657–8, 660–1,
  {iii}27–8, 46–7, 88–9, 109–10, 193–4,
  209, 215–16, 226–7, 239–40, 250, 257,
  289, 341, 352, {iv}567, 599–600,
  {v}29–30, 36, 97, 151, {vi}109–10,
  405–7, {vii}605
Gertrude, see Cooper, G.
Gesualdo, see Verga, G.
Ghandi, M., *see* Gandhi, M.
GHISELIN, BREWSTER, {vii}5, 92, 124,
  132, 135, 148
  'appeared from California – to admire
  me', {vii}118, 120, 127–8; returned to
  Oxford, {vii}137; calls himself DHL's
  'disciple', {vii}317; hated Europe,
  {vii}552
Mediterranean Fishes, {vii}553
Letters to {vii}157–8, 180–1, 264, 552–3
Ghiselin, Olive, {vii}118
Ghita, see Farbman, G.
Ghost Ship and Other Stories, The, see
  Middleton, R. B.
Ghost-Book, The, see Asquith, Lady C.
Ghosts, see Ibsen, H.
Giardini (Sicily), {iii}479, 524, 535, 618
Gibbon, Edward, {iii}233, 242, 262
  Autobiography, {iii}340;
  *The History of the Decline and Fall of the
    Roman Empire*, {iii}233, 239, 242,
    {viii}95
Gibraltar, {vii}561
Gibson, Wilfrid Wilson, {ii}2, 85, 136, 175,
  {iii}261
  will make 'an absolutely perfect
  husband', {ii}92; among 'Georgian
  party' visiting DHL, {ii}113, 116, 118;
  'a really lovable fellow', {ii}118–20; 'jolly

good' poem by, {ii}154–5; poor quality
of poems in *New Numbers*, {ii}176
'Bloodybush Edge', {ii}155;
'Solway Ford', {ii}92
Gide, André Paul Guillaume, {v}180,
{vi}100, 282, {vii}382
Corydon, {vi}282;
Les Faux-Monnayeurs, {vi}100
Gifts of Fortune, see Tomlinson, H. M.
Giglioli, Dr, {vi}2, 100, 112, 164
'best doctor from Florence', {vi}95, 109;
LCL given to, {vi}463, 513; his charges
for medical services, {vi}480, 483
Gilbert, *see* Cannan, G.
Gilbert, Sir William S., {i}5
Pirates of Penzance, {iii}556;
'Yarn of the Nancy Bell', {i}293,
{iii}573, {vi}353
Gilbert, Stuart, {vii}7
Gill, Eric, 'the fat-hipped soft fellow',
{iii}695
Art Nonsense, {vii}14
Gill, George, {i}26
Gillespie, Dr H. M., {i}187, 198
GILLETE, BARBARA ('BOBBIE',
'BOBBY'), {v}56–7, 135, 183, 312, 492,
506, 530, {vi}155, 311, 444, 448, 456,
522, {vii}219
critique of poems by, {v}118–19
Letters to {v}118–19
Gillete, Frederick W. ('Ted'), {v}56–7, 91,
96, 98, 113, 132, 135, 183, 312, 506,
{vi}12, 444
LCL sent to, {vi}448, 456, 551; 'a friend,
and a decent fellow', {vii}219
Gillott, Thomas Ignatius Joseph, {i}278,
366, {v}279
Gilly, *see* Cannan, G.
GILMAN, COBURN, {vi}10, 335
Letters to {vi}48, 181
Gin Cocktail (horse), {vii}216, 323
Gino, {v}462
see also Sansani, G.
Giordani, Giuseppe, {i}67–8
Giotto de Bondone Angiolotto, {ii}296,
{iii}341, {iv}25, {v}426, {vi}262
Giovanna, *see* Cacópardo, Giovanna

Giovanni, *see* Rossi, G.; Verga, G.
Girgenti (Sicily), {iii}506, 654, 699
Girtin, Thomas, {i}8, 89
Gissing, George Robert, {i}116, 501
'hasn't enough energy'..but is esteemed
'a good deal', {i}354; DHL read most of,
{ii}96
Henry Ryecroft, {i}107, 203;
The House of Cobwebs, {i}353–4;
New Grub Street, {i}524;
Odd Women, {i}116, 172
Giulia, *see* Pini, G.
Giuntina, *see* Tipografia Giuntina
Giuseppe, *see* Barezzi, G.
Gladstone Street School, Ilkeston, {i}83
Gladys, *see* Bradley, G.
Glaisher, Henry J. Ltd, {iii}68, {vii}124
Glaisher, William, Ltd, {iii}68
Glands Regulating Personality, The, see
Berman, L.
Glasgow (Scotland), {i}416, {ii}17, 270, 276,
330, 382, 384, 464, 466, 486, 502,
{vii}586
Glasgow Herald, {i}361, {ii}187, 456,
{iii}297
Catherine Carswell discharged from,
{iv}3, {vii}293
Glashütte (Germany), {i}432
Glenavy, Baron, *see* Campbell, Sir J. H. M.
Glorious Hope, The, see Burr, J.
Glory of Living, The, see Curwood, J. O.
Gloucester (England), {iii}252, 273, 275, 278
Gloux, Olivier, 'Gustave Aimard' (pseud.),
{iv}449, 517
Glover, William James, {v}553–6, {vi}200
Letters from {v}554
God and My Neighbour, see Blatchford, R. P.
*God: An Introduction to the Science of
Metabiology, see* Murry, J. M.
Godkins, Georgina, {iii}591–2
Godwin, *see* Baynes, H. G.
'Goethe', *see* De Quincey, T.
Goethe, Johann Wolfgang von, {i}5, 73, 430,
477, {ii}511, {iv}499, {vi}68, 157,
{vii}534
DHL dislikes, {iii}407; 'boundless ego'
of, {vi}342

Goethe, Johann Wolfgang von (*cont.*)
  Faust, {v}563;
  Iphigenie auf Tauris, {i}549;
  Wilhelm Meister, {ii}217, {vi}342;
  Werther, {vi}120
Goethe, Katharina Elisabeth, {i}477
Goetz, *see* Götsch, G.
Goldberg, Newall, Braun & Co., {ii}327,
  348, 354, 357, 377
Golden Age, The, see Grahame, K.
Golden Ass, The, see Apuleius
Golden Book, The, {v}360, {vi}606
Golden Bough, The, see Frazer, Sir J. G.
Golden Journey to Samarkand, The, see
  Flecker, J. E.
Golden Treasury, The, {i}86, 168, 192
GOLDING, LOUIS, {iii}377
  Forward from Babylon, {iii}690
  Letters to {iii}342, 690
GOLDRING, BEATRIX ('BETTY'),
  {iii}392, 404, 410, 441, 532, 625, 700,
  {vii}529
  DHL's favourite for lead part in
    Widowing, {iii}380, 483
  Letters to {iii}406
Goldring, Brendan Hugh McBride, {v}270
GOLDRING, DOUGLAS, {i}14, {iii}5-8,
  12, 16, 555, {v}270,
  invited to produce *T and G* for People's
    Theatre, {iii}371, 374-6, 385, 404, 441,
    469, 483; intermediary for *The Word*,
    {iii}391, 404; dedicates novel to DHL,
    {iii}441; 'sly journalist', {iii}469; 'such a
    shit', {iii}471; *Lost Girl* sent to, {iii}625
  Black Curtain, {iii}7, 371, 441, 531;
  Fight for Freedom, {iii}5, 7, 371, 441,
    467, 469, 471, 483;
  The Fortune, {iii}467;
  Margot's Progress, {iii}467;
  Odd Man Out, {iii}371, 404;
  Reputations, {iii}573;
  South Lodge, {iii}371;
  The Tramp, {i}136, {iii}371
  Letters to {iii}371-2, 374, 379-80, 391-2,
    403-4, 406, 410, 415, 440-1, 483-4,
    531-2, 573-4, 625, 699-700, {vii}529
Goldring, Malin, {vii}529
Goldsmith, Oliver, {i}4

GOLDSTON, EDWARD, {vii}78, 270, 337,
  416, 489, 560, 592-3, 595, 605-6, 643-4
  DHL orders books from, {vi}102, 107;
  Stephensen's partner in Mandrake
  Press, {vii}71, 82, 125, 130, 170, 253,
  285, 549, 554, 558-59, 564, 573, 578-80,
  583
  Letters to {vi}102, 107
Gollancz, Victor, {v}523, {vii}6, 448
  'good man' to do expurgated edn of
    LCL, {vii}44, 47, 59-60, 271
Gomm, Mrs, {iii}209
GOMME, LAURENCE JAMES, {vi}551
  orders 50 *LCL* without payment,
    {vi}444-5, 447-8, 456, 470, 550,
    {vii}25, 55; reports US pirated edn of
    LCL, {vi}608, {vii}20, 312; untrustwor-
    thy, {vii}25, 219; pays for 8 copies of
    LCL, {vii}274
  Letters to {vi}451
  Letters from {vi}444, 456, 550, 608
Gong, The, {i}31-2
Good Companions, The, see Priestley, J. B.
Good Housekeeping, {vi}176
Goodyear, Frederick, {ii}472
  reviewed *Trespasser*, {i}507-8
Goosens, Eugene, {ii}548
Gordon Home (Croydon), {i}97
Gordon, *see* MacFarlane, G. G.
Gordon, General Charles George, {vi}1, 513
Gordon, Jan, *Modern French Painters*,
  {vi}548
Gordon, Margaret, {vii}615
Gore Farm (Dorset), {vi}258, 298, {vii}87
Gorky, Maxim, {i}12, 278, {ii}155, 168,
  {iii}121, {iv}37
  'I'm very much of an English equivalent
    of', {i}209; DHL read widely in, {i}524;
  DHL corrects Kot's translation of
    Reminiscences, {iv}16, 478, 482, 487
  *Reminiscences of Leo Nicolayevitch
    Tolstoi*, {iii}570, 632, 640;
  Reminiscences of Leonid Andreyev,
    {iv}478, 482, 487;
  Tales from Gorky, {i}209
Gorug, Baroness, {vi}149
Goschen, Max, {ii}75, {iii}371
Gosse, Edmund, {ii}224, {iii}251

Gotham Book Mart (New York), DHL doubts honesty of, {vi}544, 547, {vii}215, 428

Gothein, Werner, {iii}658, 665

Götsch (Goetsch/Goetz), Georg, {vi}96, 259, 268, 281

Göttingen (Germany), {i}6

GÖTZSCHE, KAI GULDBRANSEN, {iv}13, 17–18, 336, 347, 354, 378, 383, 385–6, 392, 409, 413, 419, 445, 463, 470, 481, 554, 574, {v}188, 208, 211, 231, 273, 537, 652, {viii}68, 75–6
    at Del Monte, {iv}344–5, 349–52, 356–7, 359–60, 362–3, 366–7; portrait of DHL by, {iv}369–70, 373, 375, 388, 503, 519, 522–3, {viii}58–9; exhibition of paintings at Santa Fe, {iv}388–9, 406; *Captain's Doll* for, {iv}390, 453; designed jacket for *Gesualdo*, {iv}436, 439; with DHL in Los Angeles, {iv}495; travels to Mexico with DHL, {v}501–5, 507–10, 512, 515, 525–7, {viii}84–5; to England with DHL, {iv}534, 536, 538, 541; to Denmark, {iv}548; designed cover for *Palms*, {v}55; cheque from, {viii}88
    Letters to {iv}430, 434, 438–9, 459

Götzsche, V., {iv}463, 527, {viii}77

Gould, Gerald, {vi}422, {vii}294

Gourdjieff, *see* Gurdjieff, G. I.

Gow, Dr James, {i}4

Goya, Francisco, {ii}263

Grabow, Anna, *see* Bóttern, A.

Graeme, Kirsteen, {ii}384

Graham, R. B. Cunninghame, *Pedro de Valdivia*, {v}590, 601, {viii}99

Graham, Stephen, {iv}368–9

Grahame, Kenneth, *Golden Age*, {i}450, 457

Gramond, *see* Grummon, S E.

Gramophone, {v}3, 570

Granada (Spain), {vii}238, 273, 276, 282–4, 537, 541, 552

Grand Canal, Venice, {iv}195

Grand Canyon (USA), {iv}290

Grand Hotel (Annenheim), {vi}108, 125–6, 129

Grand Hotel (Chapala), {iv}436

Grand Hotel (Chexbres), {vi}425–49, 454

Grand Hotel (Le Lavandou), {vi}578, 585–8

Grand Hotel (Les Diablerets), {vi}285, 292, 527

Grand Hotel (Ossiachersee), {vi}119

Grand Inquisitor, The, see Dostoievsky, F., Koteliansky, S. S.

Grand St Bernard Pass (French Alps), {ii}185, {vi}440–1

Grant, Col. Duncan, *see* Hutchison, G. S., *The W Plan*

Grant, Duncan, {iii}103, {vii}8
    'dissipates' but DHL *'really* liked him', {ii}263–4; his 'deep inward dirt' makes DHL dream of 'beetles', {ii}319–21; 'conscientious objector' {ii}612

Grantchester (Cambridgeshire), {ii}331

Granville-Barker, Harley, {i}14, 20, 298, 509

Graphic, The, see Survey Graphic

Grasse (France), {vii}14, 104, 109, 116–17, 119, 132, 615

Graves, Clotilde Inez Mary, 'Richard Dehan' (pseud.), *Dop Doctor*, {i}221–2

Graves, Robert, {iii}363, {v}204, {vi}17, 180, 301
    My Head! My Head!, {v}383;
    The Owl, {iii}452

GRAY, CECIL, {iii}2, 167, 199, 235–6, 269, 294
    scorn for 'Goats and Compasses', {ii}558; DHL acquires furniture for, {iii}128, 130, 133; 'nice', {iii}154; 'He is music', {iii}163; lends *Songs of the Hebrides* to DHL, {iii}164; candidate for Andes, {iii}173–4; regarded DHL as object of female cult, {iii}179; interrogated by C.I.D. about DHL, {iii}188; DHL not at ease when with, {iii}224; 'wandering round like a lost infant', {iii}344; 'behaving wretchedly', {iii}349; Hilda Aldington 'went off with', {v}475; at Bosigran, {viii}25
    Peter Warlock, {ii}442, 542, 558
    Letters to {iii}128–30, 133–4, 138, 151, 167, 169–72, 174–6, 178–81, 197–9, 223–5, 229–30, 232–3, 236–7, 261–2, 265–6

Gray, Mrs, {iii}169, 171

Graz (Austria), {iii}711

Grazia, *see* Cacópardo, G.

Grazio, *see* Cervi, O.

Grazzini, Anton Francesco ('Lasca'), {vi}4, 595, {vii}19, 21–2, 141, 541, 588
 Second Cena, {vii}394, 573;
 The Story of Dr Manente, {vi}4, 595, 598, 605, 611, {vii}19, 21, 410, 415–16, 432, 446, 477, 492, 502, 504, 526–7, 536, 557–9, 565

Greasley (Nottinghamshire), {i}67

Great American Ass, The, see Edson, C. L.

Great Australian Bight, {iv}241–2, 244

Great Central Railway, {i}130, 319

Great Cham, Heinemann, {i}262, 326;
 Kippenberg, {v}558, 621

Great Expectations, see Dickens, C.

Great Hat, The, see Kouyoumdjian, D.

Great Kingshill, *see* Hawthorn Cottage

Great Neck (Long Island, USA), {vii}377

Great Northern Railway, {i}216

Great Ormes Head (Carnarvonshire), {i}294

Great Stories of All Nations, {v}451

Greatham (Sussex), 'the Meynells' place', {ii}255–89 *passim*, 304, {iii}145–6, 251; DHL preparing to leave, {ii}347; 'special atmosphere', {ii}374; DHL doesn't want to visit 'ever again', {ii}566, 635; charades at, {ii}663; Ottoline Morrell at, {vii}235

Grecian Isle, *see* Syra

Greco, El, {vii}566

Greece, {iii}488, 492, 505, 539, {iv}100, 131, 205, 212, {v}343, 345, 444, 530, 562, 595, 608, {vii}170, 508, 523, 616
 DHL would like to see, {v}484, 519, 586, 613, 617, {vii}235, 290

Green Ring, see Koteliansky, S. S.;
 Merizkowsky, Z.

Green, Russell, {vii}60–1, 88, 95, 144

Greenhill, John, {i}124

Greenland, {iv}14, 361–2, 373, {vi}183

Greenslet, Ferris, {ii}246, 562

Greenwich Village (New York, USA), {iv}4–5, 592, {v}107

Gregory the Great, {vi}298

Gregory, Alyse, {iv}560

Gregory, Lady Augusta, {i}364, {iv}105

Gregory, Richard, {vii}117

Greiffenhagen, Maurice, {ii}627, {iii}131
 An Idyll, 'the splendid uninterrupted passion of', {i}103; DHL copies, {i}234–5, 242–3, 245, 252, 282, 341, 488, 498

Grenfell, Ivo, {iii}182

Grenoble (France), {vi}421–5

Grenzen der Seele, see Lucka, E.

Grétry, André-Ernest-Modeste, {iii}136

Grey, Harry, Earl of Stamford, {iii}130, {viii}25

Grey, Sir Edward, {ii}379

Grieg, Edvard, {i}174
 DHL heard *Peer Gynt*, {i}99; 'not keen on', {i}306

Grierson, (Sir) Herbert, {iv}146–7, 157

Grimm's Fairy Tales, {i}126

Grimsbury Farm (Newbury, Berkshire), {iii}413, 449, 452, 529, 724, {iv}28, 79

Grimthorpe, 2nd Baron, {iii}712, {v}406, {vi}36
 see also Beckett, R. W. E.

Gringoire, {vii}602

Grisha, *see* Farbman, M.

Grit, *see* Cooper, G.

Gross, Dr Otto, {i}395, 409, 424, {ii}415, {iii}623, {iv}39

Gross, Frieda, {iv}39

Grosseto (Italy), {v}651, {vi}32–3, 43

Grosz, George, *Ecce Homo*, {vii}8

Groves & Michaux, {vii}207–10, 214, 219

Groves, Frank A., {vii}207–9, 214–15, 219

Grummon, Stuart E., {v}225

Grundy, Mrs, {i}64, {vi}99

Gstaad (Switzerland), {vi}451–68 *passim*

Gsteig (Switzerland), {vi}1, 3, 13, 451–568 *passim*, 570, 573–4, {vii}105, 128, 379, 418, 424, 427, 436

Guadalajara (Mexico), {iv}15, 17, 20, 416, 419, 430–9, 441–3, 445, 449, 455, 470, 473, 506–34 *passim*, {v}55, 66, 235, 261, {viii}61, 85
 'burnt dry town', {iv}442; 'pleasant', {iv}526; 'not at all a moon-city', {iv}531
 'about the best place' in Mexico, {v}219, 273

Guadalupe (Mexico), {v}154, {vi}211

Guardia, Ernesto, {vii}328

Guardian, see Nottinghamshire Guardian, The

Guatemala, {v}161

Guaymas (Mexico), {iv}17, 501, 507, {viii}85–6

Guelph, {iii}676–7, 680

Guernsey, {iii{628, {v}289
  see also Channel Isles

Guest, Stephen, *see* Haden-Guest, S. H.

Guild Theatre, *see* Theatre Guild

Guild-Socialism, {ii}489

Guildford (Surrey), {iii}52–3

Gulf of Aden, {iv}124

Gulf of Mexico, {viii}85

Gull, Cyril Arthur Edward Ranger, Guy Thorne (pseud.), {ii}564, 571, 575, 669

Gurdjieff Institute, {iv}375, 386, 555, 568, {v}422, {vii}175

Gurdjieff, Georgei Ivanovitch, {v}422–3, 431, 439, 441–2, 457, 471, 486, 540, {vi}258, {vii}206
  'not interesting' to DHL, 'a good deal of a charlatan', {vi}57; 'imaginary incarnation of Lucifer', {vii}175

Gusdorf, Gerson, {iv}354, 411, {v}51, 53, 57, 68–9, 72, 82–3, 88, 102, 128, 281, 295, 417, 425, 429, 476

Gussy, *see* Cooper, G.

Gusterl, {vii}75

Gutiérrez de Lara, L., {iv}394, 409
  The Mexican People: Their Struggle for Freedom, {iv}394

Gwen, *see* Mond, A. G.

'Gynecologia', *see* Cannan, G.

H. D., *see* Aldington, H.

Haas, Mr, {v}339, 377, 461

Haas, Mrs, {v}339–40, 377, 461

Haberman, Roberto, {iv}410, 456, {viii}71

Hadaffah, *see* Andrews, E.

Haden-Guest, Dr Leslie Haden, {iii}716

Haden-Guest, Stephen Haden, {iii}716

Hadrian the Seventh, see Corvo, Baron

Hadu, *see* Schreibershofen, H. von

Hagedorn, Hermann, {ii}416

Haggard, Sir Henry Rider, {v}591

Haggs Farm (Nottinghamshire), {i}9, 22, 35, 41, 64, 68, 90, 500, {vi}18

affection for 'old evenings' at, {i}138; DHL will 'never forget', {vi}618

Hague, The (Netherlands), {iii}6, 379, 391, 404–5, 489, {iv}314, {vi}501, {vii}341

Haig, Sir Douglas, {iii}3, 118

Hain, Kate, {viii}25

Hain, Lady Catherine, {viii}25

Hain, Sir Edward, {viii}25

Hajji Baba, Adventures of, see Morier, J. J.

Hal, *see* Bynner, H. W.

Hale, Margaret, {v}90, 277, 280, 295

Hale, Swinburne, {v}74, 90, 105–6, 115

HALÉVY, DANIEL,
  Letters to {vii}223

Haleys, {i}354

Hall, Alice Beatrice, {i}283, 532
  'Alice Gall', {i}68, 71, 232, 236–7

Hall, Elsie Stanley, {i}155, 324

Hall, Harry Reginald, *Ancient History of the Near East*, {ii}528

Hall, Marguerite Radclyffe, *The Well of Loneliness*, {vi}595, {vii}115, 132, 484

Hall, Mr, {i}281, 283–4, 287

'Halliday', *see* Heseltine, P.

Halm, Ada, {vi}398

Halm, Mr and Mrs, {vi}207, 398

Halstead (Essex), {iv}193, 320

Hamburg (Germany), {iii}714, 730, {iv}25, 36, 39, 433–4, 529, 536, 538, {v}152, {vii}633

Hamburg-Amerika Line, {iv}433–4, 538–9, {v}215–17

Hamilton, Alexander, *The Federalist*, {iii}66

Hamlet, see Shakespeare, W.

Hamlin, Chauncey J., {iv}331, {v}302

'Hammers, The', *see* Lowell, A.

Hammerslaugh, Mr, {iv}471–2, 476, 478, 501, 519

Hampshire (England), {i}349, {vii}200

Hamsun, Knut, {iv}157
  Love's Tragedy, {iii}532;
  Hunger, {v}314

'Hand, The', *see* Skinner, M. L.; Tietjens, E. S.

Handel, George Frederick, {i}67
  Messiah, {vi}207

Hankinson, Jessica, *see* Young, J. B.

Hanley (Staffordshire), {i}459, {ii}380

Hannah, *see* Krenkow, H.

Hannibal, {i}114

Hans, *see* Jaffe, H.

Hansard, Luke, {iii}506, 535, 609, 616, 640, {iv}43, 49

Hansard, Réné, {iii}496, 506, 508, 609 624, 640, 648, 687, {iv}43, 49, 244, 366
liked when she 'dropped her social tiresomeness', {iii}526; 'plans to open an English library at Cannes', {iii}553; DHL sends lace to, {iii}568; hoping to make fortune 'growing tube-roses', {iii}665
The Tavern, {iii}535, 554, 609

Hapgood, Hutchins, {vi}230

Harbottle, see Hargrave, J.G.

Harcourt, Brace & Co., {iv}485, {vii}528

Harden, Elmer, {viii}81

Hardenberg, Friedrich Ludwig von, *see* Novalis

Hardie, James Keir, {i}3, {vi}231–2

Hardy, Godfrey Harold, {ii}309

Hardy, Thomas, {i}12, 138, 277–8, 544, {ii}3, 15, 198, 247, 433, 502, 567, {iii}41, 94, 167, 224, {vi}276, {vii}256
Marsh sends complete set of, {ii}199; 'doesn't rank so terribly high, really', {vi}471; 'our last great writer', {viii}18
Jude the Obscure, {i}205;
The Woodlanders, {iii}223
see also Abercrombie, L.; Lawrence, D. H., 'Study of Thomas Hardy'

Hare, Elizabeth Sage ('Betty'), {vi}10, 16, {vi}393, 437
invites DHL to lecture in New York, {iv}330, 338; DHL visits on Long Island, {v}304, 306; invited to subscribe for *LCL*, {vi}335; proposes exhibition of DHL's paintings in New York, {vi}381, 445; Brett sold DHL MSS to, {vii}10, 343–4

Hargrave, John Gordon, {vi}279, {vii}88
'White Fox: Headman K.K.', {v}67–8; DHL has some sympathy for, {vi}267–8

Harbottle: A Modern Pilgrim's Progress, {v}67;
Kibbo Kift, {vi}258–9, 267, {vii}88

Harich, Walther, *Jean Paul*, {vi}183

Harington, Sir John, *Metamorphosis of Ajax*, {vii}85, 123

Harland, Henry, {vi}169

Harmsworth, Desmond, {iv}19

Harold, *see* Hobson, H.; Mason, H.

Harper & Bros, {iv}196, 200, 219, 232, {vii}304

Harper, Allanah, {vi}422, 438, 461, 504, 515, {vii}291

Harper's Bazaar, {ii}160, {v}400, 508

Harper's Magazine (Harper's), {ii}274, {iv}192, {vi}591

Harrap, George & Co., {v}520, 575

Harrap, George S., {vi}476, 480

Harris, James Thomas Frank, {i}16, 241, 305, {v}457, 527, 533
My Life and Loves, {v}457

Harris, Robert, {viii}103

HARRISON, AUSTIN, {i}12–13, 15, 19, 162, 301, 327, 372, 381, 384, 533, {ii}6, 135, 446, 670, {iii}15, 102, 159, 211, 266, 310, 315, 319, 327, 382–3, 397–8, 635, 645, 690
edits *English Review*, {i}152; publishes DHL's poems, {i}156, 179, 254, 375, 380, {ii}90, {iii}115, 120, {iv}380, 428; praises *White Peacock*, {i}240; publishes DHL's prose, {i}245–6, 248, 258, 275, 299, 345, 348, 351–2, {ii}26, 66, 87, 127, {iii}102, 104, 106–8, 110–11, 113–14, 164–5, 191, 270, 286–7, 299, 324–5, 357, {iv}55, 197, 226 ; DHL supports protest by, {i}277–8; friendly towards DHL, {i}304–6, 365; 'wishy-washy noodle', {i}430; commends DHL to Fisher Unwin, {i}458, {ii}216; failure to pay for 'The Blind Man', {iii}635, 645, 690, {viii}40; 'mean', {iii}383
'Puntilla', {i}152
Letters to {i}377–8, {ii}66–7, {iv}226
Letters from {i}240, 254, {ii}81

Harrison, Frederic, {i}152, {ii}384

Harrison, Jane, *Ancient Art and Ritual*, {ii}90, 114, 119

HARRISON, MABEL, {v}12, 403, {v}407, 410, 517, 532
   DHL visited Perugia and Ravenna with, {v}412; 'a very nice woman', {v}435; in Villa la Massa near Mirenda, {v}616, 643–6, {vi}39, 62, 78; *Mornings* for, {vi}69; *WWRA* for, {vi}396; *LCL* sent to, {vi}448; *Pansies* for, {vii}347
   Letters to {viii}100–1
Harrow-on-the-Hill (Middlesex), {i}132
Harry, *see* Bull, H.; Dax, H. R.
Harte, Francis Bret, {i}6, {iv}290
Harvest in Poland, see Dennis, G. P.
Harvest Moon, see Peabody, J. P.
Harwich (Essex), {ii}22, 24, {iii}406
Harwood, *see* Brewster, H.
HARWOOD, ELIZABETH CASE ('LUCY'), {iv}359–60
   Letters to {iv}363
Haskard & Casardi Ltd, DHL's bank in Florence, {iii}482, 519, {iv}91, 179, 201, {vi}375, 444, 449, 461, 465, 469–70, 478, 483, {vii}21, 63, 159, 183, 339, 565, 588
   Letters from {iii}482–3
Hassall, John, {v}518–19
Hastings, Hubert de Cronin, {vii}269, 295
Hastings, Mr, {iv}103, 214
HATHAWAY, RUFUS H., {ii}17–18
   subscribed to *Signature*, {ii}515, 518
   Letters to {ii}517–18
Hauptmann, Gerhart, {vii}563
   Elga, {i}164–5;
   Einsame Menschen, {i}171;
   Versunkene Glocke, {i}168
Haus Vogelnest (Wolfratshausen), {i}425, 431, 441
Häuslmair (Häuslmeyer, Häuselmaier),Therese, {vi}149–50
Havana (Cuba), {iv}539, 541, {v}216, {vii}146, 342
Haven (Bournemouth), {i}357
'Haw, Richard', {iii}381
Haweis, Hugh Reginald, {i}5
   Music and Morals, {i}99–100
Hawk family, {v}51, 59, 73, 83, 218, 233, 239, 412
HAWK, ALFRED DECKER, {iv}13, 343, {v}155, 157–8, 165, 185, 202, 219–20,

222, 257, 299, 303, 358, 430, 439, 467, {vi}293
   owned Del Monte Ranch, {iv}336, {v}39, 135, 137–8; pays local taxes for DHL, {v}187, 192, 208, 212
   Letters to {v}126–7, 156–7, 169–70, 183, 187, 208, 221–2, 224, 227–8, 247–9, 251, 264, 293, 311–12
Hawk, Betty, *see* Cottam, E.
Hawk, Bobbie, *see* Gillete, B.
Hawk, Elisabeth Moore, {iv}13, 343, 345, 348, 358, 362, {v}57
HAWK, LUCY MOORE WALTON, {iv}13, 343, 351, 426, 525, {v}127, 157, 165, 187, 208, 222, 228, 233–4, 249, 251, 293, 299, 303, 358, 430, 439, 652
   joint owner of Del Monte Ranch, {iv}336, {v}39
   Letters to {v}311–12
HAWK, RACHEL WOODMAN, {iv}13, 343, 345, 348, 362, 367, 438, 524–5, {v}39, 96, 137–8, 165, 191–2, 204, 212, 222, 234, 253, 299, 303, 338, 345, 358, 362, 366, 370, 395, 440, 492, 494, 503, 510, 514, 530, 586, 595, {vi}5, 155, 176, 212, 217, {vii}475
   leaving Del Monte Ranch, {v}364; should supervise Brett's spending, {v}429, 467; DHL's ranch offered to, {v}442, 466, 470, 475–6, 480, 485, 537; leaves ranch, {v}541; returns to Del Monte, {vi}293
   Letters to {v}305–6, 428–30, 438–9, 466–7, 506–7, 537, 652–3
   Letters from {v}440
Hawk, Shirley Glenn, {v}253, 394, 439, 467, 470, 652
Hawk, Walton, {iv}524, {v}44, 137–8, 165, 192, 212, 296, 358, 467, 470, 480, 485, 506–7, 652
HAWK, WILLIAM, {iv}13, 354, 359–60, 364, 367, {v}42, 127, 137–8, 156–7, 187, 204, 208, 212, 222, 234, 295, 299, 303, 333, 344, 364, 379, 421, 426, 438–9, 506, 586, 652–3, {vi}155, 176
   in the 'big house' at Del Monte, {iv}343–5, 348, 350–1, 362; DHL sends money for horses' upkeep, {v}211, 293,

HAWK, WILLIAM (*cont.*)
358, 394, 417, 428; asked by DHL to
look after ranch, {v}429, 440, 442,
466–7; buys Del Monte, {vii}475
Letters to {iv}426, 438, 524–5, {v}39, 44,
98, 149, 152, 154, 164–5, 182, 191–2,
211–12, 274, 305–6, 335, 357–8, 394–5,
428–30
Hawke, Mrs, {ii}559
Hawken, Mr, {ii}495, 520
Hawker, Robert Stephen, {vi}408
Hawthorn Cottage (High Wycombe), {v}9,
19, 226, 247, 313, 332, 401–2
Hawthorne, Nathaniel {v}308
Blithedale Romance, {iii}66, {iv}55,
197;
Scarlet Letter, {iii}66, 346, 350;
Twice Told Tales, {iii}66
see also SCAL
HAYWARD, JOHN DAVY, {v}3, 382
Letters to {v}382
HAYWOOD, J. H. LTD.,
Letters to {i}21
Haywood, John Harrington, {i}21
Haywood, John Shrewsbury, {i}21
Heal & Sons Ltd, {vii}81, {viii}111
HEALTH, 'I have the inevitable cold', {i}46,
135, 352, 355, 490, 527, 542, {ii}258,
476–9, 501, 539, 648, {iii}81, 179, 256,
310, 327, 469–70, 696, {iv}122, 406,
545–7, {v}315, 352, 582, {vi}51–2, 268,
530; Louie Burrows inherited 'good
blood and good health', {i}113; DHL
'convalescent from a sickness', {i}155;
DHL's mother's fatal illness, {i}176–202
passim; DHL like 'croaking crow' with
cold, {i}223; 'damned cold..hangs on
abominably', {i}243; 'My health is so-
so', {i}272; 'a cold like hell..as if my long
pipe were a stove chimney got red hot',
{i}306; 'quite good health', {i}310;
DHL critically ill with pneumonia,
{i}328–42; doctor warns 'I shall be
consumptive', {i}337; 'churlish after an
illness', {i}345; 'illness changes me a
good deal', {i}360; DHL breaks engagement to Louie Burrows: 'my health is so
precarious', {i}361; DHL loses salary

for long absence due to illness, {i}367–8;
'ever so well in health', {i}480; when
DHL ill 'sheer distress and nerve
strain..have let go on my lungs', {ii}73,
583; 'English autumn' causes cough,
{ii}226; 'feeling seedy', {ii}256; 'cold in
the stomach..like a sore throat in..one's
belly', {ii}314–16; 'my old winter
sickness and inflammation', {ii}507–9;
though 'ill for weeks', 'no organic illness'
but 'mucous in the bronchi etc are weak',
{ii}512; 'better in health' and regaining
strength, {ii}531, 599, 663; 'my beastly
health, I hate it', {ii}560; typing novel
makes DHL ill, {ii}638; DHL exempt
from military service 'on account of',
{ii}666; 'miserable, damnable', {iii}19;
better 'because I don't work', {iii}46;
recovery after sudden 'sickness and
diarrhoea', {iii}117; London causes
'cold in throat and chest', {iii}173;
'cough and heart-pains', {iii}329;
'miserably ill with the Flu and..compli-
cations', {iii}333; 'nearly died with that
damned Flu', {iii}337–8; 'might go to
Italy - for health', {iii}401; 'all right.
People like to exaggerate my delicacy',
{iii}540; 'a bit of flu', {iv}161;
'Ceylon..makes me feel ill all the time',
{iv}225; in New Mexico 'sore chest and
throat which doesn't get better quickly',
{v}124–5; DHL desperately ill with flu
'tangled up with *malaria*', {v}210, 217,
230, 245; DHL 'looked like the shadow
of a white rose-leaf' (Frieda), {v}218;
'now I am much better', {v}253, 269;
London fog 'gives me a cough', {v}313;
better 'but still bronchial', {v}413;
'much better', {v}478; 'England seems
to suit my health', {v}514; 'always
risky..chest-bronchial troubles and
pneumonia after-effects', {v}591; 'health
better than a year ago', {v}605–6;
'haven't had a bad cold yet this winter'
(1926–7), {v}622; 'nervous of sickness',
{v}643, {vi}42; on Gertie Cooper's
operation, 'Why save life in this ghastly
way?', {vi}42; 'Between malaria and

continual bronchial trouble, I'm a misery
to myself..as miserable as a wet hen',
{vi}59, 64; better to endure bad health
than to be 'healthy and limited like the
peasants', {vi}87; 'the cough is a
nuisance', {vi}125–6, 144; 'my one
desire, to get well as soon as possible',
{vi}183; doctor says DHL better than on
previous examination, {vi}190; cough 'a
good deal psychological in its origin',
{vi}204; 'still feeble, too much cough -
but better', {vi}220; 'never felt so near
the brink of the abyss', {vi}247; 'far
from satisfactory', {vi}264; 'only half
myself', {vi}278; 'too gaspy' to ski,
{vi}287; 'my chest is the very devil',
{vi}323; cough worse in Mirenda than
Diablerets, {vi}344, 579; 'coughing and
spitting go on just the same', {vi}350;
'really getting stronger', {vi}378; being
'vulgarly *physically* selfish' helps to avoid
illness, {vi}409; hotel proprietor
excludes DHL because of cough,
{vi}428; 'no danger' in cough, {vi}457;
DHL cannot travel while cough bad,
{vi}468, 498, {vii}203, 205; 'tired of not
being well', {vi}504, 536; 'not a death
cough..but an unspeakable nuisance',
{vi}522; 'two days hemorrhage',
{vi}598, 601; 'better in myself',
{vii}26–7, 38–9, 79. 116, 138, 282;
'cough like a brute', {vii}80, {viii}111;
'nothing so wearisome as prolonged ill-
health', {vii}203; DHL longs for 'a
dashing body that doesn't cough',
{vii}207, 214; cities bad for DHL's
health, {vii}241; 'I'm a tough and
stringy bird', {vii}293; health a nuisance
but 'I have no idea of passing out',
{vii}295; 'inside..upset..makes my chest
sore', {vii}359; 'never felt so
down..depressed..ill', {vii}399; cough
causes 'general annoyance or cold
commiseration of a nervous universe',
{vii}427; doctor says DHL's lungs
better but asthma bad, {vii}431; 'fed up
with my health', {vii}461, 464; health
worse at Rottach, 'I *must* go to the sea',

{vii}490; DHL feels 'much serener and
better' at Bandol, {vii}518; health
'devilish bad..Am miserable', {vii}529;
DHL faces prospect of sanatorium, 'No
use dying just yet', {vii}530, 623; 'my
real trouble..chronic inflammation of the
bronchials and..breathing passages',
{vii}538; 'I lie in bed and look at the
islands..think of the Greeks, and cough',
{vii}552; DHL feeling better, {vii}558;
Europe excites 'inward rage that keeps
my bronchials hellishly inflamed',
{vii}574; DHL not thinner or weaker
but asthma 'maddening', {vii}591; 'my
health..enough to depress the Archangel
Michael', {vii}605; 'a bout of bronchi-
tis', {vii}608; 'I feel my life leaving
me..old moribund Europe just killing
one', {vii}617; doctor orders complete
rest for DHL, {vii}631–3, 640; 'I have
been losing weight badly', {vii}647;
DHL worse, 'awful bad nights, cough
and pain', {vii}650–1; 'perfect hell of a
time..with bronchials', {viii}102; DHL
misses *David* production because of
'return of malaria', {viii}102–3;
'bronchial hemorrhage' recurs,
{viii}105

Heanor (Derbyshire), {i}57, 174, {iii}333
Hearn, Lafcadio, {v}646
Hearst, William Randolph, {vii}636
Hearsts International Magazine, {iv}58, 287,
    298, 302, 341, 371, 379–80, 383, 389–91,
    399, {v}459
Heath, Ellen Maurice, {ii}54, 68
Heath, Frederick, {i}29
Heath, Richard, {ii}54
Heber, Bishop Reginald, 'From Greenland's
    Icy Mountains', {ii}615, {iv}110, 191,
    {vi}588, {vii}510
Hebridean Songs, *see* Kennedy-Fraser, M.
Hecht, Ben, {iv}407
    DHL reviews *Fantazius Mallare* by,
        {iv}321, 331, 345
Hecht, Hans, {v}35
Heckscher, Maurice, {v}425, 442
Heckscher, Mrs, {v}425, 442
Hedda Gabler, see Ibsen, H.

Heidelberg (Germany), {i}539, {ii}186, {v}331, 486, 514, {vi}142–3, 145, 147, 150, 237, 243, 259, 275, 281, 356, 366, 599, {vii}332, 362, 392, 618, 622; University, {i}391, 413, 415, {iii}443, {iv}6, {v}417, {vi}34, 76, {vii}409

Heidenstam, Karl Gustaf Verner von, *The Tree of the Folkungs*, {v}256

Heidi, see Spyri, J.

Heidin, Die, see Mohr, M.

Heine, Heinrich, {i}450, {iii}303

Heinemann, Donna Magda Stuart, {v}175

HEINEMANN, WILLIAM, {i}14, 19, 148, 158, 162, 235, 297, 306, 310, 323, 327, 344, 387–8, 430–2, {ii}165, {iii}381, 392, {iv}27–8, 533, {vii}368, 386, 391, 396, 445, 455, 514–15, 518, 520, 533–4, 539–40, 602, {viii}3

accepts *White Peacock*, {i}152–3, 166, 175, 180, 200, 210, 231, 233, 315, 471, {v}119, 122, 175, {viii}2 ; DHL contracted to, {i}161; *Trespasser* and, {i}182, 184, 200, 236, 239, 276, 330, 339, 345, 351; 'Great Cham', {i}262, 326; 'the little bear', {i}316; possible publisher for DHL's poetry, {i}317, 319, 321, 325, 348, 352, 355–6, 368, 370–1, 378; 'notoriously dilatory', {i}335; 'cock of Bedford St', {i}365; DHL regards *S and L* as 'Heinemann novel', {i}405, 409, 415–16; refuses *S and L*, {i}421–3, 455; 'rotten little Jew', {i}424; refuses DHL's poems, {i}442, 447; abhors DHL, {iii}77; firm serves 'proper public', {vii}448

Letters to {i}148–9

Letters from {i}421

Helen Comes of Age, see Lindsay, J.

Helen: A Tale of Ancient Troy, see White, E. L.

Heliogabalus, {vii}323

Hemingway, Ernest, {vii}514, 520, 534

In Our Time, {v}647

HENDERSON, ALICE CORBIN, {iv}290, 325–6, 331–2, 547, 555, 578, {vi}228, 320

Collected Poems for, {vii}387; *Pansies* for {vii}414

'Music', {vi}320;

The Turquoise Trail, {vi}228–9, 321

Letters to {iv}307–8, {vi}228–9, 320–1

Letters from {vi}228–9

HENDERSON, ALICE OLIVER ('CORBINETTA'), {iv}308, 332, 360, 444, 547

Letters to {iv}339

Henderson, Frank, {vii}310

Henderson, Lawrence Joseph, *The Fitness of the Environment*, {ii}509

Henderson, Mrs, {vii}629, 643

Henderson, Philip, {vii}334

Henderson, Professor Amos, {i}49 persuaded DHL to take Arts degree, {i}31; offers but fails to teach DHL Latin {i}34; referee for DHL, {i}77;'Pa', {i}79

Henderson, Rev. Alexander Roy, {i}4, 40

Henderson, William Penhallen, {iv}12, 290, {vi}228–9

Henley, William Ernest, DHL doesn't much care for, {ii}34

'England', {vii}379;

'Invictus', {i}154, 224, 248;

Poetry of Robert Burns, {i}504;

'Pro Rege Nostro', {i}482

Hennef (Germany), {i}398

Henning, Udo von, {i}404, 406, {ii}221

Henry IV, see Shakespeare, W.

Henry VIII, {i}114

Henry, Leigh Vaughan, {iii}279, 299, 322, 325 'Poems of a Prisoner', {iii}262, 265, 269, 319

HENRY, NANCY, {iii}3, 262, 292, 372 DHL prepares 'Poems of a Prisoner' for, {iii}263, 269, 319; *Movements* and, {iii}268–9, 276, 298, 322, 326; critique of story by, {iii}285–6

Letters to {iii}263, 268–9, 276, 279, 285–6, 298–9, 306, 322, 325–6

Henselt, Adolf von, {i}324

Henty, George Alfred, {ii}588–9

Hepburn, Edith Alice Mary, *see* Wickham, A.

Heraclitus, {ii}364–5

Herald Tribune, see New York Herald Tribune

Herald, The (Paris), {vii}612

Herbert, Agnes, *The Moose*, {iii}649
Herbert, Annie, {i}288
Herbert, Emma, {i}308
Herbert, John, {i}35
Herbert, Mary ('Marie'), {iii}177
Herbertson, Andrew John, {i}122
Hercules, {i}158, {ii}530, 665, {vi}79, 164, 252
Herédia, Carlos de, {v}462
Heretics (Cambridge society), {v}3, 382
Hergesheimer, Joseph, {iv}407, {v}63, 263
   From an Old House, {v}291
HERLITSCHKA, HERBERTH EGON, translator of *LCL*, {vii}567, 571–3, 596–7, 601, 609; DHL commends as translator, {vii}598, 604, 609
   Letters to {vii}571–3, 596–7, 609–10
   Letters from {vii}571–2, 596–7, 609–10
Herm (Channel Isles), Mackenzie leases, {iii}594, 608, 616, 628, 656, 662–4, 671, 702, 708, {iv}36, {vi}105
   see also Jethou
Herman Melville, Mariner and Mystic, see Weaver, R. M.
Hermesdorf, Frau, {i}393
Hermesdorf, M., {i}393, 396
Hermitage (Chapel Farm Cottage, Berkshire), {ii}316, 476, 478, 663–5, {iii}7, 37, 96–7, 117–20, 188–241 *passim*, 274–5, 293–8, 304–5, 314, 331–2, 335–6, 339–41, 344–5, 348–76, 380, 382–4, 388, 392–409, 411, 413, 449, 542, 581, 617, 649, {iv}28, 79, 223, {vii}529, {viii}27–9
Hermon-Hodge, Sir Robert Trotter, {i}123
Herodotus, {ii}572, 654
Heron, Matilda, {i}5
Herrenalb (Herrenalp) (Germany), {v}487–9, {vii}384
Herrick, Robert, {v}397, 563
Hertford (Hertfordshire), {iii}248
Heseltine, John Postle, {ii}549
HESELTINE, PHILIP ARNOLD (PETER WARLOCK), {ii}12–13, 18, 463, 496, 512, 520, 533, 552, {iii}5, 124, 128, 130, 134, 163, 185, 196, {iv}6, {v}532, {vi}480, {viii}23
   'one of the men who will count', {ii}442, 507–8; writes to Delius for DHL, {ii}444, 446, 450; DHL proposes invitation to Garsington for, {ii}449, 452, 476; might accompany DHL to USA, {ii}462, 465–6, 481; *Rainbow Books and Music* and, {ii}472, 532, 540, 542, 547–51, 554–5, 605, {iii}153; 'a bit backboneless..needs stiffening up', {ii}473, 501–2, 505; and Puma, {ii}504, 517, 530, 539, 546,557, {iii}36, {viii}17, 25; anxious about conscription, {ii}522–5, 542, 551, {viii}17; subscribes for *Signature*, {ii}529; DHL invites to Cornwall, {ii}564, 567–9, 578, 580; relationship terminated, {ii}598; 'I don't like him any more,' {iii}122; claims to be libelled as Halliday in *W in L*, {iii}628, {iv}87–9, 93–4, 105, 108, 113–14, 116, 123, 126, 129–30, 138, 169
   Letters to {ii}447–8, 480–1, 551, 598
Hesiod, {vii}560, 578
   Hesiod, The Homeric Hymns and Homerica, {ii}510, 517, 572, 580
Hesse, Hermann, *Demian*, {iv}576
Hester Rainsbrook, see Cramb, J. A.
Hewlett, Maurice Henry, {i}116, {ii}3, 212–13, 224–5
   Forest Lovers, {i}120;
   Spanish Jade, {i}271
Heyward, Du Bose, *Mamba's Daughters*, {vii}649
Hibbert Journal, The, {i}359, {ii}398
Hicks, (Sir) Edward Seymour, {i}144
Hicks, Mr, {iv}504
Hicks, Rosamond, {iii}267
Hicks, Sir William Joynson ('Jix'), 1st Viscount Brentford, {vii}5–6, 77, 132, 239, 274, 308, 319, 327
   authorised seizure of *Pansies* MS, {vii}163, 171, 195, 197, 204, 221, 227–8, 241, 249, 256; in Low cartoon, {vii}198–9, 202, 206–7; Rebecca West's riposte to, {vii}252; *P and O* in same series as pamphlet by, {vii}468, 559, 580, 584; DHL's proposed squib on, {vii}484–5; 'mealy-mouthed worm..maggot', {vii}582, 584
   Do We Need a Censor?{vii}468, 584;

Hicks, Sir William Joynson ('Jix') (*cont.*)
  'How the Censorship Works',
  {vii}584
Higgins, Sarah Parsons, {iv}360–1, 373,
  {v}73
Higgins, Victor, {iv}347, 360–1, 373
High Court (Divorce Division), {i}514, 516
High Germany, see Hueffer, F. M.
High Wycombe (Buckinghamshire), *see*
  Hawthorn Cottage
HIGHAM, DAVID, {vi}29, 565
  Letters to {vi}565
Highbury (Birmingham), *see* Chamberlain, J.
Higher Tregerthen (Cornwall), {ii}583–670
  passim, {iii}19–168 *passim*, 197–200,
  221–5, 229, 235–6, 244, 251, 255, 261,
  265, 268–9, 294–5, 308, 314, 317,
  319–20, 344, 435, 541, 712
  see also Zennor
Highland Mary, *see* Campbell, M.
Hilda Mary, *see* Jones, H. M.
Hilda, *see* Aldington, H.; Shaw, H.
Hill of Cloves, The, see Wilson, F. R. M.
Hill, Carrie J., {vi}370
Hill, George W., {i}9, 11, 82, 84, 91, 116
Hill, Mabel, {iii}10, 491, 532, {iv}139
Hills, Misses, {v}572, 611
HILTON, ENID, {iv}231, {v}631,
  {vi}12–13, 15, 60, 62, 64, 533, {vii}62,
  90, 319, 489
  married to Laurence Hilton, {iv}194;
  wearisome, {v}539; 'all of a work with
  discontent, like brewers' yeast', {v}548,
  583; invited to Mirenda, {vi}380; 'rather
  boring..but not *bad*', {vi}406, 413–14;
  helps DHL over exhibition of paintings,
  {vi}466–7, 536, 557–8, {vii}394, 460,
  469–70; assists with clandestine distribution of *LCL*, {vi}477–8, 486–7, 489–97,
  499–503, 510–11, 511–15, 518–19,
  529–30, 535–6, 544, 552, 575, 594,
  {vii}47–9, 124, 148, 372, 416; 'awfully
  good and smart delivering' *LCL*,
  {vi}511; arranges typing of *Escaped
  Cock*, {vi}528, 539–40, 569, {vii}290,
  292; 'tragedy up her sleeve', {vi}564;
  Paintings for, {vii}321–2, 332; Lahr's
  Pansies for, {vii}380, 412; painting
  promised to, {vii}425, 512

  see also Hopkin, E.
Letters to {iv}194–5, {v}536–7, 656,
  {vi}379–80, 417, 427, 441–2, 454, 467–8,
  477–8, 489–90, 492–4, 497, 499–501,
  503, 511–13, 528, 534–5, 539–40, 557–8,
  569, 576–7, 588, 594, 611, {vii}46–7,
  148, 267–7, 291–2, 299–30, 332, 372,
  394, 403–4, 460, 470, 512–13
Letters from {vii}322
Hilton, Laurence, {iv}194, {v}536, 539, 656,
  {vi}60, 417, 427, 468, 558, {vii}46–7,
  148
  'very nice, but ordinary', {v}548,
  {vi}406, 413–14, 564; 'rather nonde-
  script', {vi}62, 64; to be reassured over
  distribution of *LCL*, {vi}477–8, 493
Himalayas (India), {iv}239, 279
Hindenburg, Paul von, Field Marshall,
  {vi}184, {vii}510
HINDUISM/HINDUS, like Christians
  and Mohammedans, Hindus faced East,
  {ii}248; 'I detest things Hindu
  and..Buddhistic', {ii}351; 'living clue of
  life' not to be found in, {iv}219; antago-
  nism of Indian religions ('Hindu and
  Mohammedan - and then Buddha')
  might prolong British influence,
  {iv}246; Forster doesn't understand
  Hindu character in *Passage to India*,
  {v}142; DHL 'much prefers Hinduism'
  to Buddhism, {v}390; 'it is the Hindu,
  Brahmin thing - that queer
  fluidity..those lively, kicking legs, that
  attracts me', {v}613; Hindus 'a bit false',
  {vi}510; DHL appreciated massage by
  Hindu Boshi Sen, {vi}519, 542, 547;
  Spaniards 'self-contained and calm..the
  very reverse of those soft, gibbering
  Hindus', {vii}250–1; 'Hindu philoso-
  phy..big enough for anything', {vii}465
Hinke, Anita von ('Annie'), {iv}258,
  {vii}422–3, 433, 436, 450
Hinke, Ernest von, {iv}76, 120, 136, 147,
  162, 258, {vii}422, 433
Hippius, Zinaida, *see* Merizkowsky, Z.
Hiroshige, Andō, *Mannen Bridge*, {v}175
History and Practice of Psychoanalysis, The, see
  Bjerre, P.C.
History of Egypt, see Petrie, W. M. F.

History of Rome, The, see Mommsen, T.
History of the Decline and Fall of the Roman Empire, The, see Gibbon, E.
History of the East, see Hall, H. R.
History of the Peloponnesian War, The, see Thucydides
Histriophone, see Dobrée, B.
Hitchcock, Frederick Hills, {iii}657
Hoang (Hwang)-Ho, River (China), {i}251
Hobbema, Meindert, {i}124
Hobbes, Oliver *see*, Craigie, P. M.T.
Hobson, Coralie, {i}443, 530; pseud. Sarah Salt, {vii}516
Hobson, Harold, {i}20, 451, 483, 507, 516, 521, 523, 533–4, 546, {ii}46, 60, 175, 322, {vii}516
   'ripping fellow', {i}443; crosses Alps with DHL, {i}443–6; visits DHL in Italy, {i}488, 491, 493–8, 500–1; 'a lazy devil', {i}506; to be married, {i}530
Hobson, John Atkinson, {i}446, 491, 493, 500
Hocking, Mabel, {iii}64, 320, {viii}25
Hocking, Mary, {iii}64, 256, 295, 317, 320, {viii}25
Hocking, Mrs, {ii}652, {iii}64, 200, 235–6, 261, 295, 317, 320, 634
HOCKING, STANLEY, {iii}64, 88, 200, 315, {viii}20, 25, 27
   DHL taught French to, {iii}295; offers keepsake to, {iii}320
   Letters to {iii}294–5, 319–20, 333–4, 418
HOCKING, WILLIAM HENRY, {ii}14, 642–3, {iii}64, 79, 89, 200, 223, 236, 315, 319–20
   'rather a burden', {ii}647–8; wants to visit London, {ii}652, 663–4, {iii}181; candidate for Andes, {iii}173–4; has married, {iii}261, 634
   Letters to {iii}317
Hodge, *see* Hermon-Hodge, Sir R. T.
Hodgkinson, George, {i}234, 325
Hodgson, Ralph, {ii}92–3, 131, {iii}281
Hofmannsthal, Hugo von, *The White Fan*, {iii}532
Hofrath, Herr, *see* Schreiber, M.
Hogarth Press,The, {ii}205, {iii}381, 570, 727, {iv}29, 274, 322, 462, 584, {vi}175
Hogarth, Dr Margaret, {ii}407

Hogarth, Mrs J. H., {v}246
Hohenlinden (Germany), {i}540–1
Holbein, Hans, {ii}296, {v}496
HOLBROOK, MURIEL MAY, {i}32
   'the essence of things is stored in books..Read, my dear', {i}96; 'Jont(y)', {i}377, 445; proposing to emigrate, {i}425, 499, {ii}148; DHL tells about Frieda, {i}499
   Letters to {i}41, 90–1, 96–8, 115–16, 134, 297, 311–12, 330–1, 346–7, 360, 371, 377, 390, 397, 408, 412, 416, 425, 499–500, 508–9, {ii}77, 148–50
HOLBROOK, WILLIAM ('BILL', 'WILL'), {i}32, 91, 98, 116, 331, 347, 360, 371, 377, 397, 408, 412, 416, 425, {ii}77, 149
   emigrating to Canada, {i}499, {ii}148
   Letters to {i}387, 444–5
Holbrooks, Mrs, {i}132
HOLDERNESS, EDITH ('KITTY'), {i}24, 274, 283–4, 287, 295
   Letters to {i}24–5
HOLDERNESS, ELLEN MARY, {i}25
   Letters to {i}35
Holderness, George, {i}24–6, 77, 295
Holdich, White, {i}232, 237
Holland, {ii}24–5, 593, {iii}379, 391, 489, 505, 620–1, 637, 711, 721, {iv}47, 51,66, 87, 193, 240, {v}32, {vii}227, 230, {viii}21
   see also Hook of Holland
Holland, Josiah Gilbert, {vi}484
HOLLAND, TERENCE B., {vii}551
   copies of *LCL* ordered for, {vi}444; additional copies ordered, {vi}518, 560–1, 566, 591, {vii}35, 62, 135; cheque received from, {vi}579, {vii}230; stigmatised as 'cheat', {vii}42, 97; DHL recants, {vii}176–7; alleged to sell pirated *LCL*, {vii}308
   Letters to {vi}568, {vii}176–7
   Letters from {vi}518, 567, {vii}176–7
Holland, Vyvyan Beresford, {vi}491
Hollow, Mr, {ii}652
Holly Bush House (Hampstead), {ii}204, 227, 567, {iii}210, 406, {iv}193, 513, {viii}28
Holman, Grace, {ii}55

Holme Lea (Worcestershire), {iv}481

Holme, Charles, *English Water-Colour*, {i}88, 196, 273

Holmes, Miss, {i}228

Holms, Mrs, {v}55

Holms, Percy Grenville, {v}55

Holofernes, {i}476, {vi}411–12

Holroyd-Reece, John, DHL negotiates for Paris edn of *LCL* by, {vii}75, 89, 95, 109, 115, 153, 159, 161–2, 172, 194
    see also Pegasus Press, The

HOLT, AGNES, {i}10, 160, 208, 234
    DHL almost decided to marry, {i}139, 143, 146; 'very nice', {i}141; 'tired of her', {i}153; will marry and live in Isle of Man, {i}249, 313, 333, 526; copy of *Idyll* for, {i}282, 286
    Letters to {i}140, 146

Holt, Guy, *Bibliography of the Writings of James Branch Cabell*, {v}63–4

Home Secretary, *see* Clynes, J. R.

Homer Singing His Iliad, see Le Thière, G.

Homer, {ii}298, {iv}115, {vii}525, 527, 544
    DHL seeks Chapman's trans. of, {ii}253, 315; 'terrible glamour of camaradérie in', {ii}618; widespread knowledge of, {iii}679
    Iliad, {ii}253, 330, 644, {v}343; *Odyssey*, {ii}253, 315, {iv}89

Homeric Hymns, see Hesiod

HOMOSEXUALITY, 'nearly every man that approaches greatness tends to', {ii}115; 'principle of evil' plain in homosexual Keynes, {ii}311; Plato and Wilde not denounced but David Garnett's Cambridge 'set' bitterly attacked over, {ii}320–1; 'horrible little frowsty people, men lovers of men' exude 'sense of corruption', {ii}323; 'I like men to be beasts – but insects – one insect mounted on another – oh God!', {ii}331; heterosexual love 'the great *immediate* synthesis', homosexual produces 'reduction, disintegration', {ii}448; 'Goats and Compasses' said to deal largely with, {ii}558; 'sworn, pledged' homosexual 'friendship' as 'eternal as the marriage bond, and as

deep', {iii}302; 'manly love' (Whitman) 'as sacred a unison as marriage', {iii}478; DHL suspects '*all* young Englishwomen instinctively homosexual', {vi}554

Honde, Miss, {v}387

Hondo, *see* Arroyo Hondo

Hondo, River, (New Mexico), {v}70, 72, 277–8, 530

HONE, JOSEPH MAUNSEL, {iii}371
    possible publisher for *W in L* {iii}183–5; refuses *W in L*, {iii}187; shows interest in DHL's essays, {iii}187, 191
    Letters to {iii}183, 195–6

Honolulu, {iii}522, {iv}142, 239, 249, 259

Hood, Hon. Alexander Nelson (Duca di Brontë), {iii}10, 491, 532, 535, 616, 620, 636–7, {iv}51, 105, 125, 139, 218, 365
    'the gaga Duca di Brontë, alias Mr Hood', {iii}496; DHL visits Castello di Maniace, {iii}509, 518, 526

Hood, Thomas, {i}3, 5
    'The Bridge of Sighs', {ii}108; 'The Death-Bed', {i}192

Hook of Holland, {ii}22, {iii}698, 721, 723, 725, {iv}61, 78
    see also Holland

Hope, see Watts, G. F.

Hope-Johnstone, John, {ii}288

Hopi Indians, {v}5–6, 89, 91–3, 96–7, 99–100, 106, 109–10, 113; snake dance and DHL's article, {v}6, 82, 92, 99–101, 103, 115–16, 142, 150, 173, 193, 195, 197, 211, 218, 241, 581, 636, {vi}31, 36, 91, 354

HOPKIN, ENID, {i}176, 211, 232, 261, 442, 490, 493, {ii}42, 56, 58, 123, 196, 237, 259, 391, 467, 514, {iii}3, 9, 115, 126, 258–9, 267, 312
    see also Hilton, E.
    Letters to {ii}76, {iii}170–1, 271, 273, 276

Hopkin, Henry, {ii}124, {v}631, 634

Hopkin, Olive ('Lizzie'), {v}279, 394, {vi}64, 499, {vii}451, 469

HOPKIN, SARAH ('SALLIE') ANNIE, {i}18, 176, 232–3, 324, {ii}7, 18, 57, 123, 237, 259, 391, 467, {iii}3, 9, 223, 276, {iv}194–5, {v}279, 548, 634,

{vi}12, 60, 558, {vii}46, 469
member of Eastwood discussion group,
{i}53; tragic dramas sent to, {i}260–2;
'good news' about Frieda sent to,
{i}412–14; 'one of the very, very few'
sympathetic to DHL and Frieda,
{i}440–2, 490; *Rainbow* for, {ii}514;
invited to Cornwall, {iii}126; visits
Middleton-by-Wirksworth, {iii}243,
258–9; condolence on death of, {iv}327
Letters to {i}211, 260–1, 412–14, 426,
440–2, 490, 492–3, {ii}41–2, 196, 200,
401–2, 514, {iii}115–16, 123, 126, 243,
246–7, 257–8, 267–8, 311–12, 446,
450–2, {iv}231

HOPKIN, WILLIAM EDWARD
('WILLIE'), {i}3, 18, 176, 211, 261,
442, 490, 493, 541, {ii}7, 18, 42, 196,
{iii}115–16, 126, 243, 247, 258, 268, 328,
{iv}194, 231, {v}13, 548, 656, {vi}12,
60, 442, 492, 499, {vii}46
member of Eastwood discussion group,
{i}53; supports DHL in furore over
White Peacock, {i}233, 237; 'good old
crusty Eastwood gossip'from, {ii}122;
proofs of *Prussian Officer* volume sent to,
{ii}259; and subscribers to *Signature*,
{ii}391, 401; *Rainbow* for, {ii}467, 514;
New Poems sent to, {iii}292; condolences
on wife's death, {iv}327; remarries
{v}279, 634, {vi}64; wind-bag, {vii}458;
Socialism damaged, {vii}468–9
Letters to {i}176, 232–3, {ii}56–8, 72,
122–4, 236–7, 258–9, 391, 401–2, 467,
514, {iii}222–3, 259, 292, 450–2, 464,
{iv}327, {v}394, {vii}450–1
Hopkins, Kenneth, {vii}3
Horace, {i}5, {ii}63, 105
writings generally known, {iii}679
Odes, {i}46–7, 56, 224, {ii}36, 46, 352,
{iii}65, {v}387, 466
Horatius, *see* Macaulay, T. B.
Horne, Maisie, {ii}213, 230, 409, {iii}346,
{v}355
Horne, William K., {ii}205–6, 210, 213,
220–2, 227, 229–31, 236–7, 250–1, 268,
287, 329, 409, 615, {iii}340, 342, 346
Hornsey (Middlesex), {i}82, 116

Horse, see Johnson W., and *Laughing Horse,
The*
Horton, Dr Robert Forman, {ii}477, {iii}61
Hotel (Kurhaus) Plättig (Baden-Baden),
{vii}9, 359, 380, 382–403, 407, 410, 423
Hotel Adlon (Berlin), {iv}91
Hotel Arzapalo (Chapala), {iv}436, 457, 467,
473, 511, {viii}81
Hotel Bear (Gsteig), {vi}451
Hotel Beau-Rivage (Bandol), {vii}5, 17–215
passim, 418, 453, 482–3, 490–4, 501, 523,
553, 562, 564, 570, 576, 579, 581, 588,
591–2, 594, 598, 604–5, 607, 610–13,
619–21, 624, 626, {viii}111
'small and inexpensive', {vii}31;
'pleasant' and food good, {vii}46, 54, 80,
169; 'filled up with strangers', {vii}107;
awkward guests, {vii}190–1
Hotel Beau-Séjour (Monaco), {v}397, 417
Hotel Bella Vista (Capri), {vi}92, {vii}28, 56,
250
Hotel Belle Vue (Thumersbach), {iv}59, 69,
77–8
Hotel Brandes (Tepic), {iv}511
Hotel Como (Milan), {iv}194
Hotel Cosmopolita (Chapala), {iv}435
Hotel de France (Mazatlan), {v}509–10
Hotel de Vargas (Santa Fe), {v}97, 103, 151,
211, 226–7, 342, 650
Hotel de Versailles (Paris), {iv}582–3,
587–91, {vii}208, 210, 213–17, 220–1,
224–5, 521
Hotel dei Cappuccini (Amalfi), {iii}464, 633
Hotel del Cervo (Gargnano), {i}466, 474,
520, 532, {iv}189
Hotel des Touristes (St Nizier de Pariset),
{vi}423
Hotel du Louvre, (Marseille), {vii}302–3
Hotel du Nord (Milan), {iii}584, {iv}194–5
Hotel Eden (Baden-Baden), {vi}168–73,
176–8, 181–2, 186–7, 192, 556–7, 562
Hotel Fischer (Villach), {vi}117–37,
{viii}105
Hotel Francia (Oaxaca), {iv}424, {v}162–74,
183, 185, 212
Hotel Garcia (Guadalajara), {iv}508, 511–16,
519–27, 529, 532–3
Hotel Great Britain (Valetta), {iii}529–31

Hotel Imperial, *see* Imperial Hotel (Mexico City)

Hotel International (Capri), {v}369, 420

Hotel Jardin (Puebla), {iv}424

Hotel Krone (Ebersteinburg), {iii}710, 714, 720, 723–6, 728–9, {iv}2, 25, 29–51

Hotel la Palma (Palm Springs), {iv}504

Hotel Lauro (Capri), {vii}56

Hotel Les Goëlands (Bandol), {vii}501, 510–11

Hotel Lohninghof (Thumersbach), {iv}61, 64, 69, 78

Hotel Löwen (Baden-Baden), {vi}562, 564–73, 576–84, {vii}378, 381–2, 384, 391, 398–437, 444–7

Hotel Lucchesi (Florence), {iii}575, {iv}80, 82, {v}418, 427–36, 441–6, 618

Hotel Miramare (Spotorno), {v}334–5

Hotel Moderno (Florence), {vi}415, {vii}154, 354–5

Hotel Monte Carlo (Mexico D. F.), {iv}414–35, 534–5, 538, {v}152–60, {viii}78

Hotel National (Gstaad), {vi}451–2

Hotel Nouvel (Vence), {vii}641–2, 644–7

Hotel Oriente (Barcelona), {vii}251

Hotel Palmera (Chapala), {iv}436

Hotel Palumbo (Ravello), {v}402, 406, 414, 427, 573, 650

Hotel Panorama (Vallombrosa), {iii}575, {vi}135

Hotel Panormus (Palermo), {iv}199

Hotel Porta Rossa (Florence), {vii}21, 369, 371, 373, 375

Hotel Principe Alfonso (Mallorca), {vii}259–86, 290–337 *passim*

Hotel Regis (Mexico City), {iv}414–16, 421, {v}152

Hotel Royal (Palma), {vii}251–9, 267

Hotel Sanetsch (Gsteig), {vi}451

Hotel Santa Lucia (Naples), {iv}197–9

Hotel Stephanie (Baden-Baden), {iii}728, {vii}423–4

Hotel Victoria (Viktoria) (Gsteig), {vi}451–2, 454–6, 458–9, 464, 468, 498, 506–7, 510, {vii}105

Hotel Webster (Capri), {v}323, 338, 342, 383

Hotevilla (Arizona, USA), {v}101

Houghton Mifflin Co., {ii}223–4, 246, 562, {iv}276, {vi}229

Houghton, Henry Oscar, {iv}276

Hound of Heaven, The, see Thompson, F.

Hours of Fiammetta, The, see Taylor, R. A.

House by the Medlar-Tree, The, see Craig, M.

House in Demetrius Road, The, see Beresford, J. D.

House of Cobwebs, The, see Gissing, G.

House of Commons, *see* Parliament

'House of Ellis, The', *see* Skinner, M. L. and Lawrence, D. H., *The Boy in the Bush*

House of Mirth, The, see Wharton, E.

House of the Dead, The, see Dostoievsky, F.

House with the Green Shutters, The, see Brown, G. D.

House with the Mezzanine, The, see Chekhov, A.

Housman, Alfred Edward, {vi}276, {viii}15
  sings only 'stale tale of the bankruptcy of life', {i}103; 'rotten' poet, {i}106
  The Shropshire Lad, {i}102–3, 106, {ii}13, 502

Housman, Clemence, *The Unknown Sea*, {iii}75

Houston, Lady, {i}381

Hove (Sussex), {i}213–14, 216–17, {iii}603

HOVEY, CARL ('HUFFEY'), {ii}475, {iii}571
  'Vin Ordinaire' rejected by, {ii}216; 'Wintry Peacock' accepted by 'Huffey', {iii}493, 548, 559, 590–1; *very* sweet' to DHL, {iii}562, 564–5, 572, 576
  Letters to {iii}590–1

How about Europe, see Douglas, G. N.

'How the Censorship Works', *see* Hicks, Sir W. J.

Howard and Son, see Beresford, J. D. and Richmond, K.

Howard de Walden, Baron, {iii}316

Howard, Keble, *see* Bell, J. K.

Howards End, see Forster, E. M.

Howe, Percival Presland, {v}318, 320, 638, {vii}381, 391
  Letters from {v}270, {vii}413

Howitt, Mary, {ii}114
Hube, Baron Rev. Rodolph von, {i}67
'Hubert', {i}102
Hubrecht, A. A. W., {iii}489
HUBRECHT, MARIE ('TUTTIE'),
    {iii}10, 481, 489, 491, 494, 637, 663, 730,
    {iv}3
    'vendetta' between Mary Cannan and,
    {iii}496, 526, 532, 535, 553; splendid
    villa, Rocca Bella owned by, {iii}506–7,
    527, 533, 554, 580, 658, 686; *Lost Girl*
    for, {iii}621, 640; *W in L* for, {iv}87,
    193; *S and S* for, {iv}193
    Letters to {iii}505–7, 526–7, 532–3, 553–4,
    580, 606–7, 619–21, 639–40, 657–8,
    665–7, 686–7, 726–7, {iv}51–2, 139–41,
    192

Huch, Ricarda, {i}513
Hudson, Nancy, {ii}360, 393
Hudson, William Henry, {i}12
    Nature in Downland, {i}334, 342, 344;
    South American Sketches, {i}151
HUEBSCH, BENJAMIN W., {ii}17, 190,
    224, 426, {iii}8, 12, 15–17, 143, 348, 365,
    367, 369–70, 376, 425, 428, 433, 486,
    503, 510–12, 516, 520, 529, 553, 575,
    612, 627, 653, 661, 690, 693, {iv}15, 134,
    390–1, 403, 406, 437, {v}18, 146, 624,
    {vi}538, 607, {vii}320, 526, 569,
    {viii}72, 77
    publishes *Rainbow*, {ii}294, 420, 429,
    441, 446, 479, 514, 518, 561, {iii}129,
    318, 388, 427, 457, 544, 613, 644–6, 651,
    673, {iv}82, 106, 150, 156, 170, 173, 182,
    399, 408, 431, 474; publishes *Twilight*,
    {ii}398, 610, {iii}129, 323; sailed on
    'peace ship', {ii}475; publishes *Amores*,
    {ii}610, {iii}129; publishes *Prussian
    Officer*, {iii}129, 323, {iv}247–8; 'a Jew',
    {iii}144, 675; publishes *LWHCT*,
    {iii}149, 238, 254, 323; *New Poems*
    published by, {iii}361, 385–8, 399, 456;
    MS of *SCAL* sent to, {iii}405, 423, 456,
    501, 519, 543, 545, 576, {viii}36; cheque
    from, {iii}413, 441, 445, 472, 508, 511,
    {iv}388; and *W in L*, {iii}457, 466–7,
    473, 477, 492, 508, 518, 543, 545, 565,

643, 646, {iv}411–12; 'terrible payer',
    {iii}500, 545; Mountsier's critical
    account of, {iii}643–4; Mountsier told to
    'make a bit of friends with', {iii}678;
    kept DHL 'in the dark', {iv}108, 394;
    DHL curses, {iv}445; *Rainbow* sales,
    {viii}51; DHL returns $200 and
    terminates contact with, {viii}79–80
    Letters to {iii}323–4, 356–8, 364, 386, 388,
    399–401, 405, 409, 413, 422–3, 426–7,
    429–30, 445–6, 455–7, 466, 468, 472–3,
    484, 492–3, 501, 508, 511, 543–4,
    {iv}106, 182–3, 229–30, 248, 387, 402,
    408–9, {viii}79–80
    Letters from {iii}356–7, 364, 385, 399, 409,
    445, 455–7, 544, {iv}106, 229, 402,
    {viii}51
HUEFFER, FORD MADOX, {i}9, 11–15,
    20, 22, 139–40, 146, 165, 167, 169,
    182–3, 200, 226–8, 276, 286, 301, 309,
    311, 323, 336, 353, 376, 379, 381, {ii}31,
    75, 132, 232, {iii}102, {v}450
    'kindest man on earth', {i}138; promotes
    publication of *White Peacock*, {i}144,
    148–9; DHL submits stories to, {i}147;
    finishes as editor of *English Review*,
    {i}152; DHL at party given by,
    {i}170–1; judges *Trespasser* 'rotten work
    of genius', {i}178, 330, 339, 417, 485; on
    Widowing, {i}199, 298; 'marries' Violet
    Hunt, {i}309, 313, 315–16, 327, 363–4;
    commends Secker to DHL, {i}433–4,
    442; regarded DHL as 'a genius',
    {i}471; critique of *White Peacock* by,
    {viii}2–3
    'A Call', {i}141;
    High Germany, {i}359
    Letters to {i}485–6, {ii}34
    Letters from {i}433–4, {viii}2–3
Hueffer, 'Mrs', *see* Hunt, V.
Huelin, David, {vii}373
HUELIN, EDWARD SCOTTON,
    {vii}338
    Letters to {vii}373–4
Huelin, Hilda, {vii}373
Huerta, Adolfo de la, {iv}465, 536
Huffey, *see* Hovey, C.

HUGHES, CHRISTINE, {v}158, 199, 250,
    252, 259, 280–2, 285, 362, 594, 598, 600,
    616, 630, {vi}38, 56, 58, 73–4, 78, 86,
    {vii}574
    'stone blind, culturally', {vi}79; order-
    forms for *LCL* sent to, {vi}319, 357;
    subscribes for *LCL*, {vi}461; *Pansies* for,
    {vii}414
    Letters to {vi}39–40, 319–20
HUGHES, GLENN ARTHUR, {vii}326
    'dull and portentous', {viii}112
    Imagism and the Imagists, {vii}223
    Letters to {vii}223, 324
Hughes, Mary Christine, {v}158, 600,
    {vi}38, 56, 78, 86, 320, {vii}414
    'doing music in Rome', {v}616; 'hard to
    please', {vi}40; 'stone blind, culturally',
    {vi}79; 'Laura Philippine' based on,
    {vi}400; wedding present for, {vii}574
Hughes, Rosalind, {v}200, 259
Hughes, Thomas, *Tom Brown's Schooldays*,
    {ii}588, {v}44
HUGHES-STANTON, BLAIR
    ROWLANDS, orders *LCL*, {vi}411;
    illustrator for *BBF*, {vii}457, 503, 549,
    563; 'as kind as an angel', {vii}641
    Letters to {vi}411–12, {vii}457, 563, 640
Hughes-Stanton, Gertrude, {vii}457, 563
Hughes-Stanton, Judith, {vi}411–12,
    {vii}457
Hughes-Stanton, Simon, {vi}411–12,
    {vii}457
Hugo, Victor, {ii}34
Huitzilopochtli, {v}160
Hull, Edith Maude, *The Sheik*, {v}574
Hume, David, *Enquiry Concerning Human
    Understanding*, {iii}719
Humes, Elizabeth, ('Bettina', 'Burr'),
    {iii}567, 687, {iv}43, 138, 143, 158, 244,
    398, {vi}12, {vii}274
    Psychoanalysis for, {iii}703; Juta's
    fiancée, {iv}25; *Aaron's Rod* for, {iv}261
Humes, Mrs, {iv}391, {vii}274
Humphreys, Arthur L., orders *LCL*,
    {vi}517–18, 529, 544
Humphreys, Ernest Arthur, {i}194, 241, 245,
    304, 318–19, 342, 355, 368, {ii}91,
    {iii}61, {v}640

objects to presentation as Holiday in
    Trespasser, {i}465, 483; 'Young Man of
    the Seas', {i}523
Humphreys, Mrs {i}291, 300, 304, 318,
    483
Hundstein, Mt. (Austria), {iv}60, {viii}43
Hungary, {vii}480, 487, 511
Hunger, Ethel, {i}73, 184, 203, 234, 280, 285,
    294, 314, 338, 387, {vii}72, 141
Hunger, Max, {i}73, 184, 234, 280, 285, 292,
    308, 314, 338, {vii}141
    Collected Poems and *S and L* for, {vii}72;
    Lost Girl and *Plumed Serpent* for,
    {vii}156, 171
Hunstanton (Norfolk), {i}81
Hunt, Alfred William, {i}144
HUNT, VIOLET, {i}14, 144–6, 183, 188,
    381, 502, {ii}8, 34, {v}589
    DHL describes, {i}170–1; reviews *White
    Peacock* favourably, {i}227, 230;
    'marries' Hueffer, {i}309, 313, 315–17,
    327; 'a neat assassin', {i}364
    Letters to {i}199–200, 226–8
    Letters from {i}199, 226–7
Huntingdons, the, {ii}120, 133, 139, 168,
    173, 192, 629
Hutchie, *see* Hutchinson, St J.
Hutchinson & Co., {i}19, {iv}32, 143, 354
    offer to 'run' DHL as 'leading author',
    {i}458, 462; 'friendly' toward DHL,
    {iv}34, 36
    Letters from {i}458
Hutchinson, Barbara, {vii}227, 238,
    371
Hutchinson, Col., *see* Hutchison, G. S.
Hutchinson, Mary, {ii}591, {vi}383,
    {vii}161, 227, 330
    'nice and gentle', {v}650–1; *LCL* for,
    {vi}512, 515; to choose one of DHL's
    paintings, {vii}371, 425, 490
HUTCHINSON, ST JOHN ('HUTCHIE',
    'JACK'), {iii}103, 175–6, {vii}6, 320,
    370, 425, 435, 473, 490, 498
    'they are bad people', {ii}591; worked
    for No-Conscription league, {ii}612;
    orders *LCL*, {vi}383; consulted about
    Pansies MS, {vii}161–2, 167, 172, 176,
    183–4, 190, 192, 195, 22, 227; to advise

on legality of 'State of Funk', {vii}188; made no progress over *Pansies*, {vii}257, 302; holds on to *Pansies* MS, {vii}238, 278, 282, 301–2, 315, 318; acts for Dorothy Warren over DHL's paintings, {vii}367, 371

Letters to {vii}184, 227, 238, 371

Hutchinson's Story Magazine, {iii}13, 613, {vi}176

DHL's stories in, {iii}299, 360, {iv}32, 126, 134, 219–20, {v}50, 87; among best of popular magazines, {v}56; bought 'Border Line' for £40, {v}57, {vi}270, 272; want to cut story, {v}109, 122, 141, 148–9

Hutchison, Lt-Col. Graham Seton, *The W Plan*, {vii}450–1, 460

Hutten, Baroness Bettina von, {vi}489–90, 511, 516

Hutton, Edward, {vii}363, {viii}37

HUXLEY, ALDOUS, {ii}4, 319, 325, 452, 481, {iii}261, {v}532, 560, 565–7, 569, 585–6, 595, 597, 601, 607, 614, 647, {vi}1–6, 15, 17, 77, 81, 84–5, 89, 106, 109, 155, 180, 187, 190–1, 198, 201, 203–4, 234, 237, 259, 266, 314, 319–20, 338, 443, 445, 459–60, 505, 538, 546, 568, 575, 580, 584–6, {vii}1, 5, 7–9, 13–15, 34, 42, 75–6, 79, 85, 105, 107, 166, 171, 173, 178–9, 181, 183, 230–1, 246, 274, 300, 309, 314, 320, 360, 384, 393, 395, 420, 433, 467, 491, 498–9, 503–4, 510, 525, 527, 532, 538, 548, 552, 558–9, 563–6, 571, 577, 586, 602, 609, {viii}112

DHL invites to Florida, {ii}483; hated India, {v}519, 561; allegedly created 'unflattering character' (Kingham) of DHL, {v}563; invites DHL to Forte dei Marmi, {vi}202, {vii}335–58; in *Proper Studies* 'serious and professorial', {vi}214; Christmas with, {vi}246–7, 250, 253, 255–6; DHL to Diablerets with, {vi}261–4, 275–6, 281, 286–7, 295, 300–2, 304–5, 311; 'like a long stalky bird, all stalk and claw', {vi}275–6; *Porcupine* sent to, {vi}289, 332, 342; admires *LCL*, {vi}308–10, 316; consid-

ers 'authors publishing company', {vi}322, 342; order-forms for *LCL* sent to, {vi}332, 334, 343; offers advice on publishing *LCL*, {vi}345, {vii}58, 109; *WWRA* for, {vi}396; with DHL at Chexbres, {vi}428, 430, 433, 436–41; bought *LCL*, {vi}456; DHL seeks words of 'Green Grow the Rushes O' from, {vi}508, 541; DHL as 'gas-bag' Rampion, {vi}601, 617, {vii}27; *Collected Poems* sent to, {vi}603; Orioli's series of translations and, {vi}591, 605, {vii}20–2, 411, 416, 540, 573, 588; *LCL* as Christmas gift to, {vii}90–1, 97; and poem by Swift, {vii}106; at Bandol, {vii}123–5, 127–8, 132, 134–5, 137, 146, 148, 150–64; 'really nicer', {vii}167; in cartoon with DHL, {vii}206–7; DHL in Paris with, {vii}208–27, 234, 302, {viii}112; *Paintings* for, {vii}321; 'Moros de la Costa' (nickname), {vii}366–7, 525, 552, 586; *Pansies* for, {vii}380, 407, 576; drew 'Maria in the nude', {vii}417; possible contributor to 'The Squib', {vii}501, 516; row between Maria and, {vii}600, 604; with DHL at his death, {vii}653

'After the Fireworks', {vii}407;

Along the Road, {v}352;

'Baudelaire', {vii}537;

Do What You Will, {vii}106, 537;

Point Counter Point, {v}650–1, {vi}596, 600–1, 610, 617, {vii}20–1, 27, 39, 55, 164, 169–70, 626, 630, 633, (*Counterpane*) {vii}41; fictional character, Rampion, {vi}601, 617, {vii}27;

Proper Studies, {vi}82, 214, 225;

This Way to Paradise, {vii}626–7, 630, 633, 642, 645, 653;

Two or Three Graces and Other Stories; fictional character, Kingham, {v}563

Letters to {ii}467–8, 471, {v}574, {vi}100, 120–1, 202–3, 214–15, 315–16, 332, 342–3, 352–4, 383–5, 483–4, 507–8, 541–3, 600–1, {vii}57, 63–4, 86–7, 109–10, 118–19, 194–5, 207–8, 232–3, 238–9, 275–6, 283, 407–8, 434–5, 465–7, 536–7, 560–1, 576–7, 608, 614–15

HUXLEY, ALDOUS (*cont.*)
  Letters from {vi}345, {vii}58, 407, 608,
    627, 642
Huxley, Anthony Julian, {vi}246, 286, 311,
    315, 345, 373–5, 403, 527, {vii}79–80,
    104
Huxley, Francis John Heathorn, {vi}246,
    286, 311, 345, 374–5, 403, 527,
    {vii}79–80, 104
HUXLEY, (SIR), JULIAN SORELL,
    {ii}264, 481, 483, {vi}246, 286–7, 289,
    300, 316, 323, 332, 344–5, 375, 384, 387,
    395, 403, 460, {vii}5, 8, 14, 79–80, 104,
    107, 109, 116–18, 124, 161, 309, 372,
    608, 615
  DHL on, {vi}373; offers DHL copy of
    Essays, {vii}227
  Essays in Popular Science, {vii}227;
    The Science of Life, {vi}374
  Letters to {vii}114
Huxley, Leonard, *Elizabeth Barrett
    Browning: Letters to her Sister*, {vii}651
HUXLEY, MARIA, {v}12, 519, 563, 565–6,
    569, 595, 629, {vi}1, 3, 5–6, 9, 15, 77,
    81–2, 106, 109, 155, 187, 190, 201, 259,
    314, 319–20, 332, 338, 342, 403, 430, 433,
    538, 546, 575, 580, {vii}5, 7, 9, 13–15, 34,
    98, 107, 119, 173, 181, 246, 274, 302, 314,
    320, 338–9, 418, 436, 446, 465, 491, 510,
    527, 532, 538, 540–3, 548, 558–9, 563–5,
    571, 581, 592, 608, 630, 633
  gave canvases to DHL, {v}585, 614;
    seems ambitious, {v}651; DHL invited
    to Forte dei Marmi by, {vi}85–7, 89, 202;
    inspires Frieda to make puddings,
    {vi}214; DHL spends Christmas with,
    {vi}234, 236–7, 246–7, 250, 253, 255–6;
    shocked by DHL's painting, {vi}245; at
    Diablerets with DHL, {vi}259–311
    passim; typing *LCL*, {vi}273, 290, 294,
    303, 385; makes 'chicken-pox of mis-
    takes' in typing, {vi}293, 353; liked *LCL*,
    {vi}308–10, 316; a DHL painting for,
    {vi}353, 384, 543, {vii}370–1, 425, 435,
    487, 490, 631; to collect *LCL* MS,
    {vi}354, 384; gift of *LCL* for, {vi}428; in
    Chexbres, {vi}436–45, 459; buys copy of
    LCL, {vi}456; at Le Lavandou,

  {vi}584–6; investigates sale of pirated
    LCL in Paris, {vii}57–8, 62, 67; poem in
    Pansies for, {vii}64, 110; sends *Blue
    Guide* to DHL, {vii}86; at Bandol,
    {vii}123–167 *passim*; distressed by *Point
    Counter Point*, {vii}169–70; DHL asks
    for 'blue coat', {vii}176, 178, 183, 190,
    202; DHL anxious about health of,
    {vii}176, 182–3, 466; DHL in Paris with,
    {vii}208–27, 234; *Paintings* for, {vii}283,
    300; capable of 'gross exaggeration',
    {vii}293, 295, 299; DHL at Forte dei
    Marmi with, {vii}343–58 *passim*; drives
    DHL to Pisa, {vii}359; 'Moros de la
    Costa', {vii}366–7, 525, 552, 586; drawn
    in nude, {vii}417; *Pansies* for, {vii}487,
    576; friction between Huxley and,
    {vii}600, 604; with DHL at his death,
    {vii}653
  Letters to {v}574, 614, {vi}100, 120–1,
    202–3, 315–16, 329–30, 352–4, 371–2,
    462, 483–4, 507–8, 568–9, 573–4, 595–6,
    609–10, {vii}21–2, 41–2, 57, 63–4, 176,
    182–3, 190–1, 207–8, 232–3, 238–9,
    275–6, 363, 407–8, 419–20, 434–5,
    486–7, 500–2, 523–4, 536–7, 560–1,
    576–7, 590–1, 602–3, 614–15, 626–7,
    641–2, 645–6, 651
  Letters from {vii}57–8
HUXLEY, (LADY), MARIE JULIETTE
    ('CENDRELLA'), {vi}5, 246, 286–7,
    289, 304, 311, 323, 330, 395, {vii}5, 14,
    107, 109, 116–18, 124, 615
  'Cendrella', {ii}264; Heseltine attracted
    by, {ii}481, 539, 557; her 'Egyptian
    book', {ii}521, {viii}17; 'moral rage'
    over *LCL*, {vi}308–10, 315; embroi-
    dered Adam and Eve in Paradise,
    {vi}313, 316, 344–5, 403; proposed
    'John Thomas and Lady Jane' as title for
    LCL, {vi}315; subscribed for *LCL*,
    {vi}386, 460; DHL submits poem for
    approval to, {vii}120, 132–3, 372; *Pansies*
    for, {vii}347, 372
  Letters to {vi}313–14, 344–5, 373–5, 386–7,
    402–3, 427–8, 459–60, 527–8, 578,
    {vii}79–80, 104, 114, 119–20, 132–3,
    160–1, 227–8, 372

Huxley, Matthew, {v}614, {vi}89, 121, 202, 246, 286, 330, 345, {vii}79, 164, 190, 435
Huxley, Thomas Henry, {vi}214
Hyères (France), {vi}542, 570–600 *passim*
Hymnen an die Nacht, see Novalis

I Malavoglia, see Verga, G.
I Regionamenti, see Aretino, P.
Ibarra, Isaac M., {v}164
Ibsen, Henrik, {i}50, 96, 166, 171, 465, 509, {ii}187, {vi}49
    Louie Burrows given volume of, {i}112; Thaulow much like, {i}113; Strindberg wooden like, {i}465; Italian performance of *Ghosts*, {i}495–6, 505; DHL will not imitate, {i}509
    Ghosts, {i}495–6, 505;
    Hedda Gabler, {i}113–14;
    The Lady from the Sea, {i}113–14;
    Lady Inger, {i}112;
    Pillars of Society, {iii}646;
    The Pretenders, {i}112–13;
    Rosmersholm, {i}113–14;
    The Vikings, {i}112, 114
Icking (Germany), {i}18, 412–31 *passim*, 475–6, 515, 534, 541, {vi}149, 151, 160, 162, 164, {viii}106
Ida, *see* Rauh, I.
Idella, *see* Purnell, I.
Idiot, The, see Dostoievsky, F.
Idyll, The, see Greiffenhagen, M.; Nylander, J. W.
Il Penseroso, see Milton, J.
il Tonno, see Bacchelli, R.
Ile de Port-Cros, *see* Port-Cros, Ile de
Ile Des Pingouins, L', see France, A.
Iliad, see Homer
Ilkeston (Derbyshire), {i}67, 178, 181, 321, {v}243; Pupil-Teacher Centre, {i}4, 24, 26–9, 83, {viii}2; Station, {i}33–4
Illustrated London News, {ii}462, {v}79, 112, 619–20, {vi}32, 69, 463, {vii}336, 563
Imagism and the Imagists, see Hughes, G. A.
Imagism, *see* Lowell, A.; *see also Some Imagist Poets*
Imagistes, Des, see Pound, E.

Imperial Hotel (Mexico City), {iv}421, {v}214–26
Imperialism and the Open Conspiracy, see Wells, H. G.
Improvisationen im Juni, see Mohr, M.
Impruneta (Italy), {vii}379, 384, 400, 416
In Accordance with the Evidence, see Onions, O.
In His Own Image, see Corvo, Baron
In Our Time, see Hemingway, E.
In the Beginning, see Douglas, G. N.
Income Tax, American: {iv}355, 382–3, 387, 391–3, 400, 544, 559, 569, 572–4, 582–3, 588, {v}16, 39, 46, {vi}539, {viii}87; British: {vi}142, {vii}130, 150
Incorporated Society of Authors, Playwrights and Composers, *see* Society of Authors
India, {i}215, {ii}91, 262, 321, 466, 596, {iv}3, 8, 89, 122, 206, 214, 221, 234–5, 239, 387, 520, 541, {v}75, 80, 142, 401, 422, 437, 454, 456, 470, 484, 492, 504, 518–19, 530, 617, {vi}1, 101, 147, 174, 101, 174, 234, 307, 335, 367, 378–9, {vii}317, 436, 529, 532, 570, 652
    Forster warned not to visit, {ii}612; DHL urged to write book on, {iv}243–5, 458, {vii}170; will 'fall into chaos once the British let go', {iv}246; 'hell can have', {iv}544; antithesis of Mexico, {v}184; Huxley loathed, {v}519, 561; Brewsters and, {v}573, 586, 626, 629, 631–2, 635; DHL's visit illusory, {vi}208; Gandhi right for, {vii}424; DHL doesn't 'belong to the actual' but admires art of, {vii}465
Indian Earth see Bynner, H. W.
Indian Sculpture, see Codrington, K. de B.
Indians, *see* Pueblo Indians
Indiscretion, see Aldington, R.
Indo-China, {viii}50
INDUSTRY, 'not an industry worth the mention' near Gargnano, {i}528; 'modern industrial capitalistic system', {ii}283; men should govern 'industrial side of life', {ii}368, 371; miners understand 'only this industrial - mechanical - wage idea', {ii}489;

INDUSTRY (*cont.*)

Beardsall family ruined in crash of lace, {iii}282; 'régime of happy industrial England..melting like a dead thaw', {iii}339; coal, {iii}611, {vi}256, {vii}98; DHL predicts 'clergy-industrial-socialist' régime in Italy, {iv}124; coal-strike makes 'industrial revolution' more likely, {v}533; DHL angry at removal of industrial regions from Austria, {vi}142; 'burning industrial town' in DHL's *Flight Back into Paradise*, {vi}188; workers should awaken from 'industrial somnambulism', {vi}266; miners all right, 'It's the industrial system which is wrong', {vi}267; 'intelligent men must take over..industries and money', {vi}280; 'crisis in Italian', {vi}412; 'industrial system piling up rubbish while nobody lives', {vii}99; Kippenberg will hate 'industrial analysis' in *LCL*, {vii}114; '*curse* the industrial world', {vii}180; DHL hates '"western" machine world', {vii}465

Inferno, see Dante, A.

Ingres, Jean Auguste Dominique, {vii}417

Inguanez, Don Mauro, *Lost Girl* to, {iii}621; *Foreign Legion* to, {iv}186, {v}141; *New Poems* to, {iv}194; DHL writes to, {v}33; *Foreign Legion* written partly for sake of, {v}240, {viii}48; tells DHL of Magnus's suicide, {viii}38

Innsbruck (Austria), {i}424–322, 541, {iii}724, {iv}25, {iv}38–48, 53, 61, 72, 74, 78, 189, {vi}100, 108, {vii}463, 465–6, 477, {viii}44

INSECTS, bees 'nuzzling' into flowers, {i}57; 'bees in..lime tree, hidden altogether, so that the tree seems to be speaking and saying nothing', {i}66; townspeople 'like races of insects running over some food body', {i}80; sometimes humans 'struggle like water-beetles stranded and toiling in mud', {i}202; reviewer 'will lie on his back and kick like a black-beetle under Keatings', {i}240; observing life's inevitability 'like

watching a big beetle wander across the table', waiting for it to 'go - flop! - over the edge', {i}263; flea leapt 'into the infinite..a glorious flying jump', {ii}85; homosexuals ('little swarming selves') made DHL dream 'of a beetle that bites like a scorpion', {ii}319, 321, 323; soldiers stricken with 'sensual lust..insectwise..obscene', recall 'lice or bugs', {ii}331; 'ugly, scaly, insect-like, unclean *selfishness*' afflicts Cornish people, {ii}520; Dostoievsky characters 'teem like insects', {ii}542; Cornish with 'souls of insects', if squashed 'would be a whitey mess, like when a black-beetle is squashed', {ii}552; 'insect-like stupidity', {ii}603; Allies 'like great insatiable leeches' on body of Germany, {ii}603; 'sea-pinks like a hover of pink bees', {ii}609, 611; 'a great box of insect powder' to cleanse earth of 'creeping multitudes', {ii}650; England is 'beetle-trap of an island', {iii}335; Sicilian musicians 'twinkling on guitars and mandolins..like grasshoppers and kindred insects', {iii}514; 'bee in my bonnet [sex]..buzzes not over loud', {iii}517; Murry 'the wet flea', {iv}38; 'q-b' (Frieda) but 'no little bees', {iv}111; in London winter DHL creeps 'under a paving-stone of a sky, like some insect in the damp', {iv}550; Oaxaca market hums 'like a bee-hive', {v}164; Seltzer 'furtive little flea', {v}194; 'cold, insect-like ugliness' of Murry's letter, {v}203; Bynner 'belated sort of mosquito', {v}580; 'fireflies go winking round..like lost souls', {vi}64; cicalas noisy like 'a dozen little people..working little sewing-machines', {vi}87; 'one felt like a bee' with smell of orange-blossom in all the air, {vii}275

Insel Almanach, {iv}260, {v}252, 417, 620, {vi}616

DHL published in, {iv}257, {v}331, {vi}52

Insel-Verlag, {iii}7, 392, 601, {iv}2, 6, 40, 72, 238–9, 252, 340, 621, {vii}65

publishes DHL in translation, {iii}620, 622–3, 625, 667, {iv}89, 193, 257, 354, 428, {v}38, 92–3, 288, 314, 332, 554, {vi}275, 291; *Biblioteca Mundi* by, {iii}679–81, 715, {iv}117–18; has translation rights for all DHL's books into German, {v}364, {vii}23; DHL threatens break with, {vi}199, 421, 429, 582, {vii}51; threat disappears, {vi}616, {vii}32; refuses *LCL*, {vii}139, 383, 386, 543, 571, 597, 609
   see also Kippenberg, Dr A.

Insole, Alan, {iii}506, 535, 552, 568, 620, 624, 637, 640, 683, {iv}26, 39, 43, 49, 138–9, 141, 143, 157–8, 244, 366
   DHL to Syracuse with, {iii}508, 526; DHL at Anticoli with, {iii}580, 584–7; in Venice with, {iii}604–6, 609; in Taormina, {iii}656, 658

Insole, Violet, {iv}26, 138

Instincts of the Herd in Peace and War, see Trotter, W.

Intelligent Women's Guide to Socialism and Capitalism, see Shaw, G. B.

Interlaken (Switzerland), {ii}184–5, {iv}72, {vi}487–8

International, see Hearsts International Magazine

International Hotel, *see* Hotel International (Capri)

International Library of Famous Literature, The, see Garnett, R.

Introduction to Psychoanalysis, see Low, B.

Introduction to the Study of Medieval Indian Sculpture, An, see Codrington, K. de B.

Inverness (Scotland), {v}12, 474, 506–13, 517, {vi}93

Invocation, see Nichols, R. M. B.

Inwood, Alfred, {i}52, 77

Inwood, Alfred John, {i}84

Inwood, Ellen (Nellie), {i}9, 11, 84, 95–6, 260

Inwood, Emma, {i}84

Ionian Sea, {iii}486, {iv}4, 97, 100, 109

Iphigenie auf Tauris, see Goethe, J. W. von

Irapuato (Mexico), {iv}443, 468

Ireland, {i}312, 314, {ii}175, 179, 187, 238, 240, 340, 418, {iii}63, 184, 195–6, 318,

327, 335–6, 480, {iv}28–9, 31–2, 36–7, {vi}1, 130, 252, 302, 334, 609

Easter Rising (1916), {ii}10, 603–4, 606; DHL contemplates visit to, {ii}192, 195–6, 198, 201, 204, {iii}337, {vi}194–5, 219–20, 233, 282, 297, 302, 335, {vi}635; part of Celtic symbolism, {ii}248–9; rebels 'mostly windbags and nothings..tragically significant in death', {ii}611; edn of *Movements* in, {v}324, 336, 495, 555; DHL's jocular conception of, {vi}283–4

Iron Age in Italy, The, see Randall-MacIver, D.

Irschenhausen (Germany), {i}431, 540–53 *passim*, {ii}19–23, 32, 44, 55–74 *passim*, 82–3, 134, {iii}716, {v}404, 416, 466, 512, 515, 526, {vi}1–2, 103, 128, 132–70 *passim*, 274, 277, {vii}48, 408–9, 423, 461, {viii}7, 105–6

Irving, Washington, *Life and Voyages of Columbus*, {vii}14

ISAACS, EDITH JULIET, {v}115, {vi}10, 335
   DHL publishes with, {v}115, 189, 195, 636, {vi}354
   Theatre Arts Monthly, {v}115, 189, 195, 636, {vi}10, 31, 354:
   Theatre: Essays on the Arts of the Theatre, {v}636, {vi}354
   Letters to {v}115–16, 189, 195, 636, {vi}354–5

Isaacs, Rufus Daniel, {iv}234

Isabel (Ysabel), {iv}438–41, 443, 450, 453, 459

Isabel Hotel (Mexico City), {v}202, 206

Isar river (Germany), {i}411, 413, 416, 425, 429, 435, 475, 540, 548, {ii}60, 87, 103, {vi}520, {vii}438

Isartal (Germany), {i}411–12, 414, 417, 419, 426, 428, 441, 540, 548, {vi}46, 58, 96, 130, 139, 144, 146, 162, 187, {vii}409, 438, {viii}105

Ischia (Italy), {iii}442, 451, {vii}510

Iseo, Lake (Italy), {iii}568–9, {iv}194–5

Isis, {i}86, {ii}454, {v}636, {vi}429

Isis Unveiled, see Blavatsky, H. P.

Isle of Man, {i}2, 139, 313, 526

Isle of the Blest, *see* Rananim

Isle of Wight, {i}132, 134–5, 173, 175, 278, {iii}454, {vii}161, 318

Israelites, {i}511, {ii}466, {v}42, {vi}382, 508

Istituto Britannico, *see* British Institute, Florence

Italian Riviera, {iii}401, {v}323, 326, 334, 496, {vi}366, {vii}40

Italy, {i}1, 10, 18, 165, 426–517 *passim*, 528, 540–1, 551, 553, {ii}20, 53, 57, 60, 64–6, 69, 84, 184, 189, 207, 637–8, 670, {iii}1, 7–9, 11, 17, 20, 33, 47, 116, 174, 229, 282, 294, 388, 398, 404–5, 449–55, 480, 488, 493–7, 500–1, 504, 520, 553, 574–5, 580–8, 593, 603, 605, 624–5, 649, 668–725 *passim*, {iv}2, 6–7, 26, 30, 33, 39–102 *passim*, 146–7, 157, 162, 201, 207, 215, 228, 263, 312, 414–15, 421, 532, {v}1, 5, 13, 30, 34, 36, 90, 92, 174, 183–4, 201, 265–6, 274, 282, 287, 294, 298–9, 312–14, 325–99 *passim*, 428–9, 438, 442, 452, 472, 494–9, 513–14, 525–6, 532, 546, 552, 562–3, 568, 589, 599–600, 623, 629–31, 635, 637, 650–1, {vi}13, 28, 72, 86–7, 107, 162, 167, 181–2, 257, 276, 284, 300–2, 310–11, 334, 338, 351, 398, 413, 441–2, 472, 490, 502, 505, 528, 530, 548, 558, 586, 594, 599, 610, {vii}5, 19, 22–3, 25–6, 28, 30, 54, 72, 90, 125, 127, 137, 165, 167, 169–70, 172–5, 178, 192, 195, 197, 200, 219, 251, 253, 277, 286, 289, 296, 306, 313, 318, 326–7, 329–37, 370, 378, 394, 398, 408, 415, 424, 427, 437, 444–517 *passim*, 540, 558, 561, 563, 585–6, 595, 600, {viii}7–8, 12, 30, 95–6, 98, 105

DHL 'can't bear to be in England' when in, {i}460, 554; learning language in, {i}474; *Hamlet* and *Ghosts* in, {i}505, 508; village life in, {i}508–9, {iii}450–1, {v}357; Germany palls after, {i}543, 546–7, 552, {ii}19; not judgmental, {i}544; social change in, {ii}148–9; Chianti in memory of, {ii}243, {iv}414; DHL longs for, {ii}319, 363, {iii}35, 207; climate better for health, {iii}19,

30, 401, 413; DHL proposes group of friends to live in, {iii}214–16; returns to, {iii}407–26; expensive, {iii}441–2, 451, 524, 534, 581, {vi}43, 45, 60, 62, 64–5, 69, 74, 77, 80–1, 169; postal strike, {iii}460–1, 464, 471; 'a ridiculous kingdom, politically', {iii}462, 483, 485, 495, 608–9; 'insouciance' gone from, {iii}475; shops bare in, {iii}530; travel in, {iii}539, 541, 584, 586, {iv}166–7, 194–5; 'going socialist', {iii}611–12; 'less and less agreeable', {iii}640; DHL tired of, {iii}664; 'will not revolute or bolsh', {iii}676–7; 'impudence and disorder' of, {iii}732; 'gone a little rancid', {iv}105, 139, 201, 203, 206; hates England and France, {iv}132–3; postal system unreliable, {iv}147, 172; no copyright law between England and, {iv}188, 196; prominence of fascists in, {iv}353, {v}550, 620, {vi}308; hunting small birds in, {v}377, 560; DHL prefers to America, {v}382, 418, 425; 'nice to live in', {v}402, 419; not so 'jolly' as before, {v}436; 'wildly nationalistic', {v}465; Germany 'more peaceful' than, {v}500; people 'dreary', {v}576; peasantry in, {v}609–10, 616, {vi}238, 336, 571; 'lack of physical freedom' in, {vi}55; DHL disenchanted with countryside in, {vi}56; Austria more refreshing than, {vi}118–19, 121–3, 125–30, 142, 151–2, 159; Frieda prefers {vi}178, 191, 194–6, {vii}74, 85, 155–6, 291–3, 298–9, 301–4, 309–11, 314; DHL has 'sort of revulsion' from, {vi}194–8, 200–6, 208, 221, 229, 262–4, 271, 279, 293, 313, 317, 329, 385, 434, {vii}107, 109, 152, 338, 347, 350; has 'not enough spunk', {vi}369; 'best when it comes to living', {vii}260, 273, 282–4, 292; rather boring after Spain, {vii}344; deflated, 'like a flat tyre', {vii}360, 362, 373

Ito, {vii}251

Iver (Buckinghamshire), {iii}396, {v}24, 34, 315, {vi}77, {vii}41

see also Bridgefoot

Ivy, *see* Litvinov, I.

Ixtaccihuatl (Mexico), {iv}536, {v}158
Ixtlan (Mexico), {iv}511–13, 516

'J', {i}80
  see also Chambers, J.
Jack im Buschland, see Lawrence, D. H., *The
  Boy in the Bush*
Jack, Jackie, *see* Clarke, J.; Hutchinson, St J.;
  Lindsay, J.; Murry, J. M.; Skinner, J.;
  Young-Hunter, J.
Jacksdale (Nottinghamshire), {i}369
Jackson, Catherine, *see* Carswell, C. R.
Jackson, Holbrook, {ii}366
JACKSON, WILLIAM, LTD, {vi}12–13,
  531, 547, {vii}35, 135
  order 45 copies of *LCL*, {vi}390, 440,
  463; order increased to 70, {vi}418, 480;
  cancel order, {vi}476–8; Enid Hilton
  reclaims copies from, {vi}477–8, 486–7,
  489–90, 492–4, 496, 512, 515; 'methodis-
  ing shit-bags', {vii}309; Lahr and
  {vii}483, 517, 560
  Letters to {vi}476–7
  Letters from {vi}390, 417–18, 518
Jacob Faithful, see Marryat, F.
Jacobs, William Wymark, {i}2, 152–3
Jacobsen, Jens Peter, *Mogens, and Other
  Stories*, {iv}507
Jade Mountain, The, see Bynner, H. W.
Jaeger, Amos J., {iv}510
Jaeger, Mrs Amos J., {iv}510
Jaffa (Palestine), {v}343
JAFFE, EDGAR, {i}391, 395, 426–7, 431,
  {ii}77–8, {iv}25, {vi}34, {viii}106
  condones wife's infidelity, {i}413; at
  Irschenhausen DHL uses house of,
  {i}541, 543, {ii}19, 21, 44, 60, 63,
  {vi}138, 141–3; Bavarian Finance
  Minister, {iii}311, 314, 316, 320, 331,
  333–4, 348; death of, {iii}711, 717; had
  'gone cracked', {iii}728; rich Jew, 'died
  of funk', {vi}281–2
  *Archiv für Sozialwissenschaft und
  Sozialpolitik*, {v}486
  Letters to {ii}145–6
JAFFE, ELSE, {i}391, 393–4, 409, 411, 421,
  430, 531, 535, 537, {ii}21, 23, 25, 75,
  146, 162, {iii}26, 311, 348, 373, 375, 505,
  623, 678, 686, 714, 724, {iv}38, 40, 44,
  49, 122, 136–7, 162, 199, 206, 256, 289,
  294, 357, 396, {v}135, 178, 191, 244,
  343, 369, 489, 502–3, 514, 635, {vi}1, 34,
  38, 95, 128–30, 132–43, 145–8, 162, 166,
  187, 192–3, 215, 218, 243, 252, 281–2,
  312, 316, 329, 336, 339–40, 350–3,
  350–3, 356, 361, 366–7, 398, 429, 509,
  537, 554, 556–7, 562, 565, 569, 574, 578,
  584–6, {vii}11, 74, 360, 409, 431, 436,
  438, 450, 461, 543, 567, 588, 591–2,
  618, 621–3, 632–3, {viii}31, 53, 92,
  106
  'sort of woman one reverences', {i}395;
  mistress of Alfred Weber, {i}395, 415,
  {ii}186, {iii}716, {vi}317; infidelity
  condoned by husband, {i}413; DHL
  encourages to write for *English Review*,
  {i}513–14; 'arranges other folk's affairs',
  {i}530; dedication of *Rainbow* to,
  {ii}349, 354; death of her son, {ii}415;
  might translate for DHL, {iii}601;
  widowed, {iv}25; *Aaron's Rod* for,
  {iv}259, 264; DHL sends money to,
  {iv}311, 434, 532; *Captain's Doll* for,
  {iv}390; translating into German for
  DHL, {v}38–9, 92–3, 96, 173, 189, 252,
  331, 485, 554–5, 558, 561, 621, {vi}76,
  140, 153, 173, 189, 199, 213, 236–7, 277,
  616, {vii}51, 553, 597, 598, 609–10; 'has
  a will-to-America', {v}63; sends MS of
  S and L, {v}65; *Plumed Serpent* for,
  {v}417; kind to DHL, {vi}178, 180; *St.
  Mawr* for, {vi}275, 291, 294–5; *Collected
  Poems* for, {vi}589; pirated copy of *LCL*
  for, {vii}246; *Pansies* for, {vii}362; lacks
  'the peculiar *mastery* a translator needs',
  {vii}572; *Escaped Cock* for, {vii}630
  Letters to {i}486, 513–15, {ii}48–50, 54–5,
  415–16, {iii}344–6, 716–17, {iv}222–3,
  262–4, 282, 310–11, {v}29, 96, 404,
  416–17, 464–6, 512–13, 515, 526, 554–5,
  558–9, 621, {vi}74–6, 103, 148–50,
  156–7, 171–3, 198–9, 213, 236–7, 261–2,
  273–4, 277, 294, 368–9, 391–2, 487–8,
  586, 589, 598–9, 611, {vii}253–4,
  331–2, 422–3, 433–6, 509–10, 598–9,
  630

JAFFE, FRIEDRICH ('FRIEDEL'), {i}421,
{ii}23, 50, 58, {iii}716, {iv}25, 118,
121–2, 135–7, 161–2, 262, 311, 531–2
{v}8, 61, 63, 125, 134–5, 172, 216,
238–9, 244, 252, 285, 285, 404, 417, 465,
469, 486, 488–9, 491, 513, 555, 605,
{vi}34, 154, 173, 192–3, 237, 252, 281,
{vii}630
  stays with DHL at Kiowa, {v}254,
  258–9, 265–6, 268–9, 276–8, 280–1; in
  Paris with DHL, {vii}225, 233, 241
  Letters to {ii}24–5, {viii}91–2
Jaffe, Hans, {i}421, {ii}25, {iv}25, 135–6,
  311, 531–2, {v}466, 555, {vi}34, 237,
  {vii}422–3
Jaffe, Marianne, {i}421, {ii}25, 145, {iv}25,
  121–2, 135–6, 311, 531–2, {v}417, 465,
  555, {vi}34, 173, 192–3, 237, {vii}422,
  433–4, 510
Jaffe, Peter, {i}421, {ii}25, 58, 415–16
Jahreszeiten, see Seelig, K.W.
Jaime, *see* Angulo, J. de
Jakobsen, J. P., *see* Jacobsen, J. P.
Jalisco (Mexico), {iv}436–57 *passim*, 474,
  507, 509, 512–13, 519, 521, 529, 534,
  537–9, {v}220, 273
James, {iv}239
James and Edgar, {iii}729–30
James I, {vii}168
James Tait Black Memorial Prize, {i}315,
  {iii}573, {iv}575
  awarded for *Lost Girl*, {iv}7, 146–7, 150,
  157, 186, 304
James, Henry, {i}12, 138, 278, {ii}26, 360,
  {v}646, {vi}58, 435, 476
  view of *Rainbow* not known, {ii}440,
  446–7; his 'subtle conventional design',
  {ii}451
James, William, *Varieties of Religious
  Experience*, {iii}355
JAMESON, C. K. WALTON
  Letters to {ii}536
Jan, *see* Juta, J.
Jane Eyre, see Brontë, C.
'Jane', {i}364
Janitor's Boy and Other Poems, see Abarbanel,
  N.

Japan, {iii}658, 683, {iv}39, 43, 49, 141, 239,
  263, 279, 361, {vii}576
  see also Ito
Jardin, G., {vi}514
Jaroso (USA), {iv}389, 416
Jarquin de Monros, Doña María, {v}163, 202
Jarquin, Maruca Monros, {v}165, 203
Jaufen Wirts-Haus (Austria), {i}450
Java, {iv}138, 143, 279, 329, {v}371
Jean Paul, see Harich, W.
Jeanne d'Arc, see Garnett, E.
Jefferies, Richard, {i}405
  The Open Air, {i}137;
  The Story of My Heart, {i}337, 353,
  {ii}243
Jeffers, Robinson, {iv}12, {v}358
Jehanne, *see* Moulaert, J.
Jenbach (Austria), {vii}477
JENKINS, ANNIE LOUISA, {iv}8, 217,
  220, 228, 232–3, 235–6
  LWHCT or *New Poems* for, {iv}248;
  Aaron's Rod for, {iv}259; in London,
  {iv}309
  Letters to {iv}217–18, 222, 224–5, 237,
  240–1, 250–1, 271–2, 302–3, 474
Jenkins, Arthur George, {iv}217
Jenkins, Oliver, {iv}407
  Letters from {iv}407
Jenkinson, Elizabeth Anne, {i}352, 354, 356
JENKINSON, FRANCIS JOHN HENRY,
  Letters to {viii}27
Jenkinson, Walter, {i}351, 354, 356
Jenner, Mrs Henry (Katharine Lee),
  Christian Symbolism, {ii}242, 250,
  252–3, 293
JENNINGS, BLANCHE MAY RUST, {i}2,
  6, 11
  invited to read early version of *White
  Peacock*, {i}43–4, 48–9, 52–3, 55, 58, 61,
  63, 65–7, 92; critique of *White Peacock*
  version 'exceedingly just', {i}68–9, 72,
  85–8; 'Art and the Individual' sent to,
  {i}63, 72, 80–1; Balzac novel for, {i}89,
  91–2; photo of DHL sent to, {i}100, 104;
  sends *Shropshire Lad*, {i}102–3, 106;
  three poems sent to, {i}108–11; urged to
  read *Tono-Bungay*, {i}119–20, 128, 142,

154, {iii}166; not a subscriber to
Signature, {ii}391

Letters to {i}43–5, 47–69, 71–3, 79–81,
85–9, 91–2, 98–104, 106–11, 118–21,
126–8, 140–2, 153–4

Jennings, Richard, {vi}71

Jericho (Palestine), {ii}278, {iii}277,
{v}42–3

Jerrold, Douglas William, *Mrs Caudle's
Curtain Lectures*, {i}5, 474

Jerusalem (Palestine), {ii}258, 625, 661,
{iii}34, 150, 277, 285, 299, 716, {iv}212,
{vi}316, {vii}290; 'New' {ii}254,
{iv}460, {vii}513

Jessie, *see* Chambers, J; Young, J. B.

JESTER, DAVID, Centaur Press publishes
Bibliography, {v}241, 271; also
Porcupine, {v}241, 255, 271–2, 279–80,
284, 295; subscribes for *LCL*, {vi}363,
450

Letters to {v}255, 271, 279–80, 284

Letters from {v}241, 280, 284

Jesus Christ, {i}86, 94, 411, {ii}141, 299,
593, {iii}124, 279, 443, 521, 617, 732,
{iv}212, 532, {v}102, 363, 423, 553,
{vi}100, 109, 221, 223, {vii}332, 606
DHL on atoning power of, {i}40,
{ii}283; substitute for mother-love,
{i}62; 'infinitely good but mortal',
{i}255–6; crucifixion of, {i}422,
{ii}248–9, {vii}545; Frieda declares
liking for, {i}506; Whitman martyr like,
{ii}129; Italian peasant on death of,
{ii}163; deleterious effect of command
to love neighbour by, {ii}192, 625,
{iii}734; Phoenix symbol of
Resurrection of, {ii}253; Forster and,
{ii}275, {iii}22; on blasphemy against
Holy Ghost, {ii}407–8; weeps over
Jerusalem, {ii}625; Dostoevsky and,
{ii}314, 646; DHL justifies words of,
{iii}80, 116; DHL rejects parallel with,
{iii}179–80; 'a back number', {iii}309,
{v}635; Resurrection of, {iii}694,
{vi}37; 'disastrously wrong', {v}205;
Murry and, {v}205–6, 368, 372, 383,
475, 504, 630, {vi}67, {vii}484, 501;

'more unsympatisch..the longer I live',
{v}322; Creator more important than,
{v}328; Brett's picture of Crucifixion of,
{v}348–9, 365, 383, 390, {vi}24; *Escaped
Cock* and, {vi}50, {vii}122; DHL's
Resurrection painting, {vi}72, {vii}271;
at Christmas DHL 'sick of', {vi}237,
243

Jethou (Channel Isles), {iii}594, 608, 628,
{iv}36, {v}413, {vi}105, 111
see also Herm

Jeune Siberienne, La, see Maistre, F. X. de

Jew Süss, see Feuchtwanger, L.

JEW/JEWRY, Jehovah is idea of God for,
{i}255; Heinemann 'rotten little',
{i}424, 442; 'fat fatherly Jews' with cars
and 'bathing tents', {ii}37, 39; DHL at
'Jewish Cosher Supper', {ii}250–1;
Kot's Jewishness, {ii}305, {iii}43, 284,
{iv}24, {v}483, {vi}47, 66, 198, 203,
343, 476, 515, {vii}47, 66; printer of
Signature is 'little', {ii}385, 397; Kot
should write truthful novel of, {ii}562;
Gertler's *Merry-Go-Round* possible only
to a, {ii}660; Jews will 'utter..death-cry
of this epoch', {ii}661; 'Gertler, Jew-
like..told every detail of his life' to
Cannan, {iii}44, 50; cause of hatred of,
{iii}136–7; Jews '*know*' truth from
untruth' but betray it, {iii}144; political
Jewry, {iii}150; DHL dislikes 'Judas and
Jews very much', {iii}160; DHL shares
Gibbon's view of, {iii}242–3; Barbara
Low 'the Jewish magpie', {iii}307; Jaffe
a 'rich', {iii}316, {vi}281; Huebsch a,
{iii}318, 400, 643, 675; Jews 'capable of
the eternal detachment of judgment',
'connoisseurs' and 'dealers', {iii}400;
DHL a wandering, {iii}435, {iv}238,
255; DHL doesn't 'really like', hates and
is wary of, {iii}547, 678; 'curse *all* jews',
{iii}674; need for novel emphasising
distinctive character of, {iii}690;
German 'money hogs in motorcars',
profiteers, mainly, {iv}33, 38; Mountsier
detests, {iv}113; Stein 'a nasty, nosy,
corrupt.. shitten', {iv}127, 182; savagery

JEW/JEWRY (cont.)
    of Red Sea indelibly associated with,
    {iv}212; Seltzer 'tiny but
    trustworthy..one of the *believing* sort',
    {iv}366, 372; DHL 'sick ..of the Jewish
    monotheistic string', {v}67; 'all Judases',
    {v}165; Judas a, {v}205; Gertler marries
    a, {v}220; Knopf Jewish 'but *rich* and
    enterprising', {v}245; Jewish conscious-
    ness comprises wholly inherited images,
    {v}262; Untermeyer a wandering,
    {v}540; Burrow denies being, {v}612;
    Franchetti a, {vi}81; 'every Jew is a
    Jehovah', {vi}100; Secker 'another',
    {vi}515; *American Caravan* 'of course..a
    Jewish selection', {vii}139; *Sergeant
    Grisha* 'sort of Jewish', {vii}166;
    Goldston a, {vii}170, 253, 579; on
    Mallorca admixture of, {vii}275; Mabel
    Luhan's houses better empty than filled
    with 'Jews and Jew-gaws', {vii}276; anti-
    Semitic proverb, {vii}304; Cournos a
    miserable, {vii}482; Marks a bookseller
    and, {vii}496; Carter's drawings falsely
    inspired by, {vii}508; St John's 'Jewish
    nasal sort of style..the moral Jew-boys',
    {vii}519, 544–5; Boni 'little Jew in a big
    overcoat', {vii}521; DHL resents
    exploitation by 'little Jew booksellers',
    {vii}647
Jewish Contingent, The, *see* Palestine Zionist
    Commission
Jewish Encyclopaedia, The, see Adler, C.
'Jim Lawson', *see* Nylander, J. W.
Jinny, *see* Bolton, S. J.
Jix, *see* Hicks, Sir W. J.
JMming, *see* Murry, J. M.
Joan, *see* Farjeon, J.; King, J.
'Joanna', *see* Carswell, C.
Joconde ou les Coureurs d'Aventures, see
    Etienne, C.-G.
Joey, *see* Chamberlain, J.
Johanna, *see* Krug, J. von; Schriebershofen, J.
    von
Johannes, *see* Carswell, J. P.
Johannesburg (South Africa), {iii}663
John Bull, {ii}371, {iii}4, 60, {iv}4,
    {vii}389

    attacks *W in L*, {iv}88, 90, 104–5, 115,
    125–6; denounces *LCL*, {vi}13, 598,
    603–4, 609, {vii}19, 23–4, 34, 53, 58, 68,
    100, 141, 144, 164
    see also Bottomley, H. W.
John Chilcote, see Thurston, K. C.
'John Hop(s)', {vii}168, 292
John of Patmos, {vii}524
John Patrick, *see* Carswell, J. P.
John the Baptist, {iii}124, 670, {v}482
John, *see* Evans, J. G.
John, Augustus Edwin, {ii}208, 288, {iii}13,
    158, 176, 261, 305, {v}11, 572, {vi}283,
    {vii}8
John, Gwen, {vii}8
Johnnie, *see* Juta, J.
JOHNS, ORRICK, {vi}376
    Letters to {vi}376
JOHNS, RICHARD, *Pagany*, {vii}524–5
    Letters to {vii}524
Johnson, Dorothy, {v}403, 405
Johnson, Dr Samuel, {iv}1, {vi}6
Johnson, Harry Roland, {iv}481, 507,
    509–10, 526, {viii}85
JOHNSON, OLIVIA ROLFE, {iv}481, 507,
    526, {viii}85
    Letters to {iv}510
JOHNSON, WILLARD ('SPOODLE',
    'SPUD'), {iv}12, 15, 316, 385, 404, 436,
    484, 506, 534, 547, 579, 595, {v}3, 40,
    42, 66, 82–4, 150, 156, 158, 185, 191,
    199, 233, 235, 237, 268, 281–2, 347, 358,
    362, 379, 417, 458, 471, 511, 586, 598,
    {vi}38, 58, 74, 101, 127, 176, 224, 310–1,
    319, 357–7, 382, {viii}76, 79
    publishes DHL in *Laughing Horse*,
    {iv}321, 331, 367, 555, 561, 567, {v}27,
    66, 393, {vii}485 ; invited to accompany
    DHL to Mexico, {iv}388, 405–6; in
    Mexico, {iv}420–3, 426, 434, 441, 443,
    453, 455, 457, 473; *Kangaroo* for,
    {iv}515; invited to Del Monte, {v}54–6,
    88–9; looks after Friedel Jaffe, {v}285;
    Laughing Horse issue dedicated to DHL,
    {v}343–4, 472, 487; *LCL* for, {vi}416,
    431, 433, 436, 445, 469, 476, 518, 551,
    {vii}25; *Collected Poems* for, {vii}387,
    472; *Pansies* for, {vii}414, 472

Letters to {iv}321, 331, 366–7, 388–9,
    405–6, 424–5, 441, 468, 473, 497,
    515–16, 536–7, 554–5, 561, 567,
    {v}27–8, 47–8, 59–60, 66, 81, 100,
    127–9, 132, 151, 155–6, 280–1, 285, 484,
    497, 600–1, {vi}416, {vii}485–6
Joiner, Mr, *see* 'Journeyman'
Jokl, Katherine, {iii}243
Jolyffe, Miss, {v}589
Jones & Evans Bookshop, {ii}407,
    {viii}16
Jones, Dr Ernest, {ii}18, 258, 623, {iii}243
    subscriber to *Signature*, {ii}404; DHL's
    ideas on 'primal consciousness' given to,
    {iii}400
Jones, Hilda Mary, {i}83, 97, 115, 138, 166,
    168–9, 208, 227, 248, 298, 300, 332,
    {v}640
    comforts DHL 'inexpressibly', {i}94;
    DHL's 'soul enlarged' by contact with,
    {i}99; laughs 'like a blackbird in a bush',
    {i}102; poem addressed to, {i}108–9;
    'the prettiest youngster in England...face
    is like apple blossom buds', {i}253;
    conversation with, {i}257
JONES, JOHN WILLIAM, {i}82–3, 108,
    114, 162, 211–12, 249, 253–4, 282, 298,
    300, 312, 364, {ii}20, {iii}62, {v}640
    'affable', {i}86; 'an inflated frog' but
    'decent', {i}89; DHL plays chess with,
    {i}94; 'paints like a bird pecking crumbs
    off the doorstep', {i}207; 'mean..
    prudent..nervous', {i}263; gave
    condoms to DHL, {i}286; DHL uses
    typewriter brought home by, {i}327;
    DHL disenchanted with, {i}332, 455;
    his mode of speech, {i}450–1
    Letters to {i}498
JONES, MARIE, {i}82–3, 117, 152, 169,
    200, 211, 236, 248–9, 279, 282, 300, 302,
    315, 332, 344, 364, 455, {iii}62
    'a splendid woman', {i}86; enjoys DHL's
    sole company, {i}253–4; reveals marital
    secrets, {i}298; writes letter for DHL
    when ill, {i}328; *S and L* for, {ii}20
    Letters to {i}498
Jones, Robert ('Bobby') Edmond, {v}107,
    540, 642

Jones, Tom, {vii}325, 333, 338
Jones, Winifred, {i}83, 89, 97, 168–9, 208,
    227, 248, 257, 300, 332
'Jont(y)', *see* Holbrook, M. M.
Jordaens, Jacob, {i}124
José, {iv}325, {v}53, 585
Joseph Conrad: An Appreciation, see
    O'Flaherty, L.
Joseph, *see* Barezzi, G.
JOSEPH, MICHAEL, {v}285, {vi}482–3
    on publishing *Glad Ghosts*, {v}523,
    535–6, 539, 543; buys *LCL*, {vii}84, 131
    Letters to {v}523, 535–6, 539, 543
Journal of the Royal Asiatic Society, The, {i}8
JOURNALISM, DHL wonders how to
    'squeeze my jostled, winded way into',
    {i}52, 303; likes journalist Hubert,
    {i}102; Murry makes 'quite a lot by',
    {ii}539; Mountsier 'real journalist',
    Esther Andrews not so, {iii}27;
    Cannan's *Mendel* 'piece of
    journalism..without spark of creative
    fire', {iii}35, 44, 50; Goldring 'sly
    journalist', {iii}469; DHL confused
    with David Lawrence, 'fairly well-known
    journalist', {v}287; in story 'sub-
    conscious' must be made conscious,
    'otherwise you have', {v}294; compro-
    mise with 'journalism and commerce' in
    US stultifies creativity, {v}308; DHL's
    success in, {vi}4, 6–7, 401, 403–4; '*far
    the best way of making money*', {vii}41;
    when compared to Hardy, 'Bennett is
    only a journalist', {viii}18
    see also Daily Chronicle, *Daily Express*,
    Evening News, *Sunday Dispatch*
'Journeyman', 'Mr Joiner and the Bible',
    {iv}462
Jove, {i}228, 263, 304, 344, 397, 429, 504,
    {ii}107, 109, 431, {iii}691, {iv}365,
    {v}66, {vi}96, 157, {viii}8
Joy Go With You, see 'Kranzler, N.'
Joy, see Galsworthy, J.
Joyce, James, {vi}489, 545, {vii}233, 236,
    653
    suspected as 'trickster', {iv}275;
    generally bracketed with DHL, {iv}340;
    DHL reluctant to publish remarks on,

Joyce, James (*cont.*)
    {iv}355; provides 'a stupid *olla podrida*
    of the Bible...stewed up fragments of
    quotation in the sauce of a would-be-
    dirty mind', {vi}507–8; 'bores me stiff',
    {vi}548; on *LCL*, {vii}7; in cartoon
    alongside DHL, {vii}206
Finnegan's Wake, {vi}507, {vii}7;
    Ulysses{iv}19, 275, 306, 319–20, 324,
    330, 335–6; DHL 'can't read', {iv}340;
    DHL 'wearied' by - 'so like a schoolmas-
    ter with dirt and stuff in his head',
    {iv}344–5; {v}359, 450, 457, {vi}7,
    507–8, {vii}62, 67, 115, 229, 291, 396–7,
    601; 'wildly expensive', {viii}56
Joynson Hicks, Sir William, *see* Hicks, Sir W.
    J.
Juan les Pins (France), {iv}299
Juarez (Mexico), {iv}412–13, {viii}78
Juárez, Benito, {iv}528
Jud Süss, see Feuchtwanger, L.
Judas, {i}51, {ii}164, {iii}160, {v}203,
    {vii}298
    Russell and Lady Ottoline are like,
    {ii}381; DHL surrounded by Judases,
    {ii}500; 'Jews all Judases', {v}165;
    Murry not a genuine, {v}205
Jude the Obscure, see Hardy, T.
Judge, *see* Ford, Judge J.
Jugend, {vi}140, 149, 153, 155–6, 163, 167,
    173, 185, 350
    Else Jaffe translates 'Rex' for, {vi}189,
    277, {vii}74
Julian the Apostate, {i}114
Jumilhac (Jumiac), Comtesse de (Constance
    Atherton), {vii}217, 291, 488
Jung, Carl Gustav, {i}475, 543, {ii}322,
    {iii}301, 307, 309, 343, 623, {iv}66, 585,
    {v}23, 125, 261, {vi}57–8, 182, 214, 393
    'very interesting, in his own sort of fat
    muddled mystical way', {v}540
'Jungfrau Max', *see* Mohr, M.
Jupiter, {iii}48, 343, 395, {iv}212
JUTA, JAN ('JANNIE', 'JOHINNIE',
    'JOHNNIE'), {iii}491, 496, 506, 508,
    526, 602, 620, 624, 640, 656, 658, 666,
    683, 686–8, 699, {iv}5, 81. 89, 141, 150,

156–7, 163, 186, 192, 201, 259, 329,
    {v}264, 436, 444
    charcoal sketch of DHL by, {iii}535,
    550, 560, 577, 605, 613, 653; DHL stays
    at Anticoli with, {iii}574, 578–87; DHL
    in Venice with, {iii}603–11; visits
    Sardinia, {iii}692, 694, 697, 705, 731;
    illustrations for *S and S* by, {iv}24, 26–8,
    34–5, 39, 42, 45, 47–8, 52, 58–60, 121,
    123, 137–8, 143, 158, 168–9, 366, {v}264,
    {viii}41–2
Letters to {iii}535–6, 550–2, 567–8, 665,
    {iv}24–6, 42–3, 45, 137–9, 158–9, 244,
    366, {v}436
Juta, Réné, {iii}496, 506, 508, 568, 624, 665,
    {iv}43, 49, 244, 366
    Lost Girl for, {iii}648
    Concerning Corsica, {v}436;
    The Tavern, {iii}535

Kaffee Angermaier (Rottach), {vii}449–80
    passim
Kahane, Jack, {vii}297
KAHLER, ERIC VON, {vi}149–50, 156,
    167, 172–3, {viii}106
    Letters to {viii}106
Kahler, Josephine von, {vi}149–50, 156, 167,
    277, {viii} 106
'Kaléidoscope', *see* Verlaine, P.
Kallen, Horace Meyer, *Why Religion*,
    {vi}92
Kameny, Miss, {v}39, {viii}89
Kandy (Ceylon) {iv}7–8, 154, 171–234
    passim, 243, 256, 266–8, 278, 356–7,
    {viii}51, 54
Kandy Lake (Ceylon), {iv}216, 221
Kandy Perahera (Ceylon), {iv}8, 215–18,
    221, 234
Kansas City (USA), {iv}336
Kant, Immanuel, {vi}342
Karavan Tea, {iii}341, 347–8
Karawanken Alps (Austria), {vi}130, 134
Karlsruhe (Germany), {iii}409, {iv}29
Kastanienbaum (Switzerland), {v}339, 341,
    {vii}29
Katharine/Katherine, *see* Mansfield, K.;
    Throssell, K.

Katherina, Frau, *see* Kippenberg, K.

Katie, *see* Berryman, K.

Katzenstein, Nanette ('Nettie'), G., offers to translate *Lost Girl* into German, {viii}95–6

   Letters from {viii}95–6

Kauffer, Edward McKnight, {iii}184, {vii}585

Kaye-Smith, Sheila, {vii}516

Keate, George, *Account of the Pelew Islands*, {iii}594

Keatings, {i}240

Keats, John, {ii}223

   died of sex, {ii}101; Amy Lowell on, {iv}242–3, {v}198, 230; Murry on, {v}171, 322, 332, 335, 337, 367

   'La Belle Dame Sans Merci', {v}281; 'Ode to a Nightingale', {iii}366

Keble, John, {vi}333

Keen, Mr, {ii}429–30, 444

Kegan Paul & Co., {i}148, {v}391, {vi}90, 113, {vii}376

Keith-Johnston, Colin, {v}604

Kemmel Hill (France), {iii}2, 239

KENDRIGAN, MR, {vii}154, 341–2

   Letters to {vii}146

Kenilworth (Warwickshire), {viii}1

Kenley (Surrey), {i}300

Kennedy, Margaret Moore, {v}322, 324, 326, 332

   The Constant Nymph, {v}322, 324, 326, 332, {viii}93

Kennedy, Mrs, {iii}225

Kennedy-Fraser, Marjorie, {iii}164

   Songs of the Hebrides, {iii}164, 170, 180, {v}570; {viii}90

KENNERLEY, MITCHELL, {i}19, 188, 430, {ii}2, 17, 75, 98, 167, 175, 271, 518, {iii}128, 627, 650, {iv}15, 150, 156, {v}146, {vi}12, {vii}52, 66, 130, 320, 522, {viii}71

   publishes *Trespasser*, {i}522, 542, {viii}10; pays £12 for 'Soiled Rose' in *Forum*, {i}522, {ii}44; publishes *Love Poems*, {i}542, {vi}607; admires and publishes *S and L*, {i}542, {ii}26, 50, 67, 117, 174, {iii}547, 576, 612, 645, 651,

661; publishes *Widowing*, {i}542, {ii}55, 65, 71–2, 77, 80, 82, 127, 133, 135, 144–5, 147, 152, {iii}129, 527, 692, {vi}87; promises £25 for *S and L* royalties, {ii}99, 217, {iii}74; sends cheque for £35, {ii}165; *Rainbow* MS sent to, {ii}167, 190, 235, 243, 246, 279, {iii}644; bank refuses cheque for £10 from, {ii}174, 190, 210, 216–17, 223, 228, 243, 245–6, 256, 279, {iii}74, 612; 'swinish', {iii}653; DHL 'sees red' over *S and L* and, {iv}131, 318–19, 323, 325, {vi}64; 'that beast', {iv}170, 445; DHL through Mountsier initiates lawsuit against, {iv}376, 382, 390–2, 417–19; Mountsier and *S and L* royalties from, {viii}56, 67–8

   Letters to {ii}71–2, 77, 80–1, 144–5, 189–90, {viii}10–11

   Letters from {i}522, 542, {ii}26, 50, 72

Kent, {i}16, 241, 265, 297, 309, 314, 360, 362, {ii}24, 26–8, 31, 52–4, 70, 174, 191, 455, {iii}56, 372, {iv}116, {vi}51, 373, 520, {vii}353, {viii}11

Kent, Adrian, {vi}420, 433, {vii}19

Kent, Miss, {vi}420, {vii}19, {viii}111

Ker, William Paton, {iii}251

Kerckoff, Miss van, {vi}22

Kesselmatte (Gsteig), {vi}17, 452–568 *passim*, 593, {vii}105, 155, 299, 463–4

Keun, Odette, {vii}104, 120, 132, 160

Keynes, John Maynard, {ii}12, {vii}8

   'principle of evil' evident in, {ii}311; associated with vicious beetle, {ii}319; 'deep inward dirt' in, {ii}320–1; orders *LCL*, {vi}11, 383

Keyserling, Count Hermann, 'noble article' probably by, {iv}357; 'snobbish', {v}390; largely ignored in Europe, {vi}419; 'Mean swine' sought free copy of *Plumed Serpent*, {vii}618

   The Book of Marriage, {v}639, {vi}419

Khartoum (Sudan), {vi}1, 513

Khovántchina, *see* Moussorgsky, M. P.

'Kibbo-Kift', *see* Hargrave, J.

Kiepenheuer, Gustav, {vii}543, 567, 572, 596, 604

KILLICK, ROWENA, {vi}136, 254
  Letters to {vi}136–7, 139–40, 153–4, 167
Kimberley (Nottinghamshire), {i}176, 233,
  293, {ii}57, {vi}178
King John, see Shipley, J. T.
King Lear, see Shakespeare, W.
King, (Sir) Norman, {iv}534, 536, {v}156,
  203, 212, 218, 220
King, Ann, {i}278, {vii}562
KING, EMILY UNA, {i}36, 40, 116, 174,
  208, 224, 228, 231, 244, 257, 262, 266,
  268, 272, 278, 280, 284, 302, 316, 325,
  333, 336, 338, 340, 354, 379, 411, 454,
  {ii}323, 330, 485–6, 654, {iii}50, 56, 88,
  112, 123, 245–7, 316, 321, 339, 381–3,
  418, 426, 478, 574, 579, 595, 616, 670,
  677, 683, {iv}7, 377, 384, {v}1, 8–9,
  12–13, 37, 85, 114, 126, 193, 206, 304,
  312, 332, 352, 366, 476, 483, 489–90,
  492, 498, 501, 506, 514, 517, 527–8, 599,
  {vi}3, 5, 10, 17–18, 39, 63, 80, 87, 146,
  179, 217, 228, 235, 245, 402, 494, 562,
  597, {vii}1, 11, 107, 192, 259, 319, 346,
  352, 398, 532, 579, 592, 602, 620–1
  ignorant about DHL and Frieda, {i}497,
  {ii}42; DHL's publications sent to,
  {ii}19, 402, {iii}729, {v}80, 141, 150,
  184, 195, 197, 226, 244, 247, 258, 323,
  329, 413, 475, 590, 607, {vi}67, 69, 325,
  396, 414, {vii}128, 232, 321–2, 327, 330,
  347, 461, 530, 557, 559, 573; 'a queer
  creature..rather poor..not beautiful',
  {ii}270; nickname, 'Pamela, or *Virtue
  Rewarded*', {iii}328, {iv}60; second
  child born, {iii}550; 'Raphael Madonna'
  for, {iv}92; birthday present for,
  {iv}215–16; *Aaron's Rod* reluctantly sent
  to, {iv}261, 299, 342; cheque for,
  {iv}413, 423, 431; DHL sends £10 for
  mourning clothes on father's death,
  {v}124, 139; gifts for, {v}209, 214, 245,
  257, 350, 405, 499, 607, 654, {vi}106,
  234, 366, 457, 485, {vii}225, 510, 594;
  DHL visits, {v}530; DHL requests tea,
  {v}607, 635, 643–4, 653, {vi}147, 215,
  234, 262–3; 'lachrymose', {v}631, 633,
  {vi}387, 509, 556; 'too ladylike nowadays', {vi}287; invited to Gsteig,

{vi}457, 473, 507–9, 511, 513, 517, 519,
  527–53 *passim*; kept in ignorance of
  LCL, {vi}486, 489, 492, 533; yawning
  gulf between DHL and, {vi}530, 533,
  535, 542; transports DHL's paintings
  from Gsteig, {vi}540, 549; *LCL* revealed
  by *John Bull*, {vii}53, 68–9, 95, 97;
  advised not to read *LCL*, {vii}69, 76;
  visited paintings exhibition, {vii}351;
  forgot DHL's birthday, {vii}478, 494;
  invited to Bandol, {vii}621, 630–3, 636
  Letters to {i}416, {ii}402–3, {iii}420, 427,
  431, 436, 440, 508, 530, 583, 589, 641,
  {iv}44, 49–50, 54, 65, 87–8, 215–16, 285,
  302, 410–14, 423, 425, 431, 439, 468,
  535, 552, 564, 579, {v}100, 124–5, 139,
  149, 154, 162, 166–7, 179, 181, 195–6,
  214, 221, 227–8, 244–5, 257–8, 277–8,
  296, 309, 325–6, 328, 337, 350, 361–2,
  397, 405, 407, 474–5, 494, 499, 527, 530,
  538, 543–4, 549, 589–90, 607–8, 635–6,
  644–5, 653–4, 657, {vi}21–2, 25–6, 47,
  51, 59–60, 67, 97, 105–6, 110, 117–18,
  130–1, 134, 140–2, 177–8, 191–2, 200–1,
  215, 234–5, 262–3, 272, 285–6, 325,
  366–7, 394, 413–14, 423, 426, 441,
  454–7, 473–4, 484–5, 508–9, 564–5, 576,
  585, 589, 592, 612, {vii}17, 22, 52–3,
  69–70, 127–8, 187, 209–10, 216, 225,
  241, 254, 262, 326–7, 331, 338, 351, 364,
  366, 378, 393, 418, 436–7, 460–1, 481,
  490, 510–11, 558–9, 561–2, 581–2,
  593–4, 621–2, 641, 646–7, 652
KING, FREDERICK ALLEN, {vii}230
  Letters to {vii}226
KING, JOAN FRIEDA, {iii}706, {iv}469,
  {v}140, 167, 258, 278, 350, 352, 428, 448,
  474, 476, 480, 544, 579, 589–90, 598–9,
  635–6, 645, 657, {vi}5, 21, 39, 131, 134,
  142, 457, 474, {vii}17, 22, 327, 418, 461;
  birth of, {iii}550, 581, 595; DHL sends
  gift for, {v}112, 181, 405, 654, {vi}106,
  118, 217, 234, {vii}69, 594; ill-health of,
  {v}350, 352, 397–8, 538, 564–6, 607,
  653, {vi}25, 177–8, 191, 200, 215, 235,
  441, 509, {vii}210, 262
  Letters to {v}178, 360, 398
King, Joe, {i}228, 230

KING, MARGARET EMILY ('PEG', 'PEGGY'), {i}116, 208, 228, 243, 257, 278, 316, 325, 354, 416, {ii}403, 493, {iii}245–7, 436, 440, {iv}87, 564, {v}9, 11, 166, 214, 474–6, 549, 565, 590, 608, 636, 645, 654, {vi}5, 17–18, 21, 25, 97, 110, 134, 142, 286, 366, 592, {vii}17, 22, 259, 262, 646

DHL sends gift for, {i}231, {ii}289, {iii}434, 530, {v}112, 181, 350, 480, 499, {vi}106, 118, {vii}69, 366, 594, 621–2, 635; DHL 'very fond of', {ii}270; 'nervous overwrought', {ii}486; 'marvellous red-gold hair', {iii}328; wins scholarship to Grammar School, {iii}581, 595; Del Monte described for, {v}110–12; DHL offers help with education of, {v}124, 139–40; DHL interested in professional career of, {v}214, 258, 325–6, 337, 362, 448, 475, 479–80, 499, 538; encouraged to write in French, {v}564; told 'not to study too hard at anything', {vi}178; learning German, {vi}178, 235, 250, {vii}53; visit to Gsteig, {vi}473, 484–5, 493–4, 507–56 *passim*; 'mincing' young female, {vi}554; not to be allowed to read *LCL*, {vii}69; 'little prig' should be 'made to read *LCL* aloud and in company', {vii}127

Letters to {iii}418, 434, 463–4, 530, 588, 595–6, 610, 706, {iv}52–3, 60, 214, 289, 294, 381, 469, 493, 496–7, 502, 509, 511–12, 541, {v}30, 37, 110–12, 139–40, 178, 297, 321–2, 403–4, 409, 428, 447–8, 479–80, 493, 546–7, 564–5, 618, 641, {vi}86, 146–7, 164, 250, 493–4, {vii}299, 635–6

King, Samuel Taylor, {i}36, 244, 257, 278, 325, 416, {iii}245, {iv}44, {v}37, 474, 643, {vi}21, 80, 178, 413, {vii}17, 127, 513

in military hospital, {iii}339; shopkeeper, {v}366, 549, 564, 608, 631, {vi}25, 47, 59–60, 97, 106, 142, 366 ; not 'flush' with money, {v}476; serious deficit in shop accounts, {vi}285, 554, {vii}22, 69, 128; 'a little nonentity', {vi}556

King-Page, Douglas, {ii}615, 621–2

Kings Heath (Birmingham), {viii}1
King's Scholarship, {i}8, 25–6
Kingsley, Charles, {i}42, 210
Kingston Vale (Surrey), {i}117, 120
Kingston, William Henry Giles, {ii}588–9
Kiowa Ranch ('The Flying Heart', 'Lobo'), {iv}329, 333–6, 338–9, 342–3, {v}4–6, 8–10, 27, 40–120 *passim*, 140, 142–4, 146–50, 164–6, 169, 182, 190–1, 197, 199, 202, 208–9, 212, 215–19, 221–6, 230–96 *passim*, 298, 300, 306–7, 312–14, 333, 335, 344–5, 347, 355, 357–8, 362, 364, 379, 389–91, 395, 402, 412, 417–18, 421, 425–6, 438, 440–2, 453–5, 463, 465–7, 470, 476–8, 491–2, 497, 503–4, 506, 510, 514, 540–1, 559–60, 562, 567, 584–5, 595, 606, 613, 635, {vi}5, 58, 75, 85–6, 128, 136, 154–5, 175–6, 211, 219, 221, 232–3, 240, 242, 248, 255, 259, 264–5, 271, 276, 278, 282–3, 296, 299, 301, 310, 319, 323, 338, 349, 358–9, 362, 365, 367, 378, 382, 384–5, 436, 449, 468, 506–8, 522, 543, 550–1, {vii}5, 10–11, 29, 54–5, 96, 138, 183, 195, 197, 206, 213, 277, 287–9, 318, 506, 574, 614, 630, {viii}93, 95

legally transferred by Mabel Luhan to Frieda, {v}23, 29–30, 32, 35, 37–8; DHL moves into, {v}40; repairs to, {v}40–54, 248, 257–9; described, {v}62, 75, 110–12; MS of *S and L* given in exchange for, {v}105; DHL returns from Mexico to, {v}228; natural beauty of, {v}235–9; 'black-eyed Susan' at, {v}263, 266, 268–9, 272–3, 279, 282–3, 358; porcupines on, {v}278; 'long, weary journey' from Italy to, {v}429–30; 'a burden' to DHL, {v}457, 485; {vii}205; DHL and sale of, {v}537, 594, 600, 651–2, {vi}256, 443, 469, {vii}203, 263, 287–8, 292; 'sometimes I pine for it', {vi}208, {vii}25; DHL 'keen', Frieda not keen, on, {vi}284, 302; DHL abandons idea of returning to, {vii}312; MSS allegedly left at, {vii}342–3, 345, 472–5, 490, 505; DHL imagines 'a sort of old school, like the Greek philosophers' at, {vii}616

Kipling, Joseph Rudyard, {i}148, {ii}128,
   {iii}111, {vi}276, {vii}85, 198, 234
   'Ballad of East and West, The', {viii}25
KIPPENBERG, DR ANTON, {iii}7, 392,
   601, {iv}2, 40, 72, 84, 428, {v}252,
   {vi}52, 262, {vii}596
   offers to publish German translation of
   DHL's works, {iii}597–8, 617–18, 642;
   invited to Taormina, {iii}648–9, 667;
   sends books to DHL, {iii}679, 715,
   {iv}40, 117–18; proofs of *Rainbow*
   translation from, {iv}89, 117; payment
   for *Rainbow* to go to Frieda's mother,
   {iv}117, 132, 136, 147, {viii}48; DHL
   argues for Else Jaffe to translate *Plumed
   Serpent*, {v}332; proofs of *Plumed
   Serpent* to, {v}332, 340; 'tiresome old
   buffer', {v}558, 621; rejects claims for
   Else Jaffe, {v}561; DHL considers
   ending contract with, {vi}199, 524,
   572–3, {vii}32, 51; invites DHL to
   contribute to Carossa book, {vi}524;
   buys copy of *LCL*, {vi}612; continues as
   DHL's German publisher, {vii}51, 113;
   and possible translation of *LCL*,
   {vii}113–14, 139, 335, 375, 383, 386,
   410, 453, 517, 567; 'old twister',
   {vii}383; 'old serpent', {vii}410; 'falser
   than seventeen hells', {vii}517; 'the old
   pasha' tries to prevent any German
   translation of *LCL*, {vii}567, 615; DHL
   on relations with, {vii}571–2, 598,
   609–10
   Letters to {iii}597–8, 617–18, 642, 648–9,
   679–81, 715, {iv}40–1, 71, 80, 89,
   117–18, 132–3, 260, {v}252–3, 331–2,
   561, {vi}524, 572–3, {vii}113
   Letters from {vii}139
Kippenberg, Katharina, {iii}648, 667,
   {v}253, 561, {vi}199, 213, 262,
   {vii}113–14
   'quite snappy' in letter, {vi}236;
   'Princess' and proofs of *WWRA* to,
   {vi}275, 277, 281, 291, 294–5; buys
   LCL, {vi}612
Kipping, Frederic Stanley, {i}514
Kipping, Lily, {i}514

Kipps, see Wells, H. G.
Kirk, Adelaide, {vi}498, 507, 510
Kirk, James Prior, {i}334, 344
Kirkby (-in-Ashfield) (Nottinghamshire),
   {i}23, {vi}47
Kit(ty), *see* Holderness, E.
Kitchener (Lord), Horatio Herbert, {ii}379
Kitson, Robert Hawthorn, {iii}10, 552–3,
   620, 624, 636–7, 639–40, {iv}125
Klapps, {vi}61, 72, 78
Klatt, Fritz, *Die Schöpferische Pause*, {v}509,
   533–4, {vi}120, 136
Kleeck, Mary Abby van, {vi}10, 335
Klu-Klux-Klan, *see* Ku Klux Klan
KNOPF, ALFRED ABRAHAM, {iii}471,
   500, {iv}9, 240, 544, {v}78–9, 255, 301,
   318, 358, 384, 473, 481, 492, {vi}8–10,
   12, 504, 538–9, 548, 572, 591, 602, 607,
   {vii}3, 38, 111, 394, 453, 521–2, 534,
   588, 638, {viii}91–3, 115
   DHL considers transferring to, {v}161,
   193; publishes *St. Mawr*, {v}206–7, 213;
   'Jew...but *rich* and enterprising', {v}245;
   US edn of *Plumed Serpent* by, {v}253,
   260, 267–9, 272, 288, 320, 342, 365, 370;
   claims sole right to publishing DHL,
   {v}271, {viii}94; publication of *David*,
   {v}274–5, 336, 340, 346, 415, 421, 454,
   460, 581, 623, 638; DHL feels 'safe'
   with, {v}303, 306; will publish *Max
   Havelaar*, {v}393, 446, 449, 452, 458,
   493, {viii}56; edn of *M in M* by, {v}581,
   594, 596, 636, {vi}31, 69–70, 73, 101;
   and *LCL*, {vi}29, 222, 253, 271, 288–9,
   292, 309–10, 314–15, 335, 372–4, 395,
   448, 470, 526, {vii}383, {viii}114; and
   WWRA, {vi}152, 254, 280, 376, 432,
   462. {vii}239–40, 243, 308, 386, 391; and
   Etruscan Places, {vi}181–2, 253, 344;
   'striped trousers and ineffectual bounce'
   of, {vi}343; refuses *Collected Poems*,
   {vii}27, 174, 236, 320, 395, 568; and
   Pansies, {vii}266, 297, 301–3, 305,
   312–13, 315, 324, 328, 347, 413–14, 467,
   485, 496, 516, 552, 593; 'a bore – and as a
   publisher..on the wane', {vii}349;
   'damned slow', {vii}413, 467; 'Knopfian

gentility', {vii}463; considers collected
edn of DHL, {vii}569, 584; to publish
Assorted Articles, {vii}623–4
  see also *Borzoi, The*
Letters to {v}249–50, 274, 320–1, {vi}182,
  253–4, 372–3
KNOPF, BLANCHE, {v}243, 250, 268, 274,
  306, 392, 450, 454, 473, 492, {vi}182,
  {vii}588
  expected to be sympathetic to *LCL*,
    {vi}253–4, 309, 359, 371–2, 374–6,
    {viii}14; 'cares for' DHL, {vi}526;
  DHL refuses to transfer from Secker to
    Knopf, {vii}37, 40, 45
  see Knopf, A. A.
  see also *Borzoi, The*
Letters to {v}243–4, 251, 256, 260, 303,
  320–1, 341–2, {vi}309, 359, {vii}37
Letters from {v}251, 256
Knowlson, T. S., {ii}409
Komroff, Manuel, {vii}625–6, 637
Kosciusko, Thaddeus, {i}114
Koteliansky, Beila, {iii}632, 658, {vi}169
KOTELIANSKY, SAMUEL
  SOLOMONOVICH ('KOT'), {ii}4, 12,
  205, 221, 242–3, 274, 280, 451, 481, 531,
  549, 551, 557, 567, 570, 584, 652, 657,
  {iii}1, 4–5, 8, 11–12, 14–15, 23, 27–8, 79,
  104, 119, 175, 181, 183, 199, 226, 240,
  250, 271, 276, 301, 372, {iv}7, 16–17, 20,
  28, 261, 375, 377, 398, 481, 483, 532,
  537–41, 559, 563, 599, {v}9, 15, 36, 170,
  311, 313, 332, 344, 350, 531, {vi}2,
  11–12, 15, 17, 55, 109–10, 194, 405–7,
  414, 440, 478, {vii}1, 12, 84, 198, 319,
  346, 434, 437, 443, 489, 498, 531, 568,
  619, 635, {viii}14, 86, 98, 103
  DHL meets, {ii}205; invited to
    Chesham, {ii}210, 212–13, 237, 257;
    short of money, {ii}212–13, 251,
    {iii}214, 529, 553, {v}559, 586, {vi}198;
    types *Hardy*, {ii}220, 227–9, 233–4, 239;
    and 'Rananim', {ii}252, {iii}23, 69, 78,
    90, 173, 208, 214, 216, 316, {iv}165, 241,
    350, {v}367, 557; with DHL when war
    declared, {ii}268, 276, {v}354–5;
    unpredictable, inert and melancholy,

{ii}290–1, 305, 308, 313–14, 614, {iii}23;
invited to Greatham, {ii}290–1, 295–6,
304, 310, 312; 'bossy and overbearing
Jew', {ii}305; types DHL's 'philosophy',
{ii}313, 317, 323, 333, 343; business-
manager for *Signature*, {ii}385, 407,
409–13, 418, 427–8, 447, 455, 461, 515,
529, {iv}323, 349; quarrels with Barbara
Low, {ii}488; gifts for DHL, {ii}545–6,
{iii}35, 315, 330–1, 348, 350, 363; and
translation, {ii}577, 588, 615; probably
will not be conscripted, {ii}650; his 'dog'
howl, {ii}660; character of, {iii}43;
Gertler's portrait of, {iii}43; offers DHL
£10, {iii}73, 78, 198, 209, 214–15, 260,
263, 327; has whole MS of *W in L*,
{iii}108–9; types essays for *SCAL*,
{iii}217–18, 228, 230–1, 261, 397, 399;
'tower of strength', {iii}277; 'ultra-
conscious Jew', {iii}284; DHL repays,
{iii}441–2; DHL offers loan to, {iii}560,
{iv}113, 297, {v}558; *Lost Girl* for,
{iii}632, 640; *W in L* for, {iii}725, 728;
Psychoanalysis for, {iv}23, 29–30, 37;
'Gentleman from San Francisco'
collaboration between DHL and,
{iv}23–4, 29, 37, 39, 58, 78–9, 87, 91,
130, 149–51, 165, 275, {vi}168–9; *S and
S* for, {iv}114, 165, 171, 193–4; *Aaron's
Rod* for, {iv}282, 296, 299; *EME* for,
{iv}349; *Fantasia* for, {iv}387; will look
after Frieda, {iv}498; conceives publishing project, {iv}556–7, 571, 574–5, 579,
581, {v}16, {vi}173–5, 180–1, 190–1,
202–4, 212, 225, 233, 247, 287–8, 322,
342–3; Kangaroo not be to identified
with, {v}143; 'a more ancient Judas'
than Murry, {v}205; *Porcupine* for,
{v}374–5; application for naturalisation
initially rejected, {v}418; DHl sends gift
for, {v}602; royalties on Shestov
translation, {v}624, 627–8, 634; report
on *David* production by, {vi}66; *M in M*
for, {vi}67, 69; 'in abysses of gloom',
{vi}155, 159; 'so Jehovahish', {vi}247,
{vii}47; No. 1 of numbered *LCL* for,
{vi}346; disapproves of *LCL*, {vi}458,

KOTELIANSKY, SAMUEL
SOLOMONOVICH ('KOT') (*cont.*)
469, 476; willingly helps over distribution of *LCL*, {vi}480–1, 483, 486–92,
494–7, 499–501, 510–11, 514–19,
529–30, 532, 535, 544–5, 561, 564, 570,
575, 579, {vii}47–9, 59–62, 68, 124–5,
131, 141–4, 154, 162, 168, 209, 233, 301;
'a very real Jew', {vi}515; 'such a fusser',
{vi}528; alarmist, {vi}558, {vii}151,
528; *Collected Poems* for, {vi}603–4;
intolerant, {vii}66; *LCL* 2nd edn as
Christmas gift to, {vii}82, 97, 134, 140,
142; to store DHL's MSS, {vii}278, 282,
296–7, 302, 318; *Paintings* for, {vii}321,
330; and *Pansies*, {vii}324, 328, 330, 340,
380, 488
Bunin, *The Gentleman from San
Francisco and Other Stories* (trans.),
{iv}274–5, {v}347;
Chekhov, *Literary and Theatrical
Reminiscences* (trans.), {vi}42;
Dostoievsky, *The Grand Inquisitor*
(trans.), {vii}618, 620, 629, 643;
Dostoievsky: Letters and Reminiscences
(trans.), {iv}462;
Dostoievsky, *Pages from the Journal of an
Author* (trans.), {ii}545, {iii}53, 183;
Gorky, *Reminiscences of Leonid Andreyev*
(trans.), {iv}16, 478, 482, 487;
Gorky, *Reminiscences of... Tolstoi* (trans.),
{iii}570, 632, 640;
Hippius, *The Green Ring* (trans.),
{iii}421, 425, 428, 442, 471, 658;
Koteliansky, Beila 'Two Jewish Stories',
(trans.), {vi}169;
Kuprin, *River of Life and Other Stories*
(trans.), {ii}562, 568, 577, {vi}174;
Rozanov, *Fallen Leaves* (trans.), {vii}82,
474, 538, 556, 575;
Rozanov, *Solitaria* (trans.), {vi}30, 41–2,
52, 81, 84;
Shestov, *All Things Are Possible* (trans.),
{iii}380–1, 387, 389, 392–3, 398–405,
407, 412, 433, 441–2, 455–6, 466, 471,
486, 500, 504, 510, 512, 516, 520, 529,
553, 560, {iv}275, {vii}474;

Tchekov, *Notebooks* (trans.), {iii}727;
Tolstoi, Countess Sophie, *Autobiography*
(trans.), {iv}274, 282;
Tolstoi's Love Letters (trans.), {iv}462
Letters to {ii}205–7, 210, 212–13, 220–2,
226–31, 233–4, 236–42, 250–3, 256–7,
260–1, 264, 269–70, 276–7, 287, 289–91,
295–6, 304–6, 308, 310, 312–14, 316–17,
323, 328–9, 333, 335, 343–4, 369, 382,
404, 407–13, 418, 427–8, 447, 455,
458–9, 461, 483–4, 488, 491, 498–9,
514–15, 529–30, 536–7, 545–6, 554, 562,
568–9, 588–91, 594, 607–8, 614–16, 618,
621–3, 628, 636–9, 646–7, 649–51,
654–5, 666–8, {iii}23, 35–6, 40–1, 43, 45,
52–4, 62, 68–9, 73–4, 77–8, 89–90,
102–4, 108–9, 112, 114, 117, 121, 124–5,
136–7, 162–3, 191–5, 198, 208, 212–14,
217–20, 228–31, 235, 256–7, 260, 263–4,
267, 269–72, 275, 277, 284–5, 292, 310,
315–19, 321, 326–7, 329–32, 335–7,
339–42, 346–52, 354–6, 363, 366–7,
375–6, 380–4, 387, 392–3, 397–9, 401–5,
408, 421, 425, 428, 433, 441–2, 471, 482,
486, 500–1, 510–12, 515–16, 560, 570,
632, 640, 658, 675–6, 725, 727–8, {iv}23,
29–30, 36–8, 78–9, 87, 91, 113–14, 149,
151, 165–6, 171–2, 184–5, 194, 202, 208,
220, 228, 241–2, 253, 274–6, 282, 291,
296–7, 349–50, 386–7, 397, 410, 420,
454–5, 462, 468, 478, 482, 487, 498–9,
519–20, 539, 550, 563, 565–6, 570–1,
574–5, 579, 583, 587, 589, 597,
{v}15–16, 347, 354–5, 366–7, 374–7,
397–8, 403–5, 418–19, 454–5, 482–3,
501, 504–6, 508, 513, 516, 521–2, 524,
527–9, 535–6, 539, 546, 557–8, 601–2,
627–8, 634, {vi}30–1, 41–2, 47, 51, 66–7,
81–3, 98, 122–3, 135, 144, 159, 168–9,
173–5, 180–1, 190–1, 203–4, 224–5,
233–4, 246–7, 271, 322–3, 346–7, 356,
375–6, 401–2, 421, 424, 427, 437, 458–9,
481, 486, 488–9, 495–6, 500, 510–11,
517, 529–30, 545–6, 563–4, 579, 585,
590, 604, {vii}18, 39–40, 49, 60, 82, 125,
141–3, 147, 162–3, 167–8, 197, 209, 282,
302–3, 319–20, 330, 473–4, 518, 537–8,

575–6, 604–5, 618, 620–1, 629, 643,
{viii}86
Letters from {vi}66, {vii}592–3
Kouyoumdjian, Dikran (Michael Arlen),
{ii}476, 496, 501, 510, 516, 598, {vi}9,
223–4, 237, 253, {vii}520, 523, 534,
539–40, 648–9
'a bit blatant and pushing' but *'very
good'*, {ii}473–4; 'self-assertive.. tiresome..disintegrated', {ii}504–5; DHL
doesn't care for, {ii}507–8; gossips,
{ii}512; 'a sad dog' but highly successful, {vi}220–1, 223–5, 227, 236; model
for Michaelis in *LCL*, {vii}476
The Green Hat, {vi}9, 220, 223, 225,
227, 236, 239
Kra, *see* Soupault, P.
'Kranzler, Norman', 'Joy Go With You',
{vi}14, 525, {vii}42, {viii}115
Kravchinsky, Serge Michaelovitch, {i}12,
{iii}116
KRENKOW, ADA ROSE, {i}7, 73, 76–8,
81, 94, 128, 176–7, 203–4, 233, 258,
266–7, 275, 280, 283, 295–6, 310, 325,
328, 333, 350, 386, 454, 498, {ii}125,
426, 489–90, 558, {vi}325, 350, 482,
{vii}193
'quite nice..a bit huffy', {i}209–10;
looked 'like a bison with a skirt on',
{i}224; 'limited vision', {i}231; 'got the
needle', {i}243; DHL does painting for,
{i}263, 273–4; visits DHL, {iii}267,
269–70, 272; avid for money, {iv}76,
384; self-concerned, {v}279; moved to
Delhi, {vii}529, 532
Letters to {iii}352–3
KRENKOW, FRITZ JOHANN
HEINRICH, {i}7–8, 17, 73, 81, 308,
310, 350, {iii}290, 329, 334, 344, 426,
620, {v}279, {vi}300, 482, {vii}193
'always working away at his Arabic',
{i}77; translated Egyptian folk-songs
into German, {i}196; 'fairly well-known
orientalist', {i}230; visits DHL,
{iii}267, 269–70, 272; continuing friend
of Louie Burrows, {iii}353; avid for
money, {iv}76; appointed to professorial

chair in Delhi, {vii}529
The Poems of Tufail Ibn Auf al-Ghanawi,
{i}8
Letters to {iii}321–2, 489–90,
Krenkow, Hannah, {i}350, 394–5, 398
'the last word of respectability', {i}399;
growing affection for DHL, {i}406,
409
Krenkow, Karl, {i}350, 394, 399, 400, 405,
406, 408
Kreutzer Sonata, see Tolstoy, L.
Kristiania (Christiania) (Norway), {iii}637,
639, 657, {iv}172–3, 175
Kronprinz, *see* Franz Ferdinand, Archduke
Kropotkin, Prince Peter Alexeivitch, {i}12
Krout, John Allen, *The Origins of Prohibition*,
DHL reviews, {v}301, 321, 325, 341
KRUG, EMIL VON, {i}391, {iii}716–17,
{iv}72, 255, 258, 395–6, 597–8, {v}266,
480–1, {vi}26, 95, 192, 284, {vii}74,
{viii}42
with DHL at Villach, {vi}97–8, 108,
111, 123–4, 126, 129; 'bourgeois dulness'
in, {vi}131, 137–8, 143; gifts for DHL
from, {vi}146–8, 166, 178, {vii}610;
'intelligent..decent..nice', {vi}226, 259;
WWRA for, {vi}396
Letters to {iv}595, {vi}141, 147–8, 580–2,
{vii}610–11
KRUG, HELENE JOHANNA
MATHILDE ('NUSCH') VON,
{iv}598, {v}266, {vi}26, 141–2, 145–6,
148, 166–7, 173, 178, 180, 207, 215, 217,
238, 259, 284, 302, 397–8, 429–30, 557,
{vii}74, 422, 611, {viii}42
always 'very nice with' DHL, {v}417;
with DHL at Villach, {vi}97–8, 103,
108, 111, 118–19, 122–6; finds husband
boring, {vi}131, 137–8, 143, 226; gift for
DHL from, {vi}147
see also Schreibershofen, H. J. M. von
Letters to {v}480–1, {vi}192–3
Krustchoff, *see* Croustchoff, B. de,
Ku Klux Klan, {vi}547, 566
Kugler, Mrs, {vi}207, 556, {vii}73, 75, 422
Kühl, {iv}306
Kull, Carola, {v}174–5, 191, 213

Kull, Dr Hermann, {v}174, 191, 202, 213

Kunze, {iv}306

Kuprin, Aleksandr Ivanovich, *The River of Life and Other Stories*, {ii}562, 568, 576–7, {vi}174

Kurhaus Plättig, *see* Hotel (Kurhaus) Plättig

Kurpark (Baden-Baden), {vi}206–7, {vii}378

Kuttner, Alfred Booth, {ii}246, 655

Kyllman, O., {vi}480

L'Assommoir, see Zola, E.

L'Innocente, see Annunzio, G. d'

La Condamine, Robert Coutart de, {v}646, {vi}59, 223
    'Apple Orchard', {v}642;
    The Upper Garden, {v}642

La Fonda Hotel (Taos), {v}276, {vii}8

La Junta (USA), {iv}323

La Massa, *see* Villa La Massa

La Milo, *see* Venus de Milo

La Porte, Mlle, {vi}246, 286, 316

La Quemada (Mexico), {iv}515–16

La Rochefoucauld, Armand, Comte de, {vii}323–4, 548

La Rochefoucauld, François, {vi}90

La Salles, S. S., {iv}157

La Vernia (Italy), {vi}605, {vii}432

La Vigie (Ile de Port-Cros), {vi}18, 542, 574, 584, 588–618, {vii}17, 152

Labour Leader, {ii}357

LABOUR, war is struggle between Capital and, {ii}366–7; will produce 'ghastly chaos of destruction', {ii}366; must not be in power, {ii}368; self-interested, {iii}116; 'trunk' of body of 'destructive evil', {iii}123; 'green half' of 'poisonous apple', {iii}283; DHL wants to meet leaders of, {iii}284; contempt for, {iii}288; DHL hates, {iii}561; threatens revolution in Australia, {iv}260; 'very strong, and very stupid' in Australia, {iv}263; will create trouble in USA, {iv}277; Mexican government very, {v}164; DHL hopes Labour government will not be 'Willy wet-legs', {vii}325; if in England DHL would

support 'without hesitation', {vii}327; hostile reviews of *Pansies* expected from, {vii}413; 'a bad egg', {viii}24

'Lacquer Prints', *see* Lowell, A.

Lady B[arrie], {iii}462
    see also Cannan, M.

Lady from the Sea, The, see Ibsen, H.

Lady Inger, see Ibsen, H.

Lady into Fox, see Garnett, D.

Lady Jane, *see* Lawrence, D. H., *LCL*

Lady Sofia, see Omptede, G. von

Lagerlöf, Selma Ottilia Lovisa, {iv}157

Lago di Garda (Italy), {i}18, 165, 430, 439–544 *passim*, {ii}58, 383, 387, 398, 408, {iii}568–9, {iv}189–9, 195, {v}362, {vi}598–9, 608, 610, {vii}5, 34, 46, 52, 54, 172, 221, 260, 273, 276–7, 283, 317–18, 327, 332, 347, 354, 391, 394, 435

Lago di Maggiore (Italy), {i}430, {iii}541–2, {vi}273

Laguna (Pueblo) (USA), {iv}293, 303

LAHR, CHARLES (E. Archer), {v}11, {vi}238, {vii}1, 3–4, 6, 96, 134, 163, 167, 191, 237, 429, 514–15, 538, 545, 557, 569, 576, 593, 621
    published 'Sun' in *New Coterie*, {v}352, 572; promotes sale of *LCL*, {vi}510–12, 515, {vii}30, 39, 42–5, 47–50, 59–61, 71, 88, 112, 120, 124–6, 140–4, 147–8, 151, 153, 155, 161, 177, 202, 233–4, 301, 320; friend to Rhys Davies, {vi}533, {vii}23, 30, 43, 162, 172–3, 198, 247; nicknamed 'the Lion', {vii}3, 301–2, 319–20, 473, 538, 576, 593, 621; 'Clifford Mellors', {vii}110; offers to publish *Pansies*, {vi}111; *Pansies* MS to, {vii}233; unexpurgated *Pansies* ('Red Lion' edn) by, {vii}256, 264–5, 278, 282, 300–2, 315, 319–20 324–5, 328, 334, 336, 340, 353–4, 361–2, 365, 375–6, 380, 389, 396, 404, 433–4, 452, 461, 473, 493, 498–9, 517, 562, 638, 644, 649; 3rd edn of *LCL* by, {vii}256, 488; DHL critical of *Pansies* edn by, {vii}406, 411–12, 473; launch of 'The Squib' suggested to, {vii}447–8, 461, 484–5, 498–9, 501, 516, 578, 589; DHL seeks books from,

{vii}506–8, 519, 528, 550, 560; sells *P and O*, {vii}580; in motor accident, {vii}599, 606

New Coterie, {v}352, 572, {vi}238, {vii}121

Letters to {v}572, {vi}533–4, {vii}23, 30–1, 43–4, 47–8, 60–1, 88, 110–11, 120–1, 143–4, 147, 154–5, 161–2, 172, 197–8, 233–4, 247, 255–6, 264–5, 278, 300–2, 314–15, 324–5, 328, 333–4, 336–7, 340, 353–4, 361–2, 365, 375, 376–7, 380, 389, 404, 406, 412–13, 434, 441–4, 447, 461–2, 483–5, 488–9, 491, 498–9, 506–7, 516–17, 528, 550, 559–60, 562, 578–9, 589, 606, 627, 638–9, 643–4, 648–9

Letters from {vii}95

Lahr, Esther, {v}572, {vi}510, 515, {vii}23, 39, 121, 404, 448

Lahr, Sheila, {vii}404, 599, 606
  Natal Verses for, {vii}121

Laisné, Albert, {i}318–19

Laisné, Cecile, {i}318

Lake Chapala (Mexico), {iv}433, 435–40, 449, 453–5, 467, 474, {v}163

Lake Como, *see* Como, Lake

Lake District (England), {i}274, {v}354, 483, {vii}615

Lake Geneva (Lac Leman) (Switzerland), {iv}279, {vi}234, 236, 261–5, 427–31, 436–7, 439, 464, 474

Lake of Lucerne (Switzerland), {v}314

Lake Poets, see De Quincey, T.

Lake View Estate (Ceylon), *see* Ardnaree

Lamartine, Alphonse-Marie-Louis de Prat de, {ii}61

Lamb, Charles, {ii}240

LAMBERT, CECILY, {iii}454, 590, {iv}28, 99, 149
  one of 'those farm girls, {iii}383
  Letters to {iii}378, 382, 384–6, 406, 411–13, 416–17, 422, 430, 438, 448–9, 460, 529, {iv}166–7

Lamont, Lucy, {v}315, 529, 638, {vi}130

Lamont, Thomas Reynolds, {v}315, {vi}130

Lamy (USA), {iv}12, 288, 290, 293–4, 309, 318

Lancashire, {i}175

Lancaster, William Joseph Cosens, pseud. Harry Collingwood, {ii}589

Land and Water, {ii}352, {iii}480, 555, 559, {iv}134, 144–5, {viii}33

Land's End (Cornwall), {ii}550–1, 554, 562, 624, {iii}60

Landmarks in French Literature, see Strachey, L.

Landor, Walter Savage, {v}579

Lane, Homer Tyrrel, {ii}655

Lane, James, {i}39

LANE, JOHN, {ii}519, {iii}68, 210, 627, {iv}27–8, {v}193, 436
  invites DHL to write book on Venice, {iii}615, 620, 623, {viii}37, 39
  Letters to {viii}37

Lang, Andrew, {i}504–5

Lang, Matheson, {i}138

Langland, William, {i}49

Langley Mill (Derbyshire), {i}23, 34, {v}243, 592

Lansbury, George, {iii}213

Laocoon, {i}5, 136–7, {ii}137, {iii}64, {v}406, 611, {vii}369

Lapland, {i}525

Laredo (USA), {iv}468, 508

Larking, Capt. Dennis Augustus Hugo, {iv}299

Larking, Dorothy, {iv}299

Larumbe, Dr José E., {v}210

Larus, the Celestial Visitor, {v}655

Lasca, *see* Grazzini, A.

Lasker-Schüler, Else, {i}513

Last Judgment, The, see Michelangelo B.

Last of the Medici, The, see Acton, H. M. M.

Last of the Mohicans, The, see Cooper, J. F.

Latin, {i}213, 529, {ii}85, 163, 252, {v}374, {vi}214, {vii}564
  DHL deficient in, {i}31, 33–4; scansion 'a *horrible* fake,' {ii}105; 'form of expression comes very natural' to DHL, {ii}249

Latour, Fantin, *see* Fantin-Latour, I.

Laughing Horse, The, {iv}20, {iv}316, 537, {v}3, 72, 281, 458, 471, {vi}212
  DHL publishes in, {iv}321, 331, 366, 555, 561, 567, {v}28, 48, 103, 127, 393, 581; cover-picture of horse 'looks like a

Laughing Horse, The (cont.)
   sobbing Ass', {iv}484; special DHL
    issue of, {v}27, 66, 343–4, 472, 475–7,
    484, 487, {vi}31, 181, 326
   see also Johnson, W.
Launcelot (Lancelot), see Robinson, E. A.
Laurence, *see* Hilton, L.
Laurie, T. Werner, {ii}519
Lausanne (Switzerland), {iv}279, {v}546–7,
   557, 559, {vi}45, 388, 428, 473, 493,
   556–7
Lavengro (yacht), {iii}560, 564–6, 572
   DHL thrilled to the 'marrow' by,
   {iii}561–3, 567; Mackenzie fails to buy,
   {iii}575, 628
Law (unidentified person), {vii}162
Law and Order, Ltd., see Crichton, K. S.
Law, Andrew Bonar, {iii}39
Lawford, Evelyn, {iv}549, 553, {v}85
LAWRENCE, ALVINA ('TIM'), {i}34, 173,
   199, 452
   'young widow', {i}68; 'desolate', {i}71;
   flirtatious, {i}104
   Letters to {viii}1
Lawrence (Laurence), *see* Hilton, L.
'Lawrence Cultivates His Beard', *see*
   Sherman, S. P.
LAWRENCE, ARTHUR JOHN (father),
   {i}3, 23, 27, 218, 257, 325, 532, 541–2,
   {iv}377, {v}9, 593
   has accident, {i}132; coal-miner, {i}174,
   {iii}282; DHL born hating, {i}190; 'like
   a cinder', {i}191; drunken and 'selfish as
   a maggot', {i}220; 'working very little',
   {i}223, 316; birthday present for,
   {i}228; lives with daughter, Ada,
   {i}229–30, 232–3, 236, 243, 444; DHL's
   financial support for, {i}281, 284, 484,
   {iii}15, 478, 626, {iv}423, {v}114;
   undermined DHL's self-confidence,
   {i}351; votes for strike, {i}379; kept
   ignorant about Frieda, {i}497; colloqui-
   alisms of, {i}506, 513, 534, {vii}410;
   visits DHL, {iii}245; death and burial
   of, {v}124, 126, 139, 142–3, 193, 197;
   DHL receives photograph of, {v}208; as
   boy-chorister, {v}592
   Letters to {i}487

Lawrence, David, *True Story of Woodrow
   Wilson, The,* {v}287
LAWRENCE, DAVID HERBERT
  FICTIONAL CHARACTERS
   in *Aaron's Rod* Algy Constable, {iii}594,
   {iv}212; James Argyle, {ii}31,
   (iii)409, {iv}54, 129, 131, 167,
   {v}184; Josephine Ford, {iii}173,
   {v}426, {vi}42; Lady Franks,
   {iii}417, {vii}262; Marchesa del
   Torre, {iv}131, 167; Sir William
   Franks, {iii}417, {iv}74, 85, {vii}262;
   Walter Rosen {v}419
   in *David* David, {vi}66, {viii}103;
   Jonathan {vi}66; Michal (Mical),
   {v}8, 28, 236, 250, 277, {vi}66,
   {viii}103; Samuel, {vi}66; Saul,
   {vi}66, {viii}103
   in *Kangaroo* Benjamin Cooley, {iv}10;
   Colonel Ennis, {iv}232; Diggers,
   {iv}320; Monsell, {iii}16, 65; Richard
   Somers, {iii}6, 8–9, 11, {vii}168,
   {viii}60
   in *Lady Chatterley's Lover* Connie
   Chatterley, {v}13, {vii}121, 179;
   Duncan Forbes, {v}13–14; Michaelis
   {vii}476; Mrs Bolton, {vii}477; Oliver
   Mellors, {v}13, {vii}110, 121, 179,
   314; Parkin, {v}13; Sir Clifford
   Chatterley, {vi}579, {vii}110, 314,
   476–7
   in *Noah's Flood* Ham, {v}217; Japhet,
   {v}217; Shem, {v}217
   in *'None of That'* Cuesta, {vi}70; Ethel
   Cane, {vi}70
   in *Sons and Lovers* Clara, {ii}40; Miriam
   Leivers, {i}20, 109, 234, 531, {ii}40,
   150, {iii}720, {v}243, 592, {viii}8;
   Paul Morel, {i}21, 109, 421, 550,
   {ii}40, {vi}283; William, {i}21, 477
   in *St Mawr* Lou Carrington {iii}687
   in *The Boy in the Bush* Jack Grant,
   {iv}524, {v}25; Jane Ellis, {v}25;
   Lennie Ellis, {v}25, 193 Monica Ellis,
   {v}25; Sarah Ann Ellis, {v}25; Tom
   Ellis, {v}25, 123
   in *The Lost Girl* Alvina, {iii}9, 14, 506,
   521, 525, 555, 641; Ciccio, {iii}9, 14,

521, 525, 555, 599–600, 605, 613, 644, {v}638; Mr Tuke, {iii}555

in *The Plumed Serpent*, Mr Bell, {iv}436; Mrs Norris, {iv}421

in *The Rainbow* Anna Brangwen, {ii}480, {iii}459; Anton Skrebensky, {ii}142, 274, {vii}201; Gudrun Brangwen, {i}549; Ursula Brangwen, {i}550, {ii}16, 142, 274, 351, 402, 480, {vii}201; Will Brangwen, {ii}480; Winifred Inger, {ii}480

in *The Sisters* Ella Templeman, {i}142, 549–50

in *The White Peacock* Cyril Beardsall, {i}61, 69, 131, 141; Alice Gall, {i}68–9, 232–3; Annable, {i}69, 92, 163; Emily Saxton, {i}68, 131, 141; George Saxton, {i}65, 67–8, 92, 141, 167, 227, {v}634; Leslie Tempest, {i}66, 68, 92, 141, 163; Lettie Beardsall, {i}66–7, 69, 92, 141, 163; Meg Saxton, {i}141; Tom Renshaw, {i}131

in *The Widowing of Mrs. Holroyd* Blackmore, {v}604; Grandmother, {v}604; Holroyd, {v}604; Mrs Holroyd, {v}604

in *Touch and Go* Gerald Barlow, {iii}510

in *Trespasser, The* Allport {i}194; Louisa {i}194; Mr Holiday {i}465

in *Women in Love* Crich family, {v}243; Donald Gilchrist, {iii}44; Gerald Crich, {iii}6, 44, 57, 617; Gudrun Brangwen, {ii}649, {iii}44; Hermione Roddice, {v}243, 'suggested by' Lady Ottoline Morrell, {iii}41, 44, 95, 109, {iv}33, 38, {vi}82, {vii}235; Julius Halliday, {iii}36, 628, {iv}6, 87, 93–4, 114, 116, 123, 138; Loerke, {iii}46; Maxim Libidnikov, {vii}78; Pussum, {iii}36, {iv}87, 93–4, 114, 116, 123; Rupert Birkin, {ii}142, 164, 614, {iii}9, 660, {iv}471; Sholto Bannerman/Donald Gilchrist, {iii}44; Ursula Brangwen, {i}550, {ii}16, 142, 274, 351, 402, 480, 614, {iii}9, {vii}201

PAINTINGS AND DRAWINGS

'Adam Throwing the Apple', *see Throwing Back the Apple*

Accident in a Mine, {vi}562, {vii}135–6, 150, 152, 155, 157, 279, 285, 300; seized by police as obscene, {vii}379

Amazon, see Fight with an Amazon

'Back into Paradise', *see Flight Back into Paradise*

Boccaccio Story, {vi}188, 283, 381, {vii}136, 180, 279, 410 'scandalous' story of nuns and gardener, {v}11–12, 582, 585, 587–8, 593, 595–601; finished, {v}606, 614, 619; Frieda wants to keep, {vi}536; DHL prefers not to sell, but seized by police, {vii}345–6, 361, 368

'Cigarette', not known under this title, {vi}381

Close-up (Kiss), {vii}136, 278–9; Frieda wants to keep, {vi}536

Contadini, {vi}506, 513, 536, 543, 553, 557, 569, {vii}136, 270 offered for £20, then given to Dorothy Warren {vii}369, 425, 490, 631

Corn-Dance, The, {v}27, 66, 114, 581, {vi}31

Dance-Sketch, {vii}136, 280; promised to Elsa Weekley, {vii}425

Dandelions, {vi}557, {vii}136 'a charming picture of a man pissing', {vi}15, 339, 344, 353; omitted from *Paintings*, {vii}135, 199; Orioli wishes to buy, {vii}353, 370, 460, 490

Eve Regaining Paradise, see Flight Back into Paradise

'Family in a garden', 'Family in Garden', *see Family on a Verandah*

Family on a Verandah, {vi}381, 384, {vii}136, 280

Fauns and Nymphs, {vi}133, 196, 208, 283, 368, 381, 405, {vii}136, 279, 300, 322 reproduced in *Vanity Fair*, {vii}504

Fight with an Amazon, {v}12, 606, 614, 619; {vi}127, 283, 381, 405, {vii}136, 279, 300; may have helped to precipitate police action, {vii}361

LAWRENCE, DAVID HERBERT *(cont.)*
  Finding of Moses, {vi}15, 540, {vii}136,
    279, 285, 300
    'all negresses', {vi}81, 199, 381, 384;
    used in prospectus for *Paintings*,
    {vii}180, 199, 204, 214, 222, 243, 253;
    illustration to 'Making Pictures',
    {vii}249, 322; sold, {vii}345
  Fire in the Sands, {vii}199
  Fire-Dance, {vi}15, {vii}136, 279
    'torch-dance by daylight', {vi}313,
    318; Enid Hilton bought for £10,
    {vii}372, 490, 512
  Flight Back into Paradise, {v}12,
    {vi}381, {vii}136, 271
    'Eve Regaining Paradise', {v}637, 639,
    651–2, {vi}188, 283; not seized by
    police, {vii}361
  Harvesting, {i}88, 491
  Hay-stack, see Under the Hay-Stack
  Holy Family, A, {v}12, 578, {vi}188,
    283, 381, {vii}136, 270
    'the Unholy Family', {v}574; DHL
    wants to keep, {vii}345–6; reproduced
    in *Vanity Fair*, {vii}504
  Idyll, An, see Greiffenhagen, M.
  Jaguar Leaping at a Man, {vi}15, 207–8,
    212, 313
  Kiss, see Close-up (Kiss)
  Leda, {vii}117, 135–6, 214, 270; sold,
    {vii}345
  Lizard, The, {vi}329, 353, {vii}136, 280
  Mango Tree, The, {vi}353, {vii}136, 279
    printers reluctant to copy, {vii}198–9,
    207
  Men Bathing, {v}12, 582, 629, 635,
    {vi}283, 381
  Moses, see Finding of Moses
  Nasturtiums, {i}78
  Negro Wedding, {v}12, 623, 629
  North Sea, {vi}553, 557, 562, {vii}136,
    279
    'figures on the sand at the sea',
    {vi}543; seized by police, {vii}363;
    gift for Maria Huxley, {vii}370–1,
    425, 435, 487, 490, 603, 608, 631
  *Nymphs and Fauns, see Fauns and
    Nymphs*

Orange Market, The, see Brangwyn, F.
Paintings of D. H. Lawrence, The, cited,
    {v}574, 582, 606, 619, 637, 652, {vi}6,
    56, 81, 133, 190, 207, 283, 313, 329,
    353, 381, 543, 562, {vii}1, 4, 157, 180,
    385, 407
  Fanfrolico (Mandrake) Press to
    publish at 10 gns, {vii}48–50, 53, 55,
    60, 66–7, 70–1, 74, 76, 78, 82–3, 85–6,
    88, 92, 95, 120, 124, 126, 128, 130, 135,
    138–9, 142, 145, 148–50, 155–7, 160,
    164–5, 168–70, 175, 178, 180, 198–9,
    204, 206–7, 210, 214–15, 224–5, 228,
    235, 259–60, 268, 445, 469–70, 472,
    505, 551, 559, 583, 640; hesitation on
    part of printers, {vii}198, 206; some
    reproductions unsatisfactory in proof,
    {vii}212, 218, 221, 262–3, 269–71,
    274, 278–80, 282–3, 285, 292–3, 295,
    298–302, 304; publication of,
    {vii}305–7, 318–19, 321–3, 327–32,
    335, 337, 339, 343–5, 353; all copies
    sold, {vii}367; copies seized by police
    and court orders copies destroyed,
    {vii}8, 413, 415, 422, 435–6, 440
  Pietà, {vii}199
  Rape of the Sabine Women, {vi}15, 368,
    381, {vii}136, 279, 300; 'a Study in
    Arses', {vi}353
  Red Willow Trees, {v}12, 619, 629, 635,
    {vi}188, 283, 381, {vii}136, 280
    finished, {v}635; DHL wants not to
    sell, {vii}345–6; reproduced in *Vanity
    Fair*, {vii}504
  Renascence of Men, {vi}446–7, {vii}117,
    135–6, 214, 271; allegedly for
    Montague Weekley, {vii}425
  Resurrection, {v}652, {vi}15, 56, 67–8,
    188, 381, 405, {vii}136, 271
    finished, {vi}72, 74; Frieda wants to
    keep, {vi}536
  Singing of Swans, {vii}135, 199, 207,
    212, 214, 216, 279, 300
  Spring, {vii}135, 157, 180, 199, 214, 279
    DHL removed blue trousers in,
    {vii}150, 169, 176; sold, {vii}553
  Summer Dawn, {vii}135, 150, 157, 169,
    180, 199, 214, 271

Sun-men catching horses, {vi}460, 503, 549

Throwing Back the Apple, {vi}15, 190, 196, 212, 353, {vii}136, 271, 361

Torch Dance, The, {vi}16, 353

Under the Hay-Stack, {vi}329, 353, {vii}136, 279

Willow Trees, see Red Willow Trees

Wind on the Wold, {i}282

Yawning, {vi}329, 353, {vii}136, 279

PLAYS

Altitude, {v}102, 172

Collier's Friday Night, A, {i}50, 139, 188, 196, 199, 202, 494, 505
Hueffer mislays, {i}309, 311, 317, 323, 376, 379, 381; Iden Payne shows interest in, {i}384, 386, 389

Daughter-in-Law, The, {i}500–1

David, {v}8, 265, 281, 283, 297–8, {vi}278, 281, 295, {vii}474, {viii}96–7, 99–100
preliminary thoughts on, {v}158, 160, 174, 199; composition of, {v}226, 233, 236, 248; finished, {v}252, 257, 268; 'a good play..for the theatre', {v}270, 274; Frieda translates, {v}275–6, 379, 388–9, 464, 468–70, 473, 478, 483, {vi}204, 248, 348, 359; Ida Rauh's reaction to, {v}282; not to be published before produced, {v}285–6; Theatre Guild rejects, {v}300; limited English edn of, {v}333, 336, 339–40, 346, 370, 376, 381, 402, 413–15, 420, 422, 481; US edn of, {v}454, 460, 581, 638; irritating negotiations for London production of, {v}470, 472, 474–5, 477, 506, 509–10, 514, 516–18, 520–2, 524–6, 530, 532, 534, 538, 543–5, 548, 555–6, 562–3, 565, 576–8, 582–3, 586, 593, 595, 600, 605, 608, 613–14, 616, 621–3, 628, 630, 635–7, 648, 651, 655–6, {vi}26, 30, 39; DHL writes music for, {v}557, 559, {viii}98; production postponed, {viii}100; firm dates for production of, {vi}46–52, 55, 57; DHL absent from performance, {vi}59, 61–2, 64,

{viii}102; cuts in text agreed, {viii}102; reception of, {vi}66–8, 70–3, 75, 77–8, 80, 82, {viii}103–4 *see also* letters to Whitworth, P.

Fight for Barbara, {i}427, 466–8, 475–8, 494, 509

Married Man, The, {i}386, 477, 509

Merry-Go-Round, The, {i}67, 200, 252, 309, 311, 317, 323, 376, 379, 381, 477, 509, {viii}113

Noah's Flood, {v}8, 174, 218, 226

Touch and Go, {i}176, {iii}6–7, 11, 293, 297–300, 305, 315, 333, 338, 360, 404, 528, 533, 642, {iv}2, {viii}63–4
Goldring interested in producing, {iii}371–2, 374–5, 396; Daniel to publish, {iii}385, 400, 427, 441, 469, 482, 513, 522, 525, 531, 545, 547; Macdermott's option to produce, {iii}423, 441, 483, 510; Goldring angers DHL over, {iii}469; Seltzer's edn of, {iii}485, 539, 548, 565, {v}140; Mackenzie shows interest in, {iii}509–10; Amy Lowell reviews, {iii}593, 629

Widowing of Mrs. Holroyd, The, {ii}14, 17, 108, 201, 225, {iii}95, 374, 380, {vii}529, {viii}10
MS to Grace Crawford, {i}188; Violet Hunt reads MS, {i}199; Granville Barker and, {i}298; Edward Garnett and, {i}309, {ii}55, 58; Kennerley to publish, {i}542, {ii}65, 67, 69, 71–2, 77–80, 86, 89, 133, 136, 143–5, 152–3, 166, 174, {iii}129, {vii}52, {viii}8; Björkman writes preface for, {ii}80, 174, {v}35; Stage Society interested in, {ii}127, 136, 152; Duckworth's English edn of, {ii}135, 144, 171, {v}87, {vi}229; reviewed, {ii}173; Frieda considers translating, {ii}210; copy to Lady Ottoline Morrell, {ii}313, 315; Esmé Percy produces, {ii}382, 384, {v}576–8, 582, 586, 591, 593, 598–602, 604–5, 608, 610, 613–14, 616, 621, 637 {viii}98–9, 102; production by Altrincham Stage Society, {iii}428,

LAWRENCE, DAVID HERBERT (*cont.*)
430, 477, 483, 487, 510; Catherine
Carswell reviews Altrincham production, {iii}477, 495; Mackenzie
interested in producing, {iii}509–10;
Seltzer's edn, {iii}527, 546, 565, 576,
{viii}63–4; Carlo Linati considers
translating, {v}140; de Wit reviews,
{viii}19

POEMS

'13,000 People', {vii}389
'After the Opera', {v}273
'Ah, Muriel!', {i}179
'All of Roses', {ii}56, 138, 209
'All of Us', {iii}49, 51, 218–19, 221, 234,
338, {viii}28
'Almond Blossom', {iii}657, 667, 674,
688, {iv}177, 380, 384
'American Eagle, The', {iv}14, 407, 409,
419
Amores, {i}246, {ii}53, 513, 522–7,
531–2, 536–7, 561, 596, 598, 619,
643–5, 655, 665, {iv}325, 330, 403,
{vi}369, 541
    dedicated to Ottoline Morrell, {ii}512,
    521; in preparation, {ii}514–19;
    poems 'make a sort of inner history of
    my life, from 20 to 26', {ii}521; 'old
    poems – but good', {ii}526; Heseltine
    typed, {ii}529; Constable and
    Sidgwick reject, {ii}535, 558, 560,
    562, {iii}77, 147; Duckworth publish-
    es, {ii}576, 589, 606, 612, {iv}201,
    428–9, {v}626, {vi}168, 607, {viii}18;
    Huebsch publishes in USA, {ii}605,
    610–11, {iii}129, 356, 547, 643, 652,
    661, {iv}169, 248, {vi}607, {vii}320;
    favourably reviewed in *TLS*, {ii}640;
    to Cynthia Asquith, {ii}649, {iii}26;
    to E. M. Forster, {iii}20; to Amy
    Lowell, {iii}32; Mcleod and, {iii}61;
    noticed in *Poetry*, {iii}99; to
    Siebenhaar, {iv}435; in *Collected
    Poems*, {vi}206, 264, 269; Viking Press
    and, {vii}65
'Another Ophelia', *see* 'Ballad of Another
Ophelia'

'Apostolic Beasts', {iv}59, 123–4, 150,
154
'Apprehension', {iii}254
'Argonauts, The', {vii}509
'Ass, The', {iii}688, 693, 700, {iv}201,
319, 324
'At the Window', {ii}610
'Attila', {vii}258
Augustan Book of English Poetry, The,
{v}2, 521, 626, {vi}305, 464
'Autumn at Taos', {iv}14, 378, 407,
{vi}229
'Autumn Rain', {iii}29
'Baby Asleep After Pain, A', {v}387
'Baby-Movements', {i}94, 137, {v}86
'Ballad of a Wayward Woman', *see*
'Ballad of a Wilful Woman'
'Ballad of a Wilful Woman', {ii}66, 94,
104, {iii}162, 165
'Ballad of Another Ophelia', {i}323;
'wonderfully good', {ii}150; rejected
by Harriet Monroe, printed by Amy
Lowell, {ii}203, 209, 219, 384
'Bare Almond-Trees', {iii}657, 688
'Bare Fig-Trees', {iii}657, 667, 688
'Bat', {iv}6, 83, 85, 88, 97, 378
Bay, {iii}11–12, {v}273
    illustrated by Ann Estelle Rice,
    {ii}404, {iii}360, 362, 366; Beaumont
    publishes, {iii}212, 233, 237–8, 241–3,
    246, 248, {iv}429, {v}120, {vi}76,
    {viii}28–9; 'Impeccable Poems',
    {iii}234; dedicated to Cynthia
    Asquith, {iii}234, 237, 287, 494;
    expected to be 'hand-printed and
    beautiful', {iii}287; dedication
    omitted, {iii}465, 494; ' silly-looking
    little book', {iii}469; to Amy Lowell,
    {iii}475, 593; to Marsh, {iii}487; to
    Juta, {iii}535, 568; DHL hopes for US
    edn, {iii}585–6, 605; included in
    Collected Poems, {vi}167, 206, 264, 269
'Be a Demon', Secker omits from
Pansies, {vii}237, 296, 300, 303, 325;
in Lahr's edn, {vii}406
'Bei-Hennef', {i}19, 398, 462, {vi}84,
280
'Bells', {vii}585

'Beyond the Rockies', {v}66, 393, 581

'Bibbles', {iv}358, 375, 378, 407

Birds, Beasts and Flowers, {iv}7, 14, 16, 18, 407, 428–9, {vi}541, {vii}437, {viii}70

cited, {iii}596–7, 616, 630, 661, {iv}59, 83, 123, 174, 201, 322, 326; MS of, {iii}613, 634, 645; Ruth Wheelock types, {iii}629; frontispiece requested, {iii}653; foreword to, {iii}657; additional poems, {iii}667, 681, 700, {iv}85, 88 ; Amy Lowell perhaps jealous of, {iii}673; TS to Barbara Low, {iii}688, 692; TS to Curtis Brown, {iii}702, {iv}380; Seltzer asked to return TS, {iv}257–8, 319–20, 324, 336; Mountsier and, {iv}336, 341, 369, {viii}57; Merrild's wood-cuts for, {iv}344–5, 369, 371, 373, 406; Seltzer publishes, {iv}374, 378, 381, 383–4, 386, 399, 401, 404, 409, 419, 442, 447–9, 476, 486, 488–90, 501, 518, 523, {vi}607, {vii}27, 38, 52, 66, 111, 130, 166, 181–2, 272, 320; Merrild's book-jacket for, {iv}394, 406, 419, 436–7, 439, {viii}72; royalty on, {iv}428; Secker's English edn, {iv}454, 481, 486, 490, {vii}526; proof correcting, {iv}470–1, 473–5, 477, 480; to Murry, {iv}500; DHL designed jacket, {iv}521, 526; DHL praises appearance of, {iv}526; complimentary copies, {iv}527, 540. 547, {v}60, 106, 246, 254, 341; reviewed, {v}91, 94; French translation of, {v}286, 363, 371 444; included in *Collected Poems*, {vi}206, 269, 277, 280–1, 291; Hughes-Stanton and Cresset Press edn, {vii}457, 503, 535, 549, 563, 573

'Birth Night', {iii}145–6

'Birthday', {ii}138, 209

'Bits' *see* 'All of Us'

'Blue Jay', {iv}381, 407

'Bombardment', {v}273

'Bread upon the Waters', {iii}325

'Brooding Grief', {ii}610

'By the Isar, in the twilight', *see* 'River Roses'

'Candlemas', *see* 'Valentine's Night'

'Censors', {vii}258

'Character in a Novel', {vii}102–3

'Cherry Robbers', {i}109

'Choir {Chorus) of Women', later *New Poems*, {iii}233, 244, 255

'Coldness in Love', {i}11

Collected Poems, {iii}15, {vi}4, 6, 348, 405, 618

cited, {ii}401, 513; {iii}284; early proposal for, {iii}379, 383, 386, 394; Secker publishes, {vi}168, 195, 206, 376, 388, 546, 572, {vii}243, 303, 324, 413, 445, 457; DHL compiling, {vi}213, 223, 264, 271, 275, 279–80, 284, 287, 293; Bridges invited to write introduction, {vi}269, 305, 330, 395; proofs of, {vi}316, 318, 327, 330, 351; special signed edn, {vi}463, 471–3, 495, 505; Knopf refuses US edn, {vi}539, {vii}320, 395, 568; complimentary copies, {vi}589, 591, 593, 598–600, 602, 604, 607, 609, 614, 616, {vii}19, 21, 23, 27, 29, 67, 72, 85, 96, 385, 387, 396, 399, 472, 486, 505, 546–7; DHL keen to have US edn of, {vii}38, 52, 65–6, 174, 182, 238; reception of, {vii}41, 144, 162, 166, 294; Cape's US edn, {vii}66, 221, 236, 266, 297, 315, 320, 324, 328, 336, 387, 413, 521

'Coming Awake', {iii}254, 262, 266, {vi}280

'Constancy of a Sort', {iii}115

'Corot', {viii}15

'Craving for Spring', {iii}2, 115, 513; DHL quotes in self-parody, {iii}170; Goldring quotes in epigraph to novel, {iii}441

'Creative Evolution', {v}385

'Cruelty and Love', {i}318, {ii}401, {vi}541

'Death', {vii}398

'Demon Justice', {vii}265, {viii}112

'Discipline', {i}137, {v}86

'Don Juan', {ii}170, 202

LAWRENCE, DAVID HERBERT (*cont.*)
    'Don't look at me!', Secker omits from
      Pansies, {vii}140, 264
    'Dreams Nascent', {vi}541
    'Dreams Old and Nascent', {i}137,
      {v}86
    'Dreams Old', {vi}541
    'Drunk', {ii}513
    'Dusk-flower', {i}204
    'Eagle in New Mexico', {iv}14, 322, 324,
      368, 378, 381, 407, {vi}372
    'Early Spring', {ii}154, 162
    'Editorial Office', {vii}389, 442–3
    'Ego Bound Women', {vii}264
    'Elephant', {iv}8, 15, 378, 380, 407, 428
    'Elixir', {i}200–1
    'Eloi, Eloi, Lama Sabachthani?',
      {ii}232–4, 236
    'Emasculation', {vii}443
    'English Are So Nice!, The', {vii}415
    'Errinyes', {ii}610, {iii}61, 513
    'Evangelistic Beasts', *see* 'Apostolic
      Beasts'
    'Eve's Mass', *see* 'Birth Night'
    'Evening Land', {iv}307, 337
    'Evening', {i}385, 446, 455
    'Everlasting Flowers', {iii}283, {vi}280
    'Father Neptune's Little Affair with
      Freedom', {vii}585
    'Fig', {iii}597, 644
    'Fireflies in the Corn', {ii}138, 209
    'Fish', {iv}83, 85, 88–9, 97
    'Flapper', {i}149, {ii}154, 170, 202
    'Fooled', {ii}154, 162
    'For God's Sake', {vii}99
    'Forte dei Marmi', {vii}356
    'Frost Flowers', {iii}115, 174, 513,
      {viii}22
    'Ghosts', {iv}409
    'Giorno dei Morti', {ii}106, 154, 170,
      202; in *Book of Italy*, {ii}384
    'Gipsy', {vi}388–9
    'Gloire de Dijon', {ii}56, 59, 87
    'Goat', {iv}324, 378
    'Grapes', {iii}597, 644
    'Great Newspaper Editor and his
      Subordinate, The', {vii}442–3
    'Greeks are Coming!, The', {vii}524
    'Green', {ii}87, 138, 209, {iii}499

'Grief', {ii}120–1, 170, 202
'Gross, Coarse, Hideous', {vii}484
'Guards!: A Review in Hyde Park 1913',
    {iii}365, {viii}29
'Guards', 'Potency of Men', third part
    of, {vi}388–9
'Hands of the Betrothed, The', {i}29
'He-Goat', {iv}324
'Henriette', {vii}120, 132–3, 372
'Hibiscus and Salvia Flowers', {iii}667,
    674, 688, 693, 700; DHL liked
    'immensely', {iii}659; offered to
    London Mercury, {iii}681
'Honeymoon', {ii}154, 162
'How Beastly the Bourgeois is', {vii}111
'Humming Bird', {vii}348–9
'Husband Dead, A', {i}254
'I heard a little chicken chirp', {vii}447
'I will give you all my keys', {i}246
'Illicit', {ii}87, 138, 209
'Image-making Love', {vii}414
'In Trouble and Shame', {ii}610
'Intimates', {vii}414
'Intime', {i}362
'It's either you fight or you die', {vii}100
'Jeune Fille, The', Secker omits from
    Pansies, {vii}237, 296, 300, 303; Lahr
    includes in unexpurgated *Pansies*
    {vii}325, 406
'Kangaroo', {iv}11, 378
'Kisses in the Train', {i}29, {ii}58
'Labour Battalion', {iii}202–4, 218, 238,
    241, 465
'Last Hours', {iii}465, {v}273,
    {viii}29
Last Poems, {vii}414, 447, 484
'Late in Life', {iii}278, 283
'Letter from Town: The Almond Tree',
    {iii}284
'Lightning', {i}323–5, 335, 442, 444,
    446
'Little Town at Evening, The', {v}273
'Little wowser, The', *see* 'Old acquain-
    tance, An'
'Lizard', {vii}258
'London Mercury', {vii}376, 389, 441,
    443
Look! We Have Come Through!, {ii}66,
    209, 664, {iii}5, 11, 13, 358, 480, 513,

{iv}248, 325, 330, 378, 403, {vi}541, {viii}22, 70

'"Bei Hennef"..starts the new cycle' of, {i}462; DHL compiling, {iii}84, 90, 93–4; 'real poems', 'chief' and 'best', {iii}86, 99, 111; 'Man and Woman' early title proposed for, {iii}93; friends' reactions to, {iii}94, 102, 178, 253; 'very precious', {iii}104; MS to Pinker, {iii}111, 113, 115; problem of publishing, {iii}121, 131, 135; Chatto & Windus and, {iii}144–5, 148–9, 152–6, 172, 175, 184–6, 211, 547, {viii}27; proof-correcting, {iii}162–5; *TLS* review, {iii}186–7, 190; 'on the whole' DHL likes appearance of, {iii}187; Huebsch publishes in USA, {iii}238, 254–5, 323, 388, 399, 473, 547, 643, {vii}320; press 'spat' on, {iii}348; Chatto not to reprint, {iv}153, 176, 180–1, {vi}168; DHL keen for new edn, {iv}428–9; to be incorporated in *Collected Poems*, {vi}206, 269, 277, 280–1, 291; paltry sales in USA, {vi}539; Viking Press has rights in, {vi}607, {vii}65; catalogued in Cambridge University Library, {viii}27

'Love has crept out of her sealèd heart', {i}150

Love Poems and Others, {i}14, 19, 109, 324, 462, 488, {ii}43, 225, 401, 655, {iii}547, {vi}541, {viii}15, 19

De la Mare helped to select poems in, {i}442, 445–7; Duckworth publishes, {i}442–3, 455, 457, 513, 519, {ii}519, {iii}612, {iv}201, 428–9, {v}626, {vi}168, 369, {viii}18; DHL 'hugely pleased' by, {i}454; proofs of, {i}459–61; publication of, {i}490–1, 493, 502, 510, 512, 517, 520; David Garnett and, {i}522, 536; McLeod praises, {i}523; reviews of, {i}526, 528, 530, 548, {v}94; copy to Jessie Chambers, {i}527, 531; Kennerley publishes in USA, {i}542, {iii}129, {vi}607, {vii}52, 66, 320; disappointing sales of, {i}545–6, 548, {ii}68, {iii}398; Pound praises, {ii}131–2,

135; included in *Collected Poems*, {vi}206, 264, 269

'Love Letter', {iii}147, 164

'Love on the Farm', {ii}401, {vi}541, {vii}348–9

'Lucifer', {vii}414

'Man and Bat', {iv}88, 378

'Man and Woman', *see LWHCT*

'Man in the Street, The', {vii}585

'Man Who Died, A', {i}254, 323

'Mana of the Sea', {vii}543

'Matthew', *see* 'St Matthew'

'Mediterranean in January', {v}66, 393, 477

'Medlars and Sorb-Apples', {iii}596, 627, 675, {iv}69

'Meeting Among the Mountains', {ii}90, 399; man in poem '*extraordinarily* like Frieda's husband', {ii}154; omitted by Chatto & Windus from *LWHCT*, {iii}145–9, 152, 164, 513, {iv}378, 429

'Memories', {ii}170, 202

'Men in New Mexico', {iv}378, 407, {vi}229

'Moonrise', {iii}115

More Pansies, {vii}286

'Mosquito, The', {iv}61

'Mother of Sons, The', {ii}138

'Mountain Lion', {iv}378, 407, {vii}272

'Mowers, The', {ii}75, 209, 384

'Mutilation', {iii}480

'My Little Critics', {vii}389, 441

'My Naughty Book', rejected by *Aphrodite*, {vii}77, 180; omitted from Secker's *Pansies*, {vii}98, 264; text sent to Charles Wilson for miners, {vii}100–1

'Near the Mark', {i}196

Nettles, {vii}373, 389, 412, 424, 443 'a few stinging "Pansies" which this time are "Nettles"' {vii}400; to get DHL's 'own back', {vii}402; to 'sting the arses of' his persecutors, {vii}410–11; Faber & Faber publish as (posthumous) pamphlet, {vii}589, 606, 619, 639–40, 649; MS to Pollinger, {vii}595

LAWRENCE, DAVID HERBERT (*cont.*)

'Never had a Daddy', {vii}441–3

'New Heaven and Earth', {ii}664, {iii}104

New Poems, {i}275, {iii}11, 15, 187, {iv}26, 325, 330, {v}17

'Chorus of Women' possible title for, {iii}233; 'Choir of Women' another possible title, {iii}244; MS to Pinker, {iii}249, 255; 'Coming Awake' might be title-poem, {iii}254; Pinker seeks publisher for, {iii}262, 265–6; Secker to publish, {iii}274, 280, 287, 290, 470, 504, 547, {iv}181, 193–4; Secker provides title for, {iii}277; poems omitted from, {iii}278, 283–4; proofs to Amy Lowell, {iii}285, 304; complimentary copies, {iii}290, 292, 294, 304, 313, 325–6, 330, 348, 358, 470, 568, 586; 'decidely false title', {iii}291; Huebsch publishes in USA, {iii}356, 385–8, 399, 456, 643, {iv}248, {vi}607, {vii}320; Secker's new edn 're-set', {iii}379, 394, 475; US edn dedicated to Amy Lowell, {iii}593; included in *Collected Poems*, {iv}429, {vi}206, 264, 268–9, 280; Viking Press has rights to, {vi}539, {vii}65

'Night Songs', {i}156

'Nils Lykke Dead', *see* 'Man Who Died, A'

'No News', {iii}204–5, 218, 465

'No! Mr Lawrence', {vii}65

'Noble Englishman, The', omitted from Secker's *Pansies*, {vii}265

'Noise of Battle', {vii}348–9

'Nostalgia', {iii}325, 376, 465, {iv}540

'November by the Sea', {vii}258

'Nuoro', {iv}42–3

'O! Americans', {v}37

'O! start a revolution', {vii}99

'Obsequial Chant', {iii}325, 376

'Old acquaintance, An', omitted from Secker's *Pansies*, {vii}98, 264; text of, {vii}101–2

'Old Men', {vii}398

'Old Orchard, The', {v}617

'On the Balcony', title given to 'Illicit' in *LWHCT*

'On the March', {iii}234

Pansies, {v}11, 572, {vii}1, 3, 5–6, 23, 106, 178, 203, 259, 400, 414, 453, 457, 559, {viii}112

composition begun, {vii}22; 'Frieda calls them poems but I call them *pensées*', {vii}28–9, 51, 55, 62, 80, 115; 'a sort of loose little poem form; Frieda says...real doggerel', {vii}64–5; finished, {vii}89; first draft of introduction to, {vii}92; DHL delaying publication, {vii}95, 98; Lahr offers to publish, {vii}110–11; 'very anti middle-class', {vii}111; DHL invites Secker to publish limited edn, {vii}120–4; Stephensen enthusiastic about, {vii}128; reflects shift in public taste, {vii}131; delay in TS reaching Curtis Brown, {vii}135–6, 140, 143, 145; police seize as obscene, {vii}147–57, 160–3, 165, 167, 171–4, 197, 204–6, 221, 224, 228; barrister Hutchinson acts on DHL's behalf, {vii}161–3, 167, 172, 176, 183–4, 190, 195, 227, 238, 257; DHL re-types, {vii}169–70, 192; copy to Marianne Moore for *Dial*, {vii}173–4, 204, 257–8, 305; expurgated copy and revised introduction sent to Secker, {vii}195–6, 215; questions in Parliament about, {vii}204, 214; Secker to publish expurgated, {vii}218, 222, 228, 231, 233, 237, 241–2, 249–50, 255–6, 261, 264–7, 274, 292, 296–305, 315, 320, 324–5, 328, 335–6, 350, 352, 358, 380–1, 387, 402–3, 413, 502–3, 554; DHL refuses to produce an 'innocuous, bourgeois little book', {vii}242, 249, 256; support from Rebecca West over, {vii}252; Lahr to publish definitive edn, {vii}256, 265, 278, 282, 301–4, 315, 320, 325, 328, 336, 340, 353–4, 365, 375–6, 396, 404, 433–5, 452, 499, 538, 562, 644; Knopf to publish Secker version in USA, {vii}266, 303, 305, 312–13, 320, 324, 328, 467, 496, 552, 568; Lederhandler and Achsah Brewster given pages from MS of, {vii}306; complimentary copies, {vii}317–18, 321, 323, 327, 335, 347, 362, 376, 379–80, 414, 421, 428, 461–2, 472, 485, 493, 498, 501, 505, 532, 547, 561, 576–9; reception of, {vii}361–2, 364, 372, 424, 584, 637; DHL 'pining to see [Lahr's] *Pansies* all abloom', {vii}389; DHL critical of Lahr's edn, {vii}406–7, 411–12, 432, 473; DHL wants Lahr's edn 'kept secret', {vii}428, 440–1; DHL to get £500 from Lahr edn, {vii}445, 487; Socialists dislike, {vii}451; police interference provoked the two edns, {vii}504; Lahr's extra copies, {vii}515–16, 520, 523, 638, 648–9; news of pirated edn of, {vii}592–3, 595, 605–6, 643

'Paradise Re-Entered', *see* 'Purity'

'Passages from *Ecce Homo*', *see* 'Eloi, Eloi Lama Sabachthani?'

'Passing Visit to Helen', {i}11, 362

'Peace' ('Slopes of Etna'), {iii}630–1, 634

'Peach', {iii}597, 644

'Pentecostal', *see* 'Shades'

'People', {viii}22

'Perfidy', {ii}610

'Physician, The', {i}204

'Piano', scrutinised in Richards' *Practical Criticism*, {vii}376

'Piccadilly Circus at Night: Street-Walkers', {vii}348–9

'Poems of a Married Man', early title for *LWHCT*, {iii}84, 86

'Pomegranate', {iii}597, 657, 681, {iv}69; $20 from *Dial* for, {iii}644

'Potency of Men', *see* 'Guards'

'Punisher, The', {i}446, 455

'Purity' ('Paradise Re-Entered'), {ii}94, 104

'Purple Anemones', {iii}661, 667, 674, 681, 688, 700

'Puss-Puss', {vii}441, 443

'Rabbit Snared in the Night' ('Rabbit Snared in the Dark'), {iii}115, 152, 165, {viii}22

'Rainbow', {v}617

'Red Wolf, The', {iv}381, 407, {vi}229

'Release', {i}11

'Renaissance', {i}110–111

'Renascence', {i}110, {vii}348–9

'Repulsed', {i}11, 378

'Resurrection', {ii}417, 455, {iii}29, {viii}22

'Revolutionary, The', {iii}596, 627, 644, 675, {iv}71

'River Roses', {ii}56, 59, 87

'Rose of all the World', {vii}584

'Roses on the Breakfast Table', {ii}56, 59, 87, 103

'Running Barefoot', {i}94

'Saddest Day, The', {vii}249

'Sane Revolution, A', {vii}362

'Scent of Irises, The', {ii}209, 384

'Schoolmaster, The', {i}386, 407, 446, 459; De la Mare advises on publication of, {i}382–4, 422, 424, 442, 444

'Sea, The', {iii}115, 142

'Sea-Bathers', {vii}356

'Sea-Weed', {vii}258

'Self-Contempt', {i}196, {vi}389

'Service of All the Dead', *see* 'Giorno dei Morti'

'Seven Seals', {iii}371, 388

'Shades', {iii}390

'She Looks Back', {iii}187

'She-Goat', {iv}324

'Ships in Bottles', {vii}140

'Sicilian Cyclamens', {iii}616

'Sigh No More', {i}179

'Slopes of Etna', {iii}630–1, 634

'Snake', {iii}657, 667, 674, 688, {iv}297, 575, {vi}21

'Snap-Dragon', in first *Georgian Poetry*, {i}19, 459, 461–2, {ii}2, 35, 140, 518, 521; in *English Review*, {i}375, 401, 407, {vi}541; expresses frustrated sexual desire, {i}403

'Snowy Day at School, A', {i}113, 385

'Song of a Man Who is Loved', Chatto & Windus omit from *LWHCT*, {iii}145–9, 152, 164, 513, {iv}378, 429; restored to sequence in *Collected Poems*, {vi}280

'Song', *see* 'Flapper'

'Sorrow', {i}254

'Sphinx', {vii}414

'Spirits Summoned West', {iv}327, 407

LAWRENCE, DAVID HERBERT (*cont.*)
'St. John', {iv}59
'St. Luke', {iv}59
'St. Mark', {iv}59
'St. Matthew', {iv}15, 59, 337, 381, 404
'Still Afternoon, A', {i}137, 139, 471, {v}86
'Storm in the Black Forest', {vii}381
'Street Lamps', {iii}29
'Street-Walkers', *see* 'Piccadilly Circus at Night: Street-Walkers'
'Study', {i}31
'Teasing' ('Tease'), {i}246, {ii}53
'Ten Months Old', {i}106, 108–9
'Terra Nuova', {ii}664, {iii}104, 513; *see also* 'New Heaven and Earth'
'The Wind, the Rascal', {i}203, {ii}87, 104, 138
'There is no way out', omitted from Secker's edn of *Pansies*, {vii}264
'Things men have made', {vii}257
'Tired of the Boat', {i}179, {ii}209
'To Clarinda', for Maria Huxley, {vii}64, 110, 264
'To let go or to hold on', {vii}257
'Tommies in the Train', {iii}325
Tortoises, {iii}688, {iv}242, 304
'a little book of those *vers libres*, {iii}605, 607–9, 614, 678; tortoises lived at Villa La Canovaia near Florence, {iii}651; Seltzer publishes, {iv}7, 107, 109, 130, {vii}320; 'a chap-book', {iv}123, 131, 150; complimentary copies, {iv}153–4, 174, 181, 184–5, 190, 213; 'not a chap-book', {iv}156–7; Amy Lowell angry about, {iv}245; royalties on, {iv}388; Secker includes in *BBF*, {iv}475, {vii}38, 166; Mountsier chose print on cover of, {v}175
'Town', {viii}29
'Trailing Clouds', {i}94
'Transformations', {i}323
'Trees in the Garden', {vii}381
Triumph of the Machine, The, {vii}595; one of Faber *Ariel Poems*, {vii}585, 589
'Tropic', {iii}630–1, 634
'True Democracy', {vii}249

'True love at last', {vii}414
'Turkey-Cock', {iii}677, {iv}307–8, 317, 337
'Turning Back, The', {ii}421–3
'Twilight', {ii}90, 120
'Two Wives', {iii}283–4
'Ultimate Reality', {vii}414
'Valentine's Night', {iii}145–6
'Violets', {i}323–5, 335, 444, 446, 459, 523, {ii}58
'War-Baby', {iii}246, 325
'Weariness', {i}254, {ii}170, 202; *see also* 'Sorrow'
'What does she want?', Secker omits from *Pansies*, {vii}264
'What Matters', Secker omits from *Pansies*, {vii}296, 300, 303, 325, 406
'What would you fight for?', {vii}258
'Whatever man makes', {vii}258
'When I went to the Circus', {vii}173, 257–8, 305
'Whether or Not', {i}523, {vii}584
'Winter's Tale, A', {i}109–10, {ii}154
'Witch, The', {i}201
'Woman and Her Dead Husband, A', {i}254, {ii}138, 209
'Women want fighters', {vii}265
'Work', {vii}258
'Worm either way', {vii}266
'Young and their moral guardians, The', Secker omits from *Pansies*, {vii}264
'Young Soldier with Bloody Spurs, The', {i}434–7
'Youth Mowing, A', *see* 'Mowers, The'

PROSE
A Propos of "Lady Chatterley's Lover", {vii}1, 4, 30, 477
My Skirmish extended into, {vii}446, 531, 533, 549, 633–4, 640; *see also My Skirmish with Jolly Roger*
Aaron's Rod, {ii}31, {iii}1, 11, 576, 708, {iv}4, 6–8, 83, 212, 220, 341, {v}184, 419, 426, {vi}213, 248, 443, 600, {viii}44
composition goes 'very slowly and fitfully', {iii}216, 567; 'as blameless as *Cranford*', {iii}227; 'quite "proper"

novel', {iii}364; 'amusing', {iii}565; 'a queer mad affair', {iii}571; '⅓ done' {iii}572; 'half done', {iii}594; 'stuck half way', {iii}602, 608, 613, {iv}267; 'can't end it', {iii}626, 634; 'left off', {iii}638, 645–6; 'will not be dangerous', {iii}653; DHL intends to try to finish, {iii}688, 702, 711, 714; two-thirds done, {iii}717; DHL finishing, {iii}720, 722; Violet Monk typing first part of, {iii}724, {iv}28, 35–6, 54; only last chapter to write, {iii}728–9; 'complete', {iii}730–2, {iv}25–6, 34–5, 48, 259, {viii}41; all written 'out of doors', {iv}25; rest of MS to be typed, {iv}27–8, 39, 44, 50; 'Conclusion' to be typed, {iv}36; Secker to publish English edn, {iv}51, 69–70, 88, 96, 116, 129, 144, 159, 175, 200; Curtis Brown to have typing completed, {iv}54–5, 57, 65, 74; Seltzer to produce US edn, {iv}57, 92–3, 95–6, 104, 121, 124–5, 127, 257–9; Mountsier dislikes, {iv}57, 66, 92, 116, 121, 127, 129, 274, 277; *Dial* prints 'Episode' from, {iv}74, 130, 187, 388; 'Novara' chapters might suit magazines, {iv}85; DHL reluctant to serialise in England, {iv}85; publication postponed, {iv}85, 87, 90; 'the last of my serious English novels', {iv}92, 104; Frieda disliked, {iv}124; DHL modifies at Seltzer's request, {iv}131, 134, 138, 152, 156–7; DHL resists further alterations, {iv}167–8, 177; published, {iv}255; complimentary copies, {iv}259, 264–5, 267, 269–70, 275, 279, 282, 303, 342, 493, {v}91; DHL pleased with appearance of, {iv}260–1; sales satisfactory, {iv}261–2, 276, 278, 296, 315–16, 319; W H Smith and Boots refuse to circulate, {iv}262; reception, {iv}294, 304, 353, 483; no German translation, {vii}597–8

'Accumulated Mail', {v}243, 251, 303

'Adolf', {iii}13, {iv}168–9
    in *Dial*, {iii}536, 562, 634, {iv}123, 144, {vi}152, 176, {viii}36; excluded

from *EME*, {iv}145; Kippenberg included in *Almanach* 1924, {iv}257; in *New Keepsake*, {v}103

All Things Are Possible {iii}407, 428
    'Apotheosis of Groundlessness' appropriate title, {iii}380, 396, 398, 400, 402–3, 437; DHL edits Kot's translation of Shestov, {iii}380–1, 384, 394, 398, 400; constructed in short paragraphs, {iii}383–4; DHL completes work on, {iii}387; Secker to publish {iii}389, 391–4, 396–7, 400, 553; DHL writes Foreword to, {iii}394, 397, 433–4, 441, {vii}474; terms of Secker's agreement for, {iii}401–5, 500; proofs of, {iii}412, 434, 437, 439; Kot to have financial benefit of, {iii}442; Huebsch and, {iii}455–6, 466, 468, 471, 486, 501, 503, 508, 510–12, 516, 520, 529, 543; no US edn, {iii}508; published, {iii}521; sales disappointing, {iii}559–60, 570, {iv}275 *also see* 'Apotheosis of Groundlessness' and 'Shestov'

'America, Listen to your Own', {iii}591, 654; Mountsier calls 'Knights of Columbus' essay, {iii}627

Apocalypse, {vii}4
    Pryse's contribution to, {iii}150; Carter and, {iv}365, {vii}12, 509, 555; Burnet and, {vii}518; DHL's introduction for Carter became, {vii}555, 599, 613, 622; DHL at work on, {vii}610; completed, {vii}633; abandoned, {vii}640

'Aristocracy', {iv}357

'Art and Mortality', {v}275

'Art and the Individual', {i}5, 55, 63, 66, 72, 81
    originated as address to Eastwood group, {i}53; adverse comments on Watts in, {i}107, {vii}441

'As Far as Palermo', {iv}107, {v}104

Assorted Articles, {v}620, {vii}4
    essays collected in, {vi}400, 438, 461, {vii}29, 51, 65, 188, 269, 400, 405; DHL encouraged to 'publish a book of small prose pieces', {vii}122, 402–3,

LAWRENCE, DAVID HERBERT (*cont.*)
    568; 'book of newspaper articles',
    {vii}549, 575, 600; 'Orts and Slarts'
    DHL's preferred title, {vii}584;
    'Chips and Faggots' alternative title,
    {vii}607; DHL chooses title of,
    {vii}611, 619; Knopf to publish in
    USA, {vii}623–4
'At the Gates', {iii}165
    DHL 'writing short essays on philoso-
    phy', {iii}110–11, 152–3; developed
    out of 'Reality of Peace' articles but
    never published, {iii}143, 155; written
    four times, {iii}163; Pinker sends to
    Chatto & Windus and Secker without
    success, {iii}185, 187; rumoured that
    Maunsel might publish, {iii}191, 195,
    261; Pinker alleged to have MS of,
    {iii}472
'Au Revoir, U.S.A.', {iv}18, 555
'Autobiographical Fragment', {vi}198
'Autobiographical Sketch', {i}2, 21,
    {v}620 *see also* 'Autobiography' and
    'Myself Revealed'
'Autobiography', {vi}465
'Bad Side of Books, The', {iii}692,
    {v}110, 241
    for McDonald's *Bibliography*, {v}64,
    116, 119, 132–3, 271–2
'Bag of Cakes, A', *see* 'Christening, The'
'Becoming a Success', *see* 'On being a
    Success'
'Benjamin Franklin', {iii}299, 315,
    324
Bibliography, Introduction to, *see* 'Bad
    Side of Books, The'
'Bitter Cherry, The', *see Lost Girl, The*
Black Swans, 'Preface to', {iv}496,
    {v}20–1, 190; *see also* Skinner, M.
'Blessed Are the Powerful', originally
    entitled 'Power', {v}380
'Blind Gods that do not spare', *see*
    'Thorn in the Flesh, The'
'Blind Man, The', composition of,
    {iii}298; sent to Pinker, {iii}301; 'the
    end queer and ironical', {iii}303; in
    English Review and *Living Age*,
    {iii}633–5; DHL enquires about

payment for, {iii}645, 650, 690,
    {viii}40; fee received from *English
    Review*, {iv}32; collected in *EME*,
    {iv}134, 144, 262; referred to by
    Secker as eponymous story for
    collection, {iv}173, 299
'Blue Moccassins, The', first published
    in *Eve*, {vi}438, 454, 475; {vii}507;
    proofs of, {vi}606, 609; in *Plain Talk*,
    {vii}496
'Bogey between the Generations, The',
    see 'When She Asks Why'
'Books', {iv}549
'Border Line, The', {v}1–2
    relationship between Murry, Frieda
    and DHL reflected in, {iv}20;
    composition, {iv}564, {v}19; sent to
    Curtis Brown, {v}26; in *Smart Set* for
    $175, {v}50–51, 58–9; in *Hutchinson's
    Magazine* for £40, {v}57; MS to
    Barmby, {v}136, {vii}475; collected in
    WWRA, {vi}152, 197; proofs reveal
    end missing from, {vi}269–70, 272;
    DHL writes new ending, {vi}275,
    277, 280
Bottom Dogs, 'Introduction to', {vii}640
    Dahlberg approaches DHL about,
    {vii}65; DHL agrees to write,
    {vii}157, 160; completed, {vii}191–2,
    201; to remain DHL's property,
    {vii}218; DHL willing to modify,
    {vii}226; Dahlberg aggrieved by,
    {vii}526
Boy in the Bush, The (with Mollie
    Skinner), {iv}9, 16, 18, 236, 560, 588,
    {v}6, 44, 85, {vi}156, {vii}375
    Else Jaffe translates into German,
    {i}391, {v}71, 92–3, 95–6, 314, 332,
    485, 558, {vi}524; originally 'The
    House of Ellis', {iv}466; DHL
    prepared to read MS and make 'a few
    suggestions', {iv}467, 474, 477; 'I
    will..re-cast it, and make a book of it',
    {iv}495–6; three books of MS sent to
    Seltzer, {iv}503, 519; DHL going
    ahead to finish, {iv}517, 521, 523, 527;
    DHL gives original 'a unity, a rhythm,
    and a little more psychic develop-

ment', {iv}523–4; DHL and Skinner to 'appear as collaborators' and share royalties, {iv}524, 533, 544, 558, 596, {v}71, 95, 116, 245, 292; 'nearly done', {iv}529; 'finished', {iv}532; agent to have MS typed, {iv}533, 543, 549, 557; Secker publishes in England, Seltzer in USA, {iv}557, 559, 563, 596–7, {v}19–21, 35–8, 45, 78–80, {viii}88; original 'muddle and mess, but good stuff in it', {iv}582, {v}120; Brett designed dust-jacket for, {v}4, 32–4, 37, 92; DHL considers it 'a fine book', {v}21; Skinner's proposed alterations, {v}24–5, 31; contract sent to Skinner, {v}55; DHL given prominence in advertisement, {v}71; publication, {v}79, 91, 106, 112–13, 140, 182; complimentary copies, {v}80–1, 95, 114, 135, 141–2, 148, 173, 184, 195, 198; DHL embarrassed by unfair treatment of Skinner, {v}120–1, 123, {viii}90; encouraging sales of, {v}121–2, 161, 171; extract in anthology on Youth, {v}193; 'a *tour de force*', {vii}36 *see also Jack im Buschland*

'Burns Novel, The', 'a sort of life of Robert Burns', {i}487, 489; abandoned, {i}491, 504–5; DHL 'not Scotchy enough' to do 'a Burns book', {vi}231

'Cagliari', {iv}107, {v}104

'Captain's Doll, The', {iv}6, 258, {v}86, 93, 232, 261, 380

DHl seeks information about Scottish regimental dress for, {iv}105; DHL 'just at the end of', {iv}107; Mrs Carmichael types, {iv}107; 'a very funny long story', {iv}109; 'finished', {iv}112, 126; novelette based in Germany, {iv}121; TS for Mountsier, {iv}130–1, 134; 'a new manner' in, {iv}132; one of three novelettes for a volume, {iv}139, 143, 150; MS to Mountsier, {iv}156–7, 159; Seltzer and, {iv}258, 338, 341; *Hearst's International*' buys, {iv}287, 298–9,

302; Curtis Brown and, {iv}343; proofs of, {iv}369, 378; *Hearst's* delays and then releases, {iv}371, 379–80, 389–91, 394; scene in Zell am See in, {iv}396, 398; never serialised, {v}104; in Secker's pocket edn, {v}267

Captain's Doll, The, {ii}420, {iv}6, 18, 407, {viii}58, 62–3, 67

Seltzer publishes in USA, {iv}107, 258, 399, {v}87, {viii}57; publication delayed, {iv}325, 383, 409, 419; Merrild designs jacket for, {iv}345, 394, 406, 453; complimentary copies, {iv}392, 396, 457, 493, 519, 592, {v}23, 45, 48; reception, {iv}440, 442, 477, {v}375; errors in, {iv}442–3; DHL approves appearance of, {iv}446 *see also Ladybird, The*

'Cavalleria Rusticana', DHL's translation sent to Murry, {iv}447; Turiddu in, {vi}88

Cavalleria Rusticana, {iii}103, {iv}106, 188, {vi}4, 88, 151

'a veritable blood-pudding of *passion*', {iii}53; consists of 'short sketches', {iv}115; Cape publishes DHL's translation, {iv}447, {vi}53, 68, 70, 110, 130, 152, 168, 343, 517, {vii}66; three stories completed for typing, {vi}135, 137, 139; 'nearly done', {vi}152–4; 'finished', {vi}157; last MS and Introduction for typing, {vi}167; complimentary copy, {vi}325; Dial Press publishes in USA, {vi}343 *see also Verga, G.*

'Certain Americans and an Englishman', against Bursum Land Bill, {iv}14, 329–34, 339, 346

'Cerveteri', first published in *Travel*, {vi}48, 176, 189; completed, {vi}77, 79, 93; sent to Curtis Brown, {vi}83–4

'Chaos in Poetry', written as introduction to Crosby's *Chariot of the Sun*, {vi}4, 372, 404; MS sent to Crosby, {vi}389; first published in *Echanges* {vi}421–2, 461–2, 504, {vii}291

LAWRENCE, DAVID HERBERT (*cont.*)
'Chapel Among the Mountains, A',
based in personal experience, {i}441;
sent to De la Mare, {i}447; rejected by
Westminster Gazette, {ii}56, 60, 83;
sent to Clayton for typing, {ii}202,
204–5; rejected by *New Statesman*,
{ii}236
Chariot of the Sun, Introduction to, *see*
'Chaos in Poetry'
'Child and the Unconscious, The', *see*
Fantasia of the Unconscious
'Child Consciousness', *see Fantasia of the*
Unconscious
'Child's Book on Art', *see* 'History of
Italian Painting for Children, A'
'Choir Correspondence', *see Mr Noon*
'Christening, The', {i}420, {ii}39
first called 'A Bag of Cakes', then 'Pat-
a-Cake, Pat-a-Cake, Baker's Man',
{ii}41; submitted to and returned by
Northern Newspaper Syndicate,
{ii}44, 58; sent to Pound, {ii}60;
accepted by *Smart Set*, {ii}132;
collected in *Prussian Officer* {ii}197;
MS with Clayton, {viii}12
'Christs in the Tirol', {i}447, 548
in *Saturday Westminster*
Gazette{i}446, {ii}373, {v}119
'Climbing Down Pisgah', {v}118, 151
'Cocksure Women and Hen-sure Men',
written for but rejected by *Evening*
News, {vi}521, 541, 601; published by
Forum, {vi}609
Contemporary German Poetry, A review
of, {i}324–5
'Corasmin and the Parrots', {v}175,
178–9, 183, 193, 242, 252
collected in *M in M*, {v}186, 580, 594;
published in *Adelphi*, {v}432, 451,
575, {v}580; 'all women' like best of
Mexican essays, {vi}91
'Crown, Note to The', {ii}385, {v}284,
295
'Crown, The', {ii}17, 323, {iii}84,
{iv}323, {v}103
Henry Miller on, {ii}18; partly
published in *Signature*, {ii}293, 386;
interim titles ('Le Gai Savaire', 'The
Signal', 'The Phoenix', 'Morgenrot')
for, {ii}295, 300, 303, 312, 315;
contributions to 'a book about Life',
{ii}299, 307–9, 312–13, 325, 317, 334,
338, 351, 354; 'my revolutionary
utterance', {ii}300; DHL types own
MS, {ii}341, 343, 352; scene of
women fascinated by wounded soldier
reappears in, {ii}342; part sent to
friends, {ii}355–6, 358; DHL left off
writing, {ii}360–4; DHL will 'write all
my philosophy again,', {ii}367; six
papers completed, {ii}405; proclaims
'blasphemy of the war', {ii}407; DHL
believes three unpublished parts of
MS with Ottoline Morrell, {ii}476;
'the "Lion and Unicorn" article',
{iv}315; included in *Porcupine*,
{v}255, 280, 284, 290, 374, 575,
{vii}403 *see also* 'Crown, Note to The'
'Crucifix Across the Mountains, The',
{ii}373, 398, {v}119
'Dance of the Sprouting Corn, The',
{v}27, 36, 66, 115, 136, 241
periodicals publish, {v}57, 59, 87, 100,
114, 116; Else Jaffe translates into
German, {v}173, 189; collected in *M*
in M, {v}581, 587, 594, 623, 636,
{vi}31; Edith Isaacs reprints, {v}636,
{vi}354; MS to Barmby, {vii}474–5
'Dance, The', {ii}414
'Daughters of the Vicar', {i}288, 298,
{ii}44, 67
typed by Clayton, {ii}45, 55, {viii}12;
never serialised, {ii}65–6; collected in
Prussian Officer, {ii}197; Ottoline
Morrell admires, {ii}254 *see also* 'Two
Marriages'
'David', {iii}428
'Day of Wrath', *see Women in Love*
'Dead Pictures on the Wall', *see* 'Pictures
on the Wall'
'Dead Rose, The', {ii}197
'Dear Old Horse, A London Letter',
{iv}20
'article in the shape of a letter',
{iv}555, 561, 567, {v}28, 48

'Delilah and Mr Bircumshaw', {i}420, 430

'Democracy', {iv}324, 341
published in *The Word*, {iii}7, 391, 404–5; Mountsier's enthusiasm for, {iv}314–15, 320

'Diary of a Trip to Sardinia', *see Sea and Sardinia*

'Dies Irae', *see Women in Love*

'Do Women Change', {vi}609
intended for *Evening News*, {vi}610; extended for *Sunday Dispatch*{vii}117–18, 188, 200

Dragon of the Apocalypse, The, 'Introduction to', {vii}613–14, 622

'Dream of Life, A', *see* 'Autobiographical Fragment'

'Dull London', for *Evening News*, {vi}438, 516

'Duro, Il', {ii}408

'Education and Sex', {iv}483; *see also Fantasia of the Unconscious*

'Education of the People', written for *Times Educational Supplement*, {iii}303, 306–7, 310–11; *Times* rejects, {iii}316, 323; Unwin and, {iii}323, 553–5, 565, {viii}30–4, 37–8

'Elsa Culverwell', {i}496, 501

'England as a Man's Country', {vi}602; *see* 'Is England Still a Man's Country?'

'England, My England', 'based on Percy Lucas family', {ii}354, 386; sold to *English Review*, {ii}364, 372, 391, 395, 402, 406; about 'men at the war, and wives at home', {ii}386; Lucas killed, DHL wishes story 'at the bottom of the sea' but doesn't regret having written it, {ii}635–6; *Metropolitan* publishes in USA, {ii}406, {iii}111; DHL re-writing *English Review* version, {iv}144, 150; finished, {iv}153, 155–6; to Curtis Brown, {iv}159, 164, 176–7

England, My England, {ii}127, {iv}6, 14, 145, 328, 407, 465, {v}87, 194, {vi}173
DHL assembling stories for, {iv}100, 117, 134; Secker to publish, {iv}144, 183, 298, 302, 383, 394, 401; Secker prefers 'Blind Man' as the lead story in, {iv}262, 299; Seltzer publishes first, {iv}262; Seltzer selects title of, {iv}299, 315; DHL anxious for speedy publication in USA, {iv}324; Seltzer's edn published, {iv}335–6, {viii}56–7; sales relatively good, {iv}341; complimentary copies, {iv}342, 349, 352, 361–2, 372, 377, 392, 403; sales in Australia, {v}122, 161; issued by Tauchnitz, {vi}262, {vii}220; remaindered, {vii}66; French translation of, {vii}223; US reviewers praise, {viii}60

'Enslaved by Civilisation', {i}3, {vii}158
written for but not published by *Sunday Dispatch*, {vii}29; bought by *Vanity Fair* (as 'Manufacture of Good Little Boys') for $100, {vii}29, 251

Escaped Cock, The, {vii}4, 7, 10, 562, 604, 623
Osiris in, {ii}454; 'story of the Resurrection', {vi}40, 44, 50, 74; DHL's summary of plot, {vi}50; sent to Nancy Pearn, {vi}51; bought by *Forum* for $150, {vi}176, 196, 224, 226, 326; possible reprintings, {vi}238, 310, 358, 416; hostile reaction of *Forum* readers to, {vi}370–1, 378, 382; DHL's defence of, {vi}378; DHL writing Part II of, {vi}418, 429, 442, 469, 526; Enid Hilton arranges for typing, {vi}528, 539–40, 552, 569; negotiations with Gaige, {vi}572, 576, 598, {vii}62, 111, 121–2, 130, 202, 236, 272, 390; 'one of my best stories', {vii}122, 412; typescript to Harry and Caresse Crosby, {vii}233, 236; Crosbys to publish limited edn, {vii}239–40, 255, 285, 290, 296–7, 322–3, 339, 398–9, 417–18, 429, 445, 471, 487–8, 504, 525, 528, 634, 647; proof-stage reached, {vii}405, 411; Marks to distribute in USA, {vii}411, 417–18, 426, 471, 487–8, 496–7, 498–9, 538–9, 550, 560, 577, 586, 589,

LAWRENCE, DAVID HERBERT (*cont.*)
606–7; DHL's water-colour decorations for (Crosby) Black Sun edn,
{vii}412, 417, 426, 450, 471, 516, 531,
557–8; DHL signs vellum copies,
{vii}487, 491; *Gallo Scappato* or
Verflogene Hahn, {vii}516, 528, 555–2,
559–60, 562, 578, 617, 639;
published, {vii}530–2, 536, 548;
complimentary copies, {vii}531–2,
575–6, 582, 630, 632; 'a lovely little
book', {vii}550, 582; later title, *The
Man Who Died* emerging, {vii}638,
648–9; Lahr's interest in producing
English edn of, {vii}638, 643–4,
648–9
Etruscan Places, {v}424, 648–51
DHL contemplates book 'about
Umbria and the Etruscans: half travel-
book, scientific too', {v}412–16, 418,
420, 427, 430, 437, 442, 444, 447–9,
453, 455–6, 460–1, 464–5, 470–1;
'nothing to be said, *scientifically*, about
the Etruscans', {v}473; none of book
done yet, {v}483, 496; DHL invited to
write Etruscan essays, {v}653, 655 *see
also Sketches of Etruscan Places*
'Europe Versus America', {v}66, 344
*European History, see Movements in
European History*
'Fanny and Annie', sent to Pinker,
{iii}360, 472, 576; with Mountsier,
{iii}582, 613; rejected by two US
periodicals, {iii}644; offered to Squire,
{iii}681; routed to, then accepted by
Hutchinson's Magazine, {iv}32, 34, 36,
{v}87; collected in *EME*, {iv}134,
143; change of title to 'The Last
Straw' not implemented, {iv}152
Fantasia of the Unconscious, {i}477,
{iv}5, 14–15, 18, 341, 349, {v}93,
{viii}81
'Psychoanalysis and the Incest Motive'
early title for, {iii}730, 732; DHL at
work on, {iv}25, 28; 'nearly done',
{iv}39; being typed, {iv}82; perhaps
entitled 'Child Consciousness',
{iv}82, {viii}41; 'written for
America', {iv}85–6; DHL writes

'Foreword' to, also for separate
publication, {iv}86, 93, 96, 104, 109,
130–2, 134; 'Child and the
Unconscious' possible title, {iv}93,
96; TS finished and sent to Seltzer,
{iv}95–6, 103–4, 107, 109, 111, 130;
'Harlequinade of the Unconscious'
another title, {iv}97; final title
adopted, {iv}103–4; 'original typescript' to be followed, {iv}132; Seltzer
publishes in USA, {iv}245, 255,
298–9, 306, 315, 319–20, 322–4, 326,
328, 330, 335–6, 458, {viii}56;
complimentary copies, {iv}259, 261,
267, 269, 276, 279, 301, 305, 342, 375,
377, 387, 449, 457, 459, 486, 547,
{v}91, 105–6, 323, {vi}281, 547, 600;
Secker and, {iv}383, 394, 399, 401,
407, 427, 454; Murry prints extracts in
Adelphi, {iv}432, 437, 446, 458, 483,
{v}205, {vii}437; errors found in,
{iv}443; response 'stupid', {iv}582;
German translation of, {v}48,
{vii}553, 571, 599; sales poor, {v}262;
'some savage spirit of life' in, {vi}400;
extract in *Adelphi* as 'On Love and
Marriage', {vii}568; reception in
USA, {viii}60–1
'Fireworks', {v}482, {vii}600
'Flowery Tuscany', {vi}189, 211,
{vii}503
Nancy Pearn very fond of, {vi}52,
{vii}185, 462; prompted invitation
from *Travel*, {vii}402
'Fly in the Ointment, The', {i}345, 420
first called 'A Blot', {i}298; DHL
probably revising, {ii}39; for *New
Statesman*, {ii}44, 52, 64, 139; Clayton
typed, {viii}11
'Flying-Fish, The', {v}162, {vi}452
written when close to death, {v}8;
incomplete, {vii}424
'Fortified Germany' I and II, {i}430
'Fox, The', {i}391, {iii}6, 10, 13,
{iv}258, 341, {v}188, 232, 380,
{vi}600
being written, {iii}299, 302; 'rather
odd and amusing', {iii}307; to Pinker,
{iii}309, 319, 472, 529, 651;

Hutchinson's Magazine pays £30 for, {iii}364, 619, 621, 627, 648; {v}87; slightly shortened for publication, {iii}371, 373–4; Monk and Lambert associated with, {iii}378, {iv}28; in proof, {iii}596–7; expanded for 'a book of novelettes', {iv}121, 126–7, 131, 139, 143, 145, 150, 157, 159; in 'a new manner', {iv}132; sent to Mountsier, {iv}134, 156; serialised in *Dial*, {iv}155, {v}104; Italian translation of, {iv}232, {v}90, {vi}516, {vi}600, {vii}386; Secker publishes in *Ladybird*, {iv}369, {viii}57; Seltzer's proofs of, {iv}378; 'belongs more to the old world', {iv}447; Else Jaffe translated (*Der Fuchs*), {v}288, 554, 558, 561; French translation of (*Le Renard*), {vii}638

'Fragment of Stained Glass, A', {i}252, 258, 297
  'Legend' first title of, {i}38; submitted to *English Review*, {i}248, 275, 292, 305, 335, 345, 471, 510; 'bit of a tour de force', {i}293; admired by 'the literary people', {i}491; collected in *Prussian Officer*, {ii}197

Frau die davon ritt, Die, see WWRA, German translation

Fuchs, Der see 'Fox, The'

'Future of the Novel, The', {iv}16, 377, {v}574; later entitled, 'Surgery for the Novel', {iv}374

'Gai Savaire, Le', *see* 'Crown, The'

Gallo, see Escaped Cock, The

'Gentle Art of Marketing in Mexico, The', *see* 'Market Day'

'Gentleman from San Francisco, The', DHL collaborates with Kot as translator of, {iv}7, 23, 29, 37; typed by Violet Monk, {iv}58, 78–9, 87, 98; offered to and published by *Dial*, {iv}58, 73, 78–9, 87, 91, 108, 165, 168; eponymous story when collected, {iv}274, 322, {v}347

'Georgian Renaissance, The', review of *Georgian Poetry* 1911–1912, {i}508, 512, 519

'German Books: Thomas Mann', {i}546

'German Impressions: I. French Sons of Germany', {i}394
  in *Saturday Westminster Gazette*, {i}396, 405, 422, 424, 430

'German Impressions: II. Hail in the Rhineland', {i}404
  Hannah Krenkow in, {i}350; in *Saturday Westminster Gazette*, {i}405, 422, 424, 430

'Getting On', {v}620

'Give Her a Pattern', MS entitled, 'Oh These Women!'; in *Express* as 'The Real Trouble About Women', in *Assorted Articles* as, {vii}51

'Glad Ghosts', {v}6, 10
  as 'Gay Ghosts' written for Cynthia Asquith, {v}348, 352, 400; becomes 'Ghost of Silence', {v}362; finished as 'Glad Ghosts', {v}365; Brett types, {v}370, 380, 382, 389; to Nancy Pearn, {v}385–6, 388; in *Dial*, {v}416, 442, 504; Benn interested for 'Yellow Books' series, {v}521, 523, 535–6; collected in *WWRA*, {vi}152, 197, 236–7 *see also Glad Ghosts*

Glad Ghosts, {v}2
  in Benn's 'Yellow Books' series but unsigned, {v}523, 535–6; proofs and agreement for, {v}543; DHL receives copies, {v}575; complimentary copies, {v}588, 594, 641; DHL uses as Christmas cards, {v}596, 599, 607, 612, {viii}100, 103; good for Harwood Brewster to read, {v}637

'Goats and Compasses', {iii}219
  'a sort of philosophy', {ii}496, 498, 504–5; 'at last I have *got* it', {ii}537, 538, 556–7; plan for publishing, {ii}542; sent to Ottoline Morrell but never published, {ii}558; Ottoline Morrell regards as 'deplorable tosh', {ii}558, 580; with Heseltine, {ii}598

'Goose Fair', {i}2, 142, 144, 155, 275, 298, 345
  written and sent to an agency, {i}131–2, 136–7; MS returned, {i}139; sent to Hueffer for advice, {i}147; in *English Review*, {i}153, 510; fee shared with Louie Burrows,

LAWRENCE, DAVID HERBERT (*cont.*)
{i}156; collected in *Prussian Officer*,
{ii}197
Grand Inquisitor, The, Introduction to,
{vii}643
'Great Return, The', *see* 'Last Laugh,
The'
'Hadrian', early title of 'You Touched
Me', {iv}134, 144–5, 177–8
'Harlequinade of the Unconscious', *see*
Fantasia of the Unconscious
Hahn, *see Escaped Cock, The*
'Hay Hut Among the Mountains, A',
{i}432, 441
sent to De la Mare, {i}447; rejected by
Westminster Gazette, {ii}56; MS
mislaid, {ii}60, 83; sent to Clayton for
typing, {ii}202, 204–5; not submitted
to Squire, {ii}236
'Henry St John Crèvecœur', in *English
Review*, {iii}299, 315, 324
'Her Turn', {ii}44
originally 'The Collier's Wife Scores',
{i}375; rejected by *Daily News* {i}379;
Belloc's *Eyewitness* a possible publisher, {i}381; De la Mare assists in
placing, {i}383; DHL revising, {ii}39;
accepted by *Westminster Gazette* as
'Strike-Pay I, Her Turn', {ii}55, 67
'History of Italian Painting for Children,
A', {iv}6, 28
DHL invited to write text, Medici
Society to provide pictures, {iii}714,
723–4, {iv}24–6, 41, 43, 49; agreement signed, {iv}46–7; project
abandoned, {iv}66
'Honour and Arms', {ii}5–6
'the best short story I have ever done',
{ii}21; Harrison *English Review* and,
{ii}26, 44, 66, 81–2; DHL accepts
Harrison's offer of £15 for, {ii}87, 90,
127; collected as 'The Prussian
Officer', {ii}197–8, 223, 241; arbitrari-
ly shortened by *English*, {ii}216; sold
to *Metropolitan* for £25, {ii}222–3,
256; typed by Clayton, {viii}12 *see also*
'Prussian Officer, The'
'Hopi Snake Dance, The', {v}103, 113,
218

sent to Curtis Brown for Murry,
{v}109–10; offered to, then published
by *Theatre Arts*, {v}115–16, 193, 195,
197, 241, 584, 594–5, 636, {vi}354;
Murry and, {v}142, 150, 170, 173;
collected in *M in M*, {v}581, 584, 587,
594–6, {vi}31, 36, 91
'Horse-Dealer's Daughter, The', {iii}29,
{iv}8
'mid-winter story of oblivion', {ii}493;
MS to Pinker under original title,
'The Miracle', {iii}74, 472–3; typed in
Florence, {iv}107; collected in *EME*,
{iv}134, 144, 155; published in *English
Review*, {iv}226; included in *Best
British Short Stories of 1923* {iv}296,
464–5, {v}87
'Hymns in a Man's Life', {i}3, {vi}4,
563
written for 'Carossa book', {vi}524,
541; translated into German by
Frieda, {vi}524, 540–1, 551; in
Evening News, {vi}541, 609, {vii}28
'If Women Were Supreme', *see*
'Matriarchy'
'In Love', {vi}189
original title, 'More Modern Love',
{v}571, 573, {vi}46, 271; in *Dial*,
{v}571, {vi}46, 176, 270; collected in
WWRA as, {vi}46, 152, 197
'Indians and an Englishman', {iv}14,
298
DHL refers to as 'Pueblos and an
Englishman', {iv}332; in *Dial*,
{iv}332, 336, 340, 369, 372, 380–1,
404, 406; republished in *Adelphi*,
{iv}432, {vii}437
'Indians and Entertainment', to Curtis
Brown, {v}36, 50; accepted by
Adelphi, {v}110; MS to Barmby,
{v}136, {vii}474–5; collected in *M in
M*, {v}580–1, 584, 594–5, 636, {vi}91
'Insouciance', in *Evening News* as 'Over-
Earnest Ladies', {vi}438, {vii}28; in
Atlantic Monthly, {vii}28
'Insurrection of Miss Houghton, The',
'simmering a new work', {i}501; 80
pages done, {i}505; 100 pages, right
for 'the Meredithy public', {i}511;

'going quite fast', {i}517; 'a weird thing', {i}525; 'more than half' written', {i}526; 'has my love', {i}530; 200 pages done, then put aside, {i}536; provisionally entitled, {i}546; Frieda comments on, {i}549; MS left in Germany, {ii}580, 595; alternative title, 'Mixed Marriage', {iii}439, 458; MS arrives, {iii}476
see also Lost Girl, The

'Intimacy', {i}298–9, 301–2, 304, 345, {ii}37, {iii}473
early title of 'The Witch à la Mode', {i}16, 253; written, {i}258; probably with *English Review*, {i}275; Garnett advises on, {i}307; MS (of 'The White Woman', interim title) lost, {ii}33; found among Frieda's underclothes {ii}36
see also 'Witch à la Mode, The'

'Introduction to These Paintings', DHL willing to write, {vii}60, 82, 95; 'one of the best things I've done', {vii}117, 138, 155; DHL busy with {vii}124; written, {vii}130–1; MS sent for typing, {vii}135–6, 140; about 10,000 words, {vii}145; police action delays in mail, {vii}148–51, 154, 157; DHL keen to revise typescript, {vii}153, 158, 163, 168, 181; 'on painting in relation to life', {vii}165; DHL correcting proofs of, {vii}197, 201; final title adopted, {vii}198; DHL prepared to sell MS of, {vii}285; 'on Modern art – more or less', {vii}304; US copyright important, {vii}321, 462; possibility of periodical publica-tion, {vii}439, 469, 496, 503, 593, 640; reception of, {vii}447; good for limited edn, {vii}462

'Is England Still a Man's Country?', in *Daily Express*, {vi}602, 606, 609
'Italian Days', *see Twilight in Italy*
'Italian Studies: By the Lago di Garda', {i}512
Pietro di Paoli in, {i}458; Ibsen's *Ghosts* in, {i}495; *Hamlet* in, {i}505; sent to *English Review*, {i}533; *English* proofs, {ii}58, 67; *English* pays £25

for, {ii}66, 70, 127; Clayton types, {ii}383, 387, 398, 408
'Italians in Exile', {ii}410

Jack im Buschland (*The Boy in the Bush*), {v}173, 558, {vi}524
Else Jaffe to translate *B in B*, {v}38–9, 71, 92–3, 95–6; DHL admires, {v}332, 485

'"Jeune Fille" Wants to Know, The' *see* 'When She Asks Why'

'Jimmy and the Desperate Woman', {iv}20, {v}1, 27
composition of, {iv}564, {v}19; 'the result of Europe, and perhaps a bit dismal', {v}23, 26; sent to Curtis Brown, {v}26, 58; accepted by *Criterion* for £18, {v}85–6, 205, {vi}270; MS to Barmby, {v}136, {vii}474–5; Jimmy modelled on Murry, {v}205; included in *Best British Short Stories of 1925*, {v}270; collected in *WWRA*, {vi}152, 191, 197

'John Galsworthy', {v}601, {vi}67, {vii}23
MS of 'Scrutiny' sent for typing, {v}649, 654; proofs corrected, {vi}136; published in *Scrutinies*, {vi}342, {viii}107; MS bound, {vi}348, 359

'John Thomas and Lady Jane', {vi}333, 335, 340, 343, 410
adopted as title being 'much more suitable' than *LCL*, {vi}308–9, 314, 316; title suggested 'rather savagely' by Juliette Huxley, {vi}313, 315; DHL forced to accept as sub-title to *LCL*, {vi}318, 321, 326, 331; appears on order-forms for *LCL*, {vi}352–3; MS entitled, {vi}354; omitted from title-page of *LCL*, {vi}384, 408; DHL continues privately to use, {vi}414, 435, 440, 484, 508 *see also LCL*

'John Thomas', *see* 'Tickets, Please'
'Just Back from the Snake Dance – Tired Out', {v}101, 103, 127

Kangaroo, {iii}3–4, 6, 8–9, 11, 16, 65, 404, {iv}9–11, 14, 16, 18, 232, 281, 362, 378, 500, {v}38, 44, 416, {vii}168, 583, {viii}90

LAWRENCE, DAVID HERBERT (*cont.*)
begun, {iv}251; 'weird novel of
Australia', {iv}255, 257, 259, 264;
novel named, {iv}261; Secker
welcomed prospect of, {iv}262; about
half done, 'now slightly stuck',
{iv}268, 271; 'nearly finished',
{iv}275; finished, {iv}277–8, 280, 282;
sent to Mountsier, {iv}277, 295,
299–300, 302, 307, 315, 318–20; copy
of TS for Seltzer, {iv}318–20, 324–5;
'now..as I want it', {iv}322–3; revised
and sent to Mountsier, {iv}329–30,
335–6; revised version to Seltzer,
{iv}340–2; Merrild designs jacket for,
{iv}345, 367, 369; 'thought adventure', {iv}353; 'last page' of, {iv}367,
380; Secker and, {iv}369, 383, 389,
391, 394, 399, 401, 427–8, {v}20;
Seltzer urged to print, {iv}428, 442,
447, 449; errors found in, {iv}443;
Secker pays £125 advance, {iv}448;
proof correction, {iv}470–1, 473–7,
480; publication of {iv}486, 489–90,
501; complimentary copies, {iv}513,
515, 517, 519, 524, 527, 547, 592,
{v}23, 45, 507,556; reception of,
{iv}557; Australian edn, {v}122, 161;
'only just what I felt', {vii}322;
'*deepest*' of his novels, {viii}57;
Seltzer's enthusiasm for, {viii}59–60
Lady Chatterley's Lover, {v}451,
{vi}4–16, 430–1, 453, 458, 460, 462,
472–3, 482, 499, 543, 551–2, 570,
612–13, {vii}1, 3, 5–7, 10, 13, 23, 27,
32, 44, 80, 82–3, 87, 90–1, 96, 112,
141, 197–8, 224, 226, 254, 310, 381,
504, 574, 588, 636
DHL 'working at a story – shortish',
{v}563, 584; second version going
'nicely', {v}596, 600–1; 'a little too
deep in bits, {v}605; 'slowly pegging
at a novel', {v}620, 628–9; different
from anything before, {v}621; not
'*really*' improper, {v}623; nearly done
and 'so *absolutely* improper, in words'
but 'really *good*... in spirit', {v}638–9,
651, 655, {vi}21; finished 'for the time

being', {v}647; '*utterly* unfit for
serialising', {vi}21; MS in two
notebooks given by Brett, {vi}23;
objective 'to make the sex relation
valid and precious', {vi}29; Curtis
Brown anxious over impropriety of,
{vi}29, 46, 222, 352, 356, 358, 371,
{vii}439, 518, 522; DHL delays
sending to publishers, {vi}31, 41–3,
45, 74, 77, 130, 182, 196; private
publication and financial advantage
contemplated, {vi}223–5, 241, 253,
255, 261, 282; third version being
written, {vi}233, 237–8; improper 'for
the conventional smut-hounds' but
'very pure and tender', {vi}238–9,
241–2, 247, 253, 300, 314–15, 317;
Nellie Morrison and typing of,
{vi}245, 249, 252, 259–60; DHL
determined to publish novel 'uncas-
trated', {vi}253–4, 293, 296–7;
alternative title, 'Tenderness',
{vi}254–5, 261–2, 264–5, 275; typing
of MS, {vi}260, 274–5, 277, 281,
288–91, 294, 303, 305–6; perhaps
expurgated edn for Secker and Knopf,
{vi}271, 288–9, 291, 295, 299, 305,
310, 314; Maria Huxley will type
'worst bits', {vi}273, 290, 294, 303;
problem of copyright on 'indecent'
book, {vi}295, 329, 333, 337; DHL
tells Orioli: 'All is ready! We can
begin', {vi}307, 310; 'John Thomas
and Lady Jane' DHL's preferred title,
{vi}308, 318; expurgation proves
difficult, {vi}308, 314; TS to
Florentine printer, {vi}313–14;
Juliette Huxley initially offended by,
{vi}315–16; proofs of, {vi}316, 329,
342, 353, 364, 369, 373–4, 377–8, 382,
385, 394–7, 405–6, 410–11, 415, 418;
order forms distributed for, {vi}316,
319–20, 322–35, 337–8, 340–6,
348–50, 353, 355–8, 360, 370, 381, 387,
391, 393; 'phallic novel..but tender
and delicate', {vi}319–20, 322, 324,
326–8, 331, 340, 355; printer ignorant
of English, {vi}322, 324, 326, 330–1,

334, 337, 344; Secker believes public
sale impossible, {vi}329–30, 333–4,
337, 344, 358, 370; a 'bomb at the skull
of idealistic Mammon', {vi}332, 513;
DHL enjoys buying special paper for,
{vi}347, 357, 363; TS transferred
from Secker to Huxleys, {vi}352, 354;
orders for £70 received, {vi}357;
printer has sufficient type for only half
of text, {vi}364, 395, 401–2, 408,
{vii}30, 39; Knopf eager to publish,
{vi}371–6, {viii}114; orders from
England encouraging, {vi}375, 401,
408, 416; DHL confident of commercial success, {vi}381; no orders from
Forster or Bell, {vi}383; booksellers
and, {vi}390, 417–18, 444–5, 447,
476–82, 484, 486–93, 496, 498, 514–15,
519, 529, 545, 547, 550, 558, 579, 588,
591, 594, 603, 608, 617, {vii}25, 35,
55, 68, 97, 124, 161–2, 176–7, 202,
306–7, 309, 320, 341, 372,
{viii}108–10; American buyers
'itching, but terrified', {vi}402; no
complimentary copies of 1st edn,
{vi}405; orders for 'Mrs Clutterley's
Lover', {vi}412; 200 extra copies
printed, {vi}414, {vii}30, 42–3, 46–9,
54, 66, 123, 131, 136–7; printing
completed, {vi}417; 'all the sheets
signed and numbered, up to 1000',
{vi}420–2; copy for Maria Huxley,
{vi}428; first 200 copies ready for
USA, {vi}432–3, 436–7; DHL's
delight in 'handsome and dignified
volume', {vi}440, 442, 505; copies
mailed to USA, {vi}447–51, 461,
469–70, 475–6, 508, 521; copies to be
sent to England quickly before 'any
fuss', {vi}465–6; Kot disapproves of,
{vi}469; financial arrangements with
Orioli, {vi}470–1, 475, 478, 483, 533,
539, 544, 560–1, 573, {vii}21, 61, 63,
86; Beaverbrook and, {vi}479;
reception, {vi}484–6, 488, 498, 520,
522, 528, 548, 560, 576–7, 595, 598,
602–4, 607, 609, {vii}19, 24, 34, 105,
141, 144–5, 177, 525, 601, 610; friends

store and distribute copies of,
{vi}489–91, 494–7, 499–501, 503,
510–15, 517–18, 528–30, 532, 535–6,
564, 575, {vii}47, 90, 121, 126, 142–3,
151; rumour of suppression of,
{vi}493, 504, 547, 549, 602–3, {vii}23;
friends scandalised by, {vi}502,
{vii}106, 108, 110, 529; Vanguard
Press offer to distribute in USA,
{vi}525–7, 530, 532, 545–6, 565, 568,
572, {vii}35, {viii}115; US authorities
seize copies of, {vi}531–2, 537, 548–9,
550, 553, 555, 559–60, 568, {vii}97,
108, 132, 145; DHL disgusted by
American attitude to, {vi}575; more
courage needed for *Point Counter Point*
than to write, {vi}600; piracies,
{vi}608, {vii}20, 25, 35, 38–40, 42–6,
55–7, 67, 77, 85, 95–7, 105, 147,
161–2, 177, 202, 210, 212, 215, 219,
234, 240, 297, 307–8, 311–12, 321,
375, 381–2, 496–8; Lahr to handle
cheap paper issue, {vii}44, 47–50,
57–9, 61, 71, 85, 88, 120, 124, 140, 177,
621; Gollancz and expurgated edn,
{vii}44, 47, 59–60, 88, 271; DHL
proposes unexpurgated cheap edn
from Paris, {vii}50, 62, 75, 77, 89, 95,
109–10, 115, 118–20, 125, 131, 137–8,
142–3, 154, 159, 168, 172, 183, 190,
194, 202; 1st edn nearly sold out,
{vii}50–1, 57, 84, 146, 154, 171, 184,
202, 496, 527, 551; Sylvia Beach and,
{vii}62, 64, 75–7, 89–90, 97–8,
109–10, 118, 125, 131–2, 134, 140, 143,
150, 153, 159, 219; copies for DHL's
sisters, {vii}68–9, 76, 107, 127; DHL
denies 'perpetual sex' advocated by,
and justifies language in, {vii}106;
German translation of, {vii}113–14,
139, 245, 287, 304, 333, 335, 375, 383,
386, 410, 517, 543, 567, 571–3, 596–8,
601–2, 604, 609, 615; British authorities act against, {vii}146–57, 160–1,
165, 174, 205; DHL to Paris to arrange
cheap unexpurgated edn, {vii}208–16,
219, 224; Paris edn by Titus,
{vii}229–30, 233–4, 238, 242–4, 246,

LAWRENCE, DAVID HERBERT (*cont.*)
261, 271, 295, 339, 341, 346, 355, 386,
390, 395, 428–9, 517, 582–3; 'final
gross profit' on 1st ed, £1239,
{vii}230, 473, 547; Bradley DHL's
agent in Paris for, {vii}245; 'Our
Lady' DHL's nickname for, {vii}253,
256, 259, 268, 278, 301, 316, 335, 339,
341, 384; 3rd edn, {vii}256, 274;
French translation of, {vii}261, 382–3,
396–7, 401, 451–3, 515, 540, 601; *My
Skirmish* as introduction to Paris edn,
{vii}316, 390, 392, 396, 428–30, 439,
446, 464, 471, 481; DHL and expurgation of, {vii}368, 383–4, 391–4, 396,
399, 401, 403, 411, 414; MS not for
sale, {vii}411, 515, 541, 632; second
printing of Paris edn, {vii}432–3, 435,
451, 455, 464, 488, 515, 587; symbolism in, {vii}476–7; royalties on Paris
edn, {vii}514, 526, 568, 612, 648;
signed copy of 1st edn for Morland,
{vii}631, 650; Campbell's stinginess
over, {vii}635; third printing of Paris
edn, {vii}637–8; Maria Chambers
offers to act as US agent for,
{viii}109–10 *see also* 'John Thomas
and Lady Jane'
'Ladybird, The', {iv}6, 258, {viii}61
'Thimble' re-written as, {ii}420,
{iv}134, {v}104; for publication with
'Fox' and 'Captain's Doll', {iv}134,
139, 143, 150, 157, 159; 'nearly ready',
{iv}144; 'finished', {iv}150, 153; TS
to Curtis Brown, {iv}155, 164; TS to
Seltzer, {iv}155–7; Italian translation,
{iv}232, {v}90, 516, {vii}386;
Mountsier fails to place with *Dial*,
{iv}302, 341, 358; proofs from Seltzer,
{iv}378, 389–90, 443; 'has more the
quick of a new thing' than companion
stories, {iv}447; in form which suits
DHL admirably, {v}194, 241
Ladybird, The, {ii}420, {iv}6, 14, 107,
155, 319, 399, {v}87, 91, 104, 267,
385, {vii}413, {viii}57, 74
DHL determines contents of, {iv}134;
Secker chooses title for, {iv}262, 298,

300, 324; Secker 'making a fine book
of', {iv}369; publication, {iv}372,
389, 401; Secker confident about
success of, {iv}427; complimentary
copies, {iv}431, 449, 549, 553;
'remarkable [press] notices' for,
{v}194 *see also Captain's Doll, The*
'Laetitia', *see White Peacock, The*
'Lance Corporal Comes Home from the
War, The', *see* 'Wintry Peacock'
'Last Laugh, The', {iv}20, {v}1
first called 'The Great Return',
{iv}564; being written, {v}19–20; TS
to Curtis Brown, {v}26–7; placed with
New Decameron for £25, {v}50, 57,
{vi}175–6; MS to Barmby, {v}136,
{vii}474; collected in *WWRA*,
{vi}152, 197, 270–1
'Last Straw, The', *see* 'Fanny and Annie'
'Latter Days, The', *see Women in Love*
'Laura Philippine', published in *T.P's*,
{vi}400, 438, 460–1; based on Mary
Christine Hughes, {vi}400, {vii}414
'Legend', *see* 'Fragment of Stained
Glass, A'
'Lemon Gardens, The', in *English
Review*, {i}458, {ii}58; Clayton types,
{ii}383, 385, 398
'Lessford's Rabbits', {i}97, 275, 297,
345, {ii}30
'Lesson on a Tortoise, A', {i}97, 275,
297, 345, {ii}30
'Life', {vii}474
in *English Review*, {iii}164–5, 191,
211, 217, {v}104
*Life of J. Middleton Murry by J[esus]
C[hrist], The*, {vii}484, 501
'Limit to the British Novelist, The',
{iii}177–8
'Lion and the Unicorn, The', *see*
'Crown, The'
'Little Moonshine with Lemon, A',
{v}66, 344, 581
Little Novels of Sicily, {iii}149, {iv}8,
14, 106, 109, 447, 480, {vi}152, 167–8,
{viii}63
DHL translates 'Sketches from
Novelle Rusticane', {iv}220, 227,

231–2, 235, 245, 300; Blackwell publishes in England, {iv}300–2, {v}20, 93, 165, 247, {vi}53; 'Black Bread' early title for, {iv}367, {viii}58; Seltzer publishes in USA, {v}20, 92–3, 247, {vi}53, {vii}445; 'greeted with enthusiasm and good reviews', {viii}93 *see also* Verga, G.

'London Letter', *see* 'Dear Old Horse'

Lost Girl, The, {i}234, 501, {ii}580, 595, {iii}1, 9, 11, 14, 242, 522, 524, 580, 603, 623, 641, 700, 729, {iv}7, 129, 200, 341, 407, {vi}213, 597–8, {viii}41, 64, 95

DHL awaiting MS of earlier novel from Germany, {iii}439, 448, 458, 469; in Capri re-working MS, {iii}476–7; 'Mixed Marriage' provisional title for, {iii}485–6; 488; had 'scrapped all the novel [done] in Capri', begun again and done about 30,000 words, {iii}490; DHL amused by, {iii}494; about ½ done, {iii}495, {viii}30; 50,000 words written, {iii}497–8; about ¾ done, {iii}503–5; hopes to finish in a week, {iii}510; novel named, {iii}512; finished and being typed, {iii}515–17, 519–21, 535, 558, {iv}220; Secker to publish, {iii}516, 521; TS to be sent to Seltzer, {iii}524, 527, 535; 'quite moral', {iii}525; DHL very keen to serialise, {iii}528, 533–4, 537–8, 560, 562–5, 567, 571–2, 574, 601, {iv}68, {viii}35–6; 'The Bitter Cherry' Secker's preferred title, {iii}534, 537, 540; TS for USA by hand via Francesco Cacópardo, {iii}544–5, 551; MS by hand via Mackenzie for Secker, {iii}549–52, {viii}36; DHL correcting carbon copy, {iii}550, 552–3, 555; carbon copy to *Queen* for possible serialising, {iii}555, 559, 586, {viii}33, 35; spelling of Ciccio, {iii}555, 559–60, 605, 613, 644, {v}638; Seltzer and publication of, {iii}563–4, 573, 590; Secker enthusiastic about, {iii}564, 567–8, 571, 574, {v}320;

DHL correcting Secker's proofs, {iii}588, 594; Secker to correct proofs from *Queen* carbon copy, {iii}599; corrected proofs for Seltzer, {iii}605, 612, 619; complimentary copies, {iii}607–8, 611, 620–1, 625, 629, 632, 639, 640, 648, 681, 703, {iv}33, 196, 493, {v}23, 91, 99, {vii}156, 171; advance copy arrives, {iii}616–17; objections from lending libraries, {iii}619, 621–2, 624; DHL hopes novel 'will bring her eggs safe to market', {iii}622, 629; Seltzer's contract for, {iii}626–7, 645, 677, {vii}440, 503; 1300 copies ordered on London publication, {iii}628; English copies available in New York, {iii}633, 635, 638, 644, 646; sales of, {iii}636, 642, 647, 651, 656, 660, 662–3, 667, 722; DHL prefers *Mr Noon* to, {iii}645; Seltzer's edn better looking than Secker's, {iii}671–2, 674–5; Rebecca West not given review-copy, {iii}709; review of, {iii}734; James Tait Black prize awarded to, {iv}146–7, 150, 158; publishers' accounts for, {iv}148, 153, 169, 174, 387–8; 'unexpurgated' copies, {v}120, 122, 160; 'begins in Eastwood', {v}243; Secker publishes in 'uniform' edn, {v}576, 638 *see also* 'Insurrection of Miss Houghton, The'

'Love', {v}279, {vii}474

in *English Review*, {iii}164–5, 191, 211, 217, {v}104

'Love Among the Haystacks', incident recorded in, {i}64, 67–8; possibly written, {i}323; with Garnett, {i}327, 345, 348; *English Review* declines, {i}378, 380–1; much revised, {ii}44; DHL seeks MS from Clayton, {ii}190; DHL asks Clayton to delay typing {ii}204; MS missing, {iii}34, 472–3; Clayton asked to return MS of, {vii}632; Clayton denies ever having MS, {viii}11

Love Among the Haystacks, {i}441, {ii}21, {iii}135, {v}86

LAWRENCE, DAVID HERBERT (*cont.*)
  'Love and Marriage', *see Fantasia of the
    Unconscious*
  'Love Was Once a Little Boy', {v}279
  'Lovely Lady, The', {vi}152
    Cynthia Asquith requests murder
      story, {v}590, 613, 631, 636, 647; story
      finished, {v}654, {vi}21; Asquith
      requests cuts in, {vi}29, 51; 'shorter
      version' produced, {vi}54, 71;
      published in *The Black Cap*, {vi}347,
      {vii}507
  'Lucky Noon', *see Mr Noon*
  'Lupa, La', {iv}447
  'Making Love to Music', {vi}40
  'Making Pictures', {i}8, 89, 196, {v}574,
    {vii}251
    written for *Studio*, {vii}249, 322; fee
      of £10 for, {vii}269, 348; proofs of,
      {vii}296; reprinted in *Creative Art*,
      {vii}536; in *Assorted Articles*,
      {vii}549
  'Man is a Hunter', {ii}147, {v}377, 590
  Man Who Died, The, *see Escaped Cock,
    The*
  'Man Who Loved Islands, The', {ii}212,
    {vi}6, 76, 174, {vii}520
    DHL promises to 'write a skit on
      [Mackenzie] one day', {iii}594; 'nearly
      done', {v}482; sent to Curtis Brown,
      {v}498; in proof for *Dial* publication,
      {vi}46; in *London Mercury*, {vi}46, 52,
      69; Mackenzie 'only *suggests* the idea -
      it's no portrait', {vi}68–9, 130; copy to
      Else Jaffe, {vi}76, 103; DHL proposes
      its inclusion in Secker's *WWRA*,
      {vi}152, 197; Secker succumbs to
      Mackenzie's objection and excludes,
      {vi}205–6, 218–19, 224; DHL feels
      insulted, {vi}269; MS bound for
      Crosby, {vi}348, 359, 372, 388, 404,
      {vii}306; Knopf includes in US
      WWRA, {vii}326, 368, 386, 390–1;
      Heinemann proposal for edn. defeated
      by Mackenzie, {vii}368, 381, 396, 445,
      455, 514–15, 518, 539–40
  'Manufacture of Good Little Boys, The',
    see 'Enslaved by Civilisation'

  'Market Day', {v}6
    collected in *M in M*, {v}186; in *New
      Criterion*, {v}432, {v}580–2; in *Travel*
      as 'The Gentle Art of Marketing in
      Mexico', {v}575, 587
  'Master in His Own House', originally
    entitled, 'Men Must Rule', {vi}441
  Mastro-don Gesualdo, {iv}6, 8, 16, 18,
    105–6, 115, 200, 215, 219–20, 276–7,
    309, {viii}58, 61
    interests DHL 'very much', {iv}157,
      162; DHL 'done about one-third' of
      translation, {iv}186; 'nearly half-way
      through', {iv}188–91; first half typed,
      {iv}196; DHL translating on ship-
      board, {iv}208, 212–14, 235; corrects
      translation, {iv}245; Blackwell
      interested in, {iv}302, 401; Seltzer
      and, {iv}367, 369–70, 394, 435, 447–8;
      Götzsche designed jacket for, {iv}406,
      436, 439, 442; DHL corrects proofs of,
      {iv}470–1, 473–5, 477; Seltzer
      publishes, {iv}478, 480–1, 501,
      517–18, 523, 526, 549, {viii}72, 88;
      complimentary copies, {iv}527,
      {vi}516; Secker rejects, Cape publish-
      es, {v}165, {vi}40, 53, 68, 130, {vii}66
    see also Verga, G.
  'Matilda Wootton', {i}172
  'Matriarchy', in *Evening News* as 'If
    Women Were Supreme', {vi}461
  Max Havelaar, Introduction to, DHL
    invited to write, {v}320, 446; complet-
    ed, {v}452, 458; in proof, {v}527 *see
    also* Dekker, E.
  Memoirs of the Foreign Legion,
    Introduction to, {ii}31, {iii}409, 480,
    {iv}6, 127, 186, {v}6, 16, 32–3,
    {v}142, {vi}45, {vii}237, {viii}88;
    Secker sends revised proofs of, {v}70;
    Jester admires, {v}241; DHL gives
    'exact truth' in, {v}255; circumstances
    surrounding writing of, {v}395–7,
    {viii}48–50 *see also* Magnus, M.
  'Men and Peacocks', *see* 'Sex Locked
    Out'
  'Men and Women', *see* 'Men Must Work
    and Women as Well'

'Men Must Rule', *see* 'Master in His Own House'

'Men Must Work and Women as Well', written for *Star Review* as 'Men and Women', {vii}10, 405, 437, 499, 512; collected in *Assorted Article*, {vii}405

'Mercury', {v}503, 521, 657

'Miner At Home, The', {i}366, 375

Minnesingers, The,'A review of', {i}331, 335–6

'Miracle, The', *see* 'Horse-Dealer's Daughter, The'

'Mixed Marriage', *see Lost Girl, The*

'Modern Lover, A', formerly, 'The Virtuous', {i}275, 298; probably sent to Garnett, {i}345, 372–3

Modern Lover, A, {i}176, {ii}33, {iv}26

'Monkey Nuts', {iii}502
    to Pinker, {iii}360, 365, 472; TS to Mountsier, {iv}134; with Curtis Brown, {iv}144, 155; published in *Sovereign*, {iv}219–20

'Morality and the Novel', {v}275; in *The Golden Book*, {v}360

'More Modern Love', *see* 'In Love'

'Morgenrot', *see* 'Crown, The'

Mornings in Mexico, {iii}471, {v}6, 27, 175, 601, {vi}38, 210, 357, {viii}103
    essays collected in, {v}36, 103, 186; four essays to Curtis Brown, {v}193, 242, 252; Murry and, {v}432, 451–2, {vii}437; Secker encourages DHL with, {v}575, 580–1; DHL keen for illustrations, {v}587, 594, 596, 620, 623, 626, 636, 638, {vi}45; proofs, {v}635, 655, {vi}24, 31, 36; no illustrations, but DHL's drawing on jacket, {vi}31, 77; complimentary copies, {vi}67, 69–70, 73, 79, 98, 101, 128, 155, 547; Knopf publishes in US, {vi}73, 101; DHL admires English edn, {vi}77; reception, {vi}91, {vii}224

'Mortal Coil, The', DHL 'had in mind for a long time', {ii}82, 90, 99, 127; MSS returned by Dunlop probably included, {ii}630; in *Seven Arts*, {ii}653, {iii}142; 'one of my purest creations', sent to Pinker, {ii}669, {iii}22, 28, 472; rejected by *English Review*, {ii}670

'Mother and Daughter', {vii}390, 500, 507
    in *Criterion*, {vi}421, {vii}170, 185, 188, 200, 272, 439

Mother, The, 'Introduction to', {vi}254

Movements in European History (by Lawrence H. Davison), {ii}483, {iii}3, 11, 14, 194, 276, 279, 298, 306, 724–5, {iv}26, 85, 131, {v}105, 175, 288, {vii}90, 141, {viii}95
    Collins invited DHL to write, {iii}261; DHL in 'historical mood', {iii}262; done first essay in, {iii}263; 'first three chapters' written, {iii}268–9; 'can wait a bit', {iii}286; books used in writing, {iii}304, 315, 317, 622; DHL hates doing, {iii}307–9; 'working away' at, {iii}318, 321; DHL loathes 'broken pots of historical facts' but 'clue of developing meaning running through', {iii}322; one chapter left and will receive £50 for, {iii}323, 347; writing finished and DHL offers to use pseudonym, {iii}326, 634; revising, {iii}347, 351–2; finished proof-reading, {iii}462, 487; complimentary copies, {iii}487, 533, 696, 701, {v}272, 278, 284, 324; revised proofs awaited, {iii}525, 576, 612; additional chapter required, {iii}622; nom de plume, Lawrence H. Davison, {iii}634, 651, {iv}48; published in England, not USA, {iii}707, 710, 713, {iv}83, {v}179–80, {viii}41; new illustrated edn, {v}26, 32, 87, 117, 120–1, 133, 136, 150, 224, 272; Epilogue for, {v}117, 120, 133, 136–7, 150, 272, 279; Irish edn, {v}324, 336, 495, 555

'Mozo, The', {v}6, 175, 186, 193, 252, {vi}210
    in *Adelphi*, {v}242; German translation of, {v}331; in *Living Age* as 'Sons of Montezuma', {v}432;

LAWRENCE, DAVID HERBERT (*cont.*)
collected in *M in M*, {v}575, 580, 594

Mr Noon, {i}176, {iii}698, 701, {iv}107, {vi}12, {viii}53
composition begun, {iii}522, 537; 'comedy', {iii}626; '⅓ done - sudden stop – may go on soon', {iii}634, 638; 'rather amusing..rather scandalous', {iii}639; ⅔ done, 'peppery', {iii}645–6; alternative title, 'Lucky Noon', {iii}645–6, 648, 722, {iv}35; writing continuing, {iii}648, 651, 662; first 200 pages self-contained, {iii}653; TS of Part I to Mountsier, and Part II 'nearly done', {iii}667, 675, 678, 684, 689; TS of 40,000 words, {iii}681; TS to Barbara Low, {iii}688, 692; copy to Curtis Brown for possible serialising, {iii}700, 702, 708, 710, {iv}69; writing of Part II delayed, {iii}714, 722; Secker enthusiastic but did not publish Part I, {iii}717, 722, 730–1, {iv}26–7; Part II about ½ done, {iv}35; 'If I am to finish', {iv}150; Seltzer to return TS to Mountsier, {iv}257–8; 'nearly two years at a full stop', {iv}267; DHL doubts if will finish, {iv}319; hymn used in, {v}634; 'errant and amusing but not improper', {viii}36

'Mrs Clutterley's Lover', *see Lady Chatterley's Lover*

My Skirmish with Jolly Roger, {vii}467, 471, 525
'little peppery foreword' for Paris *LCL*, {vii}229, 404; US limited edn of, {vii}316, 390, 392, 396, 428–32, 439, 444, 446, 462, 464, 496, 504, 551; English revised edn of, {vii}504, 531, 533, 549, 583, 587–8, 640 *see also A Propos of "Lady Chatterley's Lover"* and *Lady Chatterley's Lover*

'Myself Revealed', {i}21
in *Sunday Dispatch*, {vii}64–5, 123, 127, 189, 198, 610

'Nethermere', *see White Peacock, The*
'New Eve and Old Adam', 'autobio-
graphical story', {ii}21; earlier title 'Renegade Eve', {ii}38; MS with Clayton, {ii}190, {viii}11

'New Mexico', {vii}4
in *Survey Graphic*, {vii}71, 94, 118, 123; fee of $100 for, {vii}174, 201

'Nightingale, The', {vi}110
intended for *Vogue*, {v}482, 521; 'clipped' for *Forum* {v}583–4, 625, {vi}52, 196; *Spectator* to wait for, {v}626; not collected in *Assorted Articles*, {vii}549, 600

'Noah's Ark', *see Women in Love*
'Nobody Loves Me', {vi}462, {vii}554, 556

'None of That', {vi}213, 236
'founded on fact', {vi}70, 176; collected in *WWRA*, {vi}152, 197, {vii}26; Else Jaffe's translation of *WWRA* excluded, {vi}275, 277; MS bound {vi}348, 359; Lederhandler buys MS for $15, {vii}240, 305–6

'Note to The Crown', *see* 'Crown, Note to The'

'Nottingham and the Mining Countryside', {i}466, {vii}4, 468
'Novara', *see Aaron's Rod*
'Novel, The', {v}271–2, 275, 280, 284

Novelle Rusticane, *see Little Novels of Sicily*

'Obscenity and Pornography', *see* 'Pornography and Obscenity'

'Odour of Chrysanthemums', {i}156, 162, 298, 491, {v}593
submitted to Hueffer, {i}147, 171, 471; revised for *English Review*, {i}172, 179, 246, 248–9, 257–8; revisions make story 'work quicker to a climax', {i}252; published in *English*, {i}275, 335, 345, 510; fee of £10 for, {i}281–2, 286, 313; collected in *Prussian Officer*, {ii}197

'Oh These Women!', *see* 'Give Her a Pattern'

'Oh! for a New Crusade', *see* 'Red Trousers'

'Old Adam, The', {i}276, 298, {ii}44

'On Being a Man', {iv}18, {v}241
in *Adelphi*, {iv}549, {v}87, {vii}437;
collected in *Assorted Articles*, {vii}400,
568, 575, 611
'On being a Success', {v}620, 648
'On Being in Love', {iv}549
'On Being Religious', {v}241
in *Adelphi*, {iv}549, 565, {v}17, 87,
{vii}437; collected in *Assorted Articles*,
{vii}568, 575, 611
'On Coming Home', rejected by Murry,
{iv}549, {v}94
'On Human Destiny', {iv}18
in *Adelphi*, {iv}549, {v}17, 87,
{vii}437; collected in *Assorted Articles*,
{vii}400, 568, 575, 611
'On Love and Marriage', *see Fantasia of
the Unconscious*
'On Reading a Book', *see* 'Books'
'On Taking the Next Step', {iv}549
'On the Lago di Garda', *see* 'Italian
Studies: By the Lago di Garda'
'On Writing a Book', *see* 'Books'
'Once', submitted to but rejected by
Smart Set, {ii}44, 67; Pound sends to
English Review, {ii}82; rejected by
Egoist, {ii}132; typed by Clayton,
{ii}190, 201–2, {vii}632, {viii}11;
Pinker and, {iii}34, 135, 472–3
'Our Lady', *see Lady Chatterley's Lover*
'Over-Earnest Ladies', *see* 'Insouciance'
'Overtone, The', {i}507
'Ownership', rejected by *Evening News*,
{vi}461, 602
Oxford Book of German Verse, 'A review
of', in *English Review*, {i}331, 335–6,
514
'Pan in America', {v}40, 43
'Paris Letter', {iv}20, 567, {v}66
'Pat-a-Cake, Pat-a-Cake, Baker's Man',
see 'Christening, The'
'Paul Morel', *see Sons and Lovers*
'Phoenix, The', *see* 'Crown, The'
'Pictures on the Wall', in *Architectural
Review*, {vii}269, 295; as 'Dead
Pictures on the Wall' in *Vanity Fair*,
{vii}269, 503; collected in *Assorted
Articles*, {vii}549–50

Plumed Serpent, The ('Quetzalcoatl'),
{iii}471, {iv}15, 436, 489, 515, 534,
{v}4, 6–7, 112, 160, 410, 456, 470,
{vi}70, 156, 335, 355, 499
DHL 'keen to write an American
novel', {iv}257, 259–60, 277, 385, 429;
Zelia Nuttall and, {iv}421, {v}155;
composition of, {iv}437, 442, 444,
446–9, 453–4; 10 chapters written,
{iv}450–1; 'more than half done in
first draft', {viii}81; 'two-thirds done'
of novel DHL likes 'best of all',
{iv}455; 415 MS pages of
'Quetzalcoatl', {iv}457; bull-fight
scene, {iv}458, 480; *'nearly* finished',
{iv}462, 464, {viii}81; being typed,
{iv}470, 495, 523; DHL seeks
Seltzer's advice about revising,
{iv}517, 527; to be finished, {iv}549,
559, 591, {v}24, 26, 29, 32, 45–6, 71,
75, 77, 79, 93, 114, 161, 166, 168–9,
171, 174; DHL working on second
version, {v}179, 183, 193; 'nearly
done', {v}198–200, 207; 'finished',
{v}213, 217, 230, 245; DHL reluctant
to discard title 'Quetzalcoatl', {v}250,
254, 256, 263, 267; revised TS,
{v}254, 256, 260, 263; 'lies nearer my
heart than any other work of mine',
{v}264, 267, 271–2, 332; TS for
Curtis Brown, {v}270–1, 286; Secker
publishes in England, {v}287, 297–8,
318, 320, 336, 340, 370, 576, {vi}44;
Knopf to publish in US, {v}288,
342, 365; Conways to advise on,
{v}291; publication delayed, {v}292,
297; proofs checked, {v}320, 323;
complimentary copies, {v}373–5, 379,
383, 387, 401–2, 417, 444, 472, 507,
556, {vii}156, 171, 618, {viii}103;
reception, {v}383, 393, 398, {vi}400,
466, {viii}88; 'little sketch' of Bynner
in, {v}384, {vi}278, {viii}88; Brett
designed jacket for US edn, {v}392;
Swedish translation rumoured,
{v}489, 492; German translation,
{v}555, 558–9, 561, {vi}199, 213,
{vii}553, 563, 572, 597–8, 610; Crosby

LAWRENCE, DAVID HERBERT (*cont.*)
and, {vi}301, {vii}217; the 'hero' and, {vi}321; French translation, {vii}223, 228; Brett and MS of, {vii}472–3, 475, 485
'Poe', *see Studies in Classic American Literature*
'Poetry of the Present, The', *see* 'Verse Free and Unfree'
'Porc', 'Porcupine', *see Reflections on the Death of a Porcupine and Other Essays*
'Pornography and Obscenity', in *This Quarter*, {vii}259, 268–9, 295; revised for publication as pamphlet, {vii}467–8, 481, 569 *see also Pornography and Obscenity*
Pornography and Obscenity, {vii}4, 12 periodical publication revised as *Criterion Miscellany* pamphlet, {vii}468, 470–1, 526, 560, 568–9; Faber make deletions from, {vii}509; in proof, {vii}549, 554; complimentary copies, {vii}559, 573, 579, 582–3; impact of, {vii}578. 580, 582, 584, 588, 592, 604; sales of, {vii}580, 588–9, 592, 604 *see also* 'Pornography and Obscenity'
'Power', *see* 'Blessed are the Powerful'
'Preface to *Collected Poems*', {i}14, 16, 29, 31, 462
'Prelude, A', submitted as by Jessie Chambers, {i}38, 41,297, {v}86, {vii}137
'Primrose Path, The', {ii}67, 127, 356, {iii}34
typed by Clayton, {ii}52, 55, 201, {viii}12; DHL requests return of MS, {ii}133, {iii}472–3, {iv}100; typescript to Curtis Brown and Mountsier, {iv}144, 148, 155, 159
'Princess, The', {v}4, 6, 144, 148, 242, 288, {vi}156, 198, {vii}413
being written, {v}136, 141; typed, {v}147; TS to Curtis Brown, {v}148–9, 161; in *Calendar*, {v}180, 231–2, 331; Secker to publish with *St. Mawr*, {v}194, 206–7, 214, 227, 255, 270; Jester praises, {v}241; Else Jaffe

translates, {vi}213, 236, 275, 277
'Prodigal Husband, The', {ii}493–4, {iii}22, 34 *see also* 'Samson and Delilah'
'Proper Study, The', {iv}18
in *Adelphi*, {iv}500, 572, {v}87, {vii}437, 568; $100 fee from *Vanity Fair* for, {viii}88
'Prussian Officer, The' {ii}2, 5–6, 256 'the best story I have ever done', {ii}21; 'Honour and Arms' re-titled as, {ii}197–8, 216, 241; sold to *Metropolitan* for £25, {ii}222–3, 256; evidence of 'sexual morbidities' in, {ii}246 *see also* 'Honour and Arms'
Prussian Officer and Other Stories, The, {i}38, {ii}14–15, 66, 190, 224, 246, 259, 267, 271, 431, {iv}133–4, 153, 247, {v}66, 593, {vii}413
McLeod and, {ii}187, {v}641; contents of, {ii}197; 'The Fighting Line' a possible title for, {ii}221; Duckworth publishes in England, {ii}223, 589, {iv}181, 201; Garnett 'a devil' to name book as, {ii}241; published, {ii}243; complimentary copy, {ii}250; reception, {ii}253, 255, 258; Boots rumoured to have banned, {ii}257, 280; Huebsch publishes in USA, {ii}611, {iii}129, 323, 547, 643, 646, 652, 661, {iv}169, 248, 403; sales, {iii}356; Secker's interest in, {iv}427, {vi}68; miners might read, {vi}229; spelling in, {viii}15; contains tales about 'the common people', {viii}18
Psychoanalysis and the Unconscious, {iii}11, 688, 730, {iv}15, 57, 103, 111, 114, 259, 341, {viii}60
DHL at work on, {iii}426, 476; offered to Huebsch, {iii}466, 493, 511; TS of, {iii}497; Huebsch rejects, {iii}582; Seltzer publishes in USA, {iii}703, {viii}40; Secker unsuitable for, {iii}732, {iv}27–8, 35, 383; complimentary copies, {iii}732–3, 735, {iv}23, 25, 29–30, 37, 40, 95, 342, 377, 459, {v}48, 105–6, 323, {vi}281; in *Fantasia* DHL answers critics of,

{iv}93, 104; US royalties on, {iv}388;
Secker publishes in England, {iv}399,
401, 427, 454; 'stupid' response to,
{iv}582; poor sales of, {v}262;
reviewed by Californian mystic,
{viii}57
'Pueblos and an Englishman', *see*
'Indians and an Englishman'
'Quetzalcoatl', *see Plumed Serpent, The*
'Rachel Annand Taylor', {i}180–1
Rainbow, The, {i}6, 20, 391, {ii}5–6,
8–9, 16–17, 263, 274, 382, 411, 467,
536, {iii}1, 7, 11, 13–14, 20, 76, 85,
275, 284, 372, 393, 495, 692, {iv}2, 6,
9, 71, 92, 240, {v}79, 146, {vi}11, 465,
{vii}10, 200–1, 293, 475, 505
DHL writing, 'The Sisters'; {i}530,
{ii}20, 142, 169; Society of Authors
and, {ii}41, 430, 433–5, 439–44, 452,
469; 'Wedding Ring' becomes preferred title, {ii}132, 134, 153; Dunlop
types 'Wedding Ring', {ii}152, 164,
173; DHL fears public rejection of
'improper' novel, {ii}169; title,
'Wedding Ring', replaced by,
{ii}173–4, 190, 241; typing completed,
{ii}173–4; 'old stable ego of the
character' not to be looked for in,
{ii}183; Methuen to publish,
{ii}186–7, 190, 200, 207, 294, 318,
327–8, 509, 631, {iii}58, 212, {v}175;
MS to Kennerley. {ii}190, 235, 246,
279; Pinker and, {ii}193, 227–8, 373;
re-writing, {ii}239–40, 242–3, 255–6,
260, 270, 276, 280; Kuttner's report
on 'Wedding Ring', {ii}246; book to
be split into two volumes, {ii}256;
Viola Meynell types rewritten version,
{ii}271, 293, 299, 312, 314, 348–9;
Huebsch and US edn, {ii}294, 420,
429, 453, 475, 477–9, 480, 494,
509–10, 514, 518, 561, {iii}129, 318,
388, 399, 427, 457, 467, 545–7, 643–6,
650–2, 661, 673, {iv}82, 106, 150, 156,
170, 173, 229, 382, 394, 399, 402–3,
408–9, 431–2, 474, {vi}539, {viii}51;
'finished..and set it firm', {ii}299–300,
303; revising, {ii}308; DHL certain of

quality of, {ii}308, 315; TS to Ottoline
Morrell, {ii}314, 319, 326–7, 329, 331,
334, 351–2, 415; 'final batch' of TS
of DHL's 'beloved book' ready for
printing, {ii}349; dedicated 'To Else',
{ii}349, 354; in proof, {ii}362; DHL's
response to Methuen's request for
changes in, {ii}364, 369–70; publication of, {ii}386, 394–6; 'something
new in..art of..novel', {ii}395;
complimentary copies, {ii}402, 405,
{iii}484; 'vile' jacket, {ii}402, 406;
DHL pays for proof corrections,
{ii}406; US reaction to, {ii}419–20,
429; 'one of..important novels in the
language', {ii}428; magistrate's
suppression of, {ii}428–31, 433–5,
446–7, 454, 456–7, 462, 477, 524,
{iii}183, {viii}18; questions in
Parliament about suppression of,
{ii}439–41, 443–4, 452, 463, 656;
public demand for, {ii}449–51, 616,
621, 637; reception of, {ii}456–8, 479,
487, 566, {iii}708; private edn
contemplated, {ii}458–9, 462–5, 467,
561; 'message' of, {ii}526; DHL
writes *W in L* as sequel to, {ii}602,
606, 612, 629, 649, {iii}22, 27, 29, 55,
61, 100, 400. 538, 681, {vi}443;
DHL's own critique of, {iii}142–3;
England not forgiven for action
against, {iii}391; Secker and English
edn, {iii}439, 458–60, 462, 471–2, 491,
497; DHL turns to, then rejects
Duckworth for English edn, {iii}472,
474, 477, 484, 490–1, 497; DHL
accepts Secker's terms, {iii}499–501,
512–13, 515–17, 519–21, 525–6, 538,
544–5, 574, 613, 638, 700, 714,
{iv}35, 129, 299, 341, {vii}387;
'standard' publisher unlikely to
handle, {iii}546, 635; Insel-Verlag and
German translation of (*Der
Regenbogen*), {iii}620, 622, 625, 642,
667, 715, {iv}80, 89, 117, 132, 148,
193, 354, 428, {v}38, 314, {vii}572,
{viii}48; Perth Literary Institute
has copy of, {iv}273, {v}119–20;

LAWRENCE, DAVID HERBERT (*cont.*)
  DHL engages with Seltzer for US
    edn, {iv}355, 465, {v}91–2, 113;
    actual locations of action in, {v}243;
    Beaverbrook seeks copy of, {vi}479,
    491, 497; Frieda hurt by response to,
    {vi}485; Ada Clarke finds 'hand-
    written MS' of, {vii}458–9, 515, 541;
    DHL might sell MS of, {vii}632;
    DHL signs one copy, {viii}52 *see also*
    'Rainbow Books and Music' and
    'Sisters, The'
  'Rainbow Books and Music, The' {ii}18
    Murry's involvement in, {ii}472, 532,
    548–50; Heseltine and DHL try to
    launch, {ii}532–4, 540–2, 545, 547–50,
    551, 554–5, 571; scheme fails, {ii}605
  Rawdon's Roof, {vi}6, {vii}507
    composition of, {vi}217; DHL
    prepared for alterations by magazine
    editor, {vi}232; Elkin Mathews
    publishes limited, signed edn,
    {vi}495, 526, 552, 565, 602, 605–6,
    610, {vii}18, 23, 153, 158, 175, 181,
    496; extended text sent to Curtis
    Brown, {vii}23, 45, 59, 66; compli-
    mentary copies, {vii}232
  'Real Thing, The', {vii}554, 556
  'Real Trouble about Women, The', *see*
    'Give Her a Pattern'
  'Reality of Peace, The', {iii}4–5, 7, 15,
    120, 137, 146, {v}103
    seven 'little essays' offered to *English
    Review*, {iii}100–2, 104–8, 110–11;
    Harrison accepts three, {iii}113–14;
    one being recast, {iii}125; Harrison
    accepts fourth, {iii}138; 'At the Gates'
    developed out of, {iii}143, 155
  'Red Trousers', in *Evening News* as 'Oh!
    For a New Crusade', {vi}563
  *Reflections on the Death of a Porcupine
    and Other Essays*, {ii}17, {iv}314,
    {v}10, 94, 251, 340, 622, {vi}11, 27,
    296, {vii}20
    essays collected in, {ii}385–6, {iv}357,
    {v}271, 279, 374, 380, 575, {vii}403,
    474; Mason publishes, {v}240–1, 365,
    494–5, {vi}363; title adopted, {v}284,

  290; complimentary copies, {v}296,
    319, 329, 333, 342, 373–4, 378, 387,
    393, {vi}289, 332; 'handsome…down-
    right amusing', {v}372, 387; 'gayer
    than a geranium in a pot', {v}376;
    reception, {v}381; DHL feels Mason
    untrustworthy over, {vii}159, 172,
    297, 401
  'Remarkable Russian, A', *see* Rozanov, V.
    V., review of *Fallen Leaves*
  Renard, Le, see 'Fox, The'
  'Renegade Eve', {ii}38
  'Return Journey, The', {ii}413, {viii}9
  '['Return to Bestwood']', {v}348, 620,
    {vii}9
  Reviews: *see under* Baring, M; Burrow, T;
    Byron, R; Corvo, Baron; Dos Passos,
    J; Graham, R Cunninghame; Hecht,
    B; Hemingway, E; Krout, J;
    Maugham, W; Oman, J; Pickthall, M;
    Rozanov, V; Tomlinson, H; Van
    Vechen, C; Wells, H G; White, Walter;
    Wilkinson, W; Williams-Ellis, C
  'Rex', {iii}13, {iv}168–9, 257, {vi}152,
    176
    written for *Dial*, {iii}536, 562, 627,
    634, 675, {iv}144–5, {v}104, {viii}36;
    Else Jaffe translates into German,
    {vi}153–4, 173, 189, 277, {vii}74
  'Risen Lord, The', {vii}10, 551
    written for *Everyman*, {vii}401, 500,
    512, 532; 'same idea' as in *Escaped
    Cock*, {vii}516; rejected by *Pagany*,
    {vii}524–5
  'Rocking-Horse Winner, The', {vi}152,
    154
    in *Harper's Bazaar*, {v}400, 508;
    written for Cynthia Asquith's *Ghost-
    Book*, {v}400, 415, 424–5, {vi}140,
    {vii}445, 507; MS bound, {vi}348
  'Saga (of Siegmund)', *see Trespasser, The*
  'Samson and Delilah', MS entitled 'The
    Prodigal Husband', {iii}22, 34; in
    English Review, {iii}79, 100; MS with
    Pinker, {iii}472–3; copy to Mountsier,
    {iv}134; collected in *EME*,
    {iv}143–4
  'San Gaudenzio', {ii}390, 398

'Sardinian Films', *see Sea and Sardinia*
'Scargill Street', name proposed for unwritten novel, {i}431, 466, 477
'Sea, The', {iv}107
Sea and Sardinia, {iii}1, 11, 17, 491, {iv}5–7, 15, 111, {v}88, 386, 416, 554, 556, {vi}12, 200, 254, {viii}53
preliminary thoughts on, {iii}648, 650, 653, 660, 662; Juta and illustrations for, {iii}656, 687–8, 705, 727, 730, {iv}24, 34–5, 39, 47–8, 58, 60, 123, 138, 143, 244, {viii}41–2;
provisional title, 'Diary of Trip to Sardinia', {iii}664, 667, 675, 678, 681, 686, 688, 700–2; 'nearly finished', {iii}665–7, 681; being typed (by Ruth Wheelock), {iii}667, 675, 684, 686; TS to Mountsier, {iii}695–6, 709–10; 'Sardinian Films' one alternative title, {iii}696, 705; TS to Curtis Brown, {iii}700–2; Secker and, {iii}708, 730–1, {iv}27–8, 34–5, 69, 108, 116; extracts from in *Dial*, {iii}731, {iv}58, 73, 107, 126, 130; final title used, {iv}58; Seltzer and US publication of, {iv}69, 82, 109, 114, 116, 121, 129, 131, 133, 145, 156, 328, 366, {viii}60, 88; complimentary copies, {iv}121, 123, 162, 174–5, 190, 192–6, 207, 213, 235, 275, 320, 391, 518, {v}58, 91, 264, {vi}281; DHL on appearance of, {iv}158; Secker's edn of, {iv}163, 165, 171, 174–5, 179, 183, 199, 261, 298–9, 366, 379, 389, 391, 401, 489, 549; reception, {iv}229; sales of, {iv}276, 278, 328, 341, 366, {v}104–5; US royalties on, {iv}388; errors in text of, {iv}443; Secker re-issues, {v}460, 481, 490, 576 {vi}44; TS allegedly for sale in New York, {vii}342, 472
'Second Best', {i}298
in *English Review*, {i}348, 351–2, 363, 510; collected in *Prussian Officer*, {ii}197
'See Mexico After, by Luis Q', {v}194–6; *see also* Quintanilla, L.
'Sex Appeal', *see* 'Sex Locked Out'
'Sex Locked Out', in *Sunday Dispatch* as,

{vi}602, 606, 609, {vii}28; as 'Sex Appeal' in *Vanity Fair*, and 'Men and Peacocks' in *Golden Book*, {vi}606
'Shades of Spring, The' *see* 'Soiled Rose, The'
'Shadow in the Rose Garden, The', {i}297, {ii}39, 44, {iv}11
first called 'The Vicar's Garden', {i}35; £10 from *Smart Set* for, {ii}126–7, 132; Clayton types revised version, {ii}194; collected in *Prussian Officer*, {ii}197; in *Georgian Stories*, {iv}133, 247–8
'Sick Collier, A', {i}375, 381, 383, {ii}39
sent to Northern Newspaper Syndicate, {ii}41, 44; in *New Statesman*, {ii}58, 60; Clayton and typing of, {ii}190, {viii}11; collected in *Prussian Officer*, {ii}197
'Siegmund', *see Trespasser, The*
'Signal, The', *see* 'Crown, The'
Signature, The, {ii}13, 17–18, 184, 293, 295, 461, 476, 496, 548, {iii}84, 101, {iv}315, 349, 410, {v}103, 255, 290, 295, 374, {vii}403
published with Murry and Katherine Mansfield, {ii}385–9; for 'people who care vitally about the freedom of the soul', {ii}391, 393–402, 411–12; DHL denounces Russell's contribution to, {ii}392; subscribers for, {ii}404–5, 407, 409–13, 416, 418, 427, 447, 455, 488, 515, 529, 562, 588, {viii}16; office furniture sold, venture abandoned, {ii}428
'Sisters, The', {i}16, 20, 526, {ii}5, 8, 93
46 pages done, {i}530; 'a pot-boiler', {i}536, 538; 145 pp. and DHL has 'no notion what it's about', {i}544–5; 180 pp., {i}546; 2/3 done, {i}548; Frieda in both Ella and Gudrun, {i}549; 256pp., {i}550; end of first version in sight, {i}551–2, {ii}20; two false starts, {ii}58, 66; 'new basis altogether', {ii}67–8, {viii}7; 'going well, {ii}74–6; different from anything before, {ii}82, 132, 136, 169; MS delayed in mail, {ii}83; little progress,

LAWRENCE, DAVID HERBERT (*cont.*)
  {ii}99, 118–19; becomes 'The
  Wedding Ring', {ii}132; half sent to
  Garnett, {ii}134–5; DHL's response
  to Garnett's judgment, {ii}142–3;
  begun for 'about the seventh', then
  'eleventh' time, {ii}144, 146, 153; TS
  (by Dunlop) to Garnett, {ii}164–5;
  becomes *The Rainbow*, {ii}173–4, 241;
  DHL defends himself against
  Garnett's criticism, {ii}182–3; MS
  sent to Kennerley (and lost), {ii}190;
  DHL decides to 'split the book into
  two volumes', {ii}256; finished 'in
  effect', {ii}619; title abandoned in
  favour of *W in L*, {ii}630, 639 *see also
  Rainbow, The* and *Women in Love*
'Six Novels of Thomas Hardy and the
  Real Tragedy', {ii}295
Sketches of Etruscan Places, {vi}4, 206,
  {vii}4, 462, 503
  venture proposed, {vi}29, 36; 'nothing
  scientific', {vi}33–4; to be 'Travel
  Sketches', {vi}42; preparatory reading
  for, {vi}45; DHL keen on 'thrilling
  illustrations', {vi}45, 77, 79, 83–5, 89,
  93, 98, 105, 266, {viii}104–5; *Travel*
  might publish, {vi}48; being written,
  {vi}80–2, 86; first essay to Curtis
  Brown, {vi}83–4; six essays completed, {vi}93, 105, 111, 130, 151; four
  essays in *Travel*, {vi}168, 176, 181–2,
  196, 209, 311; also in *World Today*,
  {vi}232; 'only one-half done',
  {vi}253; DHL might visit sites to
  complete, {vi}317, 344, 347, 377, 472,
  505, 566, 575, {vii}19, 21–3, 25–6, 28,
  30, 40, 49, 195; tacitly abandoned,
  {vii}197
'Smile', Brett types, {v}351; to Curtis
  Brown, {v}360; in *Nation*, {v}430,
  504, {vi}270; also in *New Masses*,
  {v}452; collected in *WWRA*, {vi}152,
  197; MS bound, {vi}348
'Soiled Rose, The', completed, {i}343,
  345, 553; accepted by *Forum*, {i}372,
  375, 378, 380, 489, 507, 510, 522, 524,
  528, {ii}44; collected in *Prussian*

Officer as 'The Shades of Spring',
  {ii}197
Sons and Lovers ('Paul Morel'), {i}1, 16,
  19–22, 42, 109, 148, 234, 260, 262,
  388–9, 399, 434, 461, 466, 468, 491,
  493, 541, 551, {ii}1–2, 5, 15–16, 23,
  33, 67, 150, 372, {iii}12, 227, 644,
  {v}4, 66, 146, 375, {vi}12, 65, 229,
  600, {vii}309, 563, {viii}70, 74
  'Paul Morel' plotted and one-eighth
  written, {i}184, {viii}4; 'belongs to'
  DHL's mother's life, {i}195; 100 pp.
  written, {i}230; begun again, {i}237,
  239–40; 'terrible but unwritten',
  {i}258; progresses slowly but steadily,
  {i}262–6, 270, 272, 275, 279, 281, 289;
  some MS to Louie Burrows, {i}263,
  273–4; 'haven't done a stroke of Paul
  for months', {i}310; Jessie
  Chambers's advice sought, {i}317;
  promised to Heinemann, {i}319, 378;
  third version begun, {i}321–2, 326–8;
  'colliery novel' 'going pretty well',
  {i}367, 369–72, 375, 381; 'finished'
  but revision needed, {i}383, 404–5,
  408, 411; 'Paul Morel' sent to
  Heinemann, {i}415–17, 419;
  Heinemann rejects and is cursed,
  {i}421–4, 455, {iii}77; De la Mare's
  opinion of, {i}424; Garnett's advice
  on, {i}426–7; DHL re-casts 'Paul
  Morel', {i}431, 439–40, 448–9, 451,
  455, 458, 460, 462; Duckworth's
  English edn, {i}445, 482, 486, 511,
  518, 526, 544–6, {ii}34, {iv}134, 201,
  427; title becomes *S and L*, {i}462;
  DHL's defence of his 'great tragedy',
  {i}476–7; Frieda's defence of, {i}479;
  Garnett cuts, {i}481–2, 489, 496, 501,
  517; complimentary copies, {i}488,
  552, {ii}19–20, 175–6, {iv}538,
  {vii}72; is 'autobiography', {i}490,
  {iii}282, 526, {v}243, 314, {vi}465;
  'Fore-word' to, {i}507, 510; proofs,
  {i}512–13, 517, 519–20, 522, 524, 536;
  'unified whole', {i}522; Jessie
  Chambers and, {i}527, 550; Collings
  designs jacket, {i}528–9, 535–6,

538–40, 547–8; £50 and agreement from Duckworth, {i}529, 531; DHL writes blurb, {i}529–30; Kennerley publishes in USA, {i}542, {ii}50, 77, 80, 82, 99, {iii}129, 547, 661, 693, {vii}52, {viii}11; publication of English edn, {i}554; reception of, {ii}20–2, 26, 40, 47, 52, 61, 86, 133, 177, 225, 655, {iii}196, {iv}133, 308, {v}92, {vi}283, {viii}19; libraries accept, {ii}21–2; £50 from Duckworth for, {ii}26; 'one sheds ones sicknesses in books', {ii}90; sales disappointing, {ii}117, 135, 165–6; its 'hard, violent style full of sensation and presentation' not to be repeated, {ii}132, 136–7, 142, 169; Frieda doesn't 'really believe in', {ii}151, 172; dispute over royalties from Kennerley, {ii}165, 174, 190, 245, {iii}74, 576, 612, 627, 645, 650–1, {iv}131, 318–19, 323, 376, {v}64, {viii}71; German translation of, {iii}598, 618, 620, 622, 625, 642, {iv}428, {v}38; alleged to have 'no construction', {iii}718; 'seems a long way back', {iv}273; Seltzer and his US edn, {iv}320, 372, 393, 417–19, 445, {v}91, {viii}56; MS to Mabel Luhan in exchange for ranch, {v}23, 65, 72–4, 105, 111, 115, {vii}205; Swedish translation of, {v}489; Secker's English edn, {vi}68, 167; MS from Mabel Luhan to Brill, {vi}365, 382; Tauchnitz edn, {vii}220

'Sons of Montezuma', *see* 'Mozo, The'

'Spinner and the Monks, The', in *English Review*, {ii}58; Clayton types, {ii}381, 398

'Spirit of Place, The', in *English Review*, {iii}270, 292, 324, 643; some 'serious alterations' for collection in *SCAL*, {iv}442 *see also Studies in Classic American Literature*

'Squib, The', {vii}4
DHL proposes anonymous lampoons for 'a bit of fun!', {vii}447–9, 461, 484–5, 498–9, 501, 516, 528; Kot

disapproves, {vii}489; idea abandoned, {vii}578, 589

'St Joseph's Ass', Verga's story in *Adelphi*, {iv}480, 500

'St. Mawr', {iii}471, {v}2, 4, 6, 8, 111, 144, 162, 180, {vi}213, 277, 452, {vii}27, 413, 424, 474
perhaps begun and being revised, {v}57–8; writing going 'slowly', {v}80; 'just winding up', {v}86, 91; Brett typing from MS, {v}118, 121–2, 126; 'more or less a horse story', {v}133; sent to Curtis Brown, {v}136, 141, 147–9; DHL foresees publication with second novelette, {v}136, 141, 148, 161, 173; Secker agrees to publish 'Princess' with, {v}194, 206, 255; Secker proofs, {v}207, 227; published alone by Knopf in USA, {v}213, 255, 342, {viii}94; reception, {v}272–3, 275, 286, 288
see also St. Mawr Together with The Princess

St. Mawr Together with The Princess, {v}2, 8
Secker publishes, {v}149, 194, 206–7, 214, 255; Secker proofs, {v}207, 227; complimentary copies, {v}226, 230–1, 235, 244–5, 258–9, 261, 410, 507, 556, {vi}275, 291, 499; reception, {v}267, 270, 272–3, 275, 286 *see also* 'St. Mawr'

'State of Funk, The', {vii}188, 200

Story of Dr Manente, The, {iii}591, {vi}4, {vii}1, 4, 10, 21, 565, 569, 575, 577
DHL translated from Lasca's Italian, {vi}595, 598, 605, 611, {vii}19; in proof from Orioli, {vii}395, 432; DHL signs 206 copies of limited edn, {vii}492; DHL's optimism over sales, {vii}504, 560–1, 578; possibility of public sale, {vii}526–7; complimentary copies, {vii}557, 579

'Story of the Saint Joseph's Ass', *see* 'St Joseph's Ass'

'Strike Pay', first published as 'Strike-Pay II', {i}375, 381, 383

'Strike-Pay I, Her Turn', *see* 'Her Turn'

LAWRENCE, DAVID HERBERT (*cont.*)
  'Strike-Pay II, Ephraim's Half
    Sovereign', {i}375, {ii}39, 55, 67 *see
    also* 'Strike Pay'
  'Study of Thomas Hardy', {ii}3, 15
  DHL to write 'little book' on Hardy,
    {ii}193–4; Hardy's complete works
    from Marsh, {ii}198–200; 'will be
    about anything but' Hardy, {ii}212,
    216; about 50pp. done, {ii}220, 222;
    Kot typing, {ii}228, 233, 239, 647,
    {iii}163; 'a sort of Confessions of my
    Heart', {ii}235, 243; DHL and Frieda
    typing, {ii}243; leads to 'Crown',
    {ii}292–3, 295
  Studies in Classic American Literature,
    {i}6, {ii}615, {iii}4, 7, 9, 214, 289,
    613, 653, 657, {iv}14, 18, 55, 201, 514,
    {v}319, 375, {viii}58, 63
  signs of interest in project, {iii}65, 73,
    151; DHL begins essays on
    'Transcendental Element in American
    Literature', {iii}155–6, 158, 160, 163,
    172, 201; 'finally going through a set
    of' *SCAL*, {iii}205–6, 209; essay on
    Poe, {iii}212–13; Kot types some
    essays, {iii}217–19, 228, 230–1, 402;
    essays 'in their last and final form',
    {iii}224; DHL continues to write,
    {iii}242; essay on Whitman, {iii}247,
    400, 405, 565; ready for typing,
    {iii}255, 261, 266, 270, 276; essays in
    English Review, {iii}270, 286–7,
    292–3, 298–9, 319, 324–5, 346, 357,
    369, {iv}55; Carswells read some
    essays, {iii}278–9, 288; Huebsch
    considers publishing, {iii}388, 397,
    399, 405–7, 423, 430, 456, 493, 501,
    519, 543, 545, 565, 576, 582; Seltzer
    keen to publish, {iii}493, 519, 543,
    545, 565, 576, 582–3; Secker and,
    {iii}537, 563, 572. {iv}323, 383, 394;
    DHL has definitive text, {iii}545, 556;
    revised version of 'Whitman',
    {iii}576–8; complete copy to
    Mountsier, {iii}582, 588, {viii}36;
    introduction for, {iii}591, 627, 644;
    Seltzer to publish in USA, {iii}612,

  {iv}177, 300, 324, 399, 405, 419, 476,
    490, 501; DHL contemplates shorter
    title, {viii}57; Lippman's response to
    'America, Listen to Your Own',
    {iii}644–5; Mountsier's copy lacks
    chapter, {iv}169; Melville essay
    missing from Curtis Brown's copy,
    {iv}196–7; more changes to Whitman
    essay, {iv}197–8, 457, {viii}81; further
    rewriting, 'Americanising' and
    shortening, {iv}306–7, 338, 340–3,
    345, 348–9, 355; 'finished..form..now
    final', {iv}358–9, 365; TS to Seltzer,
    {iv}367, 369; Secker to publish
    English edn, {iv}399, 401, 407, 454;
    Seltzer's proofs, {iv}441–2, 445, 448;
    reception, {iv}499, 518, 543, {v}198;
    complimentary copies, {iv}499–500,
    {v}80, 91, 113; essays 'all very much
    altered' from *English Review* form,
    {v}104; offered to but rejected by
    Unwin, {viii}32–3; Palmer interested
    in publishing, {viii}36 *see also
    Symbolic Meaning, The*
  'Sun', {v}10
  Brett types, {v}352, 356, 360, 362,
    365; typescript to Curtis Brown,
    {v}370, 385–6; rejected by magazine,
    {v}389; *New Coterie* accepts, {v}505,
    528, 533 *see also Sun*
  Sun, {v}10, 352, {vii}115
  Lahr prints 100 copies, {v}571–2, 594,
    599, 607, {vi}238; collected in
    WWRA, {vi}152, 197, 270; Crosby
    keen to acquire MS of, {vi}301,
    347–8, 372; 'final MS' to Crosby,
    {vi}388, {vii}342; Crosby's Black Sun
    Press publishes unexpurgated,
    {vi}404, 462, 504–5, 548, 570, 580,
    591, {vii}334; appearance
    'elegant..aristocratic..lovely', {vi}614;
    DHL receives 4000 francs for,
    {vii}119; New York Customs threaten
    ban on, {vii}145; US piracy of,
    {vii}239–40, 242–3, 297–8, 307–8, 321
    see also 'Sun'
  'Sunday Stroll in Sleepy Mexico', *see*
    'Walk to Huayapa'

'Surgery for the Novel - or a Bomb', *see* 'Future of the Novel, The'

Symbolic Meaning, The, 'Two Principles' in, {iii}357, {v}104 *see also SCAL*

'Taos', {iv}14, 369, {vii}474

'Tarquinia', {vi}48, 77, 79, 93, 176

'Tenderness', *see Lady Chatterley's Lover*

'That Women Know Best', {vi}403

'The Collier's Wife Scores', *see* 'Her Turn'

'Theatre, The', in *English Review*, {ii}58; Clayton types, {ii}383, 387; for *Twilight*, {ii}398

'Thimble, The', {ii}426, 653
   sketch of Cynthia Asquith in, {ii}418, 420; in *Seven Arts*, {iii}50, 111, 140, 142; with Pinker, {iii}472; written for publication with 'Fox' and 'Captain's Doll', {iv}134; renamed 'Ladybird', {iv}139 *see also* 'Ladybird, The'

'Things', {vi}348, 562, {vii}496

'Thorn in the Flesh, The', formerly 'Vin Ordinaire', {ii}21, 197–9; collected in *Prussian Officer*, {ii}199, 431; formerly 'Blind Gods that do not spare', {viii}12

'Tickets Please', {iv}257, {vi}173
   in *Strand Magazine*, {ii}348, {iv}144. 148, {v}87; formerly 'John Thomas', {iii}299, 309, 319, 472; TS to Curtis Brown, {iv}144; collected in *EME*, {iv}144, 150, 173, 262

'to all men who are men', {vii}103–4

'To Nuoro', {iv}107

'To Sorgono', {iv}107

Trespasser, The ('Saga') {i}10, 13, 17, 19, 129,148, 194, 389, 423, 455, 465, 468, {ii}26, 225, 372, {iii}77, {iv}201, {v}66, 146, {vi}12, 600, {vii}52, 459, {viii}10, 18, 74
   'Saga of Siegmund' begun, {i}158; about half written, {i}159; Helen Corke reads, {i}162; 'horribly poetic', {i}167; Siegmund 'hanged', {i}168; progressing, {i}169–70, 172; 'finished', {i}175; Hueffer considers erotic, 'a rotten work of genius',

{i}178, 330, 339, 434; MS with Hueffer, then Heinemann{i}182–3, 184, 186–7, 200, {viii}4; DHL reluctant to publish, {i}229–31, 236, 239–40, 276, 313, 317, 356; MS to Garnett, {i}330, 337; negotiations summarised, {i}339–40; DHL rewriting, {i}343–5, 349, 351, 358; final title adopted, {i}345, 356; revised version to Garnett, {i}352–3; submitted to Duckworth, {i}356, 367, 369, 373; 'work of fiction on a frame of actual experience', {i}359; Duckworth to publish, {i}378–9, 388, 408, 518; proofs, {i}381, 383, 442; publication, {i}411, 417; reception, {i}415, 419–20, 425, 458, 485, 507–8, 522, {vii}252; US edn (initially Kennerley), {i}430, 489, 502, 542, {iii}74, 129, 547, 653, 692; royalties, {i}448, 453, 486, 511; complimentary copies, {ii}175–6; copies in Mudie's sale, {ii}589, 594; D'Annunzio 'cruder and stupider' than, {iii}41; Secker seeks to publish, {iv}427, {vi}68

'Trip to Sardinia, A', *see Sea and Sardinia*

Twilight in Italy ('Italian Days/Sketches'), {i}495, 505, {ii}14–15, 383, 390, 394, 408, 413–14, 416, 619, {iv}73, {v}119, {vii}342, {viii}9
   Duckworth requests 'book of sketches', {ii}372–3, 405–6; 'full of philosophising and struggling to show things real', {ii}386; 'Italian Studies'/'Sketches' to Pinker, {ii}417, 419, 440; alternative titles, {ii}475; publication by Duckworth, {ii}478, 526, 536. 596, 601, 605, 607, 612, {iii}547, 598, {iv}201; DHL hesitantly chooses 'Italian Days', {ii}484, 494, 522, 524, {iv}403; proofs, {ii}513–16, 522, 524, 532; final title adopted, {ii}606; Huebsch's US edn, {ii}610–11, {iii}76, 129, 323, 643, 652, 661, {iv}169, 403; Duckworth's edn pleases DHL, {ii}613; reception,

LAWRENCE, DAVID HERBERT (*cont.*)
{ii}616, {v}637; complimentary
copies, {ii}627, 644, 665, {iii}32, 548,
612; Cape's edn, {v}460, 555–6,
{vi}68, 281, {vii}158, 265–6, 297
'Two Blue Birds', to Curtis Brown,
{v}451; Faith Mackenzie displeased
by 'portrait-sketch' in, {vi}68–9, 224;
collected in *WWRA*, {vi}152, 197;
in *Dial*, {vi}270; MS bound, {vi}348
'Two Marriages', {i}16
composition of, {i}287–8, 298;
rewitten, {i}307–8; with typist,
{i}309, 311, 321, 326; TS to Garnett,
{i}328, 345; rejected by *Century*,
{i}343; Clayton re-types, {ii}44,
{viii}12; not serialised, {ii}65–6
see also 'Daughters of the Vicar'
'Two Principles, The', *see Symbolic
Meaning, The*
'Venice story', begun but not completed,
{iv}81, 83, 93, 116
'Verse Free and Unfree' (Preface),
{iii}387, 389, 513
'Vin Ordinaire', composition of, {ii}21,
26; accepted by *English Review*, {ii}44,
66, 81–2, 90, 127, 175, 194; collected
in *Prussian Officer*, {ii}196–9; rejected
by *Metropolitan*, {ii}216 *see also*
'Thorn in the Flesh, The'
Virgin and the Gipsy, The, {iii}591,
{v}10
written and MS to Secker for typing,
{v}380–6, 388; DHL considers
recasting, {vii}236, 402, 481
'Virtuous, The', *see* 'Modern Lover, A'
'Volterra', in *Travel*, {vi}48, 93,176, 182
'Vulci', {vi}93, {viii}104–5
'Walk to Huayapa', {v}6, 175, 186, 193,
252
collected in *M in M*, {v}242, 575,
580–1; in *Adelphi*, {v}432, 452; in
Travel, {v}587, 594, 596
'We Need One Another', {vii}513, 554,
556
'Wedding Ring, The', *see Rainbow, The*;
'Sisters, The'

'When She Asks Why', in MS entitled
'The Bogey Between the
Generations', {vi}401
'Which Class I Belong To', {v}620
'Whistling of Birds', {iii}2
in *Athenaeum* (by 'Grantorto'),
{iii}100, 332, 346, {v}87, 104
White Peacock, The ('Laetitia',
'Nethermere'), {i}3, 10–11, 13, 16,
131, 165, 202, 234, 253, 275, 351, 408,
455, {ii}225, {iii}723, {v}35, 86,
{viii}70, 113
'Laetitia': DHL writing{i}43; MS to
Alice Dax, {i}48–9, 88; much is 'poor
stuff', {i}50; 'some exquisite passages', {i}52–3; Blanche Jennings's
view sought, {i}55–6, 58, 61, 63, 69,
71–2, 85–6; prototypes for fictional
characters in, {i}65–6, 68, {v}634;
Jennings returns MS, {i}87, 89;
DHL's critique of, {i}92, 106; DHL
re-writing, {i}106, 118;
'Nethermere': 'Laetitia' re-written,
becomes, {i}43; Hueffer and, {i}141,
144, 148–9, {viii}2–3; Heinemann
accepts for publication, {i}152–3, 156;
158, 161, {iii}77, 547, {v}119, 122,
175, {viii}3–4; DHL to provide new
title, {i}162–3;
White Peacock: title (hesitantly)
adopted{i}166–7, 169–70, 172, 180;
proofs of, {i}175, 177–9, 182; Duffield
publishes in USA, {i}184, 186,
{iii}547, 652, 661, 674, {iv}372;
special copy for DHL's mother,
{i}187, 191, 194, 200, {viii}4–5;
English publication, {i}220–1;
complimentary copies, {i}221, 317,
{iii}357, 548, 568; reception,
{i}222–3, 225–31, 233, 240–1, 276,
312–14, 318, 357, 458, {ii}196;
threatened lawsuit, {i}232; royalties,
{i}310, 315, 364; 'over two years to
write', {iii}36; Duckworth republi-
shes, {iii}598, 612, 653; assignment of
US copyright to Seltzer, {iv}389, 394,
401, 403, {viii}68–9, 95; Secker's edn,

{iv}427, {vi}68, 167; 'real' landscape of, {v}243, 592; German translation blocked, {vii}597–8, 610; about farming and middle-class life, {viii}18

'White Stocking, The', Louie Burrows submits for publication{i}38, 42; DHL re-writes, {i}152, 258; offered to but rejected by*English Review*, {i}275, 297, 345, 348; typed by Clayton, {ii}64, 190, {viii}11; in *Smart Set*, {ii}166; collected in *Prussian Officer*, {ii}197

'White Woman, The', {ii}33, {viii}12 *see also* 'Intimacy' and 'Witch à la Mode, The'

'Whitman', {iii}397, {iv}7
last of *SCAL* essays to be written, {iii}247; Huebsch may find it 'politic not to publish', {iii}400, 405; not appropriate for periodical, {iii}565; revised {iii}576–8; in *Nation*, {iv}55, 66, 79, 197; further rewriting, {iv}197–8, 257; DHL will 'go over' essay again, {iv}457; 'piece added', {viii}81 *see also Studies in Classic American Literature*,

'Why I Don't Like Living in London', 'Why I don't like London', *see* 'Dull London'

'Wilful Woman, The', {iv}318–19

'Wintry Peacock', {v}243
probable reference to (when titled 'The Lance-Corporal Comes Home from the War'), {iii}319–20, 474; MS with Pinker, {iii}472; revised and sent to Sadleir as, {iii}474, 493, 548; bought for $250 for *Metropolitan Magazine* {iii}559, 590, 669, {iv}7, 57–8; in *New Decameron*, {iv}11, 31, 36, 103, 117, {v}87; collected in *EME*, {iv}134, 145, 169, 262, 302

'Witch à la Mode, The', {i}253, 298, {ii}33, {viii}12
Pinker and, {iii}34, 472–3, {iv}188, 193 *see also* 'Intimacy' and 'White Woman, The'

'With the Guns', {ii}222

'Woman in Man's Image', *see* 'Give Her a Pattern'

'Woman Who Rode Away, The', {v}4, 6, 136, 147, 270, 287–8, {vi}156
being written, {v}57–8; TS to Curtis Brown, {v}71, {vii}474; DHL resists cuts for *Hutchinson's*, {v}109–10, 122, 141, 148–9; *Dial* accepts, {v}180, 255, 260; German translation of, {v}331, 515, 558, {vi}213; in *Best British Stories of 1926*, {v}481, {vi}151; in *Criterion*, {v}514, {vi}270; DHL proposes collected volume, {vi}130, 197, 236

Woman Who Rode Away, The, {vi}4, 6–7, 176, 182, 195, 526, {vii}413
stories collected in Secker's edn of, {v}20, 50, 71, 451, 571, {vi}46, 70, 152, 197, 270–1, {vii}26, 239–40, 243, 308; Secker excludes, Knopf includes, 'Man Who Loved Islands', {vi}46, 69, 218–19, 269, {vii}368, 386, 391; publication of, {vi}152, 254, 264, 269–71, 291, 295, 351, 376; German translation of, {vi}213, 236, 275, 277, 429, 616, {vii}51, 572; complimentary copies, {vi}293, 318, 396, 413–14, 422, 430, 432, 436, 445, {vii}156, 163, 171; reception, {vi}438, 502–3; Swedish translation of, {vii}32; Tauchnitz edn, {vii}220 *see also* 'Border Line, The'

'Women Don't Change', *see* 'Do Women Change'

Women in Love, {i}20, 530, {ii}5, 15, 18, 20, 190 {iii}1, 6, 8, 11–16, 32, 46, 76, 316, 543, 630, 662, 665, {iv}2, 4, 6–7, 11, 14, 19, 33, 71, 92, 319, 400, {v}2, 91, {vii}252, 620, {viii}67, 74
emergence from 'Sisters' of, {ii}256; Café Royal in, {ii}499; *Egypte* used in, {ii}521; DHL begins to write, {ii}599, 601–2, 604, 607; 'half way through', {ii}606; 'comes rapidly, and is very good', {ii}610; sequel to *Rainbow* 'but *quite* different', {ii}612, {vi}443; ²/₃ done, {ii}614; 'nearly done', {ii}617, 619, 621; 'finished' except for last

LAWRENCE, DAVID HERBERT (*cont.*)
chapter, {ii}627; DHL typing,
{ii}629–30, 632; selects title, {ii}631,
639–40; typing abandoned, {ii}637–8;
typing resumed, {ii}645, 647, 649,
653, 656, 662, 664–5; title should
perhaps be 'Latter Days', {ii}659;
DHL has typed two-thirds but 'can't
do any more', {ii}666; Katharine
Clayton offers to type remainder but
work done by Pinker's office,
{ii}668–9, {iii}28–9, 89; 'Dies Irae'
proposed as title, {ii}669, {iii}531;
DHL despondent about reaction to,
{iii}19, 22, 35, 37, 61, 67, 69, 73–4,
85–6; 'it is so end-of-the-world' and
beginning of new one, {iii}25–6;
Catherine Carswell reads TS, {iii}34,
36, 44, 57; revised TS to Pinker,
{iii}34–6; Heseltine and Lucy
Channing in, {iii}36, 196, 628,
{iv}87–8, 93–4, 113–14, 116, 123, 129,
138, 169; Ottoline Morrell and,
{iii}41, 109, 226, 317–18, {iv}38,
{vi}82, {vii}235; possibility of
Russian edn, {iii}54, 90, 102; DHL
seeks dedicatee for, {iii}55, 58;
Methuen rejects, {iii}58, 80;
Duckworth rejects, {iii}80; DHL
despairs of its ever being published,
{iii}96, 100, 111, 131, 143–4, 156, 178;
'I *know* it is a good book', {iii}112;
Palmer's interest in publishing,
{iii}129, {viii}27; Maunsel declines,
{iii}183–5, 187, 206; 'I think I'll call it
"Noah's Ark"', {iii}183; Fisher
Unwin's interest, {iii}184–5, 187, 191,
195; Beaumont's fearful interest,
{iii}206–7, 212, 216, 219–20, 228;
George Moore on, {iii}232; TS to
Seltzer, {iii}390, 400, 408–9, 428,
472–3, 476–7, 673–4; negotiations
with Secker over, {iii}391, 394–5, 408,
410–11, 426, 434, 439, 458–60, 462,
468, 470; DHL's 'best' work,
{iii}390–1, 473, 485, 519, 619, 629,
635, 700, {iv}40; TS not seen by

Huebsch, {iii}409, 413, 423, 426, 429,
466, 472, 492, 508, 545, 565, 642–3,
{iv}411–12; Seltzer sends £50
advance royalties, {iii}441, 456–8,
467; novel 'gone to print' in US,
{iii}482, 492; Seltzer contracts to
publish, {iii}484–5, 518–19, 540,
545–9, 552, 576, {viii}38; DHL agrees
with Secker for English edn,
{iii}490–1, 497, 499–501, 503–4, 508,
515–16, 519, 521, 525, 528, 537–8,
545, 572, 574, 582, 627, 672, {iv}183;
Secker's alarm at 'provocative title' of,
{iii}512–13, 517; Secker receives from
Seltzer TS of, {iii}559, 563–4, 573;
Secker's proofs of, {iii}586, 594, 606,
613, 615, 617–19, 621, 625; Seltzer's
edn published, {iii}625, 646; complimentary copies, {iii}629, 638, 681,
695, 706, 710, 715, 725, 727–9, {iv}32,
39–40, 54, 87, 115, 192–3, 233, 299,
493, 549, 553, {v}323; Secker
instructed to delay publication of,
{iii}633, 638, 644, 672, 678, 702,
708–9; Seltzer's edn 'has made us
friends for life', {iii}635; reception,
{iii}636, 693, 734, {iv}38, 40, 90, 100,
104, 126, 407; Secker requests textual
changes, {iii}647, 651, 660, 664;
advance payment from Secker,
{iii}714, 722–4, 729; Secker's
'scrubby' edn published, {iii}728, 732,
{iv}26, 31, 35; Sutro's *W in L*, {iv}30;
sales, {iv}51, 87, 174; 50 signed copies
of, {iv}163, 173–4, 200–1; Secker's
'Second Impression', {iv}173;
unsuccessful prosecution of Seltzer
for, {iv}290–2, 296, 299–300, 305–7,
314–15, 326, 379, 501, {viii}64, 71;
Seltzer's 'trade edn' of, {iv}326,
335–6; popularity in USA increases
royalty income from, {iv}353, 363,
366, 378, 385, 387–8, 392, 457–8,
{viii}60, 63; film rights on, {iv}558,
589, {viii}87; locality associated with,
{v}243; German translation of,
{v}314, 558, {vii}572, 598; Secker's

pocket edn of, {vi}44; Croustchoff
and, {vii}78; TS for sale, {vii}539,
541; errors in Seltzer galleys, {viii}36;
Seltzer describes as 'a big seller',
{viii}73
  Foreword to, {iii}144, 391 *see also*
'Sisters, The'
'Year in Flowery Tuscany, A', *see*
'Flowery Tuscany'
'You Touched Me' ('Hadrian'), MS with
Pinker, {iii}472–3; to Mountsier,
{iv}134, 177–8; to Curtis Brown,
{iv}144–5 *see also* 'Hadrian'
Letters to DHL {i}177, 240, 254, 275–6,
421, 433–4, 442, {ii}81, 381, {iii}356–7,
385, 399, 445, 455–6, 468, 544, 599, 606,
621, 626–8, 635–8, 647, 650, 660–1, 708,
722, {iv}31, 51, 69–70, 88, 106, 113, 173,
229, 262, 292, 314–15, 326, 329, 402,
464–5, {v}16–17, 21, 24, 39, 50, 57–8,
70, 79, 86, 91, 101–2, 109, 112–13,
122–3, 130–1, 180, 193, 241–2, 251, 256,
261, 270, 280, 284, 341, 360, 386, 396,
451–2, 482, 521, 551, 602–3, 612, {vi}21,
29, 52, 66, 70, 84, 115, 140, 176, 203,
222, 232, 238, 269–70, 341, 345, 347,
355, 363, 369, 401, 403, 434–5, 438, 441,
449–50, 461, 463–4, 479–80, 521, 523,
531, 541, 548, 552, 601, 610, {vii}20, 28,
57–8, 65, 70–1, 85, 90–1, 95, 97, 118,
139, 146–7, 149, 166, 177, 185, 188–9,
206, 251, 257–8, 269, 295–6, 306–7,
311–12, 329, 333, 341, 357, 367, 390,
392, 402, 429–30, 437, 451–2, 471, 476,
497, 512, 514, 520, 533–4, 539, 554, 556,
564, 568–9, 582–3, 585, 587, 592–3,
601–2, 612, 614, 625, 637, 642, 648–9,
{viii}2–3, 11–12, 47, 49–51, 54, 59–75,
87–9, 91, 93–5, 108–10
Lawrence, Edward Arthur (nephew), {i}208
LAWRENCE, EMMA MARIA FRIEDA
  JOHANNA
[NB. Only references of some interest
are recorded; casual references are omitted.]
'the most wonderful woman in all
England', {i}376; 'the finest woman I've
ever met', {i}384; DHL to Cearne with,

{i}386; to tell Weekley about DHL,
{i}388; arrangements for departure with
DHL, {i}388–90; DHL declares love
for, {i}391–4, 396, 398, 401–4, 412, 418,
421, 439, 480; DHL tells Weekley of love
for, {i}392–4, 400–2, 409; calls DHL
'Mr Lawrence', {i}393; essential to be
'business-like' in marriage with,
{i}401–2; DHL wants children with,
{i}402–3; flirts with von Henning,
{i}404, 406–7; Weekley tormented by,
{i}409, 420–1, 424, 440, 448, 484–5;
regards Garnett as 'refuge' in England,
{i}410; 'honeymoon' with, {i}412–15,
{vii}438; 'figure like a fine Rubens
woman', {i}415; has 'a great, generous
soul', {i}418; stories written under
influence of, {i}420; loss of children,
{i}421, 430, 440, 449, 467, 486, 492,
496, 510, 514, 517, 521, 531, 535, 537–8,
551, {ii}49–51, 57, 150–1, 163, 168–9,
179, 197, 219, 244–5, 281, 343–5; DHL
will 'fight tooth and claw to keep her',
{i}427; 'wonderful naked intimacy'
with, {i}440; on *S and L*, {i}449, 479,
550, {ii}151, 172; 'Bei Hennef' written
to, {i}462; 'would rather die' than lose
DHL, {i}467; on Garnett's *Jeanne
D'Arc*, {i}470–1; not keen to re-marry,
{i}489; 'not a bit stuck-up' but makes
'class distinction felt', {i}502; 'nameless
duffer at telling anything', {i}513;
consults Robert Garnett about divorce,
{ii}20, 27, 42; designated 'Mrs
Lawrence', {ii}22, 53, as 'Mrs Lawson',
{ii}244; divorce of, {ii}93, 163, 166,
168–9, 174, 327–8, 333, 348–9; thinks
DHL stupid when didactic, {ii}95; on
Middleton, {ii}96–7; hires piano,
{ii}107–8, {v}600–1, {vi}207, {vii}524,
541, 566; fictional character amalgam of
Louie Burrows and, {ii}142; DHL
'deeply happy' with, {ii}161; marriage of
DHL and, {ii}192–3, 195–7; reaction to
outbreak of war, {ii}206, 214–15; DHL
buys necklace for, {ii}228–9; sees
Weekley, {ii}237, 241–2, 244–5; likes

LAWRENCE, EMMA MARIA FRIEDA
JOHANNA (*cont.*)
Meynells, {ii}261; 'of good family',
{ii}265, {iii}282; on Forster novels,
{ii}267, 277–8; helped to see children by
Ottoline Morrell, {ii}281, 287–89; father
dies, {ii}293; advises David Garnett on
sexual relationships, {ii}322; marriage
under strain, {ii}338, 343–5; fated to be
killed by German bomb, {ii}351; 'hates
the Infinite', {ii}359; delighted by
permission to see children, {ii}377;
abhors Ottoline Morrell, {ii}398;
fluctuating relationship with Ottoline,
{ii}415, 434, 438, 452, 462, 483, 488,
510, 512, 517, 539, 558, 571, 591–2;
passport application for, {ii}418,
{iii}84–5, 384; DHL makes hat for,
{ii}454; almost ceases 'to fret about'
children, {ii}478, 639–40, {iii}26;
'jaunty tan hat' with money from
Cynthia Asquith, {ii}486–7; 'more and
more truly married' to DHL, {ii}539,
557; writes 'cross letter' to Russell,
{ii}553; 'very busy and happy' at
Tregerthen, {ii}587; letter to Heseltine
returned with disdain, {ii}598; 'great
"rumpus" with Ottoline', {ii}606; 'the
difference between us being the adventure', {ii}636; DHL unsympathetic
about children and, {ii}651; and DHL
'at peace with each other', {ii}658, 662,
{iii}63; and Murrys {ii}667–8, {iii}28,
343; prefers 'Dies Irae' as title for *W in
L*, {ii}669; occasional 'interviews' with
children, {iii}20, 232, 267, 271–2; agrees
with DHL about Rananim, {iii}25, 66,
214–16; begs money from Amy Lowell,
{iii}29; in Cannan's novel appears as
'vulgar' character, {ii}44, 52; has
ptomaine poisoning, {iii}119–127, 151;
has neuritis, {iii}153–7, 159, 162,
{viii}24; relationship with Gray,
{iii}180; 'monstrous angry unhappiness'
of, {iii}239; has pleurisy, {iii}292–4; 'the
devouring mother', {iii}302; anxious to
visit Germany, {iii}331, 333, 344, 348,
362, 367, 369–70, 388–9, 392, 397,

403–6; 'really a devil' and DHL 'could
leave her now, without a pang', {iii}337;
to Baden, {iii}407, 587–610, {v}656,
{vi}301–7, 426–8, 431, 433, 436,
{vii}208–24, 227, 234, 375ff; DHL in
Florence waiting for, {iii}416–27;
'hopeless' in spoken Italian, {iii}435;
loves Fontana Vecchia, {iii}480, 488.
494; 'a bit scared of the almighty sun',
{iii}539; homesick for Germany,
{iii}552–87 *passim*; 'enthusiastic for
Germany', {iii}613, 623; summoned to
ill mother, {iii}678–702 *passim*; 'the q-b',
{iv}111; new dresses etc, {iv}121–2, 139;
'hated' *Aaron's Rod*, {iv}124; pampered
life on *Osterley*, {iv}206; dazed by 'world
of palm trees and dark swarming
people', {iv}217, 234; disappointed by
Australia, {iv}238; 'tired of moving on',
{iv}241, 243; happy in new (Australian)
house, {iv}250. 253; wants little farm in
USA, {iv}273, 277; won whist-drive on
Tahiti, {iv}283–4; on 'iron-grey pony
jogging through the sage-brush',
{iv}301, 325; 'boiling wild plums',
{iv}303; longed for 'freedom' of USA
but discovers its 'iron ugliness',
{iv}310–11; considers last chapter of
Kangaroo 'too shallow', {iv}329; covets
ranch, {iv}333, 335–6; Mabel Sterne
regarded as antagonistic to 'living
relation' between DHL and, {iv}337;
happier at ranch, {iv}348, 353; likes
Mexico City, {iv}415; 'crazy to wash
dishes again', {iv}426; eager for Europe,
{iv}447, 458; to England, leaving DHL,
{iv}478–90; Murry and Kot to 'look
after', {iv}482–3; DHL sends books to,
{iv}499; sees Murry 'quite often',
{iv}502; whereabouts unknown,
{iv}505–6, 508, 519–20, {viii}82–6;
wants DHL to return to England,
{iv}512–15, 517–18, 522, 524; cables
DHL to return, {iv}526; DHL surren-
ders 'once more in the long fight',
{iv}528; DHL looks for 'strength' not
'love' from, {iv}532; refuses to return to
USA, {iv}537; 'Frieda is nice, but

England is hateful', {iv}542; buys clothes in Paris, {iv}562, 566, 569, 580; 'wants to come to Taos', {iv}586; with Brett and DHL sails for New York, {iv}598; 'doesn't really like the sea', {iv}599–600; in Seltzers' New York flat, {v}17; given Kiowa ranch by Mabel Luhan, {v}23, 29, 32, 43, 46, 62; her horse, Azul, {v}59, 62; gives *S and L* MS to Mabel in exchange for ranch, {v}65, 73–4, 105, 111, {viii}90; paints picture, {v}145, {vi}543; when in Mexico 'pines for her ranch', {v}165; 'sniffing Europe-wards', {v}184–5; likes *Plumed Serpent* best, {v}190; not 'a happy combination' of Brett, DHL and, {v}192; makes tentative peace with Brett, {v}215; hates Mexico, {v}219; bans Brett from living on ranch, {v}222–3, 239; friendship with Brett unlikely, {v}234; nephew visits, {v}258–9, 277; makes butter, collects eggs, {v}266, 270; German translation of *David* by, {v}275, 379, 389, 464, 472, {vi}248, 359; sees children, {v}332–3; Kot 'pet enemy' of, {v}347, 367, 375; presents from Brett for, {v}349, 352; her children 'duds', {v}362; 'implacable intention of never seeing [Brett] again', {v}390, {vi}49; DHL leaves Spotorno after 'bust-up' with, {v}401–3; writes 'more quietly and humanly', {v}406; probably 'more tolerant', {v}412; daughters treat her egotism 'with ferocity', {v}419–21; DHL 'weary to death of struggling with', {v}424; Ada Clarke can stay at Mirenda 'when F. is away', {v}448; in London while DHL in Scotland, {v}506ff; in Lincolnshire with DHL, {v}515ff; will eventually agree to sell ranch, {v}537, 652; found Ottoline Morrell 'a little faded', {v}559; 'not such a fool' as others think, {v}569; 'wonderful at giving advice', {v}570; makes stylish clothes, {v}622–3, {vi}398; returns to Mirenda, {vi}25–6; agrees never again to mix DHL's relations and hers, {vi}38; downcast about reception

of *David*, {vi}75, {viii}104; DHL does not regard as 'social soul', {vi}76; daughter Barbara arrives, {vi}150–2; her family generous to DHL, {vi}178, 180; has lorgnette, {vi}190; 'blissfully happy' in Mirenda, {vi}194–6; provides Christmas-tree for 'peasants', {vi}237; self-righteous, {vi}243, 251; DHL's health 'always an anxiety and a strain' for, {vi}253; reading Gide, {vi}282; tries skiing, {vi}286–7; refuses to go to ranch because of DHL's health, {vi}310, 365, 437; to Alassio to see Barbara, {vi}361–7, 369, 371; feels *LCL* 'might really do some good in the world', {vi}375; wants to retain Mirenda, {vi}387, 391, {viii}107; in 'nervous state' after dentistry, {vi}407; not 'the soul of patience', and 'doesn't look on [DHL] as a shrine', {vi}419; possible sale of Kiowa, {vi}443. 550, {vii}205, 288–9, 385, 472; with DHL alone at Gsteig, {vi}454–6; both affected by altitude, {vi}476; requests underclothes and eiderdown from Emily King, {vi}485, 509; flourishes 'like a dandelion in the sun' from furore over *LCL*, {vi}487; 'grand birthday feast', {vi}507; 'pines for more islands', {vi}513; translates 'Hymns in a Man's Life', {vi}524, 540; wants to keep *Close-Up* painting, {vi}536; 'doing a grape-slimming-course', {vi}557; gives up Mirenda, {vi}576–83; DHL hears nothing from, {vi}586–7; to Ile de Port-Cros with Italian flu, {vi}588–99, 604, 608; wants own house rather than live in hotel, {vii}33, 41, 46, 52, 80, 87, 104–5, 109, 152, 155, 166, 170, 197, 283–314 *passim*; to avoid censorship DHL's mail could be sent to, {vii}44; regards *Pansies* as 'real doggerel', {vii}64–5; favourably revises estimate of Rhys Davies, {vii}74; not keen on Spain, {vii}85–6, 253; not so energetic as formerly, {vii}200; marriage of daughter Elsa, {vii}241; attends concert in Palma, Mallorca, {vii}262, 264; has bottom pinched 'on the tram',

LAWRENCE, EMMA MARIA FRIEDA
    JOHANNA (*cont.*)
    {vii}309; to London to see exhibition of
    DHL's pictures, {vii}331–9, 343–4, 346,
    349–50; out of touch with DHL,
    {vii}360–5; supports DHL over fate of
    paintings, {vii}370; secretly hates
    Germans, {vii}384, 403, 416; 'bad at
    letters', {vii}386; 'fancies herself quite a
    business-woman', {vii}392, 432; 50th
    birthday celebrations, {vii}418, 420–2,
    424. 427; DHL's MSS and pictures
    would provide income for, {vii}459;
    village bone-setter 'set her foot in one
    minute', {vii}460–1, 463–6, 469–70, 474,
    478–9; rents Beau Soleil, Bandol,
    {vii}492–4, 500–1; tempted to interfere
    in DHL's publishing affairs, {vii}526;
    slightly lame, {vii}530–1, 553; 'some-
    times unstrung', {vii}547; wants to
    return to New Mexico, {vii}574, 595;
    poor correspondent, {vii}579; under-
    clothes ordered from Ada Clarke for,
    {vii}581, 592; enjoys 'Christmas fun',
    {vii}605; less generally hostile,
    {vii}616–17; sister Else at villa, {vii}623,
    630; writes bluntly to Brett, {vii}628;
    daughter Barbara at villa, {vii}630ff; in
    Nouvel Hotel, Vence, {vii}641–7; at
    Villa Robermond, {vii}652–3; anxious
    about children, {viii}6; and DHL
    'struggling on', {viii}7; fearful after
    breaking of US-German relations,
    {viii}20; still in Capri, {viii}29; 'blissful-
    ly happy', {viii}45; assures Seltzer of
    DHL's loyalty, {viii}77; DHL advises
    circumspection by, {viii}85; urged to
    join DHL in Mexico, {viii}85–6
    Letters to {i}376, 388–94, 396–407,
    {iv}435, 529, {vi}304–5, 429–30,
    {vii}346–7, 359–60, {viii}85–6
    Letters from {i}113, 400, 410, 438–9, 449,
    451, 467, 470–1, 475–6, 479, 494–5.
    497–8, 521, 531–4, 537–8, 545, 549–50,
    {ii}23–4, 48–50, 59–60, 64, 71, 96–8,
    116–17, 128, 150–1, 170, 172, 214–15,
    219, 245, 260, 264, 267, 277–8, 287–90,
    293, 303, 306, 322, 344–5, 377, 484,

545–6, 549, 553, 570–1, 577–8, 606, 619,
    628, 642–3, 664–5, 667–8, {iii}34–5, 52,
    66, 106–7, 109–10, 161, 329, 378, 571–2,
    615, 641–2, 666–7, 708, {iv}62–3, 102,
    181, 205–6, 209–10, 244, 268–9, 339,
    356–7, 383, 395–7, 450, 455, 459, 469,
    472–3, 476, 502, 567, 575, 578, 595, 597,
    {v}41, 65, 74, 83, 89, 107–8, 125–6,
    132–5, 172, 187, 190, 202, 210, 215–16,
    218, 222–3, 225, 233–5, 250, 300, 335,
    344–5, 349–50, 375, 436, 461, 470–1,
    529, 567–9, 598, 602, 605, {vi}35, 148–9,
    192–3, 246, 252–3, 374–5, 423–4, 438–9,
    484–8, 490, {vii}212, 370, 373, 385, 578,
    628, 641, {viii}10, 14, 20, 54, 77, 91–2,
    104

Lawrence, Ernest (nephew), {i}208, {vii}459
Lawrence, Florence Anne (Flossie) (niece),
    {i}208
LAWRENCE, GEORGE ARTHUR
    (brother), {i}174, 208, 229, 278, 327
    'holy man', {i}135, 376; DHL tells of
    engagement, {i}204; visit to DHL in
    Croydon, {i}302–3, 305–6, 308–11, 314;
    ignorant of DHL-Frieda relationship,
    {i}497, {ii}42; *S and L* to, {ii}19;
    'radical nonconformist', {ii}489; in
    munitions factory, {ii}662; not well off,
    {v}126; head of Lawrence family,
    {vii}459
    Letters to {i}204
Lawrence, James (uncle), {i}68, 199, {v}593
Lawrence, John (grandfather), {i}199,
    {iii}282
Lawrence, John Arthur, *see* Lawrence, A. J.
Lawrence, Lettice Ada (sister), *see* Clarke, L.
    A.
Lawrence, Louisa (grandmother), {i}199
LAWRENCE, LYDIA (mother), {i}1–2, 9,
    15, 20, 23, 27, 31, 33, 46, 49, 68, 82, 103,
    106, 135–6, 147, 173, 212, 219, 228, 234,
    {v}1, 530, 631
    DHL on holiday with, {i}70–1, 132–4,
    278; DHL corresponds weekly with,
    {i}141, 255; described, {i}174; develops
    abdomenal cancer, {i}176–7, 179, 181,
    183; DHL sends *White Peacock* proofs
    for, {i}177–8, 184; 'horribly ill',

{i}185–6, 192, 194–5, {viii}5; 'we have been great lovers', {i}187, 190; 'very near the end', {i}189; 'has had [the soul of me], and nobody can have it again', {i}190–1; copy of *White Peacock* shown to, {i}191, 194, 312–13; 'had a bloody hard life', {i}192; 'my first, great love...a wonderful, rare woman', {i}195, 199, {viii}113; hated Jessie Chambers, {i}197, 268, 531; death and burial of, {i}198–9, 220, 243; DHL 'so miserable' about, {i}202; held Reid in high regard, {i}244; sayings of, {i}248, 489; DHL dreams about, {i}272; Ada Krenkow paid medical expenses for, {i}283; birthday of, {i}289–90; Frieda on DHL's love for, {i}449; DHL gaining indepen- dence from, {i}527; her candlesticks precious to DHL, {ii}584; from 'well-to- do, puritan family', {iii}282; DHL feels continuing presence of, {iii}291; 'never wanted [DHL] to be born', {iii}333
Letters to {i}27

Lawrence, Mary Ellen ('Polly') (aunt), {i}68, 199, 231, {viii}1
prototype of Mrs Holroyd, {v}593

Lawrence, Thomas Edward, {ii}403

Lawrence, William Ernest (brother), {i}1, 4, 23
drafted letter for DHL, {i}21; owned set of *International Library of Famous Literature*, {i}50

LAWRENCE'S READING, [NB this is not an exhaustive list of everything read by DHL; it records his attitudes to books, his current reading, and his recommen- dations to others]
authors who 'seriously modified' DHL's religious beliefs, {i}36–7; 'reverence' for Richard Garnett's *International Library*, {i}50; benefitted most from 'reading what I feel I want to read', {i}59; Krenkow's house rich in books, {i}77; Charlotte Brontë highly favoured, {i}88; 'The true heart of the world is a book..essence of things..stored in books', {i}96; DHL ignorant of aristocratic life 'save from books', {i}101; 'I love..little

volumes of poetry', {i}106; wide reading in 'modern work' while DHL in Croydon, {i}118; works regarded as 'great', {i}127, 222, 261; modern novels and plays recommended, {i}142, 172; books sent to Jessie Chambers, {i}151; in DHL's home 'shelves of study-books, a book-case of reading-books', {i}174; Bible should not be read as if 'displayed in a kind of theatre', {i}244; Meredith 'wonderfully clever', {i}250; 'rather fond of Morris', {i}298; Garnett and DHL 'discussed books most furiously', {i}315; 'I love books of Short stories', {i}349, 524; 'I hate the glum silence of ranks of shut books', {i}388; Frieda 'a cormorant of novels', {i}462; admiration for Mark Rutherford, {i}481–2, {ii}146; Murray's translations have 'fearful fascination' for DHL, {i}525; *English Review* 'so piffling', {ii}21; on Wells, {ii}74, 89–90; Harrison's *Art and Ritual* 'pleases me most just now', {ii}90, 114; George Eliot admired, {ii}101; books that are 'the raw material of Art', {ii}114; Stephens a disappointment, {ii}114, 118; DHL enjoyed *Pater*, {ii}138; Crosland's *Sonnets* 'objection- able', {ii}146; *House of the Dead* 'dull', {ii}155; DHL's joy at receiving com- plete Hardy, {ii}199; Jenner's *Christian Symbolism* greatly admired, {ii}250; Palmer's *Comedy* 'very interesting', {ii}254; Van Gogh's *Letters*, {ii}296; Radford's *Poems*, {ii}350; Burnet's *Early Greek Philosophy*, {ii}364; Nichols' poetry 'beautiful', {ii}445; significance of Frazer's *Golden Bough*, {ii}470; *Ajanta Frescoes* highly regarded, {ii}488–9; *Hesiod*, {ii}517; 'I dont like six-penny chap-books', {ii}519; *Moby Dick* 'very odd, interesting', {ii}528; DHL loves Coulton's *From St. Francis to Dante*, {ii}538; 'I've gone off Dostoevsky', {ii}542–4; dictionaries important for DHL, {ii}567, {iii}40, 43, 45, 236, {vii}540; advice on children's books, {ii}588–9, {iii}340; Rolland's *Life*

LAWRENCE'S READING (*cont.*)

of Michael Angelo 'good', {ii}592, 597; Tylor's *Primitive Culture*, 'sound substantial', {ii}593; O'Shea's *Parnell* 'poignant', {ii}604; classic American authors, {ii}614–15, 645, {iii}40; Thucydides 'very present to one's soul', {ii}614, 634; Asquith's poems, {iii}28; need of 'gardening book', {iii}103, 108; 'I am reading Gibbon', {iii}233, 239; Frobenius 'tiresome', {iii}233; 'Jung book..Beware of it', {iii}301; DHL respects 'good genuine books of mankind', {iii}315, 317; Deledda and Reade 'very interesting', {iii}338; 'one has to be in the mood to read books', {iii}347; DHL's delight in De Quincey, {iii}407; books about Pacific region, {iii}566; DHL glad of 'well-printed, carefully produced book', {iii}679; popular taste in books, {iii}680, 715; 'I've no idea *what* England likes to read', {iv}99; 'too much of an insipid old stew' in Lady Gregory's plays, {iv}105; Verga 'the only Italian' to interest DHL, {iv}109–10; 'continually borrowing' Marie Hubrecht's books, {iv}141; 'One wonders if all books..parish magazines', {iv}243; Bunin's 'tales..not very good', {iv}275; after reading three books (*Passage to India* etc) 'my belly is full', {v}77; weekly *Times* and *Strand* 'bunk' and 'piffle', {v}80; DHL glad *Arabia Deserta* 'so long', {v}89; DHL 'fond of fat two-vol books with letters in them', {v}198; 'Damn "holiday reading"!', {v}275; *Natural Man* best novel about WWI, {v}315–16; Kot sends four Russian grammar books, {v}376–7; DHL buys little books in anticipation of 'yacht library', {v}383; DHL will use Vieusseux's library (Florence) for Italian books on Etruscans, {v}444; 'very dull' books in lending library, Sutton-on-Sea post office, {v}522; DHL reading Plato 'once more', {v}577; *Life of Voltaire* 'far too jammy', {v}585; 'on principle I believe in cheap books', {v}626; reading Galsworthy's novels 'nauseated me up to the nose', {v}649; Douglas's *Siren Land* essays 'good..haven't gone thin', {vi}45; 'can't read' Proust, {vi}100; DHL tired of reading 'Storm in 18 volumes', {vi}129; reads Mohr's plays, {vi}161–2, 183; *Jugend* amusing but 'a bit "shocking"', {vi}163; 'I am sick of books', {vi}183; 'I just read Darwin's *Beagle* again', {vi}214; French book on Egypt dry, abstract, {vi}302; Aretino's fiction amusing but not '*created* enough', {vi}343; 'great fun reading Hardy's stories again', {vi}471; Stendhal novel historically good but emotionally 'trashy', {vi}543; Ernst's *To the Pure* 'pertinent..curiously moving', {vi}613; Harington's *Ajax* 'fairly amusing', {vii}85, 123; *American Caravan* 'pretty awful..a *Jewish* selection', {vii}139; despite friendship with Huxley, DHL doesn't like his books, {vii}164; Renn's *War* one of best war books, {vii}326; DHL prefers Carter's prose to drawings in 'Dragon', {vii}456; hates St John's 'Jewish nasal sort of style', {vii}519; 'tiresome and jaw-cracking style' of German academic on Etruscans, {vii}570; DHL's reading in Ad Astra, {vii}649; DHL advises de Wit on novels of working-class life, {viii}18–19

Lawson, Henry Hertzberg, *Children of the Bush*, {i}376

Lawson, Jim, *see* Nylander J.

Lawson, Mrs, {vii}42

Lazarus, {i}73

Le Beausset (France), {vii}211

Le Castellet (France), {vii}211

Le Havre (France), {iii}713, {v}549

Le Lavandou (France), {vi}578, 584–7, 589, 594, 598–9, {vii}109

Le Thière, Guillaume, {i}29

LEACH, HENRY GODDARD, {vi}370, 378

Letters to {vi}226

Leader-Williams, Basil, {iv}196, {v}419

Leader-Williams, Lilian, {iv}196, {v}419

Leake, R. E., *see* Skinner, M. L.

Lear, Edward, {ii}219

Leaves of Grass, see Whitman, W.

Lecco (Italy), {iv}194

LEDERHANDLER, DAVID V., wishes to buy DHL MS, {vii}240; prospectus for *LCL* to, {vii}243; offers $60 for MS, {vii}306; learns about symbolism in *LCL*, {vii}476–7

Letters to {vii}240, 305–6, 476–7

Lee, *see* Witt, L.

Lee, Agnes, {ii}417

Lee, Vernon (Violet Paget), {i}12, {vi}46

Leek (Staffordshire), {i}373, 377, 379

Legend of Ermengarde, The, {vii}429, 431–3, 455

see also Titus, E.

Legends of Charlemagne, see Bulfinch, T.

Legends, see Lowell, A.

LEGGETT, HARRY, {iv}71

Letters to {iv}71

Leghorn (Italy), {ii}59–60, 63, 123–4, 630, {iii}19, 411, {iv}156

see also Livorno

Legion Book, The, see Minchin, H. C.

Leicester, {i}7–8, 46, 60, 73–7, 81, 128, 161, 176–8, 189–90, 193, 203, 209, 211, 225, 266–7, 273–4, 278, 291–320 *passim,* 386–8, 498, {ii}125, {iii}267, {viii}2

Leicester Galleries (London), {vi}16, 522

Leicestershire, {i}35, 38, 46, 105, 197, 210, 247, {iii}558

Leighton, Frederick W., {iv}456

Leighton, Lord Frederic, *The Garden of the Hesperides,* {i}113

Leipzig (Germany), {i}8, {iii}597, 622, 679, {iv}6, 40, 257, 428, {v}252, 331,340, 364, 646, {vi}52, 275, {vii}23, 32, 383, 596

Leith Hill (Surrey), {i}301

'Leithdale' (Darlington, Australia), {iv}9, 236, 240, 270, 496, 524, {v}20, 23–4, 114, 291

Leitner, Josef, {vi}149

Leitner, Walburga, {vi}149, 166

Lelant (Cornwall), {iii}712

Lembo, {v}627, 637

Lena, *see* Trachsl, L.

Lengel, William Charles, {v}312

Lenin, Vladimir Ilyich, {iii}570, {iv}577–8

Lenzi, Signor, {vi}418, 437, 459, 469–70, 475, 478

Leonardo da Vinci, {vi}110, 342, {viii}48

Leoncavallo, Ruggiero, {i}247

Leopardi, Giacomo, {i}9

Leopold, Mrs, {vii}286

Lerici (Italy), {ii}3–4, 8, 57, 59, 63, 77–182 *passim,* 245, 279, 478, {iii}19, 416–17, {vii}465, 478, {viii}9–10, 86

Lerner, Miss, {iv}442

Lerolle, Guillaume, {vii}601–2

Leroy, {i}75, 322

Les Diablerets (Switzerland), {vi}1, 3, 5, 7, 16, 313–14, 322–3, 325, 332, 342, 354, 375, 380, 383, 389–90, 397, 437, 483, {vii}9, 87, 207, 431

Huxleys invite DHL to, {vi}234, 236–7, 246, 248, 261–5, 268–9; DHL at Chalet Beau Site in, {vi}270–311 *passim,* 316, {vii}79–80, 161, 208, 646; did DHL's chest 'such a lot of good', {vi}337–8, 344, 350–1; Gsteig close to, {vi}456–60, 467–8, 473, 500–2, 510, 527, 545–6

Les Lecques (France), {vii}560

Leslie, Henrietta, {vii}196

Leslie, Shane, {v}315

see also Corvo, Baron, *In his Own Image*

Lessing, Gotthold Ephraim, {i}5

Letojanni (Sicily), {iii}626, 662

LETTERS (WRITING OF), 'I hate love letters', {i}203; range of DHL's 'episto-lary styles', {i}217; DHL has to force himself to write, {i}236; 'bad writer of love letters', {i}242; when Louie Burrows offended, DHL 'no good at a letter', {i}287; 'I canna write a love letter', {i}316; to Frieda DHL 'will always try..to write the truth as near the mark as I can get it', {i}403; Collings' letters 'as good as a visit from somebody nice', {i}502; 'I don't care about form in a letter', prefers 'real bust' of correspon-dent, {ii}70; DHL likes when feeling 'spiteful: it's like having a good sneeze', {ii}106; on Futurism to be kept, {ii}184; Katherine Mansfield's letters 'as jarring

LETTERS (WRITING OF) (*cont.*)
as the sound of a saw', {ii}333; DHL
wrote when 'soul..fizzing savagely',
{ii}385; of condolence, {ii}415–16,
481–2, {iii}101, {iv}327, {v}124, 292–3,
{vii}192–4; answers 'smack off..on the
spur', {iii}718, {v}293; enable
Schwiegermutter to 'travel beside..and
with us', {iv}590; Brett writes 'very
good', {v}584; rare for DHL to write
long, {vi}76; Frieda not letter-writer,
{vi}375; DHL's 'most serious contribu-
tion to literature' for six weeks, {vii}309
Letters and Reminiscences, see Dostoievsky, F.
Letters from an American Farmer, see
Crèvecoeur, M. G. J.
Letters from High Latitudes, see Blackwood, F.
T. H.
Letters from the Underworld, see Dostoievsky, F.
Letters of a V.A.D., see Skinner, M. L.
Letters on Reasoning, see Robertson, J. M.
Lettie, *see* Skinner, M. L.
Levy, Lucille, {iii}662
Lewes (Sussex), {i}423
Lewis, A. P., {ii}615, {iii}260
DHL walks across Switzerland with,
{ii}184; visits DHL at Chesham,
{ii}230; with DHL when war declared,
{ii}268, {v}354–5; subscribed for
Signature, {ii}409
Lewis, Lady, {ii}18, 409
Lewis, Lieutenant, {ii}413
Lewis, Percy Wyndham, {i}138, 315, {ii}193,
{vii}265
Lewis, Sinclair, {iv}499
Arrowsmith, {viii}93;
Babbitt, {iv}499;
Main Street, {iv}201, 499
Lewis, Sir George James Graham, {ii}18,
409
Lewisohn, Irene, {v}303, 308, 333
Lewisohn, Ludwig, *The Case of Mr Crump*,
{vii}97
Li, *see* Whale, E.
Li Po, {i}168
Liber Studiorum, see Turner, J.
Liberal Party, {i}135, {ii}48, 253, 369, 371,
{iii}57, {vi}280, {vii}161, 315, 318

Liberia, {vii}29, 130
Libermann, Dr Henri Adolphe François,
{ii}114
Librairie Castiglione (Paris), {vii}57, 67, 75,
219
Librairie du Palais Royal (Paris), {vii}208–9,
213–15, 219, 261
Librairie Shakespeare (Paris), {v}457
see also Beach, S.
Librairie Terquem (Paris), {iii}713, {iv}42
Librarian, Cambridge University Library, *see*
Jenkinson, F.J.H.
Lichtent(h)al (Germany), {vi}576–9,
{vii}398–406, 413–18, 421–38, 444,
447
Life and Voyages of Columbus, see Irving, W.
Life in Mexico, see Barca, F. E. C. de la
Life of Charlotte Brontë, see Gaskell, E.
Life of Gladstone, see Morley, J.
Life of Henry Brulard, see Stendhal, H.
Life of Jesus, see Murry, J. M.
Life of Marcus Cato, see Plutarch
Life of Michael Angelo, see Rolland, R.
Life of Robert Burns, see Carswell, C.;
Lockhart, J. G.
Life of the Bee, see Maeterlinck, M.
Life of Voltaire, see Tallentyre, S.
Light, Dr Gertrude Underhill, {v}277
Lilliencron, Detlev von, {i}513
Limb, Billy, {i}230
Limb, Emmeline ('Emmie'), {i}85, 95, 443,
541, {v}279
LIMB, MABEL, {i}35–6, 90, 93, 230,
{v}279
Letters to {i}35, 77, 82, 84–5, 91, 95, 133–4
Limb, Mrs W. T., {i}95, 443, {v}279
Limb, William T., {i}85, 95, 133, {v}279
Limerick, Mona (Gadney, Mary Charlotte
Louise), {i}384, 414
Limpsfield (Surrey), {i}194, 265, 362, 507
LINATI, CARLO, {iv}232, {v}3, 140
critical article on DHL by, {v}90–2, 141;
DHL's response to article, {v}200–1;
translates 'Fox' and 'Ladybird',
{vi}516–17, {vii}386, 517
'Giovanni Verga and the Sicilian Novel',
{v}92
Letters to {v}90–1, 200–1, {vi}516–17

Lincoln, {i}6, 23, 137, 172, 283–4, 295–6
    sets 'the soul a-quivering', {i}80; riot in,
    {i}297, 299; DHL 'used to love',
    {vi}371
Lincoln, Abraham, {i}114
    Speeches, {iii}66
Lincolnshire, {i}8, 22, 38, 59, 371, {iii}203,
    {v}1, 13, 310–11, {v}544, {vi}107
    DHL with sisters on holiday in, {v}501,
    504, 509, 512–31
LINDSAY, JOHN ('JACK'), {vii}3, 31, 53,
    60–1, 66, 70, 85, 125, 135, 168, 253, 265
    too fearful of police to publish *Paintings*,
    {vii}77; clever but 'no strength of
    character', {vii}322
    Dionysos: Nietzsche contra Nietzsche,
    {vii}94, 117;
    Helen Comes of Age, {vii}117
    see also Fanfrolico Press; *London
    Aphrodite*
    Letters to {vii}60
Lindsay, Norman Alfred William, {vii}31,
    66, 86, 92, 125
Linnell, John, {i}89, 319
'Lion', see Lahr, C.
Lipari Isles (Italy), {iii}688
Lippman, Walter, {iii}654, {iv}333–4
Lippo Lippi, Fra, {vi}79
Lit. Supp., see *Times Literary Supplement, The*
LITERARY AGENT(S) 'trafficking with',
    {ii}99; DHL pestered by, {ii}135, 174;
    poverty thrusts DHL into hands of,
    {ii}189; source of financial support,
    {ii}629, {iii}29, 207, {v}139; 'insult-
    ing..pittance' from, {iii}70; 'rather
    tiresome tyrant', {iii}142; 'dangle a
    prospective fish on the end of a line, with
    grinning patronage, and just jerk it
    away', {iii}216; negotiate agreements,
    {iii}388; DHL to act as own, {iii}458,
    466, 473–4; vague and evasive, {iii}466;
    essential in New York, {iii}476; no more
    'professional', {iii}566; take 10%
    commission, {iii}577, {v}554; not to be
    'Pinkerish', {iii}667; should not be 'too
    humble with editors, publishers..or any
    other stinkers with money or office',
    {iii}684; essential in London 'at once',

{iii}697; initial negotiation with
    publisher done by author, {iv}27; Curtis
    Brown 'more obedient than..impudent
    Pinker', {iv}29; DHL decides to
    dispense with, {iv}376; 'Damn agents
    and their delays', {v}281; DHL has 'own
    life to live' so employs, {v}368; DHL
    'awfully bored' between publishers and,
    {v}558; oppose 'right to publish works
    without any payment whatsoever',
    {vi}516; 'dead against' unexpurgated
    Pansies, {vii}111; 'useful' to writer,
    {vii}129; police threaten, {vii}147, 153,
    157, 165; DHL hates, {vii}291; 'only
    useful when things are all straight
    sailing', {vii}522; to 'arrange any
    business that is necessary' for de Wit to
    translate his works, {viii}21; DHL
    rebukes for altering text without
    permission, {viii}38; author not to come
    between publisher and, {viii}40
    see also Brown, A. C., Low, B.,
    Mountsier, R., Pinker, J. B., Pollinger, L.
    E.
*Literary Digest International Book Review,
    The*, {iv}16, 374, {vi}210–11, 290, 296,
    {vii}55, 226, {viii}108
Littel, Robert, {v}457
Little Brown & Co., rejected *W in L*, {iii}12;
    bought *Widowing* from Kennerley,
    {iii}129, 527, 546
Little Dream, The, see Galsworthy, J.
Little Lord Fauntleroy, see Burnett, F. E. H.
Little Mary, see Barrie (Sir) J. M.
Little Novels of Sicily, see DHL; Verga, G.
Little Theatre, see London 11
Littlehampton (Sussex), {ii}12, 259, 367,
    370–7
LITVINOV, IVY TERESA, {ii}187, 258,
    279, 343, 503, 595, 636, {iii}24, 41, 210,
    362, 676, {iv}23, 362, {v}97, 355, 374,
    {vi}187, 494, {vii}359, 377
    on *S and L*, {ii}1; visits DHL,
    {ii}168–9, {iii}363; marriage of,
    {ii}532–3, 555, 629–30; ought not to
    have children, {ii}635; pregnant,
    {iii}19–20
    Letters to {ii}160

Litvinov, Maxim, {ii}160, 532, 629, {iii}20,
    {iv}362, {v}97, {vi}187, {vii}359
    Soviet plenipotentiary in London,
    {iii}210; ambassador in Estonia,
    {iii}676; 'in the Seats of the Mighty',
    {v}355
Litvinov, Michael, {iii}20, 363
Live Corpse, The, see Tolstoy, L.
Liveright, *see* Boni & Liveright
Liverpool (Lancashire), {i}2, 43–5, 55, 59,
    63, 65, 69, 126, 185, 302, {ii}227, 391,
    435, 437, 606, {iv}475, 542, {vi}514, 544
    Walker Art Gallery, {i}103
Living Age, The, 'Blind Man' in, {iii}633,
    635, 690, {viii}40; 'Sons of Montezuma'
    ('The Mozo') in, {v}432
Livonius, Frau A. von, {v}556
Livorno (Italy), {vii}109, 176, 183–4, 493,
    526
    see also Leghorn
Lizzie, {i}374
    see also Booth, E.
Llandudno (Carnarvonshire), {i}127, 295,
    {iv}59
Lloyd George (Earl), David, {ii}371, 379,
    {iii}3, 282, 317, 339, 611, {v}541,
    {vi}271
    becomes Prime Minister, {iii}39, 46,
    48–9; 'clever little Welsh *rat*', {iii}48;
    'means nothing, stands for nothing',
    {iii}56–7; associated with Bottomley by
    DHL, {iii}60; 'hopeless', {iii}283;
    'wants peace', {iii}294; schemer,
    {iii}500; British India let down by,
    {iv}234; the 'balancing-pig' after
    elections, {vii}315; 'treacherous bug',
    {vii}327
Lloyd, Muriel, {iii}107
Lo Sa il Tonno, see Bacchelli, R.
Lob Lie-by-the-Fire, see Ewing, J. H.
Lobo (ranch), *see* Kiowa ranch
Locarno (Switzerland), {iii}344, {iv}39,
    {vii}509
Locke-Ellis, Vivian, {iv}565, {vi}83
    DHL 'felt a certain contempt for',
    {iv}571–2
Lockhart, John Gibson, Burns biography
    'Made me spit!', {vi}231
    Ancient Spanish Ballads, {i}205;

Life of Robert Burns, {i}487, 504,
    {vi}231–2
'Locksley Hall', *see* Tennyson, A., Lord
Lodge, Sir Oliver Joseph, {ii}16
    sympathetic about *Rainbow*, {ii}440; and
    spiritualism, {iii}358
Loeser, Charles, {v}458, {vi}332
Loisach, River (Germany), {i}413, 415, 418,
    426, {vi}144
Loisy, Alfred Firmin, *L'Apocalypse de Jean*,
    {vii}515, 519, 528, 534, 539
Lola, *see* Derby, L.
Lolly Willowes, see Warner, S. T.
London I General
    [NB Casual references are not recorded]
    'pompous, magnificent capital of
    commercialdom', {i}80; DHL 'felt
    remarkably at home in', {i}80; thick fog
    in, {i}143, {ii}461, 465; avoided 'for
    months and months', {i}180; 'scarcely
    been in', {i}335; 'left altogether', {i}378;
    'thankful to be safe out of', {i}382;
    Weekley offers Frieda flat in, {i}467; if
    DHL lives in England should be near,
    {i}502, 506, 511; 'one breathes so much
    freer out of', {ii}84; 'all smoke', {ii}90;
    'tired of', {ii}192, 204; 'like some hoary
    massive underworld, a hoary, ponderous
    inferno', {ii}339; anti-German riots in,
    {ii}340; 'ponderous incubus of false-
    hood', {ii}380; DHL sent 'into a dumb
    fury' by people of, {ii}386; bombed by
    Zeppelins, {ii}390, 396; strikes 'a blow at
    the heart', {ii}434; 'so wretched',
    {ii}465; DHL 'loathed', {ii}504, 514;
    'spiritually' repelled by, {ii}639–41, 649,
    651, 653; 'like walking into some horrible
    gas, which tears one's lungs', {ii}650;
    DHL keeps 'putting off our coming to',
    {iii}50, 59; increased rail fare makes visit
    impossible to, {iii}63–4, 72; 'a bit
    chastened and helpless', {iii}116; DHL
    had 'a little collapse in', {iii}122–3;
    DHL expelled from Cornwall, retreats
    to, {iii}168ff; DHL 'better and happier
    in the country' than in, {iii}194;
    'detestable', {iii}273, 411, 413;
    'absolutely stricken' by flu, {iii}294–5; 'a
    prayer-meeting in comparison' to Capri.

{iii}444; 'so *wearing*', {iii}495; Sydney
'half like', {iv}249; Frieda refuses to
return to America from, {iv}524–5;
DHL feels 'buried alive, under the
yellow air and vast inertia' of, {iv}542–3,
546, 550, 565; people *instinctively* hate'
DHL in, {iv}556; Paris preferred to,
{iv}561–3, 566, 569, {v}545; 'a dying
animal', {v}17; 'can be fascinating',
{v}112; Murry's letters have 'that
London stink', {v}206; more expensive
than New York, {v}312–13; DHL feels
'depressed' in, {v}324; 'London group..
absolutely no good', {v}389; 'quiet, not
unpleasant' but DHL doesn't care for,
{v}506; Midlands preferred to, {v}518,
522; DHL felt 'cooped up' in, {v}552;
'repels rather than attracts me', {vi}55;
'virtuous indignation' over *LCL* shown
by publishers in, {vi}372–3; Huxleys 'a
bit discouraging about', {vi}438, 445;
police action against *LCL* in, {vi}498,
504, {vii}160, 174; sales of *LCL* in,
{vii}35, 42–9, 51–2, 55, 57, 62, 67, 75,
89, 134, 171; Gair Wilkinson puppet-
shows in, {vii}80–1, {viii}111; *Pansies*
TS seized in, {vii}150–1, 174; 'literairy'
sets 'effete' in, {vii}157; 'no place to live
in', {vii}234; complete *Pansies* published
sub rosa in, {vii}304, 428; exhibition of
DHL's paintings in, {vii}330–3, 335–8,
350; exhibition raided by police,
{vii}363–5, 375, 379, 440; 'slimy',
{vii}411; Frieda 'sailed along so gaily
and triumphantly in', {vii}421; expensive osteopath in, {vii}461; paintings
still stored in, {vii}594; Murry and 'the
London lot' expect DHL's death,
{vii}618; Frieda considers it vile,
{viii}20; DHL fears being ill in,
{viii}103
London II Localities etc.
Acacia Road, {ii}205, {iv}23–4, 28, 39,
58, 193, 261, 299, 377, 486, {v}375, 539,
{vi}69, 198, 478, 488, 535, 603, {vii}84,
319, 321
Katherine Mansfield gives up lease to
No. 5, {ii}465; Farbman leased No. 5
and Kot moved in, {ii}570, {iii}114,
199, 250, 267, 276, 372, 398, 426, 543,
{iv}79, {v}81, {vi}30, {vii}40; DHL
uses, {iii}114–15, 218–19, 271–5, 299,
368, 370, 377, 408–15, 728, {iv}532,
537–41, {viii}23; poste restante for
Frieda, {viii}86 *see also* Cave, The,
Acton, {iii}346
Adelaide Road, Nancy Henry lives in,
{iii}292, 298, 319
Adelphi, {vi}356
Secker's publishing house in, {i}345,
434, {iii}325, {v}33, 302, 304, 387, 410;
Murry's *Adelphi* based in, {iv}448, 549,
{v}104
Albert Hall, {i}468, 491, {ii}46
Aldwych, DHL's bank in, {ii}6, 189,
{v}572, {vi}483, 493, 511, {vii}47
Alexandra Palace, {i}116
Appenrodts restaurant, {ii}378
Athenaeum (Club), {vi}289, 322, 332
Bakerloo Line, {iii}192
Battersea Town Hall, DHL at recruiting
station in, {ii}474, 623
Battersea, Whittleys lived in, {ii}590,
{iii}256, 435, 541, 713, 724
Bayswater, {i}469, {ii}98, {iv}261
Bechstein Hall, concerts in, {i}155,
308
Bedford Street, {vi}559
Heinemann's offices in, {i}162; 'divine
William [Heinemann], cock of', {i}365,
372
Belgravia, 'vicious luxury' of, {i}40;
bookseller in, {vi}603
Berkeley Hotel, DHL meets Amy
Lowell in, {ii}207, {iii}190, {iv}487,
{v}197
Bloomsbury, {iii}516
Ottoline Morell in, {ii}253; the 'group',
{ii}263, 435, {v}286, {vi}220, 506,
{vii}82, 117; Palmer's offices in,
{iii}583; David & Orioli in, {vi}564;
Fanfrolico Press in, {vii}178, 228
Bond Street, {ii}407
Warren Gallery in, {vi}155, 351, 457
Bow Street Magistrate's Court, action to
suppress *Rainbow* in, {ii}428, {iv}2;
Russell prosecuted in, {iii}239
British Museum, {i}297, {ii}205,

London II Localities etc. (*cont.*)
{iii}71, {v}475, 538, 541, 544, {vi}53,
{vii}319, 368
oriental paintings in, {i}168; DHL may
read in, {ii}175; sees Egyptian and
Assyrian sculpture in, {ii}218; Milne on
staff of, {iv}599, {v}117, 121; consulted
for *Etruscan Places*, {vi}93, 105,
{viii}104
Burlington House, *see* Royal Academy
Cadogan Square, Cynthia Asquith and,
{iii}237, 242
Café Royal, {ii}207, 221
represented as the 'Pompadour' in *W in
L*, {ii}499; DHL horrified by incident
in, {ii}649; associated with pretentiousness, {iii}342; Starr habitué of, {iii}344;
DHL's notorious dinner-party in,
{iv}20, {v}47, 205
Caledonian Market, {ii}377
Charing Cross Road, {i}165
bookshops in, {i}5, 179, {iii}43,
{iv}171, {vi}564; Beaumont's offices in,
{iii}212, 214, 216, 219, 221, 234, 547,
585–6, 595, 598, 614
Charing Cross Station, {i}307, {iii}412,
414, 569, {v}175
DHL and Frieda leave from, {i}389
Chelsea, {i}155, {ii}173, 237, 411, 536,
{iv}49, 94, 558, {vi}422
Heseltine lives in, {ii}449, 452, 555;
Esther Andrews and Mountsier live in
(Cheyne Walk), {iii}28, 36, 51, 68, 75;
Wrights in (Cheyne Row), {iii}665, 671;
DHL rents flat in, {v}468, 474, 483, 490,
493, 498–507; Frieda 'hated', {v}524;
Millicent Beveridge lives in, {v}583,
{vi}69, 334, 396, {vii}347; Wilkinsons
moved to, {vi}380; Baroness von Hutten
lives in, {vi}489
Chiswick, Weekley family move from
Nottingham to, {i}440, 448, 485,
{v}247, 381, 443, {vi}168, 375,
{vii}120, 260, 319, 321, 380
City Temple Church, {i}310
Covent Garden Market, {i}167
Covent Garden Opera House, {i}130,
253, 277, 281, 322, 327, {viii}18

Crystal Palace, {i}81–3, 124, 168, 290,
300, {vii}85
Downshire Hill (Hampstead), Garnett's
early London address, {i}315, 467, 507,
520, {ii}38, 41, 55, 238; Anna Wickham
(Hepburn) in, {ii}401, 407, 417;
Brackenbury in, {ii}407, 509
Drury Lane Theatre, {i}130, 247,
{iii}178
Earl's Court, {iii}169, 281
Embankment, {i}130, 144, {v}175
Euston Road, {i}495
Fisher Street, *Signature* published from,
{ii}389, 391, 397, 399, 407, 409, 413,
418, 428, {viii}16
Fulham Road, {ii}583
Garnett's later address (Pond Place) in,
{ii}186, 238, {iv}116
Garland's Hotel (Pall Mall), DHL stays
in, {iv}20, 589, 591–9, {v}309–11, 313;
'too dear', {v}522
Garrick Theatre, {i}146
Gower Street, DHL at Macfarlane's flat
in, {v}316–19, 321–7; Morrells moved
to, {vi}387
Gray's Inn, {ii}51, 68, 92, {iii}182
Guilford Street, {iii}182
Barbara Low's rooms in, {iii}369–70,
376, 667, 673, 688, {iv}261, {v}329, 413,
{vi}69, 432, {vii}380; Mountsier stays
in, {iv}23, 31, 37
Hampstead, {i}182, 203, 445, 485,
{ii}13, 205, 342–4, 346–7, 351, 485,
{iii}114, 192, 210, 337, 344, 455,
{iv}579, {v}117, 309, 524–6, 528, 630,
{vi}171, {viii}6, 20, 28, 88
Hungers in, {i}184, 234, 236; H. G.
Wells in, {i}144;
East Heath Road, Murrys in, {iii}297,
346;
Elm Row, Nellie Morrison in, {v}524;
Gayton Crescent, Hobson in, {i}506;
Heath Street, DHL in, {iv}18, 542–60,
{vi}188, {viii}87; Catherine Carswell in,
{v}81, 123;
Rudall Crescent, Gertler in, {ii}407,
568; {iii}71, {v}524–5, {vi}69;
Vale of Health, DHL in Byron Villas,

{ii}354, 360–2, 370–482 *passim*, 530, 566, 569, 583–4, 599, 601, 613, {iii}101, 131, {v}351, {vi}435, {viii}16; Murry in, {v}347, 349;

Well Walk, Dollie Radford in, {ii}316, {iii}114, 168–9, 289–92; Dobrées in, {v}558;

Willoughby Road, DHL in, {v}531–45, {viii}96–8

Hampstead Garden Suburb, {ii}310

Eder in, {ii}258, {iii}42, Collins in, {ii}447, 482, {iii}194, 220, {v}26

Hampstead Heath, {i}73, {ii}354, 391, 396, 412

Hampton Court, {i}84, 156, {ii}330

Harley Place, {v}333, 375

Haymarket, {iii}721, {vi}547; Theatre, {i}141, 143, 304, {ii}167, 242

Henrietta Street (Covent Garden), *English Review* offices at first in, {i}240; Duckworth's offices in, {i}307, 529, {ii}203, 223–4, {iii}651; Curtis Brown's offices in, {iii}544, 709, {iv}73, 242, 372, 474–5, 524, 533, 557, 562, 592, {v}26, 33, 186, 197, 201, 241, 287, 291, 298, 342, 484, {vi}311, 358, 421, 486, 501, 536, 608, {vii}21, 23, 35, 39, 77, 112, 129, 144, 268, 288, 308, 343–4, 395, 464, 527; publishers Chapman & Hall in, {iv}247

High Court, {vii}369, 371

High Holborn, {ii}205, 231, 557, 652, {iii}43, 54, 68, 138, 340, {iv}30, {v}355

Highgate, {vi}330, 373, {vii}79, 347

Holland Park, {i}170, {ii}186, 412, {vi}298, 334, {viii}2

Home Office, {ii}439, 457, 647, 652, {vi}595, {vii}6, 149, 171–2, {viii}20

House of Commons, {i}420, {ii}216, 342, 502, 597, {iii}56; suppression of *Rainbow* raised in, {ii}439, 441, 443–4, 452, 457, 462, 475; seizure of *Pansies* MS raised in, {vii}5, 161, 163, 171–2, 204, 214, 227, 238, 304 *see also* General Election (1929)

Houses of Parliament, {i}266

Hyde Park, {i}130, {ii}178, {iii}158,

{iv}485, {vii}199, 221

Imperial College, {ii}28, 238

Imperial Restaurant, {ii}287

John Street, Secker's offices in, {i}275, 345, 434, {iii}586, 598, 714, {iv}115, 192, {v}33, 302, 304, 314, 339, 387, 410, 587, {vi}442, 472, {viii}34 ; Robert Garnett's office in, {ii}348, 356

Kensington, {i}491, {ii}28, 238, 516, 555, 583, {v}498–9, 531, {viii}6

Murrys in, {ii}53; Pound in, {i}145, 148, {ii}56, 60, 67, 75, 132; South Lodge, {i}315; *see also* Selwood Terrace

Kings Cross Station, {i}210, 216, 320, 389–90, {iii}300

Kingsley Hotel, {vii}351–2, 360–1

Kingsway Theatre, {ii}17, 201, 384, {v}576, {viii}98

Leicester Square Station, {iii}119

London Library, {ii}13, 529, 580, 596–7

London Polytechnic (Regent Street), {i}145, 165

Ludgate Circus, {iii}452, 725, {iv}172, {v}333

Lyceum Theatre, {i}138

Maida Vale, {vii}487, 504

Marble Arch, {i}130, {vi}447

Marlborough Street Magistrates' Court, case against DHL's paintings heard at, {vii}8, 361, 373, 406–7, 413, 423

Marylebone Road, {iv}9, {v}333, 375

Marylebone Station, {i}130, 216, 218, 255, 267, 275, 320, 364, {ii}210, 213, 241, 255, {iii}114, 192–3

Mayfair, {v}332, {vi}227, 530, 533

Mecklenburgh Square, Hilda Aldington's rooms in and where DHL stays, {iii}37, 56, 94, {iii}170–86, 188–90, 232, 259, 261, 281, 728, {vii}142

Mile End Road, {ii}385, 397

National Gallery, {i}130, 266, {ii}233, 265, 388, 427, {iii}354, {iv}27, 420, 589

New Cross, {i}290–1

Oxford Street, {i}130

Paddington Station, {ii}24, 430, {iii}180, 226, 229, 359

Pagnani's (Restaurant), {i}145

Pall Mall, {ii}329, 335, {iv}20, 74, 78,

London II Localities etc. (*cont.*)
592–9, {v}309–13, {vi}289, 322
Pall Mall Restaurant, {i}304
Park Lane, Frieda consults specialist in, {vii}460, 464, 466, 474, 478–9
Parliament, *see* House of Commons
Piccadilly, {i}96, 115, 164, {ii}241, {vi}512, {vii}482
Raynes Park, {ii}73, 169
Red Lion Square/Street, {iii}422
Lahr's bookshop in, {v}572, {vii}3, 23, 39, 49, 121, 126, 301, 569, 573, 644
Regent Theatre, {v}470, {vi}26, 66
Rossetti Garden Mansions, Heseltine in, {ii}449; DHL stays in, {v}501–7; Millicent Beveridge in, {vi}47, 69, 82, 93, 334, 396, {vii}347
Royal Academy, {i}11, 103, 124, {ii}46, {iii}654, {vi}411; DHL visits Winter exhibition, {i}113–16, 120
Royal College of Science, {i}315, 485
Royal Court Theatre, {i}364, 373, {iii}6, 374
Salisbury Square (Fleet Street), {i}447
Savoy Theatre, {i}310
Scotland Yard, *see* Police
Selwood Terrace (South Kensington), Campbells in and DHL stays, {ii}50–1, 175, 179, 181, 186–207, 272, {iii}183, {vi}219, {viii}11
Somerset House, {ii}327, 348
St James's Palace, {vii}84–5
St James's Railway Bridge, {i}286
St John's Wood, {ii}205, 465, 570–1, {iii}114–15, 218–19, 250, 377, {iv}23, 79, 93, 172, {v}81, 375, 524, {vi}30, {vii}40, 282, 319, {viii}23
St Pancras Station, {i}293, 340, {iii}264, 272, 300, {vi}540
St Paul's Cathedral, {i}130, 310, 534, {v}321
St Paul's School, {ii}343
Montague Weekley attends, {i}542, 551, {ii}51, 281, 344, 640, 643, {viii}6
Strand, {i}130, 306, {ii}108, 169, 201, 319, {iii}36, {v}78, 123, 175, {vi}311 *see also* London County Westminster Bank

Tate Gallery, {i}107, 130, 133, 266, 282, {ii}211, {iii}28
Tavistock Street (Covent Garden), *English Review* office moved to, {i}533, {ii}81
Tower, {i}130
Trafalgar Square, {i}130, {vi}479
University of, {i}136, {iii}716, {vi}50, 547, {viii}15
Vale of Health *see* Hampstead
Vaudeville Theatre, {ii}17, 187
Victoria and Albert Museum, {ii}360, 578, {v}333, 498–9, {vi}26
Victoria Park, {iii}106
Victoria Station, {i}358, {iv}589, {vi}540, {vii}353
Wandsworth Common, {i}536, 539
Wardour Street, {i}386, {ii}228, {vi}71
Warwick Square, {v}117
Waterloo Station, {i}358, {iii}192, {iv}482
Wembley, {v}85, 112
Westminster Abbey, {i}269, {vi}276
Westminster Bank (Aldwych), *see* London County Westminster Bank
Westminster School, {i}4
Westminster, {i}124, 130, {ii}474
Whitechapel, {i}40
Whitehall, {i}461, {ii}68
Wimbledon, {i}117–18, 120, 143, {ii}73, 179, 208, {iii}414, {vi}601
Zoo, {i}266, {ii}233, 238, {v}527, 530, {vii}310
London, Jack, *White Fang*, {i}172, 524
London and Provincial Press Agency, 'Goose Fair' submitted to, {i}131–2, 136–7, 139
London Aphrodite, The, {vii}68, 179, 278
Lindsay edits, {vii}31, 50; DHL thinks little of, {vii}66, 265, 269, 274; rejects DHL's poems, {vii}77
London County Westminster and Parr's Bank, DHL's account at Aldwych branch with, {ii}189, {iii}519, 524, 559, 605, 709, 722, {iv}146, 148, 168, 179, {vi}483, 493, 511, {vii}47, 112
London Mercury, The, {i}318, {iv}19, 36, {v}315, {vi}67, 169, {viii}97

Squire edits, {ii}204, {iii}452, {v}91;
DHL's writings refused by, {iii}554–5,
582, 681, 700, {iv}66, {vi}76, {viii}34;
'highbrow', {v}56; DHL dismissive of,
{v}181; prints 'Man Who Loved
Islands', {v}482, {vi}46, 52, 69, 130,
174, 348; review of *Collected Poems* in,
{vi}617; *London Aphrodite* in opposition
to, {vii}31; hostile to DHL's paintings,
{vii}376–7, 389; *Nettles* poem against,
{vii}441, 443; Carter in, {vii}555; Rhys
Davies in, {vii}579–80, 607
Long Island (USA), {iv}330, {v}304, 306,
{vi}10, 335
Long John, *see* Dunn, J.
Longfellow, Henry Wadsworth, {i}4
'The Arrow and the Song', {vi}505,
558–9;
'Excelsior', {i}450, {ii}186;
'A Psalm of Life', {i}55, {iv}521,
{vi}199;
'Retribution', {ii}35, {vii}234
Look Homeward, Angel, see Wolfe, T.
Loos, Anita, *Gentlemen Prefer Blondes*,
{v}574, {vii}145
Lord Byron in his Letters, see Collins, V. H. G.
Lord, Daisy, {i}81
Lords and Masters, see Garnett, E.
Lorenzetti, Pietro, *Anacoreti nelle Tebaidi (La
Tebaide)*, {iii}622, 624, 639, 664, 670
Lorenzini, Carlo, *Pinocchio*, {iii}340
Lorna Doone, see Blackmore. R.D.
Los Angeles (USA), {i}178, {iv}17, 112,
125–7, 130–1, 134, 139, 142, 151, 333,
367, 392, 430, 434, 439, 453, 479–519
passim, 525, 548, {v}188, 232, 261, 273,
{vi}335, {vii}467, 552, {viii}60–1,82–6
Lost and Found On A South Sea Island,
{iv}287
Loughborough (Leicestershire), {i}172, 178,
193, 208–9, 243, 248, 255–7, 302–6, 310
Louie, *see* Burrows, L.; Flitter, L.
Louis Pender, *see* Carswell, C.
Louis XIV, {ii}301, {vi}342
Louis XV, {vi}391
Louis, Francis, {iv}458
  Letters from {iv}458

Louis, Miss, {ii}404
Louvre (Paris), {i}180, {ii}97, 137, {iv}563,
{viii}48
Lovat Dickson's Magazine, 'Witch `a la Mode'
in, {ii}33, {iv}188
Love and Mr Lewisham, see Wells, H. G.
Love One Another, see Rickword, E.
Love Poems, see Titterton, W. R.
'Love's Philosophy', *see* Shelley, P. B.
LOVE, for Jessie Chambers 'deep spirit
within', {i}42; Blanche Jennings
'disciple of.."Love-thyself" school',
{i}56; after religion 'love of man
for..woman' is 'next precious', {i}57–8;
DHL could love Bernhardt 'to madness',
{i}59; 'great thing is to love', {i}62;
finest when religious as well as sexual
feeling involved, {i}66; three men whom
DHL loves, {i}67; women love 'brute in
man best', {i}88; dangerous when 'no
"abandon" in', {i}103; DHL dislikes
female passivity in, {i}103; lacking
direct experience DHL does '*not* believe
in', {i}141; 'largely a physical sympathy',
{i}153; Louie Burrows' and DHL's 'first
knowledge' of their love, {i}181; DHL
and mother 'great lovers..almost with a
husband and wife love', {i}187, 190, 195,
199; Louie Burrows' love for DHL 'like
Rhoda Fleming or a commoner Anna
Karénin', {i}191; DHL's for Louie
Burrows, {i}195, 197, 206, 208, 215,
237, 285, 287, 290–1, 363, 480; DHL
could make love 'deliciously', {i}258;
Jessie Chambers 'the love of my life',
{i}268; sexual with Helen Corke,
{i}285–6; DHL could love prostitute
'because..sorry for her', {i}286; 'à la
Garvice', {i}294; 'great lot of dissatisfied
love in my veins', {i}321; 'more delicate..to make..and to win..than to declare
love', {i}344; 'I love your wife and she
loves me', {i}392; between DHL and
Frieda, {i}393–4, 396–7, 402–3, 412,
414, 421, 439–41, 490; 'much
bigger..than passion', {i}415; 'greatest
thing that can happen to a man', {i}418;

LOVE (*cont.*)

'real tragedy is..inner war..waged between people who love each other', {i}419; 'rather suits me', {i}420; theme of *S and L*, {i}476–7; 'my life work' sticking up for the love between man and woman', {i}492; 'I shall always be a priest of', {i}493; 'direct communication with the unknown' results from, {i}503, {ii}284; artist 'must endlessly go for women, and for', {ii}95; 'hate..obverse of love, the recoil of unsatisfied', {ii}101–2; between Murry and Mansfield, {ii}111, 161; suffering part of learning about, {ii}191; 'thou shalt love thy neighbour as thyself' inadequate, {ii}192, 625–6, {iii}53; from 'mutual love of.. Father and..Son' proceeds Holy Spirit, {ii}249; Forster confuses Pan with universal, Christ-like, {ii}275; satire, not writing about 'passionate love', appropriate now, {ii}283; of property or power must be destroyed, {ii}297; 'not a grain of the passion of love' in Dostoievsky, {ii}311, 314; those knowing 'how to love must know how to slay', {ii}316; of fellow-men excludes Cambridge homosexuals, {ii}318; homosexuality 'blasphemy against', {ii}321; Ottoline Morrell uses 'power instead of', {ii}326; will transform relationship between Cynthia Asquith and son, {ii}336–7; DHL's 'ideal of one man-one woman in', {ii}345; 'only permanent thing is *consummation* in love or hate', {ii}376; Holy Spirit 'both love and hate', {ii}408; is creative and integrating power, therefore anti-war, {ii}424, 443, 636, 644; 'only love matters, now', {ii}425; to love 'really and profoundly' means loving woman 'not men', {ii}448; 'very painful' when associated with past life, {ii}487; 'freedom to love' essential to happiness, {ii}491–2, 507; 'social love' absent in Cornish, {ii}505; domination inconsistent with, {ii}509; 'Christianity infinitely higher

than..family love', {ii}633; 'active love' must *be*, cannot be created, {ii}651; faith in creative spirit 'matters *more* than', {iii}98; 'bit of kindness..worth all the love of mankind', {iii}122; Murry and DHL should neither hate nor, {iii}127; knowledge between Magdalen and Christ 'deeper than love', {iii}180; post-war new life 'based neither on work or', {iii}194, 215–16; is 'heavily overweighted', self-fulfilment more important than; {iii}368, 478; 'I love my Fontana Vecchia - et pretera nihil', {iii}676; 'war ahead: not love and peace', {iii}680; one of roots of Nirvana tree, {iii}712; DHL abandons knowing about, {iii}718; 'the word..has for me gone pop', {iii}720; in Germany 'era of love..peace.. democracy' gone, {iii}732; 'a disease', {iii}734; DHL loves 'blue of lapis lazuli..inside..film of crystal', {iv}190; 'mechanical love-motion' of 'cultured Americans', {iv}226; 'stuff we mean by love' incomprehensible in India, {iv}246; 'loyalty..far before', {iv}368; man does not seek 'love from his wife, but strength..To the devil with', {iv}532; 'chiefly bunk..exaggeration of..spiritual.. individualistic..analytic side', {v}203–4; Murry's declaration of love for DHL, {v}205; from public worse than being hated, {v}289; Bynner's spurious 'love of happiness', {v}384; Maugham 'didn't love me like a brother', {v}446; Mabel Luhan's 'real old physical love' for chauffeur, {v}462; 'The young can neither love nor live', {vi}34; 'means the pre-cognitive flow', {vi}114; DHL loves 'stillness of innumerable trees', {vi}151; Beethoven 'always in love with somebody when he wasn't really', {vi}213–15; 'I love to use a title when I can', {vi}219; 'I loved it [Haggs] so', {vi}618; 'ladies..have love affairs with their chauffeurs', {vii}179; can be 'possessive', {vii}235; Murry doesn't love real DHL, {vii}294; Germans 'love things' sentimentally, {vii}384; for one's body, {vii}625

Love's Pilgrimage, see Sinclair, U.

Lovelace, *see* Richardson, S.

Lovelace, Richard, {i}124, {vi}219

LOW, BARBARA, {ii}1, 14, 18, 258, 279, 290–1, 296, 304, 308, 312, 346, 490, 519, {iii}16, 54, 138, 161, 210, 231, 307, 309, 321,323, 337, 376, 524, 687, 716, {iv}23, 114, {v}347, 374, 482, {vi}30, 110, {vii}137

    'one of the very few' who listen to DHL, {ii}280; 'I *do* rather like', {ii}310, 488, 617; 'persistent', {ii}313–14; subscribes for *Signature*, {ii}404; school-teaching, {ii}497, 589; visits Higher Tregerthen, {ii}624, 627, 631, 637, 639, 641–2; and Hocking, {ii}642–3, 647, 652; gifts from, {ii}653–4; reads *W in L* TS, {iii}41, 51, 56–7; DHL visits at Mersea, {iii}273–4; visits Hermitage, {iii}363; to be DHL's London agent, {iii}667–8, 673–4, 678, 684–5, 688, 692–3, 696, 699–700, 705, {viii}30; hands all DHL materials to Curtis Brown, {iii}707; complimentary copies for, {iv}37, 261, {v}329, 413, {vi}69, 432, {vii}380; subscribed for *LCL*, {vi}11–12, 440, 466, 517, 530

Psycho-Analysis, {ii}279, {iv}23, 27

    Letters to {ii}279–80, 289, 305–6, 496–7, 602–3, 613–14, 623–4, 641–3, 647–8, 653–4, 655, 658–9, {iii}42–3, 50–1, 55–7

Low, David, {vii}198–9, 206

Low, Ivy, *see* Litvinov, I. T.

Lowe, Bessie, {iii}362, 378, 454, 581

    DHL lodges with, {iii}217–18, 361; her pronunciation, {iii}365

Lowell, Abbott Lawrence, {iii}155

LOWELL, AMY, {ii}2, 239, 417, 562, {iii}3, 8, 14, 83, 281, 324, 357, 636, {iv}4, 6, 38, 244, 258, 316, 407, 491, {v}7, 120,

    DHL meets, {ii}203, 207; DHL's poems in, and royalties from, *Imagist* anthologies, {ii}209, 217, 509, 513–14, 643, {iii}280, 593, {iv}61, 96, 429, 488, {v}197; intervenes with Kennerley for

DHL, {ii}216–7, 223, 228. 235, 243, 245–6, {iii}75; gives DHL typewriter, {ii}222–3, 227, 230, 233–5, 394, 645, 666; complimentary copies for, {ii}243, 610, 644, 665, {iii}156, 182, 189, 290, 326, 475, 485, 538, 619, 629, {iv}259, 488, {v}230; Frieda's confrontation with Weekley dramatised for, {ii}244; subscribed for *Signature*, {ii}515; financial support from, {ii}560, {iii}29–30, 33, 69, 207, 254, 474–5, 482–3, 538, 556; critique of poems by, {iii}30–2, 105, {iv}61–2; 'not a good poetess' but 'very good friend', {iii}61; lectures on DHL, {iii}253, 280; *New Poems* dedicated to, {iii}254, 304; warns DHL against lecturing in USA, {iii}369; gifts for, {iii}539; reviews DHL, {iii}593, 629; TS of *BBF* sent to, {iii}634, 653, 657, 669; cigar-smoking of, {iii}657, 677, {iv}245; DHL disenchanted with, {iii}673, 677, 684, 689; 'just a cupboard that loves itself', {iv}298; refused help to Seltzer over court case, {iv}315; DHL consorting with 'enemies' of, {iv}325–6

    Poems: 'Aquarium', {iii}30–1, 105; 'Bath', {iii}31; 'Blackbird', {iv}62; 'Bombardment', {ii}232, 234; 'Cremona Violin', {iii}30; 'Fool's Money Bags', {ii}234; 'The Fruit Shop', {iii}30; 'The Hammers', {iii}30, 32; 'Hedge Island', {iii}295; 'Lacquer Prints', {iii}105; 'Malmaison', {iv}567; 'Many Swans', {iv}62; 'An Opera House', {iii}30–1; 'Porcelain', {iv}62; 'The Precinct Rochester', {ii}234; 'A Roxbury Garden', {iii}30–1; 'The Ship', {iii}30; 'Spring Day', {iii}31–2; 'The Statue', {iv}62; 'Stravinsky', {iii}31–2; 'Sword Blades and Poppy Seed', {ii}234; 'The Taxi', {ii}234; 'Towns in Colour', {iii}30–2, 105; 'Witch Woman', {iv}62; 'Yucca to a Passion-Vine', {iv}62

    Can Grande's Castle, {iii}295, 313, 326, 475;

    Fir-Flower Tablets, {iv}97, 229, 242;

    John Keats, {v}198, 230;

LOWELL, AMY (*cont.*)
　Legends, {iii}629, {iv}56–7, 61–2, 77, 97,
　　242;
　Men, Women and Ghosts, {ii}561,
　　{iii}29–31, 48;
　Six French Poets, {iii}475;
　Sword Blades and Poppy Seed, {ii}223,
　　234, 243, {iii}29–30;
　Tendencies in Modern American Poetry,
　　{iii}189–90
　Letters to {ii}206–7, 208–11, 216–17,
　　222–4, 234–5, 242–5, 394, 509–10,
　　513–14, 560–1, 610–11, 643–5, 665–6,
　　{iii}29–32, 47–8, 104–5, 155–7, 189–90,
　　253–4, 280, 285, 295–6, 313–14, 326,
　　347–8, 361–2, 368–9, 422, 474–6, 482–3,
　　538–9, 556–7, 593, 607, 629–30,
　　{iv}56–7, 61–2, 77, 96–7, 229, 242–3,
　　291–2, 325–6, 429, 472, 477–8, 480, 482,
　　487–8, {v}197–8, 229–30
　Letters from {iv}292, 326
Lowell, James Russell, {iii}61
Lowell, Joan, *Child of the Deep (Cradle of the
　Deep)*, {vii}649
Lowell, Percival, {iii}47
Lowenfels, Walter, {vi}603
LOWENSTEIN-WERTHEIM-
　　FREUDENBERG, LEOPOLD,
　　PRINCE OF, {vi}341, 523, 535–6
　and rights to German translation of
　　LCL, {vii}333, 335, 374, 517, 596–7
　Letters to {vii}615–16
　Letters from {vii}333
Lowndes, F. S. A., {ii}226
LOWNDES, MARIE ADELAIDE
　　BELLOC, {ii}226, 228
　Letters to {ii}471, 477, 479
Lucas, Dr Geoffrey, Gertie Cooper's
　　physician at Mundesley Hospital,
　　{v}536, 548, 565–6, 589, 599
Lucas, Edward Verrall, {ii}240
Lucas, Madeleine, {ii}333, 386, 635
Lucas, Perceval ('Percy') Drewett, {ii}333
　'England, My England' based on family
　　of, {ii}354, 386, 635
Lucca (Italy), {iv}312, {vi}85–7, 89,
　　{vii}321, 335–55 *passim*, 380, 465, 479

Lucchesi, *see* Pensione Lucchesi
Lucii Albizzi, *see* Pensione Lucii
Lucerne (Switzerland), {ii}76–7, 79, {iv}72,
　　{v}329, 333–5, 341, 371, {vi}108, 112,
　　131, {vii}29, {viii}9
Lucia di Lammermoor, see Donizetti, G.
Lucifer, {v}52
　'Germany represents', {ii}604; Gurdjieff
　　'imaginary incarnation' of, {vii}175
　'really the Morning Star', {vii}331
Lucille, *see* Beckett, L. K.
Lucius Scarfield, see Cramb, J. A.
Lucka, Emil, *Grenzen der Seele*, {iv}99,
　　116
Ludwig-Wilhelmstift (Baden-Baden),
　　{iii}489, 505, 598, 621, 642, 683, 686,
　　694, 703–33, {iv}23, 29, 32, 41, 49, 52,
　　72, 132, 262, 390, 397, 569–85, 594,
　　{v}176, 189, 247, 314, 322, 325–7,
　　331–3, 435, 493, 495, 498, 500, {vi}136,
　　164–8, 553, 557–8, 563–5, {vii}332, 358,
　　370–86, 397, 422, 433, 436, 438,
　　{viii}40, 105
　see also Baden-Baden
Lufina, *see* Archuleta, R.
Lugano (Switzerland), {ii}77, 79, {vii}416,
　　423, {viii}9
LUHAN, ANTONIO ('TONY'), {iv}4,
　　12–13, 17, 110, 277, 311, 313, 317, 319,
　　321, 323–4, 329, 332, 336–7, 341, 347,
　　350, 360–1, 515, 545, 553, 577–8, 586,
　　593, {v}5, 22–23, 39, 41–3, 51, 53, 57,
　　64, 69, 83, 108, 151, 159, 164, 233, 281,
　　468, 497, 531, 567–8, 598, 625, 650,
　　{vi}23, 86, 101, 299, 550, {vii}628
　'nice..but silent', {iv}295; DHL lives in
　　house of, {iv}346; 'fat fellow', {iv}351,
　　388; 'really married' to Mabel Luhan,
　　{iv}434, 440, 442, 444, 450, 514, {v}28,
　　{vii}96; learning to read, {iv}560;
　　friction between DHL and, {v}51, 60,
　　68, 72–3, 76; DHL to Hopi country
　　with, {v}99; comments on relationship
　　between Mabel Luhan and, {v}114,
　　129–31; Mabel in New York with,
　　{v}191, 218, 228; 'offensive', {v}237;
　　'ugly as a pancake', {v}239; shooting of

porcupine, {v}290; in California,
{v}343, 349; ill-at-ease away from
pueblo, {v}510–11, 540, {vii}204; DHL
defends against upper-class sneers,
{vi}223; his songs, {vii}277
  Letters to {iv}346, 361
Luhan, Elizabeth, {v}151
LUHAN, MABEL DODGE, {iv}4–6, 8,
  10–13, 17, 243, 265, 298, 308, 314–15,
  321, 331–2, 342, 373, 392, 410, 443, 477,
  489–90, 492–3, 534, 571–2, {v}3–6, 8–9,
  11–12, 27–8, 43, 45, 47–8, 58, 60, 81,
  116, 118, 128–9, 136, 145, 156, 159, 187,
  218, 237–9, 259, 280, 290, 370, 381, 426,
  434, 438–9, 468, 478, 497, 533, 537,
  559–60, 600, 605, 608–9, 623, 630,
  639–40, 650, 652, {vi}1, 10, 12, 23–4,
  54–5, 127, 155, 175, 211–12, 228–9, 278,
  302, 311, 358, 363–4, 436, 440, 551,
  {vii}24, 27, 54, 56, 96, 138, 173, 222,
  263, 287, 553, 628, {viii}82–3, 104
  invites DHL to Taos, {iv}110–12,
  120–1, 123, 125, 127, 138, 141–2, 150,
  152, 154, 179; DHL goes to Taos via
  east, {iv}181–2, 202, 223, 225–6, 236,
  251–2, 259–60, 267–9, 271–2, 274,
  276–9, 281, 287–93; complimentary
  copies for, {iv}181, 259, 276, 390,
  {vi}69, 73, 293, 432–3, {vii}387, 414,
  546–7; meets DHL, {iv}294; 'sort of
  queen', {iv}295–6; 'very generous',
  {iv}300, 303–5; imprisoning patronage
  of, {iv}305–6, 310–11, 316, 324–5, 330;
  described, {iv}313, 351–2; 'The Wilful
  Woman' and, {iv}317–19, 344; DHL's
  deteriorating relationship with, {iv}329,
  337–8, 343, 345, 349, 351–2, 362–3, 370,
  378–9; offers ranch to DHL, {iv}334–6;
  'liar - and false as hell', {iv}372, 470;
  'really married to Tony', {iv}434,
  439–40, 442, 450; DHL 'ready' if
  vendetta with, {iv}498; DHL 'buries the
  hatchet' with, {iv}514–15, 518, 521, 527,
  529, 537, 540–1, 548; writes story,
  {iv}545, {v}378; egoist but 'dauntless',
  {iv}555; on introverts and extroverts,
  {iv}573–4, 576–8, 585; now 'mild' and

'wiser', {v}22, 29, 38, 46; legally
  transferred Lobo ranch to Frieda, {v}23,
  {vii}205, 289; 'everlasting will' of,
  {v}52–3; rarely visits ranch, {v}62;
  motoring to 'Hopi land' with DHL,
  {v}92, 96–100; in exchange for ranch
  Frieda gives MS of *S and L* to, {v}105,
  111, 115, {vi}382; relationship with
  Tony Luhan, {v}114, 129–31, 531;
  should exercise self-discipline, {v}125,
  423; to New York, {v}132, 172, 191, 228,
  343, 358, 395, 417; and Gurdjieff,
  {v}422–3, 431, 441–2, 457, 471, 486,
  540, {vi}57, {vii}175; Nancy Pearn on
  literary talent of, {v}551; Brett and,
  {v}585–6, 594–5, {vii}170, 276–7, 317,
  342, 344–6; *M in M* dedicated to,
  {v}594, {vi}36; ambition to have 'a real
  Mabeltown...an earthly kingdom',
  {vi}37, 223, 254; urges DHL to return
  to Taos, {vi}38, 49, 76, {viii}624;
  character in 'None of That' partly
  modelled on, {vi}70; order-forms for
  LCL sent to, {vi}319, 357, 393; satirised
  in Bynner's play, {vi}365; and Gomme,
  {vi}444, 550, 608, {vii}20, 25;
  'bitch...idiotically self-important',
  {vi}476; 'such a nosy Parker', {vii}551;
  Frieda calls 'basically destructive'
  {viii}92
  'Constance', {v}471;
  'Fairy-Tale, {v}539, 560;
  Intimate Memories, {v}423, 430–1, 457,
  462–3, 485–7, 510–11, 540, 550, 567,
  578–80, 602–3, 615, 647, {vi}58, 136,
  223, 230, 393, {vii}547; Foreword to,
  {v}348–9;
  'M. Blanchard' sketch, {v}550–1, 567;
  'Plum', {v}72–3
  Letters to {iv}110–12, 127, 141–2, 152,
  181–2, 202, 223, 225–6, 236, 251–2,
  259–60, 266–9, 276, 278–9, 287–8,
  317–8, 322, 329, 333, 335, 337–8, 343,
  346–8, 357–60, 363, 368, 370, 514–15,
  527–8, 538–41, 545–6, 552–3, 555–6,
  559–60, 570, 573–4, 576–8, 584–6, 593,
  {v}40–2, 49, 51–4, 56–7, 64, 68–70,

LUHAN, MABEL DODGE (*cont.*)
72–4, 76, 82–4, 89–90, 94–6, 102–3,
107–8, 125–6, 129–31, 150–1, 158–9,
330, 378–9, 393, 406–7, 422–4, 430–1,
439, 456–8, 462–3, 471–2, 485–7,
510–11, 540–1, 550, 567–9, 579–80,
593–4, 597–8, 602–3, 615, 618–19,
624–5, 641–2, 646–7, {vi}36–8, 57–9,
73–4, 101,135–6, 222–4, 230–1, 318–19,
393, 435–6, 498, {vii}71, 94–5, 174–5,
203–4, 232, 276–7, 289–90, 344–5,
546–7, 616–17, 624–5, 628–9, 636–7
Letters from {iv}329, {v}72, 108, 130–1
Luhan, Mrs, {v}540, 567
Lungarno Acciaioli (Florence), {vi}334,
{vii}34, 177, 411
Lungarno Corsini (Florence), Orioli's shop
at No 6 on, {iii}591, {v}641, 646–7,
{vi}116, 257, 259, 345–6, 355, 362–3,
372, 389–90, 396, 448–51, 499, 514, 529,
547, 549, 603, 612, 617, {vii}44, 47, 108,
112, 146, 173, 175, 177, 204, 240, 321,
352–5, 359, 361–5, 414, 438, 464–5, 470,
476, 499, 557, 573
Lungarno Series, {vii}526–7, 540, 548,
564–5, 573, 584, 588, 595, 600
Doctor Manente in, {vi}595, {vii}526
Lungarno Zecca (Florence), {iii}575, {iv}82,
{v}427–46 *passim*
Lunn, (Sir) Arnold Henry Moore, {iv}133,
183, 247
Lunn, Beatrix ('Betty'), {vii}529
Lunn, Brian, {vii}529
Lunn, Mrs, {v}415, 427
'Lupa, La', *see* Verga, G.
Lusitania, S.S., {ii}9, 340, 394
Lute of Jade, A, see Cranmer-Byng, L.
Luther, Martin, {i}40, 114, {ii}592,
{v}324
LUTYENS, EMILY,
Letters to {vii}499
Letters from {vii}405
Lvoff, Prince George, {iii}108
Lydbrook (Gloucestershire), {iii}275–9,
298
Lyme Regis (Dorset), {iii}274
Lynch, Col. Arthur, {ii}656

Lynd, Robert Wilson, {vii}294
Lynd, Sylvia, {vii}361–2
Lynn Croft (Eastwood), {i}22–79 *passim*,
102, 135–6, 149, 169, 174–6, 189–98,
220, 229, 268, {iv}53, {v}115, 582, 631,
633, 645, {viii}1–2
Lyon(s) (France), {vi}580–1, {vii}181, 208,
213, 241, 245, 494, 513, {viii}30–1
Lyons, Alfred Neil, *Arthur's* and *Sixpenny
Pieces*, {viii}19
Lyster, Dr, {iv}421

M., P. I., {ii}487
M., Sarah, {iv}493
Mab(el), *see* Limb, M.
Mabel, *see* Luhan, M. D. S.
Mabinogion, The, {ii}495
Mablethorpe (Lincolnshire), {i}8, {iii}203,
{v}474, 476, 499, 509, 512–16, 521,
{vi}107, 458, 509–10
Mac, *see* McLeod, A. W.
Macarther, Mary Reid, {iii}5, 284
Macartney, Herbert Baldwin, Siegmund in
Trespasser, {i}129, 158, 160, 173, 239,
253
Macartney, Laura, {i}253, 279, 300, 302
Macartney, Mr, {i}279
Macaulay, Emilie Rose, {iv}31, 51, {v}324,
326, 626
Orphan Island, {v}322
Macaulay, Thomas Babington, {i}74
Macbeth, see Shakespeare, W.
MacCarthy, (Sir) Desmond, {ii}450,
{iii}317–18, {vi}11, {vii}265
MacDermott, Norman, option to produce *T
and G* sold to, {iii}423, 440, 483, 510
MacDiarmid, Hugh, {vii}3
MacDonald, George, *At the Back of the North
Wind*, {i}109
MacDonald, James Ramsay {i}3, 12, 176,
{iv}578, {vii}171–2, 315, 325
MacDowall, Arthur Sydney, reviews *Plumed
Serpent*, {v}383
MacElwee, Henry, {v}134, 209, 332
Macey, George *see* Macy, G.
Macfall, Haldane, *The Wooings of Jezebel
Pettyfer*, {v}321

MACFARLANE, GEORGE GORDON,
{iii}146–7, {v}318–19, {vi}188, 337,
385, {vii}293
buys DHL's typewriter, {iii}365, 393–4;
DHL praises novel by, {v}315–17; DHL
in Gower Street flat owned by, {v}321–6
The Natural Man, {v}315–17
Letters to {iii}393–4, {v}316–17
MacFarlane, John Grant, {vi}188
MacFarlane, Nancy ('Nannie'), {v}316, 325
MACGREEVY, THOMAS, {vi}231
Letters to {viii}106–7
Machen, Arthur Llewelyn Jones, {i}107,
{v}79, 519, {vii}556
Far Off Things, {v}79;
Things Near and Far, {v}79
Machiavelli, Niccolo, {vii}411, 416, 504, 541,
578
Machin, John S., {i}143
MACKENZIE, (SIR) EDWARD
MONTAGUE COMPTON, {ii}4,
{iii}1, 9, 398.401, 404–5, 420, 428,
446–8, 463, 471, 493–4, 497, 500, 503–4,
512, 515, 557, 573, 628, 655, 706, {iv}36,
299, {v}3, 9, 313, 326, 333, 390, 588,
{vi}6, 11, 191, {vii}62
'very flourishing and breezy', {ii}212;
'his *Sinister Street* frippery', {ii}240;
'bosh', {ii}643; boring, {iii}166; DHL
visits on Capri, {iii}436–7, 439–40; Brett
Youngs 'humble waiters on', {iii}442;
'nice' but 'can't be quite serious',
{iii}443–4, 447; 'good sort', {iii}451–2;
proposes commercial relationship for
DHL with Secker, {iii}458–60; suggests
trip to South Seas with DHL,
{iii}461–2, 522–3, 560–8, 572, 579, 653;
DHL likes as a man 'but not as an
influence', {iii}469, 476; suggests
production of two plays by DHL in
Nottingham, {iii}509–10; takes TS of
Lost Girl to England, {iii}528, 551,
{viii}36; 'swindle' over project to buy
yacht, {iii}575; leases Herm and Jethou,
{iii}594, 600–1, 603, 608, 656, 662–3,
671, 702, 708, {v}413, {vi}105, 111;
DHL slightly apprehensive over fictional

portrait of, {vi}68–9, 130; 'idiotic self-
importance' of, {vi}205; 'vain, shallow,
theatrical..somewhat ridiculous',
{vi}218; 'mortally offended' at 'Man
Who Loved Islands', {vi}224; threat-
ened legal action if 'Man...Islands'
republished by Heinemann, {vii}381,
391, 445, 455, 515, 518
Columbine, {iii}579, 616;
Poor Relations, {iii}444;
Rich Relatives, {iii}444, 504;
Sinister Street, {ii}240;
Sylvia and Michael, {iii}501, 521;
Sylvia Scarlett, {iii}501, 521;
Vanity Girl, {iii}549
see also Lawrence, D. H., 'The Man Who
Loved Islands'
Letters to {iii}436, 474, 480–1, 490–2,
501–3, 509–10, 521–3, 527–8, 549,
561–3, 594–5, 608–9, 616, 662–3,
{iv}284, 286, {v}570
Mackenzie, Faith Compton, {iii}664, 671,
706, {v}9, 313, 326, 333, 339, 344–5,
401, 407, {vii}62, 141
'unhappy soul' pretending 'to be gay',
{v}403; not pleased by 'portrait-sketch'
in 'Two Blue Birds', {vi}68–9
Mackenzie, Virginia, {iii}509, 523
Maclure, Mr, {v}110–11
Macmillan and Co., {i}306, {iii}475, {vi}471
MacNair, Miss, {i}347, 350
Macnamara, Brinsley, *Smiling Faces,* {vii}559
MacQueen, William ('Willie'), {ii}319, 323,
452
MACY, GEORGE, considered publishing
limited edn of *LCL,* {vi}376, 470,
525, {viii}114
Letters to {vi}447–8, {viii}114
Macy, John, {iv}16, 318, {viii}58, 61
laudatory review of *W in L* by, {iii}13;
DHL meets, {iv}477; 'a dead fish',
{iv}516; reviews *SCAL,* {iv}518
Macy-Masius & Co., {vi}376, 448, 470–1,
525
Madame Butterfly, see Puccini, G.
Madeira (Portugal), {iii}344
Mademoiselle, *see* La Porte, Mlle

Maderno (Italy), {i}460

Madge, *see* Dunlop, M.

Madrid (Spain), {iv}404, {vi}513, {vii}273, 276, 282–4, 565–6, 571

Maecenas, Gaius Cilnius, {ii}63

Maeterlinck, Maurice, {i}237, {ii}26, 181
  Life of the Bee, {ii}279;
  Trésor des Humbles, {i}237

Magdalene, Mary, {iii}179, {vi}72

Maggie, *see* Burrows, M.

Maggiore, *see* Mirenda, R.

Maggiore, Lake (Italy), {i}430, {iii}541–2, {vi}273

Magic Flute, The see Mozart, W. A.

Magnelli, Alberto, 'pins all his beauty on to a dead nothingness', {v}627; 'very self-important and arch-priesty', {v}629; paintings 'pretentious rubbish', {v}637; 'very feeble', {vi}61–2

Magnus, Hedwigis Rosamunda Liebetrau, {iv}179, 186

MAGNUS, MAURICE, {ii}31, {iii}6, 409, 480, 497, 552, {iv}6, 127, 188, {v}6, 369, {vi}45, 342, {viii}88
  'that cherub' descended upon DHL at Taormina, {iii}514; translates foreign plays, {iii}532; 'jewel..floating in whiskies and soda', {iii}535; DHL thought '*Legion* MS..awfully *good*', {iii}564; Mountsier to find publisher for 'Dregs', {iv}178–9, 188, 208, 220; DHL adds 'definite facts' to 'Introduction', {iv}186; DHL hears 'bad' things about, {iv}220; TS of 'Introduction' goes to Murry, {iv}549, 559, 581; 'Introduction' not be be printed apart from *Foreign Legion*, {iv}579, {v}78; TS of 'Introduction' to go to Secker, {iv}597; Secker to publish *Foreign Legion*, {v}16–17, 24, 30–1; initials, not names, of principal figures to be printed, {v}24, 70; DHL's motives in arranging publication, {v}30–3, {viii}48–50; half royalties to Borg, {v}33, 54; proofs of *Foreign Legion*, {v}39, 56, 70, 79; complimentary copies, {v}97, 179, 184, 341; 'Magnus'

book looks like a Church hymnal', {v}141; Douglas and *Foreign Legion*, {v}184–5; Douglas attacks DHL over, {v}231–2, 240, 242, 244, 255, 340; DHL insists 'nothing but the exact truth' in 'Introduction', {v}255; Secker encourages response to Douglas by DHL, {v}340, 395–7; DHL fails to persuade Unwin to publish *Foreign Legion*, {viii}30–3; DHL admires 'simple bareness..even.. amateurishness' of *Foreign Legion*, {viii}31; suicide of, {viii}38–9
  'Dregs', {iv}6, 178–9, {v}16–17, 255, {viii}50;
  Introduction to *Foreign Legion*, {iv}6, 127, 549, 571, 579, 597, {v}6, 70, 231–2, 242, 255, {vii}237;
  Memoirs of the Foreign Legion, {ii}31, {iii}409, 480, 555, 564, {iv}127, 178–9, 186, 188, 191, 208, 549, 559, 579, 581, 598, {v}16–17, 24, 30–3, 39, 54, 56, 70, 78–9, 97, 141, 179, 184–5, 231–2, 242, 244, 255, 395–7, {viii}30–3, 88
  see also Borg, M.; Douglas, N.
  Letters to {iii}555

Magnus, Mrs, {v}31

Mail, The (Paris), {vii}612

Maillol, Aristide Joseph Bonaventure, {vii}608

Main Street, see Lewis, S.

Maine (USA), {iii}595

Mainz (Germany), {iii}21

Maisie, *see* Horne, M.

Maistre, François Xavier de, *La Jeune Siberienne*, {i}75–6;
  Voyage autour de ma Chambre, {i}341, {iii}331

Maitres Sonneurs, Les, see Sand, G.

Major, *see* Mirenda, R.

Majorca (Spain), *see* Mallorca

Making a Gentleman, see Sutro, A.

Makura, S.S., {iv}11, 274, 277–9

Malaga (Spain), {vii}86, 109

Mallaig (Invernessshire), {v}511–12

Mallock, William Hurrell, *New Republic*, {iii}61, 75

Mallorca (Spain), {vii}7, 9, 53, 86, 155, 161, 163, 170, 183, 197, 200, 204–5, 238–9, 250–337 *passim*, 343, 358, 373–4, 379, 453, 501, 528, 530
'like Sicily, but not so beautiful..much more asleep', {vii}253–7, 262; 'I don't really care for it', {vii}260; 'very quiet..very dull', {vii}264, 267; people 'rather dead' and 'ugly', {vii}275, 284, 304, 313; after bottom pinched, Frieda 'despises every letter in the word', {vii}309
Malmaison (France), {iv}567–8
'Malmaison', *see* Lowell, A.
Malory, Sir Thomas, {ii}495–6
Morte d'Arthur, {ii}492
Malraux, André, {vii}223, 261
Malta, {iii}6, 17, 509, 522, 525, 527, 529–31, 538, 540–1, 548, {iv}112, 127, 172, 184, 188, 191, {v}361, 396, {viii}51
'horrible island', {iii}531; 'glaring gritty dry yellow lump with hideous villages', {iii}533–4; 'bitterly expensive.. dry chip of a place', {iii}536; DHL bought 'tussore silk suit' in, {iii}552; 'island of British beneficence and snobbishness', {iii}557; Magnus's debts in, {iv}178, {viii}49; Magnus's suicide in, {v}30–1, {viii}38–9
Malthouse Cottage (Padworth), Aldington and Dorothy Yorke lived in, {v}426, 443, 564, 568, 602, {vi}42, 221, {vii}416; DHL visited, {v}505; copies of *LCL* stored at, {vi}486, 494, 529; DHL thought it 'sinister', {vii}151
Malwa S. S., {iv}10–11, 237–40, 243–5, 249, 251
DHL met Forresters aboard, {viii}55
Mamba's Daughters, *see* Heyward, D. B.
Man and Superman, *see* Shaw, G. B.
Man of Property, The, *see* Galsworthy, J.
Man With a Hammer, The, *see* Wickham, A.
Managers' Club, {i}386
Manby, Arthur Rockford, {v}550
murder of, {vii}486, 547
Manby's Hot Springs (New Mexico), {iv}358, 373

Manchester (Lancashire), {i}27, 77, 82–3, 146, 345, 384, 469, {ii}17, 187, 382, 384, 656, {iii}342, 428, 477, 506, {iv}492, {vi}399, 503, 514
'vile, hateful, immense', {i}80
Manchester Guardian, The, {i}344, 469–70, {iii}128, 137
DHL reviewed in, {i}420, {ii}177; 'With the Guns' in, {ii}222
Mandrake Press, The, {v}574, {vii}4, 8, 78–9, 142, 179, 279, 285, 319, 490, 499, 592
Rhys Davies and, {vii}30, 448, 461; Fanfrolico Press becomes, {vii}71; Goldston and Stephensen partners in, {vii}71, 82, 125, 130, 170, 253, 549; publishes Rozanov, {vii}82, 474, 556, 559; publishes DHL's *Paintings*, {vii}95, 180, 253; DHL suspects lack of good judgment in, {vii}443, 448, 469; *A Propos* published by, {vii}446, 587–8, 633–4; disintegrating, {vii}554–5, 557–9, 562, 564, 573, 576, 578–80, 583; 'vegetable of ill omen', {vii}649
Mandrake Booklets, {vii}530–1, 556
Manhattan Transfer, *see* Dos Passos, J.
Maniace (Sicily), {iii}10, 49, 620, 637, {iv}51, 139
DHL visits Castello di, {iii}509–10, 526
Mann, Heinrich, {ii}247
Mann, Mary E., {i}256, 525, {iii}328
Mann, Thomas, {i}546. {ii}247, {vii}563, {viii}106
Mannen Bridge, *see* Hiroshige, A.
Manners, Lady Diana, {iii}27, 71
Mano Bianca, S. S., {v}630
Manon Lescaut, *see* Prévost, Abbé
Manser, {i}210
Mansfield (Nottinghamshire), {i}265, {vi}81, 107
MANSFIELD, KATHERINE, {i}510, {ii}4, 7–8, 10, 13–14, 17, 171, 205, 207, 218, 221, 226, 233, 237–8, 240, 246, 252–3, 256, 274, 296, 301, 323, 359, 390, 404, 427–8, 464–5, 525, 535, 547–8, 554–6, 647, 650–2, 655–6, 669, {iii}3, 82, 84, 114, 318–19, 356, 366, 428, 435, 683,

MANSFIELD, KATHERINE (*cont.*)

{iv}11, 23, 33, 133, 241, 349, {v}43, 203, 531, {vi}41, 511, {vii}609, 643, {viii}7–8

with Murry co-edits *Rhythm*, {i}507, 512; admires DHL's poetry, {i}530; co-edits *Blue Review*, {i}546; living with Murry, {ii}31–2; known as Mrs Murry, {ii}45–6, 50, 53, 254; go-between for Frieda and Monty Weekley, {ii}46, 51, {viii}6; DHL on relationship between Murry and, {ii}110–13, 161, 270; regarded DHL as 'interfering Sunday-school Superintendent sort of person', {ii}160; affair with Carco, {ii}270, 289, 291, 308, 313; Frieda's affection for, {ii}290, 667–8; 'her letters are as jarring as the sound of a saw', {ii}333; contributions as 'Matilda Berry' to *Signature*, {ii}385–7, 389, 393; death of brother in France, {ii}409, 481; in Bandol, {ii}476, 506, {vii}105, 200; 'dancing with happiness' with Murry, {ii}515, 521, 530; private income, {ii}539, 586; DHL's plans for Tregerthen 'settlement' with Murrys, {ii}567–72, 584–6, 588; Murrys 'our only two *tried* friends', {ii}576; at Tregerthen, {ii}591–9, 604–6; move to Mylor, {ii}607–8, 613–21, 627, 631–2, 637–9, {iii}127; unhappy with Murry, {ii}623, 628; will not visit Tregerthen, {ii}641; Café Royal incident, {ii}649; DHL renounces 'the Murries, both, for ever', {iii}23, 28, 163; Turgenev 'very critical, like', {iii}41; DHL meets in London, {iii}294; comments on *T and G* invited from, {iii}297–8; invited to Mountain Cottage, {iii}307; DHL sends books to, {iii}327, 338–40; DHL concerned for health of, {iii}330–1, 335, 344. 541; uses 'Elizabeth Stanley' as pseudonym in *Athenæum*, {iii}344, 350; 'foolish would-be-witty letters' to Frieda from, {iii}352; in Italy, {iii}401, 467; revolts DHL 'stewing in [her] consumption', {iii}470; in Menton, {iii}471, 670; 'liar out and

out', {iii}663; 'doing the last gasp touch', {iii}675; in Switzerland, {iv}38; in New Zealand DHL remembers, {iv}283; in Fontainebleau, {iv}365; death of, {iv}375, 377, 385, 387, 555, {v}422, {vi}57; *Dove's Nest* a 'waste-paper basket', {iv}503; 'delicate and touching. - But not *Great!*', {iv}521; *Letters* 'sell largely', {vii}55; writings 'belong to her day and will fade', {vii}610

Bliss and Other Stories, {i}507, {iii}633, {iv}114;

Dove's Nest and Other Stories, The {iv}503, 521;

Gorky, *Reminiscences of Leonid Andreyev*, trans. with Kot, {iv}478, 487;

Prelude, {ii}545;

'The Samuel Josephs', {iv}458

Letters to {i}507–8, {ii}451–2, 471–3, 481–2, 499, 507–8, 522–3, 533–4, 541–5, 548–50, 563–5, 569–71, 576–7, 580–1, 631–3, 658, {iii}149, 300–3, 307–9, 312–13, 324, 327–8, 338–9, 343, 421, 470, {iv}283, {viii}6, 10

Letters from {i}510, {iii}470

Manucci, Niccolao, *Storia do Mogor*, {ii}596, 601, 608;

Taimur-I-Lang, {ii}601

'Many Swans', *see* Lowell, A.

Manzanillo (Mexico), {iv}443, 506–9, 529

Manzoni, Allessandro, *I Promessi Sposi*, {iii}327

Mapledurham (Oxfordshire), {iii}386

Marama, S.S., {iv}247, 250–2

Maran, Réné, *Batouala*, {iv}342, 359, {viii}66, 73

Marcel, Gabriel, {vii}225, 383, 540 on *LCL*, {vii}223, 397

Marconi, Enrico, {i}505

Marcus, Albidia, {v}95, 249

Mardi; and a Voyage Thither, see Melville, H.

Maremma (Italy), Etruscan tombs in, {v}413, 447, 449, 465, 650–1, 653, 655, {vi}28–30, 85

Margaret, *see* King, M.; Radford, M.; Wilkeson, M.

Margarita, *see* Scott, M.

Margate (Kent), {ii}29–32, 35–6, 38–40, 60, 64, 89, 93, 172, {vi}538–9, {viii}11–12

Margot's Progress, see Goldring, D.

Marguerite, {vi}286, 345

Margueritte, Paul, *Ame d'Enfant*, {ii}100

Mari, René, {iii}594, 616

Maria Cristina, *see* Chambers, M.

Maria, *see* Huxley, M.; Mary, Virgin

Marianne, *see* Jaffe, M.

Marie, *see* Herbert, M.

Marin County (USA), {iv}585

Marinetti, Filippo Tommaso, {ii}180–3

Mark Gertler, see Gertler, M.

MARKS, HARRY F., New York bookseller and Black Sun Press agent, {vii}239–40, 308, 323, 398, 411, 417–18, 426, 471, 487–8, 496–9, 525, 530, 538, 550, 577, 586, 589, 606, 647

   Letters to {vii}498

Marks, Henry Kingdon, *Peter Middleton*, {iii}492

Marquesas Islands (Pacific), {iii}65, 83, 563, 567, 650, 655

Marquis de Villemer, Le, see Sand, G.

MARRIAGE, 'sexual love..religious..and ordinary sympathetic feeling' necessary for, {i}66; 'on strength of sex sympathy with..accompanying beauty of harmony' as in music, {i}67; DHL's parents' 'marriage life..one carnal bloody fight', {i}190; to Louie Burrows DHL seems 'on the brink of', {i}213; 'dirty coin of', {i}286; 'in heaven..no marriage nor giving in', {i}394; for DHL 'a great thing - not..to be snatched and clumsily handled', {i}401; 'common-sense' must match love in, {i}402; DHL needs solemn preparation for, {i}403–4; 'I believe in', {i}441; Italian men and women largely faithful in, {i}508; English women want 'sensation' rather than 'husbands and', {ii}47; peasant wedding at Ameglia, {ii}109; involves change, {ii}143; wedding 'mere legal contract', {ii}179; inner union essential in, {ii}191; DHL's own, {ii}198; women

should have 'absolutely equal voice with regard to', {ii}368; 'My pure relationship with one woman is marriage, physical and spiritual', {ii}634; 'live only in marriage, not elsewhere', {iii}25; Whitman's 'manly love' as 'sacred a union as', {iii}478; unsatisfactory solution to 'labyrinth' of novel, {iii}521; David Garnett's, {iv}100; the '*kindly*' union of 'mere male and female' essential for, {v}204; holds social system together, {v}639; Burrow wrong about, {vi}114; Johanna von Krug 'hates', {vi}137; Keyserling's 'silly book' on, {vi}419; 'a treacherous stimulant', {vii}291

Marriage, see Wells, H. G.

Marryat, Frederick, {ii}588

   Jacob Faithful, {iii}40;

   Peter Simple, {iii}40, 52;

   Poor Jack, {iii}40

Marrying of Hester Rainsbrook, The, see Cramb, J. A.

Marsden, Dora, {ii}131

Marsden, Thomas Haynes, {i}26, {iii}222

Marseilles (France), {ii}464, 497, {iii}673, {iv}112, 142, 145, 231, {vi}302, 608, 616–17, {vii}5, 26, 31, 56, 67, 104, 107, 144, 174, 183, 193, 196, 202, 207, 210, 213, 260, 282–4, 298–9, 301–5, 310–11, 314, 317–18, 320–1, 329–33, 335–6, 379, 408, 465, 480–2, 485–6, 490–1, 493–5, 502, 511, 526, 552, 560, 562, 566, 574, 601, 617, 628–9

MARSH, (SIR) EDWARD HOWARD ('EDDIE'), {i}19, {ii}2–3, 7–8, 12, 14, 40, 68, 87, 108, 208, 212, 330–1, 398, 417, 447, {iii}14, 55, 146, 215, 376–7, 396, {iv}305

   invites DHL to contribute to *Georgian Poetry*, {i}459, 461–2, {ii}384, 399, {iii}371; sends royalties, {ii}35–6, 39, 140, 211, 565, 668, {iii}135, 388, 486, 611, 615, {iv}297, 430; DHL meets, {ii}36, 39, 41, 43, 45; introduces DHL to Asquiths and W. H. Davies, {ii}48, 51–2, 54, 128; DHL debates poetic form

MARSH, (SIR) EDWARD HOWARD
    ('EDDIE') *(cont.)*
    and rhythm with, {ii}61–2, 84, 89, 92–3,
    102–5, 120, 176–8; 'sweet as Maecenas',
    {ii}63; visits Lerici, {ii}136, 140; 'I feel
    Marsh against me with the whole of his
    being', {ii}161; invited to witness
    DHL's marriage, {ii}195; gives DHL
    Hardy's complete works, {ii}198–200;
    gives DHL £10, {ii}213–14; Frieda
    challenges views on war of, {ii}214–15;
    supports DHL's application to Royal
    Literary Fund, {ii}224–5; 'jeered' at
    Rainbow, {ii}411, 428; gives DHL £20,
    {ii}429, 432, {iii}358–9; and Gertler,
    {ii}509, 515, 531, 602; DHL apologises
    for offence to, {ii}535–6; DHL seeks
    help to leave England from, {iii}67,
    69–72, 81, 84–5; Brett Young 'protégé'
    of, {iii}462; did not acknowledge receipt
    of *Lost Girl*, {iv}33
    Letters to {i}461, {ii}35–6, 39, 51–4, 61,
    84–6, 91–4, 102–6, 113, 119–21, 131,
    140–2, 144, 152, 154–5, 176–8, 185–6,
    194–5, 198–200, 211–15, 384, 399–401,
    406, 428–9, 432–3, 535–6, 565, 668,
    {iii}67, 81, 84, 135–6, 358, 369–71, 388,
    486–7, 611, {iv}297, 430
Marshall, I., {i}357
Marshall, Sir John Hubert, *The Bagh Caves
    in the Gwalior State*, {vi}72, 102, 208
Martens (Martinse), Camille, housekeeper at
    Villa Beau Soleil, {vii}493, 500, 509,
    511–12, 518, 530–2, 543, 553, 563, 571,
    580–1, 621–2
Martin Chuzzlewit, see Dickens, C.
Martin, *see* Secker, M.
Martin, Dr T. P., {v}88
Martin, J., *Account of the Natives of the Tonga
    Islands, An*, {iii}594
Martindale, Elizabeth, {i}14, 144, 183
Martinse, Mme, *see* Martens, C.
Martyrdom of Man, The, see Reade, W. W.
Maruca, *see* Monros, M. J.
Marvell, Andrew, 'Picture of Little T.C.',
    {iii}246
Marwood, Arthur Peirson, {i}12, 381
Marx, Karl, {i}9, {iv}577, {vii}99

Marx, Magdeleine, *see* Paz, M.
Mary and the Bramble, see Abercrombie, L.
Mary Christine, *see* Hughes, M. C.
Mary Magdalene, {iii}179–80
Mary, *see* Cannan, M.; Jones, H. M.;
    Wilkeson, M.
Mary, Lady, *see* Starr, Lady M.
Mary, Virgin, {iv}84, {vii}54, 426
Mascagni, Pietro, {i}247
Masefield, John, {ii}176, {iii}71, 363,
    {viii}15
    'horrible sentimentalist..cheap Byron of
    the day', {i}523; Pound declared DHL
    'much better poet' than, {ii}131; 'cheap',
    {vi}320; often 'spurious', {viii}18
    The Daffodil Fields, {ii}136;
    The Tragedy of Nan, {ii}254
Mason, Agnes Louise Eliza, {i}10–11, 194,
    236, 338, 382, 385, 418, 446, 499, 523–5,
    528, {ii}22, 136, {iii}62, {v}640
    introduced DHL to Helen Corke,
    {i}129; 'looks woe-begone', {i}161;
    befriends Louie Burrows, {i}338, 341–2;
    writes to DHL, {i}355, 362–3, 367, 407,
    452, 465; sends DHL Lockhart's *Burns*,
    {i}487; *Love Poems* for, {i}513
Mason, Alfred Edward Woodley, {ii}225
Mason, Anne Brakely, {v}176, 388, {vi}27,
    242, 548, {vii}172, 312
Mason, George Heming, {i}282
MASON, HAROLD TRUMP, {v}176, 295,
    580, {vi}11–14, 314–15
    publishes *Bibliography* of DHL, {v}133,
    176, 241; publishes *Porcupine*, {v}240,
    284, 329, 375, 387, 494–5, {vi}363,
    {vii}159, 172, 400–1; advice on *LCL* in
    USA sought from, {vi}242, 288–9,
    362–3, 408, 450, 547, {vii}20; copy of
    LCL to, {vi}448–9, 470; thinks *LCL*
    'magnificent', {vi}548; DHL suspects
    involvement in pirated edns of *LCL* by,
    {vii}35, 159, 161–2, 233, 240, 297–8,
    308; innocence of offence claimed by,
    {vii}311–12; 'very untrustworthy',
    {vii}401
    Letters to {v}240–1, 329, 375–6, 387–8,
    494–5, {vi}27–8, 241–2, 288–9, 362–3,
    449, 547–8, {vii}311–12

Letters from {vi}363, 449–50, 548, {vii}311–12

Maspéro, Sir Gaston Camille Charles, *Egypte*, {ii}521, 529

Massa (Italy), {ii}153, {iii}454
see also Villa la Massa

Massa-Carrara (Italy), {vii}155, 274, 283

Masses, see New Masses

Massingham, Gertrude Speedwell, {ii}350

Massingham, Harold John, {ii}350, 402
Downland Man, {vi}298

Massingham, Henry William, {ii}402

Masters, Edgar Lee, *Spoon River Anthology*, {ii}503, 533, {iii}141

Mastro-don Gesualdo, see Verga, G.

Mather, Frank Jewett, {vi}85

Mather, Margaret G., {vi}85

MATHEWS, ELKIN, LTD, {ii}519, {vi}512
and Carter, {iv}365, 431, {vii}456, 506, 508, 519; publishes signed edn of *Rawdon's Roof*, {vi}495, 526, 552, 565, 602, 606, 610, {vii}18, 23, 163, 175, 181, 496, 507
Letters to {vii}175

MATHEWS, HENRY WILLARD, {v}255
Letters to {v}255

Mathias, Ena, {vi}16, 433–4

Matlock (Derbyshire), {i}24, 368, {iii}253, 264, 307, 309, 319, 324, 351, {v}321, 324, 551, 593
'too trippery', {i}259; like Trier, {i}397

Matson, Harold, {viii}38

Maud, *see* Beardsall, M.; Drummond, M.; Villiers-Stuart, M.

Maude, Aylmer, {iii}411

Maude, Cyril, {i}97

Maugham, William Somerset, {i}148, {iii}443, {v}3, 390, 570, {vi}11
DHL dismissive of, {v}153–5, 157–8, 160–2; 'A bit rancid', {v}166; 'perhaps he's nice', {v}446; DHL avoids, {vi}239; with Wells 'rich as pigs', {vii}615
Ashenden, or the British Agent, DHL reviews, {vi}463, 516;
The Moon and Sixpence, {iii}505, 566;
Trembling of a Leaf, {iv}246

Maunsel & Co., {iii}12
DHL fails to place *W in L* with, {iii}183–5, 187, 206; and 'At the Gates', {iii}191, 195, 261

Maupassant, Guy de, {i}29, 206, {ii}162
and Balzac, {i}91; Weekley admires, {ii}244; '*obvious*' beside Fenimore Cooper or Hardy, {iii}41
'Idylle', {i}406–7

Mauriac, François, {vii}223, 382, 540
DHL meets, {vii}225

Maurice, *see* Sterne, M.

Maurice, Furnley, *see* Wilmot, F. L. T.

Maurice, Martin, *Amour, Terre Inconnue*, {vii}609

Mauro, Don, *see* Inguanez, Don M.

Maurois, André, {vii}383, 452

Mavrogordato, John Nicolas, {v}562, 573

Max Havelaar, see Dekker, E.D.

Max, *see* Hunger, M.; Plowman, M.

Maxence, {ii}632

Mayas, {iv}541, {v}139, 144, {vi}503

Mayer, Dr, {vi}156

Mayer, Elizabeth, {vi}156

Mayne, Ethel Colburn, {ii}40, 47, 314

Mayo, Katharine, *Mother India*, {vi}174

Mayrhofen (Austria), {i}430–3, 442, 445–7, 476, 489, 521, {iv}189

Mazatlan (Mexico), {iv}17, 506–10, 518–19, {viii}84–5

Mazzaro (Sicily), {iv}155

McBride & Nast, {iii}508, 512, 516, 520, 529, 543

McCarthy, John H., {iv}347, 354

McCarthy, John Russell, 'The Hero', {ii}232

McCarthy, Justin, *Proud Prince*, {i}138

McCord, Lina, {v}58, 116, 386, {vi}181, 266, 432

McCulloch, Alec, {i}113

McCulloch, George, {i}113

McDONALD, EDWARD DAVID, {ii}15, 147, 295, 536, {iii}4–5, 7, 104, 303, 396, 404, 428, {iv}3, {v}255, 284, 329, 388, {vi}11–12, 28, 242, 363, {vii}312
DHL 'bewildered' by approach from, {v}63; DHL pleased but frightened at idea of bibliography, {v}231; takes 'infinite pains', {v}241; bibliography

McDONALD, EDWARD DAVID (*cont.*)
  'almost' makes DHL 'feel important',
  {v}271; 'marvellous to make a bibliography lively', {v}272; DHL meets,
  {v}301, 323; 'really nice - like a
  Canadian farmer..quiet, with energy',
  {v}338; arranges orders for, and is
  enthusiastic about *LCL*, {vi}408, 440,
  448, 450, 470, 487, 549–50; *WWRA* sent
  to, {vi}432
  *A Bibliography of the Writings of D. H.
  Lawrence*, {ii}80, 165, {iii}692, {iv}131,
  {v}3, 40, 63–4, 92, 116, 119, 122, 133,
  231, 241, 271–2, 338, {vi}348, 370,
  {vii}20, 297
  see also Lawrence, D. H., 'Bad Side of
  Books, The'
  Letters to {v}63–4, 86–7, 103–5, 116,
  119–21, 132–3, 150, 160, 175–6, 230–1,
  271–3, 295–6, 300–1, 323, 376, 381,
  495–6, 512, 516, 520, {vi}314–15, 408,
  450, 549–50
McDonald, Marguerite Bartelle, {v}63,
  120–1, 295, 300, 323, 376, 381, 495–6,
  520, {vi}28, 242, 314–15, 408, 549
McElligott, Selma, {v}522
McKenna, Stephen, {v}522
McKinley, William, {ii}332
McLaren, Jack, {vii}531
McLeod, Alice, {i}464, {v}640
MCLEOD, ARTHUR WILLIAM,
  {i}10–11, 18, 136, 225, 279, {ii}7, 15, 21,
  30, 36, {v}3
  DHL's school relationship with, {i}192,
  246, 355, {v}640–1; sends Latin poems,
  {i}213, {viii}5; paintings for, {i}234,
  276, 341, 488, 498; on 'White Stocking',
  {i}258; and DHL give each other books,
  {i}262, 278, 299, 326, 341, 362, 456, 459,
  462, 464, 481–2, 484, 487–8, 504, 512,
  524–5, 528, 540, 543, 551–2, {ii}22, 27,
  89–91, 117, 135, 146, 155, 180, 254,
  {iii}60–1; DHL's 'fond affection' for,
  {i}356, 418; told about Frieda, {i}418;
  doesn't 'trust other people', {i}418;
  'delightful letters' from, {i}454, 460;
  urged to visit DHL, {i}464–5, {ii}48,
  86, 136, 255, 395, {iii}291; DHL sends

complimentary copies to, {i}488, 513,
  544, {ii}19, {v}641
Letters to {i}136, 192–4, 213, 259, 277–8,
  294–5, 297, 341–2, 346, 352, 355–7,
  362–3, 367–8, 382, 395, 407, 417–19,
  432, 445–7, 454–6, 459–60, 464–5,
  481–4, 487–8, 498–9, 504–6, 512–13,
  523–5, 528, 540, 543–5, 551–2, {ii}22,
  27, 47–8, 64–5, 76–7, 86, 89–91, 117–19,
  135–9, 146–7, 155–6, 162–4, 180–2,
  186–8, 193–5, 251, 254–5, 395, {iii}60–2,
  291–3, {v}640–1, {viii}5
Mead, Frederick, sits in judgment on DHL's
  paintings, {vii}361, 382, 389–90, 411,
  413
Mead, George Robert Stow, {iv}475
Mebli, Mrs, {v}625
Medea, see Euripides
Medici Press, {iii}730, *see also* Medici
  Society
Medici Society Ltd., invited DHL to write 'A
  History of Italian Painting, for
  Children', {iii}714, 717, 721, 723, 726,
  {iv}6, 24–7, 34, 41, 43, {viii}41;
  agreement accepted, {iv}39, 45–7, 49;
  project abandoned, {iv}66
Medici, Lorenzo de, {iii}429, {vi}595,
  {vii}394, 400, 416, 433
Medici, Marchese Bindo Peruzzi de,
  {v}487
Medinier, Dr, {vii}13
Mediterranean, {iii}1, 9, 448, 451, 462, 504,
  562, 655, 698, {iv}97, 203, 207, 243,
  {v}292, 310–11, 323, 337, 343, 346–7,
  368, 375, {vi}18, 87, 513, 522, {vii}11,
  25, 40, 74, 86, 170, 257, 263–4, 267, 275,
  277, 290, 391, 421, 501, 506, 508, 513
  DHL sometimes hankers for, {v}172,
  277, 305; 'blue and young', {v}341, 345;
  'always does [DHL] good', {v}366, 376,
  478; DHL not at peace until sees,
  {vii}239, 241, 247–8, 393–5, 451, 454;
  'brilliant incandescent blue mornings of
  Southern', {vii}255, 259; 'great
  comfort', {vii}283, 435, 481; 'glad to be
  back by', {vii}490–1; 'still seems young
  as Odysseus, in the morning', {vii}509
Medley, Charles Douglas, {vii}163

Mee, Sara Lois, {i}142

Meersburg (Germany), {viii}42

Meiklejohn, John M. D., {i}26

Meistersinger, {iv}543

Melba, (Dame) Nellie, {i}281

Melbourne (Australia), {iv}8, 10, 237–8, 241, 246, 265, 273, {v}80, 161

Melcher, Walther, {iv}510–11, 518–19

Mélisande, {vi}126

Mellor, Annie J., {i}294

Mellor, Vera, {i}468

MELONEY, MARIE MATTINGLY, {iii}561
  Letters to {iii}561

Melrose, Andrew, {iii}444, 468, 525, 537, {iv}533

Meltzer, Charles H., {i}168

Melville, Herman, {ii}588, {iv}383, {v}308
  'such a treasure', {iii}83; DHL's essays on, {iii}279, 288, 397, 401, 405, 565, {iv}55, 196–8, 514
  Mardi; and a Voyage Thither, {iv}345;
  Moby Dick, {ii}528, 614–15, 645, {iii}65, 68, 71, 77, 85, 104, 279, 549;
  Omoo, {ii}614, {iii}40, 65;
  Pierre; or, The Ambiguities, {iv}345;
  Typee, {ii}614, {iii}40, 566
  see also, Weaver, R. M.

Memoirs of the Foreign Legion, see Magnus, M.

Memories, see Luhan, M. D.

Men Are We, see Skinner, M. L.

Men, Beasts and Gods, see Ossendowski, F. A.

Men, Women and Ghosts, see Lowell, A.

Mencken, Henry Louis, {ii}144, {iii}399, {vii}525
  Americana 1925{v}321

Mendel, Vera, {iv}575

Mendel: a Story of Youth, see Cannan, G.

Menton(e) (France), {iii}471, 616, 636, 639, 648, 663, 670, {vii}629, 631

Meran (Austria), {i}444–5, 450, {iv}64, 189

Mercer, T. S., {vi}514

Merchant of Venice, The, see Shakespeare, W.

Mercure de France, Le, {ii}385, 387

Mercury, {vi}23, 126

Mercury, The, see London Mercury

Meredith, George, {i}52, 109, 241, 511, {ii}146, 177, 180, 255
  Modern Love{vi}46;
  The Ordeal of Richard Feverel, {i}214;
  Rhoda Fleming, {i}191;
  The Tragic Comedians, {i}250

MEREDITH, HUGH OWEN, {ii}18, 402–4, 418
  Week-Day Poems, {ii}425
  Letters to {ii}425–6

Merizkowsky, Zinaida Hippius, *The Green Ring*, {iii}421, 425–6, 428, 442, 471, 658

Merrick, Leonard, {i}524–5

MERRILD, KNUD, {iv}13, 17, 336, 351–2, 357, 359–60, 378, 370, 385–6, 392, 445, 450, 487, 574, {v}39, 55, 188, 208, 211, 231, 537, 652, {viii}76
  book-jacket designer, {iv}344–5, 367, 383, 394, 419, 436, {v}246, {viii}58, 68; portrait of DHL by, {iv}373, {viii}58; exhibition of work in Santa Fe, {iv}388–9, 406; *Capain's Doll* for, {iv}390, 453; meets DHL in Los Angeles, {iv}495; offers to accompany Frieda to Mexico, {viii}85–6
  Letters to {iv}347, 354, 413–14, 422, 426, 430, 434, 438–9, 444, 453, 459, 463, 469–70, 481, 491–2, 502, 505–9, 512, 525–6, 538, 541, 548, 562

Merrull, *see* Merrild, K.

Merry Muses of Caledonia, see Burns, R.

Merry-Go-Round, The, see Gertler, M.

Messageries Maritimes, {vi}362, 365, 367, 379, 384

Messiah, see Handel, G.

Messina (Sicily), {iii}478–527 *passim*, 540, 548, 555, 579, 618, 623, 626, 640–1, 647, 658–9, 662, 665, 695, 697–8, {iv}79, 100, 127, 148–9, 151, 153, 160, 194, 198–9, 204–5, {viii}29, 31–2, 38, 48, 51

Městrović, Ivan, {ii}157, 360, 578, {iii}13, 137, 261
  The Mother of the Jugovići, {ii}578

Metamorphosis of Ajax, see Harington, Sir J.

METCALF, PROFESSOR JOHN CALVIN, {iii}630, 634
  Letters to {iii}630–1

Methuen and Co., {i}306, 391, {ii}6, 16, 240–1, 250, 480, {iii}547, {iv}2 outbids Duckworth and secures *Rainbow*, {ii}186–7, 189–90, 193, 200–1, 207, 211–12, 225, 255, 260, 299, 318, 328, 348, 354–7, 631, {v}120, {vi}479, {vii}458–9, 505; signs of anxiety about text of *Rainbow*, {ii}270, 294, 327, 364, 370, 372; 'swine' to have chosen book-jacket for *Rainbow*, {ii}402, 406; and suppression of *Rainbow*, {ii}428–31, 434–5, 439–40, 456–8, 462, 561; 'the skunk left the book entirely in the lurch', {ii}441, {iii}635; 'what a snake in his boiled-shirt bosom!', {ii}630, {v}175; agrees to cancel agreement for *Rainbow*, {iii}58, 74, 80, 212

Methuen, Sir Algernon, {ii}240

Metropolitan Bank, {iv}516

Metropolitan, The, {ii}475, {iv}7 DHL publishes in, {ii}6, 197, 223, 256, 406, {iii}111, 493, 559, 562, 669, {iv}31, 36, 57, 134; DHL, rejected by, {ii}216, {iii}571–2, 575–6, 582, 586, {iv}187, 219, {viii}35; regards DHL 'with a very favorable eye', {iii}477, 564–5

Metz (Germany), {i}17, 385–412 *passim*, {ii}206, 418, {viii}6

Mexican People: Their Struggle for Freedom, The, see Gutierrez de Lara, L. and Pinchon, E.

Mexicans, {iv}158, 280, 313, 352, 410, 452, 463, 536, {v}105, 111, 125, 178, 191, 197, 229, 250, {vii}204

Mexico, {iv}1, 13–18, 95, 97, 125, 138, 141–3, 159, 316, 366–562 *passim*, 581–2, 591, 595–6, {v}1, 5–6, 8, 24, 29, 40, 45–6, 50, 54–5, 59, 67, 71, 77, 79, 82, 85, 92–3, 98, 105–6, 109, 113–14, 116–18, 121–291 *passim*, 587, 596, {vi}3, 211, 346, 356, {vii}108, 184, 246, 424, 645, {viii}61, 69–70, 72, 76, 86, 90 'much pleasanter than U.S.', {iv}414, 469, 473, 479, 522; 'so few pretences of any sort', {iv}420; DHL 'had about enough of', {iv}425; 'much rougher even than Sicily', {iv}439; 'very savage

underneath', {iv}442, 445; 'some strange raw splendour in', {iv}516; London seems dead after 'brightness' of, {iv}550; DHL hankers for, {v}75; 'a bit uneasy and depressed', {v}160–1; 'rather stupid people', {v}172; 'politically..a mess', {v}174; DHL 'awfully ill' in, {v}245, 253, 269; 'a sort of nausea' associated with, {v}254, 262–4; 'gruesome', {v}290; DHL not recovered after illness in, {vi}59, 154; US recognises, {viii}85

'Mexico, Why Not?', *see* Quintanilla, L.

Mexico City, {iv}15, 150–427 *passim*, 535, {v}3, 7, 45, 75, 116, 132–231 *passim*, 258, 268, 271, 287, 306, 445–6, {vi}348, {vii}202, {viii}61, 70–2, 75 'mongrel town', {iv}417; 'a bit depressed and depressing', {iv}537, {v}156; 'not so bad', {v}229; British Consulate in, {v}133, 136–42, 144, 149, 156, 158, 160, 208, 212, 217; on plateau, not too hot, {viii}78

Meynell, Alice, {ii}255, 259, 342, 345–6, {iii}145, {v}589

Meynell, Francis, {iv}575, {vi}174, 337

Meynell, Monica, *see* Saleeby, Monica

MEYNELL, VIOLA, {ii}1, 12, 160, 264, 287, 343, 345, {v}77 lends Greatham cottage to DHL, {ii}255–6, 258–9, 261, 269, 316, 374; types MS of *Rainbow*, {ii}271, 293, 299, 312, 323, 327, 331, 348; admires Cynthia Asquith, {ii}368, 372; DHL breaks with, {ii}566, 595

Letters to {ii}299, 373–4

Meynell, Wilfred, {ii}255, 259, 261, 342, 345–6

Michael, Archangel, {iii}293

Michelangelo Buonarroti, {ii}130, 592–3, 597, 602, {vi}342

David, {iii}428, {vi}79;

The Last Judgement, {ii}593

Mickie (cat), {vii}537, 570, 590, 599, 603, 608

Middleton Murry, *see* Murry, J. M.

Middleton, Richard Barnham, {ii}28–9,
34–6, 41, 117, 179
'stupid about women' {ii}94; suffered
from self-hatred, {ii}95, 101–2, 115;
Frieda on, {ii}96–7
'The District Visitor', {ii}115;
Ghost Ship and Other Stories, The, {ii}36;
Monologues, {ii}94–7;
Poems and Songs, {ii}29, 34
Middleton-by-Wirksworth (Derbyshire),
{iii}241–352 *passim*
see also Mountain Cottage
Midgley, Eve
Letters from {vii}20
Midland (and Great Central) Railway,
{i}284
Midland (London, Midland and Scottish)
Railway, {i}172, 293, 319, {iii}252, 264,
273, 723, {iv}547
Midlands, {i}345, 349, {iii}113, 192–3, 195,
223, 226–7, 230–2, 240, 262, 330, 406–7,
{iv}552–3, {v}1, 9, 13, 310–13, 527, 535,
{vii}58, 190, {viii}5
DHL hates, {iii}114; 'full of the fear of
death' from flu, {iii}302, 304, 306;
dialect, {iii}657; life-style in Thirroul
recalls, {iv}253; 'filthy air' in, {v}332;
coal strike in, {v}515; DHL prefers to
London, {v}517–18, 521–2; 'little novel'
set in, {v}584, 601; 'gruesome',
{vii}176, 180, 183
Mifflin, George Harrison, {iv}276
'Mignonette', *see* Wilkinson, Mrs
Milan (Italy), {i}464, 524, {ii}78, 93, 124,
135, 139, 629, {iii}19–20, 523, 568–9,
574, 578, 581, 584–7, 602, 687, {iv}85,
98, 167, 186, 188, 194–5, {v}92, 201,
442, 488–9, 545–7, 638, {vi}169, 185–91,
270, 301, 303–8, 312–13, 347, 573–4,
594–5, {vii}350–2, 354–5, 360, 366, 374,
527
'beastly..with its imitation hedge-hog of
a cathedral', {ii}88
Miles, Susan, *see* Roberts, U.
Milford, Sir Humphrey, {iv}31, 68, {v}322
and publication of *Movements*, {iii}326,
696, 707, {v}105, 137

Military Service Act, {iii}92, 106, 108–9,
130, 160, 294
Mill on the Floss, The, see Eliot, G.
Mill Valley (California), {iv}573, 580, 585,
{v}156, 158
Millais, Sir John Everett, {i}113, {ii}4, 147
Miller & Gill Ltd, order copies of *LCL* but
reluctant to pay, {vi}512, 515, {vii}68,
124, 199, 274, 372, 394, 403, 416
Miller, Donald Gazley, {v}163, {vi}10, 324
Miller, Edgar {v}107–8
Miller, Henry, {ii}18
Millgate Monthly, {vi}399
MILNE, HERBERT JOHN MANSFIELD,
{iv}599, {v}117, 121, 344
Letters to {v}117
Milner, Viscount Alfred, {iii}294
MILNES, J. N.,
Letters to {ii}510
Milo, {i}505
Milton, Ernest, {v}119, {viii}97
produces *David*, {v}470, {vi}26,
{viii}102
Milton, John, {ii}448
Shelley far more 'beautiful' than,
{ii}120; his God 'the great Absolute, the
Eternity', {ii}350; idiosyncratic spelling
in poetry of, {viii}16
'Il Penseroso', {iv}355;
'Lycidas', {iii}57;
'Ode on Christ's Nativity', {i}86;
Paradise Lost, {ii}176, 390, {vi}91;
Paradise Regained, {viii}16
Minas Nuevas (Mexico), {iv}506–7, 510
Minchin, Humphrey Cotton, *The Legion
Book*, {vii}84–5, 111, 122
Miners' Relief Fund, {vii}98–9
Miners Federation, {viii}24
Ministry of Education, {iii}287
Ministry of Labour, {iii}307
Ministry of Munitions, {iii}307
Minnesingers, {i}331, 411
Minnie, {i}231
Minorca, {v}373, {vi}513
Mirabar, Jerry, {iv}347
Miranda Masters, see Cournos, J.
Mirenda, *see* Villa Mirenda

Mirenda, Raul ('Maggiore', 'Major'),
{v}459, 473, {vi}398, 573, 577, 583,
{vii}33, 281

Mirsky, Prince, *see* Svyatopolk-Mirsky, D.

Miss Julia, see Strindberg, A.

Mississippi, River (USA), {iv}470,
{viii}82

Mistress of Husaby, The, see Undset, S.

Mitchell-Thomson, Sir W., {vii}228

Mitla (Mexico), {v}163, 182–3, 197

Mitrinović, Dimitrije, {iii}5, 137

Mixtec Indians, {v}178, 184, 195

Moby Dick, see Melville, H.

Modane (France), {iii}415–16, 424, 523, 541,
569–70

Modern French Painters, see Gordon, J.

Modern Love, see Meredith, G.

Modotti, Tina, {v}186

Moeller, Philip, {v}276

Moffat, Graham, *Bunty Pulls the Strings,*
{i}304

Moffatt, James, *The New Testament,* {vii}550

Mogens, and Other Stories, see Jacobsen, J. P.

Mohr, Eve (Eva), {vi}205, 227, 249, 265, 285,
421, {vii}48, 51, 535, 537, 571

MOHR, KÄTHE, {vi}184, 205, 227, 239,
248, 285, 304, 339, 421, {vii}48, 51, 139,
461, 537, 544
Letters to {vii}534–5, 566–7, 603–4

MOHR, MAX, {vi}10, 156, 218, 281,
{vii}11, 74, 364, 412, 422, 433–5, 444,
446–7, 537, 558
thinks DHL 'the greatest living novelist', {vi}157; critique of writings by,
{vi}161, 338–9; visits DHL, {vi}167,
{vii}501, 510–11, 532, 534–5; 'good and
interesting, but..at the very end of the
road', {vi}173; and German translation
of *David,* {vi}204, 248; visits Les
Diablerets, {vi}294, 297; *WWRA* to,
{vi}396; *LCL* for, {vii}48, 50–1; and
German translation of *LCL,* {vii}114,
178, 202, 245, 287, 304, 333, 335, 354–5,
386, 596; *Pansies* for, {vii}380; DHL
visits, {vii}449–90; *P and O* for,
{vii}573, 604
Die Heidin ('Jungfrau Max'), {vi}339,
431, {vii}51;

Improvisationen im Juni, {vi}183;
Platingruben in Tulpin, {vi}183;
Ramper, {vi}161–2;
Venus in the Fishes, {vi}304, 338–9
Letters to {vi}160–2, 183–4, 204–5, 226–7,
238–9, 248–9, 265, 285, 292, 304, 338–9,
421, 431, {vii}50–1, 113–14, 139, 245,
286–7, 304, 327, 333, 335, 349–50,
354–5, 365–6, 374–5, 387–9, 408–10,
430–1, 438, 543–4, 566–7, 569–71,
603–4, 633, 642–3

Moleschott, Jacob, {iii}381

Molière (Jean Baptiste Poquelin), {viii}15
Le Bourgeois Gentilhomme, {ii}351;
Georges Dandin, {i}497;
Le Médecin malgré lui, {iii}395;
Le Tartuffe, {ii}351

Mollar, Miss, *see* Moller, M.

MOLLER, MURIEL, {vi}17, 334, 364, 368,
391, {vii}34, 274, 411, 493
Letters to {vi}351–2, 356–7, {vii}479–80,
584–5

Mollie, Molly, *see* Skinner, M.

Mollison, William, {i}138

Mommsen, Theodor, *The History of Rome,*
{v}465

Monaco, {iii}609, 614, {v}397–9, 417

Monasteries in the Levant, see Curzon, Lord
R.

Monck, Nugent, {v}576–7, {vi}30

Mond, Amy Gwen, Cannan's mistress,
{iii}90, 251, 534; marries Henry Mond,
{iii}486, 493, 500, 502–3, 664, {iv}159,
353

Mond, Henry Ludwig, marries Gwen
Wilson, {iii}486, 493, 500, 502–3, 632,
664, {iv}159, 353

Mond, Sir Alfred, {i}13, 152, {vi}280

Monet, Claude, {ii}263

Money Writes, see Sinclair, U.

MONEY, [NB production costs of, income
from, DHL's writings not included; see
under individual titles for details]
after college days DHL will write for,
{i}53; salary at Davidson Road, £95 p.a.,
{i}79–80; sister complains DHL not
sending money home, {i}143; DHL
'hasn't enough money to buy a decent

pair of boots', {i}171; father begs money from DHL for drink, {i}174; Louie Burrows' and DHL's 'wealth', {i}194; indigence delays marriage, {i}197, 199, 205–6, 230; 'magazine work' might generate income, {i}210; marriage dependent on £100 in cash and £120 (later £150) p.a. income, {i}223, 293; French holiday impossible due to lack of, {i}280; DHL supports family with, {i}283–5; calls on DHL's meagre resources, {i}286–7; success 'with literature' would increase income, {i}303; loan from Garnett, {i}337; during convalescence DHL not short of, {i}338; deduction from DHL's salary because of illness, {i}367–8; DHL has £11 when leaves for Germany with Frieda, {i}390; 'only enough money to run us a fortnight', {i}394, 401; 'at present I've about four quid', {i}408; 'we've got £23 between us'. {i}424, 430; 'enough money to live on, I think', {i}439; small loan to David Garnett to be ignored, {i}445, 451; Duckworth royalties will enable DHL to 'manage', {i}448; grievous 'to change good English money' for Italian 'trash', {i}464; if writing fails to produce enough, DHL faces return to teaching, {i}478; DHL has no sympathy for 'poor poet in garret', {i}501; will manage on £200 p.a., {i}502, 506; money from novels like manna, {i}511; DHL insists on paying Clayton proper rate for typing, {ii}30, 383; some deposited in Constance Garnett's bank account, {ii}42, 166; DHL ready to lend to Murry, {ii}45; short of, {ii}70, 82, 219, 510, 524, 527; DHL predicts £150 income for 1913, {ii}89; remonstrates with Murry about use of Mansfield's, {ii}110–12; £50 in bank, {ii}143; DHL not afraid of poverty, {ii}144, 162; friends help DHL to avoid being 'really penniless', {ii}213; 'we need little and spend little', {ii}214; £50 from Royal Literary Fund, {ii}223, 225, 228, {iii}227, 249–53, 263–5; 'I owe

£145 to divorce lawyers', {ii}226; none in Island scheme, {ii}259, 266, 272; present social system based on, {ii}280, 629; achieving social ideals requires breaking 'fetters' of, {ii}282–3; 'money spirit' must be killed, {ii}293, 376, 380; DHL depends on Pinker for, {ii}327, {iii}34, 135–6, 299; DHL faces bankruptcy over divorce costs, {ii}327–8, 346, 348, 354, 357; loan from Marsh, {ii}432, {iv}297; £30 from Ottoline Morrell, {ii}447, 593; £5 from Shaw, {ii}449; one of few things miners understand, {ii}489; Cornish live only for, {ii}520; Cornwall cheap for living in, {ii}533, 563, 574; from Amy Lowell, {ii}560, {iii}29–30, 34; '£15 between me and complete starvation', {ii}602; can manage on £150 p.a. in Cornwall, {ii}619–20; 'just enough to scratch along with', {ii}668; Dunlop offers, {iii}20; rat-like people respect only, {iii}21–2; DHL will borrow from rich not poor, {iii}46; sick of being 'up to the neck in poverty', {iii}75; 'plenty to go on with', {iii}136; 'a shy bird', {iii}163; DHL can't afford to pay for lodgings, {iii}190; all resources at an end, {iii}205–6, 209–210; £10 from Shearman, {iii}216, {vi}355–6; £5 from Cynthia Asquith, {iii}217; 'a conundrum', {iii}226; generosity from Ada Clarke, {iii}240, {vii}193; gift from Beresford, {iii}309–10; if DHL had £100 p.a. would never write again, {iii}311; world 'coldly indifferent' to artist's poverty, {iii}325–6; returns Kot's cheque, {iii}327; £20 from Marsh, {iii}358–9; $100 from American admirers, {iii}445; plan for financial partnership with Secker, {iii}458–9; 'I've got about £100..so am rolling', {iii}462; 'I am a sort of charity-boy of literature', {iii}475; sent for DHL's father, {iii}478, {iv}423; Cannan collects £75 for DHL in USA, {iii}502; costs of typing, {iii}514, 550; loan offered to Kot, {iii}560, {v}483, 558; current account

MONEY (*cont.*)

opened in New York bank, {iii}596; Mary Cannan offers £200 if required, {iii}678; DHL dreams of buying sailing ship, {iii}684, 702, 712, 714; 'doubt if I make more than £400 p.a.', {iii}734; 'money hogs..mostly Jews' in post-war Germany, {iv}33, 38, 433; DHL's English money almost gone, has dollars in USA, {iv}110, 152, {viii}70; royalties on German *Rainbow* for Frieda's mother, {iv}132, 136, 147; 'the blood of an Italian', {iv}162; cost of moving from Australia to USA, {iv}256–7, 260; better to travel, spend 'and feel one moves in life, than to sit still in nothingness', {iv}258; DHL's English earnings (a 'crust') about £120 p.a., {iv}299; £10 for Elsa Jaffe's children, {iv}311, 532; 'a fine cement', {iv}312; with £500 in hand DHL can lend, {iv}312; US strong because world wants its money, {iv}352; DHL's income tax statement, {iv}400; 'We're rather better off', {iv}444; prime concern for white Americans, {iv}452; DHL will pay half costs connected with father's death, {v}124, 126; Else Jaffe given DHL's earnings on German periodicals, {v}173; for sisters, {v}277, 405, 499, {vi}106, 234–5, {vii}69, 330, 366, 510, 594, 621–2; for Frieda's mother, {v}354, 489, {vi}616, {viii}80; Brett offered loan, {v}435, 441, {vii}27; inadvisable to 'make one's life out of', {v}489; £300 p.a. would be enough, {v}492; Voltaire's huge income astonishes DHL, {v}585; Italian peasantry have wages in kind, {v}609; tourism leads to 'endless money-grabbing', {vi}26; DHL manages 'to scramble through, but no more', {vi}90; 'the stake through the bowels of the societal suicide', {vi}99; Austrians don't 'struggle very hard to make', {vi}130; DHL offers secretly to pay Gertie Cooper £50 p.a., {vi}137; 20% tax on expatriate authors, {vi}142, {vii}26; DHL cannot afford to visit

Dobrées in Egypt, or make long sea-voyage {vi}177, 202, 227; 'money-fear and money-lust' must be rejected, {vi}240, 267, 280, {vii}99, 103–4; round-world voyage if money available, {vi}365, 367; offer to pay for sister to visit Gsteig, {vi}456–7; DHL demands recompense for signing copies of *Collected Poems*, {vi}472–3, {vii}297; 'I can't associate my pictures with', {vi}536, 546; 'I don't expect money success', {vi}608, {vii}38; 'I've got all I need', {vii}26; newspaper articles 'best way of making', {vii}41, 251; cheque for Giulia Pini, {vii}81–2; important to live 'within decent bounds of economy', {vii}93; 'a disease upon humanity', {vii}99; most men 'wage-slaves', {vii}103; making money 'the ruin of a man', {vii}121; DHL 'hates', {vii}179; Ada Clarke's generosity repaid, {vii}193–4; offered to Mohr, {vii}245; DHL ready to 'stand a few quid' to launch 'Squib', {vii}448; limited edns 'only way to make money', {vii}457, 462; sale of MSS would provide income for Frieda, {vii}459; DHL has plenty, {vii}476, 489, 505; Seltzer's debt to DHL of '$4000–odd', {vii}521; essential to be honest about, {vii}542; 'As I grow older, money bores me', {vii}547; Crosby corrupted by 'too much', {vii}607; writers who are 'mere incomes on two legs', {vii}615; £10 for Barbara Weekley's 'housekeeping', {vii}641; DHL resents exploitation by 'little Jew booksellers', {vii}647; loan from Sutro, {viii}12–13; 'always hopelessly poor' when dependent on writing, {viii}18

MONK, VIOLET, {iii}383, 385–6, 406, 413, 417, 449, 452, 460, 529

types first part of *Aaron's Rod*, {iii}724, {iv}28, 36; types 'Gentleman from San Francisco', {iv}58, 78–9, 87, 98

Letters to {iii}453–4, 589–90, {iv}98–9, 149

Monmouth (Monmouthshire), {iii}278

Monnier, Adrienne, {vii}397

Monologues, see Middleton, R. B.
Monreale (Sicily), {viii}53
MONRO, HAROLD, {ii}2–3, 68, 92, 180,
    {iii}261, {v}626
    DHL offers poems for publication by,
    {ii}53, 150, {vii}348–9, 352, 583; 'a bit
    of a fool', {ii}69; supports DHL's
    application to Royal Literary Fund,
    {ii}224; DHL doesn't care for,
    {ii}518–19, 525
    Twentieth Century Poetry, {vii}348–50
    see also Poetry and Drama
    Letters to {ii}53, 150, 427, {vii}349
MONROE, HARRIET, {ii}8, 18, 222, 509,
    665, {iii}8, 139, 141, 326, 634, 657,
    {iv}12, 330, {v}119
    'rather nice woman', {ii}167; DHL's
    poems published by, {ii}170, 202–3, 209,
    219, 417, {iii}325, {iv}307–8, 317, 381,
    {viii}22; DHL critical of, {ii}232–3;
    subscribes for *Signature*, {ii}394, 412,
    416
    Poetry: A Magazine of Verse, {ii}170,
    202, 209, 219, 416–17, {iii}99, 280, 285,
    304, 325, 331, 388, 399, {iv}290, 307–8,
    326, 381, 404, 540, {v}15, 87, {vi}10,
    327–8, {viii}22
    Letters to {ii}170, 202–3, 219, 232–3,
    393–4, 416–17, {iii}99, 304–5, 324–5,
    330–1, {iv}307, 317, 380–1, 404, 540,
    {v}15, 28, 115, {vi}327–8, {viii}22
Monros, Maruca Jarquin, {v}165, 203
Montagu, Edwin Samuel, {ii}54
Montague, *see* Mountsier, R.
Montaigne, Michel E. de, {i}306
Monte Carlo, {iii}624, 632, 636, 658, 664,
    {iv}80, 224, {v}10, 203, 357, 378,
    392–4, 397–9, 407, 417, 420, {vi}180,
    542
Monte Cassino (Italy), {iii}489, 514, 568,
    583, 602, 621, {iv}186, 194, {v}173, 240,
    255, {viii}38, 46, 49
Monte Diretto (Sicily), {iv}160–1
Monte Guffone, *see* Castello di Montegufoni
Monte Solaro (Capri), {iii}451, 454
Monte Venere (Sicily), {iii}498, {iv}158,
    160–1
Monte, Dr, {vi}22

Montecatini (Italy), {vii}356, 358, 363, 384,
    393, 407
Montenegro, {v}323, 373
Monthly Criterion, {vi}211
Montigny (Germany), {i}393, 400
Montreux (Switzerland), {vi}248, 285, 440,
    452–3, 456, 473–4, 487–8, 493, 502
Monty, *see* Mackenzie, E. M. C.; Weekley,
    C. M.
Moody, Dwight Lyman, {i}288
Moody-Manners Opera Co., {i}306
Moon and Sixpence, The, see Maugham,
    W. S.
Moore, Albert, {i}86
MOORE, GEORGE, {i}162, {iii}75,
    {viii}107
    reported praise for *W in L* from,
    {iii}191, 196, 232
    Esther Waters, {i}154;
    Evelyn Innes, {i}142, 154;
    Salve, {i}512, 524, 528;
    Sister Teresa, {i}154
    Letters to {iii}196
    Letters from {iii}196
MOORE, MARIANNE CRAIG, publishes
    DHL in *Dial*, {vi}46, {vii}257–8, 305;
    Pansies for, {vii}173, 196, 204
    Letters to {vi}46, (vii)173–4, 257–8, 305
    Letters from {vii}257–8
Moore, Thomas Sturge, {i}140
Moorgreen (Nottinghamshire), {i}116, 397,
    500, {v}243, 592–3
Moors, {vii}275, 367
Moose, The, see Herbert, Agnes
Morality Play Society, {i}364
Morand, Paul, {vii}42–3, 539–40
Mordaunt, Elinor, {v}522
Mordkin, Mikhail, {i}310, 429
Moréas, Jean P., {i}300
Morel, Auguste, {vii}396–7
Moreno, Stephano, {iv}233
Moret, Alexandre *Le Rituel du Culte Divin*
    Journalier en Egypte, {vii}515, 519, 534,
    539, 568–9
Morgano's café (Capri), {iii}438–9, 443,
    446
Morgenröte, see Nietzsche, F. W.
Mori (Austria), {i}456

Morier, James Justinian *The Adventures of
Hajji Baba of Ispahan, The Adventures of
Hajji Baba of Ispahan in England,*
{v}379, 386
Morison, Mary, *Lonely Lives,* {i}171
Morland, Dorothy, {vii}575, 618–21, 631
MORLAND, DR ANDREW JOHN,
{vii}12–13, 643, 652
persuaded by Gertler and Kot to visit
DHL, {vii}575, 605, 618–21; advises
sanatorium for DHL, {vii}623–34, 636,
639–40, 645–6; copy of *LCL* for,
{vii}631, 650
Letters to {vii}630–1
Letters from {vii}13–14
Morley, Frank Vigor, {vii}650
Morley, John, {i}4, 504
Morning Post, The, {ii}162, {iii}50
reviews of DHL in, {i}228–30, 420, 528;
adverse comment on Garnett's play,
{i}414; McLeod sends to DHL, {ii}135;
'frightfully *decent*', {ii}147; on DHL's
paintings, {vii}424
Morocco, {v}343, {vii}170
Moros de la Costa, *see* Huxley, A. *and*
Huxley, M.
Morrell, Julian, {ii}308, 360, 390, 434, 449,
463, 481, 488, 492, 502, 513, {iii}683
MORRELL, LADY OTTOLINE VIOLET
ANNE, {ii}2, 4, 9, 12–14, 205, 229, 265,
270, 277, 287, 292, 305, 347, 368–9, 377,
481, 514, 519, 525–6, 530–1, 545, 569,
598, 611, {iii}12, 270, 658, 683, 695,
{iv}33, 375, 387, {v}565, 569, {vi}3, 11,
17, 467, {vii}24, 55, {viii}16
admires DHL's stories, {ii}253–4; DHL
visits, {ii}260, 355, 427, 430–1, 433, 454,
456–9; urged to be 'nucleus of a new
community', {ii}271–3, 277, 372; visits
DHL, {ii}273–5, 291, 293, 442; and
Garsington cottage for DHL, {ii}276,
296, 308–9, 317–18, 323–5; introduces
DHL to Russell, {ii}276–8; and access to
Frieda's children, {ii}281, 287–9;
Morrells 'good, genuine souls–but not
fighters or leaders', {ii}302; DHL's
'philosophish book' offered to, {ii}303,

308, 312, 358–9, 556, 558, 580; reads
Rainbow MS, {ii}314, 319, 327, 329,
331, 338–9, 342, 351, 415, 435; scolded
for wanting to dominate, {ii}326; should
be linch-pin between Russell and DHL,
{ii}359; traitor to 'real truth', {ii}380;
Frieda 'abhors', {ii}398; 'a bond'
between DHL and, {ii}436; 'a big
woman – something like Queen
Elizabeth at the end', {ii}437, 448; gives
DHL £30, {ii}447; DHL and
Garsington, {ii}459–60, 465–6; encourages friendship between Huxley and
DHL, {ii}467–8; DHL gives *Ajanta
Frescoes* to, {ii}488; friction between
Frieda and, {ii}512, 517, 571, 591–2,
606; *Amores* dedicated to, {ii}521–2,
610, {viii}17; borrows from London
Library for DHL, {ii}529, 580, 597;
sends invalid foods to DHL, {ii}530,
536, 541, 557; gives DHL counterpane,
{ii}538, {viii}26; offers financial help,
{ii}593; 'her world is over', {ii}600;
very cool, {ii}612; DHL has 'done
with', {iii}23; and Hermione Roddice in
W in L, {iii}41, 44, 56, 95, 104, {iv}38;
'in a frenzy over the novel', {iii}87,
89–90, {iv}599; threatens legal chal-
lenge, {iii}109, 112, 220, 226, 317–18;
is loved as 'someone who is dead',
{iii}213; returns MSS to DHL,
{iii}229–30, {vii}459; DHL's tentative
approaches rebuffed, {iii}257, 260;
DHL repays loan from, {iv}297, 305;
writes to DHL, {iv}353–4; 'a little
faded', {v}559; Maria Huxley 'like a
very small edition of', {v}586; DHL
sympathetic towards, {vi}82, 375, 387,
406, 409–10, 438–9, {vii}164–6, 168;
correspondence resumed, {vi}394;
DHL justifies language of *LCL* to,
{vii}106; 'still coughing *a little* over'
LCL, {vii}110
Letters to {ii}253–4, 257, 262–4, 271–5,
278, 280–2, 287–8, 291, 296–9, 303, 308,
310–15, 317–20, 324–6, 329–31, 334–5,
338–40, 342–6, 351–5, 358–60, 362–3,

366–7, 371–2, 374–5, 388–90, 393, 415,
427–8, 434–6, 438–9, 449–50, 452–3,
459–63, 468–9, 473–6, 482–3, 488–90,
492, 501–4, 506–7, 510–13, 517–18,
521–2, 528–9, 538–40, 556–9, 572–3,
580, 591–3, 596–8, 603–4, 608–10,
656–7, 659, {iii}230–1, {iv}305,
{vi}394, 409–10, 438–9, {vii}105–6,
158, 164–6, 234–5, 248, 254, 623,
{viii}14, 16–18

Letters from {ii}253–4

MORRELL, PHILIP EDWARD, {ii}16–17,
253, 264, 302, 360, 390, 393, 434, 448,
476, 479, 490, 492, 502, 504, 512–13,
{iii}23, 112, 695, {vii}235

and proposed accommodation for DHL
at Garsington, {ii}309, 311, 324–5; asks
questions about *Rainbow* in Commons,
{ii}439–41, 443–4, 452, 456–7, 463, 475;
'sheep-faced fool', {iii}220; 'nauseous
Morrellity', {iii}270

Leaves from the Greville Diary, {vii}166,
623

Letters to {ii}324

Morris Plains, *see* Birkindele

Morris, William, {i}298–9, {viii}3

Morrison, James, {i}147

MORRISON, NELLIE, {v}454, 511, 517,
524, 534, 571, {vi}9, 61, {vii}274, 358,
479

introduced DHL to Brewsters, {iii}720;
DHL uses flat in Florence belonging to,
{iv}48, 81; and typing of *LCL*, {vi}245,
249, 252; ceases typing on grounds of
indecency, {vi}259–61; 'Dirty bitch!',
{vi}260; DHL objects to 'tone of
judgment', {vi}268; in 'green fury',
{vi}309; apparent reconciliation,
{vi}364

Letters to {iv}81, {v}454, 525, 572, 610–11,
{vi}112, 245, 249, 252, 259–61, 268,
{vii}34

Morte d'Arthur, see Malory, Sir T.

Mortimer, Mr, {iv}500

Mortimer, Raymond, {v}286

Morton, Nathaniel, *Chronicles of the Pilgrim
Fathers*, {iii}340

Morvah (Cornwall), {iii}128, {viii}25

Mosciano, *see* San Paolo Mosciano

Moscioni, Romualdo, {vi}85, 89–90,
{viii}104

Moscow (Russia), {i}443, 534, {iii}679,
{iv}96, 595, {v}363, 405, 461

Mosel, River, {i}395, 398, 413

Moseley (Birmingham), {viii}1

Moseley, Sir Oswald Ernald, {vii}161–3,
227, 238

Moserboden (Austria), {iv}75–6

Moszkowski, Moritz, {i}324

Mother Eva, {iv}576

Mother India, see Mayo, K.

Mother of the Fugovići, The, see Městrović, I.

Motley, John Lothrop, *Rise of the Dutch
Republic*, {i}37

Mott, Adrian Spear, {v}260

Mott, Herbert H., {i}76

Mott, Mrs Walter, {iv}502, 507, 509, 526

Mott, Walter, {iv}502, 507, 526

Motte, Madame, {ii}632

Mougins (France), {iv}49

MOULAERT, JEHANNE, {vii}487, 502,
591

'down on her luck', {vii}435; arranged
typing for DHL, {vii}541, 602

Letters to {vii}541–3

Moulaert, René, {vii}541

Moulaert, Sophie, {vii}542

Moulder, Mr, {vii}194, 202, 207–8

Moulin du Soleil, Le (Ermenonville), {vii}7,
115, 231–3, 241, 246, 284, 323–4, 471

Moult, Bessie, {iii}377, 389, 452

MOULT, THOMAS, {iii}376, 453

publishes DHL, {iii}376, 380, 387, 389;
reviews *T and G*, {iii}376, 513

Voices, {iii}376, 380, 387, 452

Letters to {iii}376–7, 380, 387, 389, 452,
513

Mount Sinai, {iv}208, {iv}210–11

Mount Tamalpais (California), {iv}290

Mountain Cottage (Derbyshire), {iii}235–6,
238–42, 247, 251, 259, 278, 287, 300,
305, 312, 334, 336–7, 339, 351, 354,
{vi}482, {vii}193

see also Middleton-by-Wirksworth

Mountsier, Mabel, {iv}316, {viii}1332a

MOUNTSIER, ROBERT ('MONTAGUE', 'MONTY'), {ii}475, {iii}11, 16–17, 540, 578, 601–2, 646, 721–2, 732–3, {iv}1–3, 5–6, 8, 10–11, 15–16, 23, 37, 45, 47, 52, 54–5, 58, 75–6, 79, 91, 110, 138, 153, 157, 159, 163, 173, 175–7, 182, 188, 229–30, 243, 248, 250, 253–4, 260–1, 264, 267, 269, 275, 282, 298–9, 302, 317, 337, 349, 360, 362–3, 369–71, 389–90, 395–6, 402, 409, 412, 428, {v}2, 16, 20, 33, 175, {vi}12, 95, 470, {vii}204, 375, {viii}19–20, 24, 39, 43–4, 49, 57, 79
subscribes for *Signature*, {ii}410; with Esther Andews visits DHL, {iii}24–5, 27–8, 64; '*very nice fellow*', {iii}36–7; questioned (as if spy) at Scotland Yard, {iii}65, 67–8, 70, 713; 'lovable' but 'old worldly male' underneath, {iii}93; DHL's agent in US, {iii}476–7, 504, 607, 650, 681, 690, 700–1, 705, 707, 709, {iv}29, 31–5, 65, {viii}35; copies of DHL's works for, {iii}485, 618–19; 'business' instructions for, {iii}544–8, 572, 575–7, 582–6, 591, 596–7, 605, 611–13, 626–8, 633–4, 642–5. 650–3, 656–7, 667, 673–5, 677–8, 692–3, 695–7, 714, 730, {iv}27–8, 36, 68, 85–6, 88–9, 95–6, 107–8, 130, 134, 144–5, 150, 155–6, 168–70, 178–9, 186–7, 196–8, 219–20, 245–7, 277, 300, 314–15, 318–19, 323–5, 328–9, 334, 336, 340–3; and Seltzer, {iii}635–6, 672; DHL seeks advice about USA from, {iii}667–8, 672–3, 678, 684, 688–9; urged to treat editors and publishers as 'enemies' and 'dirt', {iii}684, 689, 710; keen to acquire ship, {iv}25, 33, 49; visits DHL, {iv}49–50, 72; doesn't like *Aaron's Rod*, {iv}57, 66, 92, 116, 129, 131; 'rather overbearing', {iv}61; DHL requests money from, {iv}112–13, 121, 142, 149, 221. 232, 246, 256–8, 268, 277, 288–9, 291–2; friction between Seltzer and, {iv}315–16, 328, 367, 376, 382–5, {viii}58, 62–7, 72–3; arrives in Taos, {iv}366; DHL no longer feels friendship for, {iv}374; agency for DHL terminat-

ed, {iv}376–7, 380–1, 410; and DHL's income-tax, {iv}382, 387, 391–4, 400; 'finally settled with', {iv}406–7, 431, 464, 516, 521, 523, 534, 550, {v}128; DHL 'will have no more to do with', {iv}544; 'right' about Seltzer and DHL 'wrong', {v}127; accused of lying, {v}145; rebuts charge, {v}146; proposes anthology with DHL, {viii}59, 62; accepts DHL's dismissal terms, {viii}74–5

Our Eleven Billion Dollars, {iv}257

Letters to {iii}65–8, 70–2, 77–9, 83, 85, 88, 92, 476–7, 504–5, 523–4, 544–8, 566, 571–2, 575–7, 582–6, 588, 591, 596–7, 605, 611–13, 626–8, 632–4, 642–5, 650–7, 659, 661–2, 667–9, 672–5, 677–8, 684–5, 688–9, 692–3, 695–9, 704, 707–10, 712–15, 723–5, 729–31, {iv}24, 27–8, 36, 38–9, 41–4, 46, 59–60, 69, 74, 78, 80, 82–3, 85–6, 88–9, 95–6, 103–4, 106–8, 112, 126–7, 130, 134, 144–5, 148–50, 155–6, 168–70, 172, 178–9, 186–7, 196–8, 200–1, 214–15, 219–21, 227–8, 231–2, 235–6, 244–7, 252, 256–8, 268, 273–4, 276–8, 283, 286–7, 289–93, 295–6, 300, 306–7, 314–16, 318–25, 328–30, 334–6, 338–44, 348, 355, 358–9, 364, 374–6, 382, 387–8, 391–3, 400, 403–4, 407–8, 411, 427, 431–2, 464, 477, 489, 521, 534, 550, 569, {v}127–8, 145–6

Letters from {iii}626–7, 642–4, 685, {iv}328, 341, 387–8, {v}128, 146, {viii}74–5

Mousecliffe/Mousehole, *see* Ratcliffe-on-the-Wreake

Moussorgsky, Modeste Petrovich, *Khóvan-tchina*, {iii}179

Movers and Shakers, see Luhan M.D.

Mozambique, {iii}702

Mozart, Wolfgang Amadeus, {i}67
DHL's 'favourite composer', {v}570
The Magic Flute, {iii}181;
Seraglio, {iii}182

'Mr Joiner and the Bible', *see* 'Journeyman'

Mrs Caudle's Curtain Lectures, see Jerrold, D. W.

Mudie's Lending Library, {i}158, {ii}410, 589
  and *Lost Girl*, {iii}512, 517, 619, 621–2, 624, 647; and *W in L*, {iii}660; and *Aaron's Rod*, {iv}262
Mugello (Italy), {vi}605, {vii}305, 432
Muir, Edwin, {vi}46, 173, 342
Muir, Willa, {vi}46, 173
Mukerdji, *see* Mukhopādhyaya, D-G.
Mukhopādhyaya, Dhana-Gopàla, {vi}392, 485, 506–7, 510, {vii}170
  Caste and Outcast, {v}77
Mullan-Feroze, Dr Dhunjabhai Furdunji, {iii}603, {v}541, 545, 583, {vi}244
  wild party given by, {iii}313; treats DHL, {iii}340
Mulock, Dinah Maria, *John Halifax Gentleman*, {ii}162
Multatuli, *see* Dekker, E. D.
Mumba, see Heyward, D. B.
Mundesley Sanatorium (Norfolk), Gertler treated in, {v}9, 311, 516, {vii}12, 538; Gertrude Cooper treated in, {v}521, 536, 541, 545, 548, 560, 579, 609–10, 630, 632, {vi}25, 63, 69, 125, 137, {vii}538; DHL seen by Morland from, {vii}575, 605, 621
Munich (München) (Germany), {i}18, 385, 401–55 *passim*, 513, 520, 530–50 *passim*, {ii}74–6, 83, 97, 331–2, 334, 344, 348, 373, 505, 594, 658, 710–11, 717, 724, 28, 38, 40, 44, 49, 61, 78, 259, 390, 404, 574–7, 579, {v}26, 38, 48, 67, 92, 106, 503, {vi}58, 96, 100, 104, 112, 130–67 *passim*, 183, 187, 541, 551, {vii}11, 365, 431, 433–5, 438, 461, 466, 469, 474, 553, 558, {viii}105–6
  'easy-going and lively', {ii}66; 'town of pictures', {ii}69
Munro, Harold, *see* Monro, H.
Murdoch, Walter, {iv}517
Muriel, *see* Chambers, J.
Murillo, Bartolomé E. {i}124, {ii}97
Murray, F. E., {vi}512, 515, 532
Murray, George Gilbert Aimé, {i}141, {ii}384, 593, {iii}71
  'fearful fascination' of translations by, {i}525, {ii}130, 136

Bacchae, {i}261, {vi}24;
The Four Stages of Greek Religion, {ii}556, 558;
The Frogs, {i}525;
Medea, {i}543, {iii}24;
Oedipus, {i}261, 525;
Rhesus, {ii}136;
Trojan Women, {i}261
Murray, John, Ltd, {i}384, {v}588
Murray, Mrs, {vii}286
Murray, Scott, {v}137–8, 208, 247, 249, 251, 253–4, 264–6, 358, 395, 426, 429, 440, 442
MURRY, JOHN MIDDLETON ('JACK'), {i}507, 519, 546, {ii}1, 4–7, 8, 11–14, 17, 47, 53, 55, 83, 207–8, 217–18, 220–1, 226–7, 233, 237–8, 240, 246, 252–4, 256, 270, 274, 296, 308, 313, 323, 344, 357, 365, 382, 413, 427–8, 431, 435, 490–2, 499, 506, 508–9, 515, 521, 524–5, 530, 535, 539, 556, 571, 580–6, 588–90, 593, 606, 628, 631–2, 658, {iii}3, 48, 112, 285, 294, 317, 352, 356, 433, 435, 470, 486, 560, 573, 670, {iv}17, 20–1, 34, 283, 354–5, 386–7, 486, 539, 560, 565, 569, 571, 589, {v}24, 31, 36, 42, 47, 119, 343–4, 347, 349, 353–4, 362, 365–6, 370, 470, 483, 503, 531, 559, {vi}17, 41–2, 82–3, 155, 191, 212, 346, 357, 459, 511, 604, {vii}105, 201, 206, 618, 643, {viii}6, 86–7
  early career of, {ii}31–2; DHL offers money to, {ii}45–6; DHL 'sermony' on relationship with Katherine Mansfield, {ii}110–13, 160–2; copies of DHL's works for, {ii}173, {iv}377, 481, 500, {v}226, 372; witness at DHL's wedding, {ii}195, 198; stays with DHL, {ii}289–90, 292; 'one of the men of the future..the only man who quite simply is with me', {ii}291, 402, 501; publishes *Signature* with DHL, {ii}293, 385–91, 393, 397, 407, 411, {iii}84, {v}290, 295; DHL, Campbell and, {ii}301–3; has 'genuine side to his nature', {ii}359; distrusts 'political ideas, {ii}379–80; DHL proposes 'life in common' with Murrys, {ii}452, 482, 508, 533, 547–8,

MURRY, JOHN MIDDLETON
('JACK') (*cont.*)
555; philosophical differences emerge between DHL and, {ii}472–4; 'homeless infant', {ii}476; piqued over Heseltine and publishing scheme, {ii}548–50, 554; Rananim at Higher Tregerthen, {ii}564, 567–70, 572, 591, 594–6; DHL 'Blutbruder' with, {ii}570, 576; and conscription, {ii}597, 599, 601, 604–5, 616, 639; leaves Tregerthen, {ii}607–8, 610, 613–19, 621, 624, 627; DHL disillusioned with, {ii}617, 623, {iii}103; works in Home Office, {ii}647, 652; DHL wants to be free of, {ii}650, 661–2, 666–7, {iii}23, 28, 90, 117; 'small stinker..little muckspout', {iii}53–4; incapable of '*new* thought', {iii}63; loathed but DHL still 'fond of him', {iii}83; DHL's move to reconciliation with, {iii}127, 163, 300–3, 307, 309; DHL 'can't believe any more in', {iii}194, 343, 683, {iv}149; irony directed at, {iii}321, 339; edits *Athenæum*, {iii}332, 335–6, 344, 346, 349–50, 387, 663, {v}103–4; visits DHL, {iii}366, {v}326; 'David' (?) rejected by, {iii}428, 467; 'dirty little worm', {iii}467–8, 470–1, 541, 665, 675; threatens to 'hit [DHL] in the face', {iii}468; DHL insulted by, {iii}681; 'abject apologies' from, {iv}33; 'wet flea', {iv}38; 'too rotten to kick' over hostile review of *W in L*, {iv}79; 'patronising' review of *Aaron's Rod*, {iv}353; DHL's condolences on death of Katherine Mansfield, {iv}375; edits *Adelphi* and DHL's association with it, {iv}432, 437, 446–8, 481, 585, {v}17, 26, 94, 109–10, 116, 118, 170, 173, 242, {vii}400, 402, 437, 568, 575; *Adelphi* 'feeble..knock-kneed' with 'beggar's whine', but improves, {iv}458, 462, 480, 483, 500, 520, 522, {v}170, 231, {viii}81; may travel with DHL, {iv}544–9, 553–6, 559, 572–4, 576, 581–2, 598; 'an uncertain fish', {iv}554; 'seriousness..an awful disease in',

{iv}555; unreliable, {iv}593; remarries, {v}43; reviews *Passage to India*, {v}74; and Molly Skinner, {v}121, 351, 419; DHL's 'ways go wide apart' from, {v}143, {vi}195; 'introspective sentiment' the vice of, {v}170; and Brett, {v}202–5, 408; bitter denunciation of teachery of, {v}205–6; 'got Jesus badly, and nastily', {v}313; DHL rejects future connection with *Adelphi*, {v}368, 370, 372, 374, 380, 385–6, 389, 432, 451–2; spiteful about *Porcupine*, {v}375, 380; writes 'with sneaking impudence', {v}418; 'underhand', {v}453; 'defeated', {v}455; 'a pantheist: without a Pan..fryingpantheist!', {v}504; 'lamb of Jesus', {v}630; closes *Adelphi*, {vi}47, 55; 'Jesus' biographer and better', {vi}67; DHL 'can't stand *him* at any price', {vi}445; 'whines about poverty', {vii}55; reviews *Collected Poems*, {vii}144, 162–3, 165–6, 294; 'we belong to different worlds, different ways of consciousness', {vii}295, 302, 334; *Life of J.M.M. by J.C.*, {vii}484, 501; hypocrisy of, {vii}518; his belief that there is no God proves His existence, {vii}576; affectionately invited to visit DHL, {viii}8–10
Anton Tchekhov and Other Essays (Shestov), {iii}392;
The Bet and Other Stories (Chekhov), {ii}447, {iii}183;
Fyodor Dostoevsky, {ii}545, 646, {iii}318;
God: An Introduction to the Science of Metabiology, {vii}518;
Keats and Shakespeare, {v}322, 332, 335, 337–8;
Letters of Katherine Mansfield, {vii}55;
Life of Jesus, {v}313, 322, 383, 475, 504, {vi}67, {vii}484;
Pages from the Journal of an Author (Dostoevsky), {ii}545, {iii}53, 183;
Poems, 1916–20, {iv}114;
The Problem of Style, {iii}728;
The River of Life and Other Stories (Kuprin), {ii}562, {vi}174;

'A Simple Creed', {v}328;

Still Life, {ii}161, 356, 545, 548, {iii}53, 63;

To the Unknown God, {v}313

Letters to {ii}45–6, 110–13, 160–2, 171, 451–2, 464–5, 500, 507–8, 522–3, 533–4, 541–4, 548–50, 563–5, 569–70, 646, 661–2, {iii}113, 122, 127–8, 132, 332, 467–8, {iv}364–5, 375, 397–8, 416, 425, 432, 437, 446–7, 471, 480–3, 500, 502–3, 520–1, 551, 568, 572–3, 581, 585, 600–1, {v}16–17, 43–4, 99, 109, 121, 142–4, 150–1, 154, 162, 167–8, 170–1, 205–6, 310–11, 322, 328, 337–8, 351, 363, 367–8, 372, 380, 385, 463–4, 489, {vii}200, 294–5, {viii}7–10

Letters from {iii}468, {v}451–2, {vii}294, 437

Murry, John Middleton II, {v}463, 470, 475, 483

Murry, Katherine (Mansfield), *see* Mansfield, K.

Murry, Katherine, {v}322, 326, 328, 349

Murry, Violet, {iv}432, {v}43, 142, 322, 326, 328, 338, 347, 349, 353, 362–3, 365–6, 370, {vi}41, 47, 55, 191, 212, 445, {vii}200, 294

MUSIC, DHL feels 'current of [his mother's] thoughts like an uneasy quivering note of sad', {i}46; Verlaine's 'music before everything'; DHL 'does not 'worship music or the "half said thing"', {i}63; marriage should involve 'beauty of harmony..like Handel's, Schubert's, or Verdi's music, but *not* with Mozarts organ tones', {i}67; 'to learn about music..listen to it..Wagner's operas..will run a knowledge of music into your blood better than any criticisms', {i}99; 'Absolute music..has no more meaning than the wind..or cries of sea gulls over the low surf', {i}100–101; no 'ideational meaning to the *Pastoral Symphony* - or any other', {i}101; 'Swinburnian consonant music', {i}185; DHL at concert, {i}204, 219, 306, 322, {iii}514, 733, {vii}171; Sammarco in *Traviata*, {i}253; DHL sends (sheet?)

music to sister, {i}324; DHL dances to 'queer lively Italian', {i}537; Frieda's hired piano, {ii}107–8, {v}600–1, {vi}207, {vii}524, 541, 566; Weekley behaves in 'music-hall fashion', {ii}244; Kot 'groaned Hebrew', {ii}268; should give 'utterance to the sense of the Whole', {ii}448; 'Rainbow Books and Music' likely to attract 'good music and bad books', {ii}548; ludicrous concert by Starrs, {iii}158, {viii}25–7; 'fine Hebridean songs', {iii}164; Leigh Henry's poem needs, {iii}263; DHL 'preferred ..insect noises to ..all-too-human groans of the cello..can't stand..whining modern music..hated Bach..Schubert..Wagner.. Brahms', {iii}514; DHL seeks books of 'ordinary good songs with simple', {iv}373, {v}588; DHL's for *David* needs only 'pipe, tambourines, and a tom-tom drum', {v}557, {viii}98; 'My favourite song.."Kishmul's Galley"..composer.. Mozart..singer, a Red Indian singing to the drum', {v}570; Gardiner should encourage learning 'mass music..canons..wordless music like the Indians have', {v}591; Frieda 'strums' piano and sings, {v}600, {vi}207, {vii}541, 566; in Kurpark, Baden, {vi}207, 568–9; Baden music 'a little pathetic', {vii}382; '..wherever we go', {vii}408

'Music', *see* Henderson, A. C.

Muskett, Herbert, {ii}462

Mussolini, Benito, {ii}91, {iv}125, 353, {v}334, 342, 434, {vi}307, {vii}82

DHL ironic about, {v}427, 570

Mutzenbecher, Thesi, {vii}572

My Life and Loves, see Harris, J. T. F.

My Life, see Chekhov, A.

Mycenaean Tree and Pillar Cult and its Mediterranean Relations, The, see Evans, Sir A. J.

Myers, Ralph, {iv}422, 434, 438, {v}128

Mylor (Cornwall), {ii}14, {ii}608, 631–2, 637–9, {iii}127–8, {vi}511

'Mynie', *see* Reynolds, H.

Myron, *Discus-Thrower, The*, {iv}456
Myrtle Cottage, *see* Pangbourne

Nachtgeschichten, see Stoessel, O.
Nadegin, Nicolas, {v}407
Nana, see Zola, E.
Nancy (France), {iii}698
Nancy, *see* MacFarlane, N.; Pearn, A. R.
Naples (Italy), {i}145, 509, {ii}388, 31, 407,
    412, 414, 418, 420, 423, 428, 432, 436–84
    passim, 492, 494, 497, 519, 523, 527–8,
    533, 535, 540–1, 544, 570, 595, 633–4,
    673, 682, 687, 715, {iv}5, 9, 37, 58, 92,
    97, 104, 112, 114, 137, 165, 172, 177–207
    passim, 216–17, 227, 414–15, {v}135,
    184, 299, 305, 333, 364–5, 373, 386, 404,
    416, 421, 430, 573, 630, 645, 649, 653,
    {vi}23, 410, {vii}56–7, 67, 226, 264,
    532, 537, {viii}51, 53
Napoleon I, {i}114, 485, {ii}214, {iii}282,
    425, 679, {iv}99, 568, 587, {vi}114
Napoleon, see Trench, F. H.
Narcisse (dog), {vii}291, 472, 548
Narodiczky, Mr, 'little Jew' printed
    Signature, {ii}385, 387, 389, 397, 409,
    418
Narrow House, see Scott, E.
Nash, J. Eveleigh, {i}275, {iii}12, 111,
    {v}638
Nash's and Pall Mall Magazine, {iii}576,
    597, {iv}143, {v}481, {viii}33
Natal (South Africa), {vii}28–9
Natal Verses, see Croft-Cooke, R.
Nathan, George Jean, {ii}144
Nation and Athenæum, {iii}128, 663, 675,
    {iv}7
    'Whitman' in, {iii}247, {iv}55, 197;
    Murry reviews *Aaron's Rod* in, {iv}353;
    Murry reviewed in, {v}313; 'Smile' in,
    {v}351, 430, 504, {vi}270; 'Fireworks'
    in, {v}482; 'Mercury' in, {v}521; *David*
    reviewed in, {vi}71
    see also Athenæum
Nation, The (London), {i}366, 434, {ii}47,
    402, 446, {iii}307, 381, 663, {vi}52
    DHL published in, {i}323–5, 335, 375,
    444, 446, 459; *S and L* reviewed in,
    {ii}40–1
    see also Nation and Athenæum

Nation, The (New York), {iii}399, {iv}472,
    477, 500, 518, {v}301, 375, 513,
    {viii}58
National Bank of India, {iv}214
National Chase Bank, {iv}516, 521, 588,
    {v}18
National Coal Strike (1912), {i}366, 370–1,
    379–81
National Council for Civil Liberty, {iii}4,
    113
National Purity League, {ii}477, {iii}61
National Service, *see* Military Service Act
National Union of Teachers, {i}139, 204,
    301
National Union of Women's Suffrage
    Societies, {i}122
National Westminster Bank, {ii}189
Natividad, {v}177–8, 181, 203
Natural Man, The, see MacFarlane, G. G.
Naturalist on the Amazon, The, see Bates, H.
    W.
Nature, see Emerson, R. W.
Nature in Downland, see Hudson, W. H.
Nature Poems and Others, see Davies, W. H.
Navajo Indians (New Mexico), {v}82, 91–2,
    99–101, 109, 113, 134–5
Navojoa (Mexico), {iv}17, 501, 506,
    {viii}85
Naxos (Sicily), {iii}539, 631, {iv}139
Nayarit (Mexico), {iv}17, 511–12, 529
Needles, The (Isle of Wight), {i}134
Neilson, Harold V., {ii}17, 187, 201
Nell, William, {vii}286, 316, 337–8, 346
Nellie, *see* Allam, M. E.; Inwood, E.;
    Morrison, N.
Nelson, Horatio, Viscount, {i}114, {iii}10,
    509, 518
Nelson's Sevenpenny Series, {i}116, 153,
    172, {viii}19
Nencioni, {vii}314
Nerinda, see Douglas, G. N.
'Nest, The', *see* Sedgwick, A. D.
Neuchatel (Switzerland), {vi}345, 374, 550,
    {vii}80
Neue Merkur, {v}173, 189, 288
Neue Rundschau, {v}288
Neville, Ethel Gertrude, {i}373, 379
Neville, George Henry, {i}64–5, 68, 131, 172,
    175, 283–4, 289–90, 293, 325, 379

'Don Juanish fellow', {i}373–4; 'Diddler', {i}377; *The Married Man* based on adventures of, {i}386

Neville, James, {i}374

Neville, Sarah Ellen, {i}374

Nevin (Wales), {i}283–4, 287

Nevin, Ethelbert, 'The Rosary', {iv}102, {viii}25

New Adelphi, The, {vii}201, 334
DHL reviewed in, {vii}144, 162–3; Rebecca West on DHL in, {vii}252; 'Nottingham and the Mining Countryside' in, {vii}468

New Adelphi Library, The, {v}267, 460, 576, {vii}563

New Age, {ii}258, 366, {iii}129

New Coterie (Coterie), {vi}238
'Sun' in, and later separately by publisher of, {v}10–11, 352, 482, 505, 533, 571–2, {vi}270, 347, {vii}121

New Criterion, {v}459, 514
DHL's sketches in, {v}432, {vi}52, 189, {vii}462
see also Criterion

New Decameron, The, 'Wintry Peacock' in, {iii}474, 548, {iv}11, 31, 36, 103, 117, {v}606; 'Last Laugh' in, {v}20, 50, 59, 87, 606, {vi}175–6

New England (USA), {iv}484

New Forest (Hampshire), {iii}365, 384

New Freewoman, The, {ii}131

New Grub Street, see Gissing, G.

New Hampshire (USA), {iv}455

New Haven (USA), {iv}485

New Jersey (USA), {iv}471–8, 480–2, 484, 501

New Jerusalem, *see* Jerusalem

New Keepsake for the Year 1921, *The*, 'Adolf' in, {v}103

New Laguna (USA), {v}98–100

New Machiavelli, The, see Wells, H. G.

New Masses, {v}288
'Smile' in, {v}452

New Mexico (USA), {iv}5, 11–13, 20, 93, 95, 112–80 *passim*, 239, 251–91 *passim*, 322, 326, 344, 356, 376, 421, 465, 546–8, 555, 559–60, 562, 582, 596, 599–601, {v}3, 5–6, 157–8, 189, 197, 199, 221–3, 270, 312, 314, 395, 485, 581, 585, 587, 600, 616, {vi}5, 28, 54, 67, 72–3, 86, 155, 223, 227, 229, 240, 248, 254, 269, 278–9, 282, 301, 315, 317, 393, 437, 459, 498, 504, {vii}29, 55, 94, 108, 288, 485, 547, 599, 616–17, {viii}50, 55, 58, 86–7
DHL prefers Mexico to, {iv} | 440; preferred to New Jersey, {iv}477; 'tells on the nerves in the long run', {v}652; 'nostalgia for', {vi}31, 36, 58, 208, 296; DHL wants to return to, {vi}320–3, 325, 327–8, 332, 339, 349–50, 359, 508, {vii}175, 263, 290, 594–5, 624–5, 627, 629

New Mexico Quarterly, {v}37

New Numbers, {ii}136, 152, 155, 176–7

New Orleans (USA), {vi}11, 58, 74, 408
DHL seeks ship to, {iv}112, 114, 123, 125, 134–7, 142–65 *passim*; DHL in, {iv}469–71; 'I didn't like.. at all', {iv}473; 'broken-down.. melancholy', {viii}82

New Paths, {iv}31, {v}450
DHL's poems in, {iii}13, 202, 207, 218, 237–8, 261, 263

'New Poetry Series' (Constable), {ii}519

New Republic, The, {ii}655, {iii}156, 399, {iv}128, 338, 387
'America, Listen to Your Own' in, {iii}591, 644–5; Untermeyer on DHL in, {iii}595; DHL's poems in, {iii}596, 644, 675; *LCL* reviewed in, {vii}451–2, 525
see also Mallock, W. H.

New South Wales (Australia), {i}425, {iv}9, 228, 246, 267, 269

New Statesman, The, {i}167, {ii}38, 47, 450, {iii}381, {iv}3, 6, {v}340, {vi}270
'what a measly thing', {i}551–2; DHL's stories in, {ii}39, 44, 52, 58, 60, 64–5, 197; payment from, {ii}79, 82–3; poem in, {ii}106, 118; sketch rejected by, {ii}204–5, 236; DHL reviewed in, {iv}51, {vii}12, 447, 582; DHL protests about misrepresentation by Douglas, {v}395–7, {viii}49

New Statesman and Nation, The, {iv}20

New Testament, The, see Moffat, J.

New York Call, {iv}7

New York City (USA), {i}184, 186, {iii}5, 8,
27, 129, 140, 142, 159, 318, 348, 383,
386, 394, 400, 408, 493, 501, 508, 512,
520, 527–8, 535, 540, 544, 546–8, 559,
562, 565, 575, 582, 585, 597, 603, 632–3,
635–7, 640, 645, 664, 669–70, 672–3,
678–9, 688, 717, {iv}2, 7–8, 13–18, 20–1,
36, 67, 73, 107, 112–13, 119–90 *passim*,,
219, 221–2, 224–5, 241–87 *passim*,
324–405 *passim*, 579–84, 586, 591–9,
{v}1–3, 6, 8–9, 21, 23, 30, 55, 67, 71, 83,
85, 106, 114–15, 129, 132, 136, 141, 175,
211, 228–91 *passim*, 306–9, 319, 323, 326,
333, 343, 358, 385–474 *passim*, 511, 581,
584, 594, 615, 629, {vi}1, 10–11, 13–14,
16, 31, 74, 79, 175, 208, 211, 223, 230,
266, 269, 288, 310, 318–19, 325–8, 332,
374, 376, 436, 447, 525, 530, 545, 547,
555, 560, 565, 566–8, 575–6, 579, 591,
608, {vii}24, 26, 39, 44, 54–5, 68, 71,
94–6, 118, 134, 137–8, 145, 168, 170,
174–5, 182, 201, 204, 206, 214, 232,
239–40, 266, 272, 301, 308, 311, 315–16,
318, 324, 337, 342, 353, 367, 375, 390,
412, 418, 426, 429, 446, 472, 475, 485,
488, 490, 496–7, 502, 505, 515, 517, 521,
526, 530, 532, 538, 547–8, 550–1, 557,
560, 569, 578, 582, 586, 588–9, 594, 602,
617–18, 624–5, 644, {viii}4, 35, 72–3,
79, 82, 85, 87, 90, 108, 115
DHL anxious to go to, {iii}66–86 *passim*,
357, 362, 366–7; Mountsier DHL's
agent in, {iii}473, 476–7, 485, 566,
577–8, 607, 652, 667, 681, 690. 700,
{iv}23, 29, 49; DHL's bank account in,
{iii}577, 596, 612, 646, {iv}384; DHL
shrinks from 'witches cauldron of',
{iv}326, 364; invitations to lecture in,
{iv}352; Mountsier dismissed as agent
in, {iv}376–7; DHL arrives in: 'Don't
like it', {iv}471, 477, 487; 'great stupid
city, without background or atmosphere', {iv}479; Chicago 'more alive'
than, {iv}494; Supreme Court of,
{iv}501, {viii}71; DHL feels 'certain
disgust for', {iv}523; DHL returns to
pay income tax in, {iv}569, 572–3, 583,
588; urgent for DHL to see Seltzer in,

{iv}595–6, 598; arrival in, {iv}600,
{v}15, 17, 298–303; 'no better than
London..Humanly, rather awful', {v}18;
Curtis Brown DHL's agent in, {v}33,
127, 186, 188, {vi}29; 'weariness beyond
expression', {v}302; 'horrid, hot and
sticky', {v}304–5; London 'more
expensive than', {v}312; DHL and
possible exhibition of paintings in,
{vi}340, 343, 357, 378, 381, 383–4, 393,
434, 437, 445, 467, 469, 503, 506, 522,
536–7, 553, 557, 559, 564, 580; Curtis
Brown's office 'a bit of a failure' in,
{vii}439–40, 463, 522; Crosby commits
suicide in, {vii}600, 604, 606–7
New York Evening Post Literary Review,
{iii}13, 576, {iv}494
New York Herald Tribune Books, {v}301,
317
Sherman on DHL in, {v}272–3; DHL
reviews in, {v}319–21, 341; DHL
reviewed in, {vii}224, 395, 584
New York Sun, The, {iii}24, {vi}14, {vii}27,
134, 242, 324
Seligmann reviews *LCL* in, {vi}607
New York Times, DHL's telegram in,
{iv}379
New York Times Book Review, The, {i}19,
{vii}134
DHL reviewed in, {i}313, {ii}82,
{v}381, 387
New York Times Magazine, {iv}14
Forman on DHL in, {iv}187; DHL
writes for, {iv}329, {v}36
New York Tribune, Cannan on DHL in,
{iii}475
New York World, {iv}334
New Zealand, {i}194, 507, 517, {ii}31, 321,
{iv}11, 241, 249, 254–5, 264, 278, 283,
387, {viii}54
Newbolt, Sir Henry, 'The Old Superb',
{iii}558
Newbury (Berkshire), {iii}188, 226, 229, 275,
359, 375, {iv}79, {viii}27, 29
see also Hermitage
Newman, Cardinal John Henry, {v}180
Apologia Pro Vita Sua, {v}151
Newman, Ernest, {i}100

NEWSPAPERS, 'what a treat they were', {i}482; David Garnett to watch for news of DHL and Frieda, {i}484; Capt Scott 'more poignant' in Italian, {i}517; compared to English, Italian are 'ha'penny thin miserable things', {ii}135; from friends, {ii}162, {iv}332; DHL has connections with in Glasgow and Edinburgh, {ii}384; chauvinism of, {ii}626; state of affairs presented by adverse to publication of *W in L*, {iii}72–3; world represented by 'prancing about in a meaningless sort of nightmare', {iii}305; 'stinking..false and putrid' English, {iii}495; 'heavy ocean of printed slush' at 5 Acacia Road, {iv}171–2, 185, {v}347; '*flying* all over' Thirroul (Frieda), {iv}268; reviews of *David* in, {vi}75; of world available in Baden, {vii}538; easy money to write for, {vii}26, 41; create anxiety about DHL's death, {vii}318; DHL 'insulted' in, {vii}421, 427; 'Squib' intended to ridicule absurdities in, {vii}449

Newth, H. G., {ii}230, 238

Newthorpe (Nottinghamshire), {i}275, 500

Newton, William H., {i}64

Newtonmore (Inverness), {v}474, 506–13, 517

Newtons, {iv}446

Niagara (USA), {iv}490, 492–3
'beautiful, but corrupt', {viii}82

Niagara, S. S., {iv}267, 269

Nibelunge Not-Kudrun, Der, 'Nibelung Song', {iv}40

Nice (France), {iii}558, {iv}13, 127, 351, {v}10, 363, {vi}302, 382, 554, 557, 586, 589, {vii}14, 23, 30–1, 50, 69, 74, 76, 89, 93, 104, 116–17, 128, 132, 152, 183, 185, 190–2, 194, 202, 482, 529–30, 615
DHL visits with sister, {v}397–400, 417; DHL in sanatorium near, {vii}624–6, 629, 632, 635–6, 638–40; English nurse from, {vii}652–3

Nicholas II, Czar of Russia, {i}133–4

NICHOLS, NORAH, {vii}254, 260
Letters to {vii}286

NICHOLS, ROBERT MALISE BOWYER, {ii}442, 569, {iii}182, 212
'You are a poet', {ii}444, 448; 'nerves shattered at the war', {ii}445; DHL offers to have poems typed, {ii}446; DHL visits in hospital, {ii}449, {viii}23; writes to Hone on DHL's behalf, {iii}185; lectures in USA, {iii}280–1; DHL meets again in Mallorca, {vii}254, 260; gives DHL 'Bemax', {vii}286, 501; Huxley and, {vii}407, 608
Ardours and Endurances, {ii}442, 445–6, {iii}280;
'Before Jerusalem', {ii}443–4, 446;
'Fragment of a Poem of Vision', {ii}443, 445;
'The Hill', {ii}443–4;
Invocation, {ii}442–3, 445;
'Sonnet', {ii}443, 445;
'Spring Song of Marsyas', {ii}443, 445;
'A Tryptych', {ii}446
Letters to {ii}442–6, {iii}281–2, 377, {vii}286, {viii}23

Nicoll, Sir William Robertson, {vi}231

Nieder-Lahnstein (Germany), {i}398, 414

Nietzsche, Friedrich Wilhelm, {i}9, 545
Die fröhliche Wissenschaft, {ii}295;
Morgenröte (The Dawn), {ii}315, 317;
Thus Spake Zarathustra, {ii}546;
Will to Power, {ii}489

Nigger Heaven, see Van Vechten, C.

Night Thoughts, see Young, E.

Nijhoff, Martinus, {vi}501
Letters from {vi}501–2

Nile, River, {iii}670, {vi}300–1, 513

Nina, *see* Stewart, N.; Witt, C.

Nineveh, {ii}528, {iii}144, {iv}219, {vii}547

Niobe, {iv}510, {vi}23

'Nip', {iii}416, 449, 460

Nisbet, James & Co. Ltd, {ii}193, 216, 295

Nitria, Desert of, {ii}648–9

No-Conscription Fellowship, {ii}309, 551, 612, 656, {iii}6, 175

Noa Noa, see Gauguin, E. H. P.

Noah, {iii}604, {v}571
  and Flood, {ii}9–10, 330, 339, 663,
  {iii}620, 624, {vi}2, 155, 159; and
  Rainbow, {ii}16, {iii}183; Powys's 'a
  wooden Noah's-Ark world', {vii}256
  see also, Lawrence, D. H., *Noah's Flood*
Noelith, {ii}29
Nogales (USA), {iv}498, {viii}85
Noguchi, Yone, {ii}27, 61
Noli (Italy), {v}338, 366–81 *passim*
Nonesuch Press, The, {ii}321, {iii}279,
  {iv}575, {vi}174, 337, 376
Norbury Manor School, {i}84, 136, 194, 506,
  {ii}19, 48, {v}640
Norchia (Italy), {vi}89
Nordrach-on-Dee (Kincardineshire),
  {iii}632
Norfolk (Connecticut, USA), {iii}605
Norfolk (England), {v}311, 313, {vi}472,
  {vii}538
Normandy (France), {i}254, {vi}395
Norris, Frank, *The Pit* and *The Octopus*,
  {i}172
Norta (Italy), {vi}508
North American Review, The, {ii}26–7, 44
North Downs (Surrey), {i}128, 314–15
North Sea, {iv}72, 74
Northcliffe, Alfred Harmsworth, Lord,
  {ii}357
Northern Newspaper Syndicate, stories sent
  to and rejected by, {ii}40, 44, 58, 60, 65,
  67
Norton, E. Lucy, {vi}455
Norway, {i}174, 182, {ii}69, {iii}489, 553–4,
  580, 620, 658, 666, {iv}172–3, 175
Notebooks of Anton Tchekov, see Koteliansky,
  S. S.
Nottingham 1 General, {i}8, 10–11, 19, 22,
  27, 35, 43, 58, 67, 79, 99, 135, 138, 174,
  176, 183–4, 229, 244, 256, 258, 278, 284,
  287, 296, 319–20, 327, 334, 354, 376,
  382, 388, 391, 409, 508, 523, {ii}17, 19,
  54, 56, 76, 382, 384, 510, 662, {iii}109,
  114–15, 126, 313, 434, 595, 616, 723,
  729, {iv}19, 92, 261, 299, 342, 357, {v}9,
  13, 37, 243, 326, 366, 479, 499, 524–5,
  527, 592, {vi}47, 371, 540, {vii}261,
  {viii}55

slums of, {i}40; final meeting with Louie
  Burrows, in, {i}365–6; DHL meets
  Frieda Weekley in, {i}374; Weekley
  moves family from, {i}440, 448; Frieda
  visits to see Weekley, {ii}237–9, 241;
  munitions explosion near, {iii}262;
  'gutless, spineless, brainless', {iii}510;
  'I loathe the town', {iii}609; compared to
  Buffalo, {iv}492; DHL visits, {iv}553–4,
  {v}315, 530; DHL invited to lecture in,
  {vii}212
Nottingham 11 Localities etc.
  Arkwright Street Station, {i}296
  Basford, {i}116
  Brooklands Road {v}37, 80, 141, 150,
    247, 315, 323, 329, 413, {vi}69, 216–17,
    396, {vii}68, 232, 321, 327, 347, 461,
    557, 573
  Bulwell {v}366, {vi}97, 106, 287, 366,
    {vii}22
  Carlton, {iii}434, 579, 729, {iv}92, 261,
    299, 342, {v}37, 326, 366, 549, 631,
    {vi}47, 366
  Castle, {i}23, 136; Art Gallery, {i}29,
    278, 365–6
  Castle Gate, {i}21
  Castle Gate Congregational Church,
    {i}40
  Forest, {i}278, {vi}201, 592
  Friar Lane, {i}278
  Goose Fair, {i}21–2, 179, 302–3, 305–6,
    {vi}201, 592, 597
  Grand Theatre, {iii}509–10, 579,
    587
  High School, {i}4, 21, 23, 26, 64, 174,
    {iii}282, {vi}592
  Hunger Hill Road Baptist Sunday
    School, {i}376
  Lyons' Restaurant, {i}278
  Mapperley, {i}500, {vii}636
  Midland Baptist College, {i}44
  Midland Station, {i}296
  Paton College, {i}39–40
  Radford, {i}39
  Radford Congregational Mission, {i}39
  School of Art, {i}366
  Sneinton, {i}40, {ii}258; *see also*
    Brooklands Road

St Ann's Well Road and Edwin Street
Baptist Mission, {i}135
Theatre Royal, {i}55, 138,
University College, {i}2, 4, 6, 17, 23, 29,
30, 32, 43–4, 47, 53, 64, 114, 131, 142,
147, 301, 369, 514, {iii}282, {vi}618,
{viii}2
Latin required for Arts degree course at,
{i}31, 34; DHL's reading in second year
at, {i}37; DHL's disenchantment with,
{i}49–50; Weekley at, {i}51, 374,
{ii}154, 281, {v}347; 'Laetitia' written
in DHL's first year at, {i}72; DHL's
testimonials from, {i}73; DHL's
Teacher's Certificate from, {i}79;
'Botany' Smith at, {i}146; Louie
Burrows 'my girl' at, {i}193; DHL's
poems in notebooks from, {ii}478,
{vii}532; George V opens new building
at, {vi}474; German choir in Great Hall
of, {vii}87
Victoria Station, {i}320, 365
Nottingham Evening News, The, {vii}443
Nottingham Guardian, {iii}182, {vi}474,
{vii}212
see also Nottinghamshire Guardian
Nottingham Journal, The, {v}535
Nottinghamshire County Council, {i}54, 78
Nottinghamshire Guardian, The, {i}152, 229
DHL responds to advert in, {i}21; short
story competition in, {i}38, 142, 144;
'Prelude' in, {i}38, {v}86; Weekley
divorce proceedings reported by, {i}392;
Trespasser reviewed in, {i}425
Nouvelle Heloïse, see Rousseau, J.-J.
Nouvelle Revue Française, La, {v}444,
{vi}542, {vii}7, 183, 228, 272
Marcel's 'O aunty!' review of *LCL* in,
{vii}223, 397
Nouvelles Littéraires, Les, Levinson's review
of *LCL* in, {vii}601–2, 609–10
Novalis (Friedrich Ludwig von Hardenberg),
{ii}34–5
NOVEL/NOVELIST Jessie Chambers's,
{i}22; concentration, nothing
superfluous and 'feeling of inevitable-
ness' in best French, {i}91; on *Tono-
Bungay,* {i}119; novelist reading fiction

recognises 'inanimate dumminess' of
characters and demands 'life direct like a
blow', {i}251; difficult 'to get the action
of a novel hurried along', {i}266; Unwin
'open for a good strong', {i}458;
'Meredithy public' for, {i}511; DHL's
'novel-writing fit' replaced in June by
poetry, {i}551; DHL writes only 'one
novel a year', {ii}117; 'exhaustive
method' contrasted with 'pure object
and story' in, {ii}143; begun 'seven
times', {ii}161; diamond and coal both
carbon; 'ordinary novel' traces 'history
of diamond - but I say, "diamond..This
is carbon." ..my theme is carbon',
{ii}183; entirely new conception of
character, not 'old stable ego', in DHL's,
{ii}183–4; critique of Catherine
Carswell's, {ii}188; war 'kicks the
pasteboard bottom' of '"good" popular',
{ii}240; Campbell should get '*greatest
truth*..further than death, to the glad-
ness' in his, {ii}250; accuracy of realistic
detail important in, {ii}274; in excitement of creation DHL 'like a bird in
spring..amazed at the colours of its own
coat', {ii}300; has 'definite organic form'
when completed and not to be mutilated,
{ii}327, 370; whole truth of Jewishness
needed in, {ii}562; novelist 'sits, as in a
crow's nest', immune to external chaos,
{ii}601; new novel is 'stranger' to DHL,
its ending unknown, {ii}604; 'outer
world' unreal, novel reflects world of
'inner soul', {ii}610; composition 'like a
malady or a madness while it lasts',
{ii}656; DHL loves 'big and fearless'
world of his, {ii}659; DHL's will knock
'first loop-hole' in universal prison,
{ii}663; one of 'labours of Hercules',
{ii}665; writing should be restricted to
time of 'rising tides of strength', {iii}33;
requires re-creation of life 'into art',
otherwise 'journalism', {iii}35, 44; in
English language is supreme art of,
{ii}41, 54; 'living work' doomed in
wartime, {iii}100; production costs
militate against, {iii}231; comic novel

NOVEL/NOVELIST (*cont.*)
out of control 'jumps through the port-
hole into the unknown ocean' leaving
DHL 'on deck imploring' its return,
{iii}497; influence of lending libraries
on, {iii}512, 619, 621; spasmodic
composition like car 'breaking down',
fitful progress then 'all u.p.', {iii}567;
Australians have no 'insides' to write
novel about, {iv}246; article on future
of, {iv}377; DHL wants to write 'novel
of each continent', {iv}385; article, 'The
Novel', 'what I genuinely feel', {v}272;
good to review from standpoint of
'morality', {v}275; novelist lives 'so
intensely' with characters and recorded
experiences that 'better than the vulgar
thing people *call* life', {v}293; 'too deep
in bits - sort of bottomless pools',
{v}605; Upton Sinclair's *Oil*, {vi}102;
DHL aims to restore 'phallic consciousness', source of beauty and gentleness,
through, {vi}328; 'concerned with
human beings', drama with events,
{vi}338; death easy in novels,'never kills
the novelist', {vi}533; 'Character in a
novel' (poem), {vii}102–3; Dahlberg's
novel doesn't 'whine' or look to others
for 'help', {vii}129; language of novel
needs freeing from 'artificial taboos on
words and expressions', {vii}308; 'a
great lark, a novel after all!', {vii}574
see also DHL's novels by title
Novelle Rusticane, see Verga, G.
Nuku-Hiva (Pacific), {iii}65, 418, 549
'Numberless as the Sands of the Sea',
{ii}669
Numea (New Caledonia), {iii}418
'Nurse', {i}330–8 *passim*
'Nusch', *see* Krug, J.; von Schreibershofen, J.
Nuthall (Nuttall) (Nottinghamshire), {v}592
NUTTALL, ZELIA MARIA
MAGDALENA, {v}263
Mrs Norris in *Plumed Serpent*, {iv}421;
offers DHL house in Coyacan,
{iv}421–3; lunches with DHL,
{v}155–7, 236; *BBF* sent to, {v}246, 254
Letters to {v}155, 235–6, 246
Nuwara Eliya (Ceylon), {iv}217–18, 227, 266

Nyasaland, {iv}158
Nylander, John Wilhelm, DHL seeks
support for, {iv}172–3, 175–6, 195
'Die Frau auf dem Southern Cross',
{iv}173;
'Idyll', {iv}173;
'Jim Lawson', {iv}173;
Seevolk, {iv}172–3, 175
Nys, Maria, {ii}325–6, 360, {v}519, {vi}77,
246, {vii}21
see also Huxley, M.
Nys, Rose, {vi}120, 202, 286, 289, {vii}190,
487, 502

O'Shea, Katharine, *Charles Stewart Parnell*,
{ii}604
Oakley, Richard Bannerfield, {iv}364, 367
Oaxaca (Mexico), {iv}423, 545, 582, 596,
{v}3, 5–7, 23, 138–9, 144, {v}153–220
passim, 252–3, {vi}210, {vii}108
DHL arrives in, {v}162; 'perfect
climate: sun and roses', {v}164–6,
183–4; pronounced 'Wa-há-ka: like
tomato', {v}209; DHL seriously ill in,
{v}210–21, 229–31, 269, 282, {vi}310,
{viii}92; 'Wish we'd never gone to',
{v}235, 263–4, 273
Ober-Ammergau (Germany), {i}411–13
Obregón, Álvaro, {iv}465, 511, {v}59, 155,
{vii}108
O'Brien, Edward Frederick Joseph
Harrington, *Best British Stories of* 1923,
{iv}296, 464, {v}87;
Best British Stories of 1925, {v}270;
Best British Stories of 1926, {v}481,
{vi}151;
see also Golden Book, The
Letters from {iv}464–5
O'Brien, Frederick, *White Shadows in the
South Seas*, {iii}563, 566–7, 571
Obscene Print Act, *see* Obscene Publications
Act
Obscene Publications Act, {ii}16, 456, {iv}2
Observer, The, {i}225, 230, {ii}458, {iii}537,
638, {vi}617, {vii}41, 531
Occult (Occultist) Review, The, {iii}299,
{iv}171, 184, 365
Ocotlan (Mexico), {iv}459
Octavian Augustus, {v}342

Octopus, The, see Norris, F.

Odd Women, The, see Gissing, G. R.

'Ode to Duty', *see* Wordsworth, W.

Odette, *see* Keun, O.

Odle, Alan, {iii}244, {vi}54

Odle, Dorothy, *see* Richardson, D.

Odysseus, {vii}509

Odyssey, see Homer

Oedipus, see Sophocles

Oedipus, {i}449, {ii}1

Oeuvre de E. H. Brewster et Achsah Barlow Brewster, L', see Brewster, A. B. *and* Brewster, E. H.

O'Flaherty the Great, see Cournos, J.

O'Flaherty, Liam, {vi}283, {vii}3, 531; *Joseph Conrad: An Appreciation,* {vii}639

Oil!, see Sinclair, U.

O'Keeffe, Georgia, {iv}499, {v}319, {vi}14, 381, 506, 551, 559, {vii}24, 36, 138, 346

Old Coast Guard Station (Abbotsbury, Dorset), Murry's home, {v}142, 226, 311, 329

Old Lynell Farm, {iii}659, 668, 672
    see also Thrasher's Farm

Old Mexico, *see* Mexico

Old Moore's Almanack, {ii}609

Old Rowe, {viii}25

'Old Vicarage, Grantchester, The', *see* Brooke, R.

Old Wives' Tale, The, see Bennett, E. A.

Oldershaw, John William, {i}116

Oldmeadow, Ernest James, *A Babe Unborn,* {iii}75

OLIVER, NORAH DOREEN, {v}84
    Letters to {v}84–5

Oliver, Wade Wright, {iv}452

Olivier, Brynhild, {ii}230, 321–2, {v}475

Olivier, Daphne, {ii}230, 321–2

Olivier, Hon. Noel, {i}451, {ii}230, 321–2

Olivier, Lord Sydney, {i}451

Olivier, Margery, {ii}230, 321–2

Olivier, Sir Sidney, {ii}321

Olley, Arthur E., {vi}6–7
    publishes DHL's articles in *Evening News,* {vi}400–1, 403, 438, 460, 516; rejects article, {vi}521, 601

Olufsen, Ole, *Through the Unknown Pamirs,* {ii}631–2

OLWAY, JOCELYN,
    Letters to {vi}78

Oman, John Wood, DHL reviews *Book of Revelation* by, {iv}20, 583, 585

Omar, R.M.S. {viii}51

Omoo, see Melville, H.

Omptede, George von, *Lady Sofia,* {iii}532

One or Two Graces, see Huxley, A., *Two or Three Graces*

O'Neill, Eugene, {iii}423, {v}107
    Desire Under the Elms, {v}309

Onions, Oliver, *In Accordance with the Evidence,* {v}79;
    Whom God Hath Sundered, {v}325;
    Widdershins, {v}339

Oos, River, {vii}382

Open Air, The, *see* Jefferies, R.

Open Court Co., {i}306

Open Spaces, see Van Dyke, J.

Open the Door!, see Carswell, C.

'Opera House, An', *see* Lowell, A.

Ophelia, {iii}156, {vi}147

Oppenheim, Edgar, {iii}675

Oppenheim, James, {iii}357, {iv}407

Oppenheimer, Fanny, {vi}386

Oppenheimer, George, {vii}112, 129

Oppenheimer, Josef Süss, {v}388

Orage, Alfred Richard, {v}567
    New Age, {ii}258, 366, {v}457, 483, {vii}206

Orbita, R. M. S, {iv}17, 479–80, 482–5, 487

Orchard, Mrs, {ii}265

Orczy, Baroness Emmuska, {i}223

Ordeal of Richard Feverel, The, see Meredith, G.

Order of Silence, The, {iii}453

Orestes, {ii}107

Origins of Prohibition, The, see Krout, J.

ORIOLI, GUISEPPE ('PINO'), {iii}591, {iv}19, {v}11, 380, 534, 563, {vi}2, 4–5, 7, 9, 12, 14–15, 78, 257, 259, 337, 357, 363, 365, 372, 389, 411, 430, 435, 521–2, 543, {vii}1, 4–5, 6, 8, 10, 30, 82, 175, 180, 204, 226, 243, 258, 281, 344, 351–5, 381, 407, 414, 435, 438, 454, 456, 464–5, 469–70, 476, 494, 514, 522–3, 586, 591, 602, {viii}110
    invited to Mirenda, {v}450–1, 571, 602, {vi}88, 108–9, 249–50, 312, {viii}103;

ORIOLI, GUISEPPE ('PINO') (*cont.*)
DHL socialises with, {v}606, 611,
{vi}214, 368; and books for Mabel
Luhan, {v}619, 625, 641–2, 646–7,
{vi}37, 58–9, 101, 222–3, 476; Carletto
and, {vi}88, 249, 252, 261, {vii}63, 219,
230, 274, 561; goes to Vallombrosa,
{vi}111–12, 131, 494, 496; DHL uses
flat belonging to, {vi}116, {vii}358–68;
DHL seeks help over publishing *LCL*,
{vi}224, 289; 'All is ready! We can begin'
with *LCL*, {vi}307; MS of *LCL* to
printer by DHL and, {vi}315; forwards
proofs of *LCL*, {vi}328, 364, 369, 387,
412, 415–16; failed to see error in order-
forms, {vi}329; keen to publish after
LCL, {vi}342; responsible for despatch
of and payment for orders of *LCL*,
{vi}344, 346, 373, 375, 377, 382, 385,
390, 412, 418–19, 428, 433, 436–7,
448–51, 455–6, 458–9, 461–3, 465–6,
468–71, 475–82, 486–7, 489–96,
499–502, 511–20, 529–33, 535, 539,
544–5, 547, 552, 559–61, 564–7, 572–5,
579–80, 602–3, 607, 612, 617, {vii}24,
32, 35, 42–54, 57–63, 66, 68, 70–1, 75–7,
83–91, 95–8, 107–12, 120–6, 131–2,
134–7, 140–6, 150–5, 159–60, 171,
177–8, 184, 201–2, 233, 246, 253, 306–7,
320, 496, 650, {viii}110; arranges
binding of DHL's MSS, {vi}348, 359;
10% of profits on *LCL* for, {vi}381, 471,
475, 480, 533, 544, {vii}63, 178, 219,
230, 403; copies of DHL's works for,
{vi}396, 603, {vii}19, 300, 321, 339,
376, 493, 498–9, 548, 573, 588; banks
money for DHL, {vi}410; pays printer,
{vi}420; handles transporting of DHL's
paintings, {vi}432–3, 443–4; DHL
congratulates on appearance of *LCL*,
{vi}440; arranges false cover for *LCL* to
USA, {vi}525, 561, 575; in 'Lungarno
Series' publishes DHL's *The Story of
Doctor Manente*, {vi}595, {vii}395, 410,
415–16, 432–3, 446, 477, 492, 502, 536,
557, 560–1, 569; DHL's efforts to
promote 'Lungarno Series' for, {vi}596,
605, {vii}20–2, 416, 504, 527, 540–1,
548, 564–5, 578, 588, 595, 600; DHL's
concern about health of, {vii}33–4,
39–40, 42, 650; agent for DHL in sale of
MS, {vii}240, 306; visits DHL in Forte
dei Marmi, {vii}346, 348, 351; to buy
DHL's *Dandelions*, {vii}370, 460, 490;
DHL consults over 'public' edn of *LCL*,
{vii}383–4, 393–4; 'on the holiday
razzle', {vii}614; 'obscure satellite' to
Douglas, {vii}615; reprimanded about
behaviour, {vii}629–30
Publishes: *Apocalypse*, {vii}555; *In the
Beginning*, {vii}62; *The Last of the Medici
[Gastone de Medici]*, {vi}470, 591;
Nerinda, {vii}62, 141, 178, 246, 252,
274; *Some Limericks*, {vi}591, 598,
{vii}62, 134, 142
see also Davis & Orioli Ltd
Letters to {v}500–1, 516–17, 532, 549, 571,
602, 606, {vi}88–9, 104, 112, 116, 123,
131–2, 135, 163–4, 186–7, 224, 249–50,
273, 289, 306–7, 312, 328, 334, 359–60,
364, 369, 387, 391, 410, 412, 414–16,
420, 425–6, 428, 431–3, 440, 442–4,
448–9, 453, 455–6, 461–3, 465–6,
469–71, 475–6, 478–80, 483, 486–7,
490–1, 494, 496–7, 500–2, 514–20, 525,
531–3, 544–5, 559–61, 565–7, 569–70,
573–5, 579–80, 587, 590–1, 594–5,
597–8, 603, 605, 611, {vii}19–21, 32,
42–3, 45, 48–9, 56, 59, 61–3, 68, 70–1,
76–7, 90–1, 95–8, 112, 124–5, 134–5,
137, 140–1, 146–7, 150–1, 153–4, 159,
177–8, 184, 186, 201–2, 214–15, 218–19,
229–31, 246, 252–3, 273–4, 305, 320–1,
334–5, 339–40, 348, 354–7, 380, 383–4,
393–6, 399–400, 410–11, 415–17, 432–3,
446, 455, 477–8, 480, 492–3, 502, 526–7,
540–1, 548, 557–8, 561, 565, 577–8, 588,
600–1, 629–30, 642, 650
Letters from {vi}450, {vii}306
Orioli, Signora, {vii}400, 416
Orizaba (Mexico), {iv}416, 420–7, 432, 441,
471
Orléans (France), {vii}246
Orologio (restaurant), {vi}356
Orpheus the Fisher, see Eisler, R.
Orphics, {vii}544

Orsova, R. M. S., {iv}224–5, 227, 232–3, {v}80, {vi}335

Orvieto (Italy), {v}426, 453, 461, 465, 487, 650, {vi}42–3, 48, 75, 79, 86, 88–9, 93–4, 182, 302, 508, 538, 566

Osborne House (Isle of Wight), {i}134

Osborne, Walter Carl Henry, {v}48, {vii}553, 599

Oscar II, {ii}475

Osgood, J. R., {iv}200

Osiris, {ii}454, {vi}301, {vii}519

Ossendowski, Ferdinand Antoni, *Beasts, Men and Gods*, {iv}586, {v}77

Ossiacher, Lake (Austria) {vi}108, 111, 116–19, 122–6, 129, 131

Ostend (Belgium), {v}324, 502–3

Osteria Hotel (Vingone), {vi}31, 34–5, 37–8, 407

Osterley, R. M. S., {iv}5–8, {iv}177–217 *passim*, 243, {viii}51

Ostia (Italy), {viii}101

Otero-Warren, Maria Adelina ('Nina') Emelia, {v}108

Otford (Kent), {iii}372–3, 375

Ott/Ottoline, *see* Morrell, Lady O.

Otway, Eva M., {vi}391–2, 475, {vii}90

Ouida (Marie Louise de la Ramée), {vi}37

Our Eleven Billion Dollars, see Mountsier, R.

Ouspensky, Peter, {iv}568, 573

Outer Hebrides, {v}474

Outlines, see Collings, E. H. R.

Outlook, {ii}38

Overtoun, Lord (John C. White), {vi}231

Ovid, {iii}242

Oxford (Oxfordshire), {ii}355, 461, {iii}149, 257, {iv}103, 159, 169, 300, {v}49, 558–9, {vi}30

Oxford Book of Ballads, {viii}69

Oxford Song Book, The, {iii}279, {iv}373, {v}588, {viii}69

Oxford University, {i}4, 122, 146, {ii}2, 32, 48, 105, 253, 319, 442, 445, 472, 477, 593, {iii}202, 287, 585, {v}562
    perhaps harmed Murry, {ii}112; Ghiselin at, {vii}118, 120, 124, 127, 137, 158, 181, 264

Oxford University Press, {iii}14, 121, 474, 480, {iv}31, {v}180, {vii}502, 504

Collins on staff of, {ii}447, 483, 653, {iii}194, {v}26, 32, {vii}90, 585; publishes *Movements*, {iii}261–2, 269, 308, 321, 323, 326, 533, 576, 612, 622, 696, 701, 707, 710, 713, 725; Ely on staff of, {iii}276, 724; Milford and Ely insist on nom de plume for *Movements*, {iii}326, 634, 651; 'They are slow', {iii}634; with Medici Society, 'Art Pictures for Children' tentatively proposed by, {iii}714, 723. 725, 730. {iv}24–6, 48; illustrated edn of *Movements* by, {v}26, 32, 87, 105, 117, 120–1, 133, 136, 150, 224, 272; DHL visits Milford at London office of, {v}322, 324; publishes Irish edn of *Movements*, {v}324, 336, 555

Oxted (Surrey), {i}311, {ii}22–3

P.E.N., {v}3, 187, {vi}184
    DHL joins 'club', {v}88; DHL feted in Mexico City by, {v}157; supports fund-raising by, {vii}196; renews membership of, {vii}458
Letters to {vii}196

P.I.M.,
Letters to {ii}487

Pach, Walter, {viii}69–70

Pacific Islands, *see* Pacific Ocean; South Sea Islands

Pacific Ocean, {ii}639, {iii}579, {iv}239, 256, 272, 278, 285, 292, 433, 437, 440, 509, 534, {v}167
    DHL longs for voyage to, {ii}527, 529, {iii}25, 65, 67, 78, 80, 83, 417–18, 504, {iv}25, 483, 497, 499; wants to approach USA from, {iv}95, 126, 225, 228, 246; 'Wyewurk' on edge of, {iv}247, 249, 251–4, 261, 268, 270–1; 'almost unearthly and quite inhuman' light from vastness of, {iv}510–11
see also South Seas

Paddy, *see* Dunlop, M. H.

Padstow (Cornwall), {ii}484–519 *passim*, 529, 536, 551, 559, {iii}160

Padua (Italy), {iv}189, {v}597

Padworth (Berkshire), {v}426, 443, 505, 564, 568, 602, {vi}42, 486, 494, {vii}151, 416

Paestum (Pesto) (Italy), {v}343
Pagany, see Johns, R.
Page, George H., {i}176
Pages from the Journal of an Author, see
    Dostoievsky, F.
Paget, Miss, {ii}333
Paget, Violet, *see* Lee, V.
Pagliacci, see Leoncavallo, R.
Pago Pago (Samoan Islands), {iv}259, 287
Pain, Barry, {i}74
PAINTING, 'enjoying myself immensely'
    with water-colour landscape, {i}88–9; an
    'amusement', {i}94; DHL's intense
    response to, {i}103; Academy Winter
    Exhbition 'full of magnificent', {i}116,
    120; 'old' pictures show 'divine sorrow
    of fruitfulness', new 'cruel sorrow of
    destruction', {i}124; water-colour
    decorations on DHL's Christmas card,
    {i}149; scenery for school play, {i}186;
    DHL copies 'impressionist, decorative',
    {i}196; Jones 'paints like a bird pecking
    crumbs off the dorstep', {i}207; 'when I
    can write I can't paint, and vice versa',
    {i}245; sketching in water-colour
    'healing', copying is 'soothing.. refresh-
    ing', {i}491; 'silly experiments in the
    futuristic line', {ii}263; picture impossi-
    ble from 'geometric figures..Painting is
    not architecture', {ii}263; on boxes,
    {ii}287; DHL uses Rowney's paints,
    {ii}306; 'stark truth' essential whether
    'paint or books or life', {ii}657; 'obsceni-
    ty..the truth of our passion today'
    therefore 'only stuff of art', {ii}660;
    'painter's emerald green..beautiful
    shade', {iii}44; 'much subtler than
    sculpture..finer medium', {iii}46; during
    convalescence DHL 'happy to paint',
    {iii}341; 'not *my* art', only 'amusement',
    {iii}342, {v}590, 599; 'no serious work,
    but painting a picture', {iii}624;
    Australian lanscape recalls, {iv}265;
    Tuscan landscape 'very paintable, so
    many nooks', {v}473, 617; domestic,
    {v}474, 563, 568, 571, 588; 'fun' to paint
    'one's own ideas and..feelings.. change
    from writing', {v}585; 'suddenly

interests me seriously', {v}595; costs less
    and might pay better than writing,
    {v}601, 619; 'more fun and less soul-
    work than writing', {v}620–1; critique of
    Magnelli's, {v}629, {vi}62; Persian,
    {vi}154; Alpine stark whiteness 'offends
    the painter' in DHL, {vi}277; nude
    photographs useful for 'water-colour
    studies', {vi}302, 318, 506; 'gone clean
    off', {vi}311; DHL 'not fond of water-
    colour', {vi}357; Dorothy Warren on
    DHL's, {vi}523; DHL can't associate
    his paintings with money, {vi}536;
    'something very dramatic about paint',
    {vi}543; 'proper place' necessary for,
    {vii}25–6; 'thought of the Great British
    Public' puts DHL off, {vii}505
Palace Hotel (San Francisco), {iv}287–92,
    314
Palazzo Atenasio, {viii}48
Palazzo Cimbrone (Ravello), {v}406, {vi}49,
    56
    'a bit too much of a good thing', {v}648;
    'Grimthorpe's place', {v}651; Brewsters
    stay in, {v}651, 655, {vi}61, 80, 89, 107,
    123, 132–3, 155, 211, {viii}100; DHL
    visits Brewsters in, {v}657, {vi}21–5;
    'full of junk and statuosities', {vi}43;
    statues in grounds of, {vi}126
Palazzo Ferraro (Capri), {iii}438–78 *passim*,
    {v}344
    DHL describes apartment and location,
    {iii}442–3, 446, 451
Palenque (Mexico), {iii}144
Palermo (Sicily), {iii}469, 506, 526, 541, 570,
    656, 662, 673, 678, 682–4, 687, 689, 696,
    701–2, 715, 730, {iv}35, 111–12, 114,
    125, 127, 138, 148, 150, 154, 156–8, 163,
    194–5, 198–200, 414–15, {v}299, 427,
    {viii}52
    US Consulate in, {iii}629, 648, 651, 653,
    {iv}107, 264, 391, {viii}53
Palestine, {iii}8, 346, {vii}377
    Eder and, {iii}150, 214, 245, 332, 511,
    687, 716; DHL's interest in, {iii}316,
    332–4, 336, 340, 689; DHL's advises
    Eder about, {iii}353–4
Palestine Zionist Commission, {iii}150, 716

Pall Mall Magazine, {iii}459, {vi}270, 348

Palm Springs (USA), {iv}14, 372–3, 390, 392, 403, 430, 476, 481, 498, 504–5, 537, 567, {viii}85–6

Palma (Mallorca), {vii}197, 250–338 *passim*, 346, 355, 358

PALMER, CECIL, {iii}12
   possible publisher for *W in L*, {iii}129, 135, 137, 147–8, {viii}27; returns MS of novel, {iii}149, 151; and 'At The Gates', {iii}152–3; asks to see MS of *SCAL*, {iii}556, 563, 565, 572, 576–8, 582–3
   Letters to {iii}151–2, 556, 577–8

Palmer, John Leslie, {ii}254

Palms, see Weatherwax, I.

Palumbo, *see* Hotel Palumbo

Pam, *see* Reynolds, P.

Pamela, *see* King, E. U.

Pamela, or Virtue Rewarded, see King, E.U.; Richardson, S.

Pamphlet Poets, see Bynner, H. W.

Pan, {iv}556
   Stephens belittles, {ii}114; critique of Forster's presentation of, {ii}275–6; in DHL's 'The Last Laugh', {v}50; and DHL in Brett's painting, {v}348, {vi}23–4; Murry and, {v}504
   see also Lawrence, D. H., 'Pan in America'

Panama Canal, {iv}126, 529

Pandora Books, {iii}715, {iv}117–18

Pangbourne (Berkshire), {iii}377–87, 414, 521, 580, {v}475

Pankhurst, Christabel, {i}123

Paoli, Pietro di, {i}453–4, 458

Papa, see Akins, Z.

Papeete (Tahiti), {iv}254–5, 259, 303
   'dead, dull, modern', {iv}285–6; 'spoilt', {viii}55

Paquin, Isidore, {v}622

Paradise Lost, see Milton, J.

Paradise, {i}111, 165, 430, {ii}415, 452, {iii}296, {iv}565, {v}199, {vi}15, 96, 138, 190, 196, 367
   childhood's, {i}97, 195; Jophiel at gate of, {ii}242; bird of, {ii}254. 643, {vii}207; USA not a, {iii}70, 160, {v}278, {vii}94; 'Germany a bit of a fool's', {iii}680; allegedly once existed in Ceylon, {iv}185–6, 207; Mt Sinai 'like something dreadful, between man and his lost', {iv}211–12; Chapala is, {iv}435; Syra is Brewster's, {v}586; Baden not, {vi}185; Juliette Huxley's embroidery and, {vi}313, 316; Gaelic serpent imagined in, {vi}334
   see also Lawrence, D. H., *Flight Back into Paradise* and *Throwing Back the Apple*

Paraf, Robert, {vii}341

Paraguay, {iii}173–4

Pareto, Vilfredo, {vi}214

Parigi, see Viani, L.

Paris (France), {i}55, 165, 254, 301, 500, {ii}54, 110, 124, 139–40, 157, 171, 214, 263, 303, 311, 329, 360, 561, 632, {iii}183, 412, 415–16, 424, 516, 541, 569, 658, 679, 682, 687, 698, 711, {iv}13, 19–20, 61, 74, 78, 89, 141, 166–7, 275, 351, 404, 407, 592, {v}67, 264, 282, 294, 316–17, 319, 321–2, 324, 327, 378, 390, 410, 433–4, 439, 441–2, 450, 461–2, 473, 526, 528, 532–4, 538–45, 557, 564, 572, 622, {vi}101, 112, 135, 163–4, 323, 349, 361, 402, 405, 419, 422, 428, 434, 436–9, 445, 448, 461–2, 473, 499, 503, 505–6, 529, 549, 556, 574–5, 579–80, 591, 609, 614, {vii}1, 4, 7–9, 13, 15, 17, 43–4, 50, 64, 105, 113, 118–20, 126–8, 139, 155, 160, 163, 168, 175–8, 181–2, 190, 193, 202, 251, 264–5, 286, 314, 316, 321, 323, 334–5, 346–7, 359, 385, 398, 401, 408, 415–16, 425, 432, 444, 460, 470, 486–8, 495, 501, 509, 515, 519, 521, 535–6, 543, 545, 558–9, 561–2, 565, 571, 584, 586, 588, 601, 606, 644, 652–3, {viii}35, 43–4, 97–8, 100, 107
   Mansfield and Carco in, {ii}270, 289, 291, 296, 308, 313, 333; Conard might publish *Rainbow* in, {ii}453, 458–9, 464; Esther Andrews in, {iii}140, 142, 159; 'Matisse crowd' in, {iii}362; 'nasty city', {iii}417; Cannan in, {iii}493; Mountsier in, {iii}522–3, 540, 566, 575, 707, 710, 713, 715, 721, 723, {iv}28, 36, 39, 41–2, 44, 46, 72, 76, 79, 85–6; Millicent

Paris (France) (*cont.*)
  Beveridge in, {iii}683, 686, 701,
  {v}435, 517; Juta in, {iv}366; Mansfield
  buried near, {iv}385; DHL to, {iv}542,
  544–50, 553, 555, 558–75, 579–84,
  587–91, 596, {v}545–7; 'better than
  London', {iv}561–7, 578; Sylvia Beach
  in, {v}457, {vi}489, {vii}98, 115, 131,
  142–3; 'modernissimo periodical'
  transition from, {vi}507; 'steady orders'
  for *LCL* from, {vi}547; *Sun* produced
  by Black Sun Press in, {vi}570,
  {vii}145, 240, 243, 308, 342; Huxleys at
  Suresnes near, {vii}27, 34; pirated edns
  of *LCL* sold in, {vii}55–8, 62, 67, 162,
  212, 234; Pegasus Press in, {vii}95,
  109–10, 115, 159; DHL visits about edn
  of *LCL* to undercut pirates,
  {vii}207–47; DHL stays with Huxleys,
  {vii}218–28; 'dirty air' of, {vii}221,
  225, 227, 238; DHL meets writers in,
  {vii}223, 225, 228; 'doesn't suit' DHL,
  {vii}227, 229, 234, 293, 295; Titus and
  Paris edn of *LCL*, {vii}229–30, 232–3,
  244, 268, 274, 355, 390, 392, 395–6,
  452, 455, 464, 471, 525, 551, 597; 'no
  longer gay - no élan', {vii}238; Bradley
  and translation rights to *LCL* in,
  {vii}245, 273, 297; 'city of dreadful
  night', {vii}248; Black Sun edn of
  Escaped Cock from, {vii}412, 429, 445,
  496, 516, 525, 528, 530–2, 582, 604,
  607, 644
Parke, Mr, {vii}551, 586
Parker, Sir Gilbert, *The Trespasser*, {i}379
Parker, W. G., {ii}28, 99
Parliament, {i}266, {ii}264, 463, 557,
  {iii}56, 107–8, 116, 118, 227, 716,
  {vii}204, 214, 304, 315, 569
  Parliamentary Reform Bill, {i}420
Parma (Italy), {ii}78, 93, 124, 139–40,
  {v}433
Parmenter, Dr John, {v}424, 462, 486
Parnell, Charles Stewart, *see* O'Shea, K.
Partage de l'enfant, Le, see Daudet, L.
Partridge, Eric, {vii}3
Partridge, Ralph, {ii}508
Pasquale, {iii}606

Passage to India, A, see Forster, E. M.
'Passion-Vine', *see* Lowell, A.
Passmore, Walter, {vi}567, 579
Pastoral Symphony, see Beethoven, L.von
Pater, Walter, {ii}111, 138
Pathfinder, The, see Cooper, J. F.
Patmore, Derek, {vii}151
PATMORE, ETHEL ELIZABETH
  ('BRIGIT'), {vi}18
  prototype for Clarissa Browning in
  Aaron's Rod, {v}589; on Ile de Port-
  Cros, {vi}590, 592–3, 596, 600, 604,
  {vii}17; and Aldington, {vi}590,
  {viii}112; typed *Rawdon's Roof*,
  {vii}66; stores copies of *LCL*, {vii}90,
  112, 121, 124–6, 134, 140, 142–3, 146–7;
  copies seized by police from, {vii}151,
  153
  Letters to {v}589, {vii}126, 143
Patmos (Turkey), {iii}395, {vii}524
Paul et Virginie, see St Pierre, B. de
'Paul Morel', *see* Lawrence, D. H., *Sons and
  Lovers*
Paulhan, Jean, {vi}542, {vii}17, 183
Pauvre Fauvette, see Bastien-Lepage, J.
Pavlova, Anna M., {i}310, 429, 519, {ii}68
PAWLING, SYDNEY S., {i}14, 148, 158
  and *White Peacock* ('Nethermere'),
  {i}158–9, 169–70, 194, 200, {viii}3–4;
  sends cheque, {i}177; and *Trespasser*,
  {i}182–7, 200, {viii}4–5
  Letters to {i}158–9, 177, 184–7, {viii}3–5
  Letters from {i}177
Payne, Ben Iden, {i}344, 384, 386, 389,
  414
Paz, Magdeleine, *Woman*, {iii}662, 733
Peabody, Josephine Preston, *Harvest Moon*,
  {iii}99
Peacock Hotel (Rowsley), {v}321
Peacock Pie, see De la Mare, W. J.
Peacock, Percy, {ii}409
Peacock, Walter, {iii}385, 396, 425, 485
Pearl, Cora, {vi}61
PEARN, ANNIE ('NANCY') ROSS, {v}2,
  388, 424, 449, 545, 581, 595, {vi}4, 6–8,
  71, 130, 136–7, 140, 154, 217, 269, 272,
  305, 465, 524, 565, 597, 617, {vii}1, 6,
  15, 77, 131, 136, 189, 198, 257, 272,

348–9, 391, 400, 405, 430, 500, 513, 536, 549, 568, 585, {viii}103
places DHL's stories, articles etc with publishers, {v}50, 57–8, 86, 109, 180, 430, 590, 657, {vi}84, 176, 232, 461, {vii}269, 390; DHL relies on judgment of, {v}109, 118, 149, 242, 452, 498, 551, 613–14, 620, {vi}29, 40, 54, 70, 120, 200, 226, 401, 463–4, 541, {vii}118, 285, 554; defends DHL's interests, {v}341, 360, 482; Curtis Brown's 'golden..magazine girl', {v}459, {vi}245; meets DHL and Frieda, {v}505, 513; disapproves of *LCL*, {vi}21, 29, 222, 347; enthusiast for 'Flowery Tuscany' articles, {vi}52, {vii}185, 462; thought *David* 'tremendously well done', {vi}70; use of Mirenda offered to, {vi}128, 134–5, 139, 144, 152, 157, 165, 167, 199, 252; 'didn't like Firenze', {vi}170; encourages DHL to re-write story for sale of MS, {vi}347; encourages DHL as journalist, {vi}401; her '"periodical" efforts' important to DHL's income, {vi}438; addresses DHL as 'Dear darling Mr Lawrence', {vi}464; advocated broadcasting as 'useful and dignified bit of publicity', {vi}552; *Collected Poems* for, {vii}23, 29; MS of *Pansies* 'strictly privately for you and your use', {vii}51, 65, 124, 195; present for, {vii}94; DHL extracts in Soroptomist magazine edited by, {vii}185–6; sends Low cartoon for DHL's signature, {vii}206; anxious about DHL's health, {vii}295–6; continuing 'love' for DHL's stories, {vii}402; 'believes in my work, and works for it accordingly', {vii}439; didn't 'much like' Kot, {vii}593; 'very depressed' about DHL, {vii}634
Letters to {v}57–8, 85–6, 109–10, 118, 148–9, 242, 310–11, 317, 319–20, 331, 341, 360, 385–7, 400, 415–16, 430, 432–3, 451–2, 477, 481–2, 487, 494, 498, 505, 513, 515, 520–1, 528, 551, 570–1, 573, 583–4, 590, 601, 606–7, 613–14, 617, 620, 625–6, 647–9, 654–5, 657, {vi}21, 29–30, 40–1, 51–2, 54, 70, 84–5,
110, 119–20, 128, 134–5, 199–200, 232–3, 238, 252–4, 266, 270–1, 347, 400–1, 403–4, 421–3, 425, 427, 438, 441, 453–4, 460–1, 463–4, 475, 516, 521, 541, 551–2, 563, 594, 601–2, 606, 610, {vii}29, 51, 64–5, 94, 117–18, 123–4, 185–6, 188, 191–2, 200–1, 206, 211–12, 216, 249, 251, 268–9, 295–6, 310, 329, 401–2, 404–5, 437, 500, 512, 554, 556, 613–14
Letters from {v}50, 57–8, 86, 109, 180, 242, 270, 283, 341, 360, 386, 482, 521, 551, {vi}21, 29, 52, 70, 84, 140, 176, 222, 232, 238, 270, 347, 401, 403, 438, 441, 461, 463–4, 521, 541, 552, 601, 610, {vii}28, 51, 65, 118, 185, 188–9, 206, 251, 269, 295–6, 329, 402, 437, 512, 554, 556, 585, 614
Pears' Soap, {i}252, 269
Pearsall Smith, Logan, {ii}360
Pearse, Miss, *see* Pearn, A. R.
Pearses, the, {ii}120, 133, 139, 146, 149, 168, 173, 175, 629
Pearson, Dr Sidney Vere, {v}610, 643–4
Pecksniff, Mr, *see* Dickens, C.
Pecora, Ferdinand, {viii}71
Pedro de Valdivia, see Graham, R. C.
Peel (Isle of Man), {i}59
Peep Show, The, see Wilkinson, W.
Peer Gynt, see Grieg, E.
Peg, *see* King, M. E.
Pegasus Press Man, *see* Holroyd-Reece, J.
Pegasus Press, The, and Paris edn of *LCL* to undercut opirates, {vii}75, 77, 89, 90, 95, 97, 109–10, 115, 118, 125, 134, 140, 146, 150, 153–4, 159, 162–3, 167, 178, 183, 194, 202, 224, 230
Peggy, *see* King, M. E.
Pem, *see* King, E. U.
Pencil Drawings, see Blake, W.
Pendeen (Cornwall), {iii}128, {viii}25
Pendennis, The History of, see Thackeray, W. M.
Pendleton (Lancashire), {i}236
Pennsylvania (USA), {iv}103, 276, 287, 409, {v}104, 122, 290–1, 296
Pensione Balestri (Florence), {v}656, {vi}415

Pensione Casali (Florence), {vi}415
Pensione Giuliani (Forte dei Marmi),
    {vii}338–57 *passim*
Pensione Lucchesi (Florence), {iii}575,
    {iv}80, 82, {v}418, 427–46 *passim*,
    618
Pensione Lucii (Florence), {v}581, 587–8
Pentrich (Derbyshire), {i}541
Penzance (Cornwall), {ii}550, 562–3, 570,
    606, 610, 624, 641, 648, 652, 665, {iii}28,
    44, 49, 51, 97, 122, 126, 128, 130
    DHL required to 'join the colours' in,
    {ii}616, 618, 625
People's Theatre (Society), {iii}5–6, 385,
    396, 404, 531
    DHL finds idea 'attractive', {iii}371–2,
    374–6, 379–80
    see also 'Plays for a People's Theatre'
Perahera, *see* Kandy Perahera
Perceval, Deane, {iii}575, {iv}41, 79, 189,
    {vi}328, {vii}48
PERCY, ESMÉ SAVILLE, {ii}17, {viii}97
    and production of *Widowing*, {ii}382,
    384, {v}576, 604–5, {viii}98
    Letters to {ii}384, {v}604
P'Ermo di Camàldoli (Italy), *see* Camàldoli
Perpignan (France), {vii}245, 247–8
Persephone, {ii}330, {v}373
Persevalli, Enico, {i}505
Persia/Persians, {i}469, {iv}460, {vi}299,
    {vii}411
Persian Atrocity, The, *see* Browne, E. G.
Perth (Australia), {iv}9–10, 214, 218, 220–48
    passim, 254, 259, 272, 390, 496, {v}23–4,
    55, 120
    copy of *Rainbow* in Literary Institute at,
    {iv}273
Peru, {ii}639, {iii}315
    see also Prescott, W. H.
Perugia (Italy), {iii}602, {iv}65, {v}409–21
    passim, 442, 449, 453, 464, 485, 613,
    {vi}75, 79, 89, 93
Peshkov, Aleksey, *see* Gorky, M.
Peshkov, Zinovii A., {ii}155, 168
'Peter Bell', *see* Wordsworth, W.
Peter Middleton, see Marks, H. K.
Peter Simple, see Marryat, F.
Peter the Great, {i}114

Peter the Hermit, {i}193
Peter Whiffle, see Van Vechten, C.
Peter, *see* Skinner, M. L.
Peterborough (Northamptonshire), {i}23,
    {viii}1
Peterich, Costanza (Fasola), {vi}5, 246–7,
    {vii}346, 420, 435
Peterich, Eckart ('Ekkie'), {vi}5, 246–7,
    {vii}346, 420
Peters, Rev. Arthur, {i}377
Pethick-Lawrence, Frederick William, {vii}5
Petit Pierre, Le, see France, A.
Petit Trianon, Le, {iv}589–90
Petrie, Sir William Matthews Flinders,
    History of Egypt, {ii}538, 556, {iv}240,
    264
Petrograd (Russia), {iii}124
Petronius, Caius, *Satyricon*, {ii}510, 521,
    {viii}17
Pettit, Hilda, {i}541
Pfitscher Joch (Austria), {i}445, 450
Phaidon-Verlag, {vii}572
Pharos and Pharillon, see Forster, E. M.
Phelps, Cassandra O. {v}288
Phelps, Mary, {ii}404
Philadelphia (USA), {iii}281, {iv}296,
    {v}10, 92, 104, 122, 133, 263, 290, 300,
    319, 323, 338, 374, 414, 580, {vi}12, 124,
    288, 296, 363, 440, 448, 450, 608,
    {vii}20, 25, 35, 159, 161–2, 239–40, 242,
    297, 308, 311–12, 382, 401, 648
Philip, *see* Smith, P. F. T.; Trotter, P. C.
Phillips, Lisle M., {ii}162
Phillpotts, Eden, {i}552, {ii}96
    The Farm of the Dagger, {i}172
'Philosophy of Social Reconstruction', *see*
    Russell, B. A. W.
Phoebus Apollo, {ii}330–1, {vi}404
Phoenix, {iii}718, {vi}8, {vii}349
    Frieda refers to 'Phoenix L.', {ii}24;
    DHL's personal symbol and 'badge' of
    Rananim, {ii}252–3, 275; DHL paints
    on box, {ii}261, 273, 275; interim title
    for 'philosophy', {ii}295, 303; on seal for
    Murry, {iv}551, {vi}346, 357; in Villach
    DHL 'the only', {vi}131; 'rising from
    the nest in flames' on cover of *LCL*,
    {vi}329, 331, 333, 342, 360, 371, 376–8,

382–3, 388, 408; 'just the right bird for the cover', {vi}440; on cover of Lahr's edn of *Pansies*, {vii}336, 340, 365; on cover of *Escaped Cock*, {vii}411

PHOTOGRAPHS, of DHL:
in *Teacher*, {i}25; for Chambers family, {i}30; in College, {i}98, 100; by W. G. Parker, {ii}28, 99–100; for passport, {iii}383, {v}327; of Juta portrait, {iii}535, 560, 586, 605, {iii}535, 560, 586, 605; of Beveridge portrait, {iii}686, 694–6; by Bynner in Mexico, {iv}429; for Seltzer, {iv}486; by Weston, {v}176; in *Eve* and *Tatler*, {v}415–16; resisted as frontispiece to *Collected Poems*, {vi}405; no 'photograph is me, or even "like" me', {vi}409, {vii}189; by R. H. Davis, {vii}134, 324; by Guardia, {vii}328; as 'bright young prig', {vii}620; by Carmelo Cacópardo, {viii}53 not 'very much of a revelation' of Collings, {i}504; 'Rathe Primrose' a 'faded photograph of *S and L*', (Frieda), {i}550; of Gertler's *Merry-Go-Round*, {ii}660; 'so beautiful' of Diana Manners, {iii}27; of Kot's portrait by Gertler, {iii}43; of Catherine Carswell, {iii}524; DHL copies photograph of Uffizi picture, {iii}639; DHL uses photograph as notecard, {v}34, 176, 179, 184, 296; Brett took to photography, {v}183; of DHL's father, {v}208; photographic illustrations for *Etruscan Places*, {v}461, {vi}48, 85; x-rays of Gertie Cooper, {v}526; 'photograph illustrations' desirable for *Mornings*, {v}587, 596, 635; of Villa Mirenda, {v}644–6; of DHL's paintings, {vi}188; of 'nude studies..for water-colour studies', {vi}302; proposal to reproduce *LCL* by 'photography process', {vi}525, 530, {vii}58, 62, 119, 131, 229–30; pirated edn of *LCL* is 'photographic replica', {vii}96
Piacenza (Italy), {v}433
Piana (Corsica), {vii}190
Piazza Signoria (Florence), {iii}614, {v}492–3, 641, 657, {vi}79

Picard, Harwood, *see* Brewster, H.
Piccoli, Raffaello, {ii}4, 18, 388, 412
   The Book of Italy, {ii}384
Picinisco (Italy), {iii}414, 422–33, 446, 456
   'the devil of inaccessibility', {iii}433; 'damned', {iii}435; 'too cold', {iii}437–8; 'beautiful' but 'primitive', {iii}442; described, {iii}450–1
Pickthall, Marmaduke William, *Saïd the Fisherman*, DHL reviews, {v}301, 319–20, 325, 385–6
Pickwick Papers, see Dickens, C.
'Picture of Little T. C., The', *see* Marvell, A.
PIEHLER, HERMANN AUGUSTINE,
   Letters to {v}243
Pierre, see Melville, H.
Pietro, *see* Pini, Pietro
Pieve a S. Stephano (Italy), {vii}433
'Pig in a Poke, A', *see* Davies, R.
Pilchard, Miss, {iii}265
Pilcher, Miss, {ii}652
Pilgrim Fathers, Chronicles of the, see Morton, N.
Pilgrimage of Festus, The, see Aiken, C.
Pilgrim's Progress, The, see Bunyan, J.
Pillars of Society, see Ibsen, H.
Pillon Pass (Switzerland), {vi}455–9, 467–8
Pinchon, Edgcumb, *The Mexican People: Their Struggle for Freedom*, {iv}394
Pindar, {iii}518
Pinder, F. S., {iv}568
PINI, GIULIA, {v}583, 602, 607, 653, {vi}17, 75, 128, 190, {vii}2, 33, 274, 416, 455
   helps with Christmas preparations, {v}608, 616, {vi}248, 253; 'amusing' letter in 'quaint spelling' from, {vi}139, 164; looked after Nancy Pearn at Mirenda, {vi}165, 199; 'growing very pretty', {vi}194; keeps key to Mirenda, {vi}380, 386–7, 543; paid 20 liras weekly and 'perfectly trustworthy', {vi}392; sews and chats with Frieda, {vi}398; sends DHL's paintings to Orioli, {vi}432–3, 446; evicted by landlord, {vi}567, 571, 573, 583; on 'new farm', {vii}33, 281, 314, 454; Christmas gift for, {vii}81–2

PINI, GIULIA (*cont.*)
  Letters to {vi}122, 133, 164–5, 185–6, 273,
    306, 445–6, 464–5, 534, 563, 570–1,
    582–3, {vii}32–4, 81–2, 280–2, 428, 454
Pini, Pierino, {vii}2, 281
Pini, Pietro, {v}607, {vi}50, 104, 369, 573,
    {vii}2, 82, 281
    modelled for DHL, {v}616; steals
    Christmas tree for DHL, {v}619,
    {vi}235, 248, 252–3, 255–6, {vii}33;
    DHL's handyman, {vi}392, 431–3
Pini, Stellina, {vii}2, 281
Pini, Teresina, {vi}398, {vii}2, 82, 281
Pinker, Eric, {ii}241, 294, {iii}35
PINKER, JAMES BRAND, {ii}4–7, 13,
    15–17, 31, 60, 197, 299, 319, 326, 329,
    351, 434, 459, 463, 510, 536, {iii}12,
    14–17, 36, 41, 69, 72, 77, 89, 93–4, 96,
    100, 102, 107, 129, 163–4, 177, 183, 237,
    269, 309, 332, 372, 484, 627, {iv}176–7,
    296, {v}459, {viii}11–12, 21
    offers to be DHL's agent, {i}478, 501,
    {ii}98, 117, 135, 165–6, 174, 182; used
    by Garnett for DHL, {ii}31, 38, 44–5,
    58, 64, 66–7, 81, 83; sells DHL's prose
    writings, {ii}87, 166–7, 222, 364, 372,
    {iii}79, 319, 355, 360; becomes DHL's
    agent and negotiates with Methuen over
    Rainbow, {ii}189, 200, 260, 270, 294,
    327, 348–9, 354–7, 369–70, 406, 439,
    457, 480; DHL's finances and,
    {ii}201–2, 211–13, 220, 256, 293, 331,
    334, 358, 449–50, 452, 458, 627, 630,
    {iii}34, 135–6, 161, 205–6, 211, 216–17,
    299, 310, 315, 319, 355, 364, 473, 593,
    {viii}13; and DHL's US publishers,
    {ii}223, 246, 279, 417, 419–20, 429, 453,
    494, 560, {iii}29, 74, 323, 358, 612,
    650–3, {iv}182; intermediary with
    Bennett, {ii}479, {iii}281, 289; and
    publication of DHL's poetry, {ii}513,
    518–19, 522, 525, 527, 531–2, 535, 558,
    561–2, 589, 610–11, 619, {iii}51, 115,
    145–9, 152, 238, 241–4, 255, 338,
    {viii}17; and *W in L*, {ii}669, {iii}58,
    73–4, 80, 95, 111, 184–5, 191, 503;
    'pittance' from, {iii}70; promotes
    DHL's attempt to leave for USA,

{iii}75–6, 85–6; 'rather tiresome tyrant'
    to DHL as far as USA concerned,
    {iii}142; 'very decent', {iii}206; lets
    DHL's debt 'stand aside', {iii}213;
    supports DHL's application to Royal
    Literary Fund, {iii}249, 255; DHL
    requests special effort to place *SCAL*,
    {iii}270; given chance to break contract
    with DHL, {iii}296; DHL's growing
    independence of, {iii}374, 385, 388, 391,
    396, 398, 401, 407–8; did not show *W in
    L* MS to Huebsch, {iii}400, 409, 429,
    457, 466, 545, 642–3, {iv}411; DHL
    ends link with, {iii}439, 442, 453,
    456–60, 471, 597, 662; 'No more Pinkers
    for me', {iii}476, 667; returns docu-
    ments and MSS to DHL, {iii}485, 493,
    546; 'sharp letter' to, {iii}633, 635, 645;
    DHL demands information about
    payment for 'Blind Man', {iii}635, 650,
    690, {iv}32, {viii}40; legal rights of,
    {iii}673, 678, {iv}181; detested by
    DHL, {iii}692–3; left agreements with
    US publishers in 'beautiful tangle',
    {iii}700–1; 'impudent', {iv}29; kept
    DHL 'in the dark', {iv}108; responsibil-
    ities transferred to Curtis Brown from,
    {iv}187, 193–4, 201; death of, {iv}220
  Letters to {ii}87, 117, 166–7, 193, 200–2,
    206–8, 212, 216, 220, 227–8, 240–1,
    245–6, 256, 260, 270–1, 278–9, 293–4,
    327, 331, 334, 348–9, 354–8, 364,
    369–70, 372–3, 376, 398, 405–6, 410,
    412, 417–18, 419, 426, 429–30, 436,
    439–40, 446–7, 450–1, 453, 457–8, 464,
    475, 478–80, 484, 494, 513, 518–19, 522,
    527, 531–2, 534–5, 558, 561–2, 576, 589,
    605–6, 619–20, 630–1, 637, 653, 668–70,
    {iii}22, 28–9, 34–5, 51, 54, 73–6, 79–80,
    85–6, 95, 104–5, 110–11, 113–15, 120–1,
    135, 140, 144–6, 148–9, 152, 155, 159,
    161–2, 165, 168–9, 171–3, 178, 181,
    184–5, 187, 191, 205–6, 211, 213,
    217–19, 222, 234, 238, 241, 243–4, 249,
    254–5, 262, 265–6, 270, 274, 277–8,
    286–7, 289–90, 296, 299–301, 319–20,
    338, 355, 360, 364–5, 371, 373–5, 385,
    396, 439, 453, 473, 485, 527, 529, 593,

597, 619, 635, 645, 651–2, 689–90,
{iv}32, 164, 180–1, 193, {viii}40
Letters from {iii}249, 650, 661
Pinkerton, Percy, {ii}33
Pinner, {iii}154
Pino, *see* Orioli, G; Wilkinson, W.
Pinocchio, see Lorenzini, C.
Pioneers, The, see Cooper, J. F.
Pips ('Bibbles', 'Bubastis', 'Pipsey') (dog),
{iv}358, 360, 367, 384, 395–6, 408–9,
422, 434, 438–9, 470, {v}59, 62–3,
{viii}76
Pirates of Penzance, see Gilbert, W. S.
Pisa (Italy), {ii}57, 93, {iii}424, 523, 541,
592, {iv}82, {v}10, 378, 389, 651,
{vi}26, 82, 86, 369, 420, {vii}355–6, 359
Pit, The, see Norris, F.
Pixton Park (Minehead), {iii}237–8
Pizarro, Francisco, {ii}639
Plain Talk, {vii}496
Plain(s)field (Connecticut, USA), {iii}668,
672
Platingruben in Tulpin, see Mohr, M.
Plato, {ii}285, 320, 448, 470, {v}262, 577
Plättig, *see* Hotel (Kurhaus) Plättig
Playboy of the Western World, The, see Synge,
J. M.
'Plays for a People's Theatre', {iii}6, 421
Touch and Go in series, {iii}371–2, 374,
385, 469, 471, 531
Plisch und Plum, see Busch, W.
Plowman, Dorothy Lloyd, {iii}393, 423
PLOWMAN, MARK ('MAX'), {i}528,
{iii}6, 393, {vii}334
Letters to {iii}393, 410–11, 423, 430, 455
Plutarch, {vii}560, 589
Life of Marcus Cato, {vii}422
Plymouth (Devon), {i}168, 175, 225, {iii}44,
126, {iv}18, 529, 535–6, 538–9, 542, 548,
{v}148, 202, 214, 216–18
Plymouth Brethren, {i}249, 253
Po, River, {i}505
Poe, Edgar Allen, {i}463, {iii}630, 634;
'Bells, The', {viii}25–6;
Tales of Mystery and Imagination,
{iii}66, 212–14
Poel, William, {i}469
Poems, see Radford, D.; Radford, M.

Poems and Songs, see Middleton, R. B.
'Poems of a Prisoner', *see* Henry, L. V.
Poems of Tufail Ibn Auf al-Ghanawi, The, see
Krenkow, F. J. H.
Poems to Pavlova, see Cull, A. T.
POETRY, now 'a sort of plaster-cast craze,
scraps sweetly moulded in easy Plaster of
Paris sentiment', {i}63; DHL delights in
'modern verse' and 'minor', {i}103;
DHL loves 'little volumes of', {i}106;
country best for, {i}117; 'my beastly
long curls of', {i}167; *S and L* will not
be 'florid prose poem', {i}184; silence
poetic, {i}202; Meredith's 'very fine',
{i}242; DHL admires *Bacchae* for 'its
flashing', {i}261; 'poetic feeling' in
Bone's stories, {i}353; takes DHL 'a
long time to re-cast', {i}371; 'Snap-
Dragon' would never be written to
Frieda, {i}403; 'formless poetry..seems
to me so truthful', {i}406; 'at the *back*' of
Collings' verse, not 'much inside the
lines', {i}471; 'To write poetry one has
to let oneself fuse in the current', {i}488;
Frieda hates 'Celtic pretence of', {i}512;
DHL's father calls it 'pottery', {i}513,
536; 'everybody was talking about'
DHL's, {i}530; Collings' design for *S
and L* jacket has 'poetic quality', {i}535;
'I like any poetry, even bad..but not very
strutting stuff', {ii}34; DHL's knuckles
rapped for 'faults and transgressions' in,
{ii}70; politics hasn't got much to do
with, {ii}91; Hodgson's poem is
'currency of poetry, not poetry itself',
{ii}92–3; scansion and rhyme in,
{ii}102–5; poem facile when doesn't 'get
at the reality', {ii}116; 'I always remember poetry wrong', {ii}118; very
important to DHL, {ii}129; English
have 'loathsome superior knack of
refusing to consider [DHL] a poet at all',
{ii}146; Marsh DHL's 'poetic adviser',
{ii}154; critique of Georgian poets,
{ii}176–7; critique of Monroe's 'Poems
of War', {ii}232–3; poet's function in
war to focus on specifics not generalities,
{ii}233; critique of Lowell's, {ii}234–5;

POETRY (*cont.*)
  'poetic Meynell family', {ii}255; 'real
  passion' will 'smelt out' sentimental
  dross from, {ii}341, 493; 'the other-
  world..is world of', {ii}350; 'muse has
  gone, like the swallows in winter',
  {ii}393; 'such need of poets..world will
  all perish, without them', {ii}443;
  Nichols writes 'real', {ii}444;
  'verse..corseted in rhymed scansion',
  {ii}502; 'stark, bare, rocky directness of
  statement..alone makes poetry, today',
  {ii}503; DHL has 'poetic repute' in
  USA, {ii}513; living comes 'to perfec-
  tion and..unchanging absoluteness' in,
  {ii}516; about death needs '*opposition* of
  life to give it form', {ii}638; censorship
  of DHL's, {iii}145–6; DHL writes in
  'blind and hypnotic fashion', {iii}239;
  untrue that DHL likes only 'subjective',
  {iii}295; 'a great freemasonry', {iii}331;
  of future 'is rhymeless, naked, spontaneous rhythm', {iii}348; best when 'pure
  speech goes straight into poetry, without
  having to put on Sunday
  clothes..affectations and showing off'
  wearisome, {iv}185–6; DHL expects
  criticism of his, {iv}326; only second-
  rate when from 'general, generalised
  feelings', {v}119; DHL dislikes 'abstract
  poetry..even Blake', {v}356; 'poetic
  intelligence' essential for men to be men,
  {vi}280; 'real poet..not a strummer on a
  suburban piano', {vi}301; 'phallic
  consciousness..the root of', {vi}328;
  DHL defends poem from criticism,
  {vi}400; 'pansies, a sort of loose little
  poem form', {vii}64–5, 80, 98; 'frail
  poetry needs to be safeguarded between
  covers', {vii}121; critique of Wilson's,
  {vii}203; DHL rejects 'bourgeois
  "inoffensive" *Pansies*', {vii}242, 249;
  'not quite so dead as..reported',
  {vii}349; DHL 'riled' by Richards on
  'Piano', {vii}376; 'last thing the world
  will bear..the touch of a genuine poet',
  {viii}18
Poetry (Chicago), {ii}167, 416, {iii}99, 141,
  304, {iv}12, 15, {v}15, 87, 119
  DHL's poems in, {ii}87, 103, 120, 138,
  144, 146, 170, 202, 209, 219, 417, {iii}29,
  246, 325, 499, 677, {iv}307–8, 326, 404,
  540; payment from, {ii}138, 170, 232,
  {iii}330, 336–7, 391; 'War Number'
  infuriates DHL, {ii}232–4; *LWHCT*
  reviewed in, {iii}280; not acknowledged
  in *Bay*, {iii}331, 361, 586; acknowledged
  in US edn of *New Poems*, {iii}388, 399,
  586; liked DHL's verse, {iii}597, 657;
  acknowledged in *BBF*, {iv}381
  see also Monroe, H.
Poetry and Drama, {ii}224, 427, {vii}348
  DHL's poem in, {i}246, {ii}53; DHL's
  Collings' poems in, {ii}68; DHL's
  poems rejected by, {ii}150; Futurist
  writing in, {ii}180
Poetry Bookshop, {ii}2, 53, 92, 334, 447, 518,
  {vii}348
Poets on Poets, see Faber & Faber
Poggio a Caiano (Italy), {vii}432
Poggio Gherardo (Settignano), {vi}371
Pogmore, Richard, {i}65, 532, {v}583, 634
Point Counter Point, see Huxley, A.
Police, {ii}474, 544, {iii}16, 177, {v}334,
  {vi}12–14, 595, {vii}2, 5–6, 13, 142–3,
  169–70, 448, 557
  rumour of action against *Prussian Officer*
  by, {ii}280; suppression of *Rainbow* and,
  {ii}431, 434, 439, 456–7, {iii}212;
  'busybodiness' of, {iii}65; raid Higher
  Tregerthen, {iii}167–8, 189, 251; DHL
  reports to, {iii}169–70, 175, 264; under
  surveillance by, {iii}281; *John Bull*
  demands *W in L* banned by, {iv}88, 126;
  LCL and, {vi}483–4, 489–90, 492–3,
  498, 518, 521. {vii}47, 77, 97; copies of
  LCL and MS of *Pansies* seized by,
  {vii}146–57, 160–1, 165, 167, 174, 190,
  204–5, 304, 315; intercepting correspondence, {vii}149, 186, 419; exhibition of
  paintings delayed by fear of, {vii}214,
  327; DHL faces arrest by, {vii}222, 293;
  'publishers terrified of', {vii}319, 321,
  323; exhibition raided, pictures and
  books seized by, {vii}345, 361, 363, 365,
  367, 370, 373, 379, 385, 395, 407, 443,

472–3, 652; 'fierce', {vii}428; 'squibby bit of poetry' about, {vii}484; two versions of *Pansies* 'entirely' due to 'dirty', {vii}504

see also Scotland Yard; Warren Gallery

Polignac Prize, {ii}131–2

POLITICS, 'fervent politics are religion', {i}40; not 'much to do with poetry', {ii}91; DHL no democrat 'save in', {ii}254; State defined, {ii}254; individualism rejected, {ii}266; corollaries to essential 'revolution in the state', {ii}282, 347; 'collective vision' of nation is religion, not, {ii}301; proposed lectures on political reconstruction, {ii}359, 362, 378; 'aristocracy of people [with] wisdom' needed, {ii}364; 'Liberty, Equality and Fraternity' rejected and 'new constructive idea' of state required, {ii}366; ideal electoral system, {ii}368; Duckworth rejects early title for *Twilight* on grounds of, {ii}484; object of nation maximum individual liberty with collective search for truth, {ii}629; 'mongrel, currish desire' for absolute equality, {iii}60; DHL 'utterly bored' with English, {iii}323; taken 'with wine' in Italy, {iii}417; Italy ridiculous in, {iii}462; Italy shaky, Europe insecure, {iii}483; should be 'deadly revolution very soon', {iii}649; *Movements* 'too narrowly political' for USA, {iii}713; political world league sought by Catholic Church, {iv}124, 219; *Kangaroo* 'political..thought adventure', {iv}353; of 'white consciousness' will destroy US Indians, {iv}527; 'chimaera', {iv}528; with 'self-assertiveness' make people wearisome, {v}164; DHL doesn't like or believe in, {v}314; Germans chauvinistic and politically sensitive, {vi}96; jocularity about Irish, {vi}283; leadership and, {vi}307, 321; 'Squib' to expose 'ridiculous points' in, {vii}449

see also Capitalism, Conservative(s), Democracy, Labour, Socialism

Pollard, Emma, {ii}494–6, 501, 505, 507,

515, 519, 523–5, 533, 552, 559–60, 564, 581

Pollinger, Gerald John, {vi}552

POLLINGER, LAURENCE EDWARD, {iv}1, {v}576, {vi}6, 11, 15, 54, 152, 176, 271, 291, 346, 376, 471, 594, {vii}1, 3, 5,18, 92, 12, 129, 186, 201, 310, 346, 405, 437, 439, 457, 488, 515, 532, 539, 554, 614, 618, 629

takes over 'book side' of DHL's work with Curtis Brown, {vi}29; Secker writes to, {vi}68, 105; and publication of *LCL*, {vi}77, 295, 343–4, 526; TS of *LCL* to, {vi}305, 308, 352, 354; negotiates with publishers over *LCL*, {vi}333, 343–4, 471–3, 495, 526, 538–9, 552, 572, 602, 605–6, 610, {vii}23, 45, 52, 65–7, 77–8, 84–5, 111, 122, 130–1, 158, 163, 168, 181–2, 191, 212, 218, 221–2, 225, 231–2, 242–3, 257, 266, 272–3, 295–8, 326, 348–9, 386–7, 429–30, 445–6, 462–3, 470–1, 526, 549, 643–4, 648; orders and sells *LCL*, {vi}422, 432, 473, 476, 480, 482–3, 486–7, 489–90, 493, 501–2, 510–12, 514–15, 518, 526, 539, 552, 561, 570, 572, 598, 602–3, 613, {vii}20–1, 52, 59–63, 66–8, 71, 90–1, 112, 122–5, 131, 134, 140, 233; MSS of *Pansies* to, {vii}122–3, 136, 140, 143; police seize copies of *LCL* and *Pansies* MSS addressed to, {vii}146–50, 153, 156, 167, 172, 221; 'nice man and does things very willingly', {vii}228; and Paris edn of *LCL*, {vii}229, 232, 390, 401; and Boni, {vii}231, 236, 257, 265, 375, 468, 520–2, 533, 536; and edns of *Pansies*, {vii}242, 266–7, 272, 296–8, 303, 312–13, 324–5, 328, 350, 352, 358, 381, 502–4, 592–3, 605–6; believes he 'knows how to handle DHL', {vii}257; copy of Lahr's *Pansies* for, {vii}380; proposes volume of 'collected pieces' (*Assorted Articles*), {vii}402–3, 549–50, 568, 584, 611; 'pretty good, on the English side', {vii}522; offers help with 'Lungarno Series', {vii}527, 541, 564–5, 573, 578, 588, 595, 600; visits DHL in Bandol, {vii}620–2

POLLINGER, LAURENCE EDWARD (*cont.*)

Letters to {vi}333, 343–4, 352, 422, 432, 442, 447, 472–3, 482–3, 493, 495, 525–7, 538–9, 552–3, 572, 578, 597, 602–3, 605–6, 610, {vii}18, 23, 45–6, 52, 59, 65–7, 83–5, 111, 122, 130–1, 136, 140, 153, 158, 163–4, 166–7, 181–2, 218, 221–2, 225, 231–2, 236–7, 242–3, 257, 265–7, 272–3, 296–8, 303, 312–13, 328–9, 336, 348–9, 350, 352–3, 358, 368, 375–6, 381–2, 386–7, 390–1, 400–1, 404, 406–7, 413–14, 429–30, 445–6, 462–3, 467–8, 470–1, 481, 491, 502–5, 509, 526, 533, 535–6, 546, 549–50, 564–5, 568, 573, 583–4, 587–9, 592–3, 595, 619, 633–4, 639–40, 644, 649–50

Letters from {vi}480, {vii}61, 85, 146–7, 149, 257, 390, 521, 564

Pollinger, Russell Martin, {vi}552

Polyglots, The, see Gerhardie, W.

Pompeii (Italy), {viii}79

Pontesbury (Salop), {iv}542, 554, {vii}579

Pontius Pilate, {i}321

Poole (Dorset), {i}352, 355–8

Poole, Mrs, {ii}409

Poor Jack, see Marryat, F.

Poor Relations, see Mackenzie, E. M. C.

Popayan (Colombia), {iii}174, 179

Pope, Alexander, {i}5, 552

Pope, the, {iv}52, 250, {v}324

Popham, Arthur ('Hugh') Ewart, {ii}230, {v}475

Popham, Rosalind, {v}475, {vi}440 *see also* Baynes, R.

Popocateptl (Mexico), {iv}536, {v}158, 227, {viii}78

Popular Science, see Huxley, J. S.

'Porcelain', *see* Lowell, A.

Port Said (Egypt), {iv}7, 108, 203–13 *passim*, 234, {v}436, 484, 613, {vi}379

Port-Cros, Ile de (France), {vi}1, 3, 18, 519, 529, 537–8, 542–3, 551, 569–618 *passim*, {vii}5, 17–19, 21–2, 40, 87, 126, 152, 183

Porta Catania (Taormina), {iv}175

Porthcothan (Cornwall), {ii}13, 484, 490–559 *passim*, 641, {iii}229

Portland, Duke of, {ii}253, 265, 281, 447–8, {v}292

Porto Maurizio (Italy), {v}490

Portrait of Mabel Dodge, see Stein, G.

Portraits and Speculations, see Ransome, A. M.

Portsmouth (Hampshire), {i}132, {ii}286–7, {iii}192

Possessed, The, see Dostoievsky, F.

'Pot of Broth, A', *see* Yeats, W. B.

Potter, James Pead, {iii}267

Potter, Louie, {i}232

Potter, Maria, {iii}267

POTTER, STEPHEN MEREDITH, *D. H. Lawrence: A First Study*, {vi}68, {vii}201, 620

Letters to {vii}620

POUND, EZRA, {i}14, 19, 138, 155–6, 315, {ii}53, 56, 135, 193, 203, 295, {iv}59, {v}90, {vi}560

'his god is beauty, mine, life..good bit of a genius', {i}145; DHL stays with, {i}147–8; described, {i}165–6; 'down at the mouth', {i}335; reviews *Love Poems*, {i}523, {ii}131; and DHL's stories in *Smart Set*, {ii}26–7, 60, 67, 74–5, 82, 132, 135; places DHL's poems in *Egoist*, {ii}156; imagism 'an illusion of', {vii}223

Des Imagistes, {ii}334

Letters to {ii}131–2

Letters from {ii}75

Poussin, Nicholas, {i}124

Powell, Mrs, {ii}581, 632

Powys, Laurence, *At the Harlot's Burial: Poems*, {vii}644

Powys, Theodore Francis, {vii}3, 256

Pracchia (Italy), {v}548

Practical Criticism, see Richards, I. A.

Practice and Theory of Bolshevism, The, see Russell, B. A. W.

Prague (Austria), {viii}106

Prairie, The, see Cooper, J. F.

Prato (Italy), {vi}197, 202–3

PRAYER, DHL prays that the living be not sacrificed, {i}486; great events created by 'pure desire..like the prayer of the Saints', {iii}37; London is 'prayer-meeting' compared to Capri, {iii}444; US lawyer Curtin offers prayer of thanks for *LCL*, {vii}177

Prazer Presse, {iv}133
Precipitations, see Scott, E.
Prelude, see Mansfield, K.
Prentice, Charles, {vii}62, 109
Prescott, William Hickling, *History of the Conquest of Peru*, {iii}327
Press Agency, *see* London and Provincial Press Agency
Press Cuttings Co., {i}226, 241
Prestatyn (Flintshire), {i}289–90, 294
Preston, Edward Hayter, {ii}131
Preston, James H., {i}147
Pretenders, The, see Ibsen, H.
Prévost, Abbé, *Manon Lescaut*, {i}5, 55, 59, 126
Prewett, Frank, {v}204
Prezzolini, Giuseppe, {iv}274
   Letters from {iv}273–4
Price, {i}116
Prichard, Katharine Susannah, *see* Throssell, K.
Priestley, John Boynton, *The Good Companions*, {vii}640
Primitive Culture, see Tylor, Sir E. B.
Prince Hempseed, see Schiff, S.
Princeton University (USA), {viii}106
Principles of Social Reconstruction, see Russell, B. A. W.
Prior, Ernie, {iii}454
Prior, James, *see* Kirk, J. P.
Priory Church, Worksop, {i}371
Private Papers of Henry Ryecroft, The, see Gissing, G. R.
Pro-Italia Committee, {ii}384
Procris, {iii}103
Procter, Basil, {ii}329, 335
Profiles from China, see Tietjens, E. S.
Promessi Sposi, I, see Manzoni, A.
Prometheus Bound, see Aeschylus
Prometheus Unbound, see Aeschylus; Shelley, P. B.
Proper Studies, see Huxley, A.
Proud Prince, see McCarthy, J.
Proust, Marcel, {iv}14, {vi}41, 100, 214, 342, {vii}561, 572
Provençal, {i}145, 165, {ii}295, {vii}431
Provence (France), {vii}5
*Providence, S. S., {iv}156–7
Provincial Tales, see Bone, G.

Pryse, James Morgan, *The Apocalypse Unsealed*, {iii}150, {iv}461, ['The Apocalypse Unveiled'] {vi}92
Przemysl (Austria), {iii}89
Psycho-Analysis, see Low, B.
'Psychoanalysis in Theory and in Life', *see* Burrow, T.
Psychoanalytic Review, {ii}655, 659, {v}261, {vi}100
PUBLIC, THE, DHL feels 'daft' appearing through published verse before, {i}139; danger of 'being stuck in the stocks' of derision by, {i}181; writer has to barter with, {i}235; if 'Paul Morel' published DHL fears stoning by British, {i}239; 'nice to get away from the British', {i}420; 'Meredithy', {i}511; no point in offering books to 'swinish', {ii}276; DHL hates to be read by, {ii}294; unfair to ask writer to cut novel because not liked by, {ii}327; DHL hostile to whole of public life, {ii}328; DHL's social aims attainable only through direct appeal to, {ii}381; *Signature* not exposed for sale to, {ii}387, 389; DHL will try to change his, {ii}429; books overlooked when 'flung into the trough before the', {ii}542; DHL hates, {ii}593; 'taste averse from' DHL, {iii}69; DHL wants to secure an American, {iii}73, 427, 473, {vii}503; DHL unlike, {iii}82–3; DHL disbelieves '*utterly* in', {iii}143; *W in L* deemed 'too strong for an English', {iii}156; DHL's 'speculation..beyond the common' (Nichols), {iii}185; DHL's 'genius appeals to ..very small' (Beresford), {iii}249; DHL's 'outspo-kenness' cuts him off from English (Lowell), {iii}296; with £100 pa DHL wouldn't write for, {iii}311; 'I am not a public man', {iii}357, 476; Goldring's public would reject DHL, {iii}467; 'I am not interested in', {iii}486, 522; reading *Lost Girl*' Mary Cannan will represent, {iii}498; DHL's 'horror' of, {iii}509–10; no trust in British, {iii}621; *W in L* to 'find its public' solely through bookshops (Secker), {iii}660; 'famous but not well-known' foreign

PUBLIC, THE (*cont.*)

books appeal to, {iii}680; 'damned public' will pay for *S and S*, {iv}82; DHL 'feels hopeless about', {iv}111; not to be feared, {iv}132; 'may the general public die of colic', {iv}138; Juta perfect for American, {iv}157; 'can go to hell in any way it likes', {iv}168; should be left 'to stew in its own juice', {iv}245; 'monster with a million worm-like heads', {iv}277; expected to buy 'waste-paper basket' of Mansfield's stories, {iv}503; 'canaillerie', {iv}517, 526; new for DHL in Australia, {v}123, 161; DHL longs to kick posterior of, {v}288; 'smallness and fatuity' of, {v}292; 'weary' but must 'grow up', {v}320; wanted neither Murry alone nor 'Punch and Judy show of him and me', {v}374; 'tuppenny hands of the tuppeny', {v}387; DHL seeks wider, {v}575, 596; *M in M* should have pictures for 'wishy-washy', {v}638; DHL unable to judge taste of, {v}655, {vi}338, {vii}349; would regard *LCL* as 'pornographic', {vi}41; asinine, {vi}77; Nonesuch 'stuff for..pretty-pretty', {vi}174; 'dreary', {vi}180; DHL suggests magazine for 'decently educated', {vi}181; 'only wants foolish realism: Hamlet in a smoking jacket', {vi}204; none for 'merely "good" stuff', {vi}233; DHL may 'castrate' *LCL* for, {vi}279, 293, 296, 299, {vii}45, 50; 'pure and un-diluted' edn for 'non-vulgar', {vi}297; *LCL* 'too fine and sensitive for..gross', {vi}324, 327; 'hypocritical and snaily tails' of 'good', {vi}332; Knopfs to publish *LCL* if in shape for, {vi}374–5; DHL's paintings will be disliked by British, {vi}377; complete *Sun* ready for 'more educated', {vi}388; DHL's journalism accurately aimed at 'Great British' (Pearn), {vi}403; magazine editors afraid of, {vi}516; unaware of implications of *Point Counter Point*, {vi}600; DHL wants cheap edn of *LCL* for, {vii}75; Julian Huxley aims at

'penny-in-the-slot', {vii}117; 'godless Sabbath public' has 'more spunk than the "refined"', {vii}189; *Bottom Dogs* easy for, {vii}192; DHL fears unpleas-antness from American, {vii}203; over *Pansies* DHL will not 'haul down [his] flag' to placate, {vii}249; DHL cannot understand why war books liked by, {vii}326; Richards tried to harm DHL in eyes of, {vii}376; 'weary to death I am of the Brit.', {vii}394, 467, 505; 'I loathe the gobbling', {vii}399; DHL reluctant to produce expurgated *LCL* for, {vii}403; paintings insulted by 'meek or gloating', {vii}425, 489; 'enormous "proper" public..improper' probably bigger, {vii}448; 'esoteric public within..stupid exoteric', {vii}462; Carter not readable for vulgar, {vii}507, 544, 555–6; DHL loth to appear before, {vii}549; 'wants to be..on side of the angels', {vii}645; bare account of life in Foreign Legion 'too strong for an English', {viii}30; enthusiasm for DHL among American, {viii}60

Publisher's Weekly, {v}271, 300

PUBLISHERS, DHL ignorant of publish-ing, {i}149; 'brutal', {i}181; reception of book depends on, {i}223; Heinemann 'Great Cham of', {i}262, 326; 'more sickly than lepers', {i}382; have 'right to dispense with decency', {i}423; DHL views possibility of reading for, {i}502, 506, 510; 'procrastinators', {i}512; DHL 'safe speculation for', {ii}370; scheme for authors to be, {ii}472; DHL wants 'connection' with US, {iii}70; DHL 'reluctantly' prepared to alter MS to suit, {iii}144, 218, {iv}179; 'fools, one wants to spit on them', {iii}148; because of cost prefer 'little slight things', {iii}231; in 'present state of opinion and tyranny' DHL daren't offer *SCAL* to, {iii}255; DHL nauseated by, {iii}332; DHL hesitates to offer *SCAL* to 'promiscuous', {iii}407; agreements must be 'precise and explicit' with, {iii}458; DHL favours being 'one in a real guild' of, {iii}458; treated DHL as if 'aimiable imbecile', {iii}466; DHL firm believer in 'sticking to one', {iii}466, {viii}36; 'the publisher's veil', {iii}484; 'publishing is a disease in itself', {iii}525; DHL dislikes 'semi-gentleman, successful, commercial', {iii}547; when 'big..are excellent sellers of old hat, but fatal for new', {iii}635; 'unique' novel a 'misfortune' for, {iii}646; DHL '*never*' frets about, {iii}650; 'stinkers..enemies' to be treated like dirt but 'politely', {iii}684; '*Canaille*' to be fought with, {iii}689; wail about costs, {iv}48; can any be '*really*' trusted?, {iv}150, {viii}57; DHL loathes '*thought*' of publishing, {iv}159; DHL demands 'firm' support from his, {iv}380; do not print till 'last minute', {iv}428; 'Damn Seltzer and all', {iv}582; 'in despair', {v}34; for publicity use known and suppress unknown name, {v}71; to use only one unwise, {v}214, {vi}524; 'Never bother about', {v}292; DHL hates 'signing books for', {v}482; DHL gets bored between agents and, {v}558; 'publish too many books by half', {v}563; either dilatory or so hurried seem to have 'taken salts', {vi}40; DHL 'tired of never getting anything from', {vi}241; *LCL* to be kept from those 'who hope for something bawdy', {vi}333; when rejecting MSS 'cover their nakedness' with clichés, {vi}352; 'paradise' when beyond reach of, {vi}367, 384; 'baby terrors' of, {vi}372; fearful for profit, affect 'pious horror' about *LCL*, {vi}373; publication by author condemned by 'combine' of, {vi}408; need financial success, {vi}608; always nagging for '"a book"', {vii}26; delighted if independent author in 'tangle', {vii}31; 'damn all', {vii}261; allowed 'huge margins..author whittled down', {vii}266–7; French difficult, {vii}273, 517; DHL 'hates *all*', {vii}291; 'I have *struck*..will not be merely made use of by', {vii}297; deserve bankruptcy,

{vii}304; 'terrified of the police', {vii}319; DHL 'sick to death of', {vii}467; DHL refuses 'to do them down', {vii}488; like limited edn, {vii}589; author not to come between agent and, {viii}40; author and publisher 'men first..contractors of business second', {viii}58, 62; earning royalties not collecting charity money is duty of, {viii}79

Puccini, Giacomo, *La Bohème*, {i}281; *La Fanciulla del West*, {i}277; *Madame Butterfly*, {iii}178

Puebla (Mexico), {iv}420–4, 439–40

Pueblo/Pueblo Indians, {iv}4–5, 13, 125, 138, 252, 260, 274, 277, 303, 321, 325, 381, 410, 586, {v}9, 22, 34, 37–8, 41–6, 62, 75, 94–7, 99, 134, 149, 228, 232, 236, 251, 258–9, 263, 283, 307, 367, 378, 491, 510, 591, 594, {vi}36, 468, {vii}317 'grain-growing Indians' in Taos, {iv}301; pueblo 'earth-brown, and in a soft, sun-soaked way aboriginal', {iv}304; described, {iv}310, 313; 'very american - no inside life', {iv}362; 'poisonous white consciousness' will destroy, {iv}527–8; only way to help is to '*leave 'em alone*', {iv}545; 'school and education will finish them', {v}47; '"Savages" are a burden', {v}269

Pug and Peacocks, see Cannan, G.

Pulitzer, Joseph, {i}166

Pulley, Mrs H., {ii}413

Puma, *see* Channing, M. L.

Punch, {i}474, {v}56, 79, 91, 113, 121

Pupil-Teacher Centre, *see* Ilkeston

Puritans, {vii}253

Purley (Surrey), {i}253, 265, 279, {v}81

PURNELL, DR GEORGE EDWARD, {iv}17, 435, 441, 446, 452, 506–7, 518, 522–3, 538, 545, 562, 579, {v}55, 132, 219, 223, 235, 273, {vi}212–13 hospitality from, {iv}470, 515, 536 *Letters to* {iv}470, 508–9, 511, 535–6

PURNELL, IDELLA, {iv}17, 435, 441, 470, 508–9, 511, 515, 535–6, 567, {v}55, 66, 183, 220, {vi}10, {vii}485–6 DHL requests books from, {iv}445–6,

PURNELL, IDELLA (*cont.*)
452; *St. Mawr* for, {v}235, 261; prints
DHL's poems in *Palms*, {v}273; marries
Weatherwax, {vi}212; subscription
forms for *LCL* sent to, {vi}319, 335,
357; *WWRA* for, {vi}432
Palms, {iv}17, 435, 452, 508, 538–40,
{v}55, 260, 273, {vi}212, {vii}485
Letters to {iv}445–6, 452, 538, 544–5, 562,
579, {v}55, 132, 159, 219, 223, 225, 235,
261, 273, {vi}212, 236
Pushkin, Alexander, {i}104
'Pussum', *see* Channing, M. L.
PUTNAM'S SONS, G. P., {iv}247–8
Dahlberg's *Bottom Dogs* with DHL's
Introduction published by, {vii}157,
182, 191–2, 201, 218, 272
Letters to {vii}192
Puvis de Chavannes, Pierre, {iv}265, 273
Pwllheli (Carnarvonshire), {i}280–1, 283

Quarant'ore, {vi}361
Quarant'otto bazaar, {vi}241
Quaretaro (Mexico), {iv}468
Quattro Madonna Church, {vi}362
Queen, The, possible serialisation of *Lost Girl*
in, {iii}555, 559, 564, 572, 574, 576, 582,
599, {viii}33, 35–6; refuses serialisation,
{iii}586
Queensland (Australia), {i}425
Quemada, La (Mexico), {iv}511, 515–16
Querceta, {vii}357
Querido, Israel, *Toil of Men*, {i}341
Querschnitt, Der, {vi}233
Questa (USA), {iv}344, 348–411 *passim*,
{v}39–148 *passim*, 185, 221–97 *passim*,
{vi}69, 216–17, 432, {vii}287, {viii}90,
94, 110
'Question, The', *see* Shelley, P. B.
Quetzalcoatl, Temple of, (Mexico), {iv}418
Quick, Mary, {iii}261
Quiller-Couch, Sir Arthur Thomas, {ii}643,
{iv}490, {viii}69
Quintana, Richard ('Pablo'), {v}38, 40
Quintanilla, Jane, {v}163, 183, 187, 195, 225
QUINTANILLA, LUIS, {v}7–8, 157
introduces DHL to Weston, {v}176;

DHL polishes 'Mexico, Why Not?' by,
{v}194–6
Letters to {v}162–3, 182–3, 186–7, 194–6,
220–1, 225
QUINTANILLA, RUTH, {v}162, 183, 187,
195–6, 204, 221
Letters to {v}225
Quinton, *see* Minchin, H.
Quorn(don) (Leicestershire), {i}15–16
Burrows family home in, {i}35, 46, 60,
76, 90, 128, 134, 147, 161, 171, 176, 179,
190, 193, 209, 216, 218, 265, 267, 270,
274–5, 283, 295–6, 301, 311, 313,
315–16, 319–20, 328, 338; Louie
Burrows headmistress of school in,
{i}271, 279–81; Krenkow lives in,
{iii}322, 558, 620

Ra, {vi}301
Rabelais, François, {vi}288
Rachel, *see* Hawk, R.
Rackham Cottage (Greatham), {ii}316, 333,
342, 344, 346
Radcliffe, Anne, {vii}196
Radford, Anne, {iii}275
RADFORD, DOLLIE, {ii}333, 367, 372,
429, 476, 525, 567, 642, 655, {iii}102,
113, 132, 275, 292, {v}426, {vii}576
DHL meets, {i}491; DHL's critique of
Ransom by, {ii}316; DHL stays in
Hampstead with, {ii}361, {iii}168–9,
171, 289; subscribes for *Signature*,
{ii}404; DHL admires poems by,
{ii}515–16; packs and sends DHL's
belongings to Cornwall, {ii}567–8,
577–9, 582–4, 599, 601; gift for,
{ii}584–5, {iii}59; visits Tregerthen,
{ii}618–19, 624–5, 627, 631, 639;
'Reality of Peace' essays sent to, {iii}107,
114, 120; DHL at Chapel Farm Cottage
owned by, {iii}117, 119, 188, 191–218;
cottage required by, {iii}206–10, 218,
232; DHL returns to cottage,
{iii}219–41; has 'stinking impudence' to
ask DHL to leave cottage, {iii}367
Poems, {i}491, {ii}515–16, 596;
The Ransom, {ii}316

Letters to {ii}316, 346, 377, 430, 444–5,
    493–4, 515–16, 540–1, 547–8, 565–6,
    568, 577–9, 582–5, 596, 604–5, 618–19,
    624–5, 651–2, 663–5, {iii}37, 59–60,
    96–7, 101, 107–8, 120, 134, 153–4
Radford, Ernest, {i}14, 491, {ii}316, 372,
    577, {iii}37, {v}426
    mentally unstable, {iii}218, 274
Radford, Hester, {ii}652
RADFORD, MAITLAND, {ii}377, 430,
    548, 565, 577, 585, 605, 618–19, 624,
    652, 665, {iii}107, 108, 120, 292
    on DHL's physical state, {ii}511–12,
    516, 523, 526, 530, 533–4; hospital post
    for, {ii}540–1; marriage of, {iii}154;
    daughter born, {iii}274–5
Letters to {iii}275
RADFORD, MARGARET, {ii}316, 333,
    341, 346, 377, 494, 541, 566, 596, 605,
    652, 664–5, {iii}97, 107, 120, 154, 192,
    275, 352, 375–6, 378, 425, 449, {vii}576
    her best poems 'belong to the eternal
    world', {ii}350; gift for, {iii}101;
    'impossible', {iii}226, 228, 230; 'very
    seedy', {iii}274; 'horrible', {iii}277;
    DHL ironic about, {iii}349–50, 354;
    'wretched', {iii}382–4; let down Yorkes
    'so nastily', {iii}422; 'don't mention',
    {v}426; 'threatens' to visit DHL,
    {v}539
    Poems, {ii}350, 605
Letters to {ii}350
Radford, Muriel, {iii}107, 275
Raffalovich, George, {v}620
Ragionamenti, I, see Aretino, P.
Ragusa (Austria), {v}299, 311, 321, 323, 373
Rainusso, Eva, {ii}149, 478, 629
Raleigh, Lucie Gertrude, Lady, {ii}51, 63
Raleigh, Sir Walter Alexander, {ii}2, 48, 51,
    63, {iii}728
Ralph, *see* Myers, R.
Ramal, Walter, *see* De La Mare, W.
Ramée, M. de la, *see* Ouida
Ramie, Marian, {ii}232
Ramper, see Mohr, M.
Rampion, *see* Huxley, A.
Ramsay, *see* MacDonald, J.

Ramsey, Isle of Man, {i}139, 249, 313, 333,
    526
Ramsgate (Kent), {i}233, {vi}512, 515
RANANIM, {ii}11, {iii}8, 252, 571, {iv}20,
    241, {v}3, 6, 47
    origin of, {ii}252–3, {iv}165, 350;
    community established on 'assumption
    of goodness' in members, {ii}259;
    changed to 'Island' scheme, {ii}266, 292;
    to be built out of 'fulfilled individualities
    seeking greater fulfilment', {ii}266;
    'sacred duty' to create, {ii}271–2; to be
    started in England, {ii}277; 'a little
    Community..a new life..*together*, in a new
    spirit', {ii}485; Tregerthen possible
    location for, {ii}564; 'Where is our',
    {ii}650; DHL's continuing belief in
    versions of, {iii}23, 69–70, 74, 78, 87,
    90, 309, 316; Typee as, {iii}66, 87–8,
    566, 653; potential recruits for Andes,
    {iii}173, {vii}377; 'weak-kneed' not to
    create, {iii}208; 'something to look
    forward to', {iii}214; 'sunk out of sight',
    {v}367
    see also Andes, Florida
Randall, (Sir) Alec Walter George, {vi}532
Randall-MacIver, David, *The Iron Age in
    Italy*, {vi}298
Randazzo (Sicily), {iii}506, 509, 526
Random House, {vii}456, 468, 640
    published *My Skirmish*, {vii}316, 390,
    392, 396, 401, 411, 428–9, 439, 444, 446,
    462, 464, 496, 504, 551
Ransom, The, see Radford, D.
Ransome, Arthur Michell, *Book of
    Friendship, Book of Love*, and *Portraits
    and Speculations*, {i}552, {ii}27
Ransome, Cyril, {i}26
Rapallo (Italy), {vii}286
Raphael, Enid, {vi}530, 532–3
    Letters from {vi}530
Raphael, J. E., {i}122
Raphael, Sylvia, *see* Raphael, E.
Rarotonga Island, {iv}11, 249, 255, 259, 272,
    282–4, 286
Rassmussen, Joe, {v}438, 440, 466–8, 586
Rassmussen, Maudie, {v}438, 467–8

Rasputin, see Fueloep-Miller, R.
Ratcliffe-on-the-Wreake (Leicestershire),
   {i}105, 117, 209, 211, 295;
   'Mousecliffe'/'Mousehole', {i}105, 121,
   129
'Rathe Primrose, The', *see* Chambers, J.
Raton (USA), {iv}322–3, 325, 338, 344,
   {v}252, 281, 297, {viii}95
Rauh, Florence, {v}299
RAUH, IDA ('MRS DASBURG'), {v}8, 42,
   158, 248, 253, 285, 298–300, 302, 313,
   417, 510–11, 568, {vi}224, 231, 366,
   {vii}277, 547, 551, 574, 581, 586, 604,
   624, 636, {viii}95
   'very nice', {v}28; DHL promises to
   write play for, {v}160, 174, 199, 217–18,
   226, 233; Michal in *David* intended for,
   {v}236, 250; TS of *David* sent to,
   {v}268, 275; feels too old for Michal,
   {v}282; copy of *David* for, {v}413;
   relationship with Dasburg broken off,
   {vii}24, 345; in Bandol, {vii}588, 591,
   593, 598–9, 614, 616; 'belongs to
   civilisation and to society', {vii}594;
   DHL 'depended on her a bit', {vii}627,
   629; 'very good' companion for DHL,
   {vii}650–1, 653
   Letters to {v}174, 199, 217–18, 223–4,
      226–7, 232–3, 236–7, 250, 252, 268–9,
      275–7, 281–2, 303–4, 308–9
RAVAGLI, ANGELO ('TENENTE'),
   {v}10, 337, 490, 576, {vi}377
   Letters to {v}645–6
Ravello (Italy), {v}10, 401–9, 414–15, 421,
   427–30, 573, 612, 648–57, {vi}21–2,
   25–6, 30, 43, 133, 368, {viii}100
Ravenna (Italy), {iii}399, {v}10, 409–12,
   414–15, 420–1
Rayner, Edward ('Teddy'), {i}508
Rayner, John, {vi}13
   reviews *LCL*, 'fine novel, bold and -
   stark', {vi}576–7
READ, JAMES B., {vi}469, 550, {vii}342–4
   Letters to {vi}443
Reade, Charles, *The Cloister and the Hearth*,
   {ii}305, {iii}309
Reade, William Winwood, *The Martyrdom of
   Man*, {iii}338

Reading (Berkshire), {iii}226, 229, 382, 407
Readings from the New Poets, see Ellsworth,
   W. W.
Realist, The, {vii}117
Reclining Nude, see Gertler, M.
*Recollections of the Last Days of Shelley and
   Byron, see* Trelawny, E. J.
Red Cross, The, {viii}27
Red Lion, *see* Lahr, C.
Red Magazine, The, {i}172
Red Sea, {ii}648, {iv}7, 205, 210–13
Redhill (Surrey), {i}236, 291, 345, {ii}404
Reece, Holroyd, *see* Holroyd-Reece, J.
Reed, John, {iv}4–5, {v}76, {vi}230
   Tamburlaine and Other Poems, {v}76;
   Ten Days that Shook the World, {iv}4,
   {v}76
Reeve, Alvina ('Tim'), *see* Lawrence, A.
Reeve, Robert Henry, {i}68
Reeves, Mr, *see* Frere-Reeves, Mr
Reform Club, The, {i}144, 286
Reggie, *see* Turner, R.
Reid, Forrest, *The Bracknels,* {i}462
Reid, Mary, {i}220, 244
REID, REV. ROBERT, {i}3, 7, {v}631
   referee for DHL, {i}21, 77; DHL seeks
   tuition in Latin from, {i}31; DHL's
   tuition from other than, {i}34; views on
   'great religious topics of the day'
   debated with, {i}36–7, 39–41; help to
   control DHL's father's misbehaviour
   sought from, {i}219–20; leaves
   Eastwood, {i}236; DHL's high regard
   for, {i}243–4
   Letters to {i}31, 34, 36–7, 39–41, 219–20,
      244
Reid, Robert, {i}244
Reigate (Surrey), {i}90–1, 291
Reinhardt, Max, {i}310
Reitz, Deneys, *Commando: A Boer Journal of
   the Boer War,* {vii}650
Relativity, see Einstein, A.
Religio Medici, see Browne, Sir T.
RELIGION, DHL seeks Church's position
   on 'great religious topics of the day',
   {i}36–7; Pauline conversion not experi-
   enced by DHL, {i}39, 49, 51; consists in
   whatever man strives for

'earnestly..unselfishly', {i}40; DHL accepts 'Cosmic God' but not divinity of Jesus, {i}40–1, 255–6; DHL rejects 'fiats and decrees' in, {i}41; DHL respects, {i}50, 58; 'comforting companion', {i}57, 62; 'waxen religious look' of lilies, {i}63; love finer when attuned to 'religious feeling', {i}66; DHL's 'rather deep religious faith' lost at College, {i}72; 'I have my own', {i}215; sister Ada not to 'meddle with', {i}236; necessary to work out one's own, {i}256; Stendhal omits, {i}262; pictures in Beuerberg church 'savagely religious', {i}418; 'belief in..blood..flesh..wiser than the intellect' is DHL's 'great', {i}503; 'One has to be so terribly religious to be an artist', {i}519; art springing from 'religious yearning', {ii}90; Whitman's vision not, {ii}130; in Italy scarcely any, {ii}149; DHL 'passionately religious' and novels plumb depths of 'religious experience', {ii}165; DHL's idea of 'great religious Vision', {ii}247–50; must be lived in community, {ii}271–2; Irish feel no 'religious passion' preferring 'ecstasies', {ii}288; not 'private little concern', {ii}301; *'religious belief which leads to action'* essential, {ii}359, 361; DHL's 'christian religiosity' abandoned, {ii}365, {vi}114; *Signature* seed of 'new religious era', {ii}399; Ottoline Morrell essentially religious, {ii}448; 'easy slough of the Roman', {ii}497; DHL believes in supernatural which is not of, {ii}501; on Dostoievsky's theology, {ii}543–4; *'All religion is bad'*, {ii}612; used by Jews for 'personal..gratification', {iii}136–7; 'living clue of life' - religious - in Englishmen, {iv}219; 'rat-hole religion' of Buddha, {iv}234; young countries 'more devoid of', {iv}264; American Indians Catholic but keep old, {iv}310; 'older vision of life' grounded in, {v}68; 'religious relationship' primary, {v}77; 'animistic religion' living, 'ours..corpse of', {v}109; music for *David* to convey

'primitive religious passion', {v}557; 'Indian religious dances' profoundly moving, {vi}80; *'principle* in universe' to which 'man turns religiously', {vi}114; renewal of 'religious sense of atoneness' needed in England, {vi}258; DHL's stance in *LCL* 'truly..religious', {vi}260; real value of gold 'religious', {vi}378; 'all-round consciousness' includes, {vii}103; for the young expressed in 'The Risen Lord', {vii}401; doctrine of Fall late development in, {vii}544; Christian incompatible with State, {vii}618; effect of *David* to be 'rather slow and archaic-religious', {viii}102
Religious Drama Society, {i}469
Religious Experiences, see James, W.
Rembrandt, Harmenszoon Van Rijn, {i}130, {ii}130, 263, 301, 549, {iv}47
Remington (typewriter), {v}237, {vii}587, 601–2
Reminiscences of Leo Nicolayevitch Tolstoi, see Gorky, M.
Reminiscences of Leonid Andreyev, see Gorky, M.
Reminiscences of the English Lake Poets, see De Quincey, T.
Renaissance, the, {i}418, {ii}296, {iv}459, {vi}4, 217, {vii}4
Roman rationalism and materialism became supreme in, {ii}163; 'great collective vision' must replace analytic individualism in art since, {ii}301, 448; 'Art was holy' in, {ii}593; American Hugheses ignorant of, {vi}79; DHL suggests series of novelists of Italian, {vi}594, 598, 605, {vii}21–2, 141, 564; epoch of 'great psychic change', {vii}179
Renan, Ernest, {i}5, 36–7
Song of Songs trans. by, {i}219
RENDÓN, EDUARDO BOLIO, {v}254, 268
Letters to {v}254, 287
Rendón, Mrs, {v}254
Rene, *see* Secker, C. M.
Reni, Guido, {i}124
Renishaw Hall (Derbyshire), {v}468, 476, 532, {vi}579

Renn, Ludwig, *War*, {vii}326
Renshaw, Mary Ellen ('Polly'), {i}68, 199, 231
Renshaws, {i}116
Renwick, Professor William Lindsay, {v}603
Reparation, {iii}411
Reputations: Essays in Criticism, see Goldring, D.
Resolute, S.S., {v}9, 304–8
Return, The, see De La Mare, W.
'Revelation', *see* Davies, R.
Revermort, J. A., *see* Cramb, J. A.
REVIEWERS/REVIEWS [NB: for reviews of individual works, see under title; for authors reviewed by DHL himself, see Lawrence, D. H., Reviews]
DHL keen to see, {i}220, 223; reviewing procedure described, {i}223; DHL's gender mistaken in, {i}229; DHL invited by *English Review* to write, {i}305, 365, 380; afraid to praise DHL in case rebuked for immorality, {i}548; in Italy DHL loves 'to flounder among English news, and', {ii}135; in *Morning Post* have 'decent, honorable tone', {ii}147; of DHL bring dismissal of reviewer, {ii}456, {vi}607; have legal consequences, {ii}462, {iii}459; 'bloody fools; or..fools without blood', {ii}560; not sought by Huebsch for *Rainbow* to avoid censor, {iii}457; DHL advises not to issue *W in L* for, {iii}625, 628, 638, {iv}35; DHL rebukes, {iii}734, {iv}518, {vi}502, {vii}294; DHL seeks for his works, {iv}488, {v}121; DHL offers to write, {v}198, 289, 292, 301, {vii}448; 'good to review a novel from standpoint of..morality', {v}275; DHL likes to 'go for other men's' books in, {v}325; some books not worth, {v}359; DHL responds in public to, {v}395; DHL 'rather likes doing a serious review..now and then', {v}514; freedom of speech demanded in, {v}551; DHL will review only if book of interest, {v}571; no objection if editors omit 'any bit' from, {vi}52; better as 'waitresses in Lyons'
Cafés..all they've got spunk for', {vi}71; 'eunuchs..no balls..haven't enough spunk to hear a cow bellow', {vi}72–3; help author, {vi}120; *LCL* not sent out for, {vi}222, 288; 'I enjoy slanging a book when it gets my goat', {vi}502; hostile to *LCL*, {vi}598, {vii}141, 144; *Paintings* not sent out for, {vii}321; misquotation by reviewer harmful, {vii}362; 'impotent and elderly', {vii}395; DHL hopes for 'real Labour or Socialist or red reviews of *Pansies*', {vii}413; 'Squib' should print 'imaginary', {vii}484, 501; cease to affect sales of *LCL*, {vii}601, 610; DHL admits Murry's superiority as writer of, {viii}7
'Revistas Vanguardistas', {vii}146
Revnes, Maurice S., {iii}546–7
Letters from {iii}546
Revolution in Tanner's Lane, The, see Rutherford, M.
Revue des Deux Mondes, {iii}502, 533
Reynolds, Diana, {v}627, {vi}367, 609, {vii}378
Reynolds, Hermione ('Mynie'), {v}627, {vi}22, 367, 609, {vii}378
Reynolds, Lilian, {i}236, 245, 284, 291, 316, 322, 341, 345, {ii}18, 404
Reynolds, Mrs, {i}322, 345
Reynolds, Pamela ('Pam'), {v}627, {vi}22, 367, 609, {vii}378
Reynolds, Paul Revere, {ii}653, {iii}29, 111
Reynolds, Richard William, {vi}22, 588, {vii}28
Reynolds, Sir Joshua, {i}124
Reynolds, Stephen, {i}12
Alongshore, {i}488
Rheingold, see Wagner, R.
Rheinprovinz (Germany), {i}400, 405, 408–12, 417
Rhesus of Euripides, The, see Murray, G.
Rhine, River, {i}385, 395, 397–8, 407–8, 411–12, {ii}76, {iii}698, 720, 726, 728, {iv}25, 33, 38, {v}328, 330–1, 499, 503, {vii}397
Rhoda Fleming, see Meredith, G.
Rhys, *see* Davies, R.

Rhys, Ernest, {i}14, 141, 144, 148, 156, 491, {iv}303

Rhys, Grace, {i}14, 141, 144, 147–8, 156, 180, 491, 502, {iv}303

Rhythm, {i}489, 510, 512, 546, {ii}31, 112, 254
    'nasty' review of *Trespasser* in, {i}507–8; DHL reviews in, {i}519, 524; bankrupt, {ii}32

Rice, Anne Estelle, {ii}404
    cover and decorations of *Bay* by, {iii}238, 331, 360; 'absurd and unsuitable wood-cuts' in *Bay* by, {iii}362, 366

Rice, Dr John Dyer, {iii}130–2

Rice, F. C., {i}512, 524

Rich Relatives, see Mackenzie, E. M. C.

Rich, Edwin G., {vi}310, 447, 525, {vii}27, 117, 130, 173, 188, 308, 359, 377, 385, 387, 414, 472, 524–5, {viii}114–15
    replaces Barmby in Curtis Brown's New York office, {vi}222; unreliable in negotiations with publishers, {vi}538–9, 572, 602, {vii}35, 551; 'damn feeble at making a contract', {vii}312; DHL has 'very little faith in', {vii}439–40, 463, 496; attitude to *LCL* 'sheer funk', {vii}462; 'sort of kitten who only wants to be loved: a real dud', {vii}522; deliberately unhelpful, {vii}649

Richard, *see* Aldington, R.; Quintana, R.

Richard I, {i}114

Richard III, see Shakespeare, W.

Richards, Arthur, {ii}213

Richards, Grant, publishes Anna Wickham, {ii}400, 417; showed interest in *Foreign Legion*, {iv}178, {viii}50; not 'much good as a publisher', {v}316

Richards, Ivor Armstrong, *Practical Criticism*, {vii}376

Richards, Mrs Arthur, {i}218

Richardson (Odle), Dorothy Miller, {iii}244, 255, {vi}54, {vii}137

Richardson, Samuel, *Clarissa Harlowe*, {i}217, 524;
    Pamela, or Virtue Rewarded, {iii}328

Richmond (Surrey), {i}117–18, 120, 156,
    285, 292, 338, {iii}198–9, 276, 292, {v}317–18

Richmond, Kenneth, *Howard and Son*, {ii}640

Richter, Jean Paul, {vi}183
    Flower, Fruit and Thorn Pieces, {iii}38

Richthofen, Baron Friedrich von, {i}384, 391, 395, 429, {ii}160, 206
    'fierce old aristocrat', {i}409; 'very ill', {ii}221; death of, {ii}293

RICHTHOFEN, BARONESS ANNA VON, {i}448, {ii}74, 199, {iii}311, 316, 331, 488–9, 505, 542, 574, 581, 587, 620, 639, 642, 666, 701–5, {iv}2, 13, 20, 25, 30, 32, 38, 43–4, 48, 78, 258, 262, 316, 320, 488, {v}9–10, 12, 41, 184–5, 191, 193, 195, 197, 202, 208–9, 215, 218, 252, 277–8, 312, 314, 322, 326, 331, 366, 371, 405, 418, 435, 471, 476, 479, 554–5, 616, 657, {vi}5, 75, 103–4, 136, 147, 164–5, 167–9, 175, 199, 215, 237, 301, 429–30, 439, 441, 529, 553, 557–8, 562–3, 565, 598, 609, 611, {vii}9–10, 209–10, 332, 347, 358–9, 364, 366, 370–2, 374–5, 428, 433–4, 436, 493–4, 621, {viii}105
    'utterly non-moral, very kind', {i}409; DHL 'schimpfed' by, {i}429–30; corresponds 'amicably' with Weekley, {i}542; Frieda gets embossed notepaper from, {ii}79, 106; feels 'twilight of death in the air', {iii}26; Frieda anxious to see, {iii}348, 370, 392, 678, 682–4, 686–9, 693–4, 698; food to be sent to, {iii}476; Kippenberg to transfer DHL's translation fees to, {iii}601. 623, {iv}117, 132, 136, 147–8, {viii}48; DHL visits, {iii}706–{iv}52, {iv}569–86, {v}327–36, 494–503, {vi}175–93, 568–83, {vii}377–449; DHL sends money to, {iv}84, 122, 256, 289, 397, 434, 598, {v}63, 138, 239, 354, 489, {vi}95, 217, 243, 616, {viii}80; copies of DHL's works to, {iv}390, {v}189, 247; DHL praises 'steed-like spirit' of, {v}63; 'failing a bit', {v}176; noticeably older, {v}328, 330; 'Duchess of the Stift', {v}354; 'grows younger all the time',

RICHTHOFEN, BARONESS ANNA
VON (*cont.*)
{vi}173. 179; diabetic, {vi}510; restive,
{vi}582; 'afraid..of her age', {vii}72;
'rather awful now..hideous terror of
having to die', {vii}397–8, 400, 402;
'nice' again, {vii}421; DHL offers to
buy shoes for, {viii}31; DHL sends
spices from Ceylon to, {viii}54
Letters to {iii}447–8, 601, 623, 685–6,
{iv}56, 62–3, 72, 75–7, 83–5, 118–22,
135–7, 146–7, 160–2, 198–9, 203–6,
208–12, 237–8, 248–50, 254–6, 280–1,
288–9, 293–4, 350–2, 356–7, 395–7, 415,
433–4, 450–2, 469, 478–9, 504, 520,
529–32, 542, 561, 566, 586, 588–90, 594,
597–8, {v}28–9, 60–3, 133–5, 137–9,
152–3, 176–8, 215–17, 237–40, 265–7,
304, 353–4, 368–9, 411–12, 428, 469,
487–9, 507–8, 544, 621–3, {vi}32–5, 53,
94–5, 116–18, 129, 145–6, 166–7, 193–4,
206–7, 216–18, 242–4, 250–2, 311–12,
396–8, 423–4, 555–7, 583–5, 587,
614–16, {vii}72–5, 248, 311, 377, 450,
491, {viii}29, 31, 37, 39, 42–6, 48, 53–5,
75, 77–84
Letters from {viii}54
Richthofen, Hartmann von, {iii}314,
{iv}530–1
Richthofen, Manfred von, {iii}282
RICKARDS, CONSTANTINE G., 'very
attentive' British Vice-Consul, {v}153,
156, 177, 198
Letters to {v}198–9, 209–10
Rickards, Fr. Edward Arden, {v}153, 156,
167–8, 177, 181–3, 199, 282, {vi}210
Ricketts, Charles, {ii}412
RICKWORD, EDGELL, {v}311, 367, 601,
617, {vi}54, {vii}265, 531
Love One Another, {vii}559;
Scrutinies by Various Writers, {v}601,
649, 654, {vi}67, 342, 348, {viii}107
see also Calendar of Modern Letters and
Calendar
Letters to {viii}99
Rickworth, *see* Rickword, E.
'Ride a cock horse', {vii}408

Rider, William, {iii}299, {iv}171, 365
Riders to the Sea, see Synge, J. M.
Ridgways tea, {vii}348
Rifredi/Rifredo (Italy), {iii}585, {iv}66
Rigg Mill (Yorkshire), {i}36
Rignault, Homer, *The Legend of Ermengarde*,
{vii}429, 431–3
Rimbaud, Jean Nicholas Arthur, {iii}318
Rimsky-Korsakov, Nicholas Andreievich,
My Musical Life, {v}80, 112
Rina, *see* Secker, C. M.
Ring der Nibelungen, see Wagner, R.
Rings on Her Fingers, see Davies, R.
Rio Bravo, S. S. {v}216–18
Rio Grande, River (USA), {iv}339, 364–6,
373, {v}503
Ripley (Derbyshire), {i}174, 541, {ii}196,
200, 237, 391, 467, 472, 476–7, 482–90,
654, {iii}50, 55, 112–14, 123, 193–4, 232,
300–2, 307, 309, 311–13, 317, 320–1,
329–37, 340, 351, 579, 609, 682, 723,
729, {iv}64, 92, 261, 299, 311, 342, 384,
423, 554, {v}9, 13, 80, 112, 141, 150,
169, 189, 208, 243, 247, 265–6, 279, 311,
315–20, 325, 329, 363, 377, 413, 468,
524, 526–30, 535, 541, 552, 564, 583,
592, 610, 644, {vi}25, 63–4, 81, 88, 137,
201, 244, 396, 441, 509, {vii}68, 125,
181, 210, 232, 238, 261, 321, 337, 347,
380, 418, 459, 557, 573, 579, 631, 652
Ritchie, Rev. David Lakie, {i}39
Ritson, Joshua, {vii}161
Rituel du Culte Divin Journalier en Egypte, Le,
see Moret, A.
Riva (Italy), {i}447, 450, 452–7, 481, 484,
{iv}189
River of Life and Other Stories, The, see
Kuprin, A. I.
Riviera, French, {i}496, {iii}541, 553, 558,
675, {v}333, 444, 458, {vi}542, 574,
581–2, {vii}26, 99, 584; Italian, {iii}401,
{v}323, 326, 333–6, 351, 357, 386,
{vi}366, {vii}40
DHL 'not crazy about' Italian, {v}341,
364; 'means nothing to' DHL, {v}345;
boring, {v}347, 399; DHL prefers
Tuscany to, {v}468, 496

Riviere, Mrs, {ii}409
ROBERTS, ARTHUR LLEWELYN,
    DHL applies to Royal Literary Fund
    through, {ii}224–5, {iii}249–53, 255;
    sends £50, {iii}264
    Letters to {ii}224–5, {iii}249–50, 253, 264
Roberts, Chalmers, {vi}232
Roberts, Elizabeth Madox, *The Time of Man*,
    {vi}54
Roberts, Ursula (Wyllie), pseud. Susan
    Miles, {v}193
    Letters from {v}193
ROBERTS, WILLIAM HERBERT,
    requests photograph of DHL, {vi}228;
    DHL questions judgments in article by,
    {vi}399–400
    Letters to {vi}228, 237, 399–400
Robertson & Mullens, {v}113, 122, 161
Robertson, John Mackinnon, *Letters on
    Reasoning*, {i}36–7, 126
ROBERTSON, STEWART A., {i}202, 204,
    368, 386, 455, {iii}62
    Letters to {i}361
Robespierre, Maximilien, {i}114, {iii}498
Robin Hood, {i}118
Robin Hood's Bay, (Yorkshire), {i}8, 35–6,
    59, {vii}421
Robinson Crusoe, see Defoe, D.
Robinson, D. Bartlett (Barry), {i}357, 465
Robinson, Dr George E. J. Antoine, {v}525
Robinson, Edwin Arlington, *Lancelot: a
    Poem*, {iii}662
Robinson, Percy James Hall, {vii}8
    safeguards DHL's interests in legal
    battle over paintings, {vii}367–70, 421,
    425; 'charges pretty stiff', {vii}573
Rocca Bella (Taormina), {iii}10, 506–7, 514,
    527, 554, 666
    Bowdwin's massive alterations to interior
    of, {iii}637, 640, 658, 670, 686, {iv}140
Rocca Forte ('the Studio') (Taormina),
    {iii}489, 526, 532, 551, 553, 557, 580,
    606, 658, 663, 665, 670, 683, 686, 695,
    727, {iv}51, 192
Rocky Mountains (USA), {iv}93, 95, 158,
    309–10, {v}9, 117
    'aspens gold as daffodils' on, {iv}312–13,

328; Del Monte ranch at foot of,
    {iv}334–5, 349–51, 353, 362, 364, 366,
    {v}22, 34, 58, 67, 75, 190, {viii}90;
    'savage', {v}148,
Rodker, John, {vi}346, 569
Roger-Cornaz, Frédéric, {vii}261
Rogers, Dr, {iii}496
Rogers, William B., {iii}538, 540, 545, 560,
    563–4
Rojas, Fernando de, {i}414
Roland (dog), {v}59, 62–3, 73
Rolfe, Beatrice ('the Bee'), {iv}507, 509,
    526
Rolfe, Frederick, *see* Corvo, Baron
Rolland, Romain, *Life of Michael Angelo*,
    {ii}592–3, 507, 602
Rollings, Mrs, {i}116
Rollston, A., {i}194, 293, 362
Romagna, The, {iii}609
Romains, Jules, *Le Dieu des Corps*, {vi}569
Romance of Names, see Weekley, E.
Romance of Words, see Weekley, E.
Romances sans Paroles, see Verlaine, P.
Romanelli, Mr, {v}615, 618, 625, 641–2, 647
Rome (Italy), {i}182, 188, 226, 334, 458,
    529–31, 534–5, 537, {ii}93, {iii}19, 30–1,
    338, 407, 412–31 *passim*, 450, 452, 502–3,
    506, 512–28, 535, 541, 549–51, 570, 572,
    574, 578, 581–7, 602–3, 610–11, 620, 633,
    640, 658, 679–87, 695, 697, 700–5, 715,
    {iv}33, 43, 52, 61, 64, 79–80, 86, 92, 105,
    124–5, 131, 158, 166, 186, 210, 212, 264,
    404, {v}10, 361, 364–5, 401, 407–9,
    411–12, 414–15, 420–1, 425, 429, 433,
    465, 485, 491, 534, 542, 594, 598, 600,
    616–18, 625, 627, 630, 632, 645, 648–51,
    653, 656–7, {vi}22, 25, 27–8, 31, 33, 36,
    38–40, 48, 74, 85, 101, 150, 155, 241, 251,
    253, 317, 407, 508, 538, 593, {vii}54,
    367, 514, 526–7, {viii}37, 46, 104
    US Embassy in, {iii}703, {iv}261; 'very
    antipatica nowadays', {vi}41; 'stone-cold
    city', {vi}243; museums 'lovely',
    {vi}246; '*very* irritable and irritating',
    {viii}101
Romero, Candaleria, {iv}318, 444
Ronda (Spain), {vii}86

Rooke, Irene, {iii}484
Roosevelt, Theodore, {ii}416
Root, Pearl, {i}105, 122, 203
Rosalie, *see* Bull, R.
Rosalind, *see* Baynes, R.
Rosalino, {v}175, 177–8, 180–1, 184, 210, 296
Rosanov, V. V., *see* Rozanov, V.
Rosary, The, see Barclay, F. L.
'Rosary, The', *see* Nevin, E.
Rose and Vine, see Taylor, R. A.
Rose, {vi}36, 57, 61, 123, 241
    see also Nys, R.
ROSEBERY, ELFIE JULIA, {v}414, 650
    Letters to {v}414–15, 427, 573, 603, 612, 657
ROSEBERY, JOSEPH HENRY, {v}414, 573, 650
    Letters to {v}657
Rosenthal, David, {vi}335
Rosmer, Milton, {iii}484
Rosmersholm, see Ibsen, H.
Ross, F. S., {vii}134
Ross, Janet, {vi}371
Ross-on-Wye (Herefordshire), {iii}271, 273, 275–8
Rossetti, Dante Gabriel, {i}12
    'Ballad of Dead Ladies', {i}157;
    'Blessed Damozel', {i}51;
    'Mary Rose', {i}81;
    'Sister Helen', {i}159–60
Rossetti, William Michael, {i}170
Rossi, Giovanni, {v}343–4, 359, 376, 414, 432
Rota, Bertram, {vi}511–12, 515
Rotary, *see* Soroptimists
Rotch, Josephine Noyes, {vi}504, {vii}600
Roth, M., {ii}407
Rothenstein, (Sir) William, {ii}117, {v}11, 572
Rothley (Leicestershire), {i}190, 193
Rottach (Germany), {vi}396, {vii}11, 48, 178, 365–6, 374, 380, 388, 408–9, 423, 430–1, 433, 435, 518, 532, 558, 573
    DHL visits Mohr in, {vii}444–89 *passim*; 'beautiful' and 'peaceful' among the mountains, {vii}455, 459; DHL completes *P and O* while in, {vii}470–1, 604; place and people 'charming but I

feel..rotten', {vii}477; 'I loathe all mountains', {vii}486
Rottingdean (Sussex), {i}126–7, 215, 218, {ii}409
Rouen (France), {i}318, {iii}524
Rouge et le Noir, Le, see Stendhal, H. B. de
Rousseau, Henri (The Douanier), {vi}62
    La Bohémienne Endormie, {vi}183
Rousseau, Jean-Jacques, {vi}342, {vii}233
    Confessions, {ii}98;
    Du Contrat Social, {ii}312;
    Emile{iii}66;
    Nouvelle Heloïse, {i}203, 207
Rout of the Amazons, The, see Moore, T. S.
Routledge & Co., {v}391
Routledge, George, {vi}90
Rovereto (Austria), {i}456
Rowntree, Arnold, {iii}663, 675
Rowohlt, Ernst, Verlag, abortive negotiations for German version of *LCL*, {vii}335, 354–5, 374, 383, 386, 543, 567, 571–2
'Roxbury Garden, A', *see* Lowell, A.
Royal Academy, *see* London 11
Royal Carl Rosa Opera Co., {i}140
Royal Literary Fund, The, {ii}3, 9, {iii}14, 234, 238
    grants DHL £50, {ii}223–6, 228, {iii}213, 227–8, {viii}14; DHL reapplies and receives £50 from, {iii}249–55, 259–60, 263–5
Rozanov, Vasily Vasilyevich, {vi}42, 338–339, {vii}142, 147
    Fallen Leaves, {vii}474, {vii}538; DHL reviews, {vii}82, 125, 556, 559, 575
    Solitaria, {vi}30, {vii}556; DHL reviews, {vi}41, 52, 81, 84, {viii}107
Rozle, Alfred, & Willan, Ltd, {vi}514
Rubens, Peter Paul, {i}415
Rucker, Leonard, {v}237, {vi}210
Ruder, Barnet B., {vii}381, 411, 413, 515, 632
Rudge-Miller, Antonietta, {i}308
Rufina / Ruffina, *see* Archuleta, R.
Ruhleben (Germany), {iii}262
Runswick Bay (Yorkshire), {i}59
Ruskin, John, {i}54, 80, 477, {ii}616, {iv}545
Ruskin, Margaret Cox, {i}477

RUSSELL, ADA (DWYER), {ii}207,
210–11, 224, 235, 245, 645, {iii}32, 47–8,
296, 314, 362, 476, 539, 593, {iv}38, 57,
97, 243, 292, 326, 429, 478, 482, 487–8,
{v}198
  Letters to {iv}38
RUSSELL (EARL), BERTRAND
ARTHUR WILLIAM, {ii}2, 4, 11–13,
15, 17, 229, 253, 292, 305, 310–12, 314,
325, 355, 360, 362, 369, 372, 398, 411,
435, 439, 463, 466, 476, 483, 488, 545,
551, 557, 572, 592, 669, {iii}10, 71, 191,
570, {v}523, {vii}117
  'the philosophic-mathematics man',
{ii}273–4, 276–7, 289; visits DHL,
{ii}278; DHL's revolutionary politico-
sexual creed conveyed to, {ii}282–6.
294–5, 300, 347–8; DHL feels 'real
hastening of love to', {ii}297; DHL
pleads for 'connection' with, {ii}307;
disastrous visit to Cambridge and,
{ii}309, 320–1; 'powerful malignant will
in', {ii}315; Trinity College and,
{ii}347, 352, 656; DHL's 'philosophy'
sent to, {ii}356–7; DHL's plan for co-
operative activity with, {ii}358–9;
proposals for 'Social Reconstruction'
challenged by DHL, {ii}361, 363–6,
370–1, 378–80; emotionally immature
and inexperienced, {ii}366–7; betrays
'real truth', {ii}380; and *Signature*,
{ii}385–9; DHL quarrels with and
separates from, {ii}392–3, 397, 402, 612;
'not really enemies', {ii}436, 442;
'simple' aspect of, {ii}450, 474–5; told
about DHL's theory of 'blood knowledge', {ii}470–1; lectures by, {ii}506,
528, 534, 538, 546; DHL dismissive of,
{iii}49–50, 213, {iv}190; imprisoned,
{iii}239; founds school, {vii}165
  'The Danger to Civilization', {ii}392;
  'Philosophy of Social Reconstruction',
{ii}361;
  The Practice and Theory of Bolshevism,
{iv}190;
  Principles of Social Reconstruction,
{ii}505, {iii}50;
  War, the Offspring of Fear, {ii}436

  Letters to {ii}282–6, 294–5, 300, 307,
309–10, 327–8, 347–8, 352–3, 356–7,
361, 364–6, 370–1, 376–7, 386–7, 392,
436, 442, 469–71, 490, 505–6, 534,
546–7, 553, 574–5
Russell (Earl), John Francis Stanley, {ii}277,
669
Russell, Countess Dora Winifred,
{vii}165
Russell, Countess Mary Elizabeth, {ii}669
Russell Sage Foundation, {vi}10, 335
Russia, {i}5, 12, 133, 314, 469, 509, 521,
{ii}247, 464, 622, 660, {iii}4, 10, 12, 43,
45, 52–4, 69, 78–9, 102, 116–17, 174,
193, 230, 390, 399, 426, 482, 486, 543,
636, 676, {iv}5, 14, 96, 368, {v}47, 305,
339, 347, {vi}22, 24, {vii}84, 528
  'depraved', {ii}604; DHL would like *W
in L* published in, {iii}90; revolution in,
{iii}108, 284–5, {vii}99; 'chiefest hope
for the future', {iii}121, 124, 136; DHL
fancies visit to, {iv}362, 373, {v}355,
364–5, 367, 371, 373–4, 377, 379, 381,
384, 387–9, 391; 'not very desirable',
{iv}422, 440; idea of visit abandoned,
{v}418, 455, 461, {vii}29
Russian Law Bureau, {iii}43, 54, 163, 340,
{v}355
Russian Spirit, see Shestov, L.
Russo, Luigi, {vi}88
Rutherford (USA), {vii}71, 186
Rutherford, Mark (William Hale White),
{v}337
  Revolution in Tanner's Lane, {i}481–2,
{ii}146
Rutland, 8th Duke of, {iii}27
Rutland, 9th Duke of, {v}324
Rutter, Dolcie, {i}306
Ryan, Mrs, {ii}440–1, 446
Ryde (Hampshire), {i}134
Rye (Sussex), {ii}179

S. Manu, {ii}606–7, {iii}127
Sabino, {iv}336, 346–7, {v}82, 128
Sacchetti, Franco, {vii}20–2
Sackville-West, Vita, {vii}8
Sade, Comte Donatien-Alphonse,
{vi}333

SADLEIR, MICHAEL THOMAS
    HARVEY, {iii}202
    instigates DHL's meeting with Amy
    Lowell, {ii}203; publishes works by
    DHL, {iii}202, 474, 559, {iv}31, 36, 57,
    67–8, 117; introduced DHL to
    Beaumont, {iii}212; writes on DHL,
    {iii}261; wants copy of *LCL*, {vi}480
    New Decameron, {iii}474, {iv}31, 68,
    117
    New Paths, {iii}202, 212, 261, {iv}31
    Letters to {iii}202–7, 473–4, 493–4, 548,
    559, {iv}31, 57, 67–8, 116–17
    Letters from {iv}31
Sadler, Michael, *see* Sadleir, M. T. H.
Sadler, Sir Michael, {iii}202
'Saga of Siegmund', *see* Lawrence, D. H., *The
    Trespasser*
Sahara desert, {i}202, {ii}248, {iii}624, 637,
    {iv}209, 211
Saïd the Fisherman, see Pickthall, M.
Saint-Saëns, Camille, *Samson et Dalila*,
    {i}306
Saintsbury, George E. B., {i}89, 98
Sale of St Thomas, The, see Abercrombie, L.
Saleeby, Caleb W., {ii}340, 342
Saleeby, Mary, {ii}332, 342
    DHL teaches, {ii}340, 343, 346, 351,
    353, 362
Saleeby, Monica, {ii}340, 342, 344–5, 351,
    635
Salerno, Gulf of (Italy), {iii}446, 451, 462,
    {v}403, 406
Salimbene, {ii}538, 572, 580
Salisbury (Wiltshire), {iii}168, 175
Sallie, *see* Hopkin, S. A.
Salò (Italy), {i}460, 522
Salomé, see Wilde, O.
Salomonee, Walter, {v}33, 396
Salonika (Turkey), {ii}497, {iii}340
Salt Lake City (USA), {iv}492, 497, {vii}552
Salt, Sarah, *see* Hobson, C.
Salve, see Moore, G.
Salvestrini family, {vi}165, 306, {vii}274,
    400, 411, 416, {viii}107
Salzburg (Austria), {iii}721, 724, 730,
    {iv}25, 33, 50–78, {vi}135, 535, {viii}43,
    106

Sam, *see* King, S. T.
Sammarco, Mario, {i}253
Samoa, {iii}549
Samson et Dalila, see Saint-Saëns, C.
'Samuel Josephs, The', *see* Mansfield, K.
Samuelli, Signora, {i}466, 474, 476, 520,
    {iv}189
San A(u)gustin, {vii}374
San Antonio (USA), {iv}468–9
San Blas (Mexico), {viii}85
San Cristobal (USA), {iv}349, {v}39, 111,
    138, 265, 269, 277–8, 356–8, 379, 391,
    438, {vi}551, {vii}506
San Diego (USA), {iii}82
San Domenico Hotel (Taormina), {iii}491,
    502, 517, 648, 665
San Domingo (USA), *see* Santo Domingo
San Felipe (USA), {v}27
San Filippo (Anticoli–Corrado), {iii}551,
    568, 574, 578–87
San Francisco (USA), {iii}82, {iv}10–12,
    126–7, 130–1, 142, 182, 214, 220, 223,
    225, 227–30, 235, 238, 241, 246–54,
    256–60, 264–314 *passim*, 339, 367, 421,
    584, {vi}1, 86, 127, 208, 239, 365, 367,
    378–9, 382, 531, 555, {vii}97, 314, 617,
    628–9, 637, {viii}59–61
    'pleasant..not at all overwhelming',
    {iv}290; 'very noisy..iron-clanking',
    {iv}291; 'fine town, but bewildering..
    deafening', {viii}55
San Gaudenzio (Italy), {i}520, 526, 531, 535,
    537, 540, 551, {iv}189
San Gemignano (Gimignano) (Italy), {v}534,
    {vi}35, 209
San Geronimo fiesta (New Mexico), {iv}316,
    {v}134, 136, 139, 144, {vi}155
San Gervasio (Florence), {iii}520, 542, 595,
    597, 600, {iv}67
San Giovanni fiesta (Florence), {v}478–9,
    {vi}89
San Juan de Teotihuacan (Mexico), {iv}415,
    417, 423, {v}45, {viii}79
San Ildefonso (USA), {iv}370, {v}74, 96–7
San Moritz, *see* St Moritz
San Paolo Mosciano (Italy), {v}11–12,
    441–63, 503, 518, 525, 542, 643–6,
    {vi}131, 133, 139, 152, 164–5, 190, 237,

331, 380, 392, 465, 543, 582–3, {vii}33, 81, 280–2, 305, {viii}101, 111

DHL homesick for, {vi}169; his health better at Bandol than at, {vii}90

San Poggi, *see* Villa Poggi

San Polo Mosciano, *see* San Paolo Mosciano

San Remo (Italy), {iii}401, {vi}589, {vii}608

San Terenzo (Italy), {ii}63, 84, 86, 137

San Vincenzo a Torri (Italy), {v}633

Sanary (France), {vii}543

Sanborn's (restaurant, Mexico City), {iv}441

Sand, George, {iii}327–8, {vii}275
  François le Champi, {iii}327;
  Les Maîtres Sonneurs, {iii}327;
  Le Marquis de Villemer, {iii}327

Sandburg, Carl, {iii}141, {iv}407

Sandby, Paul, {i}89

SANDERS, MR,
  Letters to {vi}394–5

Sandgate (Kent), {i}381

Sandow, Eugen, {i}76

Sandown (Isle of Wight), {i}134

Sandringham (Norfolk), {i}27

Sands, Ethel, {ii}360, 393

Sanger, Charles P., {ii}411

Sangre de Cristo mountains (USA), {v}236, 252

Sanine, *see* Artsybashev, M. P.

Sankey, Ira David, {i}288, {ii}669

Sansani, Gino, {iv}81, {v}454, 517, 525, 534, 572, {vi}61, 112, {vii}34, 274

Santa Barbara (USA), {iv}497

Santa Domingo, *see* Santo Domingo

Santa Fe (USA), {iv}12, 112, 151, 290–5, 298, 303, 306–9, 316–69 *passim*, 386, 388–9, 395–6, 404–6, 408–9, 411–12, 414, 432, 434, 477, 546–7, 559, 567, 577, {v}3, 27, 36–7, 45, 64, 96–8, 100, 103, 108, 115, 128, 143, 150–2, 155–6, 158–9, 183–4, 199, 211, 219–20, 222–4, 226–8, 233, 235, 261, 276–7, 280, 297–8, 413, 434, 438, 475–6, 579, 600, 616, 650, {vi}38, 58, 181, 227, 229, 319–20, 326, 365, 393, 448, 461, 549, 555, {vii}387, 414, 574–5, 581, 591, 593, 598, 636, 651, {viii}75–7, 90

Santa Lucia, {iv}102

Santa Monica (USA), {iv}17, 495

Santo (or San) Domingo (USA), {iv}332, 335, 339, 349, {v}27, 82–3, 118, 121, 139, 263, 612, {vi}36, {viii}57

Santoro, Ellesina, {iii}407, 419, 429, 445

Sappho, {ii}105, 493
  see also Collings, E. H. R.

Sarah, *see* Higgins, S.

Sarah-Ann, *see* Wrath, S.

Sarawak, Rajah of, *see* Brooke, Sir C. V. de W.

Sardinia, {ii}123, {iii}17, 43, 608, 623, 637, 641, 662, 672, 687, 697, {iv}5, {v}372

DHL visits but not 'a place to live in', {iii}646–50, 654–6, 660, 676, {viii}39; writes 'Diary of a Trip to', {iii}664–5, 678, 688, 696, 700–2, 705, 730–1; 'very cheap', {iii}709; Juta's pictures of, {iv}24–5, 27, 35, 52

Sargent, John Singer, {i}113, 120, {ii}418–19

Sark (Channel Islands), {v}310

Sass, Mr, {iv}534

SASSOON, SIEGFRIED, {iii}363, 486
  'Fireflies', {iii}363
  Letters to {iii}363

Saturday Evening Post, {vi}176

Saturday Review, {i}420, {ii}1, 92, {v}614, {vii}118

Saturday Westminster Gazette, {i}350, 366, 375, 422, 447, 457, {ii}1, 56, 59–60, 83, {v}119

DHL's writings in, {i}382–3, 385–6, 396, 405, 407, 430–1, 434, 442, 446, 455, 459, {ii}39, 55, 67, 373, {v}87, {vi}541; review of *Trespasser* in, {i}419–20; 'anti-German' sketches rejected by, {i}443; Murry wrote for, {ii}31, 110

Satyricon, *see* Petronius, C.

Saudek, Robert, {iv}133

SAVAGE, HENRY, {i}16, {ii}10, 119

reviews *White Peacock*, {i}240–1; edits Middleton's poems, {ii}29, 34, 36; sends own poems to DHL, {ii}34–5; 'sort of amateur poet', {ii}41; 'exciting debauch' with, {ii}43; Frieda's opinion of, {ii}71; dificult for DHL to understand, {ii}73; sends books for DHL, {ii}100, 114, 138, 152; 'rum chap'; {ii}129; *Widowing* for, {ii}153; not regarded as writer by DHL, {ii}179

SAVAGE, HENRY (*cont.*)
  'Carber's Cruise', {ii}73, 98, 116, 180;
  Escapes and Escapades, {ii}35;
  Richard Middleton, {ii}28
  Letters to {i}241, {ii}28–9, 34–5, 40, 42–4,
    50, 69–74, 79, 94–8, 100–2, 113–17,
    129–30, 137–8, 152–4, 168–70, 178–80,
    192–3
Savarkar, Damodar, {ii}322
Savidge, Ann, {i}77
Savona (Italy), {v}352–5, 357, 359, 378, 382,
  389, {vii}164, 167, 169
Savonarola, Girolamo, {ii}592
Saxton, Camilla, {v}631
SAXTON, EUGENE F., {iii}691–2
  Letters to {iii}691
Saxton, Henry, {v}620, 631
Scandicci (Italy), {v}11, 447–96, 541–657
  passim {vi}26–113, 184–268, 311–422
  passim, 543, 567, {vii}19, {viii}98–105,
  107
Scandinavians, {v}274
  'flooded' Taormina, {iii}620, 624, 639,
    646, 649, 656, 658, 666, 676
Scarborough (Yorkshire), {i}70, {ii}244,
  {iii}257–8
Scarlatti, Alessandro, {i}171, {iii}370
Scarlet Letter, The, see Hawthorne, N.
Scarlet Pimpernel, The, see Orczy, Baroness
Schachermeyr, Fritz, *Etruskische*
  Frühgeschichte, {vii}569–70
Schaff, Hermann, {iii}397, 400–1, 405,
  455
Schaler, *see* Shaler, F.
Schalk, Franz, {i}327
Scheffel, Joseph Victor von, *Ekkehard*,
  {iii}315, 317;
  Der Trompeter von Säckingen, {iii}461
Scheinen, Mr, {i}346, 350, 355–6
Schiff, Jacob Henry, {iv}358
Schiff, Sydney, {iv}565, 571, {vi}323
  Prince Hempseed, {iv}565–6
Schiff, Therese Loeb, {iv}358
Schleswig-Holstein (Germany), {v}552–3
Schmalhausen, Samuel David, *Why We*
  Misbehave, {vi}564, {vii}467
  Letters from {vii}467
Schmidt, Florence, *see* Wood, F. M.

Schneider, Isidore, *Doctor Transit*, {v}359
Schnitzler, Arthur, {ii}80, 256, {iv}14
  Casanova's Homecoming, {iv}292, 296,
  501, 600
SCHOENBERNER, FRANZ, {vi}149–50,
  157, 167, {vi}551
  '*Jugend* man', {vi}149–50, 167; publishes
    German translation of 'Rex', {vi}153,
    189; introduced DHL to Carossa,
    {vi}167; 'Hymns in a Man's Life'
    written for collection by, {vi}541
  Letters to {vi}153, 155–6, 162–3, 184–5,
    188–9, 349–50, 540–1
Schoenberner, Frau, {vi}156, 163, 185, 189,
  350, 541
Schofield, Lily, *Elizabeth, Betsy and Bess*,
  {i}496, 512
Schönberg (Germany), {i}77, {iii}426,
  {iv}76
Schoolmaster, The, {i}204
Schopenhauer, Arthur, {i}5, {iv}128
Schöpferische Pause, Die, see Klatt, F.
Schreiber, Max (Hofrath, Herr), {iv}42, 45,
  47
SCHREIBERSHOFEN, HELENE
  JOHANNA MATHILDE ('NUSCH'),
  {i}391, 393, 409, 449, {iii}26, 348, 505,
  711, 716–17, {iv}3, 63, 72, 530–2, 586,
  590, 594–5, 597–8
  'in a large, splendid way – cocotte',
    {i}395; has villa near Salzburg, {iii}730,
    733, {iv}25, 33, 49–51, 66; leaves
    husband to marry Krug, {iv}254–5, 258,
    395–6; *Captain's Doll* for, {iv}390
  see also Krug, H. J. M. von,
  Letters to {iv}293
Schreibershofen, Anita von, {ii}60, {iv}49,
  63, 75–6, 254–5, 356–7
  marries Ernst von Hinke, {iv}258
  see also Hinke, A. von
  Letters from {iv}62–3
Schreibershofen, Hadubrand ('Hadu')
  von, {iv}49, 63, 75–6, 118, 121,
  135–6 147, 356–7, 374, 395–6, 531–2,
  {vi}173
  Letters from {iv}62–3
Schreibershofen, Major Max von, {i}391,
  {iv}25, 63, 65, 75–6

'brute of a swanky officer', {i}395; wife leaves, {iv}254–5, 258, 395–6, {vi}26; 'neer-do-well ex-army officer', {vi}131, 226

Schreiner, Olive, {i}5, 293
   The Story of an African Farm, {i}161; *Woman and Labour*, {i}287–9

Schubert, Franz Peter, {i}67–8, 73, 322, {iii}514, {vii}566

Schumann, Robert Alexander, {i}67–8

Schwannhild, {vi}126, 241

Schwarzwald, *see* Black Forest

Schweikharts, {vii}422

Science of Life, The, see Huxley, (Sir), J. S.

Scotland, {ii}323, 329, {iii}252, 264, 282, 323, 327, 409, 722, {v}12–13, 80, 228, 329, 342, 413, 429, 473–4, 497, 499–501, 514, 517–18, 527, 573, 644, {vi}39, 93, 188, 448, {vii}500
   DHL's visit to, {v}504–12; 'rather damp..somewhat obscured by tourists', {v}508–9; 'so-called mountains are dumpy hills', {v}510; DHL attends Church of, {v}511; 'among the islands..like the twilight morning of the world', {v}512

Scotland Yard, {vii}327
   Mountsier and, {iii}16, 65, 67–8; Cynthia Asquith's 'man' at, {iii}188; copies of *LCL* and *Pansies* MSS seized by, {vii}146–9, 151, 153, 156–7, 161, 165, 204–5, 315, 383, 390

Scott & Seltzer, {iii}390, 399, {iii}400, {iii}408, 527
   send £50 advance for *W in L*, {iii}428–9, 441, 456; 'Liars they are', {iii}470; relinquish novel, {iii}472, 476–7; bankruptcy rumoured, {iii}492–3; partnership dissolved, {iii}662

Scott, Capt. Robert Falcon, {i}517

SCOTT, CATHERINE AMY DAWSON, {vii}196
   DHL joins P.E.N.through, {v}88, 124; invites DHL to P.E.N. dinner, {vii}458
   Letters to {v}88, 124, {vii}458
   Letters from {vii}458

SCOTT, CHARLES, T., {vi}335
   Letters to {vi}297, 524

SCOTT, CYRIL KAY, pseud. for Frederick Creighton Wellman, {iii}672
   Blind Mice, {iii}672, 674, 691–2, 733–4
   Letters to {iii}692

SCOTT, EVELYN, {iii}672
   Narrow House, {iii}694, 733–5; *Precipitations*, {iii}672, 674, 692–4
   Letters to {iii}693–4, 733–5

Scott, Margaret, {iv}436, 515

Scott, Mr, {i}306 *or* {vii}195

Scott, Sir Walter, {i}101
   The Lay of the Last Minstrel, {i}517, {iii}349, {v}496, {vi}169; *The Talisman*, {i}504

Scott, Temple, {iii}390, 662, {iv}2

Scott, Winfield, {iv}436, 473, 508, 511, 515, {viii}81

Scott,Walter, {i}98, 154

Scott-James, Rolfe Arnold, {i}16, 318, 323–4, 326–7, 335

Scott-Moncrieff, Charles Kenneth, {vi}2, 257
   visits DHL at Mirenda, {vi}214; has 'obscene mind like a lavatory', {vi}220; very ill, {vii}561, 578

Scriven, Mr, {i}356, 358

Scrutinies by Various Writers, see Rickword, E.

Sea Garden, see Aldington, H.

Seabrooke, Elliott, {ii}2, 211

Seafarer, The, {ii}511

Seaman, Arthur George, {vi}92

Seaman, Bernal Edward ('Teddy') de Martelly, {v}389, {vi}26
   Elsa Weekley's fiancé, {v}568–9, {vii}69, 76, 81, 211; marriage of, {vii}241–2, 262, 282

SEAMAN, EILEEN HILDA, {v}389, {vi}31–5, 37–8, 45
   Letters to {vi}92

Seaman, Henry Chepmell, {vi}92

Seccombe, Thomas, {i}353–4

Secessionist Exhibition, {i}548

Sechehaye, Adrien, {vi}336

Secker, Adrian {iv}594, 598, {v}23–24, 80, 91, 185, 268, 286, 315, 327, 341, 346, 350–1, 444, 556, 588, 638, 655, {vi}32, 130, 305, 317, {vii}41, 72, 298, 403

SECKER, CATERINA MARIA ('RINA'),
{iv}26, 549, {v}24, 38, 91, 122, 184, 268,
315, 327, 333–6, 341, 345–6, 351, 356,
364, 379–80, 383, 390, 412, 443, 490,
513, 522, 528–9, 556, 563, 581, 588, 619,
623, 638, 655–6, {vi}21, 93, 130, 152,
168, 197, 265, 276, 295, 305, 317, 330,
377, {vii}40–1, 72, 196, 298, 403
translated Tozzi's *Tre Croci*, {iv}188;
persuaded DHL to rent Villa Bernarda,
{v}337; 'frightfully discontented',
{v}350, 352; 'how awful is a dissatisfied
woman', {vii}611
Letters to {v}497–8
SECKER, MARTIN, {i}15, 306, 442,
{iii}11–15, 187, 191, 262, 266, 452,
{iv}6–7, 11, 15, 18, 23, 32–3, 45, 155,
188, 192, 195, 207, 213, 235, 275, 282,
296, 300, 380, 397, 420, 454, 457, 464,
476, 513, 547, 575, 589, 592, {v}1–2, 8,
10, 13, 90, 120, 142, 169, 193, 198,
302–4, 321, 332, 385, 387–8, 410, 424,
492, 523, 533, 626–8, 634, {vi}2, 4, 6,
8–11, 173, 228, 294, 414, 462, 493, 526,
548, {vii}3, 66–7, 198, 209, 324, 340,
376, 395, 526, 536, 584, 588, 638,
{viii}69–70, 87–8, 97
offers to publish volume of DHL's short
stories{i}275–6, 298, 317, 319, 335, 345,
349, 367, 372, 432; what advantage 'if
Secker ran me for the rest of time?',
{i}434; and *New Poems*, {iii}274, 277–8,
280, 283–4, 287, 290, 325–6, 356, 379,
475, 504, 547, 568, {iv}181, {vi}607;
chose 'decidedly false title' for *New
Poems*, {iii}291, 294, 304; suggests
Collected Poems, {iii}379, 383, 386; and
All Things, {iii}389, 392–4, 396–8,
400–5, 412, 433–4, 437, 439, 441, 455,
470–1, 501, 503, 508, 510–12, 516, 529,
{vi}177, {vii}474, 538; and *W in L*,
{iii}390–1, 395, 408, 410–11, 426, 428,
434, 456–7, 459, 470, 472, 490, 497,
499–500, 503–4, 512–15, 517, 519–21,
525, 528, 531, 538, 540, 545, 586, 606,
619, 621, 625, 627–9, 638, 647, 660, 664,
672, 678, 708–9, 722–5, 727–9, 732,

{iv}26, 31, 35, 40, 51, {viii}47; 'scurvy
little swine', {iii}403, 651; and *SCAL*,
{iii}406–7, 537, 543, 556, 563, 565, 578,
{iv}323, 399, 401, 407; 'slippery worm',
{iii}425, 653; to publish *Rainbow* would
earn DHL's 'eternal allegiance',
{iii}439, 459, 468, 472, 474, 491, 497,
499, 500, 512–15, 517, 519–21, 525–6,
538, 545, {iv}129; Mackenzie's proposal
of partnership with, {iii}458–60; and
Lost Girl, {iii}503, 512, 515, 519–20,
528, 537, 540, 549–50, 552–3, 555,
559–60, 562–5, 567, 571–6, 580, 582,
586, 588, 594, 599–600, 605, 608,
611–12, 617, 619, 621–2, 624–5, 627–9,
632, 638, 640, 644, 646–7, 660, 663–4,
709, {v}122, 160, {viii}33, 35, 38, 47;
needs 'committee for his moral encouragement', {iii}513; DHL 'irritated' by,
{iii}514, 655–6; DHL requests money
from, {iii}605, 709, 714, 722, 724, 730,
{iv}148; DHL 'wrote him pepper',
{iii}633, 635; 'a cur', {iii}644; 'shoddy',
{iii}675; and *Mr Noon*, {iii}700, 702,
708, 717, 722, 730–1, {iv}27, 35; and
Aaron's Rod, {iii}702, 708, 722, 729–31,
{iv}25, 65, 69, 96, 116, 129, 144, 159,
177, 258, 262, {viii}47; Curtis Brown
told to 'go gently' with, {iii}705;
'useless' except as publisher of 'novels or
library books', {iv}27–8; and *S and S*,
{iv}34–5, 108, 116, 162–3, 165, 168,
171, 179, 183, 199, 328, 366, 378–9, 389,
391, 489, {v}460, 481, 490, {viii}41;
DHL wary of but fair to, {iv}54–5, 399;
threatened with libel action by
Heseltine over *W in L*, {iv}87–9, 93–4,
105, 113–14, 116, 123, 129–30, 138, 169;
and *Ladybird*, {iv}107, 145, 262, 298,
302, 324, 366, 371–2, 389–91, 401,
{viii}57; and *EME*, {iv}144, 401,
{v}87, 161; ignores DHL's instruction
over story-title, {iv}152; Curtis Brown
takes responsibility for DHL's accounts
with, {iv}153, 174, 187, 194; auto-
graphed edn of *W in L*, {iv}163, 173–4,
199–200; and *Kangaroo*, {iv}319, 383,

389, 391, 394, 401, 427–8, 486, 489–90, {v}122, 161; DHL's 5–book contract with, {iv}341; untrustworthy, {iv}369, {v}483, {viii}57; and *Psychoanalysis*, {iv}399, 401; and *Fantasia*, {iv}399, 401; and *BBF*, {iv}428, 448, 475, 481, 486, 489–90; action towards *Collected Poems*, {iv}428–9, {vi}168, 195, 206, 264, 268–9, 275, 280–1, 291, 305, 330, 351, 376, 388, 395, 405, 463, 471–2, 482, 495, 505, 539, 546, 572; and *B in B*, {iv}533, 557, 596–7, {v}19–21, 24, 31, 34, 37–9, 70–1, 78–80, 91–2, 95, 113, 123, 141, 161; and *Foreign Legion*, {v}16–17, 30–3, 39, 56, 70, 113, 133, 141, 161, 256, 340, 346, 348; rejects Skinner's *Black Swans*, {v}113–14, 121; and *St. Mawr*, {v}141, 148, 173, 194, 206–7, 214, 226–7, 244–5, 255, 267; rejects *Mastro-Don Gesualdo*, {v}165; and *Plumed Serpent*, {v}271, 286–7, 297–8, 318, 320, 340; *Porcupine* not offered to, {v}284, 290, 329, 375; and *David*, {v}285–6, 333, 336, 339, 376, 413, 623, {viii}96–7; visits DHL in Spotorno, {v}350–4, 356, 364, 366, 369–70; 'nice' but not 'sparkling', {v}354, 366, 377–80; urges DHL to write travel book, {v}448; resists DHL's being published by another English publisher, {v}535–6, 539; DHL sensitive to rights of, {v}554–6; and *M in M*, {v}575–6, 580–2, 584, 587, 594, 636, {vi}31, 67–70, 73; 'pleased' new novel 'to have Derbyshire setting', {v}577; hopes to reach 'wider public' for DHL, {v}596, {vi}44, 167, {vii}549, 553; warned that will 'probably hate' *LCL*, {v}638; eager to see *LCL*, {vi}21, 29, 42, 45; DHL anxious about 'Man Who Loved Islands' and Mackenzie's close friendship with, {vi}68–9, 130; and *Etruscan Places*, {vi}77, 84, 93, 105, 130, 168, {vii}197, {viii}104; adds *Little Novels* to list, {vi}152, 168; and *WWRA*, {vi}152, 176, 182, 191, 196–7, 254, 269–70, 272,

275, 277, 291, 295, 376; omits 'Man Who Loved Islands' from *WWRA* after pressure from Mackenzie, {vi}205–6, 218–19, 224, 269, {vii}514–15; and expurgated *LCL*, {vi}222, 265, 271, 289, 291–2, 295, 305, 308–10, 314–16, 326; believes impossible to expurgate *LCL* 'for public sale', {vi}329–34, 337, 344, 371; 'born rabbit', {vi}333; 'tightness' of, {vi}343; 'seems to have shrivelled up', {vi}372; subscribes for *LCL*, {vi}442, 472; 'another Jew', {vi}515; *Collected Poems* published, {vi}599, {vii}38, 41, 243, 272, 413, 445, 457; 'a liar', {vi}602; meagre royalties from, {vii}18; DHL refuses to transfer to Knopf from, {vii}37, 40, 45; DHL's 'obligations' to, {vii}111; and *Pansies*, {vii}122–3, 156, 195–6, 215; 'even more like a mouse than a rabbit', {vii}163; accepts expurgated *Pansies*, {vii}218, 221–2, 228, 231, 233, 237, 241–2, 249–50, 252, 255–7, 261, 264–7, 274, 278, 282, 292, 295–8, 300–5, 315, 318–20, 325–8, 334–6, 347, 350, 352, 358, 362, 380–1, 387, 396, 402, 406, 412, 414, 428, 445, 462, 467, 502, 504, 516, 592–3; *Pansies* not to be 'a perfect hymn-book' by, {vii}256; 'artful dodger of the worst sort', {vii}301; 'little meannesses from', {vii}350; first *LCL* 'may be the right one for', {vii}383, 390–1; and *Assorted Articles*, {vii}400–3, 611, 619; proposes 'Collected Short Stories', {vii}413; 'slow-coach', {viii}57 *Letters to* {i}275–6, {iii}283–4, 290, 379, 386, 389, 391, 394, 396, 398, 401–2, 404, 406–8, 410–12, 420, 434, 437–9, 458–60, 470, 490, 499–500, 503–4, 511–12, 515, 519–20, 528–9, 531, 537, 549–50, 552–3, 555, 559–60, 562–4, 572–3, 586, 590, 599–600, 605–6, 617, 621–2, 625, 628–9, 637–9, 647–8, 660, 702–3, 705–6, 708–9, 722, 729, {iv}35–6, 39, 50–1, 70, 87, 93–4, 113, 116, 129, 145, 148, 152–3, 163, 173–4, 193–4, 233, 261–2, 298–9, 391, 448–9, 486, 489, 548–9, 553, 558,

SECKER, MARTIN (*cont.*)
564, 576, 594, 598, {v}23–5, 34, 38, 56,
70, 79–81, 91, 96–7, 112–13, 121–2,
140–1,184–5, 206–7, 226–7, 267–8,
285–6, 290, 296, 312, 315, 318, 323, 327,
334–6, 340–1, 346, 379–84, 386, 388–9,
392, 399, 401–2, 412–13, 443–4, 490,
507, 522–4, 528–9, 556, 562–3, 575–6,
580–2, 587–8, 595–6, 619–20, 623–4,
628, 638, 655–6, {vi}31–2, 44–6, 51,
68–9, 77–8, 84, 93, 105, 111, 124,
129–30, 144, 151–2, 167–8, 176–7,
196–7, 205–6, 218–19, 264–5, 268–9,
272–3, 275–6, 280–1, 291–2, 295–6, 305,
308, 316–17, 330, 376–7, 395–6, 405,
424–6, 455, 463, 471–2, 495, 504–5,
546–7, 572, 590, 599–600, {vii}40–1, 72,
85–6, 122–3, 156, 171–2, 195–6, 215,
237–8, 241–2, 249–50, 292, 298, 310,
325–6, 335–6, 347, 362–3, 402–3, 553–4,
563–4, 611, 618–19
Letters from {i}275–6, 367, {iii}460, 599,
606, 621, 628, 637–8, 647, 660, 708, 717,
722, 730, {iv}51, 88, 94, 113, 173, 183,
199–200, 258, 262, 366, 389, 401, 427–8,
448, {v}16–17, 20–1, 24, 31, 38–9, 70,
78–9, 91, 112–13, 122, 161, 165, 173,
184–5, 194, 206–7, 267, 285–6, 297, 320,
340, 460, 576–7, 624, {vi}269, {vii}237,
296–7, 303, 413, {viii}47
Seco, *see*, Arroyo Seco
Secolo, {ii}135
Second American Caravan, The, see Brooks, V.
W.
Second Cena, see Grazzini, A.
Second Contemporary Verse Anthology, A,
DHL's review of entitled 'A Spiritual
Record', {iv}16, 494
Secret Doctrine, The, see Blavatsky, H. P.
Sedaine, Michel-Jean, *Richard Coeur de Lion,*
{iii}136
Sedgwick, Anne Douglas, 'The Nest',
{i}139, 142
SEELIG, KARL ('CARL') WILHELM,
{v}314
DHL visits in Switzerland, {v}329,
333–4, 339; *Foreign Legion* and *BBF* sent

to, {v}341; divorce of, {v}371, 461,
{vii}29–30
*Die Jahreszeiten im Spiegel
Schweizerischer Volkssprüche,* {v}327
Letters to {v}314, 327, 333–4, 339–40, 371,
377, 398, 461, {vii}29–30
Seelig, Maria Margareta, {v}314, 333, 339,
371, 461, {vii}29–30
Seevolk, see Nylander, J. W.
SELDES, GILBERT, {iv}339–41, 355,
358–9, 379–80, 383
Letters to {iv}398
Selfridges, {i}146, {ii}418, {iii}316, 330,
373, {viii}29
SELIGMANN, HERBERT JACOB, {v}2,
{vi}14, {vii}25
suffered for favourable review of *LCL,*
{vi}607; DHL seeks help over US
copyright of *BBF,* {vii}27, 38; Brett
seeks help from, {vii}342
*D. H. Lawrence: An American
Interpretation,* {v}35, 221, {vii}620,
{viii}88
Letters to {vi}607–8, {vii}228
SELTZER, ADELE SZOLD, {iii}390,
{iv}1–2, 15–17, 267, 335, 344–5, 349,
354–5, 367–8, 370–1, 374–5, 379, 383,
389, 395–6, 437, 458, 495, 517, 519, 529,
550, 559, 585, {v}16, {vii}38
likes *Rainbow,* {iii}485; translations by,
{iii}662, {iv}342; visits DHL at Del
Monte, {iv}358–60, 363–4, 366; DHL
visits in New Jersey, {iv}471–90, 492;
'dish-washing demon', {iv}501; Frieda's
confidante, {iv}502; gift for, {iv}526,
544; despondent about financial plight,
{v}305–6, 395; hopes DHL will provide
'best seller', {v}574, 619; has high
opinion of *Gesualdo,* {viii}58, 61; gift
for, {viii}76
Letters to {iv}373, 384–6, 412, 426, 444–5,
455–6, 490–1, 503, 510–11, 522–3, 562,
{v}99, 363–4, {viii}75–7, 87–8
Letters from {iv}150, {viii}95
SELTZER, THOMAS, {iii}5, 12–13, 390–1,
408, 501, 520, 539, 585, 629, 650, 653,
657, 677, 689, 693, 704, 709, 717, 722,

730, 735, {iv}1–2, 5, 7, 11, 13–20, 26, 40,
65, 74, 80, 145, 154, 170, 179, 185, 190,
219–20, 232, 241, 243, 257, 268–9, 274,
277, 279, 290, 293, 301, 311, 330, 336,
385, 387–8, 391–2, 396–400, 402–5,
425–9, 431, 439, 444–5, 449, 455–6,
461–2, 470, 485, 494, 496–500, 505–6,
508–9, 515–16, 521, 529, 533, 535, 539,
553, 563, 566, 571–4, 579–83, 587, 591,
593, 596–8, {v}1–2, 9, 18–19, 87, 90–1,
145, 161, 179–80, 198, 364, {vi}610,
{vii}85, 111, 204, 320, 413, 467, 539,
{viii}79, 82, 87, 95, 114
enquires about publishing *W in L*,
{iii}390–1; negotiations over publication
of *W in L* between Huebsch and,
{iii}408–9, 456, 457–8, 466–7, 472–3,
543, 643, 646, {iv}411–12, {viii}72, 77;
DHL accepts offer for *W in L* from,
{iii}484–5, 492; and *T and G*, {iii}485,
547–8, 565; and *SCAL*, {iii}493, 519,
543, 545, 565, 576, 612, {iv}177, 197–8,
306, 338, 341–2, 349, 355, 367, 369, 399,
419, 441–2, {viii}36, 57, 68, 81; irritates
DHL by delays in sending *W in L* TS to
Secker, {iii}500, 503–4, 508, 511–12,
519, 537, 540, 545, 549, 552, 564, 573,
586; and *Lost Girl*, {iii}519, 524, 528–9,
540, 563, 572–3, 575–6, 590, 605,
612–13, 619, 645, 662, 671–2, {iv}68,
{viii}35–6; money from, {iii}518, 520,
539–40, 564; and *Widowing*, {iii}527,
565, 576; 'sort of private edn' of *W in L*
by, {iii}537–8, 540, 545–7, 613, 618–19,
621, 625, 672, 673–4, {iv}200, {viii}35,
38; DHL doesn't 'mind if he is a Jew and
a little nobody' if treated 'decently' by,
{iii}547, 678; 'the swine', {iii}555; 'very
decent so far', {iii}627; edn of *W in L*
'has made us friends for life', {iii}635,
638; considers *W in L* not merely DHL's
best novel 'but one of the best ever
written', {iii}636; DHL needs money
from, {iii}646, 672, {iv}235, 246, 409,
419, 501, 588–9; *Psychoanalysis* looks
'nice', {iii}732; and *S and S*, {iv}45, 47,
58, 60, 69–70, 82, 107, 109, 114, 116,

129–31, 137, 156–7, 162, 165, 168, 175,
262, 299, 549; and *Aaron's Rod*, {iv}50,
57, 71, 92–3, 104, 131, 134, 152, 167,
265, {viii}41; and *Movements*, {iv}83;
and *Fantasia*, {iv}103–4, 111, 131–2,
134, 245, 299, 306, {viii}41; publishes
Tortoises, {iv}109, 123, 130, 156–7, 242;
finds *Aaron's Rod* 'wonderful, over-
whelming', {iv}121, 124–5, 127, 129,
138; suggests book on India by DHL,
{iv}244; getting known 'as a merely
erotic publisher', {iv}245, 258; and
Captain's Doll, {iv}258, 338, 341, 345,
369, 371–2, 378, 389–90, 399, 446,
{viii}57, 68, 74; and *EME*, {iv}262;
'may be dodgy', {iv}276; and *Kangaroo*,
{iv}278, 318–20, 322, 324, 335, 340–3,
367, 369, 383, 394, 399, 428, {viii}57–60;
successful against indictment over *W in
L*, {iv}292, 296–7, 300, 305–7, 314–15,
326, 379, 501, {viii}71, 73; at 'daggers
drawn' with Mountsier, {iv}298, 300,
316, 328, 374, 376–7, {viii}62–7, 72–3;
and *BBF*, {iv}324, 336, 345, 369, 371,
373–4, 378, 380–1, 383–4, 399, 406–7,
419, 428, 526, {vii}27, 38, 45, 66, 130,
181–2, 272, {viii}68, 70, 72; produces
trade edn of *W in L*, {iv}326, 335,
{viii}73; visits DHL for Christmas,
{iv}357–66; 'tiny Jew, but trustworthy',
{iv}366; and *Little Novels*, {iv}367,
{v}93, 247; if 'faithful' DHL will remain
with, {iv}378, {viii}58, 77; Kennerley, *S
and L* and, {iv}376, 417–18, {viii}57,
67–8, 71; and *Gesualdo*, {iv}436, 442,
475–6, 478, 526, {viii}58, 61, 72; DHL
visits, {iv}471–91; arranges typing of
Plumed Serpent, {iv}495, 517, 523; 'a bit
arbitrary', {iv}515; and *B in B*, {iv}523,
543–4, 549, 557, 559–60, {v}20–2, 35,
37, 71, 78, 80, 95, 123, 171; DHL 'a bit
annoyed with', {iv}550; to accept offer
for film rights on *W in L*, {iv}558,
{viii}87; 'hateful...that dog', {iv}580;
'business in low water', {iv}600, {v}16,
42, 78–9; and *Foreign Legion*, {v}31–2,
78; 'not born for success in the Knopf

SELTZER, THOMAS (*cont.*)
    sense', {v}79, 92, 147, {viii}92; 'very
    slowly pays up', {v}114, 139–40, 249,
    298, 307; DHL fears bankruptcy of,
    {v}126–7, 135–6, 148, 175, 292, 305–6,
    347; Curtis Brown transfers DHL to
    Knopf from, {v}169, 194, 213, 253, 269,
    271, {viii}91, 93–5; 'staggering',
    {v}245; 'like a creaking gate', {v}269;
    court action against, {v}342–3; 'at his
    last gasp', {v}395; unreliable, {v}458;
    DHL refuses to promise return to,
    {v}574–5; as person, DHL prefers to
    Knopf, {vi}526; DHL feels affection
    and sadness for, {vi}607–8, {vii}38;
    transfers rights in DHL's books to Boni,
    {vii}222, 236, 265, 375, 440, 445, 496,
    503, 520–2, 533, 612, 624; enthusiasm
    for DHL, {viii}60, 64; 'swelled head'
    (Frieda), {viii}92; feels DHL belongs
    'naturally' to his list, {viii}94; wants to
    reestablish 'old relations' with DHL,
    {viii}95
    see also Scott & Seltzer
   Letters to {iii}390–1, 408–9, 457–8, 467,
    484–5, 518–19, 527, 539–40, 543, 564–6,
    571, 590, 618–19, 624–5, 635, 646, 662,
    671–2, 703, 732–3, {iv}50, 57–8, 68, 71,
    86, 92–3, 104, 131–2, 156–8, 167, 172–3,
    196, 201, 258–61, 267, 278, 292, 294–5,
    297–8, 306, 320, 322, 335, 342, 344–5,
    348–9, 354–5, 367–72, 374–9, 382–4,
    389–91, 393–5, 401, 403, 406–12,
    416–19, 435–7, 441–2, 446–8, 454,
    457–9, 464–8, 492–3, 495, 501, 503–4,
    516–19, 523, 526–7, 542–4, 549–50,
    558–9, 569, 588–9, {v}22–3, 32–3, 35,
    37–40, 45–6, 48, 58–60, 78–9, 92, 99,
    105–6, 140, 213, 221, 253, 574,
    {vii}38–9, {viii}35–6, 38, 40–2, 56–9,
    81, 87
   Letters from {iii}635–6, {iv}314–15,
    {vii}166, {viii}59–73, 89, 91, 93–5
Semmering (Austria), {iv}398
Sen, Boshi ('Boshy'), {vi}521, 538, 542, 600
    gives DHL massage, {vi}519, 547;
    returned to India, {vii}436
Senard, Marcelle, {v}487

Seneca, {i}5
Sensani, Signor, {vii}358
Sentimental Education, see Flaubert, G.
Sentimental Journey, see Sterne, L.
Sentimental Tommy, see Barrie, (Sir) J. M.
Seraglio, see Mozart, W. A.
Serao, Matilde, {iii}43
Sergeant Grisha, see Zweig, A.
Sermione (Italy), {i}165
Servia, {i}474, 478
Settignano (Italy), {ii}167, {iii}425, 463,
    592, {iv}111, 128, {v}419, {vi}371,
    {vii}206, 363
Seven Arts, {iii}13, 29, 140–1, 357, {viii}24
    'The Thimble' (subsequently 'The
    Ladybird') published in, {ii}420,
    {iii}50–1, 111, 142, {iv}134, {v}104;
    'Mortal Coil' in, {ii}653, {iii}22, 142;
    merged with *Dial*, {iii}653
Seven Sleepers, The, {viii}24
Severino, {ii}116, 140
Seville (Spain), {vii}273, 276, 282–4,
    559–60
SEXUALITY, relationship between man
    and man, man and woman
    differentiated, {i}65–6; heterosexual
    love finest when 'sex notes' attuned to
    religious and sympathetic feeling,
    {i}66–7; 'sex matters' not among things
    DHL cares 'deeply for', {i}71; Jessie
    Chambers moves DHL's 'sex fire',
    {i}173; between DHL and Helen Corke
    'is sex' but 'sex relationship' will never
    be sought again, {i}285–6; in love 'sex
    passion becomes calm..steady sort of
    force, instead of a storm', {i}403; love
    bigger than passion, 'woman *much* more
    than sex', {i}415; 'sex lust fermented
    makes atrocity', {i}469, 543–4; sexual
    conflict at centre of *S and L*, {i}477;
    Middleton and, {ii}94–7; 'Most poets
    die of sex..self hate and self-murder',
    {ii}101; 'Sex is the fountain head, where
    life bubbles up..from the unknown',
    {ii}102; 'nearly every man that
    approaches greatness tends to homosex-
    uality', {ii}115; 'female influence'
    essential to 'fertilise the soul of man to

vision or being', {ii}218; Kuttner's
report on DHL's sexual obsessiveness in
'Sisters', {ii}246; 'men loving men' give
sense of 'triumphant decay', carrion,
beetles, {ii}320–1, 323; 'I like sensual
lust - but insectwise..it is obscene',
{ii}331; sex 'not living till it is unconscious', {ii}426; heterosexual love
produces 'the great *immediate* synthesis',
homosexual disintegration and 'immediate reduction', {ii}448; 'blood consciousness' and 'sexual connection',
{ii}470–1; 'licentious profligacy'
perhaps preferable to 'mental licentious-
ness', {ii}504; detestation of homosexuality in 'Goats and Compasses', {ii}558;
complex 'not simply a sex relation',
{ii}655; 'tearing asunder' of sexes,
females assuming male roles in war,
leads to 'universal death', {iii}78; DHL
tired of 'eroticism and sex perversions'
in Italian books, {iii}103; 'awful working
of sex' distinguished from 'abnormal
sex', {iii}140–1; Chatto & Windus object
to 'continuously sexual tone' of
LWHCT, {iii}148; 'woman must yield
some..precedence to a man', {iii}302; in
Lost Girl sex, 'the bee in my
bonnet..buzzes not over loud', {iii}517;
some elderly women suffer from
'megalomaniac sexual conceit', {iii}552;
Kangaroo hasn't 'so much as the letter S
of sex', {iv}258, 268; 'No sex' in *Plumed
Serpent*, {iv}457; mistake to put 'sex into
a spiritual relation', {v}203; 'sex in the
head..evil and destructive', {v}204;
'sheer physical flow..healing and
sustaining..is true sensual sex', {v}462;
books that 'treat of sex *honestly* and
with..sincere reverence', {v}637; some
young people treat sex as 'secret, dirty
thing', {v}638; 'one's proper sex life'
threatened by modern life, {v}648;
'phallus..great sacred image', {v}648;
DHL labours 'to make the sex relation
valid and precious', {vi}29; 'societal
instinct much deeper than sex instinct',
{vi}99; DHL admires Burrow's views

on 'sex and sexuality', {vi}113; 'mental
cognitive mode and..sexual mode of
consciousness' at odds, {vi}114; 'sexual
cynicism' characteristic of modernity,
{vi}156; *LCL* about 'direct sex',
{vi}295, 310; sex can be mere 'cerebral
reaction', 'real phallic..consciousness' (as
in *LCL*) quite different, {vi}319–20,
324–7, 331, 335, 337–9, 355; phallic
consciousness the source of 'real
beauty..and gentleness', {vi}328; the
'grand perverts..intellectualise
and..falsify the phallic consciousness',
{vi}342; 'Was your mind a sexual blank
at sixteen?', {vi}373; *LCL* 'like a bomb
against..false sex and hypocrisy',
{vi}513; modern society must 'embrace
the emotions and passions of sex',
{vi}614; DHL against 'perpetual
sex..Nothing nauseates me more than
promiscuous sex in and out of season',
{vii}106; for many upper class ladies
'chauffeur is the favorite fucker..a
machine à plaisir, {vii}179; 'silly twid-
dling with girls..isn't even really sex',
{vii}180; language should be freed of
'various artificial taboos on words and
expressions' associated with sex,
{vii}308; DHL on Barrie's and
Galsworthy's books inciting to 'private
masturbation', {vii}503; in *P and O*
'appreciation of the realities of sexual
morality and sexual honesty and
decency' (Barclay), {vii}582
Shakespeare and Company, {iv}19, 275, 569,
{v}457, {vii}62
Shakespeare, William, {i}5, 185, 261,
{ii}384, {iii}94, 506, {iv}99, {v}337,
524, 630, {vi}2, {vii}206
As You Like It, {i}167, 227, 242, 245,
259, 516, {iii}49, 447, {iv}73;
Hamlet, {i}207, 269, 504–5, 508, 546,
{iii}156, 517, {iv}90, 243, 253, {v}423,
464, {vi}147, 204, 384, {viii}24;
2 Henry IV, {vi}23;
Julius Caesar, {i}150, 163, 207, {iii}214,
461, 502;
King Lear, {iii}82, {v}423;

Shakespeare, William (*cont*.)
  Macbeth, {i}44, 54, 60, 74, 81, 185, 227,
    269, 483, 496, 516, {ii}37, 107, 129,
    {iii}300, 514, {v}199, 423;
  The Merchant of Venice, {iii}518,
    {iv}355;
  A Midsummer Night's Dream, {i}419,
    {ii}339, {iii}366;
  Much Ado About Nothing, {i}48;
  Othello, {i}417, {ii}162, {iii}156;
  Richard II, {iii}366;
  Richard III, {vi}329;
  Sonnets, {i}49;
  The Taming of the Shrew, {i}419;
  The Tempest, {i}419, {iii}156,
    {vii}110;
  Twelfth Night, {ii}466, {vi}158;
  The Winter's Tale, {i}202
Shaler, Fred, {iv}110, 125
Shanklin (Isle of Wight), {i}24, 129, 131–6,
  175, 283
Shaw, George Bernard, {i}12, 20, 80, 278,
  {ii}13, 97, 187, 366, 384, 430, 444,
  {iii}423, {v}3, 570, {vi}276, {vii}206
  like a jester tapping 'folks on the
  head..with a grotesque stick', {i}53;
  grins 'suavely or satanically 'after 'some
  contortion in honor of his own pet cult',
  {i}101; gives 'exquisite pleasure of
  falling out with him wholesomely',
  {i}103; in theatre 'time for a reaction
  against', {i}509; helps to found *New
  Statesman*, {i}551–2; DHL 'due to
  meet', {ii}402; sends DHL £5, {ii}449;
  'pamphleteer rather than..artist',
  {v}370; praises dialogue in *Widowing*,
  {v}605; DHL suggests Dobrée for
  'Scrutiny' on, {vi}67; Wilkinsons 'a bit
  Bernard Shawey', {vi}128; as a man,
  harmed by Socialism, {vii}468
  Arms and the Man, {i}452;
  'Common Sense About the War',
    {ii}236;
  Don Juan In Hell, {i}373;
  *Intelligent Women's Guide to Socialism
    and Capitalism*, {vi}471–2;
  Man and Superman, {i}373, 377;
  Pygmalion, {iii}305

Shaw, Hilda, {i}114, 118, 265, 267, 301,
  480–1
SHEARMAN, MONTAGUE, {iii}14, 52,
  103, 315, {vi}5
  about expulsion from Cornwall, DHL
  seeks help from, {iii}175–6, 189; sends
  £10, {iii}214–16, 251; £10 regarded as
  loan and DHL repays, {vi}355–6
  Letters to {iii}175–6, 181, 189, 216,
    {vi}355–6
  Letters from {vi}355
Shearman, Sir Montague, {iii}103
Sheerness (Kent), {i}27
Sheffield (Yorkshire), {ii}17, 391, 401, 463
Sheffield Telegraph, The, {i}52
Sheik, The, see Hull, E. M.
Shelley, Percy Bysshe, {i}52, 95, {ii}85, 101,
  115, 223, 488, 493, 625, 654, {iii}196,
  {vii}383
  at San Terenzo, {ii}63, 84, 86; scansion
  of verse by, {ii}105; far 'more beautiful
  than Milton', {ii}120; accepted 'princi-
  ple of Evil, coeval with the Principle of
  Good', {ii}315
  'Love's Philosophy', {ii}595;
  Prometheus Unbound, {v}262;
  'The Question', {ii}624;
  'To Music', {i}248;
  'To Night', {i}64
Sheppard, Elizabeth Sara, *Charles Auchester:
  A Memorial*, {iii}340
SHERMAN, STUART PRATT, {iv}499,
  {v}325
  DHL reviews, {iv}355, 398, {viii}59;
  DHL amused by article by, {v}272–3,
  275
  Americans, {iv}16, 355, {viii}59;
  'Lawrence Cultivates His Beard',
    {v}272, 275
  Letters to {v}275–6
Sherwood Forest (Nottinghamshire), {i}344,
  {v}592
Shestov, Leo, {iii}4, 11
  DHL edits Kot's translation of,
  {iii}380–4, 387, 389, 394, 455; 'writes
  atrociously', {iii}380; can achieve 'a kind
  of pathetic beauty', {iii}384; Secker and
  All Things, {iii}391–3, 396–8, 400,

402–3, 407, 428, 433–4, 441, 470–1, 500,
516, 529, 559, {iv}275, {vi}177,
{vii}474, 538; DHL will 'do the *real*
proof correcting', {iii}412, 437, 439; Kot
and royalties from translation of,
{iii}442, 516, 553, 560, 570, {v}483,
624, 627–8; Huebsch and *All Things*,
{iii}455, 466, 468, 471, 486, 501, 503,
508, 510–12, 520, 543–4
All Things Are Possible, {iii}380, 383,
428, 521, {iv}275, {v}483, 624, 627–8
{vi}177, {vii}474, 538;
'Russian Spirit' or 'Apotheosis of
Groundlessness', {iii}380, 382, 387, 397,
400, 403, 437
see also Lawrence, D. H., *All Things are
Possible*
Shevky, Eshref, {iv}339
'Ship, The', *see* Lowell, A.
Shipley (Derbyshire), {i}33, 57
Shipley, Joseph Twadell, *King John*, {v}359
Shirebrook (Derbyshire), {i}2, 44, 69, 295–7,
369–72, 374
Shirley (Surrey), {i}553
Shirley Glenn, *see* Hawk, S. G.
Shirley, *see* Brontë, C.
Short Stories, *see* Boyle, K.
SHORT, CAPT. JOHN TREGERTHEN,
{ii}13, 590, 631–2, {iii}122, 244, 317,
319–20, 334, 344, 435, 541, 639, 682,
697–8, 713–14, {iv}217
'soft like a child, with a mania for
fussing', {ii}576–7; DHL's landlord,
'perfect dear', {ii}579, 581; refurbish-
ments necessary at Higher Tregerthen,
{ii}585–7, 620–1; DHL renegotiates
cottages belonging to, {iii}221–3, 225,
235–6, 255–6, 265, 314–15; allegedly '*not*
straight' with DHL, {iii}266, 268; 'wise
and wary old bird', {iii}712; 'always'
liked by DHL, {iv}24
Letters to {ii}575, 585–7, 620–1,
{iii}221–2, 225, 235–6, 255–6, 266, 268,
314–15
SHORT, LUCY, {ii}575, 620–1, 642,
{iii}122, 222, 236, 256, 268, 315, 435–6,
569, 682
Letters to {iii}244, 488–9, 505, 587, 639

Short, Westyr, {iii}268, 315
Shorter, Clement King, {ii}462, {iii}459
Shrewsbury (Shropshire), {iv}542, 553–4,
{vii}579
Shropshire Lad, A, *see* Housman, A. E.
Shulamite, {i}227
Sicily, {ii}123, {iii}9–11, 16, 423, 469–71,
478, 480–583 *passim*, 585–6, 608,
611–702 *passim*, 706, {iv}33, 52, 57, 80,
84–5, 88–206 *passim*,232, 266, 439, 447,
520, 532, {v}12, 67, 170, 278, 287, 299,
314, 345, 357–8, 373, {vi}12, 538, 542,
{vii}63, 523, {viii}29–30, 33–5, 37–9,
48–51, 100
'touch of Saracen and the East in it,
{iii}482; 'brink of Europe', {iii}487–8,
494; 'so green and living', {iii}489;
'humanly too degraded and degrading',
{iv}51; DHL's nostalgia for, {iv}247–50,
254, 416, 444; Spring 'so lovely' in,
{v}343; Mallorca not so beautiful as,
{vii}253–5, 257, 262
Sickert, Walter Richard {i}380, {ii}54,
{iii}261
Sidgwick & Jackson Ltd, {ii}527, 535,
558
Sidgwick, Frank, {ii}525, 531, 558, {iii}77
Siebenhaar, Lydia Bruce, {iv}240, 270, 281,
309, 328, 386, 435, 449, 518, {v}32, 34,
393, 420, 446
SIEBENHAAR, WILLIAM, {iv}9, 240–1,
474, {v}9
DHL encourages over translation of
Max Havelaar, {iv}270, 309, 327–9, 383,
435, 496, {v}32, 452–3, {viii}56;
complimentary volumes for, {iv}390,
517, {v}81; DHL's introduction to *Max
Havelaar*, {iv}449, {v}320, 446, 452,
458, 527; Knopf to publish, {v}393;
DHL met in Monte Carlo, {v}420;
'bore, but inoffensive', {v}538
Dorothea, {iv}240, 251, 272;
Sentinel Sonnets, {iv}240, 251
see also Dekker, E.
Letters to {iv}240, 269–70, 281, 309, 326–8,
386, 435, 449, 517–18, {v}34, 393, 397,
420, 446, 449, 452–3, 458, 493, 527, 531,
539, 542, {viii}56

Siegfried, see Wagner, R.

'Siegmund', *see* Macartney, H. B.

Siena (Italy), {iii}520, {iv}44, 65, 86,89, 92, 105, 151, {vii}465, {viii}46

Sierre (Switzerland), {iv}38, {vi}374, 380, 384

'Silence Ladies', *see* Order of Silence

Silling, Alan, {ii}638

Silling, Mr, {ii}638

Simmonds Yat, *See* Symonds Yat

Simon & Schuster Inc., {vii}526

Simon, Sir John, {ii}439, 456–7, 462

Simpkin & Marshall Ltd, {iii}638, {v}290, {vi}486, 517–19, 532, 544–5, 574, {vii}66

Simpson, Joseph, {vii}189, 334

Sinai, {iv}210, 212

Sinaloa (Mexico), {iv}518

Sinclair, May, {ii}267
   'quite friendly' to DHL, {iii}692; 'funny little marm', {viii}41
   The Three Brontës, {ii}267;
   The Three Sisters, {ii}639, {iii}391

SINCLAIR, UPTON BEALL, {i}424, {ii}519, {vi}335
   Love's Pilgrimage, {i}424;
   Money Writes!, {vi}230;
   Oil!, {vi}102
   Letters to {vi}102

Sinister Street, see Mackenzie, E. M. C.

Sir Galahad, {i}118, 494, 503

Siracuse (Sicily), {iii}506, {iv}127

Siren Land, see Douglas, G. N.

Sister Teresa, see Moore, G.

Sitwell, (Dame) Edith Louisa, {iii}13, 261, {v}468, {vi}17, 180, 579, {viii}103
   not affected or 'sidey' on visit to Mirenda, {vi}60, 65, 67–8, 73

Sitwell, (Sir) Osbert, {iii}13, 261, {v}468, {vi}17, 180, {viii}103
   not affected or 'sidey' on visit to Mirenda, {vi}60, 65, 67–8, 73; and *LCL*, {vi}579
   Discursions on Travel, Art and Life, {vi}68;
   Triple Fugue, {vi}68

Sitwell, (Sir) Sacheverell, {iii}13, 261, {v}468, {viii}103

Sitwell, Lady Ida Emily Augusta, {v}12
   DHL lunches with, {v}468, 470, 472, 474, 483; DHL invited to Renishaw, {v}476, 503, 532

Sitwell, Sir George Reresby, {v}12
   DHL invited to lunch with, {v}468, 470, 472, 483; 'collects *beds*', {v}474; DHL invited to Renishaw by, {v}476, 503, 532

Six French Poets, see Lowell, A.

Skegness (Lincolnshire), {i}22, {vii}393, 398, 436, {viii}1

Skinner, James Tierney, {iv}449

Skinner, Jessie Leake, {iv}449, 467, 474

Skinner, John ('Jack') Russell, {iv}558
   character Jack Grant based on, {iv}524, {v}114, 123; death of, {v}292

SKINNER, MARY LOUISA ('MOLLIE'), {iv}9, 16, 18, 236, 270, 449, {v}6, 85, 110, 178, {vii}4
   DHL enquires about 'that novel', {iv}466; 'House of Ellis' sent to DHL, {iv}474; 477, 489; DHL offers to re-write 'House of Ellis', {iv}495–6; composition of *Boy in the Bush*, {iv}503, 517–19, 521, 523–4, 527, 529, 532–3, 543, 582, {v}120; 'thrilled' by collaboration, {iv}544; DHL likes *B in B* 'immensely', {iv}557; DHL shares royalties on *B in B* with, {iv}558, 596, {v}19–21, 71, 78, 112–14, 120, 123, 292; DHL respects her rights in text of *B in B*, {v}20–5, 31, 38; Brett designs and DHL modifies jacket for *B in B*, {v}32–4, 37, 92, 95; *B in B* published, {v}91–2, 95, 106; *TLS* review of *B in B* ignores contribution by, {v}121–3, 141, {viii}90; Cape publishes *Black Swans* by, {v}171, 245; DHL sends condolences on death of her brother, {v}292–3; German translation of *B in B*, {v}314, 332, 485; 'foolish facility' of *Black Swans*, {v}351, 359, 419; critique of 'Eve in the Land of Nod', {vii}36–7
   Black Swans ('Lettie', 'Letty'), {iv}9, 496, 558, {v}71, 78, 80, 91, 95, 113–14, 120–3, 171, 190, 245, 292, 351, 359, 419–20, 542, {vii}36; DHL's Preface to, {iv}496, {v}20–1, 190;

Boy in the Bush, The ('House of Ellis'),
{iv}9, 16, 18, 236, 466–7, 474, 477, 489,
495–6, 503, 517–19, 521, 523–4, 527,
529, 532–3, 543–4, 549, 557–60, 563,
582, 588, 596–7, {v}6, 19–25, 31–2,
34–8, 44–5, 55, 70–1, 78–80, 85, 91–3,
95–6, 106, 112–14, 116, 120–3, 135,
140–2, 161, 171, 173, 182, 184, 193, 195,
245, 292, 314, 332, 485, {vii}36,
{viii}90;
'Eve in the Land of Nod', {v}21,
{vii}36;
'The Hand', {v}351, 419;
Letters of a V.A.D. (by 'R. E. Leake'),
{iv}9, 533;
Men are We, {v}245, 419;
Tucker Sees India, {v}245;
W. X.- Corporal Smith, {v}245
Letters to {iv}466–7, 495–6, 523–4, 532–3,
557–8, 566, 596–7, {v}20–2, 71, 95, 123,
171, 190, 245–6, 291–3, 419–20,
{vii}36–7
Letters from {v}123
Skye, Isle of, {v}511–13
Skylark Bookshop (New York), {vi}575
Slack, Olive Lizzie, {i}176, {v}279, 634,
{vi}64, {vii}451
Slade School of Art, {ii}211, 214, 263, 427,
508, {iii}35, 112, 304, 368, 491, 654,
{iv}546, {v}29, 364, {vi}22, 406, 548
Slaley (Derbyshire), {iii}328
Slater, Mary E., {i}301
Slatkowsky, R. S., {ii}231, 268, 623, 655,
{iii}43, 53, 208, {v}355
Sleeping Together, see Crosby, H. G.
Sloan Electric Co. (Santa Fe), {v}98, 132
Sloan, Mr, {v}98, 132
Slonimsky, Henry, {vi}124–5
Small, Maynard & Co., {iv}464
Smart Set, {ii}305, {v}2, 312
Pound agent for, {ii}26, 132; W. H.
Wright editor of, {ii}26, 58, 132, 144;
DHL's writings in, {ii}39, 58, 75, 126–7,
166–7, 187, 197, 209, 637, {v}50–1,
58–9, {vii}549; Wright rejects 'Once',
{ii}67, 72, 82, 202, {iii}135
Smart, William Marshall, {ii}617
Smerdyakov, *see* Dostoievsky, F.

Smiling Faces, see Macnamara, B.
Smillie, Robert, {iii}5, 284
Smith & Son, {vii}341
Smith, Al, {vii}96
Smith, Alfred, {i}283
SMITH, ALICE, {i}218, 327, 348, 382,
385–6, 407
Letters to {i}348
Smith, Doris E., {i}218, 382, 386
SMITH, ERNEST ALFRED, {i}7, 146
Letters to {i}146–7
Smith, F., {i}123
Smith, Frederick Edwin (Earl of
Birkenhead), {ii}593, {iii}118
Smith, Leonard, {ii}407
Smith, Mr, {i}90, 93
Smith, Naomi Gwladys Royde, {v}119
SMITH, PHILIP FRANK TURNER,
{i}121, 129, 136, 193–4, 214–15, 218,
243, 246, 250, 252, 265, 319, 327, 355,
407, 455, 464–5, 484, 499, 506, 512, 524,
{ii}48, 589
'weak kneed windy fool', {i}84; 'nice,
but very flabby', {i}93, 97; on DHL as
art-teacher, {i}303; 'grieves' over DHL's
absence from school, {i}337; DHL
resigns from school, {i}368, 382, 385–6;
DHL hated, {i}419; enlisted, {iii}61;
DHL contributes to retirement present
for, {v}640–1
Letters to {i}382, 385–6
Smith, Sheila K., *see* Kaye-Smith, S.
SMITH, THOMAS ALFRED, {i}6–7, 147,
156, 172, 280, 369, 379
visits DHL in London, {i}142; 'no lady-
killer..lonely', {i}274; DHL visits in
Lincoln, {i}283, 295–6
Letters to {viii}2
SMITH, THOMAS R., {iii}601, 605
Letters to {iii}601–2
Smith, W. H. (library), refuses to stock
Sinclair's *Love's Pilgrimage*, {i}424;
insists on revision to *Lost Girl*, {iii}619,
621–2, 624; refuses to circulate *Aaron's
Rod*, {iv}262
Smithard, Mrs, {i}224
Smiths of Surbiton, The, see Howard, K.
Smyrna (Turkey), {v}436

Smyth, Ethel Mary, {iii}492
Snake Charmer, The, see Bierbaum, O. J.
Snowden (Viscount), Philip, {i}3, 176,
　{ii}593, {iii}5, 284
Snowdonia (Carnarvonshire), {i}294
Social Basis of Consciousness, The, see Burrow,
　T.
SOCIALISM, in Eastwood, {i}2, 176; 'true
　Socialism is religion', {i}40; language
　can hide 'little shades of untruth' in,
　{i}101; 'Old Socialism..application of a
　lyrical idea and passion to an inert
　object', so 'false', {ii}301; 'Guild-
　Socialism' inevitable 'in the long run',
　{ii}489; Cambridge socialists to be
　avoided at all costs, {iii}49–50;
　Goldring, 'People's Theatre' and,
　{iii}371, 379, 391, 483; DHL losing
　'remaining belief' in, {iii}486; Italy
　'going socialist', {iii}611; DHL would
　join 'revolutionary socialists', {iii}649;
　self- interest foundation of, {iii}680;
　DHL suspects 'clergy-industrial-
　socialist move' to exert influence in
　Europe, {iv}124; 'theoretic' irritates
　DHL, {iv}190; in Australia, {iv}249;
　DHL 'cynical' about Mexican, {v}156,
　166–8; Wilkinsons and, {v}568; govern-
　ment 'will end in some sort of', {vi}215;
　Mabel Luhan and, {vi}230, 319, 393;
　'dead materialism' of Marxist, {vii}99;
　'socialists will hate me most of all' for
　Pansies, {vii}413, 451, 460; 'socialists are
　merely little bourgeois over again',
　{vii}451; kills joy and true self-aware-
　ness, {vii}468–9
Society and Solitude, see Emerson, R. W.
Society for the Suppression of Vice, {iv}14,
　19, 292, 379, {viii}71
Society of Authors, {ii}16, 226, 430, {iii}213,
　227, 643
　DHL invited to join, {ii}41; DHL
　applies to join, {ii}433; response to
　suppression of *Rainbow,* {ii}439–44,
　452, 469, {iii}459; advises on Tauchnitz
　edn rights {vi}354
　The Author, {ii}433, 469

Socrates, {v}466, 577
Soeur Philomène, see De Goncourt, J. and E.
Soffici, Ardengo, {ii}180
'Soldier, The', *see* Brooke, R.
Solent, {i}133–4
Solitaria, see Rozanov, V.
SOLITUDE, recovering from illness
　requires withdrawal into 'very real',
　{ii}594; desirable to spend time in
　labour and, {iv}95; DHL longs for 'a bit
　more', {v}35; travel to be preceded by
　three months', {vi}502
Soller (Mallorca), {vii}275
Solovyov, Vladimir, *War, Progress and the End
　of History,* {ii}343, 345
'Solway Ford', *see* Gibson, W. W.
Some Imagist Poets, {ii}334, 394
　DHL's poetry in, {ii}150, 203, 209, 339,
　384, 509, 513–14, 610, 664–5, {iii}61,
　513, {viii}23; royalties from, {ii}643–4,
　{iii}104–5, 207, 280, 593, {iv}61, 96,
　488, {v}197
Some Limericks, see Douglas, G. N.
Somercotes (Derbyshire), {i}27
Somme, River, {iii}39
Song for Simeon, A, see Eliot, T. S.
Songs of Childhood, see De La Mare, W.
Songs of the Hebrides, see Kennedy-Fraser, M.
Sonia Issayevna, Sonya, *see* Farbman, S. I.
Sonnets, see Crosland, T. W. H.
Sonoma, S.S., {iv}247, 252, 267, 272, 274,
　276
Sonora (Mexico), {iv}17, 480, 505, 510
'Sophie', *see* Farbman, S. I.
Sophocles, {v}201
　Antigone, {ii}316;
　Oedipus, {i}235, 261, 525
Sorani, Aldo, {v}3, 472
Soroptimists, {vii}185–6
Sorrento (Italy), {iii}439, 442, 451, 633,
　{vi}26
Soskice, David, {i}12–13, 171
Soskice, Juliet M., {i}170–1
Sotheran, Henry, {vi}512, 515
Soul of Kol Nikon, The, see Farjeon, E.
Soupault, Philippe ('Kra'), {vi}430, 465,
　507, {vii}245

South Africa, {i}236, 356, {iii}168, 491, 609,
    655, {iv}138, 141, 143, 159, 163, {v}448,
    {vii}28–9
    see also Africa
South America, {i}509, {iii}173–4, 179, 315,
    {iv}503
South American Sketches, see Hudson, W. H.
South Lodge, {i}315–16, {v}589
South Pasadena (USA), {viii}82
South Sea Islands, {iv}239, 241, 243, 246–7,
    284, 286, {vii}29
South Seas, {iii}70, 418, 462, 481, 490,
    504–5, 522–3, 560–3, 565–6, 571–2, 587,
    653, 655, 659, {iv}127, 243–4, 247
    see also Pacific Ocean
South Wales Miners' Federation, {ii}366
Southampton (Hampshire), {ii}175, {iv}17,
    20, 478–80, 482–5, 487, 529, 594, {v}9,
    15, 299, 305–6
Southey, Robert, {iii}349
Southsea (Hampshire), {i}134, {ii}287
Southwell (Nottinghamshire), {i}295,
    {vi}371
Southwest Review, {v}40, {vi}10, 335
Sovereign, {iv}220
Soviets, *see* Russia
Sowerby, Olivia, {ii}323
Spain, {iii}562, 658, 679, {iv}66, 180, 191,
    419, 539, 544–6, 548–50, {v}170, 174,
    202, 372, 394, 398, 436–7, 630, {vi}41,
    43, 146, 302, 398, 474, 513, 516, 538,
    551, 608, {vii}5–6, 344, 486, 502, 523,
    525, 527, 532, 538, 540–1, 561, 564–5,
    576, 578, 617
    DHL and Spanish language, {iv}138,
    152, 280, 306, 314–15, 320, 339, 406,
    438, 442, 445, 534; DHL wants to visit,
    Frieda resists, {vii}37–123 *passim*, 148,
    152, 155–61; revolutionary disturbances
    and 'great deal of police-watching going
    on' in, {vii}166–7, 169–72; DHL's
    planned visit again delayed,
    {vii}193–219 *passim*, 231, 234–5; 'going
    south in stages to', {vii}237–8, 240–1,
    243, 245–6, 248; DHL in (Barcelona and
    Mallorca), {vii}249–337; 'foul, cat-piss
    is champagne compared', to wine in

{vii}260, 310; 'Spaniards seem like
    boxes of something shut up and gone
    stale', {vii}283; DHL drinks 'canary be-
    pissed beer' in, {vii}310
Spalato (Austria), {v}323, 373
Spalding, Percy, {iii}148, 155, 238
    Letters from {iii}238
Spanish Jade, see Hewlett, M.
Spanish Lovers, The, see Garnett, E.
Spanish Main, The, {iii}561, 567
Spare, Austin O., {ii}400
Sparrowdust, *see* De Gourmont, R.
Spectator, The, {i}12, 324, 339, {v}102,
    {vi}71
    DHL signs *English Review* protest
    against, {i}277; 'Nightingale' in,
    {v}584, 626, {vi}52
Speedwell, *see* Massingham, G. S.
SPEISER, MAURICE B., {vii}307
    Letters to {vii}307–8
Spencer, Gilbert, {vii}585
Spencer, Herbert, {i}36–7
Spencer, Stanley, {v}11, 49, 572
Spencer, W. K., {i}303
Spencer-Churchill, Lord Ivor Charles,
    {vi}127, 155
Spender, John Alfred, {i}375, 424
Spenser, Edmund, {i}5
    The Faerie Queene, {i}74, 85, 203, {v}52,
    {vi}59
Spettri, see Ibsen, H.
Speyer, Sir Edgar, {iv}123–4
Spezia, La (Italy), {ii}4, 77–182 *passim*,
    {iii}19, 260, 415, {vi}94, 371, 417,
    {vii}465, 478, {viii}9–10
Sphere, {v}186
    hostile review of *Rainbow* in, {ii}462,
    {iii}459
Spiers, Mr, {ii}642, 648, {iii}42
Spiez (Switzerland), {vi}485, 488, 493
SPIRITUAL, (THE), 'sudden spiritual
    conversion', {i}39; London has nothing
    of, {i}80; Helen Corke's eyes, {i}164;
    Jessie Chambers and, {i}545; artist
    needs satisfaction both physical and,
    {ii}95; pride, {ii}130; 'perambulators of
    a parson' DHL knew, {ii}267; Ottoline

SPIRITUAL, THE (*cont.*)
Morrell 'sort of spiritual home in England', {ii}435; Heseltine's need for 'spiritual connection', {ii}539; Dostoievsky's desire for spiritual 'consummation', {ii}543; 'spiritual disaster' in militarism, {ii}622, 625; need to satisfy 'most spiritual desire', {ii}634–5; Lucas 'spiritual coward', {ii}635; Swinburne and Shelley 'full of philosophic spiritual..revelation', {ii}654; *Signature* aimed to prepare for 'moral and spiritual "revolution"' (Murry), {iii}84; energy in Russia, {iii}136; English public's need of 'spiritual athletics', {iii}156; post-war spiritual atmosphere 'unpleasant', {iii}345; 'spiritual journalists' on *Athenæum*, {iii}350; DHL hates 'Oliver Lodge spiritualism', {iii}358; Hinke lacks strength of, {iv}136; 'voluptuous-ness' of East alien to DHL, {iv}233; 'great spiritual freight' of Europe absent in Australia, {iv}256; equal importance of sensual and, {v}203; spiritual 'soreness' associated with 'change of life', {vi}37, {vii}605; needs balance of 'combative', {vi}49; 'I can't stand high-browish spiritual upsoaring people', {vi}61; 'blur of spiritual admiration' in DHL's view of leader (Bynner), {vi}321; Achsah Brewster's 'most spiritual and purely pure friends', {vi}340; lust devoid of, {vi}379; Ghiselin's 'spiritual sort' of admiration for DHL, {vii}120; Huxleys seem 'finished in some spiritual way', {vii}653

Spithead (Hampshire), {i}134
Spoleto (Italy), {v}413
'Spoodle', *see* Johnson, W.
Spoon River Anthology, see Masters, E. L.
Sportsman's Sketches, see Turgenev, I.
Spotorno (Italy), {v}6, 10, 333–436 *passim*, 443, 468, 655, {vi}32, 152, 168, 361, 366, 377, {vii}40–1, 554
Sprague, Alice Louise, {v}56, 59–60, 64, 107, 302, 309

'Spring Day', *see* Lowell, A.
'Spud', *see* Johnson, W.
Spurrier, Stephen, {vi}609
Spyri, Johanna, *Heidi*, {iii}340
'Squib, The', *see* Lawrence, D. H.
SQUIRE, (SIR) JOHN COLLINGS, {ii}204–5, {iii}452, 486, 582, {iv}87, {vii}31, 265, 389, 443, 580
rejects 'Chapel Among the Mountains' for *New Statesman*, {ii}236; DHL (unsuccessfully) offers 'Education of the People' for *London Mercury* to, {iii}554–5, {viii}34; poems offered to, {iii}681, 700; 'that swine', {iv}36; 'suburban rat', {v}91, 94; 'sniveller', {vi}617; among those who 'instinctively' dislike DHL, {vii}294; 'dirty dog' prints hostile review of DHL's paintings, {vii}376–7
Letters to {ii}236, {iii}554–5, 681
St Agnes (Cornwall), {iii}607
St Anthony, {i}114, {ii}648–9, {iii}670
St Augustine, {i}40
Confessions, {ii}572
St Bernard, *Some Letters of St Bernard*, {ii}633
St Catherine of Siena, {i}114
St Cyr-sur-Mer (France), {vii}560, 566, 581
St Erth (Cornwall), {iii}126
St Francis of Assisi, {i}114, {ii}538, {iii}720, {iv}577, {v}426, 441, 558, 560, {vi}342
St George, {i}463, 494, {ii}122, 376, {vii}371
St Gotthard Pass (Switzerland), {ii}76, 79, {vi}191, {vii}410, {viii}9
St Helena, {i}485
ST HELIER, MARY, LADY, {ii}4
DHL invited to lunch by, {ii}147, 189
Letters to {ii}147–8
St Ives (Cornwall), {ii}550–669 *passim*, {iii}3, 19–168 *passim*, 177, 200, 222, 435, 712–13, {iv}24, 86, {vi}520, {viii}18, 20–5
St Ives Times, The, {iii}3, 122, 158
St Jerome, {i}114

St John the Baptist, {ii}374
St John the Divine, {ii}254, {iv}460,
 {vii}544–5, 555
'St Joseph's Ass', *see* Verga, G.
St Lawrence, {i}463, 519
St Louis (USA), {iii}662, {vi}555, {vii}345
St Margaret's-on-Thames (Middlesex),
 {i}280, 285, 292–3, 387
St Merryn (Cornwall), {ii}484, 490–559,
 {iii}160
St Michael, {i}470, {vii}331
St Moritz (San Moritz) (Switzerland),
 {vi}236–9
St Nizier de Pariset (France), {vi}3, 423–8,
 430
St Paul, {i}39, {ii}648
St Peter, {i}97, 450, {ii}252, {v}522
St Pierre, Bernadin de, {i}205
St Raphael (France), {vi}581, 588–9
St Thomas à Becket {i}114
St Trond (Belgium), {vii}58, 87
St Tropez (France), {vi}519, 537
Stafford, {i}373, {iv}554
Staffordshire, {i}23, 373, 378–9
Stage Society, {ii}127, 136, 152, {iii}425
 see also 300 Club and Stage Society
Stahl, Dr Ernst, {ii}98
Stallings, Laurence, {v}375
Stamford, Earl of, {iii}130, 154, 158,
 {viii}25
Standard, The, {ii}1
 DHL reviewed in, {i}228, 230, 420,
 {ii}21, 457–8
Standing, Aubrey, {i}322
Stanley, *see* Clarke, S.
Stanley, Beatrice Venetia, {ii}54, 63
Stanley, Edward George Villiers (Earl of
 Derby), {ii}495–6, {iii}49
Stanley, Elizabeth, *see* Mansfield, K.
Stanley, Sir Henry Morton, *In Darkest
 Africa,* {ii}107, 631
Stanway House (Gloucestershire), {ii}380,
 {iii}117, 282, 359, 366 {iv}32, 207,
 261
Star Review, The, {vii}4
 'Men and Women' in, {vii}405, 437,
 499–500, 512

Star, {v}386, {vi}13
 Douglas reviews *Rainbow* in, {ii}462;
 LCL reviewed in, {vi}511
Starnberg Lake (Germany), {iii}710
Starr, Jean, *see* Untermeyer, J.
Starr, Lady Mary, {iii}3, 130, 154, 163, 344
 DHL mocks behaviour of, {iii}158,
 {viii}25
Starr, Meredith, {iii}3, 130, 133, 154, 163,
 344
 ridiculous behaviour of, {iii}158,
 {viii}25
Station: Athos, Treasures and Men, The, see
 Byron, R.
'Statue, The', *see* Lowell, A.
Staynes, Ellen ('Nellie'), {i}22, 46, 184
Staynes, John Richard, {i}184
Stechert, G. E., & Co., {ii}562
Steegmann, Mary G., {vi}254
Steel, Eliza, {i}347, 350
STEELE, ALAN W., increases order for
 copies of *LCL*, {vi}390, 417–18; cancels
 order, {vi}476–8, {viii}108; 'scoundrel',
 {vi}489; Enid Hilton collects copies
 from, {vi}492
 Letters to {vi}390, 417–18, 476–7,
 {viii}108
 Letters from {vi}390, 417–18
STEFFENS, JOSEPH LINCOLN, {iv}406,
 409, {vi}230, {viii}71–2
 Letters to {iv}410
Stein, Charlotte von, {i}477, 549
Stein, Gertrude, {iv}5, 111, {v}419,
 {vi}180, 191, 507–8, 548, {vii}206
 Portrait of Mabel Dodge, {v}642, 646,
 {vi}59
Stein, Leo, {iii}463, {iv}5, 111, {vi}180,
 {vii}206
 bursts 'into a new Jewish psalmody',
 {iv}127–8; 'nasty, nosy, corrupt Jew',
 {iv}182; Walter Rosen in *Aaron's Rod,*
 {v}419
 Letters from {iv}128
Stein, Miss, {i}350
Stellof, Frances, {vii}215
Stempel, Baron, {iii}10, 636–7, 640, {iv}101,
 108

Stendhal, (Henri Beyle), {iii}21, {vi}214,
{vii}561
    De l'Amour, {iii}21, 679–80;
    La Chartreuse de Parme, {iii}21, {vi}543;
    Life of Henri Brulard, {v}321;
    Le Rouge et le Noir, {i}251, 255, 262–3,
    353, {iii}21
Stenterello Theatre, {v}607, 636
Stephens, James, {ii}114–15, 118, 131
    The Charwoman's Daughter, {ii}114;
    The Crock of Gold, {ii}114
STEPHENSEN, PERCY REGINALD,
    {vii}1, 4–5, 31, 142, 147, 186, 260, 330,
    340, 345, 381, 389, 394, 448, 451, 456,
    460–2, 470, 472, 504, 516, 533, 538, 550,
    634, 640, 644
    'a bit colonial and ramshackle', {vii}66;
    proposes volume of DHL's paintings,
    {vii}70–1, 74, 76–8, 82, 86, 95, 124–5,
    128, 130–1, 135–6, 149; 'not limp at all'
    and DHL likes, {vii}82, 85, 88; mutual
    regard between DHL and, {vii}91–3;
    visits DHL in Bandol, {vii}120, 124–5,
    128, 130; *Paintings* in production,
    {vii}149–50, 152–3, 157–8, 164, 168–9,
    178, 180–1, 197–9, 207, 218, 221–2, 228,
    243, 269–71, 274, 278–80, 282–3, 285,
    298, 300–2, 319, 321–2, 327–9;
    Paintings first publication by Mandrake
    Press, {vii}253; and third edn of *LCL*,
    {vii}256, 406–7, 433–4, 445, 499; essay
    in *London Aphrodite* by, {vii}265, 269;
    'like all enthusiasts..not entirely depend-
    able', {vii}329, 458; *Paintings* published,
    {vii}337, 350, 380, 469; 'keen on self-
    advertisement', {vii}443; fulminates
    against Dorothy Warren, {vii}489;
    'hasty and lavish at a start.. apt to fizzle
    out', {vii}549; and failure of Mandrake
    Press, {vii}554, 557, 559, 564, 573, 580,
    583
    The Bushwhackers, {vii}179, 270, 322,
    337, 531;
    see also Lawrence, D. H. *Paintings*, and
    Mandrake Press, The
    Letters to {vii}77–9, 91–3, 116–17, 135–6,
    149–50, 168–9, 178–80, 198–9, 215–16,

222, 243, 269–71, 278–80, 285, 300,
321–2, 329, 337, 353, 468–9, 530–1
    Letters from {vii}91–2, 556
Stepniak, *see* Kravchinsky, S. M.
Stepniak-Kravchinskaya, Fanny Markovna,
    {iii}116, 125
Stern & Ruben, {iv}182, 370, 391, {vii}612,
    624, 626, 637, {viii}67
STERN, BENJAMIN H., {iv}370
    'literary lawyer' protecting DHL's
    interests in USA, {iv}376, 382–3, 388,
    390–5, 400, 402–3, 406, 417, 465, 474,
    {v}18, 298, {vii}612, 624, 626, 637, 640,
    649, {viii}67–8, 70–2, 74
    Letters to {iv}391, 474
Stern, Gladys Bronwyn, *The Back Seat*,
    {iv}494;
    'I Could Not Have Married a Foreigner',
    {vi}6, 401
Sterne, Laurence, *Sentimental Journey*,
    {i}151, 398;
    Tristram Shandy, {ii}90
Sterne, Mabel Dodge, *see* Luhan, M. D. S.
Sterne, Maurice, {iv}5, 13, 110–11, 126, 138,
    317–18, 350–1, {v}28, 56, 95, 550
Sterzing (Austria), {i}443–5
Stevens, B. F. & Brown, Ltd, refuse to handle
    LCL and return copies, {vi}12, 479–81,
    486–8, 490, 493
    Letters from {vi}479–80
Stevens, C. H., {vi}336
Stevens, Mrs George W., {vi}299, 335
Stevenson, Robert Louis, {i}148, 361,
    {iii}549, {iv}290, {v}646
    Admiral Guinea {iii}87;
    The Silverado Squatters, {iv}290;
    Treasure Island, {ii}588–9
Stewart, Nina, {i}131, 133–4, 172
STIEGLITZ, ALFRED, {vi}12–14, 16,
    607, {vii}170
    praises *SCAL*, {iv}499; *Porcupine* sent
    to, {v}319; orders *LCL*, {vi}381, 448–9,
    470, 566–7; and exhibition of DHL's
    paintings in New York, {vi}467, 503,
    505–6, 521–2, 536–7, 551, 558–9;
    effusive about *LCL*, {vi}551; 'pleasant-
    spoken but cautious and canny bird',

{vii}24; concerned about pirate edns of *LCL*, {vii}35–6, 39, 42–4; advice sought over sale of *Paintings* in USA, {vii}138–9, 168, 222

Letters to {iv}499, 543, {v}319, {vi}449, 505–6, 536–7, 558–9, 566, {vii}35–6

Stift, *see* Ludwig-Wilhelmstift

Still Life, see Murry, J. M.

Stock, Ralph, {iii}654, 657, 684
'The Dream Ship', {iii}654

Stockholm (Sweden), {iii}676, {vii}6, {viii}24

Stockport (Cheshire), {i}77, 80

Stoessel, Otto, *Nachtgeschichten*, {v}371

Stoke-on-Trent (Staffordshire), {i}294

Stokes, Adrian, {i}113, {vi}17, 416, 420, 431

Stone, Remington, {iv}435, {vi}212

Stoney Middleton (Derbyshire), {v}243

STOPFORD, ALBERT, {iii}497, {iv}191 350, 354

Letters to {viii}52–3

Storia do Mogor, see Manucci, N.

Stories from the Dial, {v}104

Storm, Theodor Woldsen, {vi}129

Story of an African Farm, The, see Schreiner, O.

Story of Dr Manente, The, see Grazzini, A. F.

Story of my Heart, The, see Jefferies, R.

'Story of St Joseph's Ass', *see* Verga, G.

Stötzer, Mrs, {v}369, 488–9

Stour, River, {i}349

Stourbridge (Worcestershire), {i}373, 379

Stourport (Worcestershire), {v}123

Strachey, James, {ii}230, 321

Strachey, Lytton, {ii}272, 320, 508, 591, 612, {iii}103, 112, 392, {iv}584, {v}650, {vii}8
DHL 'still doesn't like', {ii}315; homosexuality associated with, {ii}321
Landmarks in French Literature, {ii}315

Straits of Bab-el-Mandeb, {iv}212

Straits of Messina, {iv}100, 204–5

Strand Magazine, The, {i}152, {ii}348, 419, {iii}22, 155, 576, 597, {iv}134, {v}56, 79, 87
prints 'Tickets, Please', {iii}299, {iv}144, 148; 'terrible piffle' in, {v}80

Strasbourg, (Strassburg), (Germany), {iii}723, {iv}44, 566, 568–70, 586–7, {v}324, 327–8, 330, 502–3, {vi}580–1, 584, {vii}208, 210, 630

Stratford-upon-Avon (Warwickshire), {vii}436

Strathspey, Baron, {iv}557

Straus, Oscar, *The Chocolate Soldier*, {i}452, 455

Strauss, Richard, {iii}532
Elektra, {i}157

'Stravinsky', *see* Lowell, A.

Strawberry Hill, *see* Perth (Australia)

Streatley (Bedfordshire), {iii}382

Strelley (Nottinghamshire), {i}117

Stresemann, Gustav, {vii}509

Strife, see Galsworthy, J.

Strindberg, August, {ii}80, 247
'rotten', {i}464, 467; 'unnatural, forced, a bit indecent', {i}465; DHL doesn't want to write plays like, {i}509
Miss Julia, {i}464, 488;
There are Crimes and Crimes, {i}464, 488

Stucki, M., {vi}430

Studio, The, {iii}129, {iv}192, {vii}503
DHL copies pictures from, {i}273, 277; 'Making Pictures' in, {vii}249, 251, 269, 296, 322, 348–9, 536

Stülchen, Herr, {i}399–400

Stuttgart (Germany), {iv}39, 42, 47, {vi}141

Suetonius, *De Vita Caesarum*, {iii}444

Suez Canal, {iv}7, 203–5, 208–9, 211, 213

Suffragettes, {i}2, 122–4, 277, 364, {ii}109

Suhrawardy, Hasan Shahid, {ii}452, 462–3, 465–6, 481

Suia (Crete), {iv}158

Sullivan, John William Navin, {vi}82, 86, 100, 109, 120

Sullivan, Sir Arthur, *see* Gilbert, Sir W. S.

Sumatra, {iv}141, 279

Summerhurst Green (Hampshire), {iii}375

Sumner, John S., {iv}292, 379, {viii}71

Sumurûn, {i}310

Sunday Chronicle, The, {i}102
strident attack on *LCL* in, {vi}13, 604, 609, {vii}24

Sunday Dispatch, The, {i}21, {vi}7, 188, 201,
　334
　DHL's articles in, {vi}602, 606, 610,
　{vii}28–9, 65, 117–18, 127, 131, 198,
　200, 251, 334; pays £25 for 2000 words,
　{vii}26; Simpson's 'Portrait Study' of
　DHL in, {vii}189
Sunday Times, The, {v}383
Sunday Times, The (Perth), {iv}557
Sunday Worker, The, {vii}256, 413
Sunstroke (horse), {vi}504, 549, {vii}216,
　323
Suresnes (France), {vi}330, 574, 580, 603,
　{vii}27, 63–4, 86–7, 209–10, 216–38,
　275, 491, 499, 527, 541–2, 561, 565, 577
Surrey, {i}90–1, 118, 120, 279, 319, {ii}329,
　404, 540, {iii}55, 199, {v}81
Survey Graphic, The, {vii}71, 94, 118, 201
Susan (cow), {v}8, 258, 263, 265–6, 268, 272,
　274, 279, 283, 291, 358, 492, {vi}24,
　{viii}110
Sussex, {i}126–7, 213–17, 537, {ii}255–374
　passim, 409, {iii}495, {iv}224, 301,
　{v}77, 426, {vii}142, 235, 516,
　{viii}14–15
SUTRO, ALFRED, {ii}279, {iv}30
　sends cheque for £10, {ii}213, 226,
　{viii}12–14; supports DHL's application
　to Royal Literary Fund, {ii}225,
　{iii}227, 251
　Making a Gentleman, {i}146
　Letters to {iv}30, {viii}12–14
Sutton-on-Sea (Lincolnshire), {v}515–35
　passim, {viii}96
Svyatopolk-Mirsky, Prince Dmitry
　Petrovich, {vi}177
Swain, Rosy, {v}634
Swaine, Ruth, {v}277
Swan, Annie Shepherd, {ii}588
Swan, John Macallan, {i}277
Sweden, {i}520, 533, {ii}101, 247, {v}35,
　232, 488–9, 492, 656, {vi}252, 398
Sweet, Algernon, {i}450
Swift, Jonathan, {i}5, 216, {v}314, 562,
　{vii}106, 196
Swinburne, Algernon Charles, {i}185, 450,
　{ii}614, {iii}42, 680

some parts of 'Tristram' 'barren to
　excess', {i}241; 'shallow', {i}242; 'with
　Shelley..our greatest poet', {ii}653–4
Atalanta in Calydon, {i}95, {ii}72,
　{iii}39;
'Dolores', {iii}494;
'The Garden of Proserpine', {i}224,
　{ii}317, {iii}497, 504;
'Tristram of Lyonesse', {i}241,
　{ii}492
Swinnerton, Frank, {ii}446
Swiss Family Robinson, see Wyss, J. D.
Switzerland, {i}430, 500, 540, 548, {ii}67,
　72, 75, 77–9, 147, 184, 186, 194, 481,
　497, {iii}175, 314, 322, 334, 344, 347,
　418, 420, 426, 580, 587, 704, {iv}38–9,
　66, 190, 259, 279, 502, 520, {v}334–8,
　340–1, 545, {vi}1, 3, 5, 86, 108, 194, 236,
　241, 246, 255–70, 292, 294, 304–570
　passim, {vii}28, 79, 105, 201, 327, 343–4,
　372, 375, 378, 586, {viii}107
'rather banal', {ii}84; DHL 'cured of
　that little country for ever', {ii}88; 'too
　milk chocolaty and..tourist trodden',
　{viii}9
Sword Blades and Poppy Seed, see Lowell, A.
Sydenham (Kent), {i}83
Sydney (Australia), {iv}8, 10–11, 214, 218,
　220, 222–5, 227–8, 235–82 *passim,* 301,
　{viii}55, 78
'great fine town' but 'costs too much',
　{iv}249; harbour 'one of the sights of the
　world', {iv}250
Sydney Bulletin, {iv}10, 250
Sylvia and Michael, see Mackenzie, E. M. C.
Sylvia Scarlett, see Mackenzie, E. M. C.
SYMBOLISM/SYMBOLS, Louie
　Burrows' symbol, 'pomegranate',
　{i}198; 'deep..in our soil', {i}399; 'true
　instinctive or *dream* symbolism' in
　'Ballad of Another Ophelia', {ii}203; a
　means to conception of 'the Whole', not
　mere '*subjective expression*', {ii}248;
　Celtic, {ii}248–9; 'central symbols' of
　vision of divine, {ii}249; spoiled by
　making 'subjective', {ii}250; DHL's
　phoenix, {ii}252–3, 275, {vi}378; of

dragon, {ii}261; Angels and Devils symbolise 'flower into which we strive to burst', {ii}275; in 'Thimble' story, {ii}420; wrecked ship 'symbol of something', {ii}607; in early times man's property symbolised manhood, {ii}633; symbol 'something static, petrified', of past, to be rejected when vitality lost {ii}634; chalcedony symbolises 'pure space..happy freedom', {ii}653; lambs symbolise 'Christian meekness', {iii}124; dead owl 'symbol of something', {iii}240; ancient Egyptian, {iii}530; of bull and rose, {iii}554; 'Lion of Buddha', {iv}228; of zodiac, {iv}460; of apple-blossom doesn't work for DHL, {v}53; of Centaur, {v}133; critics' reactions to symbolism in *St. Mawr*, {v}267, 272; of coal and steel reveal 'something in the soul', {v}294; 'stupa..monumental phallic symbol', {vi}208; 'People should have..phallic symbol branded on their foreheads', {vi}333; of ibis, {vi}345; 'all art..symbolic, conscious or unconscious', {vii}476; in *LCL*, {vii}476–7; 'Jewish-Jewy', {vii}544
    see also Jenner, Mrs H., *Christian Symbolism*
Symonds Yat (Herefordshire), {iii}278
Synge, John Millington, {i}509, {v}201
    'great dramatist' but 'his folk are too bodiless, mere spirits', {i}183; *Riders to the Sea* 'about the genuinest bit of dramatic tragedy..since Shakspere', {i}260–1
    In the Shadow of the Glen, {i}142;
    The Playboy of the Western World, {i}142;
    Riders to the Sea, {i}142, 260–1;
    The Tinker's Wedding, {ii}557
Syphilida, see Fracastoro, G.
Syra (Greece), {v}484–5, 519, 562, 573, 613, 617
Syracuse (Sicily), {iii}506, 508, 510–11, 514, 525–6, 542, 548
Syston (Leicestershire), {i}44

T. P.'s Weekly, {v}514, {vi}13, 15
    'unctuous', {v}513; prints pieces by DHL, {v}573, {vi}400–1; 'rag of a paper', {vi}460; comes out 'bravely' for *LCL*, {vi}576–9
Table Mountain (South Africa), {iv}157, 168
TAGGARD, GENEVIEVE,
    Letters to {vii}224
Tagore, Rabindranath, {ii}143, 608, {v}49
Tahiti, {ii}230, {iii}505, {iv}11, 238–9, 249–87 *passim*
    'lovely island – but town spoilt', {iv}285–6, {viii}55
Tahiti, S. S., {iv}11, 251–2, 254–6, 259, 267–86 *passim*, 303
Taj Mahal (India), {v}595, 608
Tal, E. P., Verlag, and German translation of *LCL*, {vii}567, 571–2, 596–8, 602, 604, 609
Tales of Mystery and Imagination, see Poe, E. A.
Tallentyre, Stephen G., *Life of Voltaire*, {v}580, 585
Talloire (France), {vi}396–7, 402
Tamaris (France), {vii}543
Tamburlaine, {ii}601
    see also Manucci, N.
Tamburlaine and Other Poems, see Reed, J.
Tampico (Mexico), {iv}529
Tanganyika, Lake, {iv}158
Tanner, Beatrice Stella, *see* Cornwallis-West, B. S.
Tansley Moor (Derbyshire), {v}593
Tante, see Clark, R.
Taormina (Sicily), {iii}1, 10, 478–583, 614–727 *passim*, {iv}1, 3–4, 6, 8, 25, 29, 31, 33–4, 39, 48, 52, 59, 64, 67, 70–1, 73, 77, 83, 86–9, 91–199 *passim*, 207, 216, 219, 231, 287, 365, 385, {v}373, 415, 419, {vii}5, 46, 52, 54, 109, 254, 423, {viii}29–39, 46, 48–52
    'a place where I can amuse myself by myself', {iii}491; 'a parterre of English weeds all cultivating their egos hard, one against the other', {iii}494; quiet, 'the natives go dead without their foreigners', {iii}552, 558; 'amusing, if one doesn't

Taormina (Sicily) (*cont.*)
take it a bit seriously', {iii}637; 'very expensive', {iii}658, 666; DHL 'tired of', {iii}664; 'thankful to be back' in, {iv}92, 98, 100; 'like a continual Mad Hatters tea-party' in, {iv}105; Mallorca 'not nearly so beautiful as', {vii}253–4; DHL 'very sick of', {viii}49

Taos (USA), {iv}2, 4–5, 11–15, 17, 20, 111–87 *passim*, 202, 223, 225, 235–91 *passim*, 302–412 *passim*, 434, 438–9, 444, 450, 464, 477, 489, 493, 521, 534, 555, 559, 572–601 *passim*, {v}3–4, 6, 8, 16–19, 43–5, 50, 54, 56, 65, 75, 85, 98, 101, 106, 111, 115, 128, 132, 140, 146–50, 164, 169, 174–5, 183, 191, 197, 224, 228, 233–4, 239, 250, 253, 259, 261, 277, 281, 425, 439, 472, 486, 497, 510, 540, 567, 580, 585, 594, 615, 620, 624, 629–30, 635, 647, {vi}1, 5, 10, 38, 49, 55–6, 74, 101, 211, 223, 227, 230, 293, 320, 518, {vii}5, 10, 24, 26, 138, 204–5, 277, 288, 317, 342–6, 473, 475, 506, 547, 553, 588, {viii}75, 93, 95, 104, 110
DHL arrives in, {iv}293–4, 296; 'tiny place' high up in the desert, {iv}301; 'in its way..rather thrilling', {iv}313; DHL moves from, {iv}346–9, 360, 362; 'unpleasing' scandal in, {iv}373; 'awful with its spite' (Frieda), {iv}385; 'a schweinerei', {iv}422; DHL has 'some beautiful memories of', {iv}514; 'better than California', {iv}539; 'heaven in comparison' to London, {iv}543, 548, 553; DHL returns to, {v}22–4, 28; San Geronimo fiesta in, {v}139; Willa Cather visits DHL from, {v}283; 'demonish *tension* in the atmosphere' in, {v}550; DHL indebted to Mabel Luhan for 'all that ensues from', {vi}36; 'Brett flourishes in', {vi}82; DHL wants to return to, {vi}296, 299, 349, 358, 366, {vii}174, 614, 616, 624

Taos Junction (USA), {iv}306, 321, 338, 354, 372, 411–12, {v}159

Taos mountain (USA), {iv}307, 310, 313

Taranto (Italy), {iii}687

Tarquinia (Italy), {v}447, 449, 453, 461, 465, {vi}28–31, 33, 36, 39–40, 42–3, 48, 51, 75, 77, 85, 88–9, 266, {vii}19, 508, {viii}104

Tarragon (Spain), {vii}109

Tarry, Mrs, {ii}599, 601, {iii}131, 294

Tartarin de Tarascon, see Daudet, A.

Tartuffe, Le, see Molière, J. B.

Tas, Emile, {iii}445, {viii}79

Tate, Henry, {iv}281

Tate, Nahum, {vii}564

Tatler, {v}3, 416

Tauchnitz, Christian Bernhard von, {i}446, 456, 512, 524, 528, {ii}72, 453, 459, {iii}715, {iv}132–3, {v}646, {vi}354
EME in edn by, {vi}262, {vii}220; *WWRA* and *S and L* in edn by, {vii}219–20, 228

Tavern, The, see Hansard, R.

Taylor, A. M., {iii}255, 265–6, 268, 308

Taylor, Geraldine, {v}215

Taylor, Lewis S., {i}142

TAYLOR, RACHEL ANNAND, {i}14
verses 'exceedingly good' by, {i}141; DHL gives paper on, {i}179–80, 191; DHL's visit to, {i}181–3, 189; *Fiammetta* more mature than *Rose and Vine*, {i}185, 188; involved in award of prize to DHL, {iv}304
'Epilogue of the Dreaming Women', {i}141, 181, 185, 378; *The Hours of Fiammetta*, {i}141, 179–80, 181–2, 185, 188, {iv}304; *Poems*, {i}141, 181; *Rose and Vine*, {i}141, 180, 183–5, 187, 189
Letters to {i}179–91, {iv}303–4

Taylor, Thomas Rawson, {vii}463

Tchaichowsky, Vera, {ii}412

Tchaikowsky, Peter Ilitch, {i}219

Tchekov, Anton, *see* Chekhov, A.

Teacher, The, {i}4

Teacher's Certificate, {i}7–8, 29, 46, 50, 54, 58, 79, 111, 114

TEASDALE, SARA, {iii}677
sends book of poems to DHL, {iii}654,

657; 'sensitive, delicate' poems by,
{viii}39
'Arcturus', {viii}39;
'August Moonrise', {viii}39;
'Blue Squills', {viii}39;
Flame and Shadow, {iii}654, 657,
{viii}39;
'White Fog', {viii}39;
Letters to {viii}39–40
Tebaide, La, see Lorenzetti, P.
Ted, *see* Gillete, F.
Teddy, *see* Seaman, B. E. de M.
Tegernsee (Germany), {vi}157, 166–7,
172–3, 396, {vii}48, 178, 365, 380,
438–81 *passim*, 558, 573
Tehuacan (Mexico), {iv}420–2, 424,
{v}162–3, 214
Tehuantepec (Mexico), {iv}388
Telegraph Sunday Magazine, {vii}394
Tellaro (Italy), {ii}78, 86, 89, 116, 119,
122–3, 140–1, 148–9, 163
DHL witness at peasant wedding in,
{ii}109, 125; notebooks containing MS
poems left in, {ii}478
Tempest, The, see Shakespeare, W.
Tempo, {iv}407
Ten Days That Shook the World, see Reed J.
Tendencies in Modern American Poetry, see
Lowell, A.
Tenente, *see* Ravagli, A
Teniers, David, {i}124, {iii}342
Tennyson, Alfred, Lord, {i}4, 536, {ii}4,
147, 255
'The Charge of the Light Brigade',
{ii}329;
'Idylls of the King', {v}42;
In Memoriam, {ii}266;
'Lady Clare de Vere', {i}506;
'Locksley Hall', {ii}608, {vii}577;
'Maud', {i}164;
'The Princess', {i}167
Teotihuacán (Mexico), {iv}15, 418, 420,
422–3, 457, 535, {v}67
Tepic (Mexico), {iv}17, 501, 508, 510–12,
514–16, {viii}84–5
Terence, *Heauton Timorumenos*, {iii}162
Teresina, *see* Pini, T.

Terriss, Mary Ellaline, {i}14, 144
Territorials, The, {i}118, 121
Terry, Ellen, {v}579
Terry, Marion, {iii}411
Terry, Thomas Philip, *Terry's Guide to
Mexico*, {iv}374, 383, 393, {viii}69
Tetrazzini, Luisa, {i}130
Texas (USA), {iv}112, 114, 123, {vi}559, 561
Thackeray, William Makepeace, {i}98, 101
The History of Pendennis, {iii}38;
Vanity Fair, {i}62;
The Virginians, {iii}38
Thais, see France, A.
Thaïs, {iv}307
Thames, River, {i}292, {ii}665, {v}51,
{vi}412, {vii}533
Thatcham (Berkshire), {iii}375
Thaulow, Fritz, {i}113
'Thayer, Mrs', *see* Moore, M.
THAYER, SCOFIELD, {iii}677, {iv}334–5,
478, {vi}46, {vii}173–4
invited to serialise *Lost Girl* but refused,
{iii}562, 564, 571–2, 576; and
'Gentleman from San Francisco',
{iv}23, 58, 73, 78–9, 87, 91, 108, 113;
prints DHL's poems in *Dial*, {iv}59; and
S and S, {iv}58–9, 73–4; and *Aaron's
Rod*, {iv}74, 130
see also Dial, The
Letters to {iv}58–9, 72–3
Theatre see Isaacs, E.
THEATRE (actors, drama etc), [NB: for
references to DHL's plays see their titles
under Lawrence, D. H.]
DHL's visits to: {i}55–6, 59, 130, 138,
140–1, 146, 304, 306, 310, 327, 364,
495–6, {ii}241, {iii}182, 514, {v}298,
502, 607, {vi}178–9; DHL teaches
orphans of actors, {i}97; DHL delights
in modern drama, {i}103; drama at
school, {i}186, 193, 245–6; 'tones'
important in 'act-able play', {i}199;
Bible 'displayed in a kind of theatre,
false-real', {i}244; 'Oedipus.. finest
drama of *all* times', {i}261; 'in plays you
have to be bald', {i}344–5; producer free
to adapt text of DHL's play, {i}384;

THEATRE (*cont.*)

landscape 'fit for', {i}398; 'queer old play done by the peasants' in 'Ober Ammergau country', {i}411–13; drama critics 'all fools', {i}414; difficult to animate historical characters in play, {i}469–70; DHL enjoys writing for, {i}501; Italian peasant productions in, {i}505, 508; DHL rejects 'bony, bloodless drama' by 'rule and measure mathematical folk', {i}509; Bennett on DHL as dramatist, {ii}136; 'one strong impulse' vital in play, {ii}145; DHL in group writing play, {ii}256, 501, 508; 'cinematograph drama and all our drama' mere 'combination of known reactions', {ii}285; critique of Dollie Radford's play, {ii}316; 'a queer thing..in its influence', {iii}443; 'pamphlet play with..detestable and inartistic motive', {iii}469; in Nottingham, {iii}509; 'any decent actor should have the liberty to alter as much as he likes' in play, {iii}510; 'a vomit-pot, and no better', {iii}587; to be labelled Christian 'like being on the stage in a costume play', {iv}125; world not a stage, 'art, especially novels..not little theatres where the reader sits aloft and watches', {v}201; DHL 'tired of plays that are only literature..playgoing [not] the same as reading', {v}274; audience and critic always perfect in own eyes, {v}604; 'Actors haven't enough *inside* to them', {vi}66; critics mainly interested in plays about 'divorces and money' {vi}75; nicer to shine on 'matrimonial stage..than.. theatrical', {vi}209; 'mise-en-scène' but 'no drama', {vi}282; novel concerned with human beings, '*what is*', drama with events,'*what happens*', {vi}338; drama 'essentially phallic' - where phallic consciousness dead, 'no essential drama', {vi}355; puppet-theatre shows by Wilkinsons, {vii}80–1; if no 'real' human relationships 'no possible development of drama', {vii}83; Huxley play 'horrible to look at, all plays are - so utterly false',

{vii}626; Huxley 'being *It*' among actors, {vii}630
see also People's Theatre Society

Theatre Arts Monthly, {v}582, 626, {vi}10, 354
drawing, *The Corn Dance* in, {v}27, 59, 87, 100, 581, 584, 636, 638, {vi}31; 'Dance of the Sprouting Corn' in, {v}27, 36, 59, 87, 100, 241, 581, 584, 594–5, 623, 636, {vi}31; 'Hopi Snake Dance' in, {v}103, 115–16, 189, 193, 195, 241, 581, 584, 594–5, 623, 636, {vi}31
see also Isaacs, E.

Theatre Guild, {v}8
David offered (but rejected) for performance by, {v}274, 276, 281, 285–6, 303, 308

Theatre: Essays on the Arts of the Theatre, see Isaacs, E.

Thebaïd, The, {iii}669–70

Theosophist Review, {iv}365

There are Crimes and Crimes, see Strindberg, A.

These Lynnekers, see Beresford, J. D.

Things Near and Far, see Machen, A.

Thirroul (Australia), {iv}9–10, 244–82 *passim*, {viii}55

This Quarter, see Titus, E.

This Way to Paradise, see Huxley, A.

Thomann, Dr, {v}622–3, {vi}217

Thomas Hardy, see Abercrombie, L.

Thomas of Celano, {i}225, {iii}531

Thomas, *see* Seltzer, T.

Thomas, Annie, {iii}122, 200

Thomas, Edward {i}12, 19, 138, 237, 405, 548, {ii}321, {iii}141, 372, {v}349

THOMAS, HELEN BERENICE, {iii}372–3, {v}349
Letters to {iii}372

Thomas, Olive ('Hermosa'), {i}170

Thomas, William Berryman, {iii}122

THOMPSON, CLARENCE E., {iv}515, 585, {v}4–5, 42, 51, 56–9, 76, 89, 102, 106, 128–9, 237, {vi}127
'nice fellow - not weak really, at all', {v}48; tension between DHL and,

{v}60, 64, 72–4; some reconciliation, {v}171–2
  Letters to {v}88, 99, 106–7, 144–5, 171–2
Thompson, Francis Joseph, {i}14, 95, {ii}255, 259, {v}626
  DHL copies 'Absence' from MS by, {i}145
  'The Hound of Heaven', {i}140, 145
Thomson, James, 'The City of Dreadful Night', {vii}248
Thorne, Guy, *see* Gull, C. A. E. R.
Thornton, Rev. Claude Cyprian, {i}67
Thornycroft, Rosalind, *see* Baynes, R.
Thornycroft, Sir Hamo, {iii}414, 463, 641
Thorogood, Evelyn, {vii}14, 652
Thousand and One Nights see Arabian Nights
Thrasher, Carlota Davis, DHL meets in Florence, {iii}600; offers lease on farm, {iii}605, 628, 659, 661–2, 664, 667–70, 672, 676; Thrasher's Farm, Connecticut, {iii}17, 605, 659, 661, 664, 667–8, 674–6, 678, 682–4, 689, 710
Three Brontës, The, see Sinclair, M.
300 Club and Stage Society, The, production of *David* by, {v}470, 524, 534, 543, 562, 570, 576–8, 582, 586, 600, 608, 613–14, 621, 636–7, {vi}26, 71, {viii}96, 98, 100, 102; *Widowing* produced by, {v}576–8, 582, 586, 598–602, 604–5, 608, 613–14, 621, 637, {viii}98, 100
Three Sisters, The, see Sinclair, M.
Three Soldiers, see Dos Passos, J.
Three Things, see Yeats, W. B.
THRING, GEORGE HERBERT, {ii}226
  and prosecution of *Rainbow*, {ii}430, 433–5, 440, 442, 469; advises DHL on Tauchnitz edns, {vi}354
  Letters to {ii}433–5, 469, {vi}354
  Letters from {ii}442, 469
THROSSELL, HUGO VIVIAN HOPE ('JIM'), {iv}251, 272–3, {v}21
  Letters to {iv}248
THROSSELL KATHARINE (KATHARINE SUSANNAH PRICHARD), {iv}251, {v}21
  'too feminine about *Kangaroo*', {v}44, {viii}90
  Black Opal, {iv}251, 281–2

Letters to {iv}272–3, 281–2, {v}44, {viii}90
Throssell, Ric, {iv}272
Through the Looking-Glass, see Carroll, L.
Through the Unknown Pamirs, see Olufsen, O.
Thucydides, 'splendid and noble writer', {ii}592; 'very present to one's soul', {ii}614
  The History of the Peloponnesian War, {ii}572, 592, 634
Thumersbach (Tumersbach) (Austria), {iv}25, {iv}50–78 *passim*, {viii}43
Thurston, Katherine Cecil, admired *White Peacock*, {i}312–14
  John Chilcote, {i}312
Thus Spake Zarathustra, see Nietzsche, F. W.
Tiajuana (Mexico), {vii}246
Tibet, {iv}239
Tidmarsh (Berkshire), {iii}392
TIETJENS, EUNICE STRONG, {ii}203, {iii}139, {iv}404
  'The Hand', {iii}139, 141–2;
  Profiles from China, {iii}139;
  'Reflections in a Ricksha', {iii}139
  Letters to {iii}139–42
Tignale, *see* Gardola di Tignale
Tim, *see* Lawrence, A.
Time and Tide, 'insignificant' but 'pays quite well, {iii}731; Rose Macaulay on *W in L* in, {iv}51; Rebecca West's 'Jixless Errand' in, {vii}252
Time of Man, The see Roberts, E. M.
Time, {v}288
Timeo Hotel (Taormina), {iii}10, 481, 487, 491, 496, 498, 502, 506–7, 514, 620, 639
  'seems a nasty impudent place..hateful', {iii}479–80; 'expensive', {iii}482, 648, {iv}141
Times, The, {i}52, 123, 277, 297, {iii}48, 57, 88, 138, 291, 293, 441, 450, 469, 654, {iv}133, 275, 353, {v}112, 340, 346, 384, {vii}81, 132, 167, 265, 334, 367–8, 395, 627
  Widowing reviewed in, {iii}477, 495; weekly edn 'on the whole such bunk', {v}80; *Corriere della Sera* superior to, {v}90

Times Book Club, The, {iv}262

Times Educational Supplement, The, {iii}291, 297–8

and 'Education of the People', {iii}303, 306–7, 310–11, 316, {viii}30

Times (Literary) Supplement, The, {i}107, 221, {iii}291, {v}245, 340, 376, 469, 518, {vi}257, 534, {vii}223

Secker sends copies to DHL, {v}619–20, {vi}32, 69, {vii}336, 563; Reviews in: *White Peacock,* {i}225, 230; *Love Poems,* {i}530; *Twilight,* {ii}616; *Amores,* {ii}640; *LWHCT,* {iii}186–7, 190; *Lost Girl,* {iii}638; *W in L,* {iv}38–40; *Kangaroo,* {iv}557; *B in B,* {v}121, 123, {viii}90; *St. Mawr,* {v}267; *Plumed Serpent,* {v}383; *Collected Poems,* {vii}41; *Pansies,* {vii}362

Timsy (cat), {viii}110

Tinker's Wedding, The, see Synge, J. M.

Tinners Arms (Zennor), {ii}561–81, {iii}122, 200, {iv}312

Tipografia, Giuntina, {vi}5, 10, 312, 605

'little printer' of *LCL,* {vi}303, 314–17, 323–4, 328, 338, 346, 353, 357, 364, 378, 382, 385, 391, 410, 414; 'nobody understands a word of English' at, {vi}322, 326, 330–1, 334, 337, 344, 350, 358; DHL cross with, {vi}394; has type for only half the novel, {vi}395, 401–2, 408, 412; extra 200 copies printed by, {vi}414, 442; name on verso of title-page, {vi}415–16; account to be paid, {vi}466, 471, 476, 480, 483; to print false covers for *LCL,* {vi}525, 561

'Tipple, The', *see* Crichton, K. S.

Tirpitz, Alfred von, {ii}392

Titans and Gods, see Branford, F. V.

Titian, {i}124

Tito (dog), {vi}170, 398, {vii}281

Titterton, George, {i}377

Titterton, John ('Jack'), {i}377

Titterton, Mrs, {i}377

Titterton, William Richard, *Love Poems,* {i}100

TITUS, EDWARD W., {vii}1, 4, 6–7, 9, 12–13, 386, 395, 445, 453, 516–17, 541, 573, 596, 638

agreement with DHL for publication of Paris edn of *LCL,* {vii}225, 229–30, 232–3, 244–6, 261; edn in production, {vii}271, 274, 337. 339, 346; and *My Skirmish,* {vii}316, 390–2, 401, 404, 429–32, 439, 462, 464, 471, 481, 551; arranges distribution of *LCL,* {vii}392, 396; opposes expurgated *LCL,* {vii}396, 432; 'nasty fellow if he cuts up rough', {vii}401; cheques from, {vii}428, 514, 526–7, 568, 612, 625, 648; sells 3000 copies of *LCL* and reprints, {vii}433, 435, 444, 446, 587; offers advance payment of royalties, {vii}476; referred to as 'Tite' and 'T', {vii}488–9; wants to buy *LCL* MS, {vii}514–15; and sale in Paris of Lahr's *Pansies* edn, {vii}515–16, 520, 638, 648–9; DHL seeks advice over the 'mess' of his 'affairs in USA', {vii}520–2, 533–4, 569, 601, 625–6; DHL resists discount sales of *LCL,* {vii}582–3, 587; financial statement on first printing of Paris edn, {vii}612; visits DHL, {vii}612, 625; proposes 3rd impression of Paris edn, {vii}637–8, 648

Legend of Ermengarde, {vii}429, 431;

This Quarter, {vii}225, 259, 268–9, 295, 341–2, 392, 429, 468, 476, 513–14, 539, 569, 601, 607, 625

Letters to {vii}244, 259, 268, 316, 337–8, 341–2, 391–2, 396–7, 428–9, 431–2, 451–2, 464, 475–6, 514–16, 520–3, 527, 533–4, 539–40, 568–9, 582–3, 587, 601, 612, 625–6, 637–8, 648

Letters from {vii}341, 392, 429–30, 451–2, 475–6, 514, 520, 533–4, 539, 568–9, 582–3, 587, 601–2, 612, 625, 637, 648–9

Tlalpam (Mexico), {iv}534, 536, {v}156, 212

'To a Louse', *see* Burns, R.

To the Stars, see Andreev, L. N.

Toil of Men, see Querido, I.

Toledo, S. S., {iv}18, 535–6, 538–9, {vii}282–3

Tolstoy (Tolstoi), Countess Sophie, *Autobiography*, {ii}205, {iv}274, 282, 462

Tolstoy (Tolstoi), Count Leo {i}5, 12, 42, 96, 118, 138, 278, 314, 536, {ii}21, 646, {iii}63
'really..or nearly' nihilist, {ii}102; DHL rejects 'moral scheme' in, {ii}182–3; relatively '*obvious* and coarse', {iii}41, 45; DHL dismissive of play by, {iii}411
Anna Karénina, {i}127, 191, 412, 463; *Kreutzer Sonata*, {ii}96, 100–1, 114; *The Live Corpse*, {iii}411; *Tolstoi's LoveLetters*, {iv}462; *War and Peace*, {i}127; *What is Art*{vii}82

Tom Brown's Schooldays, see Hughes, T.
Tom Jones, see Fielding, H.
Tom, *see* Betts, T.
Tombazis, {vii}583
Tomellin (Mexico), {v}162–3
Tomlinson, Florence Margaret, {v}205
Tomlinson, Henry Major, {iv}462, {v}205, 231, 242, 313
Gifts of Fortune, {v}573
Tommy and Grizel, see Barrie, (Sir) J. M.
Tonbridge Wells (Kent), {i}69
Tono-Bungay, see Wells, H. G.
Tony, *see* Almgren, A; Luhan, A.
Torbole (Italy), {i}453
Torey, Abel, {ii}130
Toronto (Canada), {ii}515, 518, {v}262, 612, {vi}518, 520, 574, {vii}218, 306–7
'Toronto', *see* Prewett, F.
Torre Quattro Venti, *see* Villa Torre Quattro Venti
Torrence, Frederick Ridgely, {iii}596, 627
Letters from {iii}596
Torrents of Spring, see Turgenev, I.
Toscolano (Italy), {i}483
Totemism and Exogamy, see Frazer, Sir J. G.
Totnes (Devonshire), {vii}317, 483, 581, 622
Toulon (France), {iv}203, {v}417, {vi}1, 19, 519, 529, 537, 573, 580–1, 586, 588, 594, 599, 608–9, 611, 615, {vii}5, 19, 22, 25–6, 31, 40, 104, 126, 154, 176, 183, 187, 195–6, 203, 205, 207, 209, 379, 453,

494, 502, 511, 525, 534, 543, 575–6, 584, 599
'a port, all sailors..cats..queer people', {vii}128
Toulouse (France), {vi}343, {vii}246
Tourneur, Cyril, {vii}508
'Towns in Colour', *see* Lowell, A.
Townsend, Gertrude, {ii}92
Townsend, Harry E., {ii}197
Towsey, Joseph H., {i}524
Tozzi, Federigo, *Tre Croci*, {iv}188
Trachsl, Käthe, {vi}456, 458–9, 468, 527, 562, 565, 592, {vii}105, 128
Trachsl, Lena, {vi}456, 458–9, 464, 468, 487, 565, 592, {vii}105
Tragic Comedians, The, see Meredith, G.
Tramp, The, {i}136, 172
transition, {vi}231, 300, {vii}265, 577, 607
'that Paris modernissimo periodical', {vi}507–8; 'some things good and amusing', {vi}548
Trapani (Sicily), {iii}656, 688, {iv}127
TRAVEL, Philip Smith 'lordly and continental', McLeod 'untravelled blighter', {i}464; 'voyage of discovery towards the real..eternal..unknown land', {ii}362; like Columbus with 'a shadowy America before him', {ii}362, 556; DHL longs for 'voyage into the South Pacific', {ii}527, 529; after illness 'I shall come south as soon as I can', {iii}338; DHL's eagerness to visit Palestine, {iii}353–4; 'Be careful, when you travel, of *thieves*', {iii}432; 'I shall certainly go' to Zululand if invitation serious, {iii}449; 'Why should one travel?..It costs so much, to', {iii}539; 'I always travel second in Italy', {iii}541; DHL's excitement over ship *Lavengro* with Mackenzie, {iii}561–2; on foot with Whittleys, {iii}569–70; in USA most significant experience of DHL's mature life, {iv}1; 'dead tired..don't want to travel another yard', {iv}80, 83; DHL wants to see 'more of the world', {iv}117; 'ready to travel: 4 trunks, one household trunk, one book trunk..two

TRAVEL (*cont.*)
 valises, hat-box..two quite small pieces',
 {iv}198, 206; at sea, Port Said, Suez
 Canal, {iv}208–13; '*never* travel round
 the world to look at it', {iv}221; 'second
 class' to Australia, {iv}227; 'one can
 travel perfectly second class – nicer than
 first', {iv}244; 'better to travel and spend
 the money' than to 'sit still in nothingness', {iv}258; 'would be so nice if fewer
 people travelled', {iv}284; 'splendid
 lesson in disillusion', {iv}286; 'great
 weariness, as well as..excitement',
 {iv}312; 'getting tired of', {iv}424; 'my
 soul..is like Balaam's ass..*can't* travel any
 farther..Later the ass will be able to',
 {iv}479; 'vile being shut in with all the
 people' on ocean liner, {v}18; 'I always
 want to travel southwards', {v}138;
 Americans travel so much, {v}586;
 'Travel no longer thrills me..it begins to
 bore me', {vi}26; DHL has a cold and
 'daren't', {vi}52; 'The longer I live, the
 less I like the actual process of travelling', {vi}62; 'One must either work or',
 {vi}123; sea-voyage might be cure for
 'bronchials', {vi}127, 299; everything so
 costly 'one dare hardly breathe let alone',
 {vi}198; DHL 'sick..of shifting about',
 {vi}202; impeded because of 'wretched
 chest', {vi}297; 'broncs aren't good
 enough for..long', {vi}310, 521; 'not well
 enough to travel' to Taos, {vii}625,
 628–9
 see also Lawrence, D. H., *Etruscan Places*,
 M in M, *Twilight*
Travel, {vi}10
 DHL's Mexican essays in, {v}575, 582,
 587, 596, 610, 620, 623, 626, 638; Tuscan
 essays in, {v}655, {vi}48, 83–4, 168,
 176, 181–2, 189, 196, 209, 232, 266, 311
Travellers' Library, The, Twilight in, {v}460;
 Gesualdo in, {vi}40, 53, 68, 517
Travels in Arabia Deserta, see Doughty, C. M.
Traviata, La, see Verdi, G.
Tre Croci, see Tozzi, F.
Treasure Island, see Stevenson, R. L.

Tree of the Folkungs, The, see Heidenstam, K.
 G. V. von
Tree, (Sir) Beerbohm, {i}97
Tree, Iris, {iii}304
Treesby Cottage (Knockholt), {vii}353
Tregerthen, *see* Higher Tregerthen
Trelawny, Edward John *Recollections of the
 Last Days of Shelley and Byron*, {ii}625,
 {iii}61
Trelawny, Sir Jonathan, {vi}408
Trembling of a Leaf, see Maugham, W. S.
Trench, Frederic Herbert, {ii}170, {iii}463
 visits DHL at Lerici, {ii}167, 173;
 invites DHL to Settignano, {iii}425, 592
 Napoleon, {iii}425
TRENCH, LILIAN ISABEL, {iii}425
 Letters to {iii}463
Trésor des Humbles, see Maeterlinck, M.
Trespasser, The, see Lawrence, D. H.; Parker,
 Sir G.
Tressider, W. J., {iv}86
Treveal (Cornwall), {viii}25
Trevelyan, George Macaulay, {ii}211
 Garibaldi, {iii}622;
 Lord Grey of the Reform Bill, {iv}146
Trevelyan, Robert Calverley, {ii}4, 211, 505,
 {iii}487, 494, {v}414, {vi}232
 at Lerici, {ii}113, 116–17; 'lovable
 fellow', {ii}118
Trevelyan, Sir George Otto, {vi}232
Treves, *see* Fratelli Treves (Milan)
Trial of Jeanne D'Arc, The, see Garnett, E.
Triangle, The (Chesham), {ii}208–19, 242,
 245–6, 251–60, {iv}165, {viii}12–13
Tribune, {v}551
Trient (Austria), {i}450, 452, 455
Trier (Germany), {i}393–9, 408–9, 411,
 {viii}6
Trieste (Austria), {v}299, {vi}97
Tring (Hertfordshire), {ii}407, {iii}71, 484
Trinidad, *see* Archuleta, T.; Brett, D.
Trionfo della Morte, see D'Annunzio, G.
Trip to New York, A, see Turner, W. J.
Triple Fugue, see Sitwell, O.
Tripoli (Syria), {i}474, 478, 515
Tristan, {ii}492, 494–6, 503, 507
Tristan and Isolde, see Wagner, R.

'Tristram of Lyonesse', *see* Swinburne, A. C.
Tristram Shandy, see Sterne, L.
Troisdorf (Germany), {i}398
Trojan Women, The, see Euripides
Trompeter von Säckingen, Der, see Scheffel, J. V. von
Trotsky, Leon, {ii}459, {iii}390
Trotter, Dorothy, *see* Warren, D.
TROTTER, PHILIP COUTTS {ii}504, {vi}577, {vii}8, 24, 345, 348, 370, 425, 486–7, 490, 631, 651
  and exhibition of DHL's paintings, {vii}361, 367, 477–80
  Letters to {vii}489–90, 652
Trotter, Wilfred, *Instincts of the Herd in Peace and War*, {iii}59
Trovatore, Il, see Verdi, G.
True History of the Conquest of New Spain, The, see Diaz del Castillo, B.
True Story of Woodrow Wilson, The, see Lawrence, D.
Truro (Cornwall), {i}207, {ii}495, 608
Truslove & Hanson Ltd, {vi}515, 519
Tucker Sees India, see Skinner, M.
Tule, Santa María del, {v}163
Tumersbach, *see* Thumersbach
Tunis, {iii}620, 624, 637, {v}343, {v}373, {vi}340, 367, {vii}170
Turgenev, Ivan Sergeevich, {i}178, 314, {iii}147
  DHL objects to 'moral scheme' in, {ii}182; 'sort of male old maid', {iii}41; 'insensitive stupidity' in, {iii}45; Baden-Baden belongs to time of, {iii}733, {v}330, {vi}180, {vii}382
  Sportsman's Sketches, A, {iii}41;
  Torrents of Spring, {i}334, 344
Turin (Italy), {ii}139, 184, {iii}412, 414–17, 421, 449, 469, 514, 523, 541, 569, 683, {iv}166, {v}363, 378, 389, {vi}420, 440, {vii}262, {viii}31
Turkey, {i}474–5, 478, {ii}69, 87
Turner, Francis W., {i}506
Turner, G. A., {i}303
Turner, Joseph Mallord William, {i}266, {ii}117, {vii}417
  Liber Studiorum, {vii}78

Turner, Leonard James, {i}506
TURNER, REGINALD ('REGGIE'), {iii}594, 599, {v}11, 501, 517, 532, 534, 563, 571, {vi}2, 112, 131, 164, 187, 289, 433, 440, 456, {vii}253, 274, 340, 478
  probably model for Algy Constable in *Aaron's Rod*, {iv}212; 'last of the Oscar Wilde group', {v}418; DHL socialises with, {v}435, 444, 450–1, 478, 490, 576, 585, 606, 611, {vi}214, 217, {viii}103
  Letters to {iii}600–1, 614, {iv}212, {v}434, 445–6, 450–1, {vi}108–9
Turner, Walter James, {vi}67, 82, 375, {viii}97
  Smaragda's Lover, {viii}97;
  A Trip to New York, {vii}531, 559
Turquoise Trail, The, see Henderson, A.
Tuscany (Italy), {iii}649, {v}12, 436, 443, 468, 482, 484, 496, 498, 518, 559, 617–18, {vi}100, 109, 118, 195, 212, 273, 395, {vii}40, 281, 465, 503
  cypresses incomparably beautiful 'like black flames from primeval times', {iv}84; DHL to 'stroll around' in preparation for *Etruscan Places*, {v}427, 447, 464–5; 'very pretty country', {v}456, 460; Frieda considers 'flowery mysterious', {v}470, 655; 'something eternal about it', {v}486; DHL better out of 'dry heat of', {vi}118–24, 130, 282; Frieda 'hankers after', {vii}87
Twelfth Night, see Shakespeare, W.
Twentieth Century Poetry, see Monro, H.
Twice-Told Tales, see Hawthorne, N.
Twixt Land and Sea: Tales, see Conrad, J.
Two or Three Graces, see Huxley, A.
Two Years Before the Mast, see Dana, R. H.
Tylor, Sir Edward Burnett, *Primitive Culture*, {ii}591, 593, 630
Tyneside (Northumberland), {vii}468
Typee, see Melville, H.
Typee, *see* Rananim
Tyrol, {i}18, 429, {iii}707, 721, 724, 726, 730, 733, {iv}25, 33, 39–40, 48, 51–2, 109
  beauty of Bavarian, {i}411, 413, 415; DHL's walking tour in Austrian,

Tyrol (*cont.*)
{i}424–6, 431–2, 444–6, 452; DHL stays in Austrian, {iv}54–78; Austrian 'though lovely is depressing', {iv}191; 'mountain-tramping people' with bare knees in, {vi}123–4, 127
Tyrwhitt-Wilson, Gerald, *see* Berners, Lord

Übrecht, *see* Hubrecht, M.
Uccello, Paolo, {iii}341, 352
Ufer, Mary Monrad Frederiksen, {iv}344, 347, 354, {v}23, 74, {viii}75
Ufer, Miss, {v}530
Ufer, Walter, {iv}344, 347, 354, 434, {v}23, 74, 224, {viii}75
Uffizi (Florence), {iii}419–23, 426, 595, 604, 622, {iv}48, {v}597, {vi}79, 415, {viii}45
Ukraine, {ii}205, {iii}482
Ulfelder, Dr Sidney, {v}7, 221–6, 230–1, 235, 241
Ulster (Ireland), {iii}39, {v}589
Ulysses, see Joyce, J.
Umbria (Italy), {v}10, 411–37, 447, 613
Umckaloaba, {vi}336, 350, 361, 387, 413
Under the Red Robe, see Weyman, S.
Under Western Eyes, see Conrad, J.
Underwood (Derbyshire), {i}22, 135, {v}243, 592
Undine, see Fouqué, F. de la Motte
Undset, Sigrid, *The Mistress of Husaby*, {v}256
Ungava, see Ballantyne, R. M.
Unger, Federico, {iv}510, 519
UNIDENTIFIED RECIPIENT,
Letters to {vi}443, {viii}15–16
Union Hill, *see* Birkindele
Union of Democratic Control, {ii}309, 347, 436, {iii}71
United States of America, *see* America
Unknown Correspondent, *see* Unidentified Recipient
Unknown Pamirs, see Olufsen, O.
Unknown Sea, The, see Housman, C.
UNTERMEYER, JEANETTE ('JEAN') STARR, {v}540

contributes to cheque for DHL, {iii}445, {viii}79; sends books of poems, {iv}185
Letters to {iv}185–6
UNTERMEYER, LOUIS, {iii}141, {iv}185–6, {viii}39
contributes to cheque for DHL, {iii}445, {viii}79; writes critical piece on DHL, {iii}595; example of wandering Jew, {v}540
Letters to {iii}595
UNWIN, (SIR), STANLEY, Harrison advises DHL to approach, {ii}216; invites DHL to complete book, 'Education of the People', {iii}321, 323, 553–4, 565, {viii}30–3; willing to read *Foreign Legion* but rejects, {viii}30–3; and *SCAL*, {viii}32–3; complete MS of 'Education of the People' rejected by, {viii}34, 37–8; DHL requests return of MS from, {viii}38
Letters to {viii}30–4, 37–8
Letters from {viii}30–5, 38
Unwin, Thomas Fisher, {i}19, 154, 297, {ii}41, 384, {iii}12, 210, {iv}27–8
invites DHL to submit 'a good strong novel' for publication, {i}458; seeming interest in publishing *W in L* not pursued, {iii}184–5, 187, 191, 195
Letters from {i}458
Upper Garden, The, see La Condamine, R. de
Urquhart, *see* Carswell, C.
Ussher, Arland, {iii}196
Ute Park (USA), {iv}322–3, 336
Utrecht (Netherlands), {iii}489, 506, 621, {iv}87, 193

Vagabondaggio, see Verga, G.
Vagabonde, La, see Collette
Val d'Arno (Italy), {v}443, 478, 644–5
Valdemosa (Mallorca), {vii}275
Valdez (USA), {iv}344, 374–408 *passim*, {v}40, 47–8, 54–5, 65–6, 71, 73, 82–107 *passim*, 115, 126–8, 132, 140, 144, 155, 185, 225–93 *passim*, 480
Valencia (Spain), {vii}86, 109, 238, 276, 543

Valiton, Carnot K., {v}55
Valkyrie, {v}63, {vi}136
Valle, Rafael Heliodoro, {v}287
Valletta (Malta), {iii}529–31, 533–5, 557,
    {iv}178, {v}31, 33, {viii}49
Vallette, Alfred, {ii}385
Vallombrosa (Italy), {iii}542, 558, 567–8,
    575, {v}614, {vi}78, 528, 532, 543,
    605
    Orioli at, {vi}109, 111–12, 131, 470, 476,
    491, 494, 496, {vii}95, 411, 446, 455
Vallorbe (Switzerland), {vi}473, 494
Valparaiso (Chile), {i}228
Van der Velde, Adriaen, {i}124
Van der Velde, Willem, {i}124
Van Dieren, Bernard, {iii}176, 181
Van Dieren, Frida, {iii}176, 181
Van Doren, Carl Clinton, {v}301, 325, 358
    Other Provinces, {v}358
Van Doren, Mark, {vii}584
VAN DOREN, IRITA, DHL reviews in *New
    York Herald Tribune Books* for, {v}301,
    317, 321, 325, 358–9
    Letters to {v}301, 325, 358–9
Van Dyck, Sir Anthony, {i}124
Van Dyke, John Charles, *The Open Spaces*,
    {iv}392
Van Gogh, Vincent, {iii}341
    DHL reads *Letters* of, {ii}296, 298–9,
    303
Van Stone, Mary Roberta Hurt, {iv}406
Van Vechten, Carl, {v}272, 639
    Nigger Heaven, DHL reviews adversely,
    {v}647, 652;
    Peter Whiffle, {iv}338
Vancouver (Canada), {iv}142, 269, 274,
    276–9, {v}229
Vandiveer, William, {vi}551, {vii}506
Vanguard Press (New York), {vi}14
    'want to publish and distribute' *LCL* in
    USA, {vi}525–7, 530–2, 538–9, 545–6,
    565, 568, 572, {vii}35, 39, {viii}115;
    DHL feels 'cheated' by, {vii}42
Vanity Fair (London), {i}241, {ii}29,
    {iii}363
Vanity Fair (New York) {v}185–6, 196, 459,
    {vi}461, 602, {vii}4, 513

requests photograph of DHL, {iii}535,
    550; DHL would like to appear in,
    {iv}518; DHL's essays in, {v}87, 241,
    {vi}606, {vii}29, 51, 118, 158, 188, 249,
    269, {viii}88; DHL invited to write for,
    {v}482; 'getting terribly attached to'
    DHL, {vii}251; DHL's paintings
    reproduced in, {vii}495, 503–4, 506,
    525; DHL reluctant to sign year's
    contract with, {vii}512, 525, 554, 614,
    624
Vanity Girl, see Mackenzie, E. M. C.
Vanne, Marda, {v}604
Varda, Mrs (Varda Bookshop), orders copies
    of *LCL*, {vi}512, 514–15, 544,
    {vii}124
Vasconcelos, José, {iv}432
Vathek, see Beckford, W.
Veii (Italy), {v}649, 651, {vi}89, {vii}608
Velarde (USA), {v}102
Velasquez, Diego Rodriguez da Silva y,
    {i}124, 130, {ii}159, {vi}318
Vence (France), DHL in sanatorium in,
    {vii}12–14, 630–1, 638–53
Vengerova, Zinaida Afanasevna, {ii}459
Venice (Italy), {i}312, 453, 465, {ii}89, 107,
    {iii}424, 533, 535, 542, 568–70, 572,
    575, 587–623 *passim*, 632, 707, 715,
    {iv}80–1, 167, 195, 312, {v}299, 454,
    555, 586, {vi}79, 86, 108, 127, 461–2,
    {vii}341, 354, 461, 463, 465–6, 471, 473,
    476–80, {viii}37
    lovely to look at but 'melancholic with its
    dreary bygone lagoons', {iii}590;
    'stagnant as regards life', {iii}608; Lane
    asks DHL for book on, {iii}615, 620,
    623, {viii}37, 39
Ventimiglia (Ventimille) (Italy), {v}378,
    390, 392, 400, {vi}593, {vii}548,
    558
Ventnor (Isle of Wight), {i}133–4,
    {iii}454
Ventura, S. S., {iv}252, 259, 277
Venus (statue), {vi}22, 126
Venus de Milo, {i}180, {ii}137–8
Venus in the Fishes, see Mohr, M.
Venus in the Kitchen, see Douglas, G. N.

Vera Cruz (Mexico), {iv}364, 377, 388, 425, 427, 433–4, 454, 458, 467, 508, 521–42 *passim*, {v}148, 170, 174, 185–221 *passim*, 235, 241, {vii}146
Verdi, Giuseppe, {i}67
  La Traviata, {i}253;
  Il Trovatore, {i}322
Vere, *see* Collins, H. V. G.
Verga, Giovanni, {iv}200, 273–4, 276–7, 300–1, 309, 435, 476–7, 480, 500, {v}92, {vi}40, 88, 132, {viii}70
  Cavalleria 'veritable blood-pudding of passion!', {iii}53; 'exercises quite a fascination' on DHL, {iv}105–6; 'the only Italian who does interest me', {iv}109–10; 'awfully difficult to translate', {iv}115; DHL translating *Gesualdo*, {iv}157, 162, 186, 188–91, 196–7, 208, 212–15, 219–20, 235, 245; translating *Novelle Rusticane*, {iv}220, 227, 231–3, 235, 245, {viii}58; Blackwell to publish translations of, {iv}300–2, 394, 401, {vi}53; Seltzer publishes *Gesualdo*, {iv}406, 436, 439, 442, 447–8, 475–6, 478, 517–18, 526, 549, {viii}58, 61, 72; Cape publishes English edn of *Gesualdo*, {v}165, {vi}53, 517; DHL translating *Cavalleria* for Cape, {vi}70, 110, 132, 151, 167, 325, 517
  'Black Bread', {iv}232, 367, {viii}58;
  Cavalleria Rusticana, {iii}53, 103, 115, 188, 447, {vi}53, 70, 110, 151, 167, 325, 517;
  'His Reverence', {iv}245;
  I Malavoglia, {iv}106, 115, 190, 200, 273;
  'La Lupa', {iv}447;
  Little Novels of Sicily, {iii}149, {iv}8, 14, 109, 300, 367, {v}20, 92–3, 165, 247, {vi}53, {vii}445, {viii}58;
  Mastro-don Gesualdo, {iv}6, 8, 16, 18, 106, 115, 157, 162, 186, 188–91, 196, 200, 208, 210, 212–15, 219–20, 235, 245, 276–7, 302, 367, 369–70, 394, 401, 406, 436, 439, 442, 447–8, 475–8, 480–1, 501, 517–18, 523, 526–7, 549, {v}165, {vi}516–17, {viii}58, 61, 72, 88;

Novelle Rusticane, {iv}106, 115, 220, 227, 231–2, 235, 245, 300–2, 447, {v}20, 93, {viii}58;
  'St Joseph's Ass', {iv}480, 500;
  Vagabondaggio, {iv}115
Vergine delle Rocce, see Annunzio, G. d'.
Verlaine, Paul, {i}5, 61, 64, 68, 179, {ii}101, 118
  'Art Poétique', {i}63;
  'Kaléïdoscope', {i}75;
  Romances sans Paroles, {i}320, {ii}109
Vermala Montana (Switzerland), {vi}374, 380, 384, 396, 398
Verona (Italy), {i}424–6, 464, 524, 531, 535, 537–40, {ii}120, {iii}326, 569, 592, 724, {iv}80; {vii}463, 465–6, 477, {viii}45
Verona, Guido da, {vii}386
Versailles (France), {v}435, 475, {vi}184–5, 366
  Treaty of, {iii}294, 366, {vi}142;
  'stupid..much too large for the landscape', {iv}589–91
Versunkene Glocke, see Hauptmann, G.
Vesuvius, Mount (Italy), {iii}446, 451, 454, 488, {v}466
Vetulonia (Italy), {vi}89
Vevey (Switzerland), {vi}430–1
Via dei Bardi (Florence), {iv}48, 69–89, {v}12, 454, {vii}479, {viii}45
Via Gellia (Derbyshire), {i}24, {iii}232, 236, {v}243, 593
Viani, Lorenzo, *Parigi*, {vi}257
Viareggio (Italy), {ii}153, 156, {vi}77, {vii}339, 348, 357
Vicenzo, *see* Cacópardo, V.
Vickers Maxim & Co., {ii}184, 268, {iii}260
Victor, *see* Higgins, V.
Victoria, Queen, {i}134, {iii}95, 559
Vienna (Wien) (Austria), {iii}400, {iv}59, 61, 68–9, 73–4, 78, 366, 398, {v}369, 480, 558, {vi}103, 118–19, 121, 123, 577, {vii}141, 567, 571–2, 596, 598, 601, 604, {viii}43
Vierwaldstätter See (Switzerland), {v}334
Vietri (Italy), {viii}100
Vieusseux Library (Florence), {v}11, 444

Vigie, The, *see* Port-Cros, Ile de

Vigo (Spain), {iv}539

Viking Press (New York), {ii}426, {iv}82, 474, {vi}607, {vii}84, 112, 129
    ineffective publishers of *Rainbow, New Poems, LWHCT,* {vi}538–9; DHL tries to recover copyright on poems from, {vi}610, {vii}38, 45, 52, 65, 85, 111, 130; consider publishing *Collected Poems* (but do not), {vii}167, 174, 182; DHL 'disgusted with', {vii}221

Vikings, The, see Ibsen, H.

Villa Ada (Florence), {iii}609, {iv}190

Villa Alpensee (Zell-am-See), {iv}53–78

Villa Beau-Soleil (Bandol), {vii}11, 492–650 *passim*
    'smallish bungalow..ordinary - but not poky', {vii}494; 'commonplace little bourgeois house..made by a *femme entretenue*, and is her ideal: awful', {vii}543

Villa Bernarda (Spotorno), {v}10, {v}337–436 *passim,* {v}565
    'nice, just under the Castle, in a big vineyard garden', {v}357

Villa Bianca (Florence), {v}617, 637

Villa Bombici (Giogoli), {vi}361

Villa Bronciliano (Vingone), {vii}19

Villa Canovaia (San Gervasio), {iii}609, 676
    Rosalind Baynes in, {iii}520–1, 542, {iv}67; on loan to DHL, {iii}585, 592–6, 602–3; *BBF* poems written at, {iii}596, 651, 657, {iv}190

Villa Carmen (Chapala), {iv}436

Villa Curonia (Arcetri), {iv}5, {v}5, 107, 407, 423, 458, 462–3, 487, 580, 593, 608, 615, 622–3, 625, 641–2, 646, {vi}37, 223, 435

Villa Fontana Vecchia, *see* Fontana Vecchia

Villa Fraita (Anacapri), Brett Youngs bought, {iii}496, 504, 522, 559, 567, 587, {iv}7, 138

Villa Giulia (Anacapri), {vi}246
    Brewsters rent, {v}626, 629, 636, {vi}340, {vii}22, 48, 54, 250

Villa Igéa (Gargagno), {i}453–535 *passim,* 545, {iv}189

Villa Jaffe (Irschenhausen), {i}541–54, {ii}19–23
    'lovely little wooden house in a corner of a..fir forest', {i}541; 'among the primulas and the gentian', {i}543

Villa la Massa (near Florence), {v}12, {vii}453
    Beveridges in, {v}616, 643–6, {vi}39, 78, 93, {vii}347, {viii}100, 103

Villa Leonardi (Riva), {i}447–57

Villa Maria (Spotorno), {v}336, 366, 382, 389

Villa Mirenda (San Paolo Mosciano), {v}11–13, 447–94, 500, 541–657 *passim,* {vi}1–2, 4–5, 7, 9, 16, 29–113, 155, 194–269, 311–422 *passim,* 433, 438, 440, 467, 476, 485, 513, 525, 542–3, 546, 558, 567, 577–81, 597–8, {vii}19, 25, 37–8, 50, 87, 105, 108, 200, 274, 281–2, 305, 314, 346, 370, 400, 418, 478, 560, {viii}98–107
    'on the bluff, square and a bit stark, the old church behind', {v}451; 'smells sourish, from the enormous vats of grapes downstairs', {v}551; rooms 'big and bare..stove is warm', {v}600; Christmas festivities for peasants in, {v}607–10, {vi}248–53, 255–6; bad for DHL's health, {vi}573–4; given up, {vi}583, 617, {viii}111; 'Frieda..pines for', {vii}292

Villa Palagio (Florence), {vii}454

Villa Pauline (Bandol), {ii}465, 476, 506

Villa Poggi (San Paolo Mosciano), Wilkinsons live in, {v}441, 500, {vi}35, 133, 151, 186, 306, 343, 399, {vii}314

Villa Primerose (Juan les Pins), {iv}299

Villa Proust, {v}493

Villa Quattro Venti (Capri), {iv}207, {v}345, 401, 635

Villa Robermond (Vence), {vii}14–15, 652–3

Villa Sguanci (Florence), {vii}281, 478

Villa Torricello (Capri), {vi}241

Villach (Austria), {vi}2, 4, 98–137 *passim,* 155, {viii}105

Village in the Jungle, The, see Woolf, L.

Villard, Oswald Garrison, {iv}16, 477

VILLIERS-STUART, MAUD, {i}16,
312–14
Letters to {i}312–13
Letters from {i}312
Villon, François, {i}157
Vingone (Italy), {vi}420, {vii}19, 411
Florence tram terminus, {v}445, 448,
451, 453–4, 456, 459, 618, 624, 656,
{vi}31, 34–5, 38, 104, 128, 220, 330–1,
369, 380, 392, 407, {vii}91; Mrs Seaman
stays in, {vi}31, 34–5, 38; innkeeper dies
in, {vi}361–2; Enid Hilton stays in,
{vi}413
Vinogradoff, Julian, *see* Morrell, J.
Violet, *see* Monk, V.; Murry, V.
Virgil, {ii}63, 517, {iv}235
Georgics, {ii}330, {iii}87, 161
Virginia, University of (USA), {iii}13, 630
Virginians, The, see Thackeray, W. M.
Virgins of the Rocks, The see D'Annunzio, G.
Visconte, Marco, {iv}204, 206
Visits to Monasteries in the Levant, see Curzon,
Lord R.
Vita Nuova, see Dante, A.
Viterbo (Italy), {v}427
Vivian, Philip (Harry Vivian M. Phelips),
The Churches and Modern Thought,
{i}36–7
Vogt, Nils Collett, {iii}381
Vogue, {v}286
DHL invited to write for, {v}482, 521;
review by DHL in, {vi}463, 516
Voice of Africa, The, see Frobenius, L.
Voices, {iii}342, 376, 380, 452
DHL's essay in, {iii}387, 513, 564; poem
in, {iv}540
Voigt, Frederick Augustus, {vii}32
Voigt, Hans Henning von, (Alastair, pseud.),
{ii}157
Volkhofsky, Feliks Vadimovich, {i}12,
{ii}139
Volkhovsky, Vera, {ii}139, 143, 146, 153, 229,
353
Völklingen (Germany), {vii}433
Volkov, Boris Ivanovich, {i}473
Voltaire, {i}274, {v}580, 585
Volterra (Italy), {v}426, 447, 449, 453, 461,
464, 650–1, {vi}27, 31–3, 35–6, 43, 48,

50, 89, 182, 196, 209, {vii}19,
{viii}49
Volumni (Italy), {v}427
Volunteer and Other Poems, The, see Asquith,
H.
Vosges, Mts, {iii}726, {iv}25, 33, 38,
{vii}397
Vourles (France), {v}444
Voyage Autour de ma Chambre, see Maistre, X.
de
Voyage of the Beagle, The, see Darwin, C.
Voyage Out, The, see Woolf, V.
Voyages of Discovery, see Cook, J.
Voynich, Ethel Lilian, *The Gadfly*, {i}525,
543
Vulci (Italy), {vi}27, 30–3, 36, 42–3, 48, 85,
89–90, 93, 105, {vii}19, {viii}104–5
Vulpius, Johanna Christiane, {i}477

W.X.- Corporal Smith, see Skinner, M.
Wabash College (USA), {i}145
Wade, Allan, {ii}127, 136
Wadsworth, P. Beaumont
Letters from {vii}137
Wagner, Richard, {i}9, {iii}514
'his bellowings at Fate and death',
{i}247
Lohengrin, {i}99;
Ring, {i}327;
Rheingold, {vi}22;
Siegfried, {i}327;
Tannhäuser, {i}99;
Tristan and Isolde, {i}140, 419, 535,
{ii}492
Wagner, Siegfried, {iii}733
Wailes, G. H. and Co., {i}443, 495
Wain, Louis, {i}23
Waldbröl (Germany), {i}17, 350, 385,
394–408 *passim*, 411
Wales, {i}54, 126, 280, 283–4, 289–91, 294,
{ii}65, 124, 366, 523, 548, {v}612,
{vi}534, {vii}53, 74, 447, 559, 607
Wales, Prince of, {iii}383, {iv}8, {vi}61, 321,
{vii}85
at Perahera in Kandy, {iv}215–19, 221,
234
Waley, Arthur, {ii}230
Walker, Dolores Louisa Carlo Kuster, {v}80

Walker, Dr, {iv}515

Walker, John Elder, {iv}474, {v}75, 80, {vi}10, 335

Wall Street 'Crash', {vii}565, 578, 582

Wallace, Miss, types *Lost Girl*, {iii}514, 521, 528, 535, 540, 549–51, 558

Wallace, William Vincent, {vi}220

Wallington (Surrey), {i}250, 266

Walpole, (Sir) Hugh Seymour, {ii}435, {iii}166, 573

   'nice letter' from, {i}421–2; 'simple commercial proposition' unlike DHL, {iii}547; friendly towards DHL, {iii}692; DHL refuses to join US lecture circuit like, {iv}349, 352; DHL satirises, {vii}485; one of the 'incomes on two legs', {vii}615

   The Secret City, {iii}573

Walsh, R. A., {iv}287

Walsh, Trevor, {ii}455

Walter, *see* Wilkinson, W

Walton, *see* Hawk, W.

Wanakah (USA), {iv}493, 505

WAR, DHL does not wage against Christianity, {i}41; Territorials play at, {i}118, 121; 'inner war' waged between loving couple, {i}419; 'war-like tendencies' of Richthofens, {i}475; over Tripoli, {i}478; warships, submarines etc in Spezia harbour 'really jolly', {ii}123–4; 'miserable about the', {ii}206; DHL's 'chief grief and misery is for Germany - so far', {ii}209; 'just hell', {ii}211; 'colossal idiocy', {ii}212; DHL has 'no sense of an enemy - only of a disaster', {ii}214; Frieda on, {ii}214–15, 344; the sensitive will be crippled by 'hideous stupidity of', {ii}218; DHL disdains competition for poem about, {ii}219; literature 'real fighting line, not where soldiers pull triggers', {ii}221; 'breaks my heart', {ii}232; its atmosphere now part of 'daily life..therefore much grimmer', {ii}234; survivors 'more important than those who fall', {ii}235; DHL's poverty because of, {ii}237, 255; shatters 'pasteboard bottom' of '"good" popular novel',

{ii}240; England 'thrilled to the marrow' by, {ii}243–4; those 'not needed for a new life' can enlist, {ii}255; Rananim reaction to 'world of', {ii}259, 277, {iii}23, 214–16; 'spear through the side of all sorrows and hopes', {ii}268; scene at declaration of, {ii}268; fragile hope replaces DHL's spiritual death resulting from, {ii}269, 271, 276; new hope is for 'great effort towards goodness' after, {ii}272; 'Augean stables' to be cleansed after, {ii}280; must be 'social revolution' after, {ii}292, 368; at home England insensitive to effect of, {ii}318; DHL refuses to be combatant in, {ii}330, 466; darkness of 'war horror' separates friends, {ii}347; to Asquith 'fighting line' the only reality, {ii}360; if continued Germany will win, {ii}365; developing into 'last great war between labour and capital', {ii}366–7; is 'pure destruction' of money-system, {ii}376; its 'persistent nothingness' renders DHL 'like a paralytic convulsed with rage', {ii}386; Zeppelin raid recalls Milton's 'war in heaven', {ii}390, 396; Russell 'the super-war-spirit' jabbing with words instead of bayonet, {ii}392; DHL predicts long continuation of, {ii}393–4, 467, 531; 'myriads of the wounded' from, {ii}396; 'contains a blasphemy', {ii}411; DHL will not 'commit..vast wickedness of acquiescence' in, {ii}414; love direct opposite of, {ii}424; signals 'the end', {ii}426; Nichols' nerves shattered by, {ii}445; 'stinks worse and worse', {ii}479; comes home to Cornish people, {ii}495–6, 520; DHL, Marsh and, {ii}535–6; will end soon, {ii}588, 608–9, 622; 'in one form or another..will never end', {ii}597, {iii}21, 224; 'robs one of speech', {ii}602; England fights 'meaningless war', Allies feed on her dismemberment, {ii}603, 611; DHL denies 'duty to fellow man' justifies, {ii}626; glorification of wealth led to, {ii}629; Christianity 'infinitely higher than the war' but its tenets must be

WAR (*cont.*)

surpassed, {ii}633–4; militarism death
to creative spirit, {ii}644; 'fine frenzy
of', {iii}26; 'utterly wrong, stupid,
monstrous and contemptible', {iii}32;
DHL repudiates sentiments of Brooke's
sonnet, {iii}33; early peace predicted,
{iii}37, 69, 93; 'reality of war lies
in..hearts of..people', {iii}39, 119; DHL
at war with 'whole body of mankind',
{iii}63; 'America won't declare', {iii}88,
91–2; surge of Spring stronger than,
{iii}118; government determined on
indefinte, {iii}123; having declared war
'America is a stink-pot in my nostrils',
{iii}124; did not alter *Rainbow*'s 'pre-
war statement', {iii}142; *W in L*
contains 'results in one's soul of the',
{iii}143; DHL evicted from Cornwall
though 'not warlike', {iii}189; *Bay*
comprises poems about, {iii}233,
{viii}29; pre-war 'kindliness' lost,
{iii}252; 'already a faded..half forgotten
event', {iii}345; Italy spoilt by,
{iii}418–19, 452; trials of German war
criminals 'unjust', {iii}450; 'made
cowards of us all', {iii}517; DHL finds
'peace beyond understanding..in
conflict', {iii}595; 'hate accumulates
everywhere..means war ahead', {iii}680,
732; Germany very different from
before, {iv}38; not won, 'we all lost it',
{iv}234–5; 'war episode' in *Kangaroo*,
{iv}318, 320, 322–3, {viii}59–60;
'changed me for ever', {v}50; critique of
war-novel, {v}315–16; damage most felt
after, {v}355; DHL has no belief in 'iron
resistances' since, {v}452; DHL fears
'class war' in England, {v}455, 468;
sadness, hopelessness in Germany since,
{vi}168; Falmouth always 'war region'
for DHL, {vi}511; DHL predicts
internal war in USA, {vi}549; 'all war
books' depress DHL, {vii}326; 'miners
like the war', Labour should help to stop
it, {viii}24

War, see Renn, L.

War and Peace, see Tolstoy, Count L.

War of the Worlds, The, see Wells, H. G.

War Office, {i}143, {iii}321
Murry in, {ii}647, {iii}127, 344; and
DHL's expulsion from Cornwall,
{iii}175–7, 179, 182, 186, 189, 207

War, Progress and the End of History, see
Solovyov, V.

War, the Offspring of Fear, see Russell, B. A.
W.

Ward, Mrs Humphry, {i}5, 524

Warlock, Peter, *see* Heseltine, P. A.

Warner Bros Pictures Inc., {viii}59

Warner, Susan B. (Elizabeth Wetherell), *The
Wide, Wide World*, {iv}492

Warner, Sylvia Townsend, *Lolly Willowes*,
{v}550

Warren Gallery, {vi}351, {vii}138, 293
for exhibition, DHL deciding between
Claridges and, {vi}437, 440; police raid
and prosecute, {vii}2, 7–8, 361–75, 379,
381, 385, 395–6, 398, 406–7, 411–13,
415, 417, 419–20, 423, 437, 440, 472–3,
505, 552, 652
see also Warren, D. C. W.

WARREN, DOROTHY CECIL WYNTER,
{ii}504, 591, {vi}16–17, 322, 417,
{vii}8, 161, 333, 340, 596, 603, 608
'beautiful', {ii}516; offers to show
DHL's pictures, {vi}127, 155, 329,
340–1, 353, 357, 371, 374, 377, 380–1,
383, 386, 402, 405, 408, 432, 434;
'longing' to have exhibition, {vi}435;
DHL decides to show with, {vi}442–7,
457–8, 460, 466–7, 469, 472, 474, 506,
513, 522–3, 535–7, 540, 542, 545–6, 551,
553–4, 557–8, 564, 567, 597; considers
DHL's pictures 'fine and free and
individual', {vi}523; orders three copies
of *LCL*, {vi}523, 535, 544; poor
correspondent, {vi}528, 577, 588, 604,
611, {vii}329; appears to prevaricate,
{vii}24, 26–7, 36, 40, 46, 48, 50, 53, 60,
70, 206, 222, 235, 269, 279, 282, 300,
314, 319, 322; pictures sent to, {vii}136,
180, 199; exhibition opened, {vii}330,
343–51, 385; police seize pictures from,
{vii}361; opposes but comes to accept
compromise in police prosecution,

{vii}367–73, 390, 421, 425; *Pansies* for,
{vii}380; 'very evasive and uncertain
bird', {vii}381; 'long raving screeds
from', {vii}394–6; to have *Contadini* as
gift, {vii}425, 490, 631; recovers pictures
and eventually closes exhibition,
{vii}435–6, 446, 461, 477; 'undepend-
able', {vii}458, 466, 479–80, 486–7, 489;
pays DHL for pictures sold at exhibition, {vii}489, 504, 511–12, 532; will
send remaining puctures to Ada Clarke,
{vii}631, 651–2
   Letters to {vi}340–1, 434, 446–7, 466–7,
522–3, 535–6, 553, {vii}70, 345–6, 361,
367–70, 425, 489–90, 631
   Letters from {vi}341, 434–5, 523, {vii}330,
367
Warren, Whitney, {iv}186, 191–2
Warwick (Warwickshire), {viii}1
Washington D. C. (USA), {iv}133, 471–2,
476, {v}107, 155, 220, {vii}488, 551
Washington Hotel (Florence), {viii}37
Washington, George, {i}114
Waste Land, The, see Eliot, T. S.
WATERFIELD, AUBREY, {ii}4, 174
   at peasant wedding in Fiascherino,
{ii}113, 116, 118; DHL visits castle
occupied by, {ii}120–1, 126–9, 178;
DHL visits near Settignano, {vi}371
   Letters to {ii}121, 172–3
WATERFIELD, LINA, {ii}116, 173, 178,
{vi}371
   Castle in Italy, {ii}116, 120–2, {vi}371;
Home Life in Italy, {ii}172
   Letters to {ii}122, 172–3
Waterloo, battle of, {i}485, {iii}282
Waterlow, (Sir) Sydney Philip Perigal,
{v}531
Waterlow, Sir Ernest, {i}113
Waterton, Mr, {iv}599
Watson, Elliott Lovegood Grant, *Where
Bonds Are Loosed*, {ii}502
Watson, Herbert, {ii}413, 577, 579, 582, 596,
{iii}101–2
WATSON, JEAN, {vi}429–30, {vii}375,
453, 565
   'tiresome', {vi}262; DHL supplies
autobiographical sketch to, {vi}465;

buys copy of *LCL*, {vi}612, {vii}32, 42,
45, 52, 59, 61, 71; 'manages the Foreigh
Dept' of Curtis Brown, {vii}23; negoti-
ates with foreign publishers for DHL,
{vii}32, 192, 219–20, 228, 273, 382–3,
386, 517, 567, 597–8, 602; 'difficult
person', {vii}572, 596–7, 616
   Letters to {vi}465, 612–13, {vii}32, 191,
219–20, 228, 382–3, 386, 517, 567,
597–8, 602
Watson, John Edward, {i}231, 461, 484
Watteau, Jean Antoine, {i}124, {ii}549,
{vi}543
Watts, George Frederic, {i}107–8, {ii}419
   Hope, {i}530;
   Love and Death, {i}107, {vii}441;
   Mammon, {i}107;
   Physical Energy, {vii}441
Watts, Isaac, {iii}349
Watts-Dunton, Walter Theodore, {i}12
Wauchope, Mrs, {iii}158
Waugh, Alexander Raban ('Alec'), {iii}537,
540, 545, 549, {iv}133
Waugh, Arthur, {iii}537
Way of All Flesh, The, see Butler, S.
Wayne's Farm (nr Del Monte), {v}70, 72,
82
Weald (Kent), {i}314
WEATHERWAX, IDELLA, *see*
PURNELL, I.
Weatherwax, John M., {iv}435, {vi}212–13,
431, 433
Weaver, Harriet Shaw, {ii}131, {vii}7
Weaver, Raymond M., *Herman Melville,
Mariner and Mystic*, {iv}306–7, 315,
319–20
Webb, Beatrice, {i}176, 552
Webb, Sidney James, {i}176, 552
Weber, Alfred, {i}395, 412–415, 419, 515,
{ii}186, {iii}678, 716, {iv}311, 357,
{v}417, 466, 621, {vi}76, 173, 207, 213,
312, 488, 557, 584, {vii}11, 423, 434
{viii}106
   'such a jolly fellow', {i}413; 'one of the
best-known German professors',
{vi}317, 356; suffers from 'nervous
disease..never very refined or naturally
intelligent', {vii}409

Weber, Max, {i}391, 395, 413, {v}486
Weege, Fritz, *Etruskische Malerei*, {v}465,
  {vi}50, 74–5, 88, 95, 102, 107
Week-Day Poems, see Meredith, H. O.
Weekley, Agnes, {i}440, {vi}142
WEEKLEY, BARBARA JOY, {i}421, 424,
  430, 440, 467, 475, 484, 486, 489–90,
  492, 496, 502, 506, 510, 514, 516–17,
  523, 530, 534, 549, 551, {ii}163, 199,
  244–5, 281, 288–9, 338, 343–4, 377, 639,
  651, 664, {iii}20, 26, 109, 232, 267,
  270–1, {iv}480, {v}10, 184–5, 278, 289,
  304, 326, 343, 427–8, 430, 445, 447–8,
  461, 463, 508, 521, 524, 539, 570, 628,
  645, 653, 656, {vi}16, 26, 35, 37–9,
  44–5, 49–51, 142–4, 146–52, 154, 166,
  168, 394, 397, 434, 485, {vii}5, 14–15,
  53–4, 56–7, 62, 67–9, 71–2, 74, 79, 81,
  85–6, 88–91, 93–4, 98, 104, 107, 109,
  132, 134–5, 137, 142, 148, 151, 260, 319,
  343, 360, 457, 591–2, 598, 623, {viii}111
  engaged to be married, {v}134, 209,
  332; *Little Novels* for, {v}247; DHL
  'can't stand', {v}332; in Alassio, {v}347,
  349–50, 352–3, 356–7, 362–6, 369–71,
  {vi}361, 366–7, 371, 375, 377; at
  Spotorno, {v}379, 381–3, 389–90, 392,
  394, 397–8, 402, 405–7, 411–17, 424–5;
  'very fierce' with Frieda, {v}419–21; in
  Florence, {v}432–8, 441–3; 'paints quite
  well" (Frieda), {v}470; at Villa
  Mirenda, {vi}30, 328–30, 340, 343; 'tall
  as a telegraph pole..not much life in
  her', {vi}34; 'hard to please', {vi}42–3;
  sells picture to Spencer-Churchill,
  {vi}127, 155; 'scatter-brained thing',
  {vi}417; in Bandol, {vii}115–20, 630–53
  passim; in 'very nasty state with those
  2nd rate studio-arty people',
  {vii}123–8, 155; *Paintings* for, {vii}321;
  Pansies for, {vii}380; at Beau Soleil
  'helps to keep things going.. very nice',
  {vii}632
  Letters to {v}443, 569, {vi}92, 347,
  {vii}259, 641, {viii}111
Weekley, Charles {i}440
WEEKLEY, CHARLES MONTAGUE
  ('MONTY'), {i}421, 424, 430, 440, 467,
  475, 484, 486, 489–90, 492, 496, 502,
  506, 510, 514, 516–17, 523, 530, 534,
  549, 551, {ii}163, 244, 245, 281, 288–9,
  338, 343–4, 377, 639–40, 651, 664,
  {iii}20, 26, 109, 232, 267, 270–1,
  {iv}480, {v}184–5, 304, 362, 498–9, 508,
  539, 543, 628, {vi}26
  Katherine Mansfield intermediary
  between Frieda and, {ii}46, 51, {viii}6;
  potential museum 'specimen of the
  perfect young Englishmen', {v}333;
  DHL makes friends with, {v}568–70;
  DHL's *Renascence of Men* promised to
  (but not received by), {vii}425
  Letters to {v}569–70
Weekley, Elsa Agnes Frieda, {i}421, 424, 430,
  440, 467, 475, 484, 486, 489–90, 492,
  496, 502, 506, 510, 514, 516–17, 523,
  530, 534, 549, 551, {ii}163, 199, 244–5,
  281, 288–9, 338, 343–4, 377, 639, 651,
  664, {iii}20, 26, 109, 232, 267, 270–1,
  {iv}480, {v}10, 184–5, 278, 289,
  304, 326, 343, 347, 353, 356, 362–3, 366,
  370, 382, 389–90, 392, 397–8, 402,
  405–7, 411–17, 419–21, 424–5, 427–8,
  430, 441–3, 445, 447–8, 461, 463, 470,
  508, 521, 524, 539, 598, 628, 645, 656,
  {vi}26, 32, 39, 375, 485, {vii}56, 62,
  68–89 *passim*, 104, 343, {viii}111
  S and S for, {iv}193, 320; 'doing a job
  and quite bouncy..sort of suburban
  bounce and *suffisance*, {v}332–3; in
  Spotorno, {v}394; in Florence,
  {v}432–8; engaged to Seaman,
  {v}568–9, 653; marriage of, {vii}211–12,
  241–2, 261–2, 282, 575, {viii}111;
  DHL's *Dance Sketch* promised to,
  {vii}425
Weekley, Emma Maria Frieda Johanna, *see*
  Lawrence, E. M. F. J.
WEEKLEY, PROFESSOR ERNEST, {i}17,
  374, 376, 396, 400–1, 402–4, 406, 438–9,
  442–3, 446, 457, 475–6, 488, 492, 498,
  534, {ii}37, 151, 219, {iv}480, {v}10,
  371, 433, {vi}26, 143
  'sure [DHL] is a poet', {i}51; praised
  'sky-high' by reviewer of 'book..on
  words', {i}384; 'ironic, pessimistic and
  cynical, nice, I like him', {i}388, {ii}154;
  asked by DHL to release Frieda, {i}392;

'knows everything' about DHL and Frieda, {i}394; 'loves his wife..really very decent over it', {i}409, 424; more likely to agree separation than divorce, {i}412, 420, 424, 448; 'going half crazed.. *fearfully* in love with Frieda', {i}420–1; 'whining bullying threatening', {i}430; moving children to his parents, {i}440, 448; offers Frieda London flat, {i}467; regards DHL as 'filthy hound' and threatens murder, {i}484–5; talks of divorce, {i}489–90, 493, 496, 499, 506, 514, 516–17; Frieda's plans to see children to circumvent, {i}542, 551, {ii}281, 288; 'love is dead' for, {ii}49; will calm down after divorce (Frieda), {ii}50, 174; 'unutterable fool', {ii}51, 162; secures custody of children, {ii}163; divorce ratified, {ii}168–9, 171; Frieda wants to see, {ii}237; behaviour 'very affected - penny novelette', {ii}241–2; 'conversation verbatim' between Frieda and, {ii}244–5; DHL required to pay costs of Frieda's divorce from, {ii}327–9, 357; and access to children for Frieda, {ii}377, 651; alleged hypocrisy of, {iii}109; prefers children not to stay with DHL, {v}347, 353, {vi}34; 'Founder' with DHL of *Word-Lore*, {v}381; 'gives radio lectures on words', {v}424
  Romance of Names, {ii}281;
  Romance of Words, {i}384, {ii}281
  Letters to {i}374, 392
Weekly Dispatch, The, {vi}52, {vii}95
Weekly Westminster, {v}242
Weingärtner, Creszenz, {iii}373, 375
Welbeck Abbey (Nottinghamshire), {ii}265
Well of Loneliness, The, see Hall, M. R.
Wellington (New Zealand), {iv}11, 249, 254–5, 259, 267, 271, 282–3, 375, {viii}54
Wellman, Frederick Creighton, *see* Scott, C. K.
Wellock, Wilfred, {iii}6
WELLS, AMY CATHERINE ('JANE'), {ii}1, 204, 444
  Letters to {ii}204

WELLS, DONALD, {v}369, {vii}121
  Letters to {v}348, 361
Wells, Herbert George, {i}12, 14, 16, 118, 138, 148, 318, {ii}1, 26, 97, 102, 204, 444, {iii}14, 27, 316, 573, 664, 693, {iv}133, 264, 462, {vi}11, 174, 279–80, 373, {vii}14, 80, 206, 468
lacks 'subtle soul of sympathy of a true artist', {i}119; does not present 'the Whole Truth', {i}121; writes some 'arrant rot' but *Tono Bungay* 'a great book', {i}127; DHL visits, {i}144; DHL wants to avoid being discussed in '*Ann Veronica* fashion', {i}339; admirable 'declaimer or reasoner' but looks at life 'as a cold and hungry little boy..stares at a shop where there is hot pork', {i}543; 'writer of books of manners..His folk have no personality - no passion', {ii}74; Abercrombie 'paltry' compared to, {ii}176; in decline, {ii}451, 560, {iii}166; one of the 'suburbanians', {v}94; DHL reviews *William Clissold*, {v}513–15, 544; Huxleys visit at Grasse, {vii}104, 109, 116–17, 120, 132; ostentatiously wealthy, {vii}615; visits DHL and prompts sculpture by Davidson, {vii}653; 'very good dealing with lower class life', {viii}19
  Ann Veronica, {i}154, 339, {ii}89–90;
  'The Country of the Blind', {ii}176;
  The History of Mr Polly, {viii}18–19;
  Imperialism and the Open Conspiracy, {vii}468;
  Kipps, {i}116, 127, 144, {iii}166;
  Love and Mr Lewisham, {i}127, {iii}166, {viii}18;
  Marriage, {i}528;
  Men Like Gods, {iv}462;
  The New Machiavelli, {i}456, 524, 543–4;
  The Passionate Friends, {ii}74;
  The Science of Life, {vi}374, {vii}80;
  Tono-Bungay, {i}119–20, 127, 142, 154, 159, 239, {iii}166, {viii}4, 18;
  The War of the Worlds, {i}127, {ii}102;
  The World of William Clissold, {v}513–15, 544, {vi}280

WELLS, MISS, {v}449, {vi}138
  Letters to {v}449–50, {vi}138
WELSH, ROBERT, {iv}146
  Letters to {iv}146
Wemyss, 11th Earl of, {ii}41, 51, {iii}237
Wemyss, Miss (cat), {v}165, 192, 246, 291,
  306, 358
Werner, Coralie Jeyes von, {i}443, 530
Wernham, Polly, {iii}581
Werther, see Goethe, J. von
Wesley, Charles, {i}94
West, George Cornwallis, {iii}305
WEST, REBECCA, {iii}664, {vii}2, 117,
  251, 516
  DHL meets in Florence, {iii}709;
  reviews W in L, {iv}51; supports DHL
  against Joynson Hicks, {vii}252;
  promises but does not write article on
  DHL for Titus, {vii}392, 513–15, 520,
  601
  Letters to {vii}252, 513
Westerham (Kent), {i}265
Westerland-Sylt (Germany), {iv}74
Western Australia, {iv}9, 214–72 passim, 386,
  503, 517, 533, 558, 582
Western Mail, {iv}270, {v}34
Western, Sir William George Balfour, {iii}4,
  168
Westlakes, the, {ii}632
Westminster (Connecticut, USA), {iii}659,
  668, 672
Westminster Gazette, {iii}129, {iv}51,
  {v}119, {viii}8
  see also, Saturday Westminster Gazette
Westmorland, {ii}184, 202, 268, {iii}260,
  500, {v}355
WESTON, EDWARD, Quintanilla intro-
  duces DHL to, {v}162; 'good photo-
  graph' of DHL by, {v}176, 186
  Letters to {v}185–6
Westyr, see Short, W.
Wetherbee, George, {i}273
Wetherell, Elizabeth, see Warner, S. B.
Weybridge (Surrey), {ii}404, {v}81, 189, 226
Weyhe Gallery (New York), {vi}340, 357
Weyman, Stanley John, Under the Red Robe,
  {i}258;
  The Wild Geese, {ii}640

WHALE, ELIZABETH ('LI'), {i}365–6,
  369, 372, 395, 410, 422, 433, {ii}22, 37,
  44
  Letters to {ii}22–3
Wharton, Edith, The House of Mirth, {i}481,
  524
What about Europe, see Douglas, G. N.
What is Art, see Tolstoy, L.
Whatstandwell (Derbyshire), {v}593,
  {vii}261
Wheeler, Mr, {ii}428
Wheelock, Ruth, {iv}107, 138, 264, {vi}12,
  {viii}53
  types poems for BBF, {iii}629; Lost Girl
  for, {iii}648; types Mr Noon, {iii}653;
  types S and S, {iii}667, 684; and DHL's
  search for a boat, {iii}689, 698–9;
  Captain's Doll for, {iv}391
  Letters from {iii}698–9
Where Angels Fear to Tread, see Forster, E. M.
Where Bonds Are Loosed, see Watson, E. L. G.
Whibley, Charles, {iii}187, 293
  actively supports DHL's application to
  Royal Literary Fund, {iii}227–8, 248,
  251, 265
Whistler, James Abbot McNeil, {ii}4
Whitby (Yorkshire), {i}36, 59, 452, {ii}244,
  {v}501, {vii}421
White Fan, The, see Hofmannstal, H. von
White Fang, see London, J.
White Fox, see Hargrave, J.
White Shadows in the South Seas, see O'Brien,
  F.
White Stallion, The, see Branford, F.V.
White, Edward Lucas, Helen: A Tale of
  Ancient Troy, {v}612
White, Trevor, {viii}25–7
White, Walter, DHL reviews Flight by,
  {v}647
White, William Hale, see Rutherford, M.
Whitehead, W. W., {i}4
Whitman, Walt, {i}5, 68, {iii}247, 280, 400,
  565, 576, 578, 680, {iv}7, {vii}419
  sometimes rhythm and mood harmonise
  perfectly in, {ii}61; critique of self-
  consciousness in, {ii}129–30; 'quite
  great', {ii}137; concept of 'manly love'
  in, {iii}478; 'reached a point of imagina-

tive or visionary adjustment to America', {v}308

'Calamus. A Song', {iii}478;
Leaves of Grass, {i}151, {iii}65;
'O Captain, My Captain', {i}293;
'Starting from Paumanok', {ii}153
see also, Lawrence, D. H., *SCAL*
Whitney Point (New York), {iv}546–7
WHITTLEY, IRENE TREGERTHEN, {ii}4, 587, 621, {iii}236, 244, 256, 268, 315, 505, 712, {iv}44, 96, 104
DHL proposes joint walking holiday in northern Italy, {iii}541, 569–70, 574, 585; walking with DHL 'among the hills behind Como', {iii}587–9, 602; DHL laments end of 'picnic à trois', {iii}591–2, 604; invited to Taormina, {iii}682, 705; visits DHL in Florence, {iv}79–80, 83, 86, 89
Letters to {ii}590, {iii}343–4, 433, 435–6, 541, 568–70, 592, 604, 615–16, 682, 697–8, 704–5, 713, {iv}91–2, 216–17
WHITTLEY, PERCY, {ii}590, {iii}236, 256, 315, 344, 505, 639, 697, 724–5, {iv}44, 92, 96, 104
DHL remembers in naval uniform, {iii}435; DHL proposes joint walking tour in northern Italy, {iii}541, 569–70, 574, 578–9, 584–5; walking with DHL around Como, {iii}587–90, 602; DHL *'so sorry'* walking tour over, {iii}591–2, 604; invited to Taormina, {iii}682; visits DHL in Florence, {iv}77, 79–80, 82–3, 86, 89
Letters to {iii}574, 578–9, 584, 591, 604, 610, 615–16, 721, {iv}77–9, 82, 230
Whittmore, Thomas, {vi}455
Whitworth, Geoffrey, {v}521, 524, 529, {viii}96, 99, 105
acting for Chatto & Windus objects to poems in *LWHCT*, {iii}148
Letters from {iii}148
WHITWORTH, PHYLLIS, {v}532, 538, {viii}103
and production of *David*, {v}521–4, {viii}96–7, 100; postpones production, {v}556, 623, {vi}30, 46, {viii}100;

stages *Widowing* first, {v}576–7, 604, 98–100; DHL agrees to cuts in *David*, {viii}102; Frieda's robust sympathy for, {viii}104
Letters to {viii}96–106
Whom God Hath Sundered, see Onions, O.
Why Freedom Matters, see Angell, N.
Why We Misbehave, see Schmalhausen, S.
Wickham, Anna (Edith Alice Mary Hepburn), {ii}18, 208, 322, 400–1, {iv}178, {vii}3
subscribes for *Signature*, {ii}407; DHL admires as poet, {ii}417
The Man With a Hammer, {ii}400, 417
Widdershins, see Onions, O.
Wide, Wide World, The, see Warner, S. B.
Wien, *see* Vienna
Wiesbaden (Germany), {vii}377
Wild Geese, The, see Weyman, S. J.
Wildbad Kreuth (Germany), {i}438
Wilde, Oscar, {i}166, {ii}94, {iii}443, 594, 708, {iv}54, {v}418
DHL did not consider 'very wrong', {ii}320; one of the 'grand perverts', {vi}342
The Importance of Being Earnest, {i}185, {viii}5;
Salome, {i}166;
'Symphony in Yellow', {i}169
Wilder, Thornton, {vii}571
'nothing - empty affectation', {vii}609
The Bridge of San Luis Rey, {vi}315, {vii}609
Wilhelm Meister, see Goethe, J. W. von
Wilkeson, Margaret, {iv}494, 498, 595
WILKESON, MARY, {iv}505, 537
complimentary volumes for, {iv}493–4; 'her serious eyes', {iv}498
Letters to {iv}494
Wilkeson, Mrs, {v}302
Wilkeson, Paul, {iv}333, 413, 484, 490, 537, {v}302
WILKINSON FAMILY ('WILKSES'), {v}11, 441, 447, 456, 560, 579, 581, 583–4, 596, 614, 643–5, {vi}5, 35, 104, 106–7, 109, 131, 180, 186–7, 194, 198, 224, 241, 243–4, 250–1, 253, 306–7, 380

WILKINSON FAMILY ('WILKSES')
(*cont.*)
'a bit extraordinary, but nice', {v}449;
'sort of village arty people', {v}453, 459;
'vegetarian, anti-vivisection, conscien-
tious objector, socialism etc' (Frieda),
{v}568; *A Holy Family* 'too sugestive'
for, {v}576; 'very kind', {vi}112; 'a bit
Bernard Shawey..live on a raw carrot sort
of thing - but..nice', {vi}128; DHL
driven to San Gemignano by, {vi}209;
leave Villa Poggi for London, {vi}343,
351
Letters to {v}587, {vi}398–9, {viii}111
WILKINSON, ARTHUR GAIR, {v}11, 13,
508, 588, {vi}35, 151, 168, 276, 300
welcomes DHL to Villa Mirenda,
{v}441, 444–5; 'artist - red beard,
Rucksack, violin-case..nice', {v}443;
hospitable, {v}460; DHL buys 'Busch
book' for, {vi}144, 153, 157–8, 170;
presents portfolio to DHL, {vi}246;
gives puppet-shows and shows pictures
in London, {vii}80–1, {viii}111
Letters to {v}441, 444–5, 460, 500, 502–3,
511, 518, 534–5, 541–2, 615–16, 618,
{vi}93–4, 117–19, 125, 144, 152–3,
157–9, 169–70, 189–90, 197, 246, 270,
290, 361–2, 385, 433–4, 577, {vii}80–1,
313–14, {viii}107
Wilkinson, Ellen, {vii}5
WILKINSON, FRANCES GAIR ('BIM',
'FRANCESCHINA'), {v}441, 447,
518, 534, {vi}35, 139, 399, {vii}80,
{viii}111
Letters to {vi}276
WILKINSON, LILIAN GAIR ('DIDDY'),
{v}11, 441, 443, 447, 500, 511, 518,
534–5, {vi}35, 134, 165, 169, 190, 276,
380, 399, {vii}80
'the limit of selfishness', {v}579, 583–4;
looks after Nancy Pearn, {vi}139, 157
Letters to {vi}138–9, 157–9, 186, 246,
361–2, 566–7, {vii}80–1, 313–14
WILKINSON, MARJORIE, DHL agrees
inclusion of poem in her anthology,
{viii}15
Letters to {viii}15

Wilkinson, Mrs, 'Mignonette', {i}236, 249,
253, 261
Wilkinson, Walter, {v}447, {vi}165,
{vii}80
DHL reviews *Peep Show* by, {vi}54, 128,
{viii}107; 'nice gentle soul with a bad
cockney accent', {vi}168
The Peep Show, {v}447, {vi}54, 128, 256
WILKINSON, WILLIAM GAIR ('PINO'),
{v}441, {vi}35, 169, 398–9, {vii}80,
{viii}111
Letters to {v}508, {vi}165, 274
Will to Power, see Nietzsche, F. W.
Will, *see* Holbrook, W.
WILLCOCKS, MARY PATRICIA,
{vi}68
Letters to {vi}70, 80
William Henry, *see* Hocking, W. H.
William the Silent, {i}114
William, *see* Hawk, W.
William-Ellis, Clough, DHL reviews *England
and the Octopus* by, {vi}463
Williams & Norgate, {ii}532
Williams, Ernest Edwin, {vii}405
Williams, Miss, {v}407–8
Williams, Mr, {v}407–8
Williamson, George, {vi}370
Willie, *see* Hopkin, W. E.
Willimantic (USA), {iii}668, 672
Willington (Co. Durham), {vi}230, 279, 281,
295, 428, 476, {vii}99, 124
Willoughby, Althea, {vii}585
Willy, Sidonie-Gabrielle, *see* Colette
Wilmot, Frank Leslie Thomson (Furnley
Maurice pseud.), *Eyes of Vigilance*,
{iv}281
Wilson, Amy Gwen, *see* Mond, A. G.
WILSON, CHARLES, {v}14, {vi}18
DHL advises on reading for miners,
{vi}229; invites DHL to meet 'the
Durham men', {vi}247; requests New
Year 'message' for 'the men', {vi}266–7;
sends cigarette case as gift, {vi}279;
DHL's books for, {vi}281, 295; copy of
LCL for, {vi}428, 430, 476, {vii}58–9,
97–8, 124, 134, 137, 202; 'irrepress-
ible..miner man', {vi}430; 'nuisance of a
fellow' sends books for DHL to sign,

{vi}476, 491, 499; DHL sends radical 'message' for miners to, {vii}98–104; critique of poems by, {vii}203

Letters to {vi}229–30, 247–8, 266–7, 279–80, 499, {vii}58, 98–104, 202–3

Wilson, Clyde, {v}212

Wilson, Edmund, {vii}452, 525

Wilson, Florence Roma Muir, *The Hill of Cloves*, {vii}381

Wilson, General, {v}349

WILSON, JOHN GIDEON, subscribes for *Signature*, {viii}16

Letters to {viii}16

Wilson, Professor James Southall, {iii}630

Wilson, Romer, *see* Wilson, F. R. M.

Wilson, Thomas Woodrow, {iii}88, 318, {v}59, 287, {vi}132

Wilson, William Joseph, {v}583, {vi}88

Wimbledon (Surrey), {i}117, {ii}173, 179, 208;

Common, {i}117–18, 120, 143, {vi}601

Wimborne Minster (Dorset), {i}357

Winchcombe (Gloucestershire), {iv}193, 261

Windeam, Robert, {iv}74, 189, {vi}328

Windmills: A Book of Fables, see Cannan, G.

Windsor Castle (Berkshire), {vii}325

Winesburg, see Anderson, S.

Wingfield (Derbyshire), {i}34, {v}592

Winnie, *see* Jones, W.

Wirksworth (Derbyshire), {iii}3, 252–3, 264, {v}243, 593

see also Middleton-by-Wirksworth

Wiseman, Mark, {v}321

Wishart & Co., {vi}52, 67, 348, {viii}107

'Witch Woman', *see* Lowell, A.

Withered Root, The, see Davies, R.

WITT, CORNELIA RUMSEY WILCOX ('NINA'), {iv}332, 338, 361, 370, 410, 450, 490, 493, {v}298–303, 306, 309, 313, 333, {vi}74, 209–10, {vii}27, 206 *Captain's Doll* for, {iv}390; divorced, {v}22, 237–40; 'beastly' rich, {v}239, 343; *LCL* 'good for her', {vi}327; 'self-important..on the golden pedestal of her money', {vii}547

Letters to {iv}417–18, 440

WITT, LEE, {iv}332, 361, 408, 410, 418, {v}53, 237, {vi}74 'addled', {v}22; 'blackguard', {v}239

Letters to {iv}440

Witte Huis (Doorn), {iii}489, 526, 621, 639, 726, {iv}51, 87, 192–3

Witter Bynner, see Bynner, H. W.

Wolfe, Charles, {i}342, {vii}126

Wolfe, Humbert, {v}2, 626, {vi}464

Wolfe, Thomas, *Look Homeward, Angel*, {vii}649

Wolfratshausen (Germany), {i}411–42 *passim*, 539, 552, {ii}21–2, 62–4, 74–5, 77, {vi}139–40, 144, 198

Wolfsgrube (Rottach), {vi}162, 227, 304, 339, 396, {vii}48, 51, 73–4, 139, 178, 286, 327, 349–50, 355, 380, 409, 444, 446–7, 449, 474, 534–5, 544, 566, 569–73

Wollongong (Australia), {iv}272

Woman and Labour, see Schreiner, O.

Woman, {v}141, 148 *see also* Paz, M.

'Woman's View, The', *see* Asquith, Lady C.

Women's Social and Political Union, The, {i}2

WOOD, FLORENCE MARY, {i}14, 155 *Letters to* {i}155

Wood, Francis Derwent, {i}14, 155

Wood, John R., {i}22

Wood, Mr, {iii}10, 506–7, 553, {iv}101, 143

Wood, Mrs Henry, *East Lynne*, {vii}39, 41

Wood, Rev. John, {ii}133, 136, 139, 168

WOODFORD, ERNEST JOHN, *Letters to* {i}26

Woodhouse (Leicestershire), {i}90

Woodhouse, Mrs, {v}327

Woodlanders, The, see Hardy, T.

Woodman, Dr Isaac, {iv}477

Wooings of Jezebel Pettyfer, The, see Macfall, H.

WOOLF, LEONARD SIDNEY, {ii}2, 205, 221, {iii}381, {iv}29, 301, {vi}11, 175, {vii}8 in discussion with DHL about Higher Tregerthen, {iii}198–201; collaborates with Kot, {iii}570, 727, {iv}23, 114, 165,

WOOLF, LEONARD SIDNEY (*cont.*)
274, {v}347; compares Murry's style
with Pecksniff, {v}313
The Village in the Jungle, {ii}291
Letters to {iii}199–201
Woolf, Virginia, {ii}205, 272, 427, {iii}381,
{iv}29, 134, 584, {v}651, {vi}175,
{vii}8, 571
'in treaty' with DHL about Higher
Tregerthen, {iii}198–9, 201; reviews *W
in L*, {iii}638; collaborates with Kot,
{iv}462
The Voyage Out, {ii}291
Worcestershire, {i}143, {iv}478, 480–1,
{v}123
Word, The, DHL's essays on 'Democracy' in,
{iii}6–7, 391, 404–5, {iv}314
Word-Lore, {v}381
Wordsworth, William, {vii}615
'Ode: Intimations of Immortality',
{vi}158;
'Ode to Duty', {i}270;
'Peter Bell', {iv}308;
'She dwelt among the untrodden ways',
{v}142
Workers' Educational Association, The, {i}2,
{vi}229
Worksop (Nottinghamshire), {i}371–2,
{ii}265, {viii}1
Worksop Guardian, The, {i}371
'World from a Woman's Window, The',
{iv}485
World of Today, The, {iii}320
World Today, {vi}232
World's Famous Literature, see Garnett, R.
Wörther-See (Austria), {v}480, {vi}94–5,
97–8, 108, 111, 119, 123–4
Worthing (Sussex), {ii}330–1
Wouverman, Philips, {i}124
Wrath, Sarah Ann, {v}635, {vii}127
Wright, Frank, {ii}402
Wright, John J., {iii}10, 665, 671, 686
Wright, Willard Huntington, {ii}26
publishes DHL's poems in *Smart Set*,
{ii}58; rejects stories as 'too hot', {ii}67,
72, 202; DHL dislikes 'terms of
payment', {ii}132; leaves *Smart Set*,
{ii}144

WUBBENHORST, F., lends *Ulysses* to
DHL, {iv}340, 345
Letters to {iv}340
Würzburg (Germany), {vii}480, 486, 489
Wyewurk (Thirroul), {iv}10, 247–82 *passim*,
{viii}55
Wyoming (USA), {iv}332
Wyss, Clotilde von, {i}122
Wyss, Johann David, *Swiss Family Robinson*,
{iii}340

Xaime, *see* Angelo, J. de
Xenophanes, {vii}573

Yale Review, The, {iii}13, 104, 155–6,
{iv}232, 494
Augusta de Witt's 'The Hunter' in,
{iii}95, 166–7, {viii}21; DHL invited to
respond to article in, {iii}166, 177–8
Yarmouth (Norfolk), {vi}67, 69, 80, 87
Ybrecht, *see* Hubrecht, M.
Yeats, William Butler, {i}12, 14, 138, 145,
277–8, 318, {iii}150, {iv}105, {v}626,
{vii}571
'vapourish, too thin', {i}107; DHL
meets, {i}156; writes 'queer stuff',
{i}488; 'sickly' use of Celtic symbolism,
{ii}248; 'shoddiness shows up rather
badly in translation', {vii}609
The Hour Glass, {i}186, 364;
Poems, {i}488;
'A Pot of Broth', {i}186, 246, {ii}557;
Three Things, {vii}585
Yellow Book, {ii}47, {vi}169
YORKE, DOROTHY ('ARABELLA'),
{iii}173, 199, 275, 308, 349, 422, 449,
454, 536, {v}426, 443, 468–9, 476, 518,
534, 564, 568, 578, 598, {vi}18, 65, 467,
474–5, 485, 488, 529–30, 532, 537, 542,
554, 569, {vii}17, 359, {viii}28–9
Josephine Ford in *Aaron's Rod*, {iii}173;
'elegant but poor', {iii}183; stays at
Mountain Cottage, {iii}256–7, 259–61;
Winifred in Cournos's *Miranda Masters*,
{v}433; wants to marry Aldington but
Hilda Aldington refuses divorce, {v}475;
at Villa Mirenda, {v}542–3, 548–50,
552; wants copy of *LCL*, {vi}491, 497,

513–14; helps distribute *LCL*, {vi}528, 535; on Port-Cros, {vi}573, 581, 584–7, 589–90, 592–4, 596, 600, 604; *Rawdon's Roof* for, {vii}232; 'not in a good way', {vii}415; in Paris, {vii}415, {viii}112
Letters to {vi}42–4, 124–5, 220–1, 491–2, 513, {vii}151–2
YORKE, SELINA, {iii}308, 449
Letters to {iii}308, {viii}28–9
Yorkshire, {i}208, 356, {v}16, {vii}421 proverb from, {i}511; DHL would like to visit, {v}501, 509; dialect in stories from, {viii}15
Yosemite Valley (USA), {iv}287–8, 290
Young Earnest, see Cannan, G.
Young Girl's Diary, A, {iv}416 prosecuted with *W in L*, {iv}292, 296, 501, {viii}64, 71
Young, Edward, *Night Thoughts,* {i}103
Young, Emily Hilda, *Corn of Wheat,* {i}222
Young, Eric, {iii}492, 528
YOUNG, FRANCIS BRETT, {iii}438, 446–8, 451–2, 458, 496, 502, 522, 557, 567, 602–3, 624, {iv}138–9, {v}349, 401, {vi}191
'humble waiter on Compton Mackenzie', {iii}442; Marsh's 'protegé', 'pas grande chose', {iii}462; 'like a fretful.. pragmatical..dictatorial infant', {iii}481; 'sly dog', {iii}504; goes to South Africa, {iii}655, 663, 702; 'pompous Brummagen', {v}362; lecturing in USA, {v}630; 'gone awfully soft', {vi}111; one of 'mere incomes on two legs', becoming 'last lake poet instead of a mere puddle poet', {vii}615; 'How are the puny risen', {vii}619
The Black Diamond, {iii}708
Letters to {iii}438, 440, 479–80, 513–15, 587, 626, 655–6
Young, Henry, & Sons, {vi}514, 535, 544, 565
YOUNG, JESSICA BRETT, {iii}438, 440, 442, 451, 462, 481, 513, 587, 624, 655–6, {iv}138, {v}349, 362, 401, 630, {vi}111, {vii}615, 619
Letters to {iii}438, 496–7, 530, 557–9, 566–7, 579, 602–3
Young-Hunter, Eva ('Eve'), {v}89, 102

YOUNG-HUNTER, JOHN ('JACK'), {v}89 interested in buying Kiowa Ranch, {vii}287–9, 475
Letters to {vii}287–8
YOUTH and AGE, 'assurance and inflatus of youth', {i}37; 'wilfulness of youth', {i}41; one of 'youth's follies', {i}50; DHL's youth 'acute and painful', {i}119; verbosity of youth, {i}141; 'old, over seventy', {i}302; 'poetry of youth', {ii}105; Whitman's 'Youth' stereotypical, {ii}130; Futurists 'young, infantile' student-like, {ii}180; Russell's 'inexperience of youth', {ii}366; '33rd birthday - the sacred age', {iii}281; 'Youth is vain' (Coleridge), {iii}502; Murry 'renewing his bald youth like the vulture', {iii}728; Australia's 'almost coal-age pristine quality', {iv}271–2; European youth should smash rotten 'elderly bunk' of status quo, {v}94; extracts from *B in B* in *Anthology of Youth*, {v}193; 40 'a very big age!', {v}376; DHL at age when sensible to have fixed abode, {v}485; 'the *âge dangereuse* for men', {v}648; Englishmen liable to bronchial trouble at DHL's age, {vi}154; Frieda's mother 76, 'spontaneous and young', {vi}169; over 70 'the only affliction-free time of youth', {vi}173; German youth capable of 'fighting unity..against the world..English are older, and weary even of victory', {vi}259; at 42 'sort of change of life', {vi}296; 'Are *all* young Englishwomen instinctively homosexual?', {vi}554; DHL's nostalgia for youth at Haggs Farm, {vi}618; young girls - 'Little prigs' - should read *LCL* aloud, {vii}127; selling ranch 'like parting with..one's youth', {vii}288–9; 'insane selfishness' of great age, {vii}398, 436; Frieda's mother told: 'Rejoice over your age', {viii}81
Ypres (Belgium), {ii}319, {iii}2, 239
Ysabel, *see* Isabel
Yucatan (Mexico), {iv}388, {v}155, 161, 166, 209

'Yucca to a Passion-Vine', *see* Lowell, A.
Yung, *see* Jung, C. G.
Yvonne, *see* Franchetti, Y.

Zaira, {vi}94, 397–9, 573, {vii}280–1, 455
Zangwill, Israel, {i}524
Zanotti, Carlo ('Carletto'), {vi}5, 249, 289,
    416, 426, 443, 466, 470, 487, 496, 519,
    591, 598, {vii}274, 340, 359–60, 400
    Orioli's 'boy', {vi}88, 104, 131, 252; on
    errands for DHL, {vi}224, 369, 391,
    579–80, {vii}190; DHL rewards,
    {vi}471, 475, 478, 480, 544–5, {vii}63,
    219, 230; writes to DHL, {vi}491,
    {vii}91, 561, 630
Zapata, Emiliano, {iv}419
Zapotec Indians (Mexico), {v}139, {v}144,
    168, 170, 175, 178, 195, {vi}210
    'small but proud..alert and alive',
    {v}162, 164, 166–7; 'strutting', {v}176;
    'sympatico', {v}184
Zaragoza, Calle, *see* Chapala
Zell-am-See (Austria), {iii}724, {iv}2–3, 6,
    15, 25, 28, 36, 38–78 *passim*, 89, 93, 119,
    121, 130, 189
    'Captain's Doll' and, {iv}396, 398
Zennor (Cornwall), {ii}4, 13, 548–669
    passim, {iii}3, 19–177 *passim*, 197, 200,
    261, 294, 334, 634, {iv}312–13,
    {viii}18–23
    'very lovely', {ii}553–5; 'gorse all
    yellow..sea a misty, periwinkle blue',
    {ii}602; 'country..simply wonderful',
    {ii}609; DHL 'daren't come out of',
    {ii}641, {iii}57, 97; DHL 'less stressed'
    in London than in, {iii}172; Starrs'
    concert 'greatest event in Zennor for
    some time', {viii}27
    see also Higher Tregerthen
Zillertal (Austria), {i}432–3, 438, 440, 442–3,
    {iv}189
Zimmern, Helen, {v}12, 611
Zionism, {iii}690
    Eder and, {ii}258, {iii}42, 150, 214;
    DHL might write 'a Zioniad', {iii}340;
    offers to write 'Sketch Book of Zion',
    {iii}687
Zola, Emile {i}91, {ii}462
    L'Assommoir, {i}258, {iii}38, 40;
    La Débâcle, {i}258, {iii}38;
    Germinal, {iii}38;
    Nana, {iii}38, 40
Zululand (South-East Africa), {iii}8, {vii}5
    DHL contemplates visit to, {iii}413,
    416–17, 449, {vii}27–8
Zuni (USA), {iv}332, 361, {vi}36, 404
Zurich (Switzerland), {ii}76, 79, {iii}623,
    {iv}61, 78, 585, {v}23, 125, 261,
    {vi}108, 562, {vii}409, {viii}9, 96
    'dreary-souled city', {iv}66
Zweig, Arnold, *The Case of Sergeant Grischa*,
    {vii}123, 166